Measurement, quantification and economic analysis

Numeracy in economics

Edited by Ingrid H. Rima

London and New York

First published 1995
by Routledge
11 New Fetter Lane, London EC4P 4EE

Simultaneously published in the USA and Canada
by Routledge
29 West 35th Street, New York, NY 10001

© 1995 Selection and editorial material Ingrid H. Rima
Individual chapters to their authors

Typeset in Times by Solidus (Bristol) Limited
Printed and bound in Great Britain by
Biddles Ltd, Guildford and King's Lynn

British Library Cataloguing in Publication Data
A catalogue record for this book is available from the British Library

Library of Congress Cataloging-in-Publication Data
Measurement, quantification and economic analysis : numeracy in
  economics / edited by Ingrid H. Rima.
       p.   cm.
  Simultaneously published in the USA and Canada.
  Includes bibliographical references and index.
  1. Economics, Mathematical.   2. Econometrics.   I. Rima, Ingrid
Hahne, 1945–   .
HB135.M423   1994
330'.01'51—dc20   94–14956
                                                                  CIP

ISBN 0–415–08915–8

Contents

Figures

Tables

Contributors

S. Ambirajan, Indian Institute of Technology, Madras, India

Bradley W. Bateman, Grinnell College, Grinnell, Iowa, USA

Randall Bausor, University of Massachusetts at Amherst, Amherst, Massachusetts, USA

John B. Davis, Marquette University, Milwaukee, Wisconsin, USA

Robert W. Dimand, Brock University, St Catherines, Ontario, Canada

Mohammed H. I. Dore, Brock University, St Catherines, Ontario, Canada

Robert S. Goldfarb, George Washington University, Washington, DC, USA

Shaun Hargreaves Heap, University of East Anglia, Norwich, Great Britain

James Henderson, Valparaiso University, Valparaiso, Indiana, USA

Sherryl D. Kasper, Maryville College, Maryville, Tennessee, USA

Donald W. Katzner, University of Massachusetts at Amherst, Amherst, Massachusetts, USA

Judy L. Klein, Mary Baldwin College, Staunton, Virginia, USA

Philip A. Klein, Penn State University, University Park, Pennsylvania, USA

Jinbang Kim, University of California, Riverside, California, USA

Sandra Peart, Baldwin-Wallace College, Berea, Ohio, USA

Robert E. Prasch, University of Maine, Orono, Maine

Ingrid H. Rima, Temple University, Philadelphia, Pennsylvania, USA

John Smithin, York University, Toronto, Ontario, Canada

Vincent Tarascio, University of North Carolina, Chapel Hill, North Carolina, USA

Yanis Varoufakis, University of Sydney, Sydney, Australia

Murray Wolfson, California State University, Fullerton, California, USA

Nancy J. Wulwick, Binghamton University, Binghamton, New York, USA

Chapter 1

From political arithmetic to game theory

An introduction to measurement and quantification in economics

Ingrid H. Rima

Contemporary economists have only limited appreciation of the extent to which early practitioners recognized that, by their very nature, the problems in which they were interested required them to measure, quantify and enumerate. From the seventeenth century onwards inquiring minds had already learned to distrust information and ideas that derived from the then traditional qualitative approach to science, which described the sensations associated with objects and events. Much like Galileo, who saw the universe as "written in mathematical characters" (Galileo 1628: 232), so William Petty, responding to the directives of nationalism and commerce, undertook "to express myself in Terms of Number, Weight or Measure, to use only arguments of sense and to consider only such causes as have visible foundations in Nature; leaving those that depend upon the mutable Minds, Opinions, Appetites and Passions of particular Men, to the considerations of others" (Petty 1690). He called his method "political arithmetick" and aimed not simply to record and describe reality in terms of numerical variables, but to use them as mental abstractions for the purpose of understanding whether there is a relationship between them and to use the information to accomplish some purpose.

Petty's pioneering work is by no means unknown, even by some who are not specialists in the history of economic thought.[1] There are also numerous more or less well known studies relating to the work of individual contributors, Cournot, Walras, Jevons, Edgeworth and Fisher, among others, who relied heavily on mathematics and/or statistics long before economics reached its present stage of mathematical formalism and model building.[2] Yet concern with measurement and quantification tools *per se* and their development in tandem with economic description and analysis is a relatively new area of economic research. Historians of economics, historians of science and philosophers whose interests extend to issues of methodology are finding new connections among their research interests. The conjoining of academic disciplines which have, in the past, been separate and distinct fields of investigation is, in part, a reflection of the discomfort which many economists feel about the methodology of their discipline and its status as a science. It lends perspective to recognize that econometrics is simply the most recent (though no doubt the most powerful) quantitative tool to have been pressed into service by those who study economic phenomena. Political economists of the seventeenth and eighteenth centuries, and the analytical economists who followed them, borrowed or refined whatever measurement and quantification tools they found useful, and supplemented them with some of their own invention. Thus the myopia underlying the popular view among many contemporary economists that their predecessors were literate but not numerate is curious to those who have greater historical perspective.[3]

It is also relevant, as a matter of perspective, to recognize that criticisms of the uses of measurement tools are quite as old as their applications. Specifically, what sort of empiricism is appropriate to the study of economics? Every writer who has sought to provide methodological guidance for scientific practice in economics – Adam Smith, W.N. Senior, J.S. Mill, J.E. Cairnes, W.S. Jevons, J.N. Keynes, Lionel Robbins, J.M. Keynes and Terence Hutchison – all struggled with this still unresolved question. Contemporary methodologists are revisiting their arguments, especially as they have resurfaced in the context of present day formalism, econometric practices and gaming experiments. The "measurement without theory controversy" that pitted early twentieth-century empiricists against one another, along with the "value judgments" controversy that came to the fore as a byproduct of the measurability of utility issue, and the empirical verification arguments that arose in the context of logical positivism, of which the Lester–Machlup controversy about maximizing assumptions was a prime example, have reappeared in new contexts and in modern garb. Their writings suggest that some of the issues that are central to contemporary theoretical and methodological controversy are embedded in contemporary measurement and quantification tools in ways which historians (Epstein 1987; Mirowski 1990; Morgan 1990; Schabas 1990) and philosophers (Hausman 1992) have only begun to discern. To continue and extend their research agendas in a broader context is essentially to give further momentum to interdisciplinary inquiry into the epistemology of measurement and quantification in economics.

Because the research that is the focus of this anthology cuts across a whole range of historical and contemporary topics of interest to economists, it exceeds by far the agenda of any single researcher. Thus it became the product of intellectual networking with many researchers who, in some cases, were unaware of elements of commonality amongst their individual efforts. Many though by no means all of the contributors to this volume share an interest in the history of economic analysis. Others have research interests that relate chiefly to contemporary microeconomics and/or macroeconomics and their applications. Yet all have thought deeply about the purported capability of mathematics as a more precise means of expression than language (Samuelson 1947). They have also reflected on the conventional wisdom that hypothesis testing to confirm theories (and their implied policies) and infer new theoretical relationships from them is the optimal vehicle for establishing linkages between economic theory and empirical reality.

From Petty's political arithmetic to Lucas's rational expectations models and von Neuman's growth theory, empiricism and deduction have vied for pride of place as the critical instrument for discovering and evaluating knowledge and the question of their relationship has been central to the methodological literature of the last half century.[4] Yet, general methodological discussions do not offer the same contextual perspective as inquiries that are more specifically concerned with measurement and quantitative techniques *per se*. That is the advantage of the papers in this volume. Their first concern is to offer an analytical and technical account of particular measurement and quantification tools, and to examine them within the theoretical framework of their development. Each paper stands on its own; yet each also contributes to a broad-based epistemological inquiry. Three broad stages can be identified as having taken place in tandem with the development of economic theory.[5] During the first relatively brief stage which roughly coincides with latter day mercantilism, the essential role of measurement and quantification tools was to serve as a policy instrument. During the second stage the chief concern of measurement and quantification techniques was the discovery of static economic laws. In the present third and still ongoing stage, economics is perceived to have emerged, at last, as a true science; mathematical formalism is relied on to create economic models which are joined to gaming experiments and econometric tests to evaluate whether the outcomes they generate from data are consistent with the model's predictions. Much of the tension about methodology today derives from questions relating to the effectiveness of these instruments for gaining knowledge about economic behavior and outcomes.

STAGE ONE: MEASUREMENT AS A POLICY INSTRUMENT

As early as the seventeenth century, political arithmeticians identified with the empiricist view that the natural world exists separately from human beliefs, philosophies and preferences. Although the first stage in the development of measurement and quantification techniques was relatively brief, its practitioners left a legacy to economics that is important both for its own sake and because it captures so clearly the essentially quantitative nature of early political economy in the service of the policy aspects of English mercantilism. Together with John Graunt and Gregory King, William Petty established much of what is now known about the behavior of crops, livestock and human population during the eighteenth century. Their best remembered French counterparts include François Bois Guilbert and Marshall Vauban, who were particularly concerned with the practical problems of France's agricultural sector, and collected much of the statistical information about the French economy that later served as a basis for the Physiocratic single tax proposal.

Their concern was to focus on formulating the kinds of economic and social reforms that would contribute toward making France's economy more efficient, just as England's political arithmeticians were concerned with making their nation wealthier and politically more powerful.

It is not without relevance for contemporary practitioners of economics that the *political* objectives of mercantilism and Colbertism became the source of their undoing as an intellectual tradition. As Robert Dimand argues in his chapter "'I have no great faith in political arithmetick'": Adam Smith and quantitative political economy", political arithmetic is the first major example of a tradition that was criticized and rejected chiefly because of the political objectives its findings were used to support. Smith's disenchantment with the political arithmetic of his contemporaries was less a reflection of his critical assessment of their methods or findings (which he did not hesitate to use in support of some of his arguments) than it was a reflection of the changing political environment and methodological perspective of the eighteenth century. In keeping with the natural order philosophy of the enlightenment, political economists from Smith onward came to rely on deductive logic to articulate a vision that the economy is composed of self-interested individuals whose actions will bring about beneficial results for all market participants. Smith's commitment to deduction was critical in bringing about an early end to the first stage of the development of measurement and quantification techniques. It also set the pattern of ongoing methodological conflict about the role of measurement and quantification tools in relation to economic method and the search for an understanding of the functioning of the economy.

STAGE TWO: QUANTIFICATION TECHNIQUES AND ECONOMIC LAWS

Data collection and induction

It was not until the Industrial Revolution transformed the relatively bucolic social order of the Smithian era and imposed new hardships on the working classes that the practical necessity for data collection and measurement tools arose again. Two factors were critical: one was the concern of inductivists to counter what they perceived as the failure of Ricardian deduction to develop hypotheses consistent with the real world and the need to provide a factual basis for policy. The second was the need for information, especially by businesses. The establishment of "The Statistical Section" of the British Association for the Advancement of Science (later Section F) and the Statistical Society of London (later the Royal Statistical Society) and the development of techniques to represent and analyze empirical data relating to virtually all areas of social existence marks the onset of the second stage in the development of measurement and quantification tools. The Association's hierarchical classification of the sciences became central to establishing the scientific authenticity of inductive political economy by virtue of the connections that the then maturing discipline of statistics was expected to establish between economic theory and the real world. Leading nineteenth-century British thinkers were cognizant that the classification of branches of knowledge lays the foundation for power to arrive at truth. They envisioned this classification as having the potential for even greater impact if the moral, political and metaphysical as well as the physical portions of our knowledge could become encapsulated in it (Whewell 1847: V.II, p. 113). James Henderson's chapter "Ordering society: the early uses of classification in the British statistical organizations" examines the relationship between statistics and economics as the first of the nonphysical "portions of our knowledge" to gain admittance among the categories of science.

Henderson's particular focus is on the role of data collection and statistical science not only to establish "correct views" about the moral sciences and their relationship to the physical sciences, but also to substantiate the impoverished nature of Ricardo's system of deduction *vis-à-vis* the process by which science is established. The methodological attack against Ricardian deductive economics was thus accompanied by both a renewed urgency for fact-gathering (reminiscent of the political arithmeticians) and a concern about establishing a basis for deriving economic laws and for mounting a social policy.[6]

Jeremy Bentham, along with other philosophical radicals, confronted the problem of defining and measuring the "greatest good" in order to provide a basis for reforms intended to increase the "sum of happiness" by means of social policy. Of necessity they concerned themselves with the practical possibility of interpersonal utility comparisons and the related problem of evaluating the "quality" of pleasures so that a hedonic balance sheet might be drawn up for the guidance of policy makers. It was largely on the stumbling block of evaluating the subjective gains and losses that would be associated with any policy measures that might be adopted that utilitarians floundered. These difficulties are the focus of Sandra Peart's chapter "Measurement in utility calculations: the utilitarian perspective". While some, F.Y. Edgeworth among them, envisioned the possibility of a "hedonometer" to lend precision to the measurement of pleasure, nineteenth-century British economists ultimately disassociated themselves from the notion that utility is measurable, and from the kinds of reform programs that depended on it.[7]

As the impracticality of the hedonic calculation in economics became apparent, the potential for appropriating the measurement and quantification tools that had already been used successfully in other fields became challenging. Analytical geometry and graphic representations had long been in use in physics, ballistics and meteorology, but, as Judy L. Klein points out in "The method of diagrams and the black arts of inductive economics", they were seldom used in economics until the early nineteenth century. Daniel Bernoulli's curve (1738) represented the utility of additional income logarithmically and was a forerunner of later works which addressed practical economic problems such as the demand for rail and other public utility services with the help of techniques borrowed from other disciplines. Many of these lent themselves to record keeping and data analysis from which numerical and graphic representations were undertaken.

By the end of the nineteenth century, the techniques developed by engineers as economists included the convention of plotting time on the horizontal axis to represent changes in related quantities. Because there was no apparent methodological need for distinguishing between static data points and data changes over time, the essential difference between logical time and historical time typically became blurred; for example, it is now recognized that the numerical facts underlying a demand curve only have meaning in terms of logical time. Yet the relevance of this point would not become apparent until the general equilibrium paradigm focused attention on the conceptual problem of time in economics (Robinson 1974).

Statistical causality and economic laws

Early data collection practices also derived from business needs for information. The business press, in particular *The Economist* and the *Commercial and Financial Chronicle*, reported changes in such critical business magnitudes as imports, exports, rail traffic, commodity prices, bank reserves and so forth on a weekly and monthly basis. Judy Klein's chapter "Institutional origins of econometrics: nineteenth-century business practices" notes that descriptive terms such as "animated", "depressed" or "fair" were typically combined with numerical averages to describe market conditions. William Stanley Jevons used these as key data sources in his studies of the causal relations that underlie the temporal phenomena of commerce. The "law of seasonal variation" which he represented in tabular and graphic form was an early technique for transforming the "rule of thumb" knowledge of merchants into statistical plots of seasonal variations by using the concepts of statistical populations and the commercial practice of calculating arithmetic differences. These later became the foundation for rate charts, the representation of successive averages as a trend, and the statistical technique of index numbers. While the path from political arithmetic to statistical methods for discerning cause–effect relationships was neither continuous nor smooth, by the nineteenth-century the operative premise was that careful data collection coupled with methods appropriate to data utilization can generate "true" theories about observable economic phenomena and thus direct economics towards "exact" laws that are analogous to those of the natural sciences.

There were, nevertheless, those who, like John Cairnes, continued to cling to the contrary view, very largely learned from J.S. Mill, that economics is and always will be an inexact science. This is the focus of Jinbang Kim's chapter "Jevons versus Cairnes on exact laws in economics". Jevons's immediate concern was the then critical question of the implications of the probable increase in England's coal consumption. He believed that it was not necessary to rely on *a priori* principles of evaluation because the principle of probability could serve as a basis for establishing economic laws. Though Jevons may be faulted for his inadequate understanding of probability theory and his failure to use Laplace's superior technique of least squares estimates, he did manage to establish the viability of a statistical approach to economic theorizing.

The latter is much in evidence in the development of the theory of demand and statistically generated demand curves. Nancy J. Wulwick's chapter "A reconstruction of Henry L. Moore's demand studies" reviews and reconstructs Moore's estimates of the demand for pig iron in order to set straight the still misunderstood reason why Moore's estimates generated upward-sloping curves which led to the criticism that Moore "misunderstood Marshall". Her replication of Moore's estimates establishes that it was Moore's critics who misunderstood; their failure was that they did not understand the identification problem he confronted. The supply and demand data which are the basis for his scattergrams can only generate what Klein would describe as "fact curves" in logical time, whereas Marshall's demand diagram is a "law curve" in logical time. Wulwick's reconstruction of Moore's study has thus disentangled the identification problem which his critics failed to discern as the root of their criticism. Her reconstruction is all the more useful from a methodological perspective because it bears so directly on the concerns of many contemporary economists about the phenomenon of time.[8]

Economic statistics and dynamics

Since Marshall economists have overwhelmingly been preoccupied with equilibrium tendencies, despite their awareness that the dynamics of capitalistic economics generate wide fluctuations in the level of prices, output and employment. The problem of changes in the general price level, which they conceived to be suitably proxied by the price of gold, was of particular concern. Both Ricardo and Jevons had already approached the matter of the price level theoretically, and the practical problem of constructing an index number to evaluate changes in prices was a matter of controversy between academics and economic analysis associated with the business press. Robert Prasch offers an account and an analysis of their methodological dispute about base weights in his chapter "The probability approach to index number theory: prelude to macroeconomics". He identifies the roots of their disagreement as deriving from the weighting problem that is inherent in index number construction. The price indices generated by the business press used a weighting scheme that was based on the quantities bought in a given base year. This is an approach that implicitly assumes a constancy over time in commodity use, and associates price level changes with changes in the quantity of money. It has simplicity on its side in that it circumvents the problem of establishing relative weights to reflect the importance of the individual commodity components. But it is also problematic, in that an index generated by calculating the change in the mean of the prices of goods comprising the index may not accurately represent the "true" measure of price change. The credibility of the index reflects the strength of the belief (or probability) that the relative weight of the components will remain the same over time.

While Alfred Marshall's chain index was designed to overcome the difficulty inherent in the problem of weighting, it did not anticipate the basis on which J.M. Keynes would later express his reservations about index numbers. Keynes's reservations would relate to his perception that relative commodity and factor prices are not independent of one another. The implication for Keynes was that, because the conventional quantity theory of money could not account for relative price changes or relate them to changes in the value of money, it did not offer a theoretically adequate basis for computing price indices or conceptualizing the notion of a general price level. He was thus led toward the importance of disaggregated indices and recognition that intersectoral imbalances must be central to the study of business cycles. For Prasch it was, at least in some measure, Keynes's reservations about the methodology of index number construction that led him in the direction of recognizing the role of the financial sector. This focus led to his later study of monetary theory and the subsequent development of macroeconomics.

Keynes nevertheless retained a "static prejudice" that led toward equilibrium analysis, and helped undermine the profession's interest in business cycle theory and in the vast opportunity it offers for measurement and quantification. The idea that capitalist economies have an inherent tendency toward business cycles, which are generated as a part of the operational process of free enterprise, is at the center of the research agenda of modern institutionalists. Much of this work is under way at the National Bureau of Economic Research (NBER), where contemporary followers of Wesley Mitchell are building on the work of intellectual forbears who compiled voluminous historical records to test the hypothesis that patterns of change can be identified from empirical data. Their ultimate objective is thus nothing less than to construct a general theory of business cycles consistent with the facts of the cyclical experience which their empirical research identified.

Philip A. Klein's paper "The indicator approach to monitoring business fluctuations: a case study in dynamic statistical methods" offers the perspective that many of the early statistical innovations developed by Geoffrey Moore and his associates at NBER are now in such general use that their origins are largely forgotten. The diffusion index is but one example; so too is the calculation of "average duration of run" which evaluates the length of time, on average, over which month to month changes in a given series are in the same direction. The Bureau's technique for making adjustments for "amplitude" changes along with their development of recession–recovery turning points are among the techniques developed by NBER associates for coming to grips with the question how today's cycles are similar to or different from cycles of the past. These developments were all forerunners of specialized indicators such as Moore's leading index of inflation and the Moore–Cullity indicator of employment, which are tools for monitoring US business cycles in the tradition of the Bureau's institutionalist forbears.

Although the institutionalist tradition is chiefly, if not uniquely, American, its aims nonetheless harken back to the business cycle research of Jevons who recognized the existence of periodicity at a time when business cycle study was in its infancy. Understandably, the Bureau's work also set loose a new round of anti-inductionist criticism, highlighted by the well-known charge that their work was empiricism without benefit of theory (Vining 1949). Irrespective of the merits of the arguments pro and con, institutionalist research, particularly of business cycles, stands both as a high point and as an end point. It is the high point of the long tradition of induction which, in an institutional sense, can be dated from the founding (1833) of the Statistical Section (later Section F) of the British Association for the Advancement of Science and the Statistical Society of London. It is an end point in the sense that disenchantment with statistical techniques led in the direction of an extensive borrowing of mathematical formulas by economists to facilitate the development of economics as a logical deductive science (as had already been the successful practice of natural scientists) capable of yielding empirically testable conclusions. Ragnar Frisch's formulation of mathematical laws of economic behaviour (1929) is, in retrospect, a bridge between the second and third stages of the development of measurement and quantification techniques in economics. It stands apart from earlier works on cycles, less for being based on statistical data than for envisioning the possibility of establishing economics as a predictive science. It thus anticipates the subsequent marriage of regression analysis and general equilibrium theory as the essential building blocks for the present stage of econometric model building and mathematical formalism.

STAGE THREE: ECONOMICS EMERGES AS A PREDICTIVE SCIENCE

From mathematical expectations to rational expectations

With the development and refinement of the statistical/mathematical method the potential emerged for joining them with general equilibrium theory to generate econometrics, in a sense, as a "super" tool. The four most important mathematical ideas on which econometricians rely are regression analysis (i.e. the method of least squares), probability distributions, simultaneous equations and matrix algebra. These have long been well established and widely used techniques; equally, the collection of data useful for students of the moral sciences has been pursued in an organized fashion since the development of Section F. Yet, as S. Ambirajan explains in his chapter "The delayed emergence of econometrics as a separate discipline", given that the requisite mathematical and statistical tools were at hand well before the middle of the nineteenth century, the late development of econometrics is more than a little surprising. Ambirajan hypothesizes that economists have been deterred in the use of statistical analysis by their concern that, unlike errors in logic, statistical errors are difficult to discover. More particularly, economists have been inhibited by their concern that the best they might generate with their statistics is a static picture of reality. They also feared that their quantitative findings might be put to nefarious uses by the state. This is essentially the same reservation that Adam Smith had about political arithmetic. Given the magnitude of these impediments, it is indeed a puzzle to Ambirajan that, by the 1950s, econometrics had become "nearly cotermi-nous with the entire field of economics".

The puzzle is compounded by the intellectual power of "high theory" during the post-Marshallian era. This theme is pursued more fully in Ingrid H. Rima's chapter "Some conundrums about the place of econometrics in economic analysis". Her inquiry proceeds by recalling the theoretical "anomalies" or "puzzles" in which economists were interested before the era which George Shackle dubbed the years of "high theory". The urgent theoretical puzzles that became apparent in the 1920s were (1) the incompati-bility between increasing returns and industry-wide equilibrium under pure competition, (2) the questionable reliability of flexible prices for achieving market equilibria, (3) the distinction between flow magnitudes *ex ante* and their values *ex post* and the related puzzle (4) of incompatibility between imperfect knowledge and successful prediction. The innovative theoretical breakthroughs made during the high theory era undertook, each in their own way, to address the impediments to equilibrium market outcomes, the problem of prediction and the phenomenon of time. The question why these innovative breakthroughs failed to bring about a "scientific revolution" (to use Kuhn's terminology) or (in Lakatosian terms) a theoretically progressive SRP is one whose answer Rima locates in the dominance which econometric techniques came to exert.

J.R. Hick's general equilibrium IS–LM representation of an economy predisposed toward optimizing outcomes is seen as a first step in the direction of establishing econometrics as the sister-discipline of economics. More important, however, was Tinbergen's (1939) statistical verification of alter-native business cycle theories for that work pioneered the application of the method of least squares and regression analysis. This method subsequently became the hallmark of the Cowles Commission approach, encouraging the perception that economics had successfully become a predictive science in a sense which is fundamentally different from Keynes's concept of mathemat-ical expectation.

The notion of mathematical expectation is another among the innovative concepts of the high theory era. It is embedded in the understanding which the Cambridge School had about the economy's macroeconomic behavior even though Keynes had reached the conclusion in his *Treatise* (1921) that expectations are relatively unimportant and that the cause of the cycle lies in the difference between natural and market rates of interest. Nonetheless, Bradley W. Bateman argues that Keynes should be credited with introducing an analytical model of expectations into economics. Keynes's intellectual encounters with Frank Ramsey convinced him to discard his earlier belief that probability has meaning only in an objective sense (1921). In Bateman's chapter "The right person, in the right place, at the right time: how mathematical expectations came into *macroeconomics*", Keynes emerges as one of the founders of the modern theory of subjective probability. Bateman maintains that by the 1930s Keynes had adopted a conception of probability that explicitly allowed for measurement. Prompted by the severely depressed business expectations of the period, he was led to think in terms of representing expectations mathematically when he conceived the major functions of the *General Theory*. Because he conceived of business expectations as being governed by the "state of confidence", Keynes was concerned with using his new model to show how fiscal and monetary policy could avoid "mistaken expectations" and economic instability. This is very different from the subsequent reinterpretation of the concept of mathematical expectation as rational expectations by the so-called New Classical theorists.

Sherryl Kasper's chapter "The New Classical macroeconomics: a case study in the evolution of economic analysis" undertakes the task of showing how the concept of mathematical expectation became the basis, in the hands of a generation of economists trained in probability theory, for recasting economic theory as a "physical analogue" or "robot imitation" of the actual economy. For Robert Lucas and others trained to think of economics as a science of choice to be studied in a general equilibrium framework "purely technical developments" in the use of equilibrium modeling techniques have been essential ingredients in the "progress" which economics has made as a scientific discipline. Mathematical models are needed for economists to "get behind terms like *theory* or *equilibrium* or *unemployment* ..." (Lucas 1981: 17). Lucas credits Samuelson with advancing "the main ingredient for a mathematically explicit theory of general equilibrium as ... an artificial system in which households and firms jointly solve explicit, static maximizing problems, taking price as parametrically given" (Lucas 1980: 277–8). Equilibrium is predicated on a wage–price sector model (attributable to Lucas and Rapping) in which the optimizing agents are wage earners who are able to discern and use the distribution of wage offers implied by market equilibrium as a basis for their subjective expectations about employment probabilities. Expectations are endogenous variables in a model which envisions the convergence of employment to a "natural rate" at which there is a tradeoff between employment and inflation.

The policy inference is that models are essentially useless for evaluating the effect of prospective changes in policy, for the "rational expectations" of the public will always enable them to correctly anticipate likely policy changes and respond with maximizing behavioral changes of their own. Thus, the utility maximizing premise on which economic models have been predicated since Bentham and Mill has been carried over as an integral component of the way in which measurement and quantification tools are now being used.

The "New Classical" paradigm has modernized the traditional utility maximizing principle by reinterpreting it in terms which focus on the actor's knowledge of the world. All phenomena are perceived and all questions are posed in terms of what actors "know" or "believe" as a basis for their expectations about external developments and the likely consequences of their own actions (Machlup 1946: 40). The task of the economist is thus to decipher the meaning, in terms of market outcomes, of the choices individuals make as they adopt their behaviors to changes in their perceptions of the market in which they operate.

Measurement and other aspects of choice

The relatively new field of "experimental economics" purports to offer an improved way for studying how individuals choose under varying conditions. The prospects for gaining new insight by setting up carefully designed experiments are examined by Shaun Hargreaves Heap and Yanis Varoufakis in their chapter "Experimentation with neoclassical economics: a critical review of experimental economics". They are generally excited about the prospects for experimental economics, but are cognizant of serious limitations which derive, in part, from the typical reliance of such studies on university students who have been taught in economics classes to think along lines that are consistent with the predictions of neoclassical theory. The sometimes unavoidable practice of paying participants also raises the possibility of attracting persons who are more likely to behave in accordance with the predictions of instrumental motivation.

Though Hargreaves Heap and Varoufakis in no way dispute the usefulness of empirical testing, it is their view that experimental evidence strongly establishes that actions reflect the "context" of particular decisions which expected utility theory regards as extraneous information. The evidence of course requires careful interpretation for if "context" matters in this way, then there must be doubt about the applicability of experimental findings to settings outside the laboratory.

There are other grounds for questioning the appropriateness of utility theory as a foundation for constructing economic models. Murray Wolfson's chapter "The Carnot engine and the working day" draws on field theory for perspective, for utility theory has essentially the same structure as do the field theories in physics. More specifically, utility theory envisions the attraction of individuals to higher levels of satisfaction in a commodity space in essentially the same way as gravity attracts objects in three-dimensional space. As is the case with field theory, utility theory serves well for certain problems and has serious limitations for others. Wolfson notes numerous examples of economic processes to which the comparative utility maximizing paradigm is relevant; for example, the acquisition of information and investment in human capital are processes in which an individual can be envisioned as reaching a state of process completion (i.e. utility is maximized). However, the notion that an individual *ever* achieves a state of rest with respect to his/her labor supply is inappropriate. Wolfson argues that, during the course of the daily cycle of work and rest, the worker contracts to spend part of the working day providing labor services and the remainder in consumption and rest in order to be able to work again the following day. Analogously, the capitalist directs his property for use in the production of goods from whose value the capital stock must be replenished. These examples lead us away from the traditional conception of the labor market as a pure exchange of labor for leisure, or of the capital market as a pure exchange of future income for present consumption. At best, the equilibrium model of utility is a special case of a broader dynamic theory. The further the examples and problems that interest us depart from static equilibrium, the greater are the limitations of the utility model.

Another conceptual problem that is inherent in the utility maximization model and which continues to bedevil contemporary theorists is the inevitable interdependence which exists among individual maximizers. Even Pareto, who along with the Austrians is the source of contemporary perceptions of economics as a science of choice which identifies individual optimization in a straightforward way with equality between marginal rates of substitution and the price ratios of goods, recognized that this relatively simplistic approach presents problems. As Vincent Tarascio points out in his chapter "The problem of interpersonal interaction: Pareto's approach", the issues involved in measuring utility and making interpersonal comparisons were not circumvented by the construction of the indifference curve, because it is the underlying model of man which is the untenable component of utility theory. This led Pareto toward sociological analysis as the inspiration for an alternative model capable of taking interactions among persons and the interdependence of their individual welfares into account.

Elaborating his own earlier work, Tarascio (1969, 1978) demonstrates that individual and societal maxima do not necessarily coincide. The problem of how to arrive at a political welfare function which can, at least in principle, serve as a basis for public policy confronts the same problem of measuring and aggregating utilities as were confronted by proponents of a hedonic calculus.

Prediction and model testing

Most contemporary economists have adopted the natural science model as their inspiration for discovering lawlike generalizations for predicting behavior. This is a quest which raises the possibility of inconsistencies between observed behavior and the outcomes inherent in the assumptions of economic choice theory. It also raises the question whether probability theory, which is now an integral part of choice theory, offers a vehicle for economic prediction and whether the concern of model testing ought to extend to falsification rather than simple confirmation. John Davis's chapter "Is emotive theory the philosopher's stone of the ordinalist revolution?" rejects choice theory altogether as an acceptable basis for explaining human behavior and maintains that humans do not, in fact, behave in certain and thus predictable ways. Davis's contention is fundamental to the currently controversial matter of model testing.

"Sign testing" and "coefficient evaluation" techniques are concerned simply with "goodness of fit". The conventional textbook method (following Koopmans) is to impose *a priori* restrictions as the econometric analogue of theoretical arguments. The problem with *apriorism* as a research strategy is that it does not necessarily lead either to a progressive development of models or knowledge. While this is the conventional method of model testing, it does not facilitate what might be termed a "severe test".

Economists may be failing to severely test their theories because the discipline is more concerned with doing "normal science" (in the Kuhnian sense) than with questioning hard core assumptions (in the sense of Lakatos), for the latter threatens an existing paradigm or research program. This is the critical point of Robert Goldfarb's chapter "If empirical work in economics is not severe testing, what is it?" He analyzes the empirical research literature of two important areas of applied macroeconomics with a view to evaluating whether severe testing is an objective. Empirical research in the labor area is interpreted as concerned chiefly with conventional "sign testing" and is not concerned with testing the underlying model of labor supply. By way of contrast Goldfarb also examines empirical work in the field of industrial organization which *does* have a serious theory-testing component. This characteristic is an important departure for empiricism in economics, which has generally not been concerned to test theories according to standards that are capable of producing falsificationist outcomes.

Nevertheless, economic theories *do* become discarded; the field of macroeconomics offers powerful examples. But these are in no sense the consequence of empirical falsification in an econometric sense. As John Smithin points out in his chapter "Econometrics and the 'facts of experience'", it has been *fact* in the sense of experience rather than empirical falsification that has demonstrable power to undermine widely accepted economic theories. The widespread and unrelenting experience of involuntary unemployment during the late 1920s and 1930s enabled Keynes's *General Theory* to successfully displace the classical school. Similarly, the credibility of the Walrasian synthesis, which followed after the so-called Keynesian revolution, was effectively undermined by the phenomenon of "stagflation" and not by failure to confirm the theory empirically. The experience of double-digit unemployment coupled with inflation facilitated the success of monetarism as an alternative paradigm capable of explaining both the inflation–unemployment "tradeoff" of the 1960s and 1970s and the depression of the 1930s. Monetarism directed the blame for these "facts of experience" at misguided central bank policy and offered "New Classical theory" and its accompanying policy irrelevance proposition with great success as a refined version of the neoclassical synthesis that displaced Keynes's *General Theory.*

Yet, the theoretical viability of the micro-foundations of the rational expectations model remains a central problem, especially as regards its premise that individuals can assess probabilities in terms of the expected outcomes of the choices they confront. This is a perspective which Donald W. Katzner categorically rejects on the ground that it derives from a model that is anchored in *logical* time, while the problem at issue involves *historical* time. His chapter "Simultaneous economic behavior under conditions of ignorance and historical time" argues that, because time only proceeds forward, standard statistical methods which rely on repeated sampling from a probability distribution must be discarded. The best that an individual can be conceived as doing is *imagining* future outcomes. This is a perspective which Katzner encapsulates in a model of a two-person, two-commodity exchange economy in which choice options and their imagined outcomes are unique to the decision-maker and the moment of time in which his decision is made.

Randall Bausor takes an alternative approach to Katzner's for reexamining the implication of the distinction between logical and historical time by comparing the general competitive analysis of economics with classical thermodynamics. He starts with the observation that the theories of dynamic stability which Liapunov developed between 1881 and 1892 offer an approach which frees static equilibria from their initial condition so that equilibria emerge by attracting non-equilibria states. As he expresses it in his chapter "Liapunov techniques in economic dynamics and classical thermodynamics: a comparison", Liapunov's method concentrates on the attractor at journey's end, instead of mapping the journey. This is analogous to the concern which competitive general equilibrium analysis has about the characteristics of equilibrium rather than the process of getting into equilibrium. Thus, the critical distinction between the past and the present is absent from general equilibrium models so that the distinction between logical and historical time is also obliterated. General equilibrium thus has essentially the same limitation as is associated with model solution by least squares regression techniques.

Is mathematics simply more convenient?

Nancy J. Wulwick's chapter "The Hamiltonian formalism and optimal growth theory" approaches the very complex and controversial issues raised by new growth theory on several levels. The most basic of these relates to the premise is that the sharing of mathematical techniques among the sciences is appropriate so long as rational analogies exist between economics and the science on which it is drawing, and that the suitability of the transfer can be tested empirically. In particular, the chapter focuses on the adoption by New Classical economists and their neo-Walrasian predecessors of the Hamiltonian dynamic system, which originated during the development of nineteenth-century energy physics, to elaborate the theory of optimal growth. What one is intended to learn from the New Classical growth model is the answer to the question "What sort of economic structure generates growth as we know it?" The preferred answer is that an intertemporal Arrow–Debreu model with increasing returns encapsulates the necessary properties to supply the answer. This "New Classical" model envisions economic growth in a framework that assumes a competitive economy in continuous equilibrium that is marching along a predetermined path.

It is Wulwick's contention that this is a framework that is inconsistent with a conception of growth as a developmental, time-dependent process. She also maintains that the Hamiltonian formulation of the New Classical growth models is internally inconsistent. The New Classical economists specify production functions that yield increasing returns to knowledge. Advances in the state of knowledge, which takes time, are irreversible. Yet the Hamiltonian dynamical system produces an optimal path that is time-independent and reversible. Thus Wulwick argues that the New Classical growth theorists provide little insight into the real growth process and that growth is far less determinate than their mathematics would suggest. This is a conclusion which substantially echoes those which were offered by Bausor, Katzner and Rima in other contexts which relied on mathematics considerably less sophisticated than the mathematics employed by the new growth theory.

It seems clear that new growth theory models are using mathematics as a problem solving technique so that it is not simply the more precise mode of communication that Samuelson envisioned. If mathematical theorems are indeed to serve as a basis for economic interpretation, there are philosophical as well as practical issues at stake. M. H. I. Dore's paper "The impact of John von Neumann's method" makes the fundamental point that, while mathematical theorems are without empirical content, it is nevertheless the objective of inductive mathematics to establish empirical content. There are, Dore argues, three requisites that must be met if mathematical theorems are to serve successfully as a basis for economic interpretation. First, any given interpretation must be consistent; that is, it must not lend itself to contradictory interpretations. Second, a one-to-one correspondence must exist between the theorem and its application. Third, an implicit solution to a fixed point theorem that is embedded in a family of problems can be avoided by means of a constructionist approach.

Dore evaluates von Neumann's growth model on the basis of these strictures. He notes that the model was built on the mathematics of convex structures and von Neumann's own minimax game theory theorem. Their use led to a bilinearity of output and prices which was rejected by Sraffa. von Neumann's linear methods are also found to be unstable, which makes them suitable only for representing "snapshots" of the economy. This leads Dore to suggest the use of nonlinear methods. But these require even more complex mathematical structures which poses the risk of a further widening of the distance between mathematical theorems and their economic interpretation. This is a danger which Dore argues can be minimized by using finitary methods and a constructionist approach.

The long view of history

The conventional wisdom among contemporary economists is that the mathematization and quantification of their discipline – for better or for worse – is their own unique achievement, dating back approximately to Samuelson's *Foundations of Economic Analysis* (1947) and Tinbergen's *Statistical Testing of Business Cycle Theories* (1939). While it is beyond question that mathematical and econometric techniques have virtually become the *sine qua non* of economic research and discourse, it is equally the case that their intellectual forbears have always relied on measurement and quantification as essential observational tools and on graphs, numbers and symbols as modes of representation. Measurement has dominated the natural sciences, at least since the scientific revolution of the seventeenth century when its success promoted encouragement to those in other fields to borrow or adapt its tools.

Even though economics was styling itself in the tradition of the natural sciences by mid-nineteenth century, the deductive method remained at least as powerful in economics as is the method of induction. No single spokesperson for the power of the deductive method put this matter into clearer perspective or practice than J. S. Mill, who maintained that economics is inherently an *inexact* science capable of generating laws that are only interpretable as *tendencies* that are "insufficient for prediction", though they can be "valuable for guidance" (1843: VI. 9, p. 3). Mill's deductive method is unique in the adroitness with which inductive evidence is shown to be the critical first step of scientific reasoning. A law is first established by induction; the circumstances under which it applies is then established by deduction.[9] Finally, the deductive results must be verified to provide confirmation of the inductively established laws on which they are based. The role of verification is not to test basic laws; these are already established and are not nullified by disturbances and interferences that might have been omitted from consideration. Mill's method thus renders untenable the demand put forward by many contemporary practitioners for the kind of empirical testing which has become known as "falsificationism". This is a methodological issue which has become the stuff of intense methodological controversy (Blaug, Caldwell, Hausman). It is of concern here chiefly within our admittedly narrow question whether and to what degree progress in economics is critically dependent on the power of measurement and quantification tools.

It is Kuhn's (1970) argument that progress in the natural sciences has taken place in consequence of paradigm destruction in response to inexplicable anomalies which call forth a new paradigm. This interpretation compromises the power of empiricism even in the realm of the natural sciences to which it has always been regarded as uniquely applicable. What then can empiricism contribute to economics, given the differing beliefs and expectations of individual agents about their world? Are its empirical tests not inherently indecisive and limited by the ever present *ceterus paribus* condition? If so, we are led in the direction of a social science perspective which, unlike that of the natural sciences, seeks understanding (in the comprehensive sense that is conveyed by the *Verstehen* of the German Historical School) to investigate how human expectations and beliefs generate empirically observable outcomes.

Because these outcomes will necessarily relate to commodities and prices which lend themselves naturally to quantification, it is both efficient and precise to represent them as points in the price and commodity space. But it is important to recognize that these cannot properly become the departure point for timeless models of causal regularity which draw their inspiration from the natural science models whose mathematical formulas they borrow. This suggests that a still closer interpenetration of the natural sciences into economics is less promising for progress in acquiring economic knowledge than is a greater affinity with the other social sciences.[10] It also behooves economists to recognize that mathematics becomes more than a universal metalanguage when it is borrowed without careful acknowledgement of the context from which it is drawn. It also implies that the prerequisite for progress in empirical economics is a new creativity to develop non-probabilistic predictions and models that are relevant to specific historical time periods. This kind of approach to induction would harken back to Mill's view of economics as an inexact science, and have something in common with the kind of empiricism envisioned by the German historicists and the American institutionalists.[11]

NOTES

1 See, for example, R. Musgrave, *The Theory of Public Finance* p. 66, which references *The Economic Writings of Sir William Petty*, ed. C.H. Hall, (London: Cambridge University Press, 1899). Donald Katzner offers historical perspective

about the obsession "We Moderns" have "to measure everything". See "Our mad rush to measure: how did we get into this mess?", *Methodus* 3(2) (1991), 18–26.

2　The most recent among these is Margaret Schabas's *A World Ruled by Numbers: William Stanley Jevons and the Rise of Mathematical Economics* (Princeton, NJ: Princeton University Press, 1990). As is also the case with the works of Morgan (1990) and Epstein (1987), Schabas's study of the rise of mathematical economics reflects the important new trend towards interdisciplinary research among historians of economics and historians of science. This sets them apart from works which are more specifically focused on individual contributors to the rise of mathematical economics. See for example John Creedy "Edgeworth and the development of neoclassical economics", Fritz Machlup's review of the Cournot–Bertrand–Edgeworth solutions to the duopoly problem in *The Economics of Sellers' Competition* (Baltimore, MD: Johns Hopkins University Press, 1952) and George Stigler's assessment of Jules Dupuit's contribution to marginal cost pricing in "Development of utility theory", *Journal of Political Economy* 18 (1950).

3　The charge of myopia is equally applicable to the rise of statistics. In *The Rise of Statistical Thinking 1820–1900* (1986), Theodore M. Porter traces the German origin of the term "statistics" and attributes its first use to Professor Gottfried Achenwall at the University of Gottingen *c.* 1749, noting also that its anglicized form was introduced by Jon Sinclair in the *Statistical Account of Scotland*. In both cases it was used in the context of the collection of numerical information. Unlike political arithmetic, statistics was not undertaken with policy objectives in mind (pp. 23–8).

4　The derivation of hypothesis testing techniques from nineteenth-century mathematical statistics is epistemologically important but beyond our scope. But see Stephen M. Stigler, *The History of Statistics* (1986).

5　Henry K. H. Woo's critique "What's wrong with formalization in economics?" also conceives of the growth of scientific knowledge as emerging in "cycles" (pp. 57–60). His chief concern is to appraise the "equilibrium archetype" and the significance of formalization in economics. Our complementary concern is the development of measurement and quantification tools in tandem with theoretical analysis with a view to exploring whether tool "borrowing" or creation was driven by the problem needs of the discipline or whether, and if so, as Woo argues is the case, why the availability of quantification and measurement tools has come to drive the discipline.

6　It was the French statisticians of this period, however, in particular Adolph Quetelet, who pioneered statistical techniques. Although France did not yet have a statistical society, Quetelet was present at the founding of Section F of the British Association for the Advancement of Science (Porter 1986: 33).

7　As a practical matter, economists eventually reconciled themselves to following Marshall in using units of money as a proxy for units of utility, even though this simplification required them to neglect "the fact that the same sum of money represents different amounts of pleasure to different people" (1890: 128). This is the origin of the convention of defining and, in effect, limiting the scope of economic problems to those in which measurement can proceed in terms of money. Marshall's technique of proxying utility by money and the necessity of ignoring the fact that the marginal utility of income differs among individuals (and sometimes for the same individual: cf. Nicholson 1894: 344) was thus carried over from the nineteenth century into contemporary economics.

8　See, for example, the papers by Katzner, Bausor and Rima listed below and their appended references which direct the reader to other writings relating to time in economics.

9   It is worth noting that Jevons's estimate of the fall in the value of gold as being between 9 and 15 percent is consistent with the estimates made by Cairnes via the more traditional deductive method.
10   This observation may relate equally well to the history of science and the history of economics (cf. Shabas 1992).
11   Three approaches that offer promise for understanding situations in which ignorance and historical time are present have been suggested in Katzner (1992). The first is to collect and summarize historical data from which one may conceivably "estimate" the parameters of equations in the context of historical time. A second is to adopt a non-distributional approach to estimating and undertake non-probabilistic predictions on the basis of historical data. A possible third approach is non-statistical falsification which undertakes empirical corroboration of theoretical models on the basis of data from specific historical time periods.

REFERENCES

Blaug, M. (1980) *The Methodology of Economics: Or How Economists Explain*, Cambridge: Cambridge University Press.

Cairnes, J.E. (1875) *The Character and Logical Method of Political Economy*; 2nd edn, reprinted New York: Kelley, 1965.

Caldwell, B. (1982) *Beyond Positivism: Economic Methodology in the Twentieth Century*, London: Allen & Unwin.

Creedy, John (1986) *Edgeworth and the Development of Neoclassical Economics*, Oxford: Blackwells.

Epstein, R.J. (1987) *A History of Econometrics*, Amsterdam: North-Holland.

Frisch, R. (1929) "Correlation and scatter in statistical variables", *Nordic Statistical Journal* 8: 36–102.

Galileo, G. (1628) *Discourses and Mathematical Demonstrations Concerning Two Sciences*, Northwestern University Press, 1946.

Gigerenzer, Gerd *The Empire of Change*, Cambridge: Cambridge University Press.

Hacking, Ian (1975) *The Emergence of Probability*, New York: Cambridge University Press.

Hausman, D.M. (1992) *Essays on Philosophy and Economic Methodology*, Cambridge: Cambridge University Press.

Hicks, John R. (1979) *Causality in Economics*, New York: Basic Books.

Hutchison, T. (1938) *The Significance and Basic Postulates of Economic Theory*, reprinted with new preface, New York: Kelley, 1960.

Jevons, W.S. (1888) *The Theory of Political Economy*, reprinted New York, Kelley, 1965.

Katzner, Donald (1992) "The role of empirical analysis in the investigation of situations involving ignorance and historical time", *Eastern Economic Journal* 17(4), 297–302.

Keynes, J.M. (1921) *A Treatise on Probability*, London: Macmillan.

Keynes, J.N. (1891) *The Scope and Method of Political Economics*, reprinted New York: Kelley, 1965.

Kuhn, T.S. (1970) *The Structure of Scientific Revolutions*, 7th edn, Chicago, IL: University of Chicago Press.

Lakatos, I. (1978) *The Methodology of Scientific Research Programmes*, ed. J. Worral and G. Currie, Cambridge: Cambridge University Press.

Lester, R. (1946) "Shortcomings of marginal analysis for wage–employment problems", *American Economic Review* 36: 62–82.

Lucas, Robert E., Jr (1980) "Methods and problems in business cycle theory", in *Studies in Business Cycle Theory*, Cambridge, MA: MIT Press, pp. 271–96.

——— (1981) "Introduction", in *Studies in Business Cycle Theory*, Cambridge, MA: MIT Press, pp. 1–18.

Machlup, F. (1946) "Marginal analysis and empirical research", *American Economic Review* 36: 519–54.

Mill, J.S. (1836) "On the definition of political economy and the method of investigation proper to it", in *Collected Works of J. S. Mill*, vol. 4, ed. J. Robson, Toronto: University of Toronto Press, 1967.

——— (1843) *A System of Logic*, London: Longmans, Green, 1949.

Mirowski, P. (1990) *More Heat Than Light*, Cambridge: Cambridge University Press.

Moore, H.L. (1908) "The statistical complement of pure economics", *Quarterly Journal of Economics* 23: 1–33.

Morgan, M. (1990) *The History of Econometric Ideas*, Cambridge: Cambridge University Press.

Petty, W. (1690) "Political arithmetic", *The Economic Writings of Sir William Petty*, vol. 1, ed. C. H. Hull, Cambridge: Cambridge University Press, 1899, pp. 233–313.

Porter, T.M. (1986) *The Rise of Statistical Thinking 1820–1900*, Princeton, NJ: Princeton University Press.

Robbins, L. (1932) *An Essay on the Nature and Significance of Economic Science*, London: Macmillan.

Robertson, D. (1951) "Utility and all that", *Manchester School* May: 439–42.

Robinson, J. (1974) *History vs. Equilibrium*, London: Thames Polytechnic.

Samuelson, Paul (1947) *Foundations of Economic Analysis*, Cambridge, MA: Harvard University Press.

Senior, N.W. (1860) "Opening Address as President of Section F" *Journal of the Royal Statistical Society* 23: 359.

Shabas, Margaret (1990) *A World Ruled by Numbers*, Princeton, NJ: Princeton University Press.

——— (1992) "Breaking away: history of economics as history of science", *History of Political Economy* 24(1): 187–203.

Smith, A. (1776) *An Inquiry Into the Nature and Causes of the Wealth of Nations*, New York: Modern Library, 2 vols.

Stigler, S.M. (1986) *The History of Statistics: The Measurement of Uncertainty Before 1900*, Cambridge, MA: Harvard University Press, and London: Belknap Press.

Tarascio, Vincent J. (1969) "Paretian welfare theory: some neglected aspects", *Journal of Political Economy* 77 (January–February): 1–20.

——— (1978) "Theories of justice, social action, and the state", *Eastern Economic Journal* 4 (January) 41–9.

Tinbergen, J. (1939) *Statistical Testing of Business Cycle Theories*, Geneva.

Vickers, D. (1994) *Economics and the Antagonism of Time*, Ann Arbor, MI: University of Michigan Press.

Vining, R. (1949) "Koopmans on the choice of variables to be studied and of methods of measurement", *Review of Economic Statistics* 31(2): 77–86. Reply by Koopmans, pp. 86–91. Rejoinder by Vining, pp. 91–4.

Whewell, W. (1847) *The Philosophy of the Inductive Sciences*, London, 2 vols.

Woo, H.K.H. (1986) *What's Wrong With Formalization in Economics?*, Newark: California Victoria Press.

"I have no great faith in political arithmetick"

Adam Smith and quantitative political economy

Robert W. Dimand

Adam Smith's *Wealth of Nations* shaped classical political economy into a discipline very different from political arithmetic, the primitive quantitative economics of the preceding century. Smith was deeply concerned with the empirical relevance of his political economy, confronting predictions with observation (see West 1990, Chapter 2 on testable propositions from Smith). He engaged in extensive historical and empirical explorations, such as his discussion of the herring bounty or the pioneering sketch of the economic history of Western Europe that constitutes Book III of the *Wealth of Nations*. This interest in evidence did not, however, lead him to approve of the elaborate quantitative reasoning of political arithmeticians from Sir William Petty, John Graunt and Gregory King in the late seventeenth century to Smith's younger contemporaries George Chalmers, Sir John Sinclair and Arthur Young. Smith regarded the products of this tradition with a skepticism equal to that which J.M. Keynes and Milton Friedman displayed toward Jan Tinbergen's macroeconometric modeling. Smith's choice of topics had as large a role in shaping classical political economy as his critical comments on other approaches. Just as the decline in attention to modeling the circular flow of income and spending owed something to Smith's decision to devote but a single sentence to the Tableau Economique in his chapter on the Physiocrats, so classical inattention to political arithmetic reflected Smith's selective silences. Arthur Young's *Political Arithmetic* (1774, 1779) is largely forgotten as part of the context of the *Wealth of Nations* (1776).

Smith's remarks on the subject in the *Wealth of Nations* were brief and dismissive. In his "Digression on the corn trade" (1776: IV. v. b, pp. 534–55), after citing estimates from Charles Smith's *Three Tracts on the Corn Trade and Corn Laws* (2nd edn, 1766), he warned that "I have no great faith in political arithmetick, and I mean not to warrant the exactness of either of these computations. I mention them only in order to show of how much less consequence, in the opinion of the most judicious and experienced persons, the foreign trade of corn is than the home trade." The opening phrase of this passage is echoed in Smith's letter of November 10, 1785 (1987: Letter 249, p. 288), to the political arithmetician George Chalmers: "You know that I have little faith in Political Arithmetic and this story [Alexander Webster's varying estimate of the Scottish population] does not contribute to mend my opinion of it." Smith informed Chalmers that he considered "The late reverend Mr. Webster, of all the men I have ever known, the most skillful in Political Arithmetic" and that Webster's "Account of the Number of People in Scotland in the year 1755", compiled for a pension scheme to assist widows and children of ministers, "seemed a very accurate account". The seemingly accurate account estimated the Scottish population at 1,250,000, yet Webster later told Smith that 1,500,000 was a more likely figure.

The only other direct mention of political arithmetic in the *Wealth of Nations* (1776: I. viii, p. 95) is to an estimate of the income of laborers and out-servants in 1688 by "Mr Gregory King, whose skill in political arithmetick is so extolled by Doctor Davenant". Smith (1776: I.xi. g, p. 215) also noted that "In 1688, Mr. Gregory King, a man famous for his knowledge in matters of this kind, estimated the average price of wheat in years of moderate plenty to be to the grower 3s. 6d. the bushel, or eight-and-twenty shillings the quarter." Despite this praise of King (attributed to Davenant on the first reference, without indication that Smith was of the same opinion), Smith used King's work only as a source of two numerical estimates, without discussion of King's method. The names of Petty, Graunt and Young are absent from the *Wealth of Nations*.

Smith made extensive use of Bishop William Fleetwood's *Chronicon Preciosum* (1707, 1745) as a source of raw price data for his "Digression on variations in the value of silver" (Smith 1776: I. xi, pp. 195–275) but he did not identify Fleetwood's work with political arithmetic and he made no use of Fleetwood's pathbreaking idea of a price index. From Fleetwood (1707: 74–124), Smith (1776: 267–75) quoted wheat prices for eighty years from 1202 to 1597, converted (with a few errors) to coin of Smith's time, and took wheat prices from the Eton College accounts for 1595 to 1764 from Charles Smith (1766). As Lawrence Klein (1992: 16) observes, Smith did not notice that the Eton College figures referred to a Windsor quarter of nine bushels, rather than a standard quarter of eight bushels, and to the best or highest price wheat. Smith (1776: 201) criticized Fleetwood without justification for supposedly mistaking conversion prices (used for settlement between land-lord and tenant) for actual market prices, but made no other comment on Fleetwood's approach and achievement. He took from Fleetwood what he wanted, the raw price data, and left the price index unremarked. Similarly he took an estimate of average wheat price in a year of moderate plenty from Gregory King, but ignored King's account of the English income distribution in 1696 and the now-famous "Gregory King's law" of how wheat prices vary as the crop varies, in effect tracing the demand curve.

Smith's reticence about political arithmetic did not stem from lack of acquaintance with the literature or practitioners of the subject. Alexander Webster's work was well known to him: in 1785, he wrote to Chalmers that

"About ten years ago I had the use of this account for many months" (Letter 249). Arthur Young is not mentioned in the *Wealth of Nations*, but the first volume of Young's *Political Arithmetic*, published in 1774, attracted considerable attention. It won Young election as a Fellow of the Royal Society (as Smith was), and to the Palatine Academy of Agriculture at Mannheim and the Royal Academy of Agriculture at Florence (Kaplow 1969: ix). "A Catalogue of books belonging to Adam Smith, Esqr. 1781" (in Yanaihara 1951) lists twelve volumes by Arthur Young in Smith's library: *Political Arithmetic*, two volumes of *The Farmer's Letters to the People of England* (1767), *Six Weeks Tour through the Southern Counties of England & Wales* (1768), four volumes of *A Six Months Tour through the North of England* (1770) and four volumes of *The Farmer's Tour through the East of England* (1771). Eleven volumes of Young's works (but not *Political Arithmetic*) shared the first shelf of the left-hand bookcase of the fourth division of Smith's library with the five volumes of Charles D'Avenant's *Political and Commercial Works* (1771 edition), the source of Smith's knowledge of Gregory King.

The Nonconformist minister Dr Richard Price is best remembered as the literary executor who published Thomas Bayes's papers on probability and as the target of Edmund Burke's denunciation of English defenders of the French Revolution. He was also a political arithmetician, unmentioned in the *Wealth of Nations* but derided in a letter from Smith to George Chalmers on December 22, 1785: "Price[']s speculations cannot fail to sink into the neglect that they always deserved. I have always considered him as a factious citizen, a most superficial Philosopher and by no means an able calculator." Smith's skepticism about Price's quantitative conclusions was justified: Price's assertion in 1772 that "our people have, since the year 1690, decreased near *a million and a half*" (Glass 1978: 55, Price's emphasis) is now universally rejected in favour of belief in a growing population in eighteenth-century England. Despite his dismissal of Price, Smith owned five books by Price: *Review of the Principle Questions in Morals* (1758), *National Debt* (1772), *Civil Liberty* (1778), *Reversionary Payments* (1783) and *American Revolution* (1785) (Smith 1987: Letter 251, p. 290 and note). The 1781 catalogue of Smith's library noted "Price on Annuities" shelved two volumes away from Fleetwood's *Chronicon Preciosum*.

Smith's ownership of so many books by Chalmers, D'Avenant, Price and Young indicates acquaintance with their work. Smith also owned a collection of the London bills of mortality, the raw material of Graunt's and Petty's demographic studies, and many mathematical tomes, shelved with Price and Fleetwood: works by Laurin, by Newton and by Simpson on fluxions (calculus), Laurin, Sanderson, Simpson and Trail on algebra, Robin's Mathematical Tracts, Merville's *Lexicon de Mathematiques*, Wright's trigonometry, *Discorsi et Dimostrazioni Mathematiche*, Simpson's Euclid, Gregory on geometry and on arithmetic and algebra, and Malcolm on arithmetic. Simpson's *Nature and Laws of Chance*, Simpson's geometry, another edition of Euclid, Kersey on algebra, *Trigonometria Britannica* and *Arithmetica Logarithmica* were shelved elsewhere (Yanaihara 1951: 84–5, 88, 118, 120).

Sir William Petty, originator of the term political arithmetic, was absent from Smith's library as well as from the *Wealth of Nations*. Smith once referred admiringly to Petty, in a letter in 1759 to the Earl of Shelburne: "tho' you are not negligent either of the elegance or magnificence of your country Villas, you do not think that any attention of that kind dispenses with the more noble and important duty of attempting to introduce arts, industry and independency into a miserable country [Ireland], which has hitherto been a stranger to them all. Nothing, I have often imagined, would give more pleasure to Sir William Petty, your Lordship's ever honoured ancestor, than to see his representative pursuing a Plan so suitable to his own Ideas which are generally equally wise and public spirited" (1987: Letter 30, p. 32). Smith is not known to have expressed such an opinion of Petty to anyone other than the head of the noble Petty-Fitzmaurice family, but the letter indicates some knowledge of Petty by Smith.

Smith's failure to cite political arithmeticians such as Price in the *Wealth of Nations* was in line with his not mentioning Sir James Steuart's *Principles of Political Economy* (1767), a recent and prominent treatise with a much larger role for state intervention than Smith could approve. "Without once mentioning it," wrote Smith in 1772 (Letter 132), "I flatter myself, that every false principle in it, will meet with a clear and distinct confutation in mine." He would provide what he considered true principles, and not guide readers to expositions of falsehood. At least one of the writers ignored in the *Wealth of Nations* remained bitter against Smith, according to a young German, Theodor von Schon, who dined at Arthur Young's home in 1798, eight years after Smith's death.

> Mr Young ... spoke extremely against A. Smith, but could not bring any particular thing against him, but that he had written against the plough. I objected that the whole book was written only for the plough against the commercial system of England, and he must agree with me in it. He declared than that A. Smith would have been a bad farmer. I desired particular objections, and he declared himself against the land tax, praised by A. Smith.
>
> (Mingay 1975: 9–10)

Smith objected to the uncritical use of insufficiently supported numbers in political arithmetic. Such careless use of numbers was common. Gregory King's work has been characterized by D.V. Glass (1978: 14) as "peculiarly inexplicit both as regards the sources of the data used and the methods of estimation". Sir George Clark (1946: 192) prefaced King's table of social structure and income distribution by remarking that King's "tables of the population and economic resources of England and Wales in the late seventeenth century ... do not all inspire confidence; his estimates of a million rabbits and 24,000 hares and leverets must be guesses". George Chalmers, the recipient of Smith's declaration of lack of faith in political arithmetic, could be rashly overconfident about data for remote periods, writing of his population estimates for 1377 that "We can now build upon a rock; having before us proof almost equal in certainty to actual enumerations" (Glass 1978: 14).

Ekelund and Hébert (1990: 84) cite Pierre le Pesant de Boisguilbert for having "estimated that between 1665 and 1695 the national income of France declined by about 50 percent" due to oppressive taxation and regulation, yet recent scholarship summarized in D.C. Coleman's *New Palgrave* articles on Colbert and Colbertism concludes that Colbert's policies in the late seventeenth century provided an initial stimulus to economic growth, with growth continuing in the next century despite the taxes and restrictive rules. Ekelund and Hébert also follow Boisguilbert in stating that "The wine tax came to be so oppressive that French workers practically ceased drinking wine (the ultimate sacrifice for a Frenchman)." They do not compare Boisguilbert's numbers with the equally extreme, but opposite, figures of his contemporary, Marshal Sébastien de Vauban, which imply a wine harvest in 1690–1701 of "340 litres of wine per year for every man, woman and child in the kingdom of France" or Gregory King's assertion that the French spent nearly nine-tenths as much on wine as on cereals (see Emmanuel Le Roy Ladurie 1972 on "The Fantastical Accounts of Gregory King"). Such numbers represented wild guesses, not empirical knowledge.

William Kruskal has investigated Thomas Paine's estimate in 1770 and again in 1791 of an English and Welsh population of 7 million. Paine's probable source, John Chamberlayne in 1755, took an estimate by John Houghton in 1693 of the number of houses and multiplied by six persons per house. If Houghton based his estimate on hearth tax returns, Paine's estimates of 1770 and 1791 must relate to a year before 1689, while the yearly fluctuations of the hearth tax returns suggest an imperfect measure of the number of houses, and no support is offered for the figure of six persons per house (Glass 1978: 29). Arthur Young's careful criticism in his *Political Arithmetic* of the accuracy of the window tax returns, which led him to reject Price's claim of a small and shrinking population, and his advocacy of a public census received, however, no more mention from Smith than the looser quantitative speculations of Paine or Price, Boisguilbert or Vauban.

The unreliability of available descriptive statistics and the limited development of techniques for formal data analysis posed less of a problem for Adam Smith than for political economists such as Steuart who were more favorably disposed toward state regulation of the economy. Smith discharged the sovereign from the onerous duty of directing private economic activity, and so diminished his ideal sovereign's need for numerical data. If tariffs and bounties were not to be employed, one need not be concerned with how large they should be.

Smith had little success in discouraging the enthusiasm of some of his correspondents for political arithmetic. George Chalmers, recipient of Smith's Letters 249–52 (November 1785 to January 1786) with Smith's critical comments on Webster and Price, was chief clerk of the Privy Council committee on trade from 1786 until his death in 1825. Smith owned Chalmers's *Political Annals of the Present United Colonies, from their Settlement to the Peace of 1763* (1780; only the first volume, up to 1688, was ever published) and thanked Chalmers for his favorable notice of Smith's views on foreign trade in the 1786 edition of *An Estimate of the Comparative Strength of Great Britain during the Present and Four Preceding Reigns* (1st edition 1782), Chalmers's major work of political arithmetic. The 1802 fourth edition of *Comparative Strength of Britain* included as an appendix the first complete printing of Gregory King's *Natural and Political Observations*, a short life of King, and King's table of the population of Gloucester, all republished by Chalmers as a separate book in 1810 (Glass 1978: 28–9). Chalmers's publication of King's table of incomes of families inspired Patrick Colquhoun to update King's results and to prepare "elaborate and detailed estimates of national income and wealth of the United Kingdom" (Deane 1987).

John Sinclair, Bart. (from 1786), of Ulbster, president of the Board of Agriculture 1793–8 and 1806–14, received Smith's Letters 196, 221, 253, 258 and 299, a correspondence lasting at least from 1778 to 1786. It was Sinclair, lamenting the misfortunes of the American war to Smith and exclaiming "If we go on at this rate the nation *must be ruined*", who provoked Smith's famous remark "Be assured, my young friend, that there is a great deal of *ruin* in a nation" (Smith 1987: 262n.). Between 1791 and 1799, Sinclair published a *Statistical Account of Scotland* in twenty-one volumes, one for each county, followed in 1826 by two volumes of *Analysis of the Statistical Account of Scotland*. This enterprise, like the country agricultural reports on England prepared for the Board of Agriculture by Arthur Young and William Marshall, bore no resemblance to the *Wealth of Nations*. Instead, Sinclair's model was Alexander Webster, of whose work Smith was so skeptical. Like Webster, Sinclair wrote to the clergy of Scotland for vital statistics on their parishes, and he adopted Webster's population estimate for 1755. Sinclair's work was in turn the model for the *Statistical Account of Upper Canada* (1822) by Robert Gourlay, who had worked under Arthur Young for the Board of Agriculture (see Dimand 1992).

Since Chalmers and Sinclair chose to follow King and Webster rather than Smith's skepticism, and in turn influenced Colquhoun and Gourlay, it might appear that Smith's lack of faith in political arithmetic had little effect. The *Wealth of Nations*, however, shaped classical political economy, while Sinclair's twenty-one volumes of parish returns were rarely read and nearly unreadable, a reference work to be consulted for information on particular localities. In the writings of David Ricardo, for example, numbers appear only in illustrative numerical examples. What Ricardo and many other classical political economists knew about the predecessors of Adam Smith was mostly limited to what they could read about them in the *Wealth of Nations*, apart from Malthus's reading of earlier demographic literature. Classical political economists, even if sufficiently avid for facts to be caricatured as Gradgrinds, began with deduction, applying theoretical principles to the facts or testing them against the evidence, and did not share the hope characteristic of political arithmetic that principles could be derived from induction from quantitative data. As Claude Ménard (1980) has shown for Say, Cournot and Walras, many nineteenth-century economists resisted statistical analysis in economics.

Phyllis Deane (1987) used the *Encyclopaedia Britannica* to chart the declining attention given political arithmetic. In 1787 the third edition had an article on political arithmetic, primarily on Petty with additional references to Davenant, King, Graunt, Halley, Brakenridge and Price, but no entry for political economy. After the end of the eighteenth century, there was instead an article on political economy, which did not even acknowledge political arithmetic as an episode in the history of political economy. Even J.R. McCulloch, more interested in numerical data and in early economic tracts than most of his contemporaries were, thought in 1847 that "during the long interval between Sir William Petty and Dr Beeke [who wrote in 1798], statistical science could hardly be said to exist" (Glass 1978: 11). He would not have thought so if Smith had given an account of the political arithmetic of the century between Petty and Beeke. Smith's silence about political arithmetic, broken by a few disclaimers of confidence, contributed to its neglect. As with his silence about Steuart's *Principles*, Smith's silence on political arithmetic did not reflect any unfamiliarity with the relevant writings.

What was lost to classical political economy when the political arithmetic tradition faded into dim recollection? Many wild guesses, presented as solid data, were lost, but so were more useful things. The King–Davenant law of demand (or Gregory King's law), first published by Davenant in 1696 in his abstract of King, gave figures for how much a given defect in the harvest would raise the price of corn above its common rate (e.g. 30 percent above the common rate for a 10 percent deficiency in the crop), embodying the notion of quantity demanded as a function of price and of a market-clearing price equating supply and demand. Fleetwood first used a price index in 1707, extended to an index with different weights for different goods by Arthur Young in 1812 (Westergaard 1932: 202–3, on Young). Without mentioning Fleetwood or Young, Arie Arnon (1990) has considered "What Thomas Tooke (and Ricardo) could have known had they constructed price indices". Had Smith presented Fleetwood's price index rather than just using his raw data, economists might well have constructed such indices long before Jevons.

Phyllis Deane (1955) and M.O. Piquet-Marchal (1965) showed that national income and expenditure accounts can be reconstructed from the estimates of Gregory King, Joseph Massie and Arthur Young. Leroy Ladurie (1972) has shown the weaknesses of King's income, consumption and population estimates for France, whose population in 1695 was between 19 and 20 million (judging from a national survey after the famine of 1693, and some provincial censuses in the 1680s) rather than the $13\frac{1}{2}$ million estimated by King. His figures for England and Wales, based on such sources as hearth tax returns and a house by house survey of the parish of Harefield in Middlesex, have held up much better under later scrutiny. The sporadic efforts at construction of national accounts in the nineteenth century were undertaken outside classical political economy, and received little attention from leading economists.

Classical political economy thus failed to pursue several aspects of political arithmetic of subsequent importance: national income and expenditure accounts, price index numbers, and the King–Davenant law of demand. All of these were represented in Adam Smith's library, but he left them out of the *Wealth of Nations*. He was rightly skeptical of many of the numbers advanced in the political arithmetic literature, but took no part in promoting the availability of more reliable statistics, for instance by supporting Young's 1771 proposal for a census. Smith's attitude to political arithmetic has received little attention. Lawrence Klein (1992), writing on Smith's use of data, concentrates on the corn prices that Adam Smith took from Fleetwood and Charles Smith, testing whether the data are cyclical. Smith's selective silence, together with his few critical comments on political arithmetic, helped limit the role of quantification in classical political economy.

NOTE

I am grateful to Mary Ann Dimand, Spencer J. Pack and Edwin G. West for helpful comments.

BIBLIOGRAPHY

Arnon, Arie (1990) "What Thomas Tooke (and Ricardo) could have known had they constructed price indices", in D.E. Moggridge (ed.) *Perspectives on the History of Economic Thought*, vol. 4, Aldershot: Edward Elgar, pp. 1–19.

Chalmers, George (1782–1802) *An Estimate of the Comparative Strength of Great Britain during the Present and Four Preceding Reigns*, London, 4th edn 1802.

Clark, G.N. (1946) *The Wealth of England from 1496 to 1760*, London: Oxford University Press (Home University Library).

D'Avenant, Charles (1771) *Political and Commercial Works*, ed. Sir Charles Whitworth, 5 vols, London.

Deane, Phyllis (1955) "Implications of early national income estimates for measurement of long-term economic growth in the United Kingdom", *Economic Development and Cultural Change* 4: 3–38.

——— (1987) "Political arithmetic", in J. Eatwell, M. Milgate and P. Newman (eds) *The New Palgrave: A Dictionary of Economics*, London: Stockton Press.

Dimand, Robert W. (1992) "Political protest and political arithmetic on the Niagara frontier: Robert Gourlay's *Statistical Account of Upper Canada*", *Brock Review* I: 52–63.

Ekelund, Robert, and Hébert Robert, (1990) *A History of Economic Theory and Method*, 3rd edn, New York: McGraw-Hill.

Fleetwood, William (1707, 1745) *Chronicon Preciosum*, London; 2nd edn reprinted New York: Kelley.

Glass, D.V. (1978) *Numbering the People*, London and New York: Gordon & Cremonesi.

Gourlay, Robert (1822) *Statistical Account of Upper Canada*, 3 vols, London: Simpkin & Marshall, reprinted East Ardsley, Yorks: S.R. Publishers, and New York: Johnson Reprint, 1966.

Kaplow, Jeffry (1969) "Introduction", in Arthur Young, *Travels in France*, New York: Doubleday Anchor.

Klein, Lawrence R. (1992) "Smith's use of data", in Michael Fry (ed.) *Adam Smith's Legacy*, London: Routledge

Ladurie, Emmanuel Leroy (1972) "The fantastical accounts of Gregory King", trans. P. Wexler, in Marc Ferro (ed.) *Social Historians in Contemporary France: Essays from Annales*, New York: Harper & Row.

Ménard, Claude (1980) "Three forms of resistance to statistics: Say, Cournot, Walras", *History of Political Economy* 12: 524–41.

Mingay, G.E. (1975) *Arthur Young and his Times*, London: Macmillan.

Piquet-Marchal, M.O. (1965) "Gregory King, précurseur de la compatibilité nationale", *Revue économique* 212–45.

Smith, Adam (1776) *Wealth of Nations*, ed. R.H. Campbell, A.S. Skinner and W.B. Todd, Indianapolis, IN: Liberty Classics, 1981.

——— (1987) *Correspondence*, ed. E.C. Mossner, and I.S. Ross, Indianapolis, IN: Liberty Classics.

Steuart, Sir James (1767) *An Inquiry into the Principles of Political Economy*, ed. A.S. Skinner, Edinburgh: Oliver & Boyd for the Scottish Economic Society, 1966.

Webster, Alexander (1755) "An account of the number of people in Scotland in 1755", reprinted in James Gray Kyd (ed.) *Scottish Population Statistics*, Edinburgh: Scottish Historical Society, 1952.

West, Edwin G. (1990) *Adam Smith and Modern Economics*, Aldershot, and Brookfield, VT: Edward Elgar.

Westergaard, Harald (1932) *Contributions to the History of Statistics*, London: P.S. King; reprinted New York: Kelley, 1969.

Yanaihara, Tadao (1951) *A Full and Detailed Catalogue of Books Which Belonged to Adam Smith*, Tokyo: reprinted New York: Kelley, 1966.

Young, Arthur (1774, 1779) *Political Arithmetic*, London. Part I: W. Nicoll, reprinted New York: Kelley, 1967. Part II, T. Cadell.

Chapter 3

Ordering society

The early uses of classification in the British statistical organizations

James P. Henderson

Man in society is the subject of our study; to detect the influences which bear upon his welfare, our ultimate aim; inductive reasoning from phenomena observable and observed with mathematical precision, our method; and to make use of all evidence of this character which may be turned up in the daily working of society, as well as to collect new data, our necessity.

(*Journal of the Statistical Society* May 1849: 98)

INTRODUCTION

This statement was adopted as the epigraph to this chapter because it is the most eloquent explication of the mission of the Statistical Society. As their science became more sophisticated and as statisticians developed new analytical tools, the role of classification changed. In nineteenth-century Britain science was regarded as an adornment to culture as a form of systematic knowledge. Classification of the branches of knowledge was thus an important feature of scientific endeavor. William Whewell maintained that: "The classification of knowledge has its chief use in pointing out to us the extent of our powers of arriving at truth, and the analogies which may obtain between those certain and lucid portions of knowledge ... and those other portions" (Whewell 1847: vol. II, p. 113). Whewell believed that "The classification of human knowledge will ... have a more peculiar importance when we can include in it the moral, political, and metaphysical, as well as the physical portions of our knowledge" (Whewell 1847: vol. II, p. 113). Statistics and economics were the first of these nonphysical "portions of our knowledge" to be admitted into the halls of science by those who demonstrated that they had a proper place in the classification *of* sciences.

The role of classification in a systematic inductive approach to science was first detailed by John F. W. Herschel in *A Preliminary Discourse on the Study of Natural Philosophy* 1830. Herschel's book included four chapters devoted to "the rules by which a systematic examination of nature should be conducted ..." (Herschel 1830: 75). These chapters outline four steps in the inductive approach to science: (1) "Of the Observation of Facts and the Collection of Instances", (2) "Of the Classification of Natural Objects and Phenomena, and of Nomenclature", (3) "Of the First Stage of Induction. – The Discovery of Proximate Causes, and Laws of the lowest Degree of Generality, and their Verification" and (4) "Of the Higher Degrees of Inductive Generalization, and of the Formation and Verification of Theories" (p. xxvi). Whewell praised Herschel's "rules by which true science must be conducted" as a

> most valuable addition to our philosophical literature; for it is, we believe, the first attempt since Bacon to deliver a connected body of rules of philosophizing which shall apply alike to the conduct of all researches directed to the discovery of laws of nature.
>
> (Whewell 1831: 398)

Whewell read into Herschel's "rules by which a systematic examination of nature should be conducted" applications beyond the sphere of physical phenomena, believing that the inductive method could be applied to social and moral sciences.

In June 1833, Whewell spoke to the General Meeting of the British Association detailing the philosophy of science that he was developing. The role he assigned to classification stemmed from his view of the alleged antithesis between theory and facts.

> It has of late been common to assert that *facts* alone are valuable in science; that theory, so far as it is valuable, is contained in the facts; and so far as it is not contained in the facts, can merely mislead and preoccupy men. But this antithesis between theory and facts has probably in its turn contributed to delude and perplex; to make men's observations and speculations useless and fruitless.
>
> (Whewell 1833: xx)

Classification resolves the "antithesis between theory and facts". For Whewell, "facts can only become portions of knowledge as they become classed and connected; that they can only constitute truth when they are included in general propositions" (ibid., p. xxi).

In 1841, Dr William A. Guy outlined the "best Method of Collecting and Arranging Facts" (Guy 1841: 353–65). He designed a "Common-place Book" to aid the investigator in classifying data. In explaining the benefits to be gained by systematic classification, he illustrated Whewell's conception of the role of classification. Guy noted the correlation between classification and

> the mental process by which sciences are built up. First, a single fact is observed, then many others resembling it in some general features; then, with accumulation of observations, confusion, and an effort at subdivision; then the formation of smaller groups, and lastly the re-union of the several

groups with others formed by similar a process, and the construction of separate sciences.

(ibid., p. 360)

Whewell did not restrict "the term 'science' to the sphere of physical phenomena" for he believed "that the intellectual processes which [science] involved could be extended to other areas", in particular, political economy (Yeo 1991: 178). Unfortunately, the deductively derived political economy of David Ricardo and his followers was riddled with errors due to its faulty method. Whewell forcefully declared that "*all deductions from theory for any other purpose than that of comparison with observation* are frivolous and useless exercises of ingenuity" (Whewell 1833: xxii, his italics). Whewell asserted that investigators

if of active and inventive minds, *will* form theories whether we wish it or no. These theories may be useful or may be otherwise – we have examples of both results. If the theories merely stimulate the examination of facts, and are modified as and when the facts suggest modification, they may be erroneous, but they will still be beneficial; – they may die, but they will not have lived in vain.

(ibid.)

Though Whewell addressed the following comments to faulty method in the physical sciences, they applied equally well to Ricardian political economy:

If . . . our theory be supposed to have a truth of a superior kind to the facts; to be certain independently of its exemplification in particular cases; – if, when exceptions to our propositions occur, instead of modifying the theory, we explain away the facts, – our theory becomes our tyrant, and all who work under its bidding do the work of slaves, they themselves deriving no benefit from the result of their labours.

(ibid.)

As early as 1831, Whewell declared that "Political economy must be a science of *induction* and not of *deduction*. It must *obtain* its principles by reasoning upwards from facts, before it can *apply* them by reasoning downward from axioms" (Whewell 1831a: 52, his italics).

Among the factors "favoring the rise of attention to classification" during the nineteenth century, Dolby identified "the related rise of an inductive philosophy of science" (Dolby 1979: 173). William Stanley Jevons later merged the process of classification directly into induction, blurring Herschel's separation of these as distinct stages. Jevons said:

The purpose of classification is the detection of the laws of nature. However much the process may in some cases be disguised, classification is not really distinct from the process of perfect induction, whereby we endeavour to ascertain the connexions existing between properties of the objects under treatment.

(Jevons 1877: 675)

This chapter examines the changing functions of classification applied to the study of society and the economy during the nineteenth century. The use of classification to establish the parameters of statistics is investigated. Then the development of heuristic classification schemes by the statistical organizations is reviewed. In the fourth section, classification in the maturing disciplines of statistics and economics is treated. Several conclusions follow.

CLASSIFICATION TO ESTABLISH THE PARAMETERS OF STATISTICS

In June 1833, at the third meeting of the British Association for the Advancement of Science (BAAS), Richard Jones and Whewell along with the Reverend Thomas Robert Malthus, Charles Babbage and Adolphe Quetelet, organized the "Statistical Section" (later Section F). They intended "to redefine the province of political economy through the incorporation of empirical material drawn from all areas of social existence" (Goldman 1983: 600).

The five founders, joined by Adam Sedgwick, President of the British Association that year, justified introducing the new subject into the system of scientific knowledge by reclassifying the five existing "Sections" or "Committees of Sciences" into a numbered, hierarchical order: "I. Mathematics and General Physics; II. Chemistry, Mineralogy, &c.; III. Geology and Geography; IV. Natural History; V. Anatomy, Medicine, &c.;" and adding a new scientific section "VI. Statistics" (*Report of the Third Meeting of the British Association for the Advancement of Science* 1833: xxxix–x1).[1] The scientific legitimacy of statistical research was established for that community by specifying a place for a section devoted to such study in the British Association's hierarchical classification of sciences.

One of the first acts of the new Statistical Section was to seek approval from the governing Council of the BAAS "to promote the formation of a Statistical Society in London" (ibid., p. 483). The founders were permitted to publish the "Prospectus of the Objects and Plan of the Statistical Society of London" in the 1833 *Report* of the British Association (ibid., pp. 492–5). The two organizations, through their affiliation with the British Association, proclaimed the interconnectedness of social and physical science.

Whewell and Richard Jones led the methodological attack on Ricardian deductive economics. While there was widespread disagreement with Ricardo on many points, "only the 'Cambridge inductivists' attacked the very method of political economy – its reliance on deduction from 'self-evident truths' of human behavior and its restriction to the existing economic state of Britain"

(Goldman 1983: 598–9). In a letter to Jones, Whewell summarized his critique of the Ricardians:

> They have begun indeed with some inference of facts; but, instead of working their way cautiously and patiently from there to the narrow principles which immediately inclose a limited experience, and of advancing to wider generalities of more scientific simplicity only as they become masters of more such intermediate truths – instead of this, the appointed aim of true and permanent science – they have been endeavouring to spring at once from the most limited and broken observations to the most general axioms.
>
> (Whewell to Jones, Whewell Papers Collection, Add. Mss. c. 51^{92}).

Only by following the percepts of induction could political economy achieve "the appointed aim of true and permanent science". This required accurate classification. Jevons later explained:

> Science can extend only so far as the power of accurate classification extends. If we cannot detect resemblances, and assign their exact character and amount, we cannot have that generalised knowledge which constitutes sciences.... A full classification constitutes a complete record of all our knowledge of the objects or events classified, and the limits of exact knowledge are identical with the limits of classification.
>
> (Jevons 1877: 730–1)

Based upon Whewell's understanding of the nature of the discovery of truth, the founders of the Statistical Society, rather than pronouncing a narrow definition of statistics, declared their mission to be "for the purposes of procuring, arranging, and publishing 'Facts calculated to illustrate the Condition and Prospects of Society'" (*Report of the Third Meeting of the British Association for the Advancement of Science* 1833: 492). Any attempt at defining statistical science must wait "until time and labour should have furnished materials that would group themselves into classes too distinctly marked to require any such formal definition" (*Journal of the Statistical Society* April 1840: 1).

In Jones's careful inductive approach to political economy, Whewell saw the opportunity to extend the intellectual processes used in "true and permanent science" into other areas of inquiry. Jones's work demonstrated that Ricardian political economy clearly lacked a body of induced empirical knowledge at its foundation. Whewell insisted upon applying the inductive method, "in order to defend the scientific status of political economy" (Yeo 1991: 184). Thus "the deductive character of Ricardo's system was not a mark of its scientific character but a symptom of its failure to appreciate the process by which sciences were established" (ibid., p. 183).

The Statistical Section and the Statistical Society were designed to serve as an institutional base of operation for the methodological attack on Ricardian economics.[2] In February 1833, in his inaugural lecture as Professor of Political Economy at King's College, London, Jones "advocated a statistical society for England", and he and Whewell "discussed strategy several months before the British Association meeting" (Cannon 1978: 242). On March 24, 1833, Whewell wrote to Jones asking "to talk to you about getting statistical information, if the British Association is to be made subservient to that, ... which I think would be well" (Todhunter 1876: II, p. 161). Though Adam Sedgwick initially rejected "the prospectus of the new section during the 1833 meeting because he found it politically controversial", he was persuaded by Whewell and the others to approve it when assured that the investigations of the section would be limited to scientific matters (Goldman 1983: 591). Thus it was important to the scientific community to control the activities of these two organizations, the intention being to control the production of scientific knowledge generated there.

In order to insure that the inquiries undertaken by the new section would meet the tests of science (and also to convince skeptics like Sedgwick) two innovations were adopted – limitations were imposed on the investigations undertaken by the Statistical Section and a formal classification blueprint was created. These innovations were also adopted by the new Statistical Society.

The Drinkwater notes of the founders gathering on June 28, 1833, at Cambridge reveal that Jones "read to the meeting a sketch of the objects" of this new section:

> In its narrowest sense considered as a subordinate to the inquiries of the political economist alone, the science of statistics would have for its subject-matter such phenomena only as bear directly or indirectly upon the production or distribution of public wealth. It is with wider views that such an association as the present would approach the subject. It may be presumed that they would think foreign to the objects of their inquiries no classes of facts relating to communities of men which promise when sufficiently multiplied to indicate general laws.
>
> (Drinkwater, quoted in Goldman 1983: 599)[3]

This last sentence, intended to expand the scope of statistics beyond political economy, was altered slightly and became instead the restriction imposed on the research activities of the new section. The formal approval for the new section was passed by the General Committee only after it was

> resolved that the inquiries of this Section should be restricted to those classes of facts relating to communities of men *which are capable of being expressed by numbers, and which promise, when sufficiently multiplied, to indicate general laws*
>
> (*Report of the Third Meeting of the British Association for the Advancement of Science* 1833: xxxvii and 483; italics in original)

This limitation made the Statistical Section the only section in the British

Association with formal restrictions imposed on it in an effort to control its inquiries. In the "Prospectus" of the Statistical Society of London a similar control was adopted:

> The Statistical Society will consider it to be the first and most essential rule of its conduct to exclude carefully all *opinions* for its transactions and publications, – to confine its attention rigorously to facts, – and, as so far as it may be found possible, to facts that can be stated numerically and arranged in tables.
>
> (ibid., p. 492)

The second innovation, designed to insure that the inquiries of the two organizations met the test of science, was the creation of a formal classification blueprint. In a letter to Whewell, written just before the founders gathered at Cambridge for the British Association meeting, Jones outlined the four "divisions I propose". These divisions defined the scope and range of the investigations that would be undertaken in Section F and the Statistical Society in order to control the production of scientific knowledge.[4] The "Prospectus of the Objects and Plan of the Statistical Society of London" included Jones's four "divisions" (see Table 3.1).

Jones's division of topics was formally instituted in the form of the Committees that constituted the Society's structure. At its inaugural meeting in May 1834, the Society's

> Council began its scientific work ... by appointing five Committees on "Economical Statistics," on "Political Statistics," on "Medical Statistics," on "Moral and Intellectual Statistics," – these four were contemplated in the Prospectus – and on "Colonial Statistics".
>
> (*Annals of the Royal Statistical Society, 1834–1934* 1934: 31)

A division of labor among the members of the Statistical Society emerged from this slightly altered version of Jones's original four categories. In January 1835, the Society designed a "great Questionnaire" which was to be used

> to furnish "interrogatories" on the branch of knowledge in which [the members] were most interested – [Nassau] Senior on "Labouring Classes," Rev. R. Jones on "Rent," Whewell on "Education and Literature," G. R. Porter on "Crime," "Savings Banks," and "Agriculture," J. E. Drinkwater on "Machinery and Manufacture," S. Jones Loyd (afterwards Lord Overstone) on "Currency." The various drafts were, a month later, referred to the four Committees or divisions of the Councils ("Economical Statistics," "Political Statistics," "Medical Statistics," and "Moral and Intellectual Statistics").... The society thus embarked on the work of "collecting fresh statistical information and of arranging, condensing, and publishing much of what already exists".
>
> (ibid., pp. 31–2)

Table 3.1 The original classification systems of Section F of the British Association and the Statistical Society

The classification scheme devised by Richard Jones – the four "divisions I propose" – for Section F of the British Association and the Statistical Society	"Prospectus of the Objects and Plan of the Statistical Society of London"
	The whole subject [of subdivisions] was considered, by the Statistical Section of the British Association at Cambridge, as admitting a division into four great classes: 1. ECONOMICAL STATISTICS 2. POLITICAL STATISTICS 3. MEDICAL STATISTICS 4. MORAL AND INTELLECTUAL STATISTICS If these four classes are taken as the basis of a further analysis, it will be found that the class of
Economical Statistics: 1. Agriculture, 2. Manufactures, 3. Commerce & currency, 4. Distribution of wealth, i.e. rent, wages, & profits	*Economical Statistics* comprehend, 1st, the statistics of natural productions and the agricultural nations; 2ndly, of manufactures; 3rdly, of commerce and currency; 4thly, of the distribution of wealth, or all facts relating to rent, wages, profits, &c.
Political Statistics: 1. Statistics of elements of institutions, jurors – electors – &c., 2. Legal statistics, number of national & local tribunals, nature of courses tried &c. &c., 3. Finance – taxes, expenditures, public establishments &c. &c.	*Political Statistics* furnish three subdivisions: 1st, the facts relating to the elements of political institutions, the number of electors, jurors, &c.; 2ndly, legal statistics; 3rdly, the statistics of finance and of national expenditure, and of civil and military establishments
Medical Statistics: 1. General medical statistics, 2. Population (the doctors say they shall want subdivisions)	*Medical Statistics*, strictly so called, will require at least two subdivisions; and the great subject of population, although it might be classed elsewhere, yet touches medical statistics on so many points, that it would be placed most conveniently, perhaps, in this division, and would constitute a third subdivision
Moral & Intellectual Statistics: 1. Crime, 2. Education & *literature*, 3. *Ecclesiastical* statistics	*Moral and Intellectual Statistics* comprehend, 1st, the statistics of literature; 2ndly, of education, 3rdly, of religious instruction and ecclesiastical institutions; 4thly, of crime. Although fourteen subdivisions have now been enumerated, it is probable that more will be required

Sources: Left-hand column, Jones to Whewell in the Whewell Papers Collection, Add.Mss.c.52[60]; right-hand column, *Report of the Third Meeting of the British Association* (1833: 492–3)

These "great Questionnaires", designed by the Reverend Edward Stanley and called "Heads for the Arrangement of Local Information", were intended to control the collection of data. The division of labor among the members of the Statistical Society now took on a new dimension, which emphasized two skill levels. While the data could be gathered by those with only modest skills, the major task of the four (or five) Committees, which required much higher scientific skills, was classification – "arranging, condensing, and publishing" the data collected.

The actual collection of data could be done by almost any amateur with minimal training. In the Society's *Proceedings* for June 15, 1835, is Rawson W. Rawson's short paper "On the Collection of Statistics" encouraging members to set about gathering whatever data to which they had access. Rawson

> compared statistics to a vast edifice, composed of many smaller parts, each requiring care in its preparation, and the arrangement of the whole demanding much sagacity and combination. In both, persons of different capacity were required for different purposes.
>
> (Rawson 1835: 41)

Rawson contended that a "person who could not complete a scheme of statistics might be the best qualified to furnish the details" (ibid., pp. 41–2). Such people, lacking the broad vision of one who could complete a scheme of statistics, might suppose that such details "were valueless; but they were like particles of gold, which, when collected and refined, furnish those precious ingots which become both the means and the emblem of wealth" (ibid., p. 42). Apparently Whewell disagreed with this aspect of Rawson's position. In his 1833 address to the British Association Whewell maintained that the act of classifying and connecting facts must be done immediately after the appropriate observations have been assembled by the very people who had gathered the data:

> It may be added – as a further reason why no observer should be content without arranging his observations ... and without *endeavouring* at least to classify and connect them – that when this is not done at first, it is most likely never done. The circumstances of the observation can hardly be properly understood or interpreted by others; the suggestions which the observations themselves supply, for change of plan or details, cannot in any other way be properly appreciated and acted on. And even the mere multitude of unanalysed observations may drive future students of the subject into despair of rendering them useful.
>
> (Whewell 1833: xxi)

For Rawson, who did believe that a division of labor was preferable, those who were delegated "to furnish the details" had three tasks to perform: "The first task was to discover the books in which authentic data were published. . . .

The second task was that of extraction.... The third task was verification"
(Rawson 1835: 42). The second of these three tasks, "extraction", seemed to
be a real problem for the Society. Rawson remarked that the Council could
not perform this task: "the small number, and the still smaller leisure of the
Council, with the absence of means to employ clerks and copyists, render the
Society dependent upon the co-operation of its members" (ibid.). Thus, "in
the collection of facts, the assistance of members became absolutely
necessary" (ibid.).[5] Their efforts were to be controlled by the Committees
"who would be most glad of the assistance of individual members" (ibid.).
Members were urged "to attend at least one meeting of a Sub-committee in
order to learn how the objects of the Society might best be promoted" (ibid.).
Here Rawson seems to move toward Whewell's position, that those who
gather the data ought also to classify it, for he appears to suggest that these
"extractors" require guidance from the Committee. Members were assured
that attending the committee meeting did not obligate the member to
participate in its work "and there was, therefore, no ground for entertaining
a fear of future inconvenience" (ibid., pp. 42–3). These pleadings suggest that
the tedious tasks of data collection were not of much interest to most
members. Moreover, it is clear from Rawson's tone that, while such efforts
were absolutely vital to the Society's success, they were viewed as menial
tasks of a much lower order of significance and prestige than those performed
by the Council. While the three tasks of discovering facts, extracting and then
verifying them were of such a nature that "all members might assist" in
performing them, the most important work was to be done by the Council. "It
remained for the Council to digest and embody the information collected"
(ibid., p. 42).

The two innovations adopted at the founding of the two statistical
organizations to control their members and the production of scientific
knowledge soon proved so restrictive that little actual scientific work was
accomplished. "The difficulty of not straying from this narrow path soon
became evident, for in March, 1836, a dispute broke out with the Medical
Committee as to the nature of their Queries" (*Annals of the Royal Statistical
Society, 1834–1934* 1934: 32). Although additional projects were being
developed, it was obvious that

> the fact-collecting machinery of the Society through the five Standing
> Committees was not working well. "The practical working of the system,"
> according to a report of a Committee of the Council on 17 February, 1837,
> "has been as follows. Out of the five Committees appointed, one never met.
> Others after a few meetings ceased to make quorums; while only one
> [Medical Statistics] continued its operation to the present day; but none
> have so far fulfilled their original intentions....
>
> (ibid., pp. 37–8)

Fearing that these two organizations would stray into the production of controversial, political knowledge, the scientific community imposed controls that proved to be so restrictive that intellectual activity was stifled. Concern over these failures and fearing that they had not adequately delineated the nature of their investigations led these organizations to reexamine their goals and activities.

HEURISTIC CLASSIFICATION AND THE HIERARCHY OF CATEGORIES

In the "Introduction" to the first issue of the *Journal of the Statistical Society*, the Council reassessed its understanding of the distinction between statistics and political economy.

> The Science of Statistics differs from Political Economy, because, although it has the same end in view, it does not discuss causes, nor reason upon probable facts; it seeks only to collect, arrange, and compare, that class of facts which alone can form the basis of correct conclusions with respect to social and political government.
>
> (*Journal of the Statistical Society* May 1838: 1)

Thus the Society characterized its mission in terms of classification – "to collect, arrange, and compare" facts. Since "Statistics is of a very extensive nature", in organizing that knowledge it is important:

> to shew how every subject relating to mankind itself forms a part of Statistics; such as, population; physiology; religion; instruction; literature; wealth in all its forms, raw material, production, agriculture, manufactures; commerce; finance; government; and, to sum up all, whatever relates to the physical, economical, moral, or intellectual condition of mankind.
>
> (ibid., p. 2)[6]

This list of "every subject relating to mankind [which] forms a part of Statistics" coincided roughly with the specifics in Jones's four "divisions" which defined the scope of the inductions of both Section F and the Statistical Society.[7]

By 1840, new challenges by the scientific community to the mission of the Society and the scope of its researches forced it again to attempt to delineate "the whole field of our labours" (*Journal of the Statistical Society* April 1840: 4). The founders agreed with Whewell, that "facts can only become portions of knowledge as they become classed and connected; that they can only constitute truth when they are included in general propositions" (ibid.). Thus:

> Any very accurate definition of the subject of our investigations was left unattempted by the founders of this Society, until time and labour should have furnished materials that would group themselves into classes too distinctly marked to require such formal definition.
>
> (ibid., p. 1)

If statistics was to take its place among the physical sciences, it must not be defined as "the mere 'method' of stating the observations and experiments of the physical or other sciences" (ibid.). Six years of experience led the Council of the Statistical Society to posit this definition of their science:

> Statistics, by their very name, are defined to be the observations necessary to the social or moral sciences, to the sciences of the *statist*,[8] to whom the statesman and legislator must resort for the principles on which to legislate and govern. These sciences are equally distinct from the purely physical, the purely mathematical, and the purely metaphysical, though the mathematical must lend aid to their pursuit.
>
> (ibid., p. 2)

The Society seemed ready to challenge the scientific community's efforts to control its inquiries. This new definition of statistics brought the Statistical Society close to violating its original canon – "to exclude carefully all *opinions* from its transactions and publications" (ibid.). In 1838, the first issue of its *Transactions* provoked John Robertson to attack the Society for adopting such a rule in the first place. In the *Westminster Review*, he listed four objections to the rule that excluded "opinions":

> It prevents the discovery of new truths; – it deprives the labours of the Society of definite purposes; – the facts of which it causes the collection and arrangement are those which are useless and irrelevant as evidence; – and lastly, the observance of this rule is irreconcilable not merely with the progress of science and knowledge, but with the actions and operations of the Society itself.
>
> (R. [John Robertson] 1838: 47–8)

Stung by Robertson's accusations, the Council clarified its interpretation of those restrictions that had been imposed on both the Society and Section F. The Council asserted that the original decision to exclude all "opinions" from its publications was not made

> with the view of discouraging the proper use of *a priori* reasoning or of hypothesis, which is essential to the profitable cultivation of almost every science, but for the purpose of devoting its publications to facts, and not to systems. Hypothesis and conjecture are necessary to individuals in their pursuit of any investigation; but it is observation and experiment which decide their truth and fullness, or demonstrate their fallacy and insufficiency; and it is the results of such observation and experiment which it is the main purpose of this Society to "collect, arrange, and publish." The facts must have been sought on some theory, of which they may prove the fallacy or truth. Labourers in the field of science must, like all other labourers, have a prospect of reward; and this reward is the advancement of some definite branch of human knowledge and power. Scientific

societies, however, possess no theories in their corporate capacity. They do not vote upon systems, and decide the truth by majorities, but simply open the way for its demonstration by facts.

(*Journal of the Statistical Society* April 1840: 6–7)

Experience had also taught the Society that its four original classes of research were too narrow to guide its actual work. So a new classification scheme was drawn up by the Council. It stipulated that the topics in the classification are arranged in the order of their importance to the welfare of the society. The classification is a hierarchy of topics fashioned "according to the great purposes of mankind in society" (ibid., p. 5). Henceforth, "the whole field of our labours appears ... to be divisible into the following chief sections" (ibid., p. 4; see Table 3.2). Since this new taxonomy was organized "according to the great purposes of mankind in society", its "chief value" was that it afforded "a system of classification equally available for the most savage or the most civilised community, in any age or country" (ibid., p. 5). This initial outline did not exhaust the possibilities. A second, more detailed heuristic classification, "arising from each of these purposes being variously pursued" in the collection of data under the first scheme, was created. The first taxonomy was determined to be all encompassing and therefore perhaps a bit too vague to be useful for those interested in launching statistical studies. The second classification was heuristic and declared to be

> useful, not only for the perspicuity which it will give to our observations, but for the facility which it affords for at once selecting for immediate pursuit the branches of statistics which illustrate particular portions of moral or social science, without doubt or confusion, leaving for future and more favourable opportunities such as now present serious or insurmountable difficulties without relaxing our efforts in the prosecution of the former [taxonomy].
>
> (ibid.)

This heuristic taxonomy was divided into "fifteen well-defined sub-divisions of Statistics, universally available for purposes of comparison, and susceptible of the minutest sub-division, according to the multifarious detail of the affairs of life" (ibid., p. 6). Like the first outline, topics are arranged in order of importance "according to the great purposes of mankind in society" (ibid., p. 5; see Table 3.2).

Throughout the nineteenth century, scientists engaged in the work of classification tended to divide into two categories – "lumpers" and "splitters" (Knight 1981: 65).

> Genera involve the recognition of similarities, and species within them the recognition of differences. At all times there have been "lumpers" who pay little attention to small differences and try to keep the number of species and genera down, and "splitters" who feel that no differences

Table 3.2 The Statistical Society's 1840 revised classification frameworks

The first system	*The second (heuristic) system*
I. The *Statistics of Physical Geography, Division, and Appropriation*; or geographical and proprietary statistics	I. The Statistics of *Appropriation*, it divides into these, – 1st. Of private tenures and private property; 2d. Of voluntary association to hold property in common use, or to the common benefit; and, 3d. Of public property, or property held by the state, or the political organisation of any whole community, to the common use and advantage, against all claimants, internal or external
II. The *Statistics of Production*; or agriculture, mining, fishing, manufacturing, and commercial statistics	II. The *Statistics of Production*, it divides into these, – 1st. Of "technography," or the arts of material production as privately pursued, including private policy in the management of land and capital, and every class of services directed to supply physical wants and comforts; 2d. Of industrial co-operation and exchanges; being the whole of the field contemplated by political economy, excepting the consumption of wealth; and, 3d. Of public works, and the influences of government upon industry and commerce.
III. The *Statistics of Instruction*; or ecclesiastical, scientific, literary, and academical statistics	III. The *Statistics of Instruction*; it divides into these, – 1st. Of private or domestic instruction, and self-instruction; 2d. Of instruction by common competition, and by voluntary associations; and 3d. Of public instruction by endowments, and by applying a political organisation to the cultivation and diffusion of religion, science, or letters
IV. The *Statistics of Protection*; or constitutional, legal, judicial, and criminal statistics	IV. The *Statistics of Protection*, it divides into these, – 1st. Of domestic organisation and discipline;

2d. Of the moral relationships of neighbourhood, of voluntary association for mutual protection or for arbitration; and of the remaining portions of *lex talionis* to be found in every society; and,
3d. Of political constitutions; of judicial, correctional, and police establishments and criminal laws; and of diplomatic services, war establishments, and the customs of war

V. The *Statistics of Consumption and Enjoyment*, or of population, distribution, consumption, diversions, life, health, and public and private charity	V. The *Statistics of Consumption and Enjoyment*, it divides into these, – 1st. Of domestic economy and manners, and private charity; 2d. Of social intercourse, combined amusements, mutual assurance, and voluntary association for charitable purposes; and, 3d. Of public amusements, or public supplies of commodities provided by public authorities; of public hospitals, and of public charity as organised by poor laws, &c.

Sources: Left-hand column, *Journal of the (Royal) Statistical Society* 3, Part 7 (April 1840): 4–5; right-hand column, ibid., pp. 5–6

should be neglected and who therefore see the need for many more groups.

(ibid.)

The Council's approach to production and consumption differs from the "lumping" of the classical economists. Of interest is the Council's explanation for "splitting" two topics "The Statistics of Production" and "The Statistics of Consumption and Enjoyment" and inserting between them two other topics – "The Statistics of Instruction" and "The Statistics of Protection".

It is very common to proceed immediately from contemplating the "production" of wealth (or commodities) to regard its "consumption"; but society has other functions to exercise besides these, or its "production" would be very insignificant, and its "consumption" very insecure. Until these are examined, in fact, no just view of distribution and consumption of wealth can be arrived at.

(*Journal of the Statistical Society* April 1840: 3)

This "splitting" emphasized the hierarchical nature of the heuristic classification. Members were advised that data within any of these subdivisions could be compared and analyzed in essentially two ways, both now familiar. The first technique was time series analysis, "an historical series relating to one or more communities"; and the second was cross-sectional analysis, "simultaneous observation in a number of communities, or in different portions of the same community" (ibid., p. 6).

The fundamental importance of classification was reasserted. Classification was vital because those engaged in the moral and social sciences are unable to perform experiments and rely instead on observation. The Council declared that

> well-directed observation, aided by analysis, would, if pursued with vigour and judgment lead rapidly to the elaboration of important truths. By analysis in moral investigations is meant that minute classification of actions and their results, which presents each group for separate contemplation, to the end that their relative force and amount may be accurately estimated.
>
> (ibid., p. 7)

In the moral and social sciences, classification must be analytical. Since the "relations of each group are exceedingly intimate", accurate classification is imperative.

> Without this process of analysis there can be no certainty as to the causes of any moral phenomenon; and daily experience presents instances of the most contradictory causes being assigned for the same phenomenon, because there exist no means by which to prove the truth or falsehood of any one assertion.
>
> (ibid.)

Moreover, unique abilities are required to execute a valuable classification of observed phenomena. While "the mere labour of observation may often be entrusted into hands of far less skill",

> it is in the facility of analysis, to those who possess the talent, cultivation, and integrity to pursue it, that the field of moral science presents advantages for study scarcely enjoyed by some of the physical sciences, even those in which experimentation can be introduced.
>
> (ibid.)

So the division of labor between observers and classifiers, endorsed by Rawson and opposed by Whewell, continued.

That the classification system adopted at the 1840 meeting was challenged is apparent from the opening remarks in the next "Annual Report" of the Council. Noting that it had "entered so fully into an examination of the field of Statistical science, and of the mode in which the Society can most efficiently aid in its cultivation", the Council declared that it simply would not "pursue the subject further on the present occasion" (*Journal of the Statistical*

Society April 1841: 69). Instead the Council asserted that its duty was "to survey what has been done during the past year towards carrying out the suggestions contained in that Report, and to shew the effect which the results are likely to have upon the influence and reputation of the Society" (ibid.).

Ongoing concern to stake out an exclusive territory for themselves led the members of the Statistical Society to repeatedly distinguish their efforts from those of the classical economists. In 1843, the Council argued that the work of its members served "as tests to, and checks upon, hypothetical reasonings in the moral and political sciences" (*Journal of the Statistical Society* May 1843: 89). Moreover, the data provided by the statisticians "exploded . . . [the] errors as to the facts which illustrate the actual condition and prospects of society" (ibid.). They supplied more accurate data for "the exertions of the philanthropist, the judgment of the legislator, and the speculations of the reasoner" (ibid.). "To make, to register, and to reduce [i.e. to put into tabular form] these observations is the express province of the *statist*" and when done properly the deductive reasoner "is compelled to amend his conjectures as often as they are irreconcilable with facts newly established by scientific observation" (ibid.). No support for such claims was offered. The next year, the "Report of the Council" asserted that: "The Labours of the statist, indeed, can alone assure us that we are really advancing in that knowledge of human interests in the aggregate to which it is no longer possible to deny the name of science" (*Journal of the Statistical Society* June 1844: 99).

Confidence in their classification framework grew when the Central Statistical Commission of Belgium adopted a set of "decrees appointing and regulating the operations" of their organization which "closely accord with those laid down by the Statistical Society" in 1840 (*Journal of the Statistical Society* June 1845: 98). When the Belgians defined "the subjects which ought to be included" in "making a general statistical account" of their own country, the result was in such close accord with the Society's own "great divisions [and] their principle subdivisions" that it afforded "a gratifying testimony to the entertainment of precisely the same views by our gifted neighbors and ourselves" (ibid.). The Belgian's scheme was then laid out alongside the Society's classification system so that the members could compare them (see Table 3.3). The Council commented how remarkable it was that there were so few differences between the two classification systems even though there were such differences in the political, religious, economic and other social institutions between the United Kingdom and Belgium.

Little practical use seems to have been made of the heuristic classification systems developed in 1840. Yet the members continued to take the work of classifying facts seriously and included references to it in the various statements of purposes and objectives issued by the two statistical organizations.

Table 3.3 The classification schemes of the Statistical Society of London and the Central Statistical Commission of Belgium

Statistical Society of London	Central Statistical Commission of Belgium
I. The *Statistics of Physical Geography, Division, and Appropriation*; or geographical and proprietary statistics	I. *Territory.* The topographical, hydrographical, and meteorological description of the country
II. The *Statistics of Production*; or agriculture, mining, fishing, manufacturing, and commercial statistics	III. *Industrial Condition.* The economical condition of the agriculture, commerce, and industry
III. The *Statistics of Instruction*; or ecclesiastical, scientific, literary, and academical statistics	IV. *Intellectual, Moral, and Religious Condition.* Public instruction, sciences, letters, fine arts, charitable institutions, crimes, &c.
IV. The *Statistics of Protection*; or constitutional, legal, judicial, and criminal statistics	V. *Political Condition.* The constitution, fundamental laws, internal administrative organization, and relations with other states
V. The *Statistics of Consumption and Enjoyment*; or of population, distribution, consumption, diversions, life, health, and public and private charity	II. *Population and its Movement.* Number of inhabitants, their physical constitution, their classification by ages and professions, births, marriages, and deaths

Sources: Left-hand column, *Journal of the (Royal) Statistical Society* 2 (12) (April 1839): 4–5; right-hand column, *Journal of the (Royal) Statistical Society* 8, Part 1 (June 1845): 98–9

CLASSIFICATION IN A MATURING DISCIPLINE

As their science became more sophisticated and as the statisticians developed new analytical tools, the role of classification changed. By 1865, fearing that "*statistics* had already come to mean rather the materials of science than the science itself", Dr William A. Guy examined the question: "Is there a Science of Statistics; and if so, what are its Nature and Objects, and what is its Relation to Political Economy and Social Science?" (Guy 1865: 483, 487). He found it difficult to define "science", given the diversity of scientific practices in the various branches of the acknowledged sciences. He declared that "I infer that there is a Science of Statistics" based on these "considerations":

> we, too, have our classifications and our nomenclature; we, too, have our numerical method; we, too, have powerful instruments of analysis in our tabular forms; we, too, have the most universal and subtle of all the means of discovery, the power of eliminating disturbing elements, of establishing

numerical equalities, and exhibiting residues as containing the cause or causes which make two or more numerical statements to differ from each other. We largely use the true Baconian method of induction, and Lord Bacon's own favourite instrument the *Tabula inveniendi*. Lastly, of the utility and dignity of our pursuit there cannot be a doubt.

(ibid., p. 491)[9]

Notice that Guy's list of the attributes of scientific statistics includes, in addition to classification, a variety of newly developed statistical tools. Classification had become part of a more sophisticated process. Statisticians could now bring to "bear the pure light of scientific method ... upon the collection, arrangement, tabulation, and analysis" of facts (ibid., p. 492). Others actively sought the assistance of the statisticians:

in almost all disputed questions, our aid is invoked, because we are believed to collect, arrange, and classify our facts in the true spirit of science, calmly and impartially, having as our primary object the discovery of truth by facts, and not the redress of grievances.

(ibid.)

Guy reassured the members that the "science of statistics" is a "science worthy of respect, encouragement, and support" (ibid., p. 491).

One last use of classification was implemented by the Statistical Society. This is the library function, using classification to bring coherence to a large collection of writings. This the Society started to do at the Twenty-first Anniversary Meeting on March 15, 1855, when the papers read and discussed at the Ordinary Meetings of the Society were for the first time classified by subject by William Guy. He chose to use Jones's four divisions, and added a fifth category "General Statistics". It is fascinating that Guy employed Jones's older, cruder divisions rather than the more comprehensive classification system that the Statistical Society had developed in 1840.[10] At the 1857 meeting another effort at classification of their papers was undertaken. Here only three categories were listed – "Vital Statistics, Economical Statistics, and Criminal Statistics" (*Journal of the Statistical Society* June 1857: 98).[11] In June 1865, those papers published in Society's "*Journal* during *the last ten years*" were

classed under eight heads, namely: (a) Commercial Statistics [14 papers]; (b) Industrial Statistics [6 papers]; (c) Financial Statistics [15 papers]; (d) Moral and Social Statistics [16 papers]; (e) Political Statistics [4 papers]; (f) Vital Statistics [12 papers]; and (g) Miscellaneous Statistics [15 papers].

(*Journal of the Statistical Society* June 1865: 232–5)

This procedure was repeated in 1876 using the same classes and the growth of the research conducted by the members can be seen in the increased numbers in all but the first category: (a) Commercial, 12 papers; (b) Industrial,

Table 3.4 Subject Index to the Journal of the Royal Statistical Society, vols
XXVIII–LVII, 1895

A. Theoretical and Historical
    I. Theories
        a. Generally (and Definitions)
        b. Political Economy
        c. Methods
        d. Graphics and Tabulations (1. Preparation of Parliamentary Papers, 2.
           Arrangement of Statistical Information, 3. Diagrams, 4. Tabular
           Analysis)
        e. Averages
        f. Utility of Statistics
    II. Machinery
    III. Historical
        a. Present State and Condition of the Science
        b. Reports of Congresses, &c.
        c. Biography
B. General
    I. Statistics of a Country
C. Demographic and Hygienic
    I. Population
        a. Censuses (Methods)
        b. Areas
        c. Population (*including* Results of Censuses)
        d. Races and Constituents of Population
        e. Migration
    II. Vital Statistics
        a. Generally (*including* Movement of Population)
        b. Births
        c. Marriages
        d. Mortality (generally)
        e. Registration
        f. Actuarial
    III. Hygiene (*including* Mortality *under each* heading)
        a. Generally
        b. Special Diseases and Causes of Death (1. Amputations, 2.
           Consumption, 3. Contagious Diseases, 4. Plague, 5. Suicide, 6.
           Small-pox, 7. Violence, &c.)
        c. Age
        d. Locality
        e. Class Statistics
        f. Army and Navy
        g. Sickness and Occupation
        h. Hospitals and Other Institutions
        j. Heredity
    IV. Dwellings
    V. Lunacy and Other Infirmities
        a. Lunacy
        b. Other Infirmities
    VI. Accidents (1. Mines, 2. At Sea)
    VII. Food

VIII. Anthropometry
D. Moral and Social
  I. Education
    a. Generally
    b. Primary
    c. Higher
    d. Examinations
    e. Books, Libraries, &c.
  II. Religion
  III. Charities
    a. Generally
    b. Hospitals
    c. Institutions
  IV. Friendly Societies
  V. Crime
    a. Generally
    b. Prisons
    c. Special Crimes (1. Murder)
  VI. Morality
    a. Generally
    b. C.D. Acts
  VII. Social Condition
    a. Locality
    b. Class (1. Working Classes, 2. Agricultural Labourer)
    c. Pauperism
    d. Civilisation, Social Reform, &c.
E. Political and Legal
  I. Administration
    a. National
      α. Generally
      β. Legislation Generally
      γ. Special Legislation (1. Banking, 2. Commerce and Tariffs, 3. Corn Laws, 4. Crime, 5. Currency, 6. Education, 7. Land, 8. Liquor, 9. Shipping Bounties)
      δ. Special Government Departments (1. Civil Service, 2. Indian Commission on Education, 3. Labour Department, 4. Statistical Offices)
    b. Local
  II. Army and Navy
  III. Representation
  IV. Law
F. Fiscal
  I. National Finance
    a. Generally
    b. Receipts
      α. Generally
      β. Taxation
      γ. Other Receipts
    c. Expenditure (1. Civil, 2. State Pensions)
  II. Local Finance
    a. Generally
    b. Receipts

Table 3.4 Continued

        c. Expenditure
     III. Public Debts
        a. National Indebtedness
        b. Government Loans
        c. Local Indebtedness
G. Financial
     I. Precious Metals
        a. Production
        b. Prices of Precious Metals
        c. Assays
     II. Money
        a. Generally
        b. Currency
        c. Foreign Exchanges
        d. Coinage
     III. Banking
        a. Generally
        b. Savings Banks
        c. Clearing
        d. Crises
     IV. Insurance
        a. Generally
        b. Life
        c. Fire
        d. Marine
     V. Losses and Casaulties
        a. Losses (1. Fires, 2. Hail, 3. Shipping)
        b. Trade Failures
     VI. Property and Credit
        a. Value of Property (1. Commercial, 2. Personal)
        b. Loans and Mortgages
        c. Stock Exchange Values
        d. Land Tenure
H. Commercial
     I. Capital and Wealth
        a. National Wealth or Incomes
        b. Individual Wealth
     II. Prices
        a. Generally
        b. Food (1. Wheat)
        c. Other Articles (1. Cotton, 2. Coal)
        d. Index Numbers
     III. Trade
        a. Generally
        b. Special Articles (1. Cotton and Silk, 2. Food, 3. Grain)
        c. Local
IV. Companies
     V. Transport and Communications
        a. Roads
        b. Railways

    c. Canals
    d. Shipping
    e. Posts and Telegraphs
J. Production and Consumption
    I. Agriculture
        a. Generally
        b. Local
        c. Food (1. Food Generally, 2. Horses, 3. Milk, 4. Sugar, 5. Tea, 6.
           Wheat)
        d. Alcohol
        e. Tobacco
        f. Other Special Articles (1. Cotton, 2. Wool)
        g. Famines
        h. Animals
    II. Fishing
    III. Mining
        a. Generally
        b. Local
        c. Special (1. Coal, 2. Iron, 3. Other Metals, 4. Diamonds)
        d. Royalties
    IV. Manufactures
        a. Generally
        b. Special
K. Industrial
    I. General Condition of Industry
    II. Occupations
        a. National
        b. Local
        c. Special (1. Coal Mining, 2. Dock Labour, 3. Hosiery)
    III. Wages
        a. Generally
        b. Special Trades (1. Coal Mining)
        c. Local
        d. Methods of Remuneration
    IV. Trade Combinations
        a. Trade Societies
        b. Strikes and Disputes
        c. Conciliation and Arbitration
    V. Co-operation
        a. Generally
        b. Distributive
        c. Productive

9 papers; (c) Financial, 29 papers; (d) Moral and Social, 36 papers; (e) Political, 14 papers; (f) Vital, 14 papers; and (g) Miscellaneous, 31 papers (*Journal of the Statistical Society* September 1876: 450–5). The last time these classes were employed was ten years later. A decline in research activity is apparent from the reduced number of articles in all categories except (e) and (f): (a) Commercial, 7 papers; (b) Industrial, 6 papers; (c) Financial, 10 papers; (d) Moral and Social, 12 papers; (e) Political, 15 papers; (f) Vital, 17

papers; and (g) Miscellaneous, 24 papers (*Journal of the Statistical Society* September 1876: 450–5).

The Society published three "General Indexes" before the turn of the century. In 1854, under the direction of Wheatley, the Society published a *General Index to the First Fifteen Volumes* (1834–52), using Jones's four divisions. These same four divisions were employed in the next two "General Indexes", for volumes XVI–XXV (1853–62) and for volumes XXVI–XXXV (1863–72). In 1895, a *Subject Index to the Journal of the Royal Statistical Society* appeared. This employed a detailed classification built around ten broad categories (see Table 3.4).

CONCLUSIONS

To those inductive scholars, like Whewell, who sought to adopt the methods of science to the study of the economy and society, classification performed several functions – establishing the parameters and controlling the new discipline, creating a heuristic classification which established a hierarchy of topics arranged "according to the great purposes of mankind in society", developing classification as part of more sophisticated processes of analysis, and, as its literature increased, classification as a library function became important. Richard Jones sketched out four divisions identifying "the objects of their inquiries" which were to include all "classes of facts relating to communities of men which promise when sufficiently multiplied to indicate general laws". Jones's classification was employed to establish the parameters in order to control the new discipline. When the rigid organizational structure and division of labor that resulted from formalizing Jones's classification interfered with the production of scientific knowledge, they reconsidered both the categories and the intent of their taxonomy. In 1840, the Statistical Society devised a new, heuristic classification, establishing a hierarchy of topics arranged "according to the great purposes of mankind in society". As the discipline matured the task of classification changed, becoming part of a more sophisticated process of analysis. Statisticians could now bring to "bear the pure light of scientific method ... upon the collection, arrangement, tabulation, and analysis" of facts. Finally, as its literature increased, the library function of classification became important.

In the nineteenth century, scholars did not appeal to "the potential applications of the new subject" but rather to "its place in the system of scientific knowledge", to justify research into new subjects within the burgeoning scientific community (Dolby 1979: 188). Yet a mere four years after he played such an instrumental role in launching it, Whewell declared that "the statistical Section ought never to have been admitted into the Association" (Morrell and Thackray 1981: 294).[12] Instead of restricting its efforts to "those classes of facts relating to communities of men which are capable of being expressed by numbers, and which promise, when sufficiently multiplied, to indicate general laws", the Section had become "an ambulatory body, composed partly of men of reputation, and partly of a miscellaneous crowd, [who] go round year by year, from town to town, and at each place … discuss the most inflammatory and agitating questions of the day" (Todhunter 1876: II, p. 291). Such unscientific behavior provoked serious questions about the activities of the Statistical Section.

Whewell was elected President of the British Association in 1841.[13] His exasperation with the Section's activities provoked the first public rebuke attacking the quality of the studies presented there. In his Presidential Address, he expressed his concern that Section F was developing a tendency to overstep the bounds of proper scientific investigation. In his view, "the collection of information respecting the habits, numbers, and education of the people, where the information is such as almost necessarily suggests legislation, or discussions having legislation for their natural end, and involving the deepest political and moral considerations" is best left to the government and not to Section F (Whewell 1841: xxxiii).

Most importantly, it is clear that Whewell exercised his influence to limit funding the research proposals coming from Section F (see Henderson, forthcoming). The early success of Section F in obtaining research funds from the British Association, during the period from 1836 to 1842, indicates support for the initial effort to put economics on a scientific footing. The controversies that arose in the early 1840s resulted in the British Association shutting off grant money to Section F research proposals. The decline in appropriations and payments began around 1843 and from 1846 until 1863 no payments were made and only one £20 appropriation was approved. Modest financial support resumes in the mid-1860s, but no actual payments were made until after Whewell's death in 1866. In *Gentlemen of Science*, Morrell and Thackray point out that the scientific community used the British Association to secure research funds and to publicize their findings. In the case of Section F, it is evident that the same scientific community was willing to restrict access to funding for research proposals which were deemed to conflict with the interests of the culture of science. No doubt Whewell resolved to impede research and its dissemination when it went beyond "those classes of facts relating to communities of men which are capable of being expressed by numbers, and which promise, when sufficiently multiplied, to indicate general laws" – the initial restriction imposed on that Section's researches.

In his recent book *Science as Practice and Culture*, Pickering notes that

while science has always commanded a considerable audience, scholars have traditionally shown little interest in scientific practice. Their primary concern has always been with the products of science, especially with the conceptual product, knowledge.

(Pickering 1992: 3)

In the early 1970s, the sociology of scientific knowledge (SSK) differentiated itself from both the sociology and the philosophy of science by insisting that "scientific knowledge itself had to be understood as a social product" (ibid., p. 1). While historians of science have made important headway in these matters, historians of economics have lagged behind in developing an understanding of the sociology of scientific knowledge in economics (the "sociology of economic knowledge" (SEK)). The central problematic of SSK is that of knowledge and begins by characterizing the technical culture of science as a single conceptual network and thus scientific "practice is the creative extension of the conceptual net to fit new circumstances" (ibid., p. 4). What holds the culture of science together is "the instrumental aspect of scientific knowledge and the agency of scientific actors: knowledge is for use, not for contemplation, and the actors have their own interests that instruments can serve well or ill" (ibid.). Pickering continues:

> On the one hand, actors can be seen as tentatively seeking to extend culture in ways that might serve their interests rather than in ways that might not. And on the other hand, interests serve as standards against which the products of such extensions, new conceptual nets, can be assessed. A good extension of the net is one that serves the interest of the relevant scientific community best.
>
> (ibid.)

Thus the emphasis of SSK is not to understand scientific knowledge as objective truth, but to consider it relative to the interests of the culture of science.

The episode examined in this chapter has interesting implications for the sociology of scientific knowledge (SSK) and the sociology of economic knowledge (SEK). These understand knowledge not so much as objective truth but as a mechanism for promoting the interests of the culture of science – "the culture of economics". Ricardian economics was based on a utilitarian philosophical foundation and employed the deductive method. The enemies of the Ricardians, the inductivists, created two organizations, the "Statistical Section" (later Section F) of the British Association and the Statistical Society of London (later the Royal Statistical Society) and sought to control the scientific study of political economy through the use of classification systems. Jones's classification sought to impose controls on both the actors and the production of new scientific knowledge. Though the Jones classification of 1833 became institutionalized in the original Committee structure of the Society and was employed to try to control both the research topics and the members' actions, it failed as a control mechanism.

That failure threatened the culture of science. In the case of Section F, the interests of the culture of science, promoted and protected by the British Association, were threatened by the interests of the culture of statistics and economics. When the research presented in Section F moved beyond science into political issues, not only was their legitimacy as a rightful part of the British Association challenged, but that benefit most likely to appeal to those with an interest in economics – funding for research – was denied them. Yet, as Pickering observed: "nothing within the net fixes its future development" since "modeling is an open-ended process" (Pickering 1992: 4). What happened in this case was what sociologists of scientific knowledge expect – scientific "practice is the creative extension of the conceptual net to fit new circumstances" (ibid.).

NOTES

1 The ordering of these six sections follows closely the hierarchy laid out in Whewell's speech to the General Meeting of the British Association. In the two meetings prior to 1833, there had been separate structures. At the 1831 meeting, there were six subcommittees (mathematical and physical science; chemistry; mineralogy; geology and geography; zoology and botany; and mechanical arts) with no number or letter assigned and no sections. At the 1832 meeting, there were four sections and four committees of science (I: Pure Mathematics, mechanics, hydrostatics, hydraulics, plane and physical astronomy, meteorology, magnetism, philosophy of heat, light and sound; II: Chemistry, mineralogy, electricity, magnetism; III: Geology and geography; and IV: Zoology, botany, physiology, anatomy) with each section having a designated chairman and secretary (see Morrell and Thackray 1981: 453–4 Table 11).

   Morrell and Thackray add to the list of the six sections established at the 1833 meeting their respective subsections: I: Mathematical and physico-mathematical sciences (astronomy, mechanics, hydrostatics, hydraulics, light, sound, heat, meteorology and mechanical arts); II: Chemistry, electricity, galvanism, magnetism, mineralogy, chemical arts and manufactures; III: Geology and geography; IV: Natural history (botany and zoology); V: Anatomy and medicine; and VI: Statistics (ibid.).

2 Jones and Whewell explored launching both a periodical and the statistical organizations. In 1831, Jones proposed to Whewell that they launch an inductivist periodical. Jones's enthusiasm for the project convinced Whewell to set aside his initial misgivings. In an April 24, 1831, letter to Jones, Whewell declared that:

   I have a very strong conviction that taking such [an inductive] line of moral philosophy, political economy, and science, as I suppose we should, we might partly find and partly form a school which would be considerable in influence of the best kind.

   (Todhunter 1876: II, p. 118)

   Whewell made a failed effort to enlist Malthus into their campaign for the periodical (see the correspondence between Whewell and Malthus in De Marchi and Sturges 1973). With Malthus's rejection of the effort to recruit him and Whewell's interests far too encompassing to devote the necessary time and energy to this project, "Jones was confronted with the dual role of rounding off a system and publicising it. The task was too much for him" (Checkland 1949: 45).

3 Like the other sections of the British Association, the Statistical Section had its "Committee of Science". At its founding, that Committee included the following members:

Chairman – Professor Babbage.
Secretary – J. E. Drinkwater, M.A.
H. Elphinstone, F.R.S. W. Empson, M.A. Earl Fitzwilliam, F.R.S. H. Hallam, F.R.S. E. Halswell, F.R.S. Rev. Professor Jones. Sir C. Lemon, Bart. F.R.S. J. W. Lubbock, Treas. R.S. Professor Malthus. Capt. Pringle. M. Quetelet. Rev. E. Stanley, F.L.S. G.S. Colonel Sykes, F.R.S. F.L.S. G.S. Richard Taylor, F.L.S. G.S.
(Report of the Third Meeting of the British Association for the Advancement of Science 1833: xl)

4   Though Jones's letter is undated, it was clearly written just before the 1833 meeting of the British Association. A companion letter written shortly after this one, on the same general topics, has been dated by an unknown hand, presumably an archivist working with the Whewell Papers Collection, as either 1833 or 1836. In the first of the two companion letters, Jones refers to a meeting which included Malthus. Since Malthus died in 1834, the 1836 tentative dating of these two letters is clearly mistaken.

5   Rawson urged the members to focus attention on the collection of facts to which they had access. Here he urged members to specialize in one, or perhaps two, classes of data.

> Some had the opportunity or inclination to collect one class, others a second – few or none could collect all. All members were, therefore, invited to transmit those with which they were familiar. Members connected with public institutions, hospitals, charities, corporate bodies, bodies administering the poor-laws, regulating markets, or employing a number of labourers, might also afford useful information.
>
> (Rawson 1835: 42)

Rawson's plea for specialization in the collection of facts was contradicted many years later, in March 1881, by Robert Giffen in his discussion of Wynnard Hooper's paper "The Method of Statistical Analysis". Giffen

> thought it was sometimes to be regretted that statisticians seemed to confine themselves exclusively to one science. If they found some people acquainted with the statistics of trade, they generally found the same people unacquainted with the facts relating to population, and so on with other things, which was greatly to be regretted. One use of the work of a society like this ought to be to stimulate the general knowledge of statistical facts apart from a particular branch of the study. One service which they could render was to bring together all the statistical data about different studies, and popularise and diffuse the information regarding them.
>
> (Giffen 1881: 49)

6   At the 1838 meeting of the British Association, the President of the Leeds Statistical Society, Samuel Hare, proposed "an Outline for Subjects for Statistical Enquiries". Hare's "Outline" was based on the need for the statistical societies to pay "strict attention, so far as is practicable, to uniformity in the designs they have in view; by general agreement in reference to the principles on which they are based, the terms and numerals employed in their investigations, and the documents necessary to their elucidation" (*Journal of the Statistical Society* November 1838: 426). Hare then "sketched an Outline of the Subjects of Enquiry, comprising a series of tables, intended to be subsequently filled up by different Societies; the arrangement of which subjects, though necessarily

complex, are classified in a comprehensive, yet condensed manner" (ibid., pp. 426–7). Here is Hare's "Outline for Subjects for Statistical Enquiries".

I.   Physical Statistics; relating to Topography, &c.
     Topography, Geology, Meteorology.
II. Vital Statistics; relating to the Physical Being of Man.
     Births, Marriages, Deaths, Population, and Medical Statistics.
III. Mental Statistics; relating to the Intellectual and Moral Being of Man.
     Education, Adult Instruction, Ecclesiastical Institutions, and Criminal Statistics.
IV. Economic Statistics; relating to the Social Condition of Man.
     Real and Personal Property, Manufactures, Trade, Commerce, Transit of Goods, Municipality, Agriculture, &c.
V.   Miscellaneous.
     Various Subjects, not embraced in the foregoing.
                         (ibid., p.427; order revised slightly for clarity)

7   The Council of the Statistical Society also set about trying to devise means of developing uniform data sets. In its "Fifth Annual Report" the Council announced that the Society's Committee on Vital Statistics had developed common "forms of registry" which "have been adopted in important public institutions – a fact which, as tending to produce a systematic completeness and uniformity of future results, is alone compensation for the labour of planning judicious forms of registration" (*Journal of the Statistical Society* April 1839: 131).
8   The term "*statist*" meant statistician.
9   "Lord Bacon's own favourite instrument the *Tabula inveniendi*" means an inventory table.
10 Dr Guy's classification of the papers read the previous year reads:

To the division of Economical Statistics belong Dr. Guy's paper, "On the relation of the Price of Wheat to the Revenue derived from Customs and Excise"; Mr. Danson's able paper on "our Commerce with Russia in peace and war"; Mr. Minasi's paper, "On the Decimal System of Coinage"; Dr. Waddilove's paper, "On the effect of the Recent Orders in Council in relation to British, Russian, and Neutral Commerce"; and Mr. Newmarch's valuable contribution, "On the Loan raised by Mr. Pitt during the French War, 1793–1801, with some statements in defence of the Methods of Funding employed." All these communications, from their direct bearing on questions of the highest interest to the Politician and Statesman, might have been classed with equal propriety under the second head of Political Statistics, to which division Mr. William Taylor's "Statistical and Historical View of the Statutes of the Realm" may also be referred. To the subdivision of Medical Statistics belong Mr. Angus's communication, "On the Movement of the Population, Mortality, and Fatal Diseases in London in the last fourteen years." Under the head Moral and Intellectual Statistics, the paper by the Reverend Robert Everest, "On Pauperism and Crime in the United States of America," and that by Mr. Horace Mann, "On the Statistical Position of Religious Bodies in England and Wales," would have to be placed. Mr. Bell's paper on the "Statistics of the Colony of Victoria," and Mr. Welton's paper on the "Statistics of the United States of America," must be arranged under the class of General Statistics, for which the classification just quoted makes no provision.
                         (*Journal of the Statistical Society* June 1855: 99–100)

11   The articles were classified as follows:

> Mr. Hodge followed up his valuable paper "On the Mortality arising from
> Naval Operations," by a similar communication, "On the Mortality arising
> from Military Operations." A paper presented by Dr. Fenwick, of Tynemouth,
> "On the Effects of Over-crowding and Want of Ventilation on Cholera"; and
> by Dr. Guy, "On the Duration of Life among Lawyers." These papers illustrate
> the subject of Vital Statistics. In the subdivision of Economical Statistics the
> Society had the advantage of a paper, "On the Bank of England: its present
> Constitution and Operations," by Mr. Jellicoe; – "On the loss sustained by
> Government in granting Annuities," by Mr. Hendricks; – and "On the Banking
> Establishment in Brussels, termed Union du Credit de Bruxelles," by Mr.
> Lumley. Under the head of Criminal Statistics the Rev. John Clay communi-
> cated a Paper "On the Connection between Crime, Popular Education,
> Attendance at Religious Worship, and Beer-houses."
>
> (ibid.)

12   The material that follows is drawn from my paper "The place of economics in
      the hierarchy of sciences: Section F from Whewell to Edgeworth", forthcoming.
13   A year earlier, shortly after the 1840 meeting of the British Association, Whewell
      had complained in private to Murchison, in a letter dated September 25, 1840,
      that

> It was impossible to listen to the proceedings of the Statistical Section on
> Friday without perceiving that they involved exactly what it was most
> necessary and most desired to exclude from our proceedings. Is there any
> objection to the President declaring in his place, in the most emphatic manner,
> that the mode in which this Section has been conducted is inconsistent with
> the objects and character of the Association?
>
> (Todhunter 1876: II, p. 289)

Whewell raised the question of "the President declaring in his place" because
Murchison had proposed that he serve as President of the British Association for
the next meeting. So annoyed was Whewell with the activities of Section F that
he made the following declaration in a letter to Murchison dated October 2,
1840:

> As to the Statistical Section scruple, I cannot get over the utter incongruity of
> its proceedings with all our professions and all our principles. Who would
> venture to propose (I put it to Chalmers, and he allowed the proposal to be
> intolerable) an ambulatory body, composed partly of men of reputation, and
> partly of a miscellaneous crowd, to go round year by year, from town to town,
> and at each place to discuss the most inflammatory and agitating questions of
> the day? Yet this is exactly what we have been doing for several years. I must
> say plainly, that rather than be concerned in such wild and dangerous
> absurdity, in defiance of solemn professions to the contrary, I would utterly
> renounce the Association with all its advantages. You have made me your
> President, with no good will of mine; in everything else I will be instructed
> by you, and labour, as well as I know how, for the advantage of the
> Association, in any way in which I can aid it: but I will make no agreement
> with you that I will not denounce, in the most public and emphatic manner,
> this gross violation of our fundamental constitution. If we offend people by
> recurring to our professed principles, I cannot help it. If our Association does

not suit them, when conducted on its only rational grounds, let them make one of their own.

(ibid., pp. 291–2)

On October 5, 1840, Whewell laid out the exact nature of his quarrel with Chalmers in a letter to Lord Northampton.

If such discussions be allowed, there is nothing in legislation or politics which can be consistently excluded. Dr. Chalmers made an attempt to justify or mask this impropriety by saying that it was an example of the value of *numbers*.... The absurdity of such a plea is, I think, undeniable, and the inconsistency of such discussions with our fundamental constitution. And this is not a question of form merely. For what kind of institution do we become, if we allow ourselves to be made an ambulatory meeting for agitating in assemblies, when both *eminent* and *notorious* men (Dr. Chalmers and Robert Owen) address a miscellaneous crowd on the sorest and angriest subjects which occur among the topics of the day? If we cannot get rid of this character, most assuredly I shall be disposed to make my connection with the Association as brief as I can do, without shewing myself indifferent to the good opinion of friends like yourself, who are good natured enough to think that I can be of service to the genuine interests of the body.

(ibid., p. 294)

BIBLIOGRAPHY

Annals of the Royal Statistical Society, 1834–1934 (1934) London.

Cannon, Susan Faye (1978) *Science in Culture: The Early Victorian Period*, New York.

Checkland, S. G. (1949) "The Propagation of Ricardian Economics in England", *Economica, New Series* 16 (61) (February): 40–52.

De Marchi, N. B. and Sturges, R. P. (1973) "Malthus and Ricardo's inductivist critics: four letters to William Whewell", Economica, *New Series* 40 (November): 379–93.

Dolby, R. G. A. (1979) "Classification of the sciences, the nineteenth century tradition", in Roy F. Ellen and David Reason (eds) *Classifications in their Social Context*, London: Academic Press, pp. 167–93.

Giffen, Robert (1881) "Discussion [of Wynnard Hooper's 'The Method of Statistical Analysis']", *Journal of the Statistical Society* March: 49.

Goldman, Lawrence (1983) "The origins of British 'social science': political economy, natural science and statistics 1830–1835", *The Historical Journal* 26 (3): 587–616.

Guy, William A. (1841) "On the best method of collecting and arranging facts, with a proposed new plan of a common-place book", *Journal of the Statistical Society* 3, Part IV (January): 353–66.

—— (1865) "On the original and acquired meaning of the term 'statistics,' and on the proper functions of a statistical society: also on the question whether there be a science of statistics; and if so, what are its nature and objects, and what is its relation to political economy and 'social science'?", *Journal of the Statistical Society* 28, Part IV (December): 478–93.

Hare, Samuel (1838) "Abstract of an outline for subjects for statistical enquiries", *Journal of the Statistical Society* 1, Part 3 (November): 426–7).

Henderson, James P. (forthcoming) "The place of economics in the hierarchy of sciences: Section F from Whewell to Edgeworth", in Phillip Mirowski (ed.) *Natural Images in Economics: Markets Read in Tooth and Claw.*

Herschel, John F. W. (1830) *A Preliminary Discourse on the Study of Natural Philosophy*; reprinted Chicago, 1987.

"Introduction", *Journal of the Statistical Society* 1 (1) (May 1838): 1–5.

Jevons, William Stanley (1877) *The Principles of Science: A Treatise on Logic and Scientific Method*; reprinted New York, 1958.

Journal of the Statistical Society, various editions, London.

Journal of the Statistical Society: General Index, various editions, London.

Knight, David (1981) *Ordering the World: A History of Classifying Man*, London.

Morrell, Jack and Thackray, Arnold (1981) *Gentlemen of Science, Early Years of the British Association for the Advancement of Science*, Oxford.

Pickering, Andrew (ed.) (1992) *Science as Practice and Culture*, Chicago.

"Prospectus of the Objects and Plan of the Statistical Society of London", *Report of the Third Meeting of the British Association for the Advancement of Science* (1833), pp. 492–5.

R. [John Robertson] (1838) "Transactions of the Statistical Society of London", *London and Westminster Review* 31 (1) (April): 45–72.

Rawson, Rawson William (1835) "On the collection of statistics", *Proceedings of the Statistical Society of London* 1 (1) (June 15): 41–3.

Report of the Third Meeting of the British Association for the Advancement of Science (1833).

Subject Index to the Journal of the Royal Statistical Society (1865–1894) (1895) London.

Todhunter, Isaac (1876) *William Whewell, D.D. Master of Trinity College, Cambridge, An Account of His Writings*, 2 vols, London.

Whewell, William (1831a) "Jones – on the distribution of wealth", *British Critic, Quarterly Theological Review, and Ecclesiastical Record* 10 (July): 41–61.

—— (1831b) "Moral science – inductive science", *Quarterly Review* 45 (July): 374–407.

—— (1833) *Report of the Third Meeting of the British Association for the Advancement of Science*, pp. xi–xxvi.

—— (1841) "Address", *Report of the Eleventh Meeting of the British Association for the Advancement of Science*, pp. xxvii–xxxv.

—— (1847) *The Philosophy of the Inductive Sciences, Founded Upon their History*, 2 volumes, London.

Whewell Papers Collection, Trinity College Library, Cambridge.

Yeo, Richard R. (1991) "William Whewell's philosophy of knowledge and its reception", in Menachem Fisch and Simon Schaffer (eds) *William Whewell: A Composite Portrait*, Oxford, pp. 175–200.

Chapter 4

Measurement in utility calculations
The utilitarian perspective

Sandra J. Peart

INTRODUCTION

In his 1981 Richard Ely Address to the American Economics Association, Lionel Robbins reasserted his conviction, originally posed in his famous 1932 essay, that policy analysis, and indeed applied economics more generally, necessarily relies on value judgments and therefore lies outside the scope of scientific ("value-free") economics. Instead of repudiating policy analysis on these grounds, however, Robbins called for the (re)creation of "political economy" – "covering that part of our sphere of interest which essentially involves judgments of value. Political economy, thus conceived, is quite unashamedly concerned with the assumptions of policy and the results flowing from them" (1981: xxvii).[1] In the face of a seemingly intractable measurement problem created by the impossibility of interpersonal comparisons of utility or welfare, Robbins's recommendation is that economists redirect their efforts away from welfare economics in the tradition of the felicific calculus and into "political economy" as such.

Not all economists, however, have shared Robbins's conviction that welfare is unmeasurable and that attention should therefore be directed to issues other than measurement; "cardinalists" have reemerged in welfare economics during the past few decades. Relying in part on the justification that economists are better equipped than ethicists or politicians to measure social welfare, these economists have attempted to estimate welfare empirically. Their procedure is to assume that individuals are the same in their *capacity* for enjoyment, but not in their *circumstances*; utility is presumed to be the same function of various determinants of utility for all individuals (or households), while parameters characterizing individual functions are allowed to differ (Tinbergen 1991:7). These empirical endeavors are grouped by Jan Tinbergen into the American procedure (associated with Dale Jorgenson), which has used a translog utility function where the log utility is a quadratic function of the logs of three or five determinants of utility (consumption goods or services).[2] Family size, age of head, region of residence, race and type of residence are the parameters that characterize groups of consumers (p. 8). The procedure of the Dutch group (associated with Van Praag) has been to specify the welfare function as a function only of income: $W = \sum a_i \ln(x_i + 1)$, where x represents income (p. 9). This functional form has the advantage of yielding diminishing marginal utilities: $\partial W/\partial x_i = a_i/(x_i + 1)$.

At the same time as the empirical measurement of "welfare" has been revived as a legitimate concern for economists, some attempt has been made further to define the nature of "social welfare". As Amartya Sen has argued recently, the pioneers of modern welfare economics (Bergson 1938; Samuelson 1947; Arrow 1951) presume that "social welfare" represents the "goodness of the social state"; the determination of that "goodness", however, is left "completely open" in the sense that neither the arguments in nor the functional form of the social welfare function is restricted in the analysis of modern welfare economics (1991: 15). The utilitarian social welfare function, $W = \sum U_i$, implies that *only* individual utilities, $\{U_i\}$, contribute to the evaluation of social good; non-utility information plays no role in the evaluative judgments concerning various social states. In addition, because the ranking of any two alternative states, such as x and y, relates only to the utility *difference* that an individual has between these alternatives, the levels of utility play no direct role in the ranking of different welfare states.[3] Thus, in traditional welfare economics, the welfare of any state is determined only by individual utilities or welfares of individuals in that state. Further, individual welfare or utility is identified with the fulfillment of individual preferences. As a result, individual preferences between any social state and another constitute the basis for ranking those two states.

In opposition to this approach, Sen argues in favor of giving "a more central and constitutive place to the freedoms and liberties of individuals in the determination of social welfare" (p. 18), an approach which implies rejecting the claim that social welfare is a function only of individual welfares, and also rejecting the identification of preference fulfillment with individual welfare. By contrast, Sen regards individual preference as intrinsically important and individual utility as secondarily so (p. 20). In his formulation, freedom is "primarily related to the specification of the *set* from which one can choose"; generally, freedom is not independent of the preference ordering over the constituents of these respective sets (pp. 21–2).[4] Thus, the evaluation of the freedom enjoyed from a given menu depends on how the elements in the menu are valued by the individual (pp. 22–5).[5]

Many of the contemporary debates concerning the nature and constituents of the "social good", as well as the measurability of utility and the relationships between individual goods, preferences and social welfare, have historical precedents in the works of nineteenth-century policy analysts. J. S. Mill and W. S. Jevons struggled with the issue of defining and measuring the "greatest good". Like Sen, Mill was ambivalent about equating welfare with preference fulfillment. Jevons, by contrast, took a step towards the approach of modern welfare economists by identifying welfare with choices made. Both Mill and Jevons explicitly considered "liberty" (carefully defined) as a constituent of the social as well as the individual good, so that in this respect their approach has something in common with the type of social judgments that Sen favors. While welfare, for Mill, was measurable in principle, he was stopped by the difficulty of reconciling different pleasures into one whole "pleasure". Jevons overcame this measurement problem by allowing that pleasures differ only in their (quantifiable) characteristics. But he was unable to define a means of measuring these characteristics, and ultimately also stopped short of recommending measurement of social happiness.

Nevertheless, in their policy evaluations Mill and Jevons made the type of explicit value judgments that Robbins unashamedly called for in the address, based on their "own estimates of the happiness afforded or the misery endured by different persons or groups of persons". Their agreement about many policy recommendations reflects the similarity of their visions of a reformed society, whose citizens were, broadly speaking, intellectually as well as economically independent. Once that vision of the basis for reform largely disappeared from economic analysis – which was accompanied by a perceptible decline in optimism about the prospects for reform via policy – the problem of *measuring* social welfare began to take precedence in utilitarian policy analysis, and the concept of social welfare became more narrowly identified with the sum of individual utilities. In this chapter we argue that the shift in focus begins in the transition of economics from Mill to Jevons.

BENTHAM, J. S. MILL AND THE SEARCH FOR A STANDARD OF "UTILITY"

As Wesley C. Mitchell has noted, what distinguished Jeremy Bentham's work was not the idea of utilitarianism *per se* – the "greatest good of the greatest number" – but rather the argument that net pleasures might be measured via the "felicific calculus" (1918: 163). Bentham described how these measurements might proceed in a passage that Jevons would return to a hundred years later:

> To a person considered *by himself*, the value of a pleasure or pain considered *by itself*, will be greater or less, according to the four following circumstances: 1 Its *intensity*. 2 Its *duration*. 3 Its *certainty* ... 4 Its *propinquity*.... But when the value of any pleasure or pain is considered for the purpose of estimating the tendency of any *act* by which it is produced, there are two other circumstances to be taken into the account; these are, 5 Its *fecundity* ... 6 Its *purity*.... [When a community is considered, it is also necessary to take account of] 7 Its *extent*; that is, the number of persons to whom it *extends*.
>
> (1789: 16)

In principle, the calculation was to proceed as follows. Intensity was to be measured in units of the "faintest sensation that can be distinguished".[6] Units of intensity are multiplied by the duration units, and then by fractions expressing certainty and proximity. If additional pleasures (fecundity), or pains (purity), are produced by an act, these are measured in the same way, and added to the measure of direct pleasure. The measurement is completed by multiplying the result by the number of individuals affected (Mitchell 1918: 165).

Bentham realized that this last step required a simplification that was generally unwarranted, because not all individuals are alike in their capacities for enjoying pleasures and pains. Health, strength, firmness of mind, occupations, income, sex, age, rank, education, climate, lineage, government, religious status and other "circumstances" all influenced the individual's "sensibility" to experience and register pleasures and pains (Bentham 1789: ch. 6). Indeed Bentham clearly recognized that measurement of social utility was approximate at best:

> 'Tis in vain to talk of adding quantities which after the addition will continue distinct as they were before, one man's happiness will never be another man's happiness: a gain to one man is no gain to another: you might as well pretend to add 20 apples to 20 pears.... This addibility of the happiness of different subjects, however when considered rigorously it may appear fictitious, is a postulatum without the allowance of which all political reasoning is at a stand: nor is it more fictitious than that of the equality of chances to reality, on which that whole branch of the Mathematics which is called the doctrine of chances is established.
>
> (cited in Halévy 1928: 495)

Thus while there was no way to measure social welfare or happiness precisely, expediency required some attempt at approximate weighing of the net balance.[7]

For J. S. Mill, like Bentham, the unifying principle of public policy was "the greatest good of the greatest number". He was much concerned, however, with the precise nature of the general rule, in particular with "what things [utilitarianism] includes in the ideas of pain and pleasure" (*Collected Works of John Stuart Mill* (*CW*), x, p. 210). Two problems emerged. First, whom to include in the maximand? – a question which, as the quotation below reveals, Mill answered on pragmatic grounds. Second, and more complex for Mill, is how to define individual, let alone social, "happiness". Here, in one of his strongest reactions against Bentham, Mill distinguished between an individual's "happiness" and "good": " 'The greatest happiness of the greatest number' is to be our invariable guide! Is it so? – the greatest happiness of men living, I suppose, not of men to come; for if of all posterity, what legislator can be our guide? Who can prejudge the future? Of men living then? – well

– how often would *their* greatest happiness consist in concession to their greatest errors" (*CW*, x, pp. 501–2).[8]

Mill reformulated the utilitarian goal, rejecting what he perceived to be Bentham's excessively narrow definition of utility (cf. *CW*, i, pp. 99–100).[9] Because he stressed man's spiritual nature, Mill argued that material gain is not the ultimate goal for society. A moral tone and a wide notion of "improvement" were therefore integrated into the utilitarian goal; "utility", he maintained, constitutes "the ultimate source of moral obligations" (*CW*, x, p. 226). This perspective had major implications for economic policy, which at the least, Mill argued, was to suit, and at best might improve, the moral character of the public.[10] Thus Mill occasionally questioned the effectiveness of institutional reforms which did not aim at moral improvement and would consequently not achieve lasting effects.

In "Utilitarianism", Mill insisted that "equal amounts of happiness are equally desirable, whether felt by the same or by different persons".[11] He championed "impartiality" and "equality" – "exalted" both "popularly" as well as by the "enlightened" – not as a corollary of utilitarianism but instead as "involved in the very meaning of Utility": a principle that is "a mere form of words without rational signification, unless one person's happiness, supposed equal in degree (with the proper allowance made for kind), is counted for exactly as much as another's" (*CW*, x, p. 257). Thus each has "an equal claim to all the means of happiness", although that right is qualified: "except in so far as the inevitable conditions of human life, and the general interest, in which that of every individual is included, set limits to the maxim" (p. 258).

The greatest-happiness notion remained problematic nonetheless, since the amount of happiness (of the same kind) was not directly measurable, as Mill's choice of verb above ("*supposed* equal in degree") reveals. An "anterior principle" of utilitarianism, it is allowed, is "that the rules of arithmetic are applicable to the valuation of happiness, as of all other measurable quantities" (*CW*, x, p. 258n.). The only measure of quantity, Mill argued, consisted of the verdict of those who had experienced different quantities of pleasurable sensations: "What means are there of determining which is the acutest of two pains, or the intensest of two pleasurable sensations, except the general suffrage of those who are familiar with both? Neither pains nor pleasures are homogeneous, and pain is always heterogeneous with pleasure. What is there to decide whether a particular pleasure is worth purchasing at the cost of a particular pain, except the feelings and judgment of the experienced?" (*CW*, x, p. 213). Unlike the cardinalists whose procedures are outlined above, Mill maintained that individuals differed in their capacity for feeling (see *CW*, viii, pp. 856ff.; De Marchi 1972).

Even more serious, Mill maintained that pleasures differed in kind as well as amount; but he was never able to provide a clear-cut means of either measuring total pleasure or, indeed, ranking types of pleasure. Thus, he argued that "It is quite compatible with the principle of utility to recognise the fact, that some *kinds* of pleasure are more desirable and more valuable than others" (*CW*, x, pp. 211).[12] Given Mill's "anterior principle" noted above, "qualitatively" and "quantitatively" different pleasures might, somehow, be combined into "total pleasure", or "social utility". But the means of this reconciliation was unsatisfactory and elicited harsh criticism from Jevons since it entailed a potential loss of individual sovereignty. The moralist like Mill who attempts to promote improvement might not accept that pleasures which attract more people are those which should be ranked more highly than ones which attract fewer people.[13] Consequently Mill maintained that popular pleasures were not necessarily ranked above less popular pleasures, and sought an alternative means of ranking pleasures. He suggested that "those who are competently acquainted" with two pleasures might pronounce judgment on their relative merits:

> If I am asked, what I mean by difference of quality in pleasures, or what makes one pleasure more valuable than another, merely as a pleasure, except its being greater in amount, there is but one possible answer. Of two pleasures, if there be one to which all or almost all who have experience of both give a decided preference, irrespective of any feeling of moral obligation to prefer it, that is the more desirable pleasure. If one of the two is, by those who are competently acquainted with both, placed so far above the other that they prefer it, even though knowing it to be attended with a greater amount of discontent, and would not resign it for any quantity of the other pleasure which their nature is capable of,[14] we are justified in ascribing to the preferred enjoyment a superiority in quality, so far outweighing quantity as to render it, in comparison, of small account.
>
> (*CW*, x, pp. 211)[15]

As a last resort, apparently, Mill relied upon the evaluation of "competent judges" who were to perform the difficult task of "valuing" the quality of pleasures. Yet Mill traveled some distance towards equating "quality" with "quantity" differences: intellectual pleasure is preferred to physical pleasure because it leads to additional future pleasure, and it is less frequently associated with pain, thus entailing, on the whole, a larger quantity of pleasure.[16] Mill maintained, also, that constancy of pleasure is to be preferred over intensity, and that active pleasures are preferred to passive pleasures (although we must bear in mind that intellectual pleasures are seen as mentally active). Here the suggestion is that intense pleasure is – by its nature – fleeting, and thus compares poorly with less intense but longer lasting pleasure. It is in this context that we must understand Mill's warning that individuals should not expect "more from life than it is capable of bestowing", meaning that one should not expect to achieve a life filled with intense pleasure:[17]

If by happiness be meant a continuity of highly pleasurable excitement, it is evident enough that this is impossible. A state of exalted pleasure lasts only moments, or in some cases, and with some intermissions, hours or days, and is the occasional brilliant flash of enjoyment, not its permanent and steady flame. Of this the philosophers who have taught that happiness is the end of life were as fully aware as those who taunt them. The happiness which they meant was not a life of rapture; but moments of such, in an existence made up of few and transitory pains, many and various pleasures, with a decided predominance of the active over the passive, and having as the foundation of the whole, not to expect more from life than it is capable of bestowing.

(*CW*, x, p. 215)

The alleviation of poverty – "in any sense implying suffering" – is not, however, expecting too much from life and constitutes a key element in the "happy" life for individuals, and for social happiness: "Poverty, in any sense implying suffering, may be completely extinguished by the wisdom of society, combined with the good sense and providence of individuals." Somewhat naively, Mill believed that education might "indefinitely" reduce disease: "Even that most intractable of enemies, disease, may be indefinitely reduced in dimensions by good physical and moral education, and proper control of noxious influences; while the progress of science holds out a promise for the future of still more direct conquests over this detestable foe" (*CW*, x, p. 216). The "present wretched education, and wretched social arrangements", Mill contends, are the "only real hindrance" to achieving social utility and progress (p. 215).

Since for Mill the moral, economic and intellectual independence of each is integral to "happiness", he emphasized "liberty" as a component in the utilitarian goal. This is a carefully specified liberty, pertaining to "self-regarding" actions ("liberty of thought and feeling"; "liberty of tastes and pursuits"; and the liberty "of combination among individuals"), and is regarded as a human need, requisite to attaining happiness: "Where, not the person's own character, but the traditions or customs of other people are the rule of conduct, there is wanting one of the principal ingredients of human happiness, and quite the chief ingredient of individual and social progress" (*CW*, xviii, p. 261). "A person", Mill contends, has no character unless his "desires and impulses are his own – are the expression of his own nature, as it has been developed and modified by his own culture" (p. 264).

As a result, so-called progress cannot be imposed on individuals; the effectiveness of institutional reforms is limited by the ability of individuals to understand and to embrace reform measures. Mill stressed that specific reforms should be encouraged but voluntary, and preferred local to central control of reforms on the grounds that this preserved liberty; his praise for the Poor Law ran along precisely these lines.[18] Further, diversity, reflecting liberty to formulate and question one's beliefs and habits, was not to be eroded by the oppression of public opinion:

> It is not by wearing down into uniformity all that is individual in themselves, but by cultivating it and calling it forth, within the limits imposed by the rights and interests of others, that human beings become a noble and beautiful object of contemplation; and as the works partake the character of those who do them, by the same process human life also becomes rich, diversified, and animating, furnishing more abundant aliment to high thoughts and elevating feelings, and strengthening the tie which binds every individual to the race, by making the race infinitely better worth belonging to.

(CW, xviii, p. 266)

In instances of "social acts", however, intervention was admissible, and here a weighing of the net benefits from intervention was required, taking into account the predicted influence of intervention on liberty (*CW*, xviii, p. 293; cf. *CW*, iii, pp. 803–4).[19] Each case required examination to determine whether intervention was warranted; if unimpeded action led to undesirable results, this behavior might be restricted on utilitarian grounds. Laws preventing fraud, and sanitary and safety regulations were justified on this basis (pp. 293–4).

Throughout, Mill's program for social reform accords conspicuous weight to the encouragement of self-reliance among laborers.[20] The distribution of rewards to labor in nineteenth-century Britain, "almost in an inverse ratio to the labour", was viewed as an impediment to the acquisition of independence among the laboring classes (*CW*, ii, p. 207; cf. "The claims of labour", iv, p. 385; v, p. 444). Education, understood in the widest sense of "whatever acts upon the minds of the labouring classes" – including "the whole of their social circum-stances" – constituted a "most obvious remedy" to the plight of the laboring poor (p. 376; cf. pp. 377ff.).[21] The attainment of high general wages should "be wel-comed and rejoiced at" (*CW*, iii, p. 929; cf. p. 930). Most importantly, "the right of making the attempt" to raise wages by trade unions was a matter of justice, and not to be denied. In short, "the improvement and elevation of the working classes" through "the liberty of association" was championed (p. 903).[22] As a preferable means of improvement, however, Mill favored cooperation, on the grounds precisely that cooperative arrangements would encourage the achieve-ment of independence among the laboring classes.[23]

In summary, Mill's utilitarian standard entailed allowance for qualitative and quantitative differences in pleasures, while equal amounts of equally ranked pleasures were to count equally for all. Measurement of social utility was nonetheless difficult, and Mill maintained that those who had wide experience with pleasures might pronounce judgment on the most "desirable" pleasures from the perspective of society. Mill's own vision of social happiness entailed a prominent role for liberty, which presupposed improved material well-being and the acquisition of self-reliant behavior among the laboring classes. Undoubtedly Mill was overly optimistic in this regard, arguing that "no one whose opinion deserves a moment's consideration can doubt that most of the great positive evils of the world are in themselves removable, and will, if human affairs continue to improve, be in the end reduced within narrow limits" (*CW*, x, p. 216). By way of contrast, as we shall see below, Jevons argued that qualitative differences in pleasures could be reduced to quantities of (Benthamite) characteristics of pure pleasure. While his own vision of social utility remained similar to that of Mill, Jevons was less willing to trust that reform could substantially alter the character of the laboring classes.

JEVONS'S DENIAL OF MILL'S STANDARD

In his review of Mill's "Utilitarianism" Jevons charged that "Mill was intellectually unfitted to decide what was utilitarian and what was not" (1879: 523). In fact, "in removing the obstacles to the reception of his favourite doctrine he removed its landmarks too, and confused everything" (p. 523). The crux of the matter was this: "Do pleasures differ in quality as well as in quantity?" (p. 525). Are there "elevated" pleasures which can outweigh large amounts of "low quality" pleasures? This question was complicated by the fact that people's estimation of pleasures must differ, there being no evident way to make interpersonal comparisons: "The tippler may esteem two pints of beer doubly as much as one; the hero may feel double satisfaction in saving two lives instead of one; but who shall weigh the pleasure of a pint of beer against the pleasure of saving a fellow-creature's life" (p. 526).[24]

Jevons sided with Bentham and opposed Mill in this matter. Thus, he contended that all types of pleasure might be reduced to quantities of: 1, *intensity*; 2, *duration*; 3, *certainty* or *uncertainty*; 4, *propinquity* or *remoteness*; 5, *fecundity* (the "chance that [pleasure] has of being followed by sensations of the same kind"); 6, *purity* ("the chance it has of *not* being followed by sensations of the *opposite* kind"); and 7, *extent* (to other people).[25] "In all that Bentham says about pleasure and pain", Jevons argued, "there is not a word about the intrinsic superiority of one pleasure to another. He advocates our seeking *pure* pleasures; but with him a pure pleasure was clearly defined as one not likely to be followed by feelings of the opposite kind" (1879: 527).[26] An impure pleasure such as "opium-eating", by contrast, leads to the pain ("evil consequence") of ill health. Jevons maintained that "the ledger and the balance-sheet" should be sufficient to measure "pleasure": "all feelings were reduced to the same denomination of value, and whenever we indulge in a little enjoyment, or endure a pain, the consequences in regard to subsequent enjoyment or suffering are to be inexorably scored for or against us, as the case may be. Our conduct must be judged wise or foolish according as, in the long-run, we find a favourable 'hedonic' balance-sheet" (p. 527).

Like Bentham, Jevons allowed, J. S. Mill regards "pleasure" as "the ultimate purpose of existence" (1879: 528), a pleasure that is distinct from "egoism" *because* it is an aggregate: "the happiness of the race, is, of course, made up of the happiness of its units, so that unless most of the individuals pursue a course ensuring happiness, the race cannot be happy in the aggregate" (p. 529). Thus, the distribution of happiness matters: the utilitarian social welfare function has been mistakenly represented by the sum of individual utilities in the form outlined above (p. 64).[27]

To achieve happiness, the individual must "select that line of conduct which is likely to – that is, will in the majority of cases – bring happiness."[28] It is here that Jevons begins to part company with Mill who, according to Jevons, erred when he argued that there are higher and lower feelings:

> Then Mill proceeds to point out, with all the persuasiveness of his best style, that there are higher feelings which we would not sacrifice for any quantity of a lower feeling. Few human creatures, he holds, would consent to be changed into any of the lower animals for a promise of the fullest allowance of a beast's pleasures; no intelligent human being would consent to be a fool, no instructed person would be an ignoramus, no person of feeling and conscience would be selfish and base, and so forth.... Mill overflows with genial and noble aspirations; he hardly deigns to count the lower pleasures as worth putting in the scale; it is better, he thinks, to be a human being dissatisfied than a pig satisfied; better to be Socrates dissatisfied than a fool satisfied. If the pig or the fool is of a different opinion, it is because they only know their own side of the question. The other party to the comparison knows both sides.
>
> (1879: 528)

Jevons objected on a number of grounds to Mill's characterization of the constituents of "happiness". First, he recoiled at Mill's description of the "good life", suggesting that, on a close reading of Mill's recommendations for achieving happiness (cited above, p. 69), the best thing for an individual to do would be to "aim at moderate achievements in life" and altogether to forgo "higher aspirations" (1879: 529, 530). "It would seem, then", according to Mill, Jevons writes, that "for the mass of mankind" there "is small prospect indeed of achieving happiness through high aspirations" (p. 530).

Just as strongly Jevons reacted against Mill's implicit suggestion, alluded to in the quotation above, that individuals are not always the best judge of their own interests and, as a consequence, that individuals are not always best able to achieve "happiness". Here Jevons referred to Mill's admission that "men often do, *from infirmity of character*, make their selection for the nearer good, though they know it to be the less valuable. Many who begin with youthful enthusiasm for everything noble, sink in later years into indolence and selfishness" (1879: 531). If that were really the case, Jevons argued, then on Mill's own terms this constitutes evidence that the baser pleasure should be ranked ahead of the noble pleasure: "If such men, with few exceptions, decide eventually in favour of the lower life, they are parties who *do* know both sides of the comparison, and deliberately choose not to be Socrates, with the prospect of the very imperfect happiness (probably involving short rations) which is incident to the life of Socrates" (p. 531). Indeed, Mill's insistence *in the face of conflicting evidence* – many individuals reverting from so-called higher to lower pleasures – that the life of Socrates entailed a "higher" pleasure, rankled with Jevons:

> Although, then, millions and millions are continually deciding against Socrates' life, for one reason or another (and many in all ages who make the ineffectual attempt at a combination break down), Mill gratuitously assumes that they are none of them competent witnesses, because they must have lost their higher feelings before they could have descended to the lower level; then the comparatively few who do choose the higher life and succeed in attaining it are adduced as giving a large majority, or even a unanimous vote in favour of their own choice. I submit that this is a fallacy probably best classed as a *petitio principii*; Mill entirely begs the question when he assumes that every witness against him is an incapacitated witness, because he must have lost his capacity for the nobler feelings before he could have decided in favour of the lower.
>
> (p. 532)

Jevons concluded that Mill's call for competent judges amounted to a verdict "in favour of his high quality pleasures" by "a packed jury", a verdict comparable with that "given by vegetarians in favour of a vegetable diet" (p. 532).[29]

Jevons himself insisted that "I am not denying the moral superiority of some pleasures and courses of life over others" (1879: 532). His objection was instead to "Mill's attempt to reconcile his ideas on the subject with the Utilitarian theory" which, he concluded, "hopelessly fails" (p. 532). Mill failed in this attempt, Jevons argued, because he departed from the Benthamite argument that pleasures differed only in quantifiable characteristics of pleasure itself. In opposition to Mill, Jevons maintained that the difference between "high" and "low" pleasures might be analyzed in terms of the (quantifiable) Benthamite characteristics of intensity, length, certainty, fruitfulness, and purity; and "when we take Altruism into account, the feelings must be of wide extent – that is, fruitful of pleasure and devoid of evil to great numbers of people" (p. 533).[30] The social happiness created by various government policies could be quantified and compared, in order then to reveal which contributed most to overall happiness. Thus "after the model of inquiry given by Bentham, [we may] resolve into its elements the effect of one action and the other upon the happiness of the community":

> It is a higher pleasure to build a Free Library than to establish a new Race Course; not because there is a *Free-Library-building emotion*, which is

essentially better than a *Race-Course-establishing emotion*, each being a simple unanalyzable feeling; but because we may, after the model of inquiry given by Bentham, resolve into its elements the effect of one action and the other upon the happiness of the community.

(p. 533)

Jevons's philosophical objections to Mill's "Utilitarianism" centred on what might, broadly speaking, be termed measurement problems. By allowing that pleasures differed qualitatively Mill created a seemingly intractable measurement problem: how was one to measure happiness if it consisted of the weighted sum of qualitatively different pleasures? How was one, indeed, to determine these weights, and how to combine weighted sums of qualitatively different pleasures? Since Mill is first and foremost reform-minded, he has a firm subjective notion of "higher" and "lower" pleasures. As an individualist reformer, he is loath to give up sovereign choice as the means to maximize pleasure. He does come dangerously close to this, however, in the suggestion that "competent judges" might be resorted to in order to rank higher and lower pleasures. Jevons strongly opposed the recommendation, insisted on the sovereignty of individual choices, and maintained, further, that pleasures differed only quantitatively, that is, in their attributes.

Jevons, however, was unable to overcome the measurement problem himself. It is by no means clear how to rank any two policies until a means of measuring "intensity", "fruitfulness" etc. for each person affected by the policy has been devised, and then a weighting scheme has been designed and justified for total pleasure, the (weighted) sum of each type of pleasure (summed across all individuals).[31] Without having measured the pleasure associated with various attributes, Jevons concluded that some pleasure attributes (such as length) contributed more to social utility than others (such as intensity). Policies that might be expected to promote these more worthwhile characteristics were, in his estimation, better than policies which did not. Thus he suggested, for instance, that the construction of a library, which entails lasting pleasure, results in "a higher pleasure" than the establishment of a race course that creates intense, short-lived pleasure (1879: 533). Despite his objections to the subjective nature of Mill's pleasure ranking (the "packed jury"), Jevons did not escape this problem; Jevons's utilitarianism was intimately bound up with subjective judgments concerning the general development of society and the amelioration of working class conditions. Here, he followed closely in the reformist tradition of Mill.[32]

Can we infer anything more precise about how Jevons proposed to measure "happiness"? On balance, although Jevons was cautious in this regard, he did take a step towards the "cardinalist" approach outlined above (pp. 63–4). He sometimes insisted that individual utility, *even in its narrowest, strictly economic sense*, was not measurable.[33] He did maintain, however, that individual utility might be measured indirectly from its effects (although he recognized that individuals differed, and that interpersonal comparisons are not possible). At the same time, social utility, entailing wider concerns than individual activity in the market place, is said to involve a (subjective) weighing of a wide range of pleasures and pains.

In the *Theory of Political Economy* (*TPE*) Jevons acknowledged that measuring pleasure and pain was no simple matter: "I hesitate to say that men will ever have the means of measuring directly the feelings of the human heart. A unit of pleasure or of pain is difficult even to conceive" (*TPE*, p. 11). Indeed, since "we can hardly form the conception of a unit of pleasure or pain", Jevons maintained, "the numerical expression of quantities of feeling seems to be out of the question" (p. 12).

But for the purposes of his theory of exchange, the measurement problem could be avoided; Jevons proposed an indirect measure of these feelings: "*it is from the quantitative effects of the feelings that we must estimate their comparative amounts*".[34] In correspondence with J. E. Cairnes, Jevons reiterated that the only feasible means of measuring utility consisted of using prices:

> The fundamental objection which you make to my theory of exchange is that I defined value by utility and then propose to use prices to measure the variation of utility.[35] This seems a *vicious circle* – but I do not think you will find it to be so really, and the method seems to me exactly analogous to that employed in other theoretical subjects such as that of light, heat, electricity, &c. . . . there is no means of measuring pleasure & pain directly, but as those feelings govern sales and purchases, the prices of the market are those facts from which one may argue back to the intensity of the pleasures concerned.
>
> (January 14, 1872, *P&C*, iii, p. 245)[36]

Notwithstanding, Jevons maintained that no attempt was or could be made to measure total utility, or to measure one total pleasure relative to another: "We can seldom or never affirm that one pleasure is an exact multiple of another; but the reader who carefully criticizes the following theory will find that it seldom involves the comparison of quantities of feeling differing much in amount. The theory turns upon those critical points where pleasures are nearly, if not quite, equal. I never attempt to estimate the whole pleasure gained by purchasing a commodity" (*TPE*, p. 13).

Further, interpersonal comparisons of utility were ruled out: "there is never, in any single instance, an attempt made to compare the amount of feeling in one mind with that in another" (*TPE*, p. 14). Indeed, Jevons maintained that this comparison was not possible: "I see no means by which such comparison can be accomplished. . . . Every mind is thus inscrutable to every other mind, and no common denominator of feeling seems to be possible" (p. 14). It is this conclusion, cited by Robbins in 1981 (p. xxi), that yields the "fundamental implication" that "all recommendations of policy involve judgments of value" (Robbins 1981: xxiv).

Finally, Jevons insisted in his *Theory* that in the evaluation of policy, when one must consider how "to employ that wealth for the good of others as well as himself", a "higher calculus of right and wrong" was required:

> It is the lowest rank of feelings which we here treat. The calculus of utility aims at supplying the ordinary wants of man at the least cost of labour.... A higher calculus of moral right and wrong would be needed to show how he may best employ that wealth for the good of others as well as himself. But when that higher calculus gives no prohibition, we need the lower calculus to gain us the utmost good in matters of moral indifference.
>
> (*TPE*, p. 27)[37]

Insistence upon a broad perspective for this "higher calculus" emerges when Jevons turned specifically to policy. In *The State in Relation to Labour* (1882) (*SRL*) he suggested that policy makers who sought general happiness must consider not only "economic" but also "moral", "sanitary" and "political" probabilities (*SRL*, p. 30). Further, interpersonal comparisons of utility (not only at a point in time, but also through time) were now explicitly called for, this being the "outcome" of utilitarian doctrine.

Did the actual policies emerging differ between Mill and Jevons? The answer is, emphatically, "No". For Jevons, like Mill, utilitarianism involved the alleviation of poverty, including its consequences "vice" and "ignorance". In *The Coal Question* (1865) (*TCQ*) he referred to "the poverty" and "ignorance, improvidence, and brutish drunkenness of our lower working classes" which he linked to rapid population growth in the face of stagnating demand for agricultural labor, and which was to be corrected by a system of general education (*TCQ*, pp. xlvii–xlviii). His 1870 Opening Address to the British Association for the Advancement of Science decried the results of over-population, "the deep and almost hopeless poverty in the mass of people", and advocated policies which would enable the laborer to become self-sufficient (*Methods of Social Reform* (*MSR*), pp. 196, 197). In 1878 Jevons called for wide-ranging social reform to eliminate "the citadel of poverty and ignorance and vice" and to secure "the ultimate victory of morality and culture" (*MSR*, p. 2).[38] Cooperation, which would enable laborers to become capitalists "in some degree", was a primary means to achieving this end (cf. *MSR*, pp. 123ff.), and one which would enable workers to become intellectually as well as materially independent.[39]

Since for Jevons as well as Mill "happiness mainly consists in unimpeded and successful energising", liberty constituted a major component of the utilitarian goal, being envisaged as both a basic requisite to happiness and a means of achieving it (*SRL*, p. 5; cf. p. 13). At the same time man is a social being, and consequently the "mere fact of society existing obliges us to admit the necessity of laws, not designed, indeed, to limit the freedom of any one person, except so far as this limitation tends on the whole to the greater average freedom of all" (p. 14). Here interpersonal tradeoffs were the norm; yet since liberty ranked highly as a pleasure, Jevons was inclined to argue that "a heavy burden of proof" was required in order to show that a liberty-reducing intervention is warranted. Although there is "on the whole, a certain considerable probability that individuals will find out for themselves the best paths in life" (*MSR*, p. 176), if evidence reveals exceptional cases to the contrary, intervention is justified.[40]

Like Mill, Jevons was characteristically reform-minded: "no social trans-formation would be too great to be commended and attempted" provided that "it could be clearly shown to lead to the greater happiness of the community" (*SRL*, p. 11). Thus on utilitarian grounds "the State is justified in passing any law, or even in doing any single act which without ulterior consequences, adds to the sum total of happiness. Good done is sufficient justification of any act, in the absence of evidence that equal or greater evil will subsequently follow" (p. 12). Interpersonal and intertemporal weighing of the net balance was required: "It is not sufficient to show by direct experiment or other incontestable evidence that an addition of happiness is made. We must also assure ourselves that there is no equivalent or greater subtraction of happiness, – a subtraction which may take effect either as regards other people or subsequent times" (p. 28; cf. p. 17). While he recognized that a policy such as a tax on matches would impose hardship upon laborers in the industry as a result of a fall in demand for their product, Jevons stressed the short-run nature of this hardship, and concluded (in what is very likely his most dogmatic utilitarian justification of policy) that "It is the law of nature and the law of society that the few must yield to the good of the many [a reference to those citizens outside the industry who benefit from the imposition of a sound tax] provided that there is a clear and very considerable balance of advantage to the whole community" (*The Principles of Economics and Other Papers* (*PE*), p. 221).

At the same time, Jevons's approach to legislation was cautious, and appreciative of the fact that policy must take public opinion into account: "The Government cannot always engage to teach people what is best for them" (*PE*, p. 223). In 1880 he stressed the limitations which popular opinion placed on policy makers, so that while Parliament might "to a certain extent, guide, or at any rate restrain, the conduct of its subjects", its "powers" were "very limited" (*MSR*, p. 261; cf. p. 256; *SRL*, p. 20). On balance, Jevons emerges as somewhat more cautious than Mill, of whom he was critical in his review of "Utilitarianism" for overestimating the malleability of human nature: "The fact is that the whole tone of Mill's moral and political writings is totally opposed to the teaching of Darwin and Spencer, Tylor and Maine. Mill's idea of human nature was that we came into the world like lumps of soft clay, to be shaped by the accidents of life, or the care of those who educate us" (p. 536).[41] In opposition to the "lumps of clay" conception of humanity Jevons maintained that

> Human nature is one of the last things which can be called "pliable." Granite rocks can be more easily moulded than the poor savages that hide among them. We are all of us full of deep springs of unconquerable character, which education may in some degree soften or develop, but can neither create nor destroy. The mind can be shaped about as much as the body; it may be starved into feebleness, or fed and exercised into vigour and fullness; but we start always with inherent hereditary powers of growth.
>
> (p. 536)

Thus, the evaluation of policy measures involved more than a simple-minded observation of prices, but Jevons refrained from specifying here or elsewhere how to measure social utility precisely, relying instead in the discussion of specific policy measures on loose evaluations concerning the net balance of good created by particular policies. His procedure contained no mechanism, or alternative to that of the competent judges, to estimate consumers' pleasures or social welfare when prices are not allowed as proxies for indicators of happiness.[42] This measurement is certainly called for, if interpersonal tradeoffs of happiness are required. Given this inadequacy, it is not surprising that in 1882 Jevons fully acknowledged that estimates of "utility" might differ: "We cannot expect to agree in utilitarian estimates, at least without much debate. We must agree to differ, and though we are bound to argue fearlessly, it should be with the consciousness that there is room for wide and *bona fide* difference of opinion" (*SRL*, p. 166).

LATE-NINETEENTH-CENTURY DEVELOPMENT ON UTILITY MEASUREMENT

Mill and Jevons were utilitarians in two broad senses. First, they both adhered to "the greatest good" doctrine, where "good" is defined quite broadly, and evaluation of the social good entails subjective weighing of the gains and losses associated with policy measures. While Jevons disagreed strongly with the evaluation process outlined by Mill and argued that qualitative differences in pleasures might be reduced to Benthamite characteristics that in principle were quantifiable, Jevons, like Mill, was aware that social happiness was at best a fuzzy and, worse still, inherently a subjective concept. But second, Jevons and Mill were utilitarians in the original sense of that word, in that both had in mind a program of social reform, according a prominent role to greater liberty – broadly defined, to include economic and intellectual independence – and, as a prerequisite to greater liberty, improved living conditions among the working classes. Jevons, at least by the end of his career, emerges as somewhat less willing to allow that policy in and of itself can effect wide-ranging improvements (though here, one must recall that Mill, too, warned against the ineffectiveness of policy that did not aim at altering *character*; see pp. 67, 69).

Since 1880, utilitarians largely disassociated themselves from the latter broad-ranging reform program and focused their attention on the narrower issue of measurement *per se*. Late in the nineteenth century it still seemed at least possible to foresee the application of Jevons's mathematical logic to policy analysis: F. Y. Edgeworth called for the development of a "hedoni-meter", whereby pleasure might be precisely measured and then, through the use of "wide averages", individual utilities might be combined into social utility (1881: 101–2). Thus he called for the creation of a "psychophysical machine, continually registering the height of pleasure experienced by an individual, exactly according to the verdict of consciousness, or rather diverging therefrom according to a *law of errors*" (p. 101). Edgeworth argued that utility units are cardinal, consisting of "just perceivable increments of pleasure". Since each person registered these units individually, however, measuring total utility presented the same type of difficulties alluded to by Bentham and Jevons (see pp. 66, 75). Edgeworth's procedure was to argue that "the greater uncertainty of hedonimetry in the case of others' pleasures" could be "compensated by the greater number of measurements, a wider average" (p. 102).[43]

In 1890 Alfred Marshall introduced the notion of consumer surplus as an approximate measure of social utility, while at the same time carefully qualifying the concept. Thus, he pointed out that in order to use consumer surplus to measure the "surplus satisfaction which the sale of tea affords, say, in the London market", one must "neglect" "the fact that the same sum of money represents different amounts of pleasure to different people" (1890: 128; cf. n. 1).[44] The importance of the assumption of equal marginal utilities of money is reiterated in a nearby passage: "This involves the consideration that a pound's worth of satisfaction to an ordinary poor man is a much greater thing than a pound's worth of satisfaction to an ordinary rich man: and if instead of comparing tea and salt, which are both used largely by all classes, we compared either of them with champaign or pineapples, the correction to be made on this account would be more than important: it would change the whole character of the estimate" (pp. 130–1).

J. Shield Nicholson strongly objected to the measurement of utility by money. But he nonetheless claimed in 1894 that "some sort of measurement [of utility] is not only possible but [also] is actually adopted in practical life" (p. 343). Nicholson opposed using money as a measuring rod for utility on the grounds that doing so added an "unreal" assumption to the analysis: "the essence of my contention is that we cannot use money as the measure, without making the problems unreal by the multiplication of hypotheses. . . . It is the appearance of exact simplicity – where from the nature of the case exactness is impossible – which seems to me illusory and misleading. . . . what we seem to gain in exactness we lose in reality" (p. 343).[45] Not only did individuals differ, so that the marginal utility of income differed for different individuals, but also "even with the same individual" Nicholson foresaw problems: "even with the same individual a change in the cost of some things must change his so-called subjective valuation of other things. The money measure, then, of the final utility of anything varies not only with his desires and means of satisfaction in respect to that thing, but [also] with his desires and means in respect of all other things" (p. 344). The difficulties were compounded, Nicholson argued, when the number of individuals was increased (p. 345).[46]

CONCLUSION

By the turn of the century many of the difficulties associated with measuring social utility had been outlined, though by no means resolved. At least in part because of the problems associated with specifying and measuring social welfare, as well as, perhaps, the increasing awareness of the complexity of achieving the reformed society – evident in Jevons's "soft lumps of clay" remarks – economists by and large disassociated themselves from the broad-ranging reform programs that served as the underpinning for policy evaluation in the mid to late nineteenth century.

The issue of utility *measurement per se* subsequently has reemerged in welfare economics. Pigou (1903), Pareto (1909), Robbins (1932), Bergson (1938), Samuelson (1939), Hicks and Allen (1934), Kaldor (1939), Hicks (1939) and, of course, Arrow (1951) all wrestled with the problems of the measurability of utility, and in increasingly technical work described the conditions under which preferences might be aggregated and the social welfare function specified. Considering the fundamental importance of measurement to policy evaluation as well as the tendency – noted by Nicholson as well as Robbins (see note 1) – for household members as well as policy makers routinely to make evaluations of interpersonal utility tradeoffs, not surprisingly debates on these issues have resurfaced. What may be surprising, however, is that recent work within the mainstream of the economics profession has sought to enlarge the notion of social utility, returning it to something closer to the nineteenth-century conception that underlies the analysis of policy by J. S. Mill and W. S. Jevons. It seems implicit in Tinbergen's approach to the empirical estimation of social utility functions which argues in favor of a wider range, as well as a larger number, of determinants of welfare – including "learning", "productive activities" and "international security" (1991: 10–11). He calls for the inclusion of some fifty categories in his determinants of well-being, only a handful of which might be described as "goods and services" as economists usually use that phrase. This has something in common, as noted above, with Sen's argument in favor of giving a more central and constitutive role to the freedoms of individuals in the evaluation and determination of social welfare. Both are effectively restoring J. S. Mill's concern with liberty and self-reliance to economic thinking about social welfare.

NOTES

I would like to thank Craig Heinicke, Ingrid Rima and participants in the History of Economic Thought Workshop at the University of Toronto for helpful discussions and comments on earlier drafts of this chapter. Any remaining errors are my own.

1 Robbins maintains that rough estimates of utility or welfare have long been commonplace: "Of course I do not deny that, in every-day life, we do make comparisons between the satisfactions of different people. When the head of a family carves up a turkey, he may take account of his estimate of the satisfaction afforded to different members by different portions; and, in more serious judgments of social relationships outside the family, whenever we discuss distributional questions, we make our own estimates of the happiness afforded or the misery endured by different persons or groups of persons" (1981: xx).

2 As Tinbergen points out, this procedure requires restrictions be placed on the utility function: exact aggregation and integrability.

3 As Sen argues: x R y implies $\Sigma[U_i(x) - U_i(y)] \geqslant 0$. Then if a constant k is added to an individual's utility function U_i, the social ranking of x and y remain unaltered, since the utility differences remain the same (1991: 16–17).

4 Sen notes that this may conflict with the Benthamite argument of basing "the social good on the good of the individuals": "If individual preferences (and choices based on them) are not geared to the pursuit of the good of the respective persons (but, partly or wholly, to other objectives and values), that – in this reformulated framework – is not a source of any embarrassment in taking preferences as constitutive of the informational base of social evaluation. If individual preference is what counts, then the role of 'the good of the individual' has to be derivative, unless, of course, the good of the individual is simply *defined* as the fulfilment [sic] of what the individual prefers (no matter what his or her motives may be)" (p. 20). Cf. note 8 below.

5 To use a simple example adapted from Sen: Suppose we compare three states of the world: one in which you can read any book and you choose to read Miriam Monfredo's *Senaca Falls Inheritance*; a second in which you can read only one book, *Senaca Falls Inheritance*; and a third in which you can read only one book, *Winnie the Pooh*. In the last two states of the world your freedom has been unequally reduced, even though you have the same number of possible things to read in both cases. In the *Winnie the Pooh* situation you have less freedom than in the *Senaca Falls* case, where you are offered the restricted reading choice that happens to be what you would choose in the unrestricted case. Thus, preference information is a key to evaluating the existence of freedom.

6 Cf. Edgeworth's phrase, cited on p. 79.

7 That Bentham knew the logical limits of his procedure has been recognized by Robbins (1970: 56–7; 1981: 5), Hollander (1985: 615ff.) and Mitchell (1918: 167).

8 This discussion has been ongoing; in 1903, Pigou remarked on the further distinction between "pleasure" and "what is desired" (p. 67). For recent treatments see Sen (1991) and Broome (1991). Arrow (1951 [1978]: 22) argues that, by identifying happiness with hedonist pleasure, utilitarians also identified good with happiness. But, since utilitarians in the tradition of Mill favored wide-ranging reform, "good" was not necessarily identical with "happiness" or with

the results (consequences) of choices made.

9   For a full discussion of Mill's vacillations regarding Bentham and utility, see Hollander (1985: 602ff.). The author argues that Mill's utilitarian position, according a prominent role to individual liberty, was in fact consistent with Bentham's original position, and that Mill realized he was returning to Bentham's position (p. 605).

10 The utilitarian standard for policy was therefore capable of changing through time. On this matter see Mill's correspondence with Edward Herford, dated January 22, 1850 (CW, xiv, p. 45), as well as "The claims of labour" (CW, iv, p. 375).

11 Hollander (1985) points out that, for Mill, this position is *not* a presupposition of the doctrine, but rather constitutes the essence of utilitarianism (p. 650).

12 Indeed, this provided Mill with a way to embrace the idea that morality was a changing standard: if moral improvement (a transition to higher pleasures) can occur, there is room for policy to encourage this transition. Mitchell argues that Bentham also allowed for pure pleasures to vary qualitatively: "Indeed in this whole treatise Bentham relies upon classification, and not upon calculation. He splits everything he discusses – pleasures, pains, motives, dispositions, offenses, "cases unmeet for punishment" etc. – into kinds, limits his quantitative comparisons to relations of greater and less, and makes even these comparisons chiefly among phenomena belonging to the same kind" (1918: 169). Thus while different pleasures are in principle commensurable, Bentham also recognized the difficulties entailed in comparing quantities of different pleasures.

13 See Steven (1900: iii, pp. 304ff.).

14 In this context, Mill does not envisage smooth tradeoffs of qualitatively different pleasures: a superior pleasure is preferred to "any" quantity of an inferior pleasure.

15 Cf. "The test of quality, and the rule of measuring it against quantity, being the preference felt by those who, in their opportunities of experience, to which must be added their habits of self-consciousness and self-observation, are best furnished with the means of comparison" (CW, x, p. 214). Mill relies on this criterion in order to argue that "the manner of existence which employs their higher faculties" is, qualitatively speaking, a superior pleasure to the pleasure entailed in a life of base animalistic pleasure.

16 See Robson (1968: 156–7).

17 Jevons interpreted this passage uncharitably. See pp. 72–3.

18 See CW, xix, pp. 606–7. Thus, for example, education should be required, and available to all, but state education should not be compulsory. See CW, xviii, p. 302; CW, xiv, p. 89; and the discussion in Robson (1968: 124–7). In the light of these recommendations, Jevons's strictures against Mill's "packed jury" (below, pp. 72–4), may have been overly harsh.

19 Cf. "I regard utility as the ultimate appeal on all ethical questions; but it must be utility in the largest sense, grounded on the permanent interests of a man as a progressive being. Those interests, I contend, authorise the subjection of individual spontaneity to external control, only in respect to those actions of each, which concern the interest of other people" (CW, xviii, p. 224).

20 Cf. "The aim of improvement should not be solely to place human beings in a condition in which they will be able to do without one another, but to enable them to work with or for one another in relations not involving dependence" (CW, iii, p. 768).

21 "We hail, therefore, the cheap Libraries, which are supplying even the poorest with matter more or less instructive, and, what is of equal importance, calculated

to interest their minds. But it is not only, or even principally, books and book learning, that constitutes education for the working or for any other class. Schools for reading are but imperfect things, unless systematically united with schools of industry; not to improve them as workmen merely, but as human beings" (*CW*, iv, p. 378).

22 Like Jevons, however, Mill insisted that unions be voluntary.
23 Cooperation, the association of laborers as equals "collectively owning the capital with which they carry on their operations, and working under managers elected and removable by themselves", would encourage independent and moral behavior among both laborers and managers by, first, ending the wage relationship that symbolized the dependent nature of the laboring classes (*CW*, ii, pp. 207ff.; cf. *CW*, iv, p. 382).
24 This is the only reference in the review, however, to the issue of interpersonal comparisons of utility.
25 The passage in Jevons is, as he puts it, an "abridgment" of Bentham's *Principles*.
26 But see note 12 above.
27 As Dimand (1991) points out, Bentham sometimes gives the impression that the simple social welfare function presented above (p. 64) is the correct representation of social utility. But in Dimand's view, implicit even in the (Benthamite) utilitarian conception is a distributional element; the social welfare function for Bentham is therefore more accurately represented by $W = \{u_1 + \ldots + u_n\}/(j + 1)$ where j is the number of individuals with lower than average utility (pp. 17–18).
28 Interestingly, Jevons allows that people make mistakes, and the course of action which *in the majority of cases* brings happiness, yields the greatest total happiness for the individual. This may constitute the basis for Edgeworth's call for the use of "wide averages"; see p. 79.
29 "By the same method of decision, we might all be required to get up at five o'clock in the morning and do four hours of head-work before breakfast, because the few hard-headed and hard-boiled individuals who do this sort of thing are unanimously of opinion that it is a healthy and profitable way of beginning the day" (Jevons 1879: 532).
30 It is not clear, however, why altruism has to enter into this calculation: altruism is not necessary for a pleasure to extend to large numbers.
31 There is yet another problem. For the transformation from individual to social pleasure is itself no simple matter: the functional form chosen to combine individual pleasures into a social total itself involves a value judgment. On this matter, see Robbins (1932) and Arrow (1951 [1978]: 16–17).
32 For a full demonstration of this point, see Peart (1990a).
33 As Stigler (1950) pointed out, however, Jevons was not entirely consistent on this matter, and sometimes seemed to argue not that utility was unmeasurable but that it was not measurable at present (p. 88).
34 Cf. "But, then, value there really means utility, because what people want ultimately is command over conveniences and luxuries. Now as I have said there is no real way of measuring and defining utility, and the only approximation we can make to a standard of value is something which shall exchange for other articles, on the average, in as nearly an unchanged rate as possible" (*P&C*, vi, p. 95).
35 For Cairnes's objections to Jevons's theory, see his review of *TPE*, reprinted in *P&C*, vii, pp. 150ff.
36 For a similar argument, see Tinbergen (1991: 9): "Clear examples can be found in physics where initially qualitative characteristics were followed by very satisfactory quantitative measurements."

37 Jevons's contemporary, T. E. C. Leslie, denied that the broader utility, encompassing "moral" questions, was quantifiable, although he apparently allowed that ordinal rankings of pleasure were possible:

> But the very reference which Mr. Jevons proceeds to make to morals militates against the assumption that "political economy must be mathematical simply because it deals with quantities," and that "wherever the things treated are capable of being greater or less, there the laws and relations must be mathematical." He instances Bentham's utilitarian theory, according to which we are to sum up the pleasures on one side and the pains on the other, in order to determine whether an action is good or bad. Comparing the good and evil, the pleasures and pains, consequent on two courses of conduct, we may form a rational judgment that the advantages of one of them preponderate, that its benefits are greater, its injurious results, if any, less; but it by no means follows that we can measure mathematically the greater or less, or that the application of the differential calculus would be appropriate or possible in the matter.
>
> (*P&C*, vii, pp. 159–60)

38 For further evidence of Jevons's concern with poverty and the link with over-population, as well as his policy recommendations to alleviate these problems, see Peart (1990b: 46–9).
39 Jevons explicitly refers to the authority of J. S. Mill in this context. See Peart (1990a: 302–4).
40 Individual interests were in all cases to be balanced against the general good, a consideration which in 1876 is said to require "the nicest discrimination" "to show what the Government should do, and what it should leave to individuals to do" (*PE*, p. 206).
41 See the remarks in Coats (1971): "as time passed there was a growing realization that the process of reforming the labouring classes would be neither quick nor easy" (p. 153). Robson (1968) has argued that during his career Mill, also, became increasingly convinced that reform would be a drawn-out process.
42 This point is reiterated by Paul (1979: 283).
43 As Dimand (1991) has pointed out, this is not a legitimate procedure, however, if the sample is not representative of the population.
44 The idea of money as a measuring rod for utility was not new in 1890. As noted above, Jevons used the idea in his *Theory*. Bentham also refers to money as a measuring rod for pleasures. He was stopped, moreover, by the problem of diminishing utility of wealth. See Mitchell (1918: 169–71).
45 This tradeoff between exactness and reality is one that troubled J. S. Mill, and led him to oppose quantification in applied economics. For an elaboration, see Peart (1993).
46 Cf. "Professor Edgeworth, like every one else, is obliged to admit that a shilling represents different degrees of utility to different people, and even to the same people at different times. If these differences are recognized I fail to see how the same measure can be applied; if they are not recognized the conclusion is unreal, for the people or their feelings are made identical" (Nicholson 1894: 345).

REFERENCES

Arrow, Kenneth J. (1951) *Social Choice and Individual Values*, reprinted New Haven, CT: Yale University Press, 1978.
Bentham, Jeremy (1789) *An Introduction to the Principles of Morals and Legislation*,

in *Works of Jeremy Bentham*, vol. 3, ed. J. Bowring; reprinted Edinburgh, 1843.

Broome, John (1991) "Utility", *Economics and Philosophy* 7 (1): 1–12.

Coats, A. W. (1971) *The Classical Economists and Economic Policy*, London: Methuen.

De Marchi, N. B. (1972) "Mill and Cairnes and the emergence of marginalism in England", *History of Political Economy* 4 (2): 344–63.

Dimand, Mary Ann (1991) "The aggregation of preferences: from Lull to Arrow", paper presented to the 1991 HES meeting, June.

Edgeworth, F. Y. (1881) *Mathematical Psychics*, reprinted New York: Kelley, 1967.

Halévy, Elie (1928) *The Growth of Philosophical Radicalism*, Boston, MA.

Hollander, Samuel (1985) *The Economics of John Stuart Mill*, Oxford: Basil Blackwell.

Jevons, William Stanley (1865) *The Coal Question An Inquiry Concerning the Progress of the Nation, and the Probable Exhaustion of our Coal-mines*, 3rd edn 1906, ed. by A. W. Flux, reprinted New York: Kelley, 1965.

—— (1871) *Theory of Political Economy*, 4th edn, ed. H. S. Jevons, reprinted London: Macmillan, 1911.

—— (1879) "John Stuart Mill's philosophy tested. iv. Utilitarianism", *Contemporary Review* 36 (November): 521–38.

—— (1882) *The State in Relation to Labour*, reprinted London: Macmillan, 1887.

—— (1883) *Methods of Social Reform*, reprinted New York; Kelley, 1965.

—— (1884) *Investigations in Currency and Finance*, ed. H. S. Foxwell, London: Macmillan.

—— (1905) *The Principles of Economics and Other Papers*, ed. Henry Higgs, reprinted London: Macmillan, 1965.

—— (1972–81). *Papers and Correspondence of William Stanley Jevons*, 7 vols, ed. R. D. Collison Black, London: Macmillan.

Marshall, Alfred (1890) *Principles of Economics*, reprinted London: Macmillan, 1930.

Mill, John Stuart (1962) *Collected Works of John Stuart Mill*, ed. J. M. Robson, Toronto: University of Toronto Press. Vols II–III: *Principles of Political Economy*, 1965; vols IV–V: *Essays on Economics and Society*, 1967; vol. X: *Essays on Ethics, Religion and Society*, 1969; vol. XIV: *The Later Letters 1849–1873*, 1972; vols XVIII–XIX: *Essays on Politics and Society*, 1977.

Mitchell, Wesley C. (1918) "Bentham's felicific calculus", *Political Science Quarterly*, 33 (2): 161–83.

Nicholson, J. Shield (1894) "The measurement of utility by money", *Economic Journal*, 4: 342–7.

Paul, Ellen Frankel (1979) "Jevons: economic revolutionary, political utilitarian", *Journal of the History of Ideas*, 40 (2): 267–83.

Peart, Sandra J. (1990a) "Jevons's applications of utilitarian theory to economic policy", *Utilitas*, 2 (2) (November): 281–306.

—— (1990b) "The population mechanism in W. S. Jevons's applied economics", *Manchester School*, 58 (1): 32–53.

—— (1993) "W. S. Jevons's methodology of economics: some implications of the procedures for 'inductive quantification'", *History of Political Economy*, 25 (3): 435–60.

Pigou, A. C. (1903) "Some remarks on utility", *Economic Journal* 13: 58–68.

Robbins, Lionel C. (1932) *An Essay on the Nature and Significance of Economic Science*, 3rd edn, New York: New York University Press, 1984.

—— (1970) *The Evolution of Modern Economic Theory*, London: Macmillan.

—— (1981) "Economics and political economy", Lord Robbins's Richard T. Ely

Lecture to the AEA; reprinted in *An Essay on the Nature and Significance of Economic Science*, New York: New York University Press, 1984, pp. xi–xxxiii.

Robson, J. M. (1968) *The Improvement of Mankind*, Toronto: University of Toronto Press.

Sen, Amartya (1991) "Welfare, preference and freedom", *Journal of Econometrics* 50 (1–2): 15–29.

Steven, Leslie (1900) *The English Utilitarians*, 3 vols, London: Macmillan.

Stigler, George (1950) "The development of utility theory", reprinted in *Essays in the History of Economics*, Chicago: University of Chicago Press, 1965, pp. 66–155.

Tinbergen, Jan (1991) "On the measurement of welfare", *Journal of Econometrics*, 50 (1–2): 7–13.

Chapter 5

Institutional origins of econometrics
Nineteenth-century business practices

Judy L. Klein

Probability theory is usually the starting point for pedagogical developments of econometrics. The ideal roots are traced to the mathematical treatment of games of chance, errors in measurement and combination of observations. The practices of merchants, bankers and captains of industry, however, had more influence on early economic statistics than did the logic of mathematical philosophers. The humbler origins of econometrics lie in the nineteenth-century rules of thumb on temporal comparisons of prices, sales and assets. Political economists adapted these tricks of the trade in their search for scientific means for investigating laws of motion.

Econometricians are not alone in glorifying the stimulus of probability theory at the expense of ignoring practical and cultural influences on the development of statistical method. As Laura Tilling (1973) and Theodore Porter (1986) have demonstrated in their respective histories of statistics, however, algorithms and interdisciplinary imagery applied to meet institutional exigencies usually preceded the theoretical applications of mathematics and probability to statistical studies in the natural and social sciences. It is likewise with econometrics. In fact it was not until Trygve Haavelmo's work in 1944, as Mary Morgan (1987) has pointed out, that probability theory was introduced into econometrics. Long before then, the temporal and multi-variate nature of economic theory and data forced nineteenth-century statisticians to look to business journals rather than Latin treatises for technique.

The legacy of statistical method from studies in games of chance, errors of measurement, social physics and eventually inheritance and natural selection was a concept of logical variation confronting cross-sectional data. Statistical population, frequency distribution and surfaces, and deviation from the mean involved a static comparison of differences. A goal of statistical investigations in social physics and natural selection had been to analyze change over time, temporal variation. The data used, however, were usually cross-sectional statistics, not time series. It was with the application of statistical method to meteorology and political economy that temporal variation was studied with temporal samples. This raised new problems and new concepts.

The early contributions of economics to the development of statistical method were attempts to reconcile the logical variation of statistical procedure with the temporal variation of economic series. Conditions for this fruitful interaction in the late nineteenth century were

- a shift in theoretical concern for long-term irreversible change to short-term fluctuations;
- a shedding of the idea of natural values in favor of normal or long-run values;
- a willingness to rely on quantitative observation and scientific method and rhetoric;
- a recognition that business practices could be used for discerning empirical laws and relationships.

Within this context, commercial tricks of the trade regarding seasonal variation, moving averages and serial differences were modified into tools of scientific method. In this adaptation, tables were transformed into graphs, rough senses of average became calculated means, and moving averages and series were given time frameworks for analytical decomposition.

TEMPORAL COMPARISONS IN COMMERCE

The major contributions of nineteenth-century political economy to statistical method are listed in Table 5.1. All of these concepts or techniques arose from the desire to analyze change over time or to overcome the statistical problems inherent in time series data. Stanley Jevons, John Norton and others turned to the quantitative skills of those in business for inspiration in tracking fluctuations. Jevons explained how his attempts to map seasonal variations mimicked the mental machinations of merchants and those in business.

> By the skill and rule-of-thumb knowledge which each one acquires in his own pursuits, they make allowances for such variations, and thus very rude comparison of prices, stock and sales enable them to detect irregular changes in their own markets, which is all they require. But this unwritten knowledge of commercial fluctuations is not available for scientific purposes, and is always of a very limited extent.
>
> (Jevons [1862] 1884: 3–4)

The rude comparisons Jevons speaks of are evident in business journals such as *The Economist* and the *Commercial and Financial Chronicle*. The former was published weekly in London starting in 1843 and the latter was published weekly in New York from 1865 onwards. These dates correspond roughly to the beginning of the critical period in industrial business that Thorstein Veblen described as "the coming of corporation finance as the ordinary and typical method of controlling the industrial output" (Veblen 1919: 13).

Table 5.1 Contributions of economic investigation to statistical method 1862–1927

Relative-time frameworks – seasonal variation

Moving averages

Serial differences – first differences, variate difference method

Scaled series – index numbers

Harmonic mean

Decomposition of time series into
    trend–trend fitting
    cycle deviation from a trend
    random components

Least squares regression
    applied to stochastic relationship in social sciences
    criteria of normal distribution applied to residual rather than variable

Stochastic sequence – statistical series

The Economist and the *Commercial and Financial Chronicle* were considered the leading business periodicals of their day, catering to industrial specialists concerned with the profit and financial side of business (Larson 1948: 440). The aim of the *Commercial and Financial Chronicle*, for example, expressed in an editorial on June 30, 1866, was to give readers

> a classified, accurate, trustworthy record of all the movements in commercial and financial affairs which are worthy of being remembered, and preserved in a permanent form for reference hereafter. This record we strive to make more valuable to the man of business; more complete, more minute and more extensive in its details than has ever been attempted before by any journal in this country.

In their reporting of the weekly and monthly conditions of exports, imports, rail traffic, commodity prices and banking statistics, these journals presented measurements of stocks and flows in tabular form. The tables enabled comparisons to be made either with the corresponding weeks in the previous few years or with the weeks or months that immediately preceded the current figures. Often the increases and decreases in the values were printed in a separate column.

The tables rarely covered more than four years in showing figures from corresponding weeks. Also it was unusual for means spanning those weeks to be calculated and printed. There were many textual allusions, however, to "rude" averages. Common phrases found in various nineteenth-century issues of the two journals include the following: "about an average business was transacted", ". . . was in fair average request", "a moderate business done for the season". Prices, if not moderate, were either "dull" or "firm" and differences gave indications of "excited", "animated", "quiet" or "depressed" markets.

The emphasis in the text and the tables was on "movements" in commerce. Differences and deviations, whether numerically specific or verbally vague, were used to recognize and judge fluctuations. Political economists took these tools, expanded time horizons, and calculated means and deviations from means to categorize, quantify and decompose the essential elements of time series.

SEASONAL VARIATION

Stanley Jevons turned to business practice in his search for a basis of scientific examination of temporal phenomena. For commercial fluctuations he argued that "every kind of periodic fluctuation, whether daily, weekly, monthly, quarterly, or yearly, must be detected and exhibited" (Jevons [1862] 1884: 4). His task was to convert the unwritten knowledge of merchants into scientific method. In his 1862 study on periodic commercial fluctuation, Jevons mapped seasonal variation for the purpose of eventually eliminating such periodic variation in order to focus on irregular or non-periodic fluctuations. Jevons argued that it was the irregular fluctuations that were the goal of merchants' comparisons and of the most interest and importance to political economists.

Ironically, Jevons's first step in eliminating periodic variation to discover irregular fluctuations was to describe and model the periodic variation by eliminating fortuitous, random variation. As financiers and business journals had done, Jevons arranged weekly figures on commodity prices and discount rates in a table according to their numerical order within the years. In place of a rule-of-thumb comparison, Jevons calculated and plotted the mean value for each month from seventeen years of January values, seventeen years of February values etc. These seventeen values for each month became a sample from which a mean was calculated and non-periodic fluctuations were cancelled out.

Jevons's next step was to connect the twelve means (or four means in the case of quarterly fluctuations) with lines that visually traced the typical path of seasonal variation. The average price of wheat was thus plotted as a function of relative or cycle time. The months on the horizontal axis were not from any one year and the image was of no historical significance, unless there was considerable structural change. The usefulness of this quantified temporal relationship was in its universality. It was an analytical image of a cyclical law of seasonal variation.

MOVING AVERAGES

In his transformation of merchant "skill and rule-of-thumb knowledge" into means of scientific investigation, Jevons applied concepts of statistical population and mean. His connection of monthly means essentially yielded a plot of averages in motion. The technique we now call "moving averages", however, is different; the mean is calculated over consecutive observations.

Moving averages were first used by bankers and financiers in order to smooth the data and thus smooth people's reactions to it. From 1832 to 1844 the Bank of England's monthly announcement of their bullion possessions was in the form of the average of the three preceding months. In his 1840 tract on *Fluctuations of Currency, Commerce and Manufactures Referable to the Corn Law*, James Wilson, who later edited *The Economist*, had to use these monthly averages in his study of recurrence of "periods of excitement and depression". As Wilson pointed out, the moving averages ensured that the public was never aware of the extremes to which reserves went and the fluctuations appeared smaller than they actually were. Making reference to Wilson's tract, Stanley Jevons used a moving average to smooth data in his presentation to a meeting of the British Association in 1878. Jevons's semi-log graph of a three-year moving average of exports of merchandise from England to India highlighted the decennial periodicity of commercial crisis which was to be a focus of so much of his later research.

A moving average obviously entailed calculating an arithmetic mean from consecutive observations, but this empirical device did not become a tool of statistics, the science of means, until deviations from a moving average were also considered. This "method of averages", or "process of averaging" as it was called, was first used for rigorous statistical analysis by John Poynting in his 1884 study investigating the possibility of a common meteorological cause in worldwide fluctuations in wheat, cotton and silk harvests. Poynting was aiming for a visual confirmation of a co-relationship between time series of three variables: the price of wheat, British imports of cotton, and imports of silk. Such a confirmation was not forthcoming from the plots of actual values. What was needed was a way to manipulate the statistics to show "the true fluctuations, whatever they may be, with the effects of war, increases of commerce, etc. as far as possible eliminated ... fluctuations freed to some extent at least from accidental irregularities" (Poynting 1884: 35).

The method he pursued to obtain "true fluctuations" was to construct a standard of a ten-year moving average, or instantaneous average as Poynting called it, and a four-year moving average. The four-year average as a percentage of the ten-year average was plotted as a time series. The results were synchronized curves; smoothed waves appeared to fluctuate over time in a similar manner.

Poynting's method raised questions in the Royal Statistical Society, such as "What is an average?" One commentator, for example, noted that "The system of averaging therefore for the purposes of economical practice was as far as he could see totally different from the system of averaging bases which commended itself to the mathematical mind" (Poynting 1884: 73). Part of the confusion was due to Poynting's arbitrary choice of ten- and four-year averages. The practice, however, did and does raise doubts about the homogeneity or singularity of statistical populations in time series.

Poynting had arbitrarily picked ten-year and four-year groupings to calculate deviations from an instantaneous mean. He made no assertion of cycles or periods. In later works (e.g. Hooker 1901) it was recognized that correlating deviations from an instantaneous average was only appropriate in series that were periodic. The interval for averaging over was determined by the period of the cycle and the symmetry of this selection gave the instantaneous mean, or moving average, a link with the subjective mean, as Ysidro Edgeworth (1887) called it, and with the law of error.

SERIAL DIFFERENCES

One of the most useful commercial practices adopted for statistical analysis of motion was the attention given to differences or deviations. In his 1902 statistical study of the New York money market, John Norton explained the importance of adopting the business focus on changes:

> it is with these changes that interesting problems in economies are connected, not with gross sums. . . . It was some chemist who said, "Never throw away your residues. Look in these for your results." This practice of studying the residues is perhaps the most common in the business world. A glance by our leading journals will convince the reader how familiar this method is outside the text-books. The mill owner and the speculator are constantly watching the net changes, the differences, and these become the motives of their actions. The economists may profitably study these differences for the verification of his laws.
>
> (Norton 1902: 34)

The study of differences became a popular tool for capturing economic "laws". Several major contributions of political economy to statistical method, such as index numbers, correlation of differences or deviations from a trend, and stochastic sequences, have their roots in the commercial attention given to net changes. Tables and textual references in nineteenth-century issues of *The Economist*, *The Statist*, and the *Commercial and Financial Chronicle*, the leading journals Norton referred to, are full of first difference calculations. First differences were the primary method of tracking movement week to week, month to month in prices and production.

As in the case of moving averages, Stanley Jevons was a pioneer in bridging the commercial focus on differences or changes with scientific investigation using time series data. One year after his first publication on seasonal variation, Jevons (1863) published a pamphlet investigating the possible depreciation in the value of gold. In this one study, Jevons introduced several new analytical tools to distinguish between a mere change in relative prices of essential commodities and a change in the value of gold. These included index numbers to focus on relative change rather than absolute level, ratio charts to compare proportional variation in prices and the harmonic mean as an average of ratios.

Jevons established likeness in unlike things by concentrating on relative change. He explained that "there is no such relation or similarity between a ton of iron and a quarter of corn as can warrant us in drawing an average between six pounds and three pounds". If, however, one measures the relative change in prices then "the ratios 100:150 and 100:120 are things of the same kind, but of different amounts, between which we can take an average" (Jevons [1863] 1884: 23). Thus Jevons created, with rates of change, a population of similar but variable (in the logical sense) observations for which a mean had significance.

The focus on rates of change enabled Jevons and others to treat such changes in each year as a sample and to compare movement in one series with that in another. The latter capacity was fully developed by Arthur Bowley in his famous study of wages (Bowley 1895). Working with a large variety of data on wages from different places, occupations and times, Bowley constructed a consistent index series from fragmented pieces. The links of the chain were rates of change.

ECONOMETRIC INVESTIGATION

The tools of moving averages and differences reached their most sophisticated forms in their application to regression analysis. With the biometricians, deviations from a mean, which were seen as the seeds of creative change not manifestations of error or imperfection, became an integral part of statistical analysis. For economists, the correlation of deviations from moving averages or of differences from one period to another became a technique for reconciling logical and temporal variation.

There was, of course, the question of which of the several tides of time were to be correlated. Many of the earliest studies mention the different movements of a variable due to forces acting in different time frameworks. Among the movements described were

- seasonal movement within the year;
- rapid, irregular movements from year to year;
- oscillations of about ten years corresponding to the "wave in trade";
- slow, secular movement, either non-periodic or periodic with a very long period.

The earliest writers saw the time correlation problem as isolating the different components and correlating only similar components of two or more variables. They soon recognized that the correlation coefficients of unmanipulated observations only indicated a relationship between the secular changes.

It was usually of greater interest to economists to investigate correlation of short-term oscillations.

Reginald Hooker's method of isolating short-term oscillations was to correlate deviations from an instantaneous or moving average. Such an average was calculated as the average of all observations over an entire period of cyclical movement, e.g. nine years of the trade cycle. Each observation successively served as a central point in the moving average calculation. It was the method suggested by Poynting, but Hooker went beyond visual confirmation to quantify correlation. Of more significance, he recognized that the statistical foundation of this method of averaging was the periodic movement of a series.

Hooker called the curve or line representing the successive instantaneous averages a "trend". The trend showed "the direction in which the variable is really moving when the oscillations are disregarded" (Hooker 1901: 486). Norton, also interested in correlating oscillations, suggested a similar method. The line from which he calculated deviations he labeled a growth axis.

When weekly observations of time series were connected on a graph of a variable plotted against time, the result was a complex polygon. Norton argued that the statistician's task was to "resolve the motion of the polygons into elements". An element was an "ideal influence which is at work in the curve in a certain motion correlate with time". Norton isolated three types of elements: specifically, a growth element in a continuous passage of time, periodic elements in recurrent periods of time, and dynamic elements.

To capture the growth element Norton graphically interpolated growth axes in each series. The growth axis was in effect similar to a trend line calculated from a moving average with a period equal to, or a multiple of, the period of cycles. Norton's primary interest, however, was not in the trend, but in the percentage of deviations of reserves, loans and deposits from the respective growth axes and the correlation of these deviations:

> In this Chart are represented the really important movements in these financial statistics. The motion of the growth element is slow and gradual. Its effect is scarcely felt. But in the deviations are the movements which are forever puzzling financiers, and upon whose often apparently eccentric movements great fortunes are made or wrecked, panics are bred and crises precipitated.
>
> (Norton 1902: 36)

The method of correlating deviations from an instantaneous or moving average was recognized as only being applicable if there was a periodic movement in a variable. Lucien March (1905) and Reginald Hooker (1905) independently suggested that correlation of first differences could be used to capture the correlation of short-term changes in cases of non-periodic variables.

A few years later the correlation of differences was modified to the variate-difference method. In the 1914 issue of *Biometrika*, Oscar Anderson and "Student" (William Gossen) argued that correlating first differences is only valid when the connection between the variables and time is linear. They suggested that the variables be differenced until the correlation of the nth difference of X and Y was the same as the correlation of the $(n + 1)$th difference. The effect of this would be "to eliminate variability due to position in time or space and to determine whether there is any correlation between the residual variations" (Student 1914: 180).

In a review of the variate-difference method, Yule (1921) pointed out the large gap between Hooker and March, and Anderson and Student. He argued that the view of the earlier writers was that the essential difficulty of correlation of time series was "the isolation, for separate study, of oscillations of different durations". In contrast, the advocates of the variate-difference method saw the problem as "spurious correlation" due to variables being functions of time. Their solution was to eliminate all components which were functions of time and to correlate the serially independent residuals. Yule questioned the usefulness of isolating random residuals and demonstrated that the variate-difference method tended to give correlations due to two-year oscillations.

The advocates of the variate-difference method had argued that the time correlation problem was that time itself was a causal factor; the variables were functions of time and were thus correlated with time. Yule disagreed with this argument and eventually came to the conclusion that the source of many problems in regressing time series was not that variables were correlated with time but that observations were correlated with previous values in the same series. He demonstrated that nonsensical results were more likely with series for which the serial correlations are positive and whose differences are also positively correlated (Yule 1926). Such series, usually displaying secular trend, were common in economic and business data.

Yule's generation of experimental data with correlated differences to investigate what is now called stationarity in time series serves as an example of the sophistication that a focus on differences eventually achieved. The roots of autoregression and time series analysis go to the mill-owner and the speculator "watching the net changes".

CONCLUDING COMMENTS

Henry Moore argued that empirical investigation with probability theory was a systematic method for mimicking the instinct of sensitive gamblers and speculators. In his introduction to *Forecasting the Yield and the Price of Cotton*, Moore described his attempts to replace the instinct of the few with a statistical system that could be used by the many:

> On the cotton Exchanges of the world there are always certain speculators, *les esprits justes* of the commodity market, who seem to know by a kind

of instinct the degrees of significance to attach to Government crop reports, weather reports, changes in supply and demand, and the movements of general prices. Mathematical methods of probability reduce to system the extraction of truth contained in official statistics and enable the informed trader to compute, with relative exactitude, the influence upon prices or routine market factors.

(Moore 1917: 2)

The mathematical methods that Moore spoke of were described by Ysidro Edgeworth as the "science of means". This science encompassed much more than empirical averages. For a mean to have a representative and scientific character there had to be concentration about a central tendency and a group identity to the observations. Once this condition was met, deviations from the mean took on an analytical significance that matched that of the typical to which they were compared.

Pioneers in economic statistics, such as Stanley Jevons and John Norton, bridged the *ad hoc* quantitative reasoning of financiers and merchants with the statistical theory that had been established in such applications as games of chance, errors in observations and biometry. Crude averages became means when nested in groups of observations from well-defined time frameworks. Data that had been published weekly in tabular form were plotted on graphs that covered decades. The resulting irregular polygons were decomposed in order to capture laws of motion. Institutional practices, such as moving averages, became part of scientific practice with an experimentation on and specification of an appropriate period for the averaging. Serial differences and deviations from moving averages were calculated, correlated and used to identify dangerous time series and model stochastic processes.

These significant contributions to statistical method were the product of a historical conjecture of a theoretical interest in short-term change, the unique nature of economic and business time series, and the institutional exigencies of profit makers facing fluctuating market phenomena. The rough analytical methods that were popular and necessary in the era when captains of finance took on the role of captains of industry eventually became the foundation for the development of econometrics as a science of observation.

NOTE

This paper, written in 1989, is an early version of my work on the history of statistics. A more recent and detailed discussion can be found in my book on the history of time series analysis to be published by Cambridge University Press.

REFERENCES

Bowley, Arthur (1895) "Changes in average wage (nominal and real) in the United Kingdom between 1860 and 1901", *Journal of the Royal Statistical Society* 58: 223–85.

Edgeworth, F. Ysidro (1887) "Observations and statistics: an essay on the theory of errors of observation and the first principles of statistics", *Transactions of the Cambridge Philosophical Society* Part II: 138–69.

Hooker, Reginald (1901) "Correlation of the marriage rate with trade", *Journal of the Royal Statistical Society* 64: 485–703.

——— (1905) "On the correlation of successive observations: illustrated by corn prices", *Journal of the Royal Statistical Society* 68: 696–703.

Jevons, William Stanley ([1862] 1884) "On the study of periodic commercial fluctuations", in *Investigations in Currency and Finance*, London: Macmillan.

——— ([1863] 1884) "A serious fall in the value of gold ascertained and its social effects set forth", In *Investigations in Currency and Finance*, London: Macmillan.

——— ([1878] 1884) "The periodicity of commercial crises and its physical explanation", in *Investigations in Currency and Finance*, London: Macmillan, pp. 206–19.

Larson, Henrietta (1948) *Guide to Business History*, Boston, MA: J. S. Cramer.

March, Lucien (1905) "Comparison numérique de courbes statistiques", *Journal de la Société de Statistique de Paris* 46: 255–311.

Moore, Henry Ludwell (1917) *Forcasting the Yield and the Price of Cotton*, New York: Macmillan.

Morgan, Mary (1987) "Statistics without probability and Haavelmo's revolution in econometrics", in *The Probabilistic Revolution*, Cambridge, MA: MIT Press.

Norton, John (1902) *Statistical Studies in the New York Money Market*, New York: Macmillan.

Porter, Theodore M. (1986) *The Rise of Statistical Thinking 1820–1900*. Princeton, NJ: Princeton University Press.

Poynting, John Henry (1884) "A comparison of the fluctuations in the price of wheat and in cotton and silk imports into Great Britain", *Journal of the Royal Statistical Society* 47: 34–64.

Student (William Gossen) (1914) "The elimination of spurious correlation due to position in time or space", *Biometrika*, 10: 179–80.

Tilling, Laura (1973) "The interpretation of observational errors in the eighteenth and early nineteenth centuries", Ph.D. Dissertation, University of London.

Veblen, Thorstein (1919) *The Industrial System and the Captains of Industry*, New York: Oriole Chapbooks.

Wilson, James (1840) *Fluctuations of Currency, Commerce and Manufactures Referable to the Corn Laws*, London: Longman, Orme, Brown, Greenard & Longmans.

Yule, G. Udny (1921) "On the time correlation problem with especial reference to the variate-difference correlation method", *Journal of the Royal Statistical Society* 84: 497–526.

——— (1926) "Why do we sometimes get nonsense-correlations between time-series? – A study in sampling and the nature of time series", *Journal of the Royal Statistical Society* 89: 1–65.

Chapter 6

The method of diagrams and the black arts of inductive economics

Judy L. Klein

There are few tools so important to economic pedagogy and analysis as graphic representation. Even a cursory comparison of economics with other social and natural sciences reveals the unusual emphasis economists place on the use of diagrams. Yet, little has been written on economists as graphic toolmakers. This exploration of early developments in economists' use of graphs addresses the temporal conjunctures of graphs and economic concepts, the developmental patterns of common forms of economic diagrams, comparisons with diagrams used in other modes of thought, and the significant contributions of economists to the technique of visual abstraction.

The process by which I examine these tools involves weaving the source of the raw material of graphs with the relevant time frame (see Table 6.1). Henry Cunynghame in *A Geometrical Political Economy*, published in 1904, classified diagrams as law-curves or fact-curves. The raw materials for law-curves are hypotheses and mental abstractions; the raw materials for fact-curves are concrete data. I have woven the law-curve/fact-curve distinction with a time-frame distinction, made by Joan Robinson (1980), between curves drawn in logical time and those in historical time. Lines imaged in logical time connect and compare static positions. The sense of logical time is created by the eye moving left to right from lower to higher values of the x variable. One can also go in the reverse direction in logical time, whereas the curves

Table 6.1 Classification of graphs

	Law-curves	Fact-curves
Logical time	Mental abstractions drawn to compare values of y, as value of x is low or high	Actual data plotted to compare values of y, as value of x is low or high
Historical time	Mental abstractions drawn to follow path or y changing over time	Actual data plotted to follow path of y changing over time

drawn in historical time attempt to pattern irreversible paths of change in temporal processes.

My first use of the four-celled structure is to review the history of graphs in sciences other than economics. I then look at the history of specific examples in the economist's tool bag, taking each cell in the following order:

law-curve, logical-time cell	demand curves
fact-curve, historical-time cell	graphs of the price of wheat
law-curve, historical-time cell	utility cycle and business cycle diagrams
fact-curve, logical-time cell	regression lines

The comparison between economics and other disciplines of thought reveals that in nineteenth-century political economy there was relatively little work on fact-curves in logical time and considerable development of curves in historical time. This contrasts with the rapid growth of experimental curves (fact-curves in logical time) during the same period in other sciences. The least squares regression line eventually enabled economists to thrive in this realm.

A superficial glance at the history of economic diagrams suggests that most law-curves in economics were in logical time and most fact-curves were in historical time. These two cells (the upper left and lower right in Table 6.1) are emphasized in my review of primarily nineteenth-century diagrams. The uniqueness of economic reasoning, however, is often revealed in the law-curves plotted in historical time and the fact-curves shaped in logical time.

Historical time and logical time frameworks became less distinct with the advent of graphs in relative time. If we take types of time plotted on a horizontal axis as examples, absolute historical time is the case where each tic mark on the axis is associated with a unique calendar date. For example, in Playfair's absolute time graph of the annual average of the price of wheat from 1560 to 1822 (Figure 6.7, later), the horizontal axis tic marks go from 1560 to 1570 to 1580 etc., whereas, in cases of relative historical time, each tic mark is a sequence in a cycle. In Jevons's relative time graph of the seasonal variation in the price of wheat (Figure 6.8, later), the horizontal tic marks go from January to February to March, ending in December, with no attachment to any one year. The value of the first coordinate Jevons plotted on the vertical scale was the mean value for seventeen Januaries.

Logical time can also be seen as a variation on the theme of relative time, though obviously not relative historical time. Relative historical time is cycle time: sequences in a diurnal, lunar, annual, business or life cycle. With logical time, however, the horizontal axis of a market diagram marks off sequences from a low value of x to a high value of x. The two are distinguished by the fact that movement along the curve is revocable and reversible only in a logical time framework. In a relative historical time framework, the movement is revocable, it can be repeated with the next cycle, but it is irreversible. In an absolute historical time framework movement is both irrevocable and irreversible.

There are historical patterns common to all four cells of the analytical matrix. Although political economists at first used diagrams as means of representation and persuasion, by the end of the nineteenth century Alfred Marshall was instructing on the "method of diagrams", and economists were using graphs as means of investigation and comprehension. This increasing use of diagrams as means of investigation coincided with the relative demise of analytical geometry and the growing popularity of projective geometry.[1] In his Gresham lectures on the geometry of statistics, Karl Pearson spoke about the power of this modern geometry and the graphical process of calculation. Until the 1870s, graphs had been seen primarily as a tool of representation for "rhetorical statistics" or the "popularization of statistics". Pearson argued, however, that geometry was now being used as a "mode of statistical research" and a "fundamental process of statistical inquiry" (Pearson 1891: 11). Unlike René Descartes, Pearson and the modern geometers thought that geometry was the best mode of dealing with arithmetic rather than vice versa. For Pearson,

> Geometry originated as a science of measurement, and up to the days of Descartes, geometry was the chief mathematical means of investigation. But Descartes invaded the province of geometry and actually made algebra – a science of number – the means of reaching geometrical truth. Newton was nearly the last of the great geometrical investigators. But in the last few years geometry has been turning the tables on arithmetic and algebra. It has not only developed itself enormously, but to crush its old antagonist it has absolutely called machinery into its service, and now we have reached an epoch when geometry has become a mode of ascertaining numerical truth. As length of lines and areas of surfaces can be represented by numbers, so numbers can be represented by lengths of lines and areas of surfaces.
>
> (Pearson 1891: 11)

There was a shift in visual impact that paralleled the change in the use of graphs from representation to investigation. The generic diagrammatic forms in economics changed from concern with shape and functional form to a focus on turning points or points of intersection. Paul Klee's classification of lines, described in his *Pedagogical Sketchbook* for art students, is useful in tracing the changing nature of diagrams in economics. Klee's cases are based on distinctions between the constructing agency of the diagrams (what he labels energy or cause) and the form of the finished visual impact (the effect). Figure 6.1 reproduces Klee's classification of three types of linear sketches, and I have added the fourth and fifth cases. In the example of economic law curves in logical time, the earliest diagrams were generally of the second case, medial lines with planar impact. By the end of the nineteenth century the fourth case, of intersecting lines with pointal impact, was more prevalent. This corresponded with the increasing importance of the concept of equilibrium to

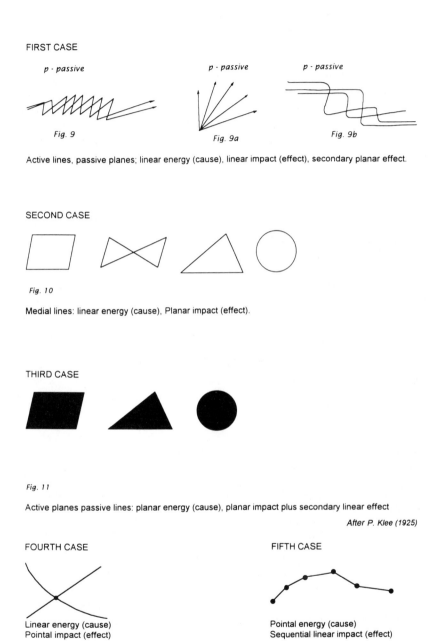

FIRST CASE

p - passive

Fig. 9

p - passive

Fig. 9a

p - passive

Fig. 9b

Active lines, passive planes; linear energy (cause), linear impact (effect), secondary planar effect.

SECOND CASE

Fig. 10

Medial lines: linear energy (cause), Planar impact (effect).

THIRD CASE

Fig. 11

Active planes passive lines: planar energy (cause), planar impact plus secondary linear effect

After P. Klee (1925)

FOURTH CASE

Linear energy (cause)
Pointal impact (effect)

FIFTH CASE

Pointal energy (cause)
Sequential linear impact (effect)

Figure 6.1 Classification of lines by cause and effect

economic theory. With the change in focus from secular trend to cycles and seasonal variation, economic fact-curves in historical time generally developed from medial lines with planar impact to the fifth case of pointal cause and sequential linear impact.

By the end of the nineteenth century, there was a tendency for graphs in logical time to be seen as plots in historical time and for graphs in historical time to increasingly use relative time on the horizontal axis. One of the goals of this history of economic diagrams is to disentangle the roots of a confusion between logical time and historical time that is still endemic in economic reasoning.

EARLY GRAPHS IN OTHER MODES OF THOUGHT

Several writers have documented the earliest developments of the art of graphic representation (see Marey 1878; Shields 1937; Funkhouser 1938; Tilling 1975; Beniger and Robyn 1978; Tufte 1983, 1990). Table 6.2 classifies some of the original graphs described in these histories.

Graphic representation was not a widely used analytical tool until the 1830s. The earliest forms were law-curves in historical time. For example, Nicole Oresme in his fourteenth-century *Tractatus de Latitudinibus Formarum*, used geometric representation to illustrate different types of natural, functional change (Figure 6.2(c)). Oresme's drawings look hauntingly similar to Jevons's marginal sketches.[2] René Descartes's *Geometria*, first published in 1637, also played an important role in the history of graphic representation (Figure 6.2(a)). Descartes argued that every equation could be represented by a curve and every curve by an equation. His analytical geometry was the foundation for law-curves plotted in logical time.

Table 6.2 Early graphical representation in other modes of thought

	Law-curves	Fact-curves
Logical time	Analytical geometry	Gases
	Descartes 1637	Watt 1764
	Atmosphere	Regnault 1847
	Halley 1686	Atmosphere
	Solar energy	Lambert 1771
	Herschel 1800	Forbes 1834
	Gases	Ballistics
	Clapeyron 1834	Thompson 1781
Historical time	Planetary orbits	Meteorology
	Tenth-century manuscript	Lambert 1779
	Functional change	Forbes 1831
	Oresme 1350	Lubbock 1830
	Social physics	Social physics
	Quetelet 1835	Quetelet 1835

The most common type of early graph was plotting experimental data, fact-curves in logical time. Edmund Halley, in the late seventeenth and early eighteenth centuries, is credited with the first graphs recording the results of observation. Halley had few followers in this particular technique, however, and a question addressed by historians of science is why the dearth of experimental graphs from the seventeenth to the nineteenth century? James Watt's description of plotting the relationship between steam pressure and boiling point, Benjamin Thompson's diagrams of ballistics experiments and Johann Heinrich Lambert's extensive use of fact-curves and law-curves in comprehending variation in temperature and magnetism stand out as rare eighteenth-century applications of this instrument.

Although there are several seventeenth-century examples of thermometer and barometer readings plotted against time (fact-curves in historical time) these were used only for description and historical narrative. Laura Tilling (1975) points out that, even when automatic recording devices plotted out indicator diagrams, the data were put into tabular form for analysis and publication. It was not until the 1830s that fact-curves in either logical time or historical time became commonly used analytical tools. J.D. Forbes's many plots of meteorological and other natural phenomena (see Figure 6.2(b)) were a prime stimulus to the acceptance of graphic analysis in this and subsequent decades. But even a decade later there were apologies accompanying scientific graphs. John Lubbock, who helped to diffuse useful knowledge through *The British Almanac*, qualified an ingenious meteorological fact-curve in relative historical time (Figure 6.2(d)) with the following:

> In order to render still more evident the coincidence between theory and observation I have drawn a diagram ..., which is nothing more than a graphical illustration of the preceding table, and must not be considered of use further than in affording facility to those who are not accustomed to mathematical calculations.
>
> (Lubbock 1830: 64)

There are many "laws" in the natural and social sciences, for example Boyle's and Engel's, for which it is difficult to imagine their origins were not in the visual, geometric forms so widely used today. Neither Robert Boyle, Edme Mariotte or Joseph Gay-Lussac, however, used curves to illustrate laws of gases. In 1834 Emile Clapeyron argued that his hyperbolic curve was a new form of representing the way in which volume of gas decreases as the pressure increases when temperature is held constant (see Shields 1937). This law-curve became a popular fact-curve with Henrie Victor Regnault's published graph of experimental data in 1847.

The historical-time/logical-time distinction is not as useful for classifying the graphs of the natural and physical scientists as it is for the social scientists. Clapeyron's hyperbolic curve, showing how volume of a gas varies with different levels of pressure, can be both a comparison of static points and an

LAW-CURVES

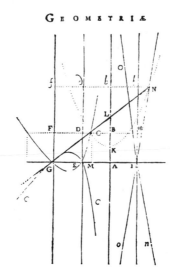

(a)

(b)

FACT-CURVES

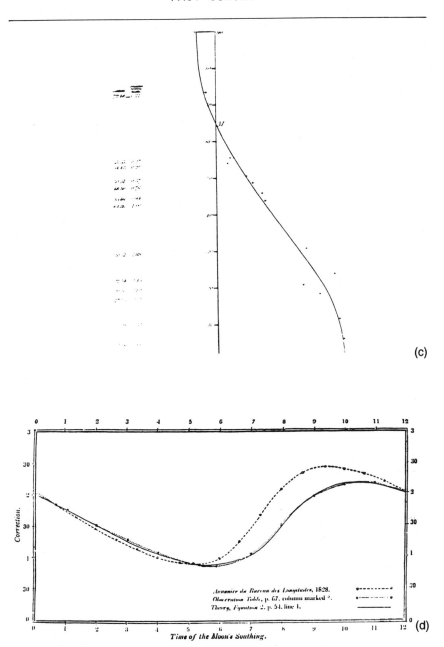

Figure 6.2 Early graphic representation in other modes of thought: (a) Descartes 1637: 42; (b) Forbes 1834: Plate VII; (c) Oresme 1350; (d) Lubbock 1830: 66

image of process of change. For example, Regnault probably collected his data by gradually, but continuously, increasing pressure, and had few problems in achieving *ceteris paribus*, that is, keeping temperature constant. Economists, however, can rarely study a phenomenon simultaneously in logical time and historical time. The "law of demand", for example, is only in logical time. Joan Robinson (1980) illustrated this limitation with a quote from Paul Samuelson: "When a mathematican says '*y* rises as *x* falls', he is implying nothing about temporal sequences or anything different from 'When *x* is low *y* is high'." This caution on interpretation of diagrammatic curves is more important for economics than for physics.

GRAPHIC REPRESENTATION IN POLITICAL ECONOMY

The use of diagrams in mathematics, engineering and meteorology obviously influenced those who sketched in political economy. The influences, however, flowed in both directions. Many of the early economic cartographers were very interdisciplinary scholars. In the eighteenth and nineteenth centuries one was never just an economist nor just a mathematician. Also the economic mode of thought called for the development of unique instruments which were subsequently modified for other types of investigations. Similarly, there were those thinkers, such as William Playfair, whose economic diagrams were so novel or so spectacular that their contribution to the art is recognized in histories of science.

Table 6.3 highlights important developments in the use of graphs in nineteenth-century political economy. A comparison between Tables 6.2 and 6.3 brings out the dearth of fact-curves in logical time in nineteenth-century economic graphs, suggesting once again that economics is different from the sciences that can rely on controlled *ceteris paribus* for inductive reasoning. Not until the marriage of least squares and regression analysis were economists able to construct fact-curves in logical time. The contrast between Tables 6.2 and 6.3 also highlights one of the main contributions of economics to graphic representation, that of diagrams in historical time.

The chronological development of applications of geometric form to political economy corresponds to that in other subjects. There were a few spectacular examples in the eighteenth century (Bernoulli 1738; du Pont 1774; Playfair 1786) and then several barren decades followed, eventually, by new applications in the mid-nineteenth century.

Within three of the cells of the analytical matrix there is often a chronological pattern of development from focus on area and shape to focus on relational lines and points of turning or intersection. The lines of the earliest curves are smoothed, continuous and relatively passive, and they serve as limits or boundaries. Later on they assume a more active role and serve as abstractions of forces or paths of change, and are often limited in their movement by points. Simultaneously, intersections of lines become more

Table 6.3 Early graphical representation in political economy

	Law-curves	Fact-curves
Logical time	Utility of income 　Bernoulli 1738 Demand curves 　Cournot 1838 　Rau 1891 　Dupuit 1844 　Lardner 1855 　Mangoldt 1863 　Jenkin 1870 　Marshall 1879	Regression 　Yule 1897 　Norton 1902
Historical time	Developmental change 　Du Pont 1774 　Gossen 1854 　Jevons 1871 Cycles and trends 　Lubbock 1840 　Trotsky 1923	Price of wheat 　Playfair 1786, 1822 　Cooke 1844 　Jevons 1862

important than overlapping planes. This qualitative change in the visual role of lines corresponds to the increasing importance of equilibrium and of turning points in economic thought.

LAW-CURVES IN LOGICAL TIME

With the earliest uses of law curves in logical time, the explanations were in the language of calculus and the images were smooth continuous functions with requisite convexity. As with other types of curves, there was an eventual shift from a comparison of different areas bounded by the curves to focus on the points of intersection and lines of force. The calculus was left behind as these tools changed from being short-hand images of functions and integrals and became means of exploration and comprehension in their own right.

Daniel Bernoulli's logarithmic curve (1738) showing that the advantage of additional income was inversely proportional to present wealth was the first published example of analytical geometry and of differential calculus applied to economic thought.[3] This very early graph and explanation of the marginal utility of income was recognized more for its contribution to probability theory than for its contribution to economic reasoning. It was not until a century later with the demand curves of Augustin Cournot and Jules Dupuit that law-curves in logical time became an integral part of the means of production of economic thought. Indeed, the chronological development of the demand curve from Cournot onwards serves as a useful path to examine these changes in economic law-curves in logical time.[4]

(a)

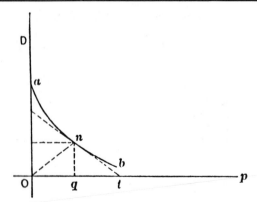

(b)

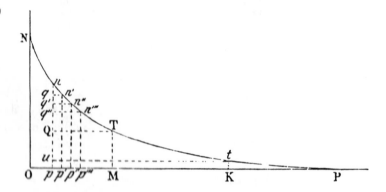

(c)

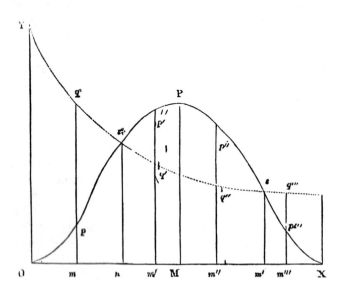

(d)

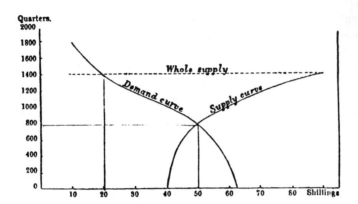

(e)

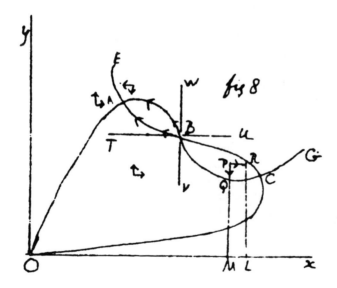

Figure 6.3 Law-curves in logical time – demand curves: (a) Cournot 1838: Figure 1; (b) Dupuit 1844: Figure 3; (c) Lardner 1850: 249; (d) Jenkin [1870] 1887: 77; (e) Marshall 1879: Figure 8

For Cournot, like Bernoulli, graphic representation was linked with differential calculus. The law of demand had been spelled out before *Recherches sur les Principes Mathématiques de la Théorie des Richesses* was published in 1838, but Cournot specified the law as a continuous function and a smooth, negatively sloped curve (Figure 6.3(a)). Cournot's Figure 6 in Chapter VIII of *Recherches...* depicts an intersection of a curve showing the rate of increase of cost of production with a curve of revenue changes. His chief use of diagrams, however, was not to illustrate determination of relative price or of market equilibrium but to explain changes in the areas underneath the curves, e.g. total revenue. In keeping with this, the demand curve of Cournot's Figure 1 in Chapter IV is a curve only of demand that results in sales, and the focus is on a comparison of total revenue rectangles.

As with Cournot, the demand curves of Jules Dupuit (1844, 1849) are more passive than those later used by Fleeming Jenkin or Alfred Marshall. The curves of Dupuit serve as boundaries that, along with the horizontal and vertical axes, determine the rectangles and triangles of total and relative utility (see Figure 6.3(b)). Dupuit held the post of *Inspecteur-Général des Ponts et Chaussées* and his approach to graphic representation is more that of an engineer than a mathematician.[5] For example, angles take on importance, and the lines are continuous, but not representations of mathematical functions. The curves were drawn for planar impact, but the areas of utility bounded by the curve and perpendiculars from the axes were interpreted geometrically rather than with algebra or calculus.

The analysis of Dionysius Lardner in his 1850 publication *Railway Economy* received praise from Stanley Jevons, in part due to the remarkably early appearance of what Jevons called a graphic representation of the laws of demand and supply. Lardner's diagram in Chapter XIII, "Receipts–Tariffs–Profits", is actually of a total receipts curve and of a total expenses curve, both drawn as functions of price, not quantity (Figure 6.3(c)). The main point of the diagram was to illustrate that the value of the rail tariff that brings in maximum receipts was not the same value as the one that ensured maximum profits. The maximization of profits is

> geometrically expressed by stating it to be the point at which the two curves become parallel to each other. After passing this point, the perpendicular representing the receipts will diminish faster than that which represents the expenses, and the profits will diminish.

> (Lardner 1850: 252)

Like Cournot, Lardner was demonstrating the relationship between total revenues and what we now call the price elasticity of demand. Like Dupuit, his analysis was practically rather than mathematically oriented. Lardner, however, plotted in a curve the concepts that Cournot and Dupuit had depicted as areas beneath their curves. There are points of intersection (zero profits), but the focus is on the height of the "perpendiculars" between the receipts and cost curves. The planar impact, so important to the demand curves of Cournot and Dupuit, prevails as well as Lardner's diagrams.

Lardner argues that, in practice, the point of maximum profits can only be determined by trial and error and the "highest managerial skill". Given his emphasis on practice, Lardner's geometric examples are more helpful than a more rigorous mathematical approach would have been in demonstrating the ironies of pricing. Lardner's diagram of receipts and expenses as functions of price is a remarkable diagram for its time. The curves are not drawn as formal representations of function, and there is no mention of calculus in the accompanying text. But Lardner was a popularizer of high order mathematics in his encyclopedias and keenly aware of the importance of the second derivative to an economic way of thinking. Not only does the revenue curve first increase and then decrease as the price is increased, but the cost curve also embodies notions of fixed costs, of increasing marginal costs and of first decreasing and then increasing average costs.

Credit for the ubiquitous demand and supply diagrams of principles texts is usually given to Fleeming Jenkin. In his 1870 study on "The graphic representation of the laws of supply and demand . . ." and his 1871 paper "On the principles which regulate the incidence of taxes", Jenkin used demand and supply curves as the primary tools of analysis and explanation of economic laws (see Figure 6.3(d)). For the first time, a real visual sense of the market is located. Pride of place goes to equilibrium price. Areas bounded by curves are ignored as attention is given to the direction and positions of lines and most of all to their points of intersection.

Mathematical functions and differential calculus become superfluous as Jenkin allows the curves to take on an active life of their own. The curves are imaginary, but Jenkin draws them not with regard to whether they are hyperbolic, logarithmic or exponential but in order to tell a story. The hypothetical numerical values that label tic marks on both axes add to the narrative effect. Jenkin shifts curves to show changes in demand and supply and repositions them to compare different elasticities. There is no diagram in Jenkin's article showing just a demand or just a supply curve. The curves are inseparable, and the point is *the point*.

Jenkin's visual method of comprehension was not just confined to economics. In 1877 he presented an important paper, "On the application of graphic methods to the determination of the efficiency of machinery". Jenkin's graphical representation of the dynamical analysis of machines was novel and is stunning. This instrument maker was also at home with drawing and sketching from observation. His portraits and landscapes are very accomplished. In a biographical memoir on Jenkin, Robert Louis Stevenson gives full credit and full blame for this talent to Jenkin's mother, who was an artist and a "drawing-room queen". Stevenson lamented:

She probably rejoiced to see the boy grow up in somewhat of the image of herself, generous, excessive, enthusiastic, external; catching at ideas, brandishing them when caught ... His thoroughness was not that of the patient scholar, but of an untrained woman with fits of passionate study.

(Jenkin 1887: xivi)

With such pursuit, market diagrams reached their maturity.

In Alfred Marshall's renditions of market curves (e.g. Marshall 1879), the focus remains on intersections and the curves appear as even more free-flowing than they were in Jenkin's diagrams. Particularly in his diagrammatic interpretation of the laws of international trade, Marshall used "contrary flexure" and directional arrows to give a sense of movement (Figure 6.3(e)). Marshall was careful to explain, however, that the drawn lines were not paths of change, and he described the exchange index as oscillating along these curves on its way toward a stable equilibrium (Marshall 1879: 19–21). The arrows indicate the stability or lack thereof at points of intersection. Thus, Marshall saw one of his chief contributions to the art of graphic representation as the recognition that there could be more than one point of intersection, and only at every alternate point of intersection could the exchange value remain in stable equilibrium (Marshall 1873).[6] This was one of what Marshall called the "fundamental laws of curves".[7]

Marshall not only spelled out the laws of curves, but also became an influential advocate of the tool of graphic research. For Marshall, all the important results of the application of mathematical methods to pure economic theory could be obtained independently by the method of diagrams (1879: 5). In most cases, he considered diagrams to be better models of real world forces than could be established by means of mathematics:

For the mathematical function introduced into the original differential equation could not, in the present condition of our knowledge, be chosen so as to represent even approximately the economic forces that actually operate in the world. And by integrating them we should move further away from, instead of approaching nearer to the actual facts of life. For this reason, among others the method of diagrams seem to me to be generally speaking of greater use to the Economist, than the methods of mathematical analysis.

(Marshall 1879: 25)

Marshall even took steps to ensure mass production of economic diagrams. He persuaded Henry Cunynghame (1873) to produce a machine for constructing series of rectangular hyperbolas with the same asymptotes. In his address before the International Statistical Congress in 1885, Marshall asked the Congress to fix standard gauges for pages and for intervals for each year on historical curves drawn as functions of time. He argued that such standardization had revolutionized many industries and would allow for easy international comparison and the use of mechanical appliances in the method of diagrams.

Given Marshall's appeal for standardization, it is ironic that he went against the mainstream in his choice of axes for independent variables. The convention of plotting demand and supply curves with price on the horizontal axis had already been established.[8] Not only did Marshall put price on the vertical axis, but also in his fact-curves plotted in historical time he put time on the vertical axis with the earliest date furthest away from the origin. The former practice stuck, the latter did not, and Marshall is now remembered only for his law-curves and not his fact-curves.

With Jenkin and Marshall, law-curves in logical time not only became the means for being understood, but also the means for understanding. They were more than representations of laws, they took on a life and a set of laws in their own right. It is significant that Marshall talked not just of graphic representation but of the process, calling it the method of diagrams.[9] According to Marshall, the method of diagrams should be seen as separate from a method of mathematical analysis. By the 1870s, graphs were not substitutes of equations or tables pegged, with apology, at the end of a work for the mathematically illiterate; they were tools for exploring and describing phenomena that could not easily be captured by algebra, calculus or words.

Even before the close of the nineteenth century the economic method of diagrams had reached considerable sophistication in the hands of such economists as Rudolf Auspitz, Richard Lieben and Ysidro Edgeworth, and in 1904 Henry Cunynghame published an entire book on geometric political economy. Their work definitely divorced economic curves from the language and rules of analytical geometry and differential calculus. This liberation, unfortunately, generated a confusion of logical time with historical time that is still with us today.

FACT-CURVES IN HISTORICAL TIME

The economist's claim to fame in the broad history of graphs is with fact-curves in historical time. Economics is a time-bound mode of thought. Economists' attempts to capture change and realize empirical laws from visual images have left stunning legacies. *A priori* expectations would suggest that in the development of tools the instruments are at first simple and crude and that with new applications and new tool-making technologies they become complex and sophisticated. But, as a history of graphs of the price of wheat shows, this generalization is at best too simplistic.

Two things revealed in the historical examination of early fact-curves plotted in historical time are the importance of wheat to society and the volatile nature of its price. No other variable is the subject of so many economic graphs from 1786 to the end of the nineteenth century. In the eighteenth century, over half a laborer's income in a year might go to buy

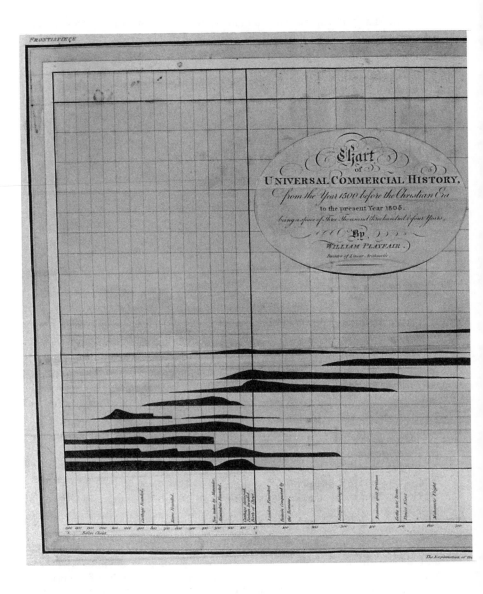

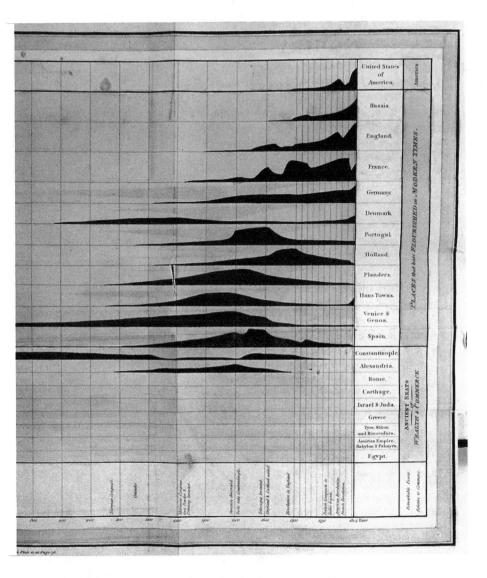

Figure 6.4 William Playfair's chart of universal commercial history. Playfair used
the shaded areas to represent the wealth and commerce and thus the strength,
longevity, rise and fall of empires. The horizontal axis measures absolute historical
time from 1500 BC to AD 1804. The bold line perpendicular to the horizontal axis
about a quarter of the way from the origin separates BC and AD. Playfair broke the
vertical axis into sections for twenty-one commercial empires
Source: Playfair 1805: frontispiece

wheat or wheat products. Wheat was important not only because of its food value and its production value in economies that were still so dependent on agriculture, but also because its price did fluctuate so much.[10] Near the end of the nineteenth century pig iron replaces wheat as the chief subject of fact-curves in historical time; perhaps oil prices or rates on financial assets would be the equivalent in our time.

The glorious beginning of economic fact-curves in historical time is with the work of William Playfair. Playfair is rarely acknowledged in histories of economic thought,[11] but few histories of graphic representation fail to sing his praises. He published beautiful, thought-provoking graphs in English and French from 1786 to 1822. He is credited with inventing the graphic method of representing statistical data and he can claim several firsts: plots of money and financial flows, graphs of social time series observations, bar charts, circle and pie graphs, and the use of statistical graphs for analysis of public policy.[12]

Playfair called his invention "linear arithmetic". He acknowledged the stimulus for that as coming from childhood experiences. His older brother, the mathematician John Playfair, taught William that whatever could be expressed in numbers could be represented by lines and he encouraged him to record daily thermometer readings graphically (Funkhouser 1938). In one of his various occupations, William Playfair worked as a draftsman in the shop of James Watt, also one of the early graph-makers. Whether Watt inspired Playfair or vice versa in this respect is not known. Whatever the case, both engineering and meteorology were a way of thinking and visualizing for this political economist.

In *The Commercial and Political Atlas*, first published in 1786, Playfair used forty-four graphs to show what was and even what might be for the economy of England. Playfair feared that the 1780s were the beginning of the end in the life cycle of Britain's commercial empire. Playfair's vision of the universal life cycle of commercial empires is reproduced in Figure 6.4. The horizontal axis tics off absolute historical time from 1500 BC to 1805 AD. The vertical axis is sectioned into twenty-one commercial empires, with the oldest, Egypt, nearest the origin, and the newest, the United States of America, furthest away. For each, there is an area chart showing the timing and relative magnitude of the rise and fall of the empire.[13] Although Playfair published this graph in 1805, one can see the late-eighteenth-century dip in England's fortune (third empire from the top of Figure 6.4) that Playfair had been concerned about in the his 1786 work. As Playfair saw it, the causes of the country's downfall were the government's growing national debt and the excess of imports over exports. Most of his graphs in *The Commercial and Political Atlas* are plots of time series data on these subjects, and one is a projection into the future of the interest burden of debt.[14]

In almost all of Playfair's early graphs the lines are passive and the focus is on areas bounded by the lines. The published graphs were colored in by hand before distribution. The color adds exquisite beauty and serves as a code. For example, in the area between the curve of exports and the curve of imports, favorable trade balances were colored blue and unfavorable were red (see Figure 6.5). For most of the graphs, the lines are smoothed over the points. This curvature and the planar impact of the color wash make the lines passive and emphasize the qualitative change that Playfair was so eager to convey:

> The advantage proposed by this method, is not that of giving a more accurate statement than by figures, but it is to give a more simple and permanent idea of the gradual progress and comparative amounts, at different periods, by presenting to the eye a figure, the proportions of which correspond with the amount of the sum intended to be expressed.
>
> (Playfair [1786] 1801: x)

The lines become more active in Playfair's later graphs. This transition is best illustrated by Playfair's various graphs on the price of wheat. The "Chart shewing variations in the price of the sack of flour at Mark Lane for 10 years", which appeared in the 1801 edition, is actually the simplest and least artistic of all the *Atlas* charts. As with most of the other charts, there are no sharp turning points, but the dramatic increase in the price of flour at the turn of the

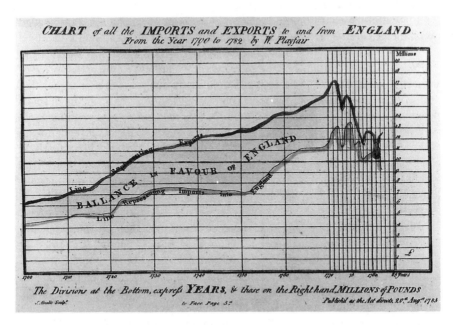

Figure 6.5 Chart of all the imports and exports to and from England from the year 1700 to 1782 by W. Playfair
Source: Playfair 1786: Plate 1

century is highlighted. In the explanation that accompanied the graph, Playfair argued for regulation of the price of wheat before the extremely high prices created any more hunger or adverse commercial relations.

Playfair's graphs in the 1821 edition of *A Letter on Our Agricultural Distress* were more complex and his statistical tools more sophisticated than those in the *Atlas*. By 1821, the problem with the price of wheat was that it was relatively too low and farmers and agricultural workers were suffering as a result. Playfair wanted to convey the idea that although the price of wheat had been high in recent years, relative to other prices it was at its lowest level. The charts in Playfair's *Letter* demonstrate not only his understanding of distinction between real and nominal values, but also his complete mastery of the graph as an instrument of persuasion. In the chart "Shewing at one view the price of the quarter of wheat, & wages of labour by the week, from the year 1565 to 1821", a five-year average wheat price is plotted with vertical bars, and average weekly wages with a smooth line. In the chart "Shewing the value of the quarter of wheat in shillings & in days' wages of a good mechanic from 1565 to 1821" vertical, colored bars of twenty-five-year averages compare the nominal and real cost of wheat (Figure 6.6). This chart demonstrates that in the 1821 a good mechanic could purchase a quarter (eight bushels) of wheat with 14 days' wages, while in Elizabethan times such a purchase had required 73 days' wages.

In light of the considerable variation in the price of wheat, Playfair pleaded with the government to regulate the market. In the 1822 edition, he included a "Chart representing the average yearly price of the quarter of wheat from 1560 to 1822" (Figure 6.7). Compared with his earlier graphs on the price of wheat, this last one emphasizes rapid, volatile fluctuation. Playfair argues that these fluctuations are not related to changes in taxation nor to the medium of payment, nor even to wars; the price of wheat was extremely irregular in its own right. The plate shows "that high prices and low have succeeded each other, nearly as rain and sunshine, substituting years for days" (Playfair 1822: 76). Graphically, Playfair's treatment of the price of wheat had gone from emphasizing gradual change to highlighting random and cyclical fluctuations. Motion rather than flow was the metaphor in this last of Playfair's published graphs.

Playfair's method of graphic representation had virtually no effect on subsequent economic analysis until nearly a century later.[15] The price of wheat, however, continued to inspire visual abstraction. Layton Cooke, a British land surveyor, used several ingenious graphs of the price of wheat to examine the value of land and to recommend a system of rent based on the share of the produce due for the use of different qualities of land.

In his graph of the price of wheat from 1829 to 1842, Cooke (1844: 54) makes use of lines parallel to the horizontal axis to show the average price during the seven years ending 1835, the average for seven years ending 1842 and the average for fourteen years. The annual average price is plotted against

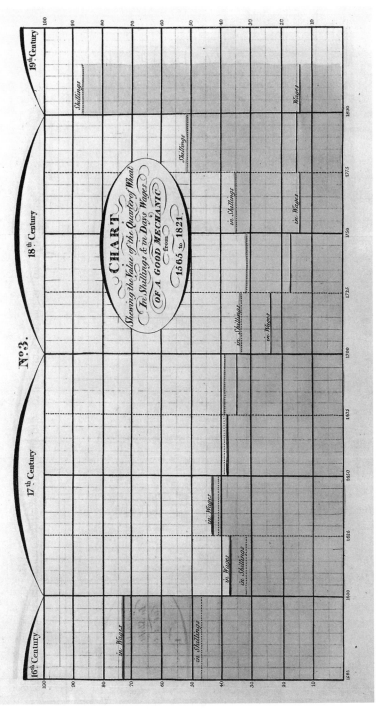

Figure 6.6 Chart showing the value of the quarter of wheat in shillings and in days' wages of a good mechanic from 1565 to 1821

Source: Playfair 1822

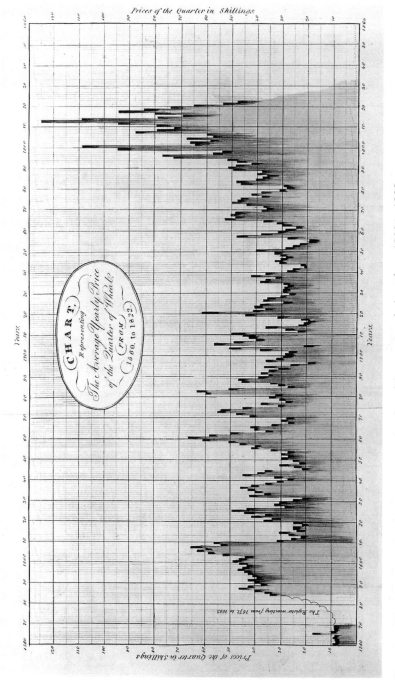

Figure 6.7 Chart representing the average yearly price of the quarter of wheat from 1560 to 1822
Source: Playfair 1822: 74

the vertical axis with a red broken line. The idea conveyed is that fixed rents based on an annual or even seven-year average price of grain would be inappropriate if not disastrous within a few years. Cooke does not explain why he chose a seven-year average to critique; perhaps it was an empirical investigation of William Petty's supposition:

> that the Remainder of the Corn is the natural and true Rent of the Land for that year; and the *medium* of seven years, or rather of so many years as makes up the Cycle, within which Dearths and Plenties make their revolution, doth give the ordinary Rent of the Land in Corn.
>
> (Petty [1662] 1986: 24–5)

Cooke's graphs in his 1844 work on the valuation of estates do not rival the beauty of Playfair's, but they convey a more theoretical approach to analysis. There are, for example, several law-curves in logical time. One delicately colored stacked bar chart (p. 65) displays the relative distribution of the value of produce, to profit, labor and rent, as functions of the price of wheat and method for calculating rent. Another (No. 7 at the end of the book), uses "isoprice" lines plotted on coordinate paper to examine the relationship between yield per acre and profit per acre.

The price of wheat was also a variable in one of Johann Heinrich von Thünen's law-curves plotted in logical time. In keeping with his very spatial approach to economic reasoning, von Thünen shows the distance of various methods of cultivation from the city center as functions of the price of wheat (von Thünen 1826: 393). The price of wheat is essentially represented as an angle rather than a length. This one picture alone gives a sense of the unique spatial reasoning of von Thünen in *The Isolated State*. von Thünen's almost apologetic insertion of his four diagrams at the end of his work indicates that graphic representation was not fully accepted as a form of scholarship in 1826.

The price of wheat and fact-curves in historical time take on more sophistication with the attention of William Stanley Jevons. He used law-curves to illustrate his theories and fact-curves to search for temporal patterns and empirical relationships. Jevons was an admirer of the work of Playfair, Lardner and John Lubbock, all of whom used graphic representation in historical time. Playfair's work, Jevons wrote to his brother, was "exactly resembling mine in principle; but in statistics, the method, never used much, has fallen almost entirely in to disuse. It ought, I consider, to be almost as much used as maps are used in geography" (H.A. Jevons 1886: 158).

Jevons worked for a couple of years on compiling a *Statistical Atlas* of more than 28 diagrams plotting variables over more than a century. He was unsuccessful at persuading a publisher to take on the expense of this unusual approach. Keynes paid high tribute to Jevons's graphic method:

> Jevons was the first theoretical economist to survey his material with the

prying eyes and fertile, controlled imagination of the natural scientist. He would spend hours arranging his charts, plotting them, sifting them, tinting them neatly with delicate pale colours like the slides of the anatomist, and all the time pouring over them and brooding over them to discover their secret. It is remarkable, looking back, how few followers and imitators he had in the black arts of inductive economics in the fifty years after 1862.[16]

(Keynes 1936: 53)

In 1862 Jevons published a diagram that measured 20 by 30 inches and pictured at a long glance over 12,000 observations from statistical tables.[17] The price of wheat, as well as several other financial and commercial variables, was plotted for each month from 1731 to 1861. The physical process of creating such works of art must have suggested, to Jevons, works of science, in particular, the decomposition of time series.

Also in 1862, Jevons presented his study of "Periodic commercial fluctuations". In this presentation, the price of wheat was plotted as a function of relative time (Figure 6.8, bottom chart). Jevons marshalled a single time series of 204 observations into twelve cross-section samples, each with seventeen observations. The plotted path of seasonal variation consists of lines connecting twelve points, which are determined by the arithmetic mean for that month based on seventeen years' statistics. In the charts on the right-hand side, the line connects coordinates determined by the means of samples for each of the four quarters of the year. With Jevons's method, historical time was transformed from absolute time into relative time. Jevons used the mapping of seasonal variation in relative time as an investigative tool for the decomposition of time series (see Klein, forthcoming). His ultimate goal was to focus on the irregular and unusual changes in the price of wheat by subtracting the typical seasonal value from the actual value.

In a lecture on the geometric statistical method for the solution of problems in commerce and industry, Emile Cheysson, Ingénieur en Chef des Ponts et Chaussées, praised the work of Jevons and others who went beyond graphical representation to graphical investigation:

The method of which I am going to speak is located midway between graphic statistics and interpolation; it participates in their advantages and escapes their disadvantages. It is sure like the first, and active like the second. It goes beyond the data, instead of limiting itself to translating and photographing them; it proposes to discover unknown elements; but in this research it leaves nothing to chance, nor to hypothesis. It is the fact itself, appropriately put into operation, which furnishes solutions that it contained implicitly in itself, and which it concerns itself with extracting, as one extracts the metal from ore .... The system then is in part experimental, in part geometric. It takes its data from observation, translates them by graphic statistics, and puts them into operation by geometry. It is therefore nothing other than a means, but a powerful means, of elaborating on these empirical data and realizes, in

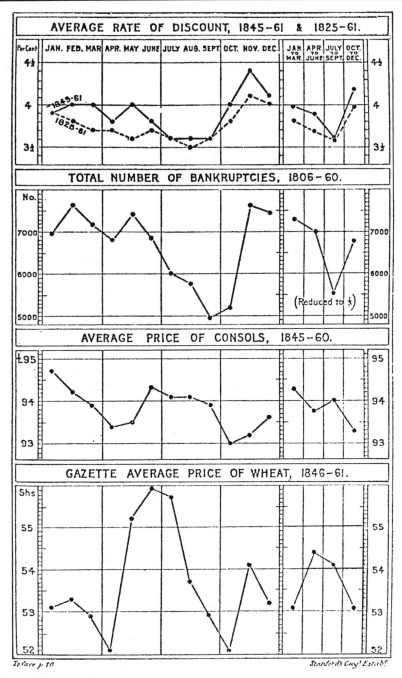

Figure 6.8 Periodic commercial fluctuations
Source: Jevons [1862] 1884: 192

relation to the resources of reasoning, the same advantages as algebra, whose operations lead straight to the goal. Only here it is not about equations to solve by the subtleties of the calculation, but about curves whose points of inflection, retrogression or intersection, answer questions posed by industrial and commercial practice.

(Cheysson 1887: 8)

From persuasive representation to investigation, from absolute time to relative time, from qualitative change to quantitative change, from shape to line, from flow to motion; these are developments in graphical representation suggested in the history of visions of patterns in the price of wheat from Playfair to Jevons.

LAW-CURVES IN HISTORICAL TIME

From the calculus of pleasure and pain to the trigonometry of systems, political economists have given geometric form to law-curves in historical time to hypothesize processes of change. I have found it useful to classify law-curves in historical time as either microeconomic or macroeconomic. The microeconomic curves, such as those of Pierre Du Pont, Heinrich Gossen and Stanley Jevons, illustrate finite, incremental change. There are beginning and end points to a process, and usually specified intervals of time between the two. These graphs are usually in a cycle time or relative time framework. There is a terminal point, but the path may be repeated by starting at the beginning again. These curves have usually been used when economists focused on the individual as an economic agent. The vertical axis measures pleasure or pain and the relative time marked on the horizontal axis is often sequences in a consumption cycle. So the curve showing total utility as a function of the number of pastries eaten would be a typical micro law-curve in historical time.

The macroeconomic law-curve in historical time is the hypothetical path of a changing economy. The ubiquitous sine waves that economists draw to represent the business cycle are examples of this. There is rarely a beginning or end point, and the pattern hypothesized is more like the mapping of a celestial cycle than a life cycle. The time marked on the horizontal axis is often absolute time, but unlike with fact-curves in historical time, no dates from a calendar serve as x axis labels.

It is ironic that discontinuity, beginnings and ends, intervals and thus a sense of epochs are usually only manifest in the microeconomic curves that apply to the individual and to very short-term phenomena, such as acts of consumption. Economists have usually only given a sense of history to law-curves that are not on the scale of history. One of the earliest examples of graphic representation is the eloquent diagram of Pierre Samuel Du Pont De Nemours circulated in 1774[18] (Figure 6.9(a)). Du Pont, a French physiocrat, was demonstrating the effects on sales price of the elimination of an excise tax. Through nine periods (epochs), measured on the x axis, the price received by the sellers gradually increases until it reaches a terminal point – the "natural" price the sellers would have received without the tax. It is a curve of "progressive repercussions" and Du Pont's explanation comes close to the language of the multiplier.

Although the visual focus is on the increments of change, the curves that bind the increments are not smooth ones. Within each increment there is exponential change with a terminal point at the end of that respective period:

> It follows that during each successive period of new profits resulting from the interdependence of supplies, services, and auxiliary works, the curve must make a wavelike movement. This movement expresses the path through which the effect of the change in prices in the trade is passed on to the farmer. In other words, the entire curve is composed of numerous particular curves, one similar to the other, but with the waves progressively becoming less pronounced as the curves approach the natural terminal point at which all must stop.
>
> (Du Pont [1774] 1955: 12)

In a letter to the Margrave Carl Friedreich of Baden, Du Pont wrote that he was sending his ideas on "economic curves" to Daniel Bernoulli. These curves were to be both rising and falling ones, produced from intuition (Du Pont [1744] 1955: 15). Neither Bernoulli's reaction to these curves nor other examples by Du Pont are known.

Rising and falling curves from deductive reasoning were a well-used tool with several writers who sought to translate the calculus of pleasure and pain into economic laws. The marginal concept is a very visual one for economists. An equation system of utility would start with the function, not the first derivative, whereas the marginal curve can give primacy to the latter. Also the incremental approach was often used to introduce the concept of decreasing marginal utility, and in such cases geometry rather than calculus was preferable.

Gossen (1854) and Jevons (1871) both used remarkably similar diagrams to describe the decreasing intensity of pleasure as a function of the increasing consumption time.[19] Jevons's line showed curvature (see Figure 6.9(c)); Gossen, for simplicity, usually used a straight line (Figure 6.9(b)); but in both their works the first figure is that of a negatively sloped curve as a function of consumption-cycle time. A few diagrams later, increasing intensity of pain as a function of labor time is introduced and there is intersection and equilibrium.

Gossen takes the time dimension a step further in his Figure 1.5 and shows the relatively lower position of a new pleasure curve if the act of consumption is repeated without interruption to satiety and then interrupted but repeated soon after. The intensity of pleasure is thus a function of time in the consumption cycle and a function of time between consumption cycles.

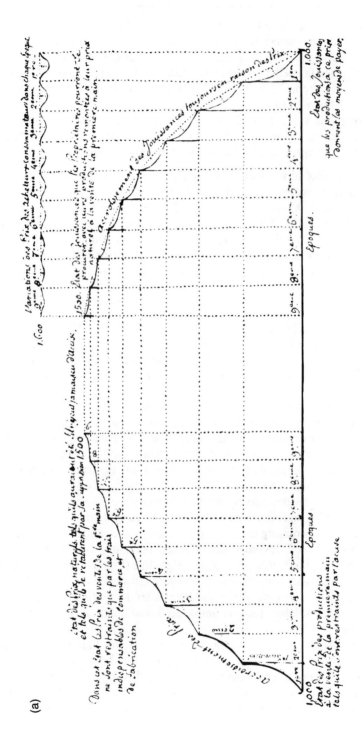

(a)

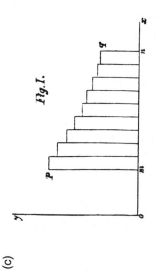

(c)

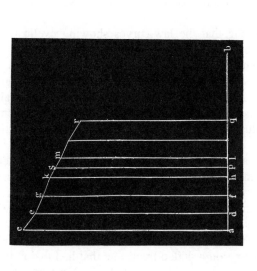

(b)

Figure 6.9 Microeconomic law-curves in historical time: (a) Du Pont [1774] 1955: Figure 2; (b) Gossen [1854] 1888: 8; (c) Jevons 1871: 36

A more macro approach in subject and a more inorganic approach in metaphor is seen in the diagrams abstracting cyclical changes. At one level, there is incremental change within these plots, but it is digital rather than analog: on/off or recession/expansion. The change is a process of oscillation between these states. John William Lubbock's anonymously published tract *On Currency* (1840) contains some of the earliest diagrams of cyclical change (e.g. Figure 6.10(a)). Lubbock used hypothetical plots to show the problem of time lags between changes in the bank notes in circulation and changes in the par metallic exchange rate. In describing one diagram on page 21, in which he assumed a time lag of six months, Lubbock stated:

> If the variation in the quantity of money does not produce its effect instantaneously ... under a system of paper issues, regulated by the exchanges, the issuer prolongs the state of oscillation, restoring the quantity of motion lost, in the same manner as the escapement of a clock supplies motion to the pendulum and prevents it from arriving at a state of rest.

(Lubbock 1840: 21–2)

Lubbock was also one of the early users of graphic representation in meteorology. For example in the same year as *On Currency* was published, Lubbock published graphs on atmospheric temperature and refraction. Even earlier, in a step rare for that time, Lubbock used the graphic form to compare empirical observations of the timing of high water in the lunar cycle with predictions from Daniel Bernoulli's theory (see Figure 2d from Lubbock 1830).[20]

It is interesting that the law-curves showing cyclical change are rarely accompanied by equations of trigonometric functions. It is also ironic that although a trend element might be included in the image there is rarely a notion of a beginning or end to a process. An exception to the latter observation is Leon Trotsky's schematic drawing of capitalist development. It appeared much later than other graphs described in this chapter, but it is an interesting illustration of the use of graphic representation in economic debate.

In his 1923 article "On the curve of capitalist development", Trotsky uses a law-curve in historical time (Figure 6.10(b)) to criticize Nicolai Kondratieff's theory of "long cycles" that was eventually displayed in fact-curves in historical time.[21] In this Russian battle of the curves, Kondratieff's smooth, cyclical curves of fifty-year periods about a continuously rising trend line clashed with Trotsky's smooth cyclical curves of eight-and-two-thirds-year periods oscillating on a dotted trend line that had major changes in slope at two key turning points. Unlike Kondratieff's, Trotsky's trend line showed a life cycle in capitalism's "moving equilibrium" that culminated in its inevitable demise.

Trotsky's curve, like Playfair's universal law of commercial history, is

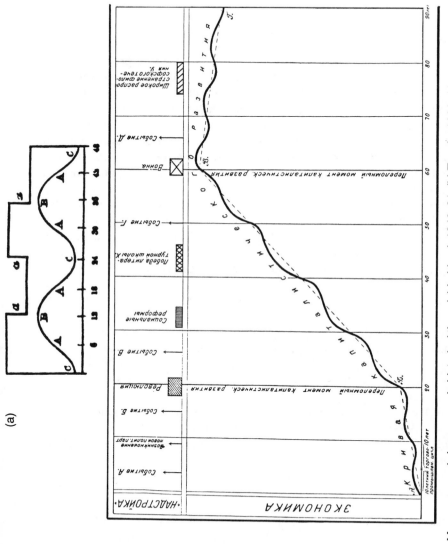

(a)

(b)

Figure 6.10 Macroeconomic law-curves in historical time: (a) Lubbock 1840: 21; (b) Trotsky 1923: 11

obviously an exception to the mainstream economic theory. According to the mainstream, capitalism suffers from nothing worse than harmonic oscillation. Economists admit the possibility of diminishing returns in the course of eating more pastries or producing more pastries with the same amount of plant, but diminishing returns or life cycles on the level of whole systems are rarely envisioned.

FACT-CURVES IN LOGICAL TIME

With all three other cells of the analytical matrix, graphic representation had been used in economic thought in the early nineteenth century and even in the late eighteenth century. Published examples of economic fact-curves in logical time, however, cannot be identified before 1850. This is in marked contrast to their use in other disciplines. By 1840, graphs of experiments that plotted observations of one variable against another were a relatively common analytical tool in the physical sciences. In fact it was in this cell that most of the development in graphic representation in the physical and natural sciences occurred.

Freedom to draw economic fact-curves in logical time only came with the application of the method of least squares to regression analysis. This could be one reason why regression so overwhelms econometric practice; a dearth of fact-curves in logical time would have been detrimental to a discipline so dependent on the method of diagrams and so concerned about appearances of science.

The history of correlation and regression itself can be seen in the development of the visual imagery that accompanied developments in mathematical statistics. In the beginning there was the surface, then came the line. The former is associated with biometrics and with correlation, the latter with econometrics and regression. Both had their origins in doodles on a bivariate frequency table. They serve as powerful examples of plotting not so much in order to be understood but in order to understand.

In 1886 Galton published a study on human stature that led him to discover, from observation, the form of the normal frequency surface. After taking the mean of four adjacent cells and then drawing lines connecting points of the same frequency, Galton noticed that he had sketched concentric contour ellipsoids (Figure 6.11(a)). These contour lines in three-dimensional form yielded a normal frequency surface and the conjugate diameters of the variate axes became the lines of regression.[22]

The subsequent approach of Galton, Raphael Weldon and Karl Pearson to correlation and regression was to work with frequency surfaces (e.g. Figure 6.11(b)). This became difficult, however, with applications to time series data in meteorology and economics, which rarely exhibited normal frequency distributions, let alone normal surfaces. In 1897 Udny Yule introduced the method of least squares regression that estimated a regression line with no

(a)

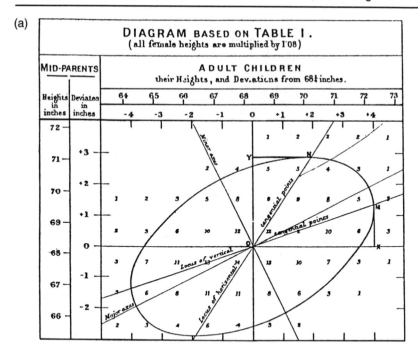

(b)

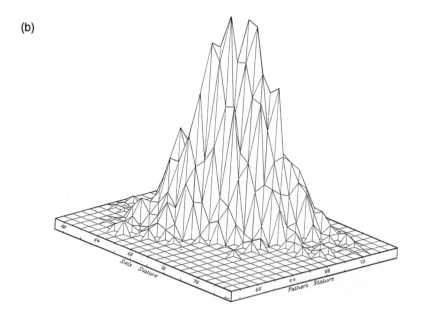

Figure 6.11 Fact-curves in logical time – correlation surfaces: (a) Galton 1886: Plate X; (b) Yule 1911: 166

(a)

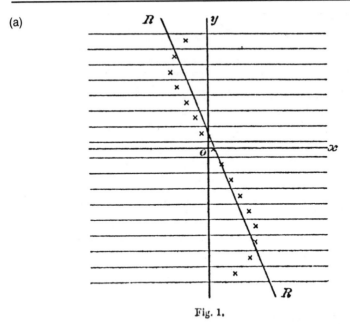

Fig. 1.

Let the diagram of fig. 1¹ represent a general correlation table

(b)

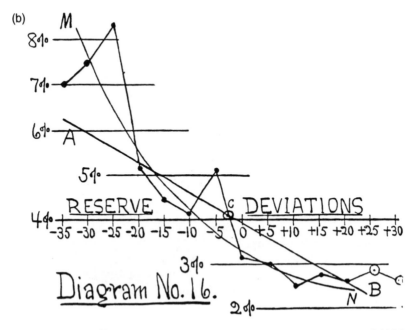

Figure 6.12 Fact-curves in logical time – regression lines and polygons: (a) Yule 1897: 813; (b) Norton 1902: Diagram 16

reference to the underlying frequency distributions or surface.

In Figure 1 of his article on the theory of correlation (Figure 6.12(a)), Yule plots out a line of regression through the mean values of successive x arrays of a correlation table. The visual image, though not the subject, of this diagram is remarkably like that of James Forbes's 1834 graph of daily barometer oscillations by latitude (Figure 6.2(b)). Forbes interpolated a curve through his observations using what he called "Legendre's method of squares". Although least squares had been used for decades for fitting lines in logical time, Yule's application was novel. Before Yule, the least squares algorithm had only been used in cases of physical science where an exact, deterministic relationship between the variables could be assumed. Forbes and scores of others used the least squares algorithm to reveal the law-curve hidden in the facts by error in measurement. Yule used the least squares criterion to fit the best-fact curve to a stochastic relationship in cases of social science.[23]

The biometricians did use a two-dimensional image to plot fact-curves in logical time, but it was usually what John Norton called the "regression polygon" not the regression line that was emphasized. The use of a "polygon" raises less confusion between logical time and historical time because it is a statement of the average value of y conditional upon a certain value of x. With the exception of John Norton (1902) (Figure 6.12(b)), however, economists have forsaken the polygon for the line.

As Yule acknowledged in the opening paragraph of his classic paper on least squares, the economic investigator can seldom make experiments or study one cause at a time. The least squares regression line that Yule formulated was to become the economist's fact-curve in logical time.

CONCLUSION

Political economists have made the diagrammatic method into an incredibly flexible and viable tool useful not just for final representation, but also for initial comprehension and investigation. There have been trade offs in this achievement, however. Specifically, in representing law-curves in logical time economists have departed from the conventions of analytical geometry and differential calculus to develop their own fundamental laws of law-curves. Therein lies their glory, but also their problem. Economists have forsaken the timeless functionality of geometry and the infinitesimal changes of calculus to use their curves to convey a sense of force and movement. But on occasion it is forgotten that, although visual construction and comprehension proceed in real time, the pictorial, theoretical comparison is necessarily simultaneous and static.

Economic curves in historical time have given art and science novel visions of change and means for discerning empirical laws. Fact-curves have developed from illustrating flow (gradual, qualitative change) to capturing motion (repeatable, predictable, quantitative change). The horizontal axis for fact-curves and law-curves in historical time now often tics off relative time, sequence in a cycle. Our curves of human commerce, however, can lull us into thinking that all change is quantitative and revocable.

With fact-curves in logical time, economists create the illusion of a laboratory where none existed before. Mission impossible, *ceteris paribus*, has been achieved; the organic surfaces of the biometricians have been replaced with the inorganic lines of the econometricians. The regression line has given economists, who work with the raw materials of non-normal distributions and time-bound data, licence for constructing fact-curves in logical time, but their predictive powers are still slight.

From the history of our method of diagrams, economists should take both pride and caution.

NOTES

A grant from the National Science Foundation, SBR-9312693, supported my work in revising this paper for publication. Figure 6.1 reproduced with permission from Paul Klee ([1925] 1984) *Pedagogical Sketchbook*, London: Faber & Faber.

1   In *Mathematical Visions: the Pursuit of Geometry in Victorian England*, Joan Richards argues that the British tradition of seeing geometry as a descriptive and applied art, rather than as a formal system of proofs, explains the zest with which British mathematicians took up projective geometry as *the* modern geometry in the latter half of the nineteenth century.

2   In addition to his work on mathematics, Oresme (also known as Nicolaus Horen) wrote on economics and in particular on money.

3   Bernoulli's marginal curve is in logical time because it is a comparison of the utility of extra income for individuals with different levels of wealth. The marginal curves of Hermann Heinrich Gossen and William Stanley Jevons depict the changes in utility as one consumes, for example, more pastries. Gossen's and Jevons's curves are thus drawn in historical time.

4   Reghinos Theocharis (1983) discusses the diagrammatic analysis of Bernoulli and Cournot. R. B. Ekelund Jr and R. F. Hébert (1983) examine Cournot's and Dupuit's contributions to demand curves. Thomas Humphrey (1992) illustrates the pre-Marshallian diagrammatic analysis of price elasticity of demand, comparative statics, market stability, tax incidence, consumer and producer surplus, dead-weight loss and price discrimination in the work of Cournot, Dupuit, Jenkin, Karl Heinrich Rau, and Hans von Mangoldt. The demand curves of the latter two are not discussed in this chapter.

5   Ted Porter (1991) has pointed out that the state engineering corps, which Dupuit directed, used the language of mathematics to garner authority, obscure, and above all to persuade. Dupuit's demand curve was part of his fulfillment of his oath of public welfare; the area underneath the curve measured the public utility, which formed part of the corps' mission statement.

6   Marshall's use of arrows to illustrate movement from intersections of unstable equilibrium to those representing stable equilibrium evokes Paul Klee's ([1925] 1984: 53) description of the role of arrows drawn at the side of spiral lines:

This direction determines either a gradual liberation from the center through freer and freer motions, or an increasing dependence on an eventually destructive center. This is the question of life and death; and the decision rests with the small arrow.

While there may be acknowledgment of the stable equilibrium as the end point of movement, the neoclassical economist perceives it not as death, but as a point of rest in a cleared market. Of course, the state of rest is a permanent one unless market forces change.

7   Another contribution of Marshall to graphic methods was his advocacy for the use of tangential lines for making it easy to see the proportional rates of increase in curves plotted in historical time.

8   Thomas Humphrey (1992) points out that although Cournot, Dupuit and Jenkin put price on the horizontal axis, Rau in his 1841 diagrams and Mangoldt in his 1863 diagrams measured price on the vertical axis.

9   In his 1891 lectures on the geometry of statistics, Karl Pearson credited Marshall with being one of the pioneers in recognizing that graphs could be a means of investigation as well as a means of representation. Similarly, Stanley Jevons acknowledged Marshall's ingenious, investigative instruction with law-curves in logical time. In a letter to Marshall on January 7, 1875, Jevons wrote of his impressions while examining Cambridge students in political economy:

> What interested me most of all however was the way in which some of them applied the graphical method no doubt according to your views.... I understood enough however to think that the way in which you had applied curves to questions of taxation and the like was very successful. I have no doubt that there is a great field open for the investigation of economy in this way and I wish that you could be induced to print what you have already worked out on the subject.
>
> (Jevons [1875] 1977: IV, p. 96)

10   Many eighteenth- and nineteenth-century political economists, including Charles Davenant, Thomas Tooke, Charles Babbage and James Wilson, have commented on the considerable fluctuation in the price of wheat. Adolphe Quetelet, who systematically studied the temporal variation of scores of variables that affected humans, noted that none varied "within wider limits than the price of grain" and it was "one of the most influential causes operating on the mortality and reproduction of the human species" (Quetelet [1835] 1842: 108).

11   He is remembered in economics not for his graphs but for his critical edition of Adam Smith's *Wealth of Nations*.

12   Evidence of the high value now placed on Playfair's graphs is indicated by the fact that a first edition of Playfair's *The Commercial and Political Atlas* was the Bank of England's retirement gift to Chairman Charles Goodhart.

13   Playfair's "Chart of universal commercial history" in someway straddles the classifications of law-curve and fact-curve. He drew the curves on the basis of historians' observations of Western civilizations, but no quantitative data existed that would enable Playfair to measure and plot the rise and fall of commercial strength for the twenty-one societies spanning 3,300 years.

14   This theme of the twin deficits (trade and budget) bringing down the world's number one economic power will sound familiar to those who have read political economic analysis on the US economy two centuries after Playfair first voiced his concern with these causes of Britain's demise.

15   Funkhouser (1938: 292) said that he found no mention of Playfair by an English statistician or economist until Stanley Jevons recognized his neglected contribution.

16 Although Jevons contributed greatly to the technique and beauty of the graphical method in inductive economics, he got a low rating in a test of the powers of mental imagery that Francis Galton gave to a hundred eminent people. In response to Galton's queries on the ability to visualize plane and solid geometric figures and spatial placement of numbers, Jevons responded:

> Though (I hope) comprehending the principles of geometric reasoning, I soon get confused by a problem of any complexity. Some parts of the figure slip out of my memory while I am thinking of the other. . . . I have tried all my life to become a mathematician under the best teachers and I flatter myself I understand the principles – but a formula of any complexity soon slips away and I have to begin at the beginning again. I have no doubt that *mathematical power* depends upon some mental conformation quite different from mine.
> (Jevons 1879: 3–4)

Galton placed Jevons's faculty for visualizing in the lower quartile of his sample.

17 By the last edition of this chart, its length was 62 inches.
18 The diagram and an explanatory letter were translated and discussed by Henry Spiegel in 1955. Reghinos Theocharis (1983) also discusses Du Pont's curve.
19 The diagrammatic method of Jevons and Gossen, and in particular the latter, are thoroughly discussed in Nicholas Georgescu-Roegen's introduction to Rudolphe Blitz's translation of *Entwickelung* . . . (Gossen [1854] 1983). Geogescu-Roegen not only discusses Gossen's curves but also creates new visual imagery to complement Gossen's analysis.
20 Lubbock's work on the analysis of tides and money flows in relative time is discussed further in Klein (forthcoming). Also James Henderson (1986) examines the contribution of Lubbock's *On Currency* to monetary and mathematical economics.
21 Richard Day has translated Trotsky's curve into English in "The theory of the long cycle", *New Left Review* (1976): 67–82.
22 "That Galton should have evolved all this from his observations is to my mind one of the most noteworthy scientific discoveries arising from pure analysis of observations." So said Karl Pearson in his "Notes on the history of correlation" (Pearson 1920: 37). Galton said that his association of a surface with the bivariate table was inspired by the contour maps of L. Lalanne in 1843 and L.L. Vauthier in 1874 (see Beniger and Robyn 1978).
23 In their use of least squares algorithms, Adrien Legendre, Carl Friedrich Gauss, James Forbes and others investigating physical phenomena had assumed that there was an exact, single-valued, deterministic relationship between the unobserved variables. The observations on these variables were subject to measurement error, however, so the observed variables were considered as independent of each other. Yule assumed that there was a stochastic relationship between the observed variables. The "errors" were not in measurement but in the relationship itself, and the least squares line showed the typical rather than the true relationship. The criterion of normal distributions was shifted from the variables or the errors in measurement to the residuals of the stochastic relationship.

REFERENCES

Auspitz, Rudolf, and Lieben, Richard (1887) *Zur Theorie des Preises*, Leipzig: Duncker & Humbolt.
Beniger, James, and Robyn, Dorothy L. (1978) "Quantitative graphics in statistics: a brief history", *American Statistician* 32: 1–11.

Bernoulli, Daniel (1738) "Specimen Theoriae Novae de Mensura Sortis", *Commentarii Academiae Scientiarum Imperialis Petropolitanae* 5: 175–92.

Cheysson, M. Emile (1887) *La Statistique Géométrique: Méthode pour la Solution des Problèmes Commerciaux et Industriels*, Paris: Publications du Journal Le Génie Civil.

Cooke, Layton (1844) *The Value of Landed Property Demonstrated by Practical Deductions and Illustrations*, London: author.

Cournot, Augustin (1838) *Recherches sur les Principes Mathématique de la Théorie des Richesses*, Paris: Hachette.

Cunynghame, Henry (1873) "A machine for constructing a series of rectangular hyberbolas with the same asymptotes", *Proceedings of the Cambridge Philosophical Society* October: 319.

—— (1904) *A Geometrical Political Economy*, Oxford: Clarendon.

Descartes, René ([1637] 1649) *Geometria*, Rome: Lugduni Batavorum.

Dupont, Pierre S. De Nemours ([1774] 1955) *On Economic Curves*, trans. Henry W. Spiegel, Baltimore, MD: Johns Hopkins University Press.

Dupuit, M. Jules (1844) "De la mesure de l'utilité des travaux publics", *Annales de Ponts et Chaussées* 8: 332–75.

Edgeworth, F. Ysidro (1881) *Mathematical Psychics*, London: Kegan Paul.

Ekelund, R.B., Jr and Hébert, R.F. (1983) *A History of Economic Theory and Method*, 2nd edn, New York: McGraw-Hill.

Forbes, James (1834) "On the horary oscillations of the barometer near Edinburgh", *Transactions of the Royal Society of Edinburgh* 12: 153–90.

Funkhouser, H.G. (1938) "Historical development of the graphical representation of statistical data", *Osiris*, 3f: 269–404.

Funkhouser, H.G. and Walker, Helen (1935) "Playfair and his charts", *Economic History* 3 (10): 103–9.

Galton, Francis (1886) "Regression towards mediocrity in hereditary stature", *Journal of the Anthropological Institute* 15: 246–63.

Georgescu-Roegen, Nicholas (1983) "Hermann Heinrich Gossen: his life and work in historical perspective, Introduction, in Hermann Heinrich Gossen *The Laws of Human Relations*, trans. Rudolph Blitz, Cambridge, MA: MIT Press.

Gossen, Hermann Heinrich ([1854] 1888) *Entwickelung der Gesetze des menschlichen Verkehrs, und der daraus fliessenden Regeln für menschliches Handeln*, Berlin: Praeger.

Henderson, James P. (1986) "Sir John William Lubbock's *On Currency* – 'an interesting book by a still more interesting man'", *History of Political Economy* 18 (3): 383–404.

Humphrey, Thomas M. (1992) "Marshallian cross diagrams and their uses before Alfred Marshall: the origins of supply and demand geometry", *Economic Review* March–April: 3–23.

Jenkin, Fleeming ([1870] 1887) "The graphic representation of the laws of supply and demand and their application to labour", in *Papers Literary, Scientific, &c.*, ed. S. Colvin and J.A. Ewing, London: Longmans, Green.

—— ([1871] 1887) "On the principles which regulate the incidence of taxes", in *Papers Literary, Scientific, &c.*, ed. S. Colvin and J.A. Ewing, London: Longmans, Green.

—— ([1877] 1887) "On the application of graphic methods to the determination of the efficiency of machinery", in *Papers Literary, Scientific, &c.*, ed. S. Colvin and J.A. Ewing, London: Longmans, Green.

Jevons, Herbert A. (1886) *Letters and Journals of W. Stanley Jevons*, London: Macmillan.

Jevons, William Stanley ([1862] 1884) "On the study of periodic commercial fluctuations", in H.S. Foxwell (ed.) *Investigations in Currency and Finance*, London: Macmillan.
—— (1871) *The Theory of Political Economy*, London and New York: Macmillan.
—— ([1875] 1977) "Letter to Alfred Marshall on 7 January, 1875", *Papers and Correspondence of William Stanley Jevons*, ed. R.D. Collison Black, London: Macmillan, pp. 95–6.
—— (1879) Letter to Francis Galton on 7 December, 1879. Galton Papers 152/2B, Archives of University College, London.
Keynes, John Maynard (1936) "William Stanley Jevons, 1835–1882", *Journal of the Royal Statistical Society* 99: 523–4.
Klee, Paul ([1925] 1984) *Pedagogical Sketchbook*, trans. Sibyl Moholy-Nagy, London: Faber & Faber.
Klein, July (forthcoming) *Statistical Visions in Time: A History of Time Series Analysis from 1662 to 1938*, New York: Cambridge University Press.
Lardner, Dionysius (1850) *Railway Economy: A Treatise on the New Art of Transport*, 2nd edn, New York: Harper & Brothers; reprinted New York: Kelley, 1968.
Lubbock, John William (1830) "The tides", in *The British Almanac 1830: The Companion to the Almanac*, London: Charles Knight, pp. 49–67.
—— (1840) *On Currency*, London: Charles Knight.
Marey, Etienne Jules (1878) *La Méthode Graphique dans les Sciences Expérimentales et Principalement en Physiologie et en Médecine*, Paris: Libraire de L'Académie de Médecine.
Marshall, Alfred (1873) "Graphic representation by aid of a series of hyperbolas of some economic problems having reference to monopolies", *Proceedings of the Cambridge Philosophical Society* October: 318–19.
—— (1879) *Pure Theory of Foreign Trade*, Private Printing: Henry Sidgwick; reprinted New York: Kelley, 1974.
—— (1885) "The graphic method of statistics", *Journal of the Royal Statistical Society, Jubilee* 251–60.
Norton, John P. (1902) *Statistical Studies in the New York Money Market*, New York: Macmillan.
Pantaleoni, Maffeo ([1889] 1898) *Pure Economics*, trans. T. Boston, London: Macmillan.
Pearson, Karl (1891) "The geometry of statistics", Lecture given at Gresham College, Pearson Papers Box 49, Archives of University College, London.
—— (1920) "Notes on the history of correlation", *Biometrika*, 13: 25–45.
Petty, William ([1662] 1986) "Treatise on taxes and contributions", in *The Economic Writings of Sir William Petty*, ed. Charles H. Hull, Fairfield, NJ: Kelley.
Playfair, William (1786) *The Commercial and Political Atlas*, 1st edn 1786, 2nd edn 1787, 3rd edn 1801, London: J. Debrett.
—— (1805) *An Inquiry into the Permanent Causes of the Decline and Fall of Powerful and Wealthy Nations*, London: Greenland & Norris.
—— (1822) *A Letter on our Agricultural Distress*, 1st edn 1821, London: William Sams.
Porter, Theodore (1991) "Objectivity and authority: how French engineers reduced public utility to numbers", *Poetics Today* 12 (Summer): 245–65.
Quetelet, Adolphe J. ([1835] 1842) *A Treatise on Man and the Development of his Faculties*, English trans, of 1835 study, Edinburgh: William & Robert Chambers.
Richards, Joan L. (1988) *Mathematical Visions: The Pursuit of Geometry in Victorian England*, Boston, MA: Academic Press.
Robinson, Joan (1980) "Time in economic theory", *Kyklos* 33: 219–29.

Shields, M.C. (1937) "The early history of graphs in physical literature", *American Physics Teacher* 5: 68–71.

Theocharis, Reghinos (1983) *Early Developments in Mathematical Economics*, Philadelphia, PA: Porcupine Press.

von Thünen, Johann Heinrich ([1826] 1966) *Der Isolierte Staat in Beziehung Auf Landwirtschaft Und Nationalökonomie*, Darmstadt: Wissenchaftliche Buchgeselschaft.

Tilling, Laura (1975) "Early experimental graphs", *British Journal for the History of Science*, 8 (30): 193–213.

Trotsky, Leon (1923) "O Krivoi Kapitalisticheskovo Razvitya", *Vestnik Sotsialisticheskoi Akademii* (4): 5–12.

Tufte, Edward (1983) *The Visual Display of Quantitative Information*, Cheshire, CT: Graphics Press.

——(1990) *Envisioning Information*, Cheshire, CT: Graphics Press.

Yule, G. Udny (1897) "On the theory of correlation", *Journal of the Royal Statistical Society* 60: 812–54.

——(1911) *An Introduction to the Theory of Statistics*, London: Charles Griffin.

Chapter 7

Jevons versus Cairnes on exact economic laws

Jinbang Kim

INTRODUCTION

William Stanley Jevons, a self-claimed revolutionary fighting against "the noxious influence of authority", brought various innovations to economic science. The marginal utility theory of exchange, of course, was among them and has been cited the most. His persistent promotion of mathematical economics has also been noticed. But there was another line of economic inquiries which occupied Jevons for the whole period of his career. It may be called statistical economics. Although Jevons has been referred to as a pioneer in the use of index numbers, it is only in a few recent studies that he is examined exclusively as a statistician (Stigler 1982; Aldrich 1987).

My examination of Jevons's statistical works will differ in some ways from these and other previous studies. Focusing on the statistical methods as he applied them to economic investigations, the examination will illuminate what he thought of such methods and what uses he made of them. In particular it will be shown that he trusted and employed statistical methods to ascertain the exact forms of economic relations. The present chapter has a further theme; his statistical works are examined in relation to the view of John Elliot Cairnes that we could never have "an exposition of economic principles drawn up in quantitative formulas". There was nothing unconventional in this view, but Cairnes advanced it in an unusually straightforward manner. And that is exactly why his argument is reviewed in the next section. Then the penultimate section will examine how Jevons employed statistics to surmount what Cairnes called an insuperable obstacle in the way of erecting economics into an exact science.

THE UNATTAINABILITY OF EXACTNESS: CAIRNES'S VIEW

In his lectures on the *Character and Logical Method of Political Economy*,[1] Cairnes made a comparison between economics and the natural sciences. In astronomy or chemistry, for instance, "the discovery of a law of nature is never considered complete till . . . an exact numerical expression [of the law] is found". "This is, however, a degree of perfection ... which it does not seem possible that Political Economy ... should ever attain," said Cairnes (1875: 108–9).

He reinforced his contention by taking a few specific cases, one of which is of particular interest to us because Jevons took the same case to make his own point. The case concerned a tabular statement about the relations of the harvest and price of corn, which Davenant had attributed to the seventeenth-century economist Gregory King. This famous table is as follows:[2]

Defect		Above the common rate
1 tenth		3 tenths
2 tenths	raises	8 tenths
3 tenths	the	16 tenths
4 tenths	price	28 tenths
5 tenths		45 tenths

So far as Cairnes was concerned, however, it was only obvious that "no reliance can be placed on the accuracy to such calculations" (1875: 116).

We shall see below how Cairnes put forth this view on the character of economics in general, and Gregory King's table in particular.

The logical method of political economy

When Cairnes defined Political Economy as the science which investigates the laws of the production and distribution of wealth, he had a specific idea of how economic laws should be established; and this idea led him to deny that Political Economy could become an exact science.

According to Cairnes, economic laws relate to the constant relations which result from the principles of human nature as they operate under the actual circumstances of the external world. At the outset of his researches the economist is already in possession of the principal of these "ultimate facts" (1875: 59, 75, 77). Cairnes took "the desire to obtain wealth at the least sacrifice" to be among these facts. This principle of human nature was claimed to be a direct knowledge depending on our consciousness, yet of paramount importance in relation to the production and distribution of wealth. Diminishing returns on land to further applications of capital were cited as another important, easily ascertainable fact. Such facts alone, he said, "afford a sound and stable basis for deducing the [economic] laws" (1875: 59).

Cairnes's prescription of the method appropriate to Political Economy, therefore, was straightforward: the economist has only to develop the consequences of those well-established facts. In doing so, the economist often employs "hypothetical cases framed with a view to the purpose of his inquiry" (1875: 77). If, for instance, his purpose is to ascertain the law governing agricultural rent, the economist might take as his hypothesis "a capacity of the soil to yield certain returns on the application of capital and labour in certain proportions". He might also make some supposition about the ownership of land and capital. He would then take account of the known principles, mental and physical, and would deduce from them, in connection with the supposed circumstances, the amount of rent which farmers should pay to landlords. This mode of investigation, which we may call the hypothetico-deductive method, was what Cairnes considered appropriate to political economy.

In light of these explications, one is almost ready to understand why Cairnes denied that economics could become an exact science. Cairnes asserted that it would never be the case that economic laws could become numerically sated for mental principles "do not ... admit of being weighed and measured like the elements and forces of the material world; they are therefore not susceptible of arithmetic or mathematical expression" (1875: 109).

This consideration was the basis for Cairnes's distrust of Gregory King's table. It had nothing to do with the data from which the table derived, or the procedure through which it had been constructed.[3] He only considered the circumstances that would determine the extent of a rise in price resulting from a deficiency in quantity. Among those circumstances was "the disposition of the people to sacrifice other gratifications which it may be in their power to command to the desire of obtaining the usual quantity of their accustomed nutriment" (1875: 116). As Jennings (1855: 259–60) seemingly suggested, an exact measure of this disposition might lead to a precise numerical statement of the rise in price. "[But] the disposition ... is not susceptible of precise measurement, and can never, like the forces of physical nature, be brought within the limits of a formulated statement," said Cairnes (1875: 117).[4]

In short, Cairnes maintained that economic laws should be deduced from the principles of human nature and the physical conditions. He also believed that the mental principles would never admit to numerical expression, primarily because they contain entities which defy measurement. It thus followed that political economy could never become an exact science.

The impotence of statistical method

If economic laws can only be ascertained by deduction from mental and physical principles, then few will be hopeful about "an exposition of economic laws drawn up in quantitative formulas" (Cairnes 1874: 110). But such deduction may not be the only method of economic inquiry. One may instead attempt to establish an exact law based on data furnished by direct observation of economic phenomena. Cairnes, however, did not trust those attempts at all.

Let us begin with a less controversial point made by Cairnes in regard to statistical inferences. It is that no economic truth can be discovered by "induction in the strict sense", as distinguished from the interpretation of facts guided by knowledge of human nature or physical conditions. Induction is impotent because economic phenomena are "the result of a great variety of influences, all operating simultaneously, reinforcing, counteracting, and in various ways modifying each other" (1875: 63).[5] It was plain to him that there is no hope for establishing inductively the connection of such phenomena with their causes and laws.[6]

The futility of pure induction as a means of discovering economic laws was not the only point made by Cairnes. As it has been noted earlier, he maintained that economic laws must and can be deduced from mental principles and physical conditions. The laws obtained by these methods were taken by him to represent, not what will actually take place, but what would take place in the absence of disturbing causes. If there are discrepancies between an economic law and the facts, it implies no more than the existence of disturbing causes or overlooked principles. He thus concluded that economic laws could "neither be established nor refuted . . . by statistical or documentary evidence" (1875: 99). In other words, he had no more trust in empirical testing than in pure induction.

But what directly concerns the present chapter is the use of statistics in combination with economic theory to attain an exact law. This is the use which Jevons made of Gregory King's table. That is, Jevons reasoned from economic principles to the price of corn before he proceeded to derive a quantitative formula from the data on price and quantity. Cairnes, however, did not distinguish this use of statistics from the pure induction which he believed to be utterly futile. "At all events," he also said, "the formula, if it were possible to evolve one, would need . . . to be altered with every change in either the amount or the distribution of purchasing power in a community" (1874: 105). This remark apparently related to the complexity of economic phenomena, which he cited as the reason for the futility of pure induction.

As a non-believer in empirical testing for the same reason, Cairnes would also not have agreed to adopt "goodness of fit" as a criterion for selecting a formula from various candidates, although he did not explicitly say so. In brief, he really meant what he said: "Beyond the merest empirical generalizations, advance from [economic] data is plainly impossible" (1875: 66).

JEVONS'S VIEW AND PRACTICE

Although Jevons found Cairnes's lectures admirable, he also held the opinion, so clearly expressed in the *Theory of Political Economy*, that

> Economics might be gradually erected into an exact science, if only commercial statistics were far more complete and accurate than they are at present, so that the formulae could be endowed with exact meaning by the aid of numerical data.
>
> (1957: 21)[7]

This conviction has much to do with the theory of probability as Jevons understood it.

Inverse probability and statistical inference

Jevons not only maintained that statistics could help erect economics into an exact science, he also engaged himself in translating the possibility into reality. We begin with a different kind of statistical investigation contained in his 1863 pamphlet on "The value of gold",[8] to which he explicitly applied the *principle of inverse probability*.

Although the pamphlet primarily purported to measure the depreciation of gold during the 1850s, it also offered a causal explanation of the event. Depreciation was attributed to the discoveries of gold in California and Australia, rather than other circumstances such as a variation in the production of commodities. It was to establish this explanation that Jevons made an "inverse or inductive application of the theory of probability", as he later called it in the *Principles of Science*.[9]

As he was conscious of the novelty involved in this attempt, he first illustrated how to proceed with a hypothetical case of five articles, of which an article A fell in its rate of exchange with each of the other articles, B, C, D, E. He made the following inference:

> *It is more likely that the alteration should have arisen on the side of A than on the side of B, C, D, E,* because one cause affecting A, will suffice to explain the change, four separate but concurring causes respectively affecting B, C, D, E, will be needed on the other side. The odds, then, are four to one in favour of the cause of alteration being in A, and not in B, C, D, E.
>
> (1909, p. 16; emphasis in the original)

He then dealt with a more realistic case, in which "the majority of B, C, D, *etc.*, had risen in value, and only a minority fallen". Though he did not elaborate how to evaluate the odds in this case, his inference was clear. "[I]t is more likely that a single cause acting on A should have led to a general rise than that the majority of B, C, D, *etc.* should have been affected by separate but concurring causes," he said (1909: 17).

Apparently, the inference was based on the presumption that a cause acting on A is no more probable than any others. In actuality, however, it was certain rather than probable that there had been a variation in the production of gold. As Laplace (1951: 16) put it, "the various causes, considered *a priori*, [were] unequally probable".[10] Jevons did not fail to take this non-uniformity of prior probabilities into consideration as he concluded the investigation.

> Joined to the fact that circumstances have occurred in the production of gold which would probably cause a considerable rise of price, it is hardly to be doubted that any general elevation of prices which we may discover is for the most part due to such circumstances.
>
> (1909: 18–19)

Jevons did not, however, apply the principle of inverse probability in a coherent and sound way. To the contrary, his evaluation of the odds in a hypothetical case of five articles is problematic, and his attempt to deal with a more realistic case is similarly deficient.[11] One may even dismiss the whole inference as a mindless application of the theory of probability. Nevertheless, it still is the case that Jevons drew an inference from economic data, which Cairnes said was plainly impossible; and the principle of inverse probability was adopted for the inference.[12] Jevons trusted that the principle would, "out of a great multitude of cases, lead us most often to the truth" (1887: 243).[13]

Average and pure effect

Periodic variations

Asserting that no advance from economic data is possible, Cairnes cited the multiplicity of causes and the intermixture of effects as the reason. But Jevons thought that there should be a way of disentangling the intermixture of effects. Otherwise, he would not have attempted to ascertain irregular variations, as distinguished from "periodic commercial fluctuations" which he again decomposed into quarterly and yearly fluctuations.[14]

Surprised that little work had so far been done in this subject, Jevons considered the accounts of the Bank of England. Taking weekly data of the years 1845–61 inclusive, he computes the week-to-week averages for the year. That is, if we represent one of the Bank accounts as $X_{52a+i} = Z_i + \varepsilon_{52a+i}$ for $a = 0, 1, \ldots,$ 16 and $i = 1, 2, \ldots, 52$, the average he drew for the ith week is

$$\bar{X}_i = \frac{1}{17} \sum_{a=0}^{16} X_{52a+i}$$

In this series of fifty-two averages, he said, "all non-periodic variations $[\varepsilon]$ seem to be nearly eliminated, and the seasonal variations $[Z]$ remain" (1909: 5).

But the yearly variation, which concerned him the most, was yet to be determined because other periodic variations were also compounded in the averages. As he was particularly concerned with the quarterly variation, he took the week-to-week averages of the quarter and subtracted them from the whole variations of the year. In our terms, presuming that $Z_{13q+j} = Y_{13q+j} + Q_j$ for $q = 0, 1, 2, 3$ and $j = 1, 2, \ldots, 13$, he computed

$$\bar{X}_j = \frac{1}{68} \sum_{a=0}^{16} \sum_{q=0}^{3} X_{52a+13q+j}$$

and subtracted it from $\bar{X}_i$ for each $i = 13q + j$. "We thus ascertain", he claimed, "the nature of the yearly variation $[Y]$ which is due to natural causes, as distinguished from the artificial distinctions of . . . quarters" (1909: 6).[15]

The value of gold

His pamphlet on "The value of gold" also used averages to disentangle the intermixture of effects. As has already been suggested, the pamphlet had two purposes, namely, measurement and explanation. The former, however, was not entirely free from the notion of cause and effect. His intent was to ascertain the variation of prices *due to* the gold discoveries, whereas the observed variation was understood as reflecting the effect of alterations in the production of commodities as well. He thus proposed to compute an intertemporal price ratio for each of a large number of commodities and take the geometric mean of these ratios.[16] In this mean, he said, "the distinct and contrary variations peculiar to [the commodities] will destroy each other more or less completely" (1909: 17).

Jevons restated this idea in another article while defending his adoption of the geometric, rather than the harmonic, mean. The statement also sounded very much like that of a model-builder.

> [The geometric mean] seems likely to give in the most accurate manner such general change in prices as is due to a change on the part of gold. For any change in gold will affect all prices in an equal ratio; and if other disturbing causes may be considered proportional to the ratio of change of price they produce in one or more commodities, then all the individual variations of prices will be correctly balanced off against each other in the geometric mean, and the true variation of the value of gold will be detected.
>
> (1909: 114)

The contention herein is so straightforward that no distortion will result if we paraphrase it as follows. The rate (R) of change in price of an article i is to be decomposed: $R_i = G \times E_i$ where G is the effect of the gold discoveries and E_i the effect of disturbing causes peculiar to the article. Trusting that

$$\frac{1}{n}\sum_{i=0}^{n} \log E_i$$

will approach zero as n increases, an estimate can be made of $\log G$ by

$$\frac{1}{n}\sum_{i=0}^{n} \log R_i$$

or of G by the geometric mean of the R_i.[17]

He also compared this statistical approach to a "searching inquiry", perhaps like that of Tooke (1838) and Newmarch (1860, 1861).

> Now there is not a single article but is affected by many circumstances besides the alteration in gold. A searching inquiry into the conditions of supply and demand of every article would result in every one being thrown

out as unworthy of reliance as a measure of the value of gold. It is only by *ignoring all these individual circumstances, and trusting that in a wide average, such as that of 118 articles, all individual discrepancies will be neutralized*, that we can arrive at any conclusion in this difficult question.

(1909: 54; emphasis added)

Besides the degree of exactitude of an average result as proportional to the size of sample, the remark above also intimates the notion of randomization, of which an exact formulation is credited to C.S. Peirce (1839–1914).[18]

To repeat, Jevons thought it possible to distinguish the effect of one cause from those of others and employed averages to do so. He also implied that the decomposition of effects will be more free from errors if averages are drawn from a larger size random sample. In such an average he ascertained the "true variation" of the value of gold, as he distinguished a kind of fluctuation in the Bank accounts from others.

The degree of exactitude

Jevons claimed that non-periodic variations of the Bank accounts were *nearly* eliminated in the week-to-week averages, while other variations attributable gold discoveries destroyed each other *more or less* completely in the geometric mean of price ratios. But these remarks can also be read to mean that the average results were not entirely free from errors. He then could have agreed that "it is further necessary to appreciate the probability that the errors of these results are comprised in the given limits" (Laplace 1951: 73–4). It finally occurred to him in 1869 that "some notion of the degree of probability" should have been added to the conclusions stated in his pamphlet on the value of gold.[19] He thus proceeded to calculate the so-called probable error. "[It] proved to be just 2.5 per cent – that is to say, *it is as likely as not that the true alteration of gold lies within 2.5 per cent of 16 per cent*; or between 13.5 and 18.5 per cent" (1909: 148–9). If we continue to use the notation introduced above, the distribution of posterior probability of G is such that prob $(13.5 < G < 18.5) = 1/2$. This calculation seems to have been based on $\sum_i (R_i - \bar{R})^2$ where $\bar{R}$ is the geometric mean.[20] Given the sum of squares he would have applied the same rule as explicated in De Morgan (1831: ch. VII) or Airy (1861: Section 3).[21]

Now it must be clear that and how Jevons disagreed with Cairnes. To the former, controlled experiment was not the only means of ascertaining the effect of a cause free from that of disturbing causes. Jevons trusted that the method of means could be substituted to measure pure effects. But his trust was not blind; it was guided by the theory of probability as it was prevalent at the time. He called the mean result "the most probable estimate".[22] He also appreciated the uncertainty involved in such estimation, although he did so more often in qualitative terms such as "nearly" or "approximately".

The method of means and exact laws

In comparison with measuring the pure effect of the discoveries of gold, that is, the *shift* in the value of gold between two points of time, Jevons's study of *The Coal Question* was a statistically more involved project since it concerned the *course of change* in the consumption of coal over a period of time. He believed that the consumption of coal in England obeyed the law of geometrical rather than arithmetic increase. In establishing this law of progress, he made it clear that he would appeal to the record. Nevertheless, there was little genius in his method and no interesting argument was offered for it.[23] It thus suffices to note the fact that, despite Cairnes's warnings, Jevons attempted to ascertain an exact law with the aid of numerical data. Having said this, we will focus on an attempt of the same kind made in the "Gold coinage", which was communicated to the Statistical Societies of Manchester and London in 1868.

In order to estimate the cost of recoinage, Jevons had to ascertain how the weight of an average coin would vary with its age. Jevons first reasoned that "coins of different age, being indifferently used in the ordinary course of circulation, would suffer equal friction, so that any difference in the amount rubbed away could only rise from the varying prominence of the impression". He thus supposed that "the wear of a sovereign would be approximately uniform and proportional to its age" (1909: 258). In other words, the weight of a coin of age T_i was modeled as $W_i = W_0 - bT_i + E_i$. Here E_i was added for two reasons: the coin as issued from the Mint could be slightly heavier or lighter than the average (W_0); and thereafter it may have been through more or less severe wear. Given this model, he tried to determine the rate of wear, b, based on a random sample of coins.

Before discussing the statistical method Jevons employed, consider how modern statistics would tackle the problem. Suppose the use of the same data that Jevons obtained from weighing 434 coins drawn from ordinary circulation. The ordinary method of least squares seems a reasonable first approach. However, because W_0 is known to be 123.26 grains, the estimation of b could be more efficient.[24] That is, a restricted regression is preferred. Proper care must be taken on the sample selection problem; overwise, b is likely to be underestimated since the sample excluded those coins which the Bank had withdrawn from circulation because of their excessive wear.[25] These are basically the steps through which Jevons went, except for the method of least squares.

Jevons estimated b by $\bar{T}/(\bar{W} - W_0)$ where $\bar{W}$ and $\bar{T}$ represent the sample means. Now that $\bar{W} = 122.71$ and $\bar{T} = 12.9$, b is estimated as 0.043 grain per annum. Apparently this estimation was based on his trust that $\bar{E}$ would be approximately zero since the sample consisted of as many as 434 coins. Note that $\bar{W} = \bar{W}_0 + bT + E$. But, as soon as Farr pointed it out,[26] Jevons admitted to have committed an error of which a consequence was underestimation of *b*. The error was said to consist in "estimating [the annual rate of wear] from the weight of *circulating sovereigns*; thus not allowing for the waste in light sovereigns withdrawn by the Bank" (Farr 1869; requoted from Jevons 1909: 260).

Now let us note that the practice above described constitutes a significant step toward the discovery of exact laws. In "The value of gold", the method of means was employed to measure the pure effect of a given change in circumstances. The inquiry concerned only the variable's value at each of two different points of time, or the ratio of such values. In comparison the "Gold coinage" employed the same method to quantify *a relation between two variables*, that is, the weight and age of coins. Further, the exact relation so obtained was applied to make predictions. "Just about eighteen years' wear", he said, "will reduce a sovereign below its point of legal currency", namely, 122.5 grains (1909: 260).

It is relevant also to note that Jevons could have used the method of least squares instead of the method of means. Leplace had already compared the two methods in relation to the same statistical problem as Jevons, namely, estimation of a single unknown coefficient in a linear equation.[27] In the comparison the least squares estimate was shown to be more "advantageous" in the sense of its precision. The same conclusion was reached by De Morgan (1838: 155–6). What is perhaps more important is that Jevons rarely appreciated the uncertainty which is inherent perhaps in estimation or prediction. The probable error, for instance, could have been calculated of the least squares estimate. The "Gold coinage" case, therefore, demonstrates that Jevons was not a master of the theory of probability. It seems in particular that he had yet to understand the notion of "the degree of exactitude", at least until it finally occurred to him in 1869.

The method of least squares and exact laws

As was quoted earlier, Cairnes denied that any reliance could be placed on the accuracy of the King–Davenant table. The same table was cited by Jevons as "our most accurate estimates" of the variation of the price of corn. A more striking contrast between the two economists is that given the estimates Jevons proceeded to ascertain the exact law relating the price of corn to harvest.

But let us digress to examine one of Jevons's non-economic works, in which he tried to discover a numerical relation between two variables based on a series of experiments. The experiment consisted in measuring the distances to which various weights could be thrown by his arm upon level ground. Noting that "good" averages were obtained from about fifty-seven experiments with each weight, Jevons reported the results:

Weight (pounds)	56	28	14	7	4	2	1	1/2
Distance (feet)	1.84	3.70	6.86	10.56	14.61	18.65	23.05	27.15

"A little consideration", he said, "proved it to be probable that these numbers would agree" which led him to an equation of the form

$$x = \frac{p}{w + q} \qquad (7.1)$$

in which x is the distance thrown and w is the weight thrown. Then he determined the "most probable values" of p and q respectively to be 115.7 and 3.9, stating that he applied the method of least squares. Finally the residuals were computed and led to an observation: "the correspondence is so close as to show that the formula is in all probability the true one".

Several points are to be made. First, he reduced the primary data to averages. We now know that it was to eliminate the effect of disturbing causes. Second, no *a priori* justification was given of the form of equation. Later he recalled that it had been discovered by "a purely haphazard trial" (1887: 490). Third, since equation (7.1) is not linear in p and q, it is not straightforward to apply the method of least squares. Nevertheless, Jevons did not disclose how he proceeded. It may thus be doubted that he applied the method at all, regardless of what he said. But I have contended elsewhere that he would have reached the numbers 115.7 and 3.9 as a result of *ad hoc* search for the least squares estimates. Fourth, he referred to his estimates of p and q as the "most probable values". This shows how he understood the method of least squares. For instance, Gauss (1809) had justified the method by proving that the posterior probability would be the highest in the neighborhood where the sum of squares is minimized.[28] Fifth and last, he related the goodness of fit to the probability of a hypothesis being true. But he failed to quantify the former and explicate its relation to the latter. Here we see both the direction and limits of his research program.

We are now in a better position to assess the attempt of Jevons to "ascertain the law to which Davenant's figures conform". First, recall that Jevons referred to the figures as an "estimate" of the variation of the price of corn. I thus suspect it to be his presumption that the figures were averages obtained from a series of data.[29] In other words, when he restated the original table in the following manner, the figures for price were thought to be of the same nature as the average distances discussed above.

Quantity of corn	1.0	0.9	0.8	0.7	0.6	0.5
Price	1.0	1.3	1.8	2.6	3.8	5.5

Second, the equation he fitted to these figures was of the form

$$y = \frac{a}{(x - b)^n} \qquad (7.2)$$

where x and y are the quantity and price of corn. Its similarity to equation (7.1) is obvious, except for another unknown quantity n. But according to him equation (7.2) was not the outcome of "a purely haphazard trial". It was chosen because it fulfilled *a priori* conditions. For instance, he had reasons to believe that "the price of corn should never sink to zero" and that "the price should become infinite before the quantity is zero" (1957: 157).

Third, he said little about how he determined the three unknown quantities. All he said is the following: "An inspection of the numerical data shows that n is about equal to 2, and, assuming it to be exactly 2, I find that the most probable values of a and b are $a = .824$ and $b = .12$" (1957: 157). However, given the similarity of equations (7.1) and (7.2), it seems to be a reasonable conjecture that he would have determined the values for a and b in the same way as he had done for p and q. That is, n being set equal to 2, he would have searched for the values of a and b to minimize the sum of squares:

$$\sum_{i=1}^{6}\left[y_i - \frac{a}{(x_i - b)^2} \right]^2 \tag{7.3}$$

Once he had somehow arrived at $(a, b) = (0.824, 0.12)$, he would have found what I have shown elsewhere: no more reduction in the sum of squares follows if a different value is taken of either a or b, although this is not the case for concurring changes in a and b. Note also that he tried to find "the most probable values", which he considered synonymous with the least squares estimates.

Finally, he prepared a table to "show the degree of approximation between the ... formula and the data of Davenant". Then "the close approximation" was taken as one of the "reasons ... for supposing that this formula is not far from the truth" (1957: 157–8). This inference, however, was still within the limits above mentioned. To repeat, he did not explicate how to determine "the degree of approximation", not to mention its relation to the probability of a formula being true. This might be too much to ask for an economist of the mid-nineteenth century, although the probable error used to be calculated for the least squares estimates.

CONCLUDING REMARKS

Jevons's use of statistics has been examined with the focus on his attempts to render economics exact, and in relation to Cairnes's arguments against the appropriateness of such attempts. Cairnes rejected any use of statistics in economic inquiry, citing the multiplicity of causes and the intermixture of effects. By denying the possibility of advancing from economic data, his view of economics as an inexact science was inevitable. Jevons, however, thought that the method of means could help disentangle the intermixture of effects. In the "periodic commercial fluctuations" he distinguished one kind of variation in the Bank accounts from another. A more sensible use of the method is found in "The value of gold", where the depreciation of gold due to a change in its production conditions was estimated. Based on the theory of probability, his arguments for this estimation also were to the point. He even measured the precision of an average result in terms of the probable error. The role the theory of probability played is more noticeable, if not admirable, in his inference as to the cause of the depreciation of gold. It thus seems that the theory of probability, as he understood it, led him to depart from Cairnes with regard to the use of statistics in economic inquiry.

Trusting that the disturbing causes would cancel each other in a wide average, Jevons made another use of such average. It was to ascertain the relation between the wear and age of coins in circulation, which he presumed was proportional. Although Cairnes would not have labeled the relation economic, Jevons's work on it illustrates how his view of economics as an exact science evolved. An exact relation between variables seemed to him as much possible to ascertain as pure effects of a cause.

The method of means, however, was not the most advantageous that was applicable to the coin problem. This might have occurred to him as he fitted a curve to data based on his weight-throwing experiment, stating that the method of least squares was employed. The same method seems to have been applied to Gregory King's data, although he hardly explicated how he proceeded. Whether these two curve-fittings constitute an improvement compared with his estimation of the annual rate of wear of coins, he again failed to calculate the probable error of estimation despite the authority of Laplace. He should also have appreciated the goodness of fit in a more specific term before citing it as a reason to trust the outcome of curve-fitting.

Jevons did not pursue the discovery of an exact law any further than we have examined above, perhaps because of his early death at the age of 46. In addition his efforts were diverted to an inductive study of the cause of business cycles. But his weakness as a mathematician might have been a more critical reason. Having the method of means in his hand, he could make a strong case with regard to the obstacle that concerned Cairnes. But erecting economics into an exact science demanded more advanced tools than Jevons could handle. He was a painstaking statistical craftsman, but not a competent master of probability theory (Aldrich 1987).

It is still a puzzle, however, that no other economists took up the project of discovering exact laws until the twentieth century arrived.[30] In so far as the technique is concerned, Jevons did not have to be a lonesome pioneer in this field. For instance, the method of least squares had been invented in 1805 and soon became a standard tool in astronomy and geodesy.[31] Further, the method was easy to understand and simple to apply. It thus seems that at least some of Cairnes's arguments were still persuasive to economists in spite of all the developments in the theory of probability and statistical methods during the nineteenth century.

NOTES

1　The lectures were delivered and published in 1857. But the present chapter quotes from the second edition that was published after Cairnes acquainted himself with Jevons's works.

2　For instance, the table appeared in the celebrated book of Tooke (1838), *A History of Prices*, vol. 1, p. 12.

3　Davenant did not disclose the empirical basis of the table, and it was even suspected that the table might not have been derived from actual observations at all. Whewell (1862) was among those who made such suggestion. See Creedy (1986).

4　Since we examine Cairnes's view in order to offer a basis of comparison with Jevons's statistical works, the following question may be raised. How could the former's statement have been interpreted by the latter? According to Jevons's theory of exchange, the quantity (x) of food demanded by a consumer, its price (m) and income (c) are such that $\phi(x) = m\psi(c)$ where ϕ and ψ represent the marginal utilities of food and money, respectively. But Jevons was told like this: the marginal utility functions are not susceptible of arithmetic or mathematical expression because the marginal utilities are not to be weighed and measured; and hence numerical accuracy is not attainable for the price of food (cf. Cairnes 1875: 109).

5　Cairnes also cited the multiplicity of causes and the intermixture of effects from Mill (1879: Book III, ch. 10), whose position he mostly adopted.

6　It was suggested that the situation would be different if the economist had the power of experimentation. But Cairnes also pointed out that the economist, whose subject matter of inquiry is human beings and their interests, is absolutely barred from controlled experiment.

7　Jevons continued to say: "These data would consist chiefly in accurate accounts of the quantities of goods possessed and consumed by the community, and the price at which they are exchanged."

8　The pamphlet was reproduced in *Investigations in Currency and Finance*.

9　The principle of inverse probability, first set forth by Thomas Bayes (1702–61) and further developed by Laplace (1749–1827), consists in computing the probability of an observed event resulting from each possible cause. The highest probability then is taken as the reason why the event should be attributed to a particular cause. To be more specific, "the probability of the existence of any of these causes is then a fraction of whose numerator is the probability of the event resulting from this cause and whose denominator is the sum of the similar probabilities relative to all the causes" (Laplace 1951: 15–16). For the development of this principle, see Todhunter (1949) and Stigler (1986).

10　In such a case, Laplace said, "it is necessary, in place of the probability of the event resulting from each cause, to employ the product of this possibility by the possibility of the cause itself" (1951: 16).

11　The following is the most favorable interpretation that I can propose. Taking Jevons to consider a case where the value of an article has fallen *at the same rate* in its rate of exchange with each of the four other articles, let $P(A)$ represent the probability that the demand or supply of an article A is so disturbed as to raise (drop) its rate of exchange with other articles during a given period of time. Apparently, he assumed such disturbances to be independent of each other: $P(BC) = P(B)P(C)$ if $P(BC)$ represents the probability that the disturbance occurs to both B and C. It also seems to be his assumption that $P(A) = P(B) = P(C) = P(D) = P(E) = p$. Then $p(1 - 2p)^4/p^4(1 - 2p)$ should be the odds which concerned him. My conjecture is that he ignored the term $(1 - 2p)^4/(1 - 2p)$ while mistaking p/p^4 to be four to one.

12   Jevons referred to the principle as a rule of inference "which common sense leads us to adopt almost instinctively" (1887: 243). In contrast, Cairnes (1875) did not even mention the theory of probability. J.S. Mill (1879), whose view Cairnes fully adopted, briefly discussed the principle of inverse probability, only to deny its applicability to scientific investigations.

13   This statement alludes to the notion of probability as long-run relative frequency. Jevons in fact said: "the most probable cause of an event really means that cause which in the greatest number of cases produces the event" (1887: 243–4). But Boole (1854) and Venn (1962) had already made it clear that the principle of inverse probability will lead to contradictions unless probability is regarded as measuring "the feeling of the mind".

14   This is one of the two papers that Jevons forwarded to the Meeting of the British Association in 1862. The other was "Notice of a general mathematical theory of political economy", which attracted little attention by developed into the *Theory of Political Economy*.

15   Jevons was not quite right. Note that $\bar{X}_i - \bar{X}_j = Y_i - \bar{Y}_j + \bar{\varepsilon}_i - \bar{\varepsilon}_j$ This difference will not approach Y_i because $\bar{Y}_j \neq 0$.

16   In fact, Jevons made two uses of averages. The first was to "guard against mistaking any temporary fluctuation due to excessive investment or credit, for the effect of gold depreciation" (1909: 30). Considering such fluctuation to constitute cycles like the tide, he first located a seven-year "commercial tide" prior to the gold discoveries. Then for each commodity he took the average price of this interval and compared it with the price after the gold discoveries. The final mean result was obtained from these ratios between averages. Later in the *Principles of Science* he called this kind of average a precise mean result, or "a result approximately free from disturbing quantities, which are known to affect some results in one direction, and the other equally the opposite direction" (1887: 359).

17   This trust, of course, would not be warranted unless the effect of disturbing causes on each article were independent of their effects on others. But Jevons seemed to suggest that there was no reason to believe otherwise: "all facts I am aware of are so inconsiderable compared with the great discoveries of gold" (1909: 54).

18   See Stigler (1986: 253–4).

19   It is a main point of Stigler (1982) that Jevons did not quantify the uncertainty in measurement with the *exception* of the 1869 article. But I would rather call it a significant improvement on his major statistical investigation.

20   According to my own calculation based on the same sum of squares, the posterior variance of G is 3.646^2 and hence the probable error 2.459. But Jevons should have used $\sum_i (\log R_i - \log \bar{R})^2$ to be consistent with his model of price change. If he had done so then he would have found the probable error to be 2.391.

21   Both books are cited in the *Principles of Science*.

22   It seemed to be so called in the sense that the posterior probability would be the highest at the sample mean.

23   He computed both the annual addition and the annual ratio of increase in the production of pig iron over twelve decades, pointing out that the annual addition had undergone a rapid and continuous increase whereas the ratio of increase had been more or less constant. But the inference drawn from this observation was *ad hoc*, although he considered how each hypothesis agreed with experience. Applying the principle of inverse probability, he could have somehow related the

degrees of agreement to the odds for the law of progress being geometric, and not arithmetic.
24 Jevons determined W_0 by a weighing of 1,000 new sovereigns.
25 Heteroskedasticity could be another issue to be raised; the variance of a coin's weight would increase more or less with its age.
26 William Farr (1807–83) was well known for his contribution as "Compiler of the Abstracts" at the General Register Office since the Office began to index and collate the returns of births, deaths and marriages in 1837. He was also a leading member of the Statistical Society of London. See Cullen (1975).
27 See Stigler (1982, ch. 4).
28 Laplace also proved that the least squares estimate ($\tilde{\theta}$) is "most advantageous" in the sense that it minimizes $\int |\tilde{\theta} - \theta| \phi(\tilde{\theta}) d\tilde{\theta}$ where $\phi(\tilde{\theta})$ is the asymptotic probability density function. But I suspect that the proof would have been beyond Jevons's comprehension. See Stigler (1982, ch. 4).
29 Jevons also said the following: "I cannot undertake to say how nearly Davenant's estimate agrees with experience" (1957, p. 158).
30 In the lack of contrary evidence, I presume that Mackeprang (1906), Benini (1907) and Moore (1911) are the earliest attempts to discover exact laws in economics since Jevons fitted a curve to Gregory King's figures. For Mackeprang's work on demand curves, see Kærgaard (1984).
31 The method of least squares was first proposed in 1805 by a French scientist named Adrien Marie Legendre. The method soon became a standard tool in astronomy and geodesy. See Stigler (1986).

REFERENCES

Airy, George Biddle (1861) *On the Algebraic and Numerical Theory of Errors and Observations and the Combination of Observations*, London: Macmillan.
Aldrich, John (1987) "Jevons as statistician: the role of probability", *Manchester School* 55 (June): 253–7.
Benini, R. (1907) "Sull' uso delle formole empiriche nell' economia applicata", *Giornale degli Economisti* 35: 1053–1906.
Black, Robert Dennis Collison (1960) "Jevons and Cairnes", *Economica* 27 (August): 214–32.
——(1972) "Jevons, Bentham and De Morgan", *Economica* 39 (May): 119–34.
Bostaph, Samuel, and Sieh, Yeung-Nan (1987) "Jevons's demand curve", *History of Political Economy* 19: 107–26.
Cairnes, John E. (1863) "Have the discoveries of gold in Australia and California lowered the value of gold", *The Economist* May 30: 592–3.
——(1874) *Some Leading Principles of Political Economy Newly Expounded*, New York: Harper & Brothers.
—— (1875) *The Character and Logical Method of Political Economy*, 2nd edn, London: Macmillan.
Creedy, John (1986) "On the King–Davenant 'law' of demand", *Scottish Journal of Political Economy* 33 (August): 193–212.
Cullen, M. J. (1975) *The Statistical Movement in Early Victorian Britain: the Foundations of Empirical Social Research*, New York: Harvest Press.
De Morgan, Augustus (1838) *An Essay on Probabilities and on Their Application to Life Contingencies and Insurance Offices*, London: Longman, Brown, Green & Longman.
Gauss, C. Friedrich (1809) *Theorie motus corporum celestium*; trans. C. H. David as *Theory of Motion of the Heavenly Bodies Moving About the Sun in Conic Sections*, Boston: Little & Brown, 1857.

Jennings, Richard (1855) *Natural Elements of Political Economy*, reprinted New York: Kelley, 1969.

Jevons, William Stanley (1909) "A serious fall in the value of gold ascertained and its social effects set forth", first published 1863; reprinted in H. S. Foxwell (ed.) *Investigations in Currency and Finance*, London: Macmillan.

—— (1865) *The Coal Question: an Inquiry Concerning the Progress of the Nation, and the Probable Exhaustion of Our Coal-mines*, London: Macmillan.

—— (1870) "On the natural laws of muscular exertion", *Nature* June: 158–60.

—— (1877) *The Principles of Science: a Treatise on Logic and Scientific Method*, 2nd edn, London: Macmillan.

—— (1957) *The Theory of Political Economy*, 5th edn, reprinted New York: Kelley, 1965.

—— (1972) *Papers and Correspondence of William Stanley Jevons*, vol. 7, ed. R. D. Collison Black, London: Macmillan.

Kærgaard, Niels (1984) "The early history of econometrics: some neglected Danish contributions", *History of Political Economy* 16: 437–44.

Kim, Jinbang. "A note on Jevons's curve fitting", Unpublished paper.

Laplace, Pierre S. (1951) *Essai Philosophical sur les Probabilités*, 6th edn, trans. F. W. Truscott and F. L. Emory, New York: Dover Publications.

Legendre, Adrien M. (1805) *Nouvelles Méthodes pour la Détermination des Orbites des Cométes*, trans. in *Edinburgh Philosophical Journal* 7 (1822): 292–301.

Mill, John S. (1879) *A System of Logic*, 10th edn, London: Longmans, Green.

Moore, Henry L. (1911) *Laws of Wages: an Essay in Statistical Economics*, New York: Macmillan.

Newmarch, William (1860) "Results of the trade of the United Kingdom during the year 1859; with statements and observations relative to the course of prices since the year 1844", *Journal of the Statistical Society of London* 23: 76–110.

—— (1861) "Results of the trade of the United Kingdom during the year 1860; with statements and observations relative to the course of prices since the year 1844", *Journal of the Statistical Society of London* 23: 74–124.

Stigler, Stephen M. (1982) "Jevons as statistician", *Manchester School* 50 (December): 354–65.

—— (1986) *The History of Statistics: the Measurement of Uncertainty before 1900*, Boston, MA: Harvard University Press.

Todhunter, Isaac (1949) *A History of the Mathematical Theory of Probability from the Time of Pascal to that of Laplace*, first published 1865; reprinted New York: Chelsea.

Tooke, Thomas (1838) *A History of Prices, and of the State of the Circulation from 1793 to 1837*, reprinted New York: Adelphi.

Venn, John (1962) *The Logic of Chance*, 4th edn, New York: Chelsea.

Whewell, William (1862) *Six Lectures on Political Economy*, Cambridge: Cambridge University Press.

Chapter 8

A reconstruction of Henry L. Moore's demand studies

Nancy J. Wulwick

Author: H.L. Moore
Statics. Theory of "static equilibrium" showing "the interdependence of all economic quantities" and through "simultaneous mathematical equations the conditions of their common determination".
Dynamics. Theory of "moving equilibria, oscillations, and secular change ... where all the variables in the constituent problems are treated as functions of time".

(Machlup 1991: 17)

MOORE'S DYNAMIC STATISTICAL LAWS OF DEMAND

In *Economic Cycles: Their Law and Cause*, H.L. Moore (1914) estimated statistical laws of demand for crops and pig iron in order to summarize the average changes that markets underwent as a result of shifts in demand and supply functions over the trade cycle. *Economic Cycles* pursued the research program that searched for the source of the trade cycle in an exogenous or natural phenomenon affecting agriculture (Peart 1991). Moore proposed that a meteorological cycle synchronous with a cosmical cycle and evident in a rainfall cycle caused a cycle in crop yields and then crop prices. The economic connection between the cycle in crop prices and the trade cycle is obscure, but Moore seemed to think that since the raw material used in making consumer goods largely came from farms and money wages varied with the price of food, the cycle in crop prices fed through into general prices, unit profits and production (Moore 1911: 32; 1914: 112; 1923: 14–17). His hypothesis led him to examine the statistical relations over time between the price and quantity of four staple commodities – corn, hay, oats and potatoes – and pig iron, an indicator of the trade cycle (Mitchell 1913: 199).[1]

Moore called the statistical relations between the price and the quantity of each good law of demand. Moore emphasized that

> the statistical laws that have just been derived apply to the average changes that society is actually undergoing. They summarize the changes in prices

that are to be expected from changes in the supply of the commodity, thus enabling one to predict the probable variation in price that will follow upon an assigned variation in the amount of the commodity.

(1914: 77)

Thus Moore used the term law as natural scientists sometimes used the term, to refer to a summary of representative facts culled from a large body of empirical observations. The observations were of market prices and quantities produced that were generated *while* national income and general prices varied over the trade cycle.

Moore estimated the relation between price and quantity by least squares, the method "most frequently used in the natural sciences" (Moore 1908: 22).[2] According to the statistical convention of the time, Moore transformed the original observations in order to remove trends in the mean of the time series, a practice intended to preclude spurious correlations and isolate the cyclical movement of the variables. The least squares equations relating price P_t and quantity Q_t appeared in terms of the year-to-year t, $t-1$ percentage changes (Figures 8.1 and 8.2):

$$P_t \equiv 100 \, \frac{p_t - p_{t-1}}{p_{t-1}} \tag{8.1}$$

$$Q_t \equiv 100 \, \frac{q_t - q_{t-1}}{q_{t-1}} \tag{8.2}$$

where the levels of variables p, q are dated observations (Figure 8.3). Another reason for transforming the observations into percentage changes was that the slope of the least squares line readily provided an estimate of an arc elasticity

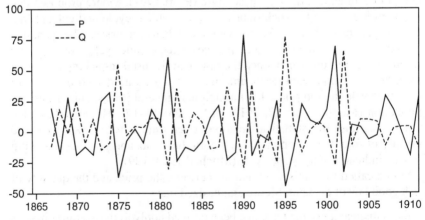

Figure 8.1 Annual percentage changes of corn 1867–1911, Moore's data

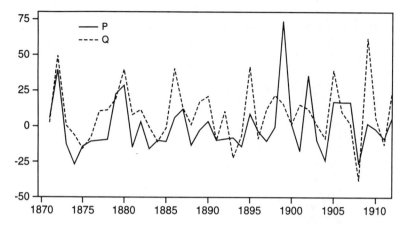

Figure 8.2 Annual percentage changes of pig iron 1871–1912, Moore's data

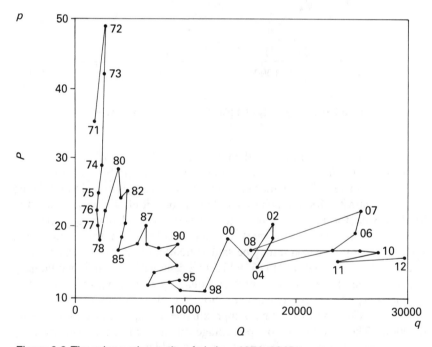

Figure 8.3 The price and quantity of pig iron 1871–1912

of quantity traded in respect to price. Thus percentage changes also increased the information readily supplied by any one estimation, an important time-saver when interpolation of a scatter diagram was a laborious task. Following Moore, the percentage change or link relative (the percentage divided by 100 and minus one) became one of the standard terms in which economists in the

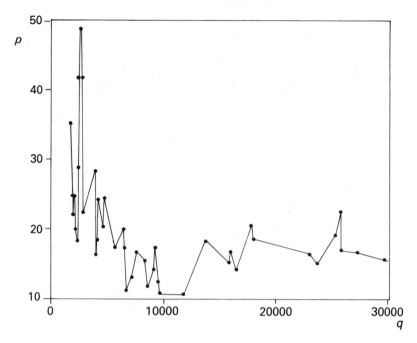

Figure 8.4 The price and quantity of pig iron out of the time domain

interwar period stated models of demand (Schultz 1938: 525).

Economic Cycles sought to treat "concrete dynamic problems" (1914: 64). Moore's estimates of elasticities thus pertained to changes in real time (Figure 8.3). In contrast, Moore emphasized, "the theory of elasticity of demand in [the] classical form ... gives the degree of elasticity of demand for a point in time, for a given state of the market assuming all other things to remain the same; and for this reason it may be said to treat of elasticity of demand from a statical point of view" (1914: 65). Figure 8.4 shows how Moore would have structured the observations of price and quantity had he wanted to estimate the elasticity of a static demand function; the observations of quantity are ordered by size, so that the figure approximates the appearance of a demand function. The definitions of percentage change in price and quantity corresponding to the static demand function would be

$$P_n \equiv 100 \; \frac{p_n - p_{n-1}}{p_{n-1}} \tag{8.3}$$

and

$$Q_n \equiv 100 \ \frac{q_n - q_{n-1}}{q_{n-1}} \tag{8.4}$$

where n refers to order of magnitude of quantity q.[3]

The author repeated Moore's estimates of the demand for corn 1866–1911 by means of ordinary least squares:

$$P_t = 7.8145 - 0.8901Q_t \tag{8.5}$$

Standard error   (2.479)   (0.106)

Two-tailed significance   (0.003)   (0) $r = -0.789$
         level

The estimate of the correlation coefficient r shows a high degree of correlation. The slope of the law of demand implies a point estimate of the elasticity of quantity traded with respect to price of –1.12 (1914: 84). The estimates of the law of demand for pig iron are[4]

$$P_t = 4.5714 - 0.5228Q_t \tag{8.6}$$

Standard error   (2.797)   (0.130)

Two-tailed significance   (0.11)   (0) $r = 0.538$
         level

implying an elasticity of 1.91 (1914: 114). (The estimate of the elasticity of demand pertaining to the undated observations in Figure 8.4 is 1.47.)[5] The estimates of the least squares lines (equations (8.5) and (8.6)) and correlation coefficients are virtually identical to Moore's estimates. Moore called the positively sloped statistical law of demand for pig iron (equation (8.2)) a "new type of demand curve" (1914: 110).

The signs of the elasticities of Moore's statistical laws (equations (8.5) and (8.6)) supported his theory of the trade cycle. Moore maintained that crop prices moved contracyclically while yields per acre, industrial prices and industrial production moved procyclically. This followed from his causal theory of the trade cycle, which stated that decreases in yields per acre in farming caused decreases in trade and the prices of producer goods, employment and general prices, and *mutatis mutandis* for a rise in yields per acre (1914: 116). The weather seemed to Moore to be the main cause of price and quantity changes. Hence Moore treated the statistical relations between price and quantity in equations (8.1) and (8.2) as evidence of correlations rather than causal relations.[6]

Moore intended the least squares analysis in *Economic Cycles* to develop a forecasting method superior to the one used by the Crop Reporting Service of the US Department of Agriculture, which had recently rejected least squares as a basis for forecasting. Recognizing that forecasts of prices were only as sound as the closeness of fit of the least squares line to the observations, he defined as a measure of fit the root mean square of the residuals S, a statistic akin to the modern standard error of the regression, $S = \sigma_y(1-R^2)^{1/2}$, where σ_y is the standard deviation of the dependent variable. The lower the value of S is, the higher the "degree of probability" (1914: 84). Moore then constructed a confidence band (based on the cumulative probability of a standard normal distribution) at the 95 percent level, or plus or minus two standard deviations S, around the statistical law of demand in order to forecast price after the sample period. Using Moore's method the author found a confidence band around the least squares line for pig iron of $\pm 2 \times 16.13$ ($S = 16.13$), which meant that the chances were 95 out of 100 that, if the law of demand for 1871–1912 (equation 2) held in 1913, then the difference between the forecast and actual percentage change in the price of pig iron in 1913 would be at most 32 percentage points.[7] The Crop Reporting Service, having become convinced after further demonstrations of the general relative accuracy of Moore's forecasts, adopted the least squares forecasting method in the 1920s (Moore 1914: 77–9; 1917: 99–100; Kaye 1956: 241).

STRUCTURAL EQUATIONS VERSUS MOORE'S "REDUCED FORMS"

Economic Cycles focused attention not on demand and supply functions but on the motion of market prices and quantities traded. Moore analyzed the relations between price and its determinants, and quantity and its determinants. He showed graphically that the cycles of general prices and the quantity of pig iron both reflected the cycles of yields per acre (1914: Figures 23, 26–7). According to Moore (a) the prices and quantities of corn each depended on rainfall and the state of industrial activity;[8] (b) prices and quantities of pig iron depended on the state of industrial activity governed by yields per acre. In light of his research on wages and strikes (Moore 1911), Moore would have recognized that the state of labor in the coal, iron and steel regions, known for their industrial warfare, also affected the price and quantity of pig iron. Equations expressing (a) and (b) provided the equilibrium solutions for prices and quantities from diagrams of demand and supply functions. But in *Economic Cycles* Moore declined to state "the problem of the relation between price and the quantity of commodity" in "the form of simultaneous [demand and supply] equations" because the equations "are never tested" within the general equilibrium system (1914: 81–2). "[W]ould it not be wise", he asked, "to ascertain first just how closely is the variation in ... price related to the variation in ... supply?" *Economic Cycles* ascertained the correlation between price and quantity. Afterwards, Moore attended to the estimation of a simultaneous equation system of demand and supply functions expressed in link relatives or similar form (Moore 1919: 152–62; 1925; 1929).

Economists since the Cowles Commission in the 1940s have referred to sets of equations expressing the Moore statements (a) and (b) as reduced form equations. The demand and supply functions that the reduced forms solve are structural equations. Moore did not attempt to estimate structural equations, but rather estimated (equations (8.5), (8.6)) the association between the dependent variables of the two reduced form equations.

The Appendix shows the author's estimates of the structural equations for corn and pig iron. All the variables appear in terms of first differences. Figures 8.5(a) and 8.6(a) show Moore's data and the laws of demand (equations (8.5), (8.6)). Figures 8.5(b), 8.5(c) and 8.6(b), 8.6(c) present the structural demand and supply functions with respect to corn and pig iron for 1873 (a year of a cyclical downturn) and 1880 (a year of cyclical upswing). In Figures 8.5(b) and 8.6(b) the demand functions slope downwards and the supply functions slope upwards because the author imposed *a priori* restrictions on the estimates of the elasticities of quantity with respect to price. Figures 8.5(c) and 8.6(c), which include a downward-sloping supply function for corn and an upward-sloping demand function for pig iron, result from unconstrained estimates. The two sets of figures ((a) versus (b), (c)) clearly distinguish Moore's statistical laws of demand as points of moving equilibria from the estimates of static demand functions.

MAY STATIC DEMAND FUNCTIONS HAVE POSITIVE SLOPES?

The statistician Yule in his review of *Economic Cycles* cautioned readers not to confuse Moore's demand curves (equations (8.1) and (8.2)) with Marshall's. As Yule stated,

> [t]o say that the regression curves of price on production over a series of years cannot be regarded as demand curves in the sense used, e.g. by Professor Marshall, does not lessen their interest or value, but does imply that they have no bearing on Professor Marshall's statement as to the uniformity of the law which he quotes.

(1915: 305)

Indeed, Moore explicitly rejected Marshall's theory of demand (Mirowski 1990). The fourth (1898) edition of Marshall's *Principles* cited by Moore maintained that the demand function for a good based on the separable utility function, where the marginal utility of each good depends only on consumption of that good, follows "one universal rule, that it is *inclined negatively* throughout", given the assumptions of diminishing marginal utility for goods and constant marginal utility of money income, or (to use an anachronism) the

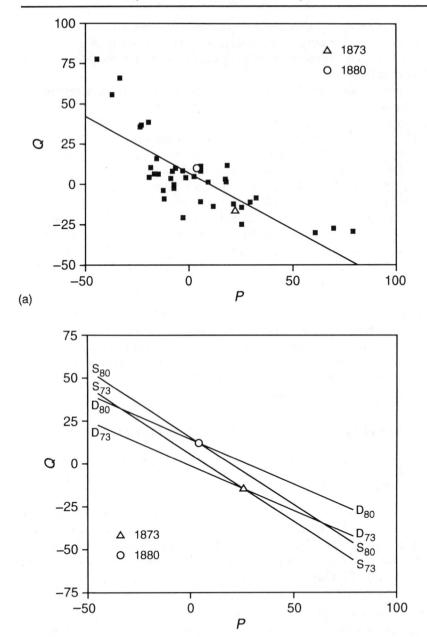

(a)

(b)

$$D_{73}: \ Q = -0.01 - 0.53\,P \qquad D_{80}: \ Q = -0.14 - 0.53\,P$$

$$S_{73}: \ Q = -0.05 - 0.79\,P \qquad S_{80}: \ Q = -0.15 - 0.79\,P$$

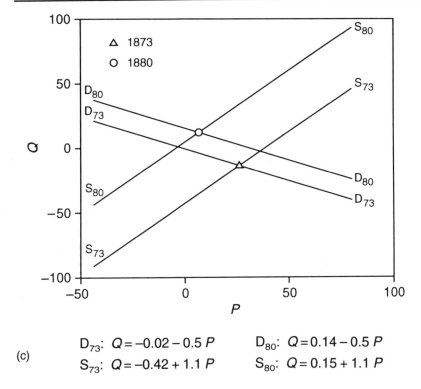

$$D_{73}: Q = -0.02 - 0.5\,P \qquad D_{80}: Q = 0.14 - 0.5\,P$$
$$S_{73}: Q = -0.42 + 1.1\,P \qquad S_{80}: Q = 0.15 + 1.1\,P$$

(c)

Figure 8.5 (a) Scatter diagram and Moore's law of demand for corn 1872–1910; (b) demand for and supply of corn in percentage terms 1873 and 1880, unconstrained estimates; (c) demand for and supply of corn in percentage terms 1873 and 1880 with restrictions on the slopes

absence of an income effect due to a change in own price (Moore 1914: 64–7; 1917: 149–51; Walker 1982). As an empirical matter Marshall knew of positively sloped demand curves but assumed that their existence was limited to subsistence (or "Giffen") goods that should be treated on their own merits (Marshall 1898: 207 and n. 1). Moore insisted in *Economic Cycles* that the *ceteris paribus* conditions implied by the assumptions of separability and constant marginal utility of money income normally went unmentioned, unenumerated and unanalyzed, which made the law of demand of the negative type impossible to estimate or test (1914: 64–7, 77, 87–8; Pigou 1930: 385–90).

If Moore never estimated demand functions, why did he and his successors use the term demand curves? The term demand, which today has a precise meaning based on the mathematical presentation available in standard microeconomics textbooks, in 1914 lacked such a definite reference. Moore himself remarked that "[t]he bewildering vagueness of economic theory is largely due to the fact that the terms used are in all ... stages of development"

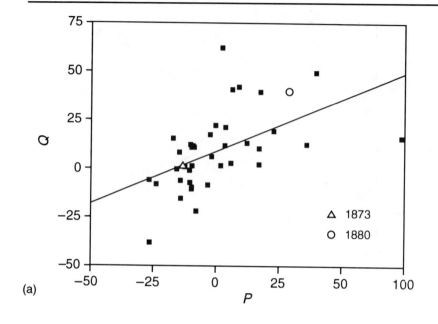

(a)

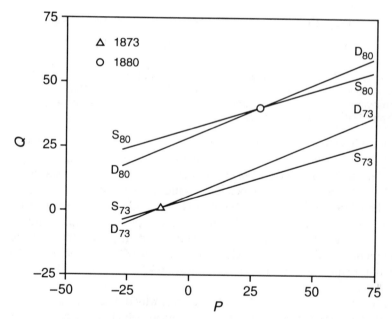

D_{73}: $Q = 5.58 + 0.41\,P$ D_{80}: $Q = 28.18 + 0.41\,P$

(b) S_{73}: $Q = 4.15 + 0.29\,P$ S_{80}: $Q = 31.46 + 0.29\,P$

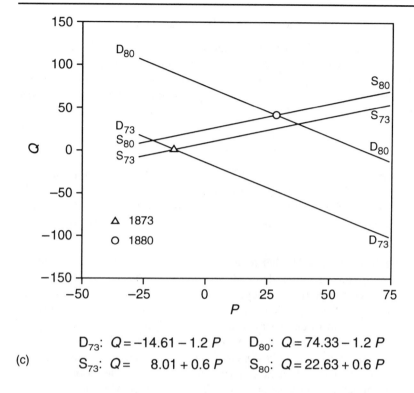

$$D_{73}: \ Q = -14.61 - 1.2\,P \qquad D_{80}: \ Q = 74.33 - 1.2\,P$$
$$(c) \quad S_{73}: \ Q = \quad\ 8.01 + 0.6\,P \qquad S_{80}: \ Q = 22.63 + 0.6\,P$$

Figure 8.6 (a) Scatter diagram and Moore's law of demand for pig iron 1872–1910; (b) demand for and supply of pig iron in percentage terms 1873 and 1880, unconstrained estimates; (c) demand for and supply of pig iron in percentage terms 1873 and 1880 with restrictions on the slopes

(Moore 1906: 211).[9] Because Marshall's law of demand was popular amongst English-speaking economists due to its simplicity and approximate correspondence to many instances of casual experience, Moore occasionally cited Marshall's *Principles* in order to engage the attention of his readers, while distinguishing his own project from Marshall's. For example, Moore stated that "[t]he statistical laws of demand for the commodities corn, hay, oats, and potatoes present the fundamental characteristic which, in the classical treatment of demand, has been assumed to belong to all demand curves, namely, they are negatively inclined" according to "Marshall: *Principles of Economics*, 4th edit., p. 174". Nevertheless, Moore continued, his statistical laws of demand were "unlike the classical theory of demand which was limited to the simple enunciation of this one characteristic *ceteris paribus*" (Moore 1906: 72, 77; Mirowski 1990).

Despite Moore's sharp criticisms of Marshall's theory of demand, the book reviews by economists mistook Moore's regressions as estimates of

Marshallian demand functions. Wright (1915) stated that

> [t]he demand curves for crops harmonize perfectly with theory: the conditions of demand remain approximately constant; there is an increased output of crops (very probably due to heavier rainfall); with the diminishing utility due to this increased supply, the marginal utility and hence [assuming constant marginal utility of money income] the price falls
>
> (1915: 638)

as shown in Figure 8.7. Lehfeldt (1915) continued that

> the curve [for pig-iron] on p. 115 [of *Economic Cycles*] is not a demand curve at all, but much more nearly a supply curve. It is arrived at by the intersection of irregularly fluctuating demands on supply conditions that, on the whole, may be regarded as steady but for a secular growth
>
> (1915: 411)

as shown in Figure 8.8. Neither reviewer thought that it was necessary to test their assumptions that the demand for corn and the supply of pig iron remained fixed during the trade cycle. Such assumptions, the econometrician E.J. Working (1927) remarked in a discussion of Wright's (1915) review, might not stand up to empirical scrutiny (pp. 222–3). Nor did Lehfeldt and Wright in any manner raise the empirical issue of whether the demand for pig iron historically was positively sloped. The two reviewers simply claimed that what they *mistook* as a demand *function* in *Economic Cycles* conflicted with the theory of demand because the function was positively sloped.

Moore never responded directly to his critics.[10] He was reclusive and independently minded, and retired from academic life in 1929 (Schumpeter 1954: 877). He let others explain the difference between his statistical demand curves, which pertained to the time domain, and static demand functions. Certainly Moore disagreed with critics who said that demand functions must be negatively declined. In *Forecasting the Yield and the Price of Cotton* (1917) Moore appealed to Pareto's theory to defend the existence of positively sloped demand functions. Moore argued that the usual statement of the law of demand based on the separable utility function did not take account of the fact that, as Marshall himself stated, "'the more a person spends on anything ... the greater is the marginal value of money to him'". Given changes in the marginal utility of money income Pareto showed that it was possible to have positively sloped demand functions (Moore 1917: 20; Pareto 1909: 424–6). Economic theory, Moore continued, should not exclude the possibility of such demand functions. In this context, Moore quoted Pareto's disciple W.E. Zawadzki (1914) that "[i]l est facile d'imaginer des cas théoriques où la demande diminuerait à la suite d'une diminution de prix. La théorie doit donc être capable d'en tenir compte.... *Dans cet exemple nous touchons, pour ainsi dire, du doigt la puissance et la faiblesse de l'économie mathématique. Nous avons la formule la plus générale ... mais nous ne*

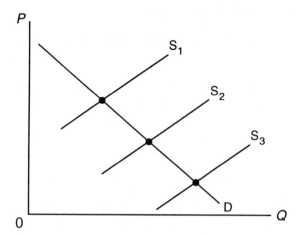

Figure 8.7 Demand and supply functions for corn according to Moore's critics

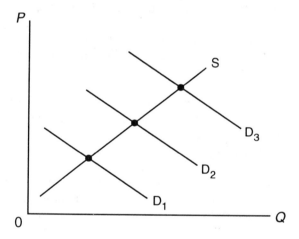

Figure 8.8 Demand and supply functions for pig iron according to Moore's critics

pouvons pas en passer aux cas particuliers, pas même distinguer ce qui est l'exception de ce qui est la règle (Moore 1917: 150 n. 2).[11] According to the theory of nonseparable utilities, as Moore knew, economists can test whether the demand function for one good is upward sloping only within the system of demand functions for all goods (Moore 1914: 81–2).[12]

THE IDENTIFICATION PROBLEM

There were economists in the interwar period who remarked on the difference between the statistical demand curves that Moore established and demand functions. Pigou (1930) and Stigler (1939) explained that demand functions implied causal relations *ceteris paribus* and shifted according to explicit conditions. Statistical demand curves showed mere correlations (Pigou 1930: 390–1; Stigler 1939: 469–70). Pigou (1932), as if aware of the folklore that Moore mistook the supply of pig iron for the demand for pig iron, further clarified that

> Marshall's elasticity, if known, would make it possible to predict how far the introduction of a new cause modifying supply in a given manner would *affect* prices; Professor Moore's to predict with what price-changes changes in supply coming about naturally, in company with such various other changes as have hitherto been found to accompany them, are likely to be *associated*.
>
> (p. 782 n. 2)

Shepherd (1950) cautioned his undergraduate agricultural economics students that the statistical "quantity–price curves for many farm products have a negative slope, and it is easy to suppose that they show the demand curves for those products. Actually ... the curves may have very little relation to demand curves. Many 'demand curves' are not demand curves at all, but only mixtures of demand and supply curves that ... leave a track of intersection points" (1950: 108). Nevertheless, Stigler (1962), in his obituary of Moore, propagated the folklore that Moore had "blundered into the positively sloping demand curve for pig iron" (p. 367). Recent histories of economics by Darnell (1984), Christ (1985), Blaug (1986), Kim (1988), Epstein (1987) and Morgan (1990) repeated the folklore.[13]

If the folklore about Moore is misinformed, why has it remained alive ninety years? "There are many ways to read a text", as historians know (Kuhn 1977: xii).[14] How historians have read Moore's book has depended on the problems which they have posed in marshalling the historical evidence. Because Marshall's law of demand has served as the point of departure for many English-speaking economists, historians commonly have interpreted that Moore was grappling with the sorts of problems that arise in a Marshallian context. However, the theoretical framework in which economic problems arose then was less well defined than in the period of the professionalization of economics following the Second World War. Hence, the readings most accessible to modern historians might be inappropriate when applied to Moore. What is the criterion which guides the choice of the superior reading(s) of historical texts? As Kuhn remarked, the "plasticity of texts does not place all ways of reading on a par, for some of them (ultimately, one hopes, only one) possess a plausibility and coherence absent from others". The maxim is "[w]hen reading the works of an important thinker, look first for the apparent absurdities in the text and ask yourself how a sensible person could have written them" (ibid.). The folklore about Moore's text says that Moore was a blunderer, that he unthinkingly called a positively sloped function in price–quantity space a demand function. Such a reading neglects the sections in the text that insist that Moore will not apply the static Marshallian demand functions, but rather will apply the dynamic theory of moving equilibria to analyze historical market data.

The folklore about Moore mistakes the nature of the identification problem.[15] The folklore assumes that formal economic theory implies empirical conclusions that it really does not imply. The folklore says that because the scatter diagram of price and quantity of pig iron 1871–1912 formed an upward-sloping band (Figure 8.6(a)), a supply function necessarily underlies the scatter diagram. But the section of the econometrics textbook on the identification problem explains that a scatter diagram results from one of two kinds of interaction of demand and supply functions: one function shifting along the other, fixed function; or two shifting functions.[16] The essay has shown that there are any number of observationally equivalent systems (such as Figures 8.5(b), 8.5(c), 8.6(b), 8.6(c)) each with a shifting demand function and a shifting supply function that could have produced Moore's scatter diagram for pig iron. Moore's statistical law of demand for pig iron then estimated the slope and the closeness of the scatter of observations as the basis for prediction.

APPENDIX

The Appendix[17] illustrates the structural equations that a modern economist might use in light of Moore's research questions. The symbols for the variables are as follows: E, workers' money earnings; F, commercial failures; I, inflation; P, nominal prices; Q, quantity supplied; R, rainfall; S, swine; Y, yield per acre of corn; t, time; α, β, elasticities; μ, η, disturbance terms.[18] All the variables appear in terms of annual percentage changes.

The unconstrained structural equations for pig iron estimated by two-stage least squares are as follows.

Demand

$$Q_t = 11.29 - 0.09F_{t-1} + 0.71I_t - 0.23Q_{t-1} - 0.35P_{t-1} + 0.41P_t + \mu_{t1}$$

The demand equation is based on Whitman's (1934) demand in speculative markets for steel (p. 591).

Supply

$$Q_t = 10.06 - 1.35E_{t-1} + 1.62I_t - 0.06Q_{t-1} - 0.29P_{t-1} + 0.29P_t + \mu_{t2}$$

The two-stage least squares estimates of the structural equations for pig iron with a restriction imposed on the elasticity of quantity with respect to price are as follows.

Demand

$$Q_t = 13.55 - 0.12F_{t-1} + 5.73I_t - 0.18Q_{t-1} - 0.58P_{t-1} - 1.2P_t + \mu_{t3}$$

Supply

$$Q_t = 9.89 - 0.52E_{t-1} + 1.26I_t + 0.0004Q_{t-1} - 0.6P_{t-1} + 0.6P_t + \mu_{t4}$$

The observed levels of significance for tests of exclusions of the four equations above are 0.78, 0.19, 0.03 and 0.003 respectively. Each structural equation excludes a number of variables that are in the reduced form equations. The smaller the observed significance level, the less the support afforded hypotheses by the data.

The unconstrained structural equations for corn estimated by two-stage least squares are as follows.

Demand

$$Q_t = 0.05 - 0.0006F_{t-1} + 0.001S_t + 0.53P_{t-1} + 0.53P_t + \eta_{t5}$$

Supply

$$Q_t = 0.06 + 0.004R_t + 0.0001Y_t + 0.32P_{t-1} - 0.79P_t + \eta_{t6}$$

The two-stage least squares estimates of the structural equations with a restriction imposed on the elasticity of quantity with respect to price are as follows.

Demand

$$Q_t = 0.05 - 0.0005F_{t-1} + 0.0008S_t + 0.5P_{t-1} - 0.5P_t + \eta_{t7}$$

Supply

$$Q_t = -0.05 + 0.004R_t + 0.008Y_t - 0.12P_{t-1} + 1.1P_t + \eta_{t8}$$

The observed level of significance for tests of exclusions of the four equations above are respectively 0.0003, 0.73, 0.0002 and 0.03.

Complete details about the estimates are available from the author.

NOTES

Another version of the essay appeared under the title "The Folklore of H. L. Moore on the demand for pig iron", *Journal of the History of Economic Thought* 14 (Fall 1992), 168–88. The author acknowledges comments of R.L. Basmann, H. Brems, D.W. Hands, T. Mayer, P. Mirowski, I.H. Rima and the participants of the Economics Department Seminar of the State University of New York at Binghamton.

1 Pig iron, or iron cast in blocks, or pigs, is used in the manufacture of steel and iron casts.
2 Moore's (1914) data appeared in Tables 1–4 of Chapter 4 and Tables 2 and 5 of Chapter 5 of Moore. Pig iron prices (in levels) appear in *Statistical Abstract of the United States 1912*, Department of Commerce and Labor, Washington, DC, p. 572, Table 281. The observations of crop prices and crop production came from the Yearbooks of the United States Department of Agriculture 1866–1911. The observations of pig iron 1870–1912 which came from *Statistical Abstract for*

1912 referred to national production and prices recorded in Pittsburgh and Philadelphia, the major centers of the iron industry. Moore treated the data on quantities supplied as proxies for quantities traded.

3 The difference between estimating demand elasticities in and out of the time domain appears in R.L. Basmann and D. Slottje's new econometrics textbook to be published by Dryden Press.

4 The estimate of the constant differs from the estimate in Wulwick 1990 (p. 174) by 0.0001 because of an error of 0.001 in inscribing one of the observations.

5 The estimates based on the definitions of variables in equations (8.3) and (8.4) are $P_t = 4.9447 + 0.6781Q_t$.

6 Following that approach Schultz (1925) chose as the best fitting line the one which minimized the sum of the mean square vertical *and* horizontal deviations (p. 581 and n. 4).

7 The 95 percent confidence band for the change in price in 1913 given the forecast change (from equation 8.2)) of −2.39 was −34.39 to 26.91, which covered the actual change of 4.34 (*Statistical Abstract of the United States 1913*, Tables 149, 267).

8 To show the effect of changes in economic activity on agriculture, Moore split the sample for crops between the long economic downswing 1866–90 and the long upswing 1890–1911, two phases that were superimposed upon numerous eight-year trade cycles. The divided sample supplied just enough observations to show that "the demand schedule [for crops] or yield–price curve is high when the general level of prices is high; and the demand schedule is low when the general level of prices is low" (Moore 1914: 57, 100–2, 125).

9 Cited in Machlup (1991: 5).

10 The early Danish econometrician E.P. Mackeprang, who in 1906 estimated positively sloped statistical demand curves for coal and metals, encountered criticism similar to that received by Moore (Kærgaard 1984).

11 Author's translation: "It is easy to imagine theoretical cases where the quantity demanded decreases with decreases in price. Theory ought to be able to take such cases into account.... This example puts, so to speak, our finger on the power and weakness of mathematical economics. We have general formulae that extend to extremely rare cases, but we cannot pass to the particulars, not even to distinguish what is the exception from the rule."

12 Ferguson and Saving (1969) derived positively sloped demand functions for producer goods given the assumption of cost minimization. The author thanks C. Colburn for this reference.

13 J.J. Heckman in his review in the *Journal of Economic Literature* of *The History of Econometric Ideas* propagated Morgan's criticism of Moore without showing any sign of having checking the primary source. "In the hands of ... Henry Moore," Heckman wrote, "the empirical analogue to Alfred Marshall's logical *ceteris paribus* operation was produced by linear regression. In a notorious episode in the history of economic thought, uncritical use of regression methods led Moore to proclaim an upward sloping empirical 'demand' curve for pig iron" (1992: 878).

   The histories of Moore's work by Schumpeter (1954: 876–7) and Mirowski (1990) are exceptional in recognizing the distinction that *Economic Cycles* drew between static (Marshallian) and dynamic (statistical) demand curves.

14 The author is grateful to T. Mayer for pointing out the Kuhn reference to her.

15 The identification problem has two meanings. The relevant meaning in the context of the essay is the problem of *locating* a relationship in the data (Morgan 1990: 162).

16 C.F. Christ, author of a classic econometrics textbook, paradoxically charged that Moore "apparently had no idea of the identification problem, and did not consider that his positively sloped elasticity for pig iron was closer to a supply elasticity than to a demand elasticity" (Christ 1985: 43, as cited in Mirowski 1990: 597; Christ 1966: 307–8).
17 The author thanks R.L. Basmann for advice on estimation by two-stage least squares.
18 *Sources*: (a) From Moore (1914): inflation, p. 133, Table VI, column 5; rainfall, p. 61, Table IV, column 2; yield per acre of corn, pp. 39, 58, Table 1, column 3; price and quantity supplied, note 2 above. (b) From *Historical Statistics of the United States: Colonial Times to 1970*, US Department of Commerce, Bureau of the Census, Washington, DC, 1975: earnings, Series D 735–8 on annual money earnings of nonfarm employees 1871–1900 and Series D 739–64 on annual annual money earnings of manufacturing employees 1900–10. (c) From *Statistical Abstract of the United States 1914*, Department of Commerce and Labor, Washington, DC: commercial failures, No. 352, p. 681; swine, No. 352, p. 661.

REFERENCES

Blaug, M. (1986) *Great Economists Before Keynes*, New York: Cambridge University Press.
Christ, C. F. (1966) *Econometric Models and Methods*, London: Wiley.
——— (1985) "Early progress in estimating quantitative economic relationships in America", *American Economic Review*, 75: 39–52.
Darnell, A. C. (1984) "Economic statistics and econometrics", in his *Economic Statistics and Econometrics*, London: Butterworths.
Epstein, R. J. (1987) *A History of Econometrics*, New York: North-Holland.
Ferguson, C. E. and Saving, T. R. (1969) "Long-run scale adjustments of a perfectly competitive firm and industry", *American Economic Review* 59: 774–83.
Heckman, J. J. (1992) "Haavelmo and the birth of modern econometrics: a review of the history of econometric ideas by Mary Morgan", *Journal of Economic Literature* 30: 876–86.
Kærgaard, Niels (1984) "The early history of econometrics: some neglected Danish contributions", *History of Political Economy* 16: 437–44.
Kaye, N. J. (1956) *Pioneer Econometric of Henry Ludwell Moore*, Unpublished Ph.D. Dissertation, University of Wisconsin.
Kim, K. (1988) *Equilibrium Business Cycle Theory in Historical Perspective*, New York: Cambridge University Press.
Kuhn, T. S. (1977) *The Essential Tension*, Chicago, IL: University of Chicago Press.
Lehfeldt, R. A. (1915) *"Economic cycles: Their Law and Cause*, by H. L. Moore", *Economic Journal* 25: 409–11.
Machlup, F. (1991) *Economic Semantics*, London: Transaction Publishers; originally published in 1963 as *Essays in Economic Semantics*.
Marshall, A. (1898) *Principles of Economics*, London: Macmillan.
Mirowski, P. (1990) "Problems in the paternity of econometrics: Henry Ludwell Moore", *History of Political Economy* 22: 587–609.
Mitchell, W. C. (1913) *Business Cycles and Their Causes*, Philadelphia, PA: Porcupine Press, 1989 reprint.
Moore, H. L. (1906) "Paradoxes of competition", *Quarterly Journal of Economics* 20.
——— (1908) "The statistical complement of pure economics", *Quarterly Journal of Economics* 23: 1–33.
——— (1911) *Laws of Wages*, reprinted Fairfield, NJ: Kelley, 1967.

———(1914) *Economic Cycles: Their Law and Cause*, reprinted Fairfield, NJ: Kelley, 1967.

———(1917) *Forecasting the Yield and the Price of Cotton*, reprinted Fairfield, NJ: Kelley, 1967.

———(1919) "Empirical laws of demand and supply and the flexibility of prices", *Political Science Quarterly* 34: 546–67.

———(1923) *Generating Economic Cycles*, reprinted Fairfield, NJ: Kelley, 1967.

———(1925) "A moving equilibrium of demand and supply", *Quarterly Journal of Economics* 39: 357–71.

———(1929) *Synthetic Economics*, reprinted Fairfield, NJ: Kelley, 1967.

Morgan, M. S. (1990) *The History of Econometric Ideas*, New York: Cambridge University Press.

Pareto, V. (1898) *Cours d'Economie Politique*, Lausanne: Rouge.

———(1909) *Manuel d'Economie Politique*, New York: AMS.

Peart, S. J. (1991) "Sunspots and expectations: W. S. Jevons's theory of economic fluctuations", *Journal of the History of Economic Thought* 13: 243–65.

Pigou, A. C. (1930) "The statistical derivation of demand curves", *Economic Journal* 40: 384–400.

———(1932) *Economics of Welfare*, London: Macmillan.

Schultz, H. (1925) "The statistical law of demand as illustrated by the demand for sugar", *Journal of Political Economy* 31: 577–637.

———(1938) *The Theory and Measurement of Demand*, Chicago, IL: University of Chicago Press.

Schumpeter, J. A. (1954) *History of Economic Analysis*, New York: Oxford University Press.

Shepherd, G. S. (1950) *Agricultural Price Analysis*, Ames, IA: Iowa State College Press.

Stigler, G. J. (1939) "The limitations of statistical demand curves", *Journal of the American Statistical Association* 34: 469–81.

———(1962) "Henry L. Moore and statistical economics", *Econometrica* 30: 1–21.

Walker, D. A. (1982) "A defense of Marshall on substitute and complements in consumption", *Eastern Economic Journal* 8: 67–78.

Working, E. J. (1927) "What do statistical 'demand curves' show?", *Quarterly Journal of Economics* 41: 212–35.

Wright, P. G. (1915) "Review: Moore's economic cycles", *Economic Journal* 29: 631–41.

Wulwick, N. J. (1992) "The folklore of H. L. Moore on the demand for pig iron", *Journal of the History of Economic Thought* 14: 168–88.

Yule, G. U. (1915) "*Economic cycles: Their Law and Cause.* By Professor H. L. Moore", *Journal of the Royal Statistical Society* 78: 302–5.

Zawadzki, W. E. (1914) *Les Mathématique appliquées à l'Economie Politique*, Paris: Rivière.

Chapter 9

The probability approach to index number theory
Prelude to macroeconomics

Robert E. Prasch

INTRODUCTION

The earliest index numbers in economics were associated with attempts to theorize about the "general price level". That the "general price level" was a distinct abstraction which existed as a quantifiable entity was a shared certainty of all the early theorists who constructed index number schemes.[1] The idea of a general level of prices, one which exists independently of relative prices, was a direct result of these theorists' prior belief in the quantity theory of money.

The problem of index number construction is to establish a number for an abstract quantity (price level or total quantity) which cannot be observed or measured in practice.[2] A pronounced difficulty with economic data is that they consist of two distinct phenomena compounded into a single observation. One is the actual quantities of goods under consideration. The other is the set of prices associated with each of these goods. For example, a number such as $4.76 does not reveal much about a specific economic phenomenon. For such a number to make sense, we must first establish both the value of the currency unit and the temporal and spatial quality and quantity of goods being offered for sale.[3] In this example, the system is underdetermined in the mathematical sense, since we have only one equation with two unknowns: $P \times Q = \$4.76$. In simple language, this means that more information will be required before we can establish the numerical value of either P or Q.

In its most simple formulation, index number theory can be thought of as a technique or method. This method enables us, by a mental exercise, to assign a number, called an index number, to either P or Q. Such an expedient allows us to resolve the problem of underdetermination and solve for the other variable. The trick is to do this in a sensible manner which does not so completely distort reality that it results in a useless set of data. The next section of this chapter will discuss the different approaches that nineteenth-century theorists used to resolve the index number problem. In particular, the chapter will focus on the evolving understanding of the theory of probability and how this change resulted in different approaches to index number theory.

This will be followed by a review of the criticism directed at this tradition by Alfred Marshall and the early works of John Maynard Keynes.

NINETEENTH-CENTURY INDEX NUMBER THEORY

The probability approach

The essential proposition which characterizes the quantity theory of money is the claim that a prior change in the supply of money is eventually and fully reflected in an equiproportional change in the aggregate price level.[4] An important corollary of the quantity theory, if it is assumed to be strongly operative in the comparatively short run, is that it relieved the early index number compiler from the arduous and abstract task of accounting for the relative weight of the quantities of the various goods being gathered in the data sample.

The quantity theorists could make this seemingly dubious assumption because they were convinced that the Q of my earlier equation, and all other Qs, would remain stationary after any change in the overall price level. They felt that it was safe to assume that, at least in the long run, all prices would rise and fall together in response to a change in the supply of money.[5] In this case it would follow that relative prices, the prices at which goods exchange for one another, could be assumed to be stable. More to the point, if relative prices did change, they could be assumed to change in a random fashion around a mean price level. This average, or absolute level, of prices is termed the "general level of prices".

The early index number theorists were not naive; they understood that quantity changes between goods would take place over time, and that a change in the money supply would initially be reflected in relative prices through temporary imbalances. However, as quantity theorists, they maintained that these changes would even out in "the long run". Driven by the arguments of elegance and simplicity, the quantity theory provided the intellectual basis for the probabilistic approach to index number theory.

The pivotal assumption upon which early index number theorists depended was a belief that in the short run any relative price changes induced by monetary phenomena could be considered, for calculating purposes, to be statistically "independent". For this reason, their major statistical concern was to ensure that enough price observations were being made to eliminate any "small sample bias".[6] Given these assumptions, all that was required of a researcher using the probabilistic approach was that they be sure that price observations were made over a relatively large number of goods; this effort would be sufficient to compile an index of the general price level.[7]

As part of an official English commission, Francis Ysidro Edgeworth made an important attempt to defend the quantity theory approach to price indices on the basis of probability theory. The idea was that if prices did not change much, and if the time periods under comparative investigation were not too distant or, equivalently, no one changed their consumption choices, then an index formed by calculating the change in the geometric mean of the prices of the goods chosen for the index would accurately represent the true underlying rate of inflation.[8] Following the theory, this calculation of the mean is made without reference to a scheme of weights. Edgeworth makes no attempt to enlist any evidence on the relative importance of specific goods in the makeup of the economy.

This aspect of the probabilistic method was a strong point in its favor. Not only was it thought to be based on sound economic principles, but it was easy to calculate – a fact which was not inconsequential given the high cost of computation at this time. As noted, Edgeworth argued that this theorem would hold if all errors of observation could be treated as if they were independent. This independence assumption was crucial and, as John Maynard Keynes later argued, problematic.[9]

The probabilistic approach to measuring changes in the general level of prices assumed, along with the quantity theory of money, that the change in any one price was composed of two independent components. The first is due to changes in the money supply. The second is attributed to changes in the relative prices of the goods traded. The problem, as stated by Keynes, was that changes in relative prices are not always, or even usually, independent.[10] In reality, prices are more typically interdependent. One can easily imagine that in a modern economy changes in the price of commodities such as crops and fertilizer, or cars and gasoline, show symptoms of strong interdependence. The existence of substitutes and complements implies that the choice of goods to be included in the index is important and that observed movements between individual prices are not independent.[11]

For these reasons the probabilistic method was not immediately accepted by all. With the exception of William Stanley Jevons, whose rhetorical style prohibited lukewarm attachment to any doctrine, most theorists accepted the probability theory of index construction only as a fallback position. Edgeworth was typical of this position in his guarded, but strong and ultimately influential, acceptance of the probability theory of index numbers. In his treatise on the subject, Edgeworth proposed the probability approach only after carefully eliminating other, seemingly more logical, candidates from consideration. His acceptance was reserved as he thought that the approach represented the best option amongst a set of poor alternatives. This reserved attitude was very much in contrast with the more enthusiastic endorsement of earlier index number theorists.[12]

At this time, an important holdout from the probability approach was the business press. This was important because they were the actual innovators in the compilation and publication of price indices.[13] The indices compiled by the press, in particular the influential index published by *The Economist*, employed a weighting scheme that was determined by the amounts of the goods purchased in a given base year.[14] The compilers assumed that the existent use pattern remained constant for the duration of the index.[15] This fixed weight index had the wonderful attribute of simplicity in calculation. The difficulty with such a method was (1) determining the initial weights and (2) the fact that, over a number of years, these weights would become arbitrary with regard to actual use patterns. In particular, such an index tends to overstate changes in the price level to the extent that it ignores the effect of consumers substituting into cheaper goods over time. For instance, an index which included a buggy whip would miss the fact that the annual expenditure on such implements has declined relative to gasoline as a proportion of the average household budget.

CRITICS OF THE PROBABILITY APPROACH TO PRICE INDICES

Marshall's chain index

Alfred Marshall, at the conclusion of a short paper published in 1887, began to develop an aggregate index that could explicitly incorporate changes in the weights of the goods that were represented in the base of the index. Marshall's innovation in overcoming the problem of base weights was through the device of a chain index. In his formulation, the changing mix and weights of goods are incorporated into the composite commodity making up the index number. In this index the base is recalculated for each year, and price changes are calculated for each period on the basis of the updated base year. The idea is that constantly changing base years can address the inherent problem of the changing state of final demands or use patterns in the actual economy.[16]

The major drawback to the chain index is that rigorous accuracy is restricted to a comparison between the price level of two consecutive years. Years that are distant from one another cannot logically be compared as they do not share a common composite commodity on which to base a calculation of the changing price level. The degree of error introduced by an index which features an evolving composite commodity varies with the rapidity and degree of change which takes place in a specific historical period. A second concern is that the index ascribes too much importance to short-term fluctuations in prices. For this reason the index can miss an underlying inflation rate by a significant margin.[17]

Keynes's critique of index number theory (1909)

It is generally agreed that Keynes's study of probability was inspired by his interest in ethics, particularly the work of Cambridge philosopher George E. Moore.[18] A proposition important to Moore's ethical theory was that the moral worth of an action depended on an estimate, by the actor, of the "total results" of the proposed action. Unfortunately, the effects of an action are uncertain and therefore cannot be known in an exact way at the time that the initial activity is conducted.[19] The temporal nature of life thus threatened to place ethical theory in an intellectual impasse to the extent that the future is unknown.[20] This problem induced Keynes to investigate the rational basis of probabilistic knowledge as part of an ongoing program in ethical research. His interest in political economy was only to develop in the course of writing his fellowship dissertation on probability. For these interrelated reasons, the final published work on probability was strongly influenced by a concern for issues of interest to the field of "moral philosophy". To the English intellectuals of Keynes's youth, this field included both ethics and economics.[21]

Keynes's essay, "The method of index numbers with special reference to the measurement of general exchange value" (1909), investigated the basis of existing index number schemes and proposed alternatives that he thought to be both theoretically informed and rigorously defensible. At the time of his essay two major index number schemes were in general use: one was Edgeworth's probabilistic method described above and the other was the method of *The Economist* which assigned fixed weights to a base year and calculated price levels while holding these weights constant over the duration of the index.

In a manner which was to typify Keynes's later rhetorical style, he allowed that both approaches were correct, but only for specific cases. As a way out of the theoretical impasse Keynes endorsed a more general approach, namely Marshall's chain index. The chain index was specifically designed to overcome the deficiencies of the probabilistic approach, while simultaneously eluding the arbitrary weighting scheme of *The Economist*.[22]

It was in the course of his critique of the probabilistic method that Keynes first began to question the empirical accuracy of the quantity theory of money. This doubt necessarily followed from his work on index numbers since the probabilistic conception of index numbers was grounded in the quantity theory of money. A byproduct of Keynes's doubt was the conclusion that an important, if not extreme, modification of the quantity theory was required to the extent that it failed to account for the relative price changes which emerged from changes in the value of money. While Keynes was not yet prepared to abandon the quantity theory of money in economic analysis,[23] he was prepared to question its capacity to provide a theoretically adequate underpinning to index number computation. Specifically Keynes continued to employ the equation of exchange in his work but was less willing to apply the quantity theory as a strict causal axiom. This was especially the case for the study of short-run phenomena. Taking a position which was to characterize his later writings, Keynes perceived the short run to be the only scientifically defensible arena for the application of index numbers.[24]

In his essay on index numbers, Keynes was critical of the casual manner in which economists had assumed the existence of a general price level.[25] Keynes maintained, in juxtaposition to Correa Walsh, that there were deep logical problems with the idea of a general price level.[26] Specifically he argued that one cannot simply assume the existence of such an abstraction and then proceed to theorize about its presumed behavior. His skepticism led him to propose that the best one can practically accomplish is to establish a particular composite commodity and discuss specific changes in that composite:

> After first arguing that general exchange value, defined as an *ensemble* of particular exchange values, is generally incapable of measurement, we decided to define it, for the purpose of index numbers, as being the exchange value of some specific composite commodity. Thus defined, its price is as satisfactory a measure as the price of a particular commodity, and has the same properties.
>
> (Keynes 1909: 95)

One obvious problem with this approach is the potentially infinite number of eligible composite commodities. Each of the composites exhibits various levels of generality and usefulness. One cannot say *a priori* that one composite is better than another. For this reason, Keynes proposed that the researcher be guided by the specific question asked, while remaining alert to the fact that bias is built into the specific composite chosen for study (1909: 126). If it is true that a host of price levels for specific composites exists, and if money neutrality cannot be thought to be the actual or typical case, a fruitful course of study could be the dynamic between the various price levels during the course of the business cycle.[27]

Keynes's reformulation of the units of economic analysis

In the course of the essay on index numbers, Keynes argued that it is important to produce a price index with an emphasis on consumer purchases. He proposed that the appropriate weights be established through extensive surveys of population and consumption data. Keynes thought that contemporary indices were overly weighted towards the mix of goods typically of interest to the "entrepreneurial classes" (1909: 103, 123). He argued that an index which embodied a more accurate weighting of consumption goods would be able to capture changes which were under-represented in current calculations.

Keynes inferred that an index based on an accurate numerical weighting of consumed foodstuffs would result in lower estimates of price changes over the course of the business cycle. This correction was important as Keynes was concerned that the underweighting of consumption goods relative to producer goods in current indices was misleading.[28] Underweighting was more than a theoretical matter, as one could reasonably argue that these errors were built into the economic policies of the day. As an example of poor policy, a high bank rate could be overly restrictive to the extent that the authorities may be relying on biased or misleading indices.

Keynes understood that the chain index method, with its ability to incorporate changes in the weight, quality and typology of goods, could cause the analyst to lose the ability to compare price levels that are too many years apart. However, he was not convinced that such comparisons were really possible with existent index number schemes.[29] He also thought that improved analysis would result if researchers had available a number of indices for the different sectors of the economy, such as trade goods, intermediate or capital goods, and consumption goods. Interestingly enough, and in a way that anticipated Dennis Robertson, he also argued that specific indices for regions would be analytically important.[30]

CONCLUSION: INDEX NUMBER THEORY AND THE DEVELOPMENT OF MACROECONOMIC THEORY

The early Keynesian position on the importance of disaggregated indices clearly anticipated the work on the business cycle still to be accomplished in the next decade by Ralph Hawtrey, Dennis Robertson and Keynes.[31] The possibility of compiling and measuring a variety of different price levels would lead to a macroeconomics which focused on the control and management of an economy that was presumed to be subject to intersectoral imbalances. The role of money in the problem of sectoral balance theories, theories which were typified by such devices as forced savings and other early macroeconomic categories, came to dominate the Cambridge scene in the 1920s.[32] For Keynes himself, this work culminated in his study of the role of the interest rate in the maintenance of sectoral balance which was the subject of the *Treatise on Money* (1930).[33]

The advent of the First World War induced an outpouring of studies on empirical economic matters and sectoral planning. Irving Fisher, Carl Snyder and others made important contributions to the theory of index numbers during the early postwar period in the United States. By the 1920s, index number theory was becoming relatively sophisticated.[34] It was with the development and refinement of the price index as a conceptual construction that the stage was set for the pursuit of monetary policies which could be designed to stabilize domestic prices and employment. This in itself was an almost revolutionary development in monetary policy. Previously, monetary policy had been limited to its traditional focus on the current account, the foreign exchange rate and the state of bullion reserves at the Central Bank. It would not be an exaggeration to say that up to this time external balance was the primary goal and purpose of monetary policy.[35]

In hindsight, it is apparent that these advances in empirical economics contributed to a growing research interest in the relationship between the financial sector and the real economy. The primary focus was on the issue of intersectoral balance and it took a number of forms before its practitioners began to develop the sense that a new area of study, namely macroeconomics, was emerging. Given the historical evidence, it would appear that this early work on the nature, meaning and proper specification of price index numbers formed an important part of the intellectual climate from which macro-economics would emerge as a distinct and independent field of economic inquiry.

NOTES

The author would like to thank Ingrid Rima, Falguni Sheth, Bent Hansen, Barry Eichengreen, Niloufer Sohrabji, the University of New Hampshire Economics Seminar, the University of Maine Economics Seminar, and participants at the 1992 and 1993 History of Economics Society Meetings for their contributions to several earlier drafts of this chapter. Research for this work was partially financed by a University of Maine faculty summer grant.

1 Jevons (1884), Edgeworth (1887, reprinted in Sections H and I of Edgeworth 1925) and Bowley (1926).
2 This is actually Bowley's (1926) definition.
3 This is true only if these goods are assumed to be capable of clear and consistent denomination in terms of their qualitative attributes for all of the years covered in the index series. In this chapter, I will abstract from the difficulties presented by qualitative differences between or within a quantitative series, but I will note in passing that changes in the qualitative nature of commodities is a significant, and in some ways fundamental, challenge to the problem of index number construction. On the problem of quality measurement see Griliches (1971).
4 It is curious to observe the tenacity of the belief in this doctrine since it has long been understood by theorists that a restrictive set of assumptions must be imposed on the matrix of prices in order to get this result. In particular, the neoclassical school has had to surmount or suppress a number of important obstacles in order to establish the assumption of long-run neutrality. An example of an intellectually honest attempt is Patinkin (1965). The New Classical school does not confront the issue. Rather it employs an extreme form of scientific positivism to defend its assumption of short period "money neutrality".
5 The modern equivalent of this doctrine is monetarism. See Friedman (1968).
6 This argument is made in Edgeworth's critique of Correa Walsh. See Edgeworth (1925: Section M).
7 Edgeworth (1925: Sections H and I). Also Jevons (1984: especially Part II, ch. II) and Bowley (1926).
8 A geometric mean is the nth root of the product of n variables. The arithmetic mean is taken by adding n variables and dividing by n. We commonly refer to this as the "average" of a group of variables, such as the mid-term grades of our students. A probability index compiled with an arithmetic mean would look like the following:

$$\frac{(P'_1 + P'_2 + P'_3 + \ldots + P'_n)/n}{(P_1 + P_2 + P_3 + \ldots + P_n)/n}$$

The numerator is the set of all contemporary prices, the denominator is the set of all base prices. Notice the absence of weights. Again, the sample of prices must be large enough to eliminate all bias due to fluctuations in relative prices.

9   John Maynard Keynes (1909). For the critique of Edgeworth's index number theory, see Section VIII, "Measurement of general exchange value by probabilities", pp. 104–20.

10   John Maynard Keynes (1909). The discussion of interdependence is on pp. 83–5.

11   Along with the difficulty presented by the existence of substitutes and complements, a further problem is presented by changes in aggregate income. While Keynes's thinking had not yet developed this far, it is clear that the independence assumption is inaccurate in the absence of a secondary belief in what has come to be known as "Say's law of markets". Any systematic unemployment would also cause price declines in wage goods, and these declines are likely to be correlated.

12   Edgeworth, "Measurement of change in the value of money" (originally published 1888), in Edgeworth (1925: Section H).

13   *The Economist* began an index in 1865, which appears to have been the first price index series to be compiled and published. See Sauerbeck (1886).

14   Suppose that the set $(a, b, \ldots, z)$ corresponds to the weights of the goods which are appropriate to the first period. P_a is the price of a in the first period, P'_a is the price in the second period. This index would look as follows:

$$\frac{P'_a a + P'_b b + \ldots + P'_z z}{P_a a + P_b b + \ldots + P_z z}$$

15   This corresponds with our modern notion of the Laspeyres index.

16   Suppose that a is the weight associated with the use of a particular good in the first period, and a' is the weight associated with the good in the second period. Further suppose that P_a is the price of this good in the first period and P'_a is the price associated with this good in the second period. Then a chain index comparing two periods, with a list of goods from a to z, would look as follows:

$$\frac{\tfrac{1}{2}(a + a')P'_a + \tfrac{1}{2}(b + b')P'_b + \ldots + \tfrac{1}{2}(z + z')P'_z}{\tfrac{1}{2}(a + a')P_a + \tfrac{1}{2}(b + b')P_b + \ldots + \tfrac{1}{2}(z + z')P_z}$$

In the next period the same index would be calculated as follows:

$$\frac{\tfrac{1}{2}[(a + a')/2 + a'']P''_a + \tfrac{1}{2}[(b + b')/2 + b'']P''_b + \ldots + \tfrac{1}{2}[(z + z')/2 + z'']P''_z}{\tfrac{1}{2}[(a + a')/2 + a'']P'_a + \tfrac{1}{2}[(b + b')/2 + b'']P'_b + \ldots + \tfrac{1}{2}[(z + z')/2 + z'']P'_z}$$

Notice that the denominator used in the comparison of the second and third periods is different from the denominator which compares the first and second periods. This means that, logically speaking, one cannot perfectly contrast the price level in the first period with that in the third period using this index. This is a distinct drawback for this index when considering the price changes which are exhibited within an index number series. Also note that, at any time, the weight associated with a commodity can drop to zero. Such a good effectively leaves the index. Others can be added in the same manner. In this way the index is open to changes in economic use patterns.

17   These issues were discussed in Edgeworth (1925) and Irving Fisher (1922).

18   The influence of Moore on Keynes's work is discussed in Skidelsky (1983: ch. 6, pp. 133–60). See also Keynes's own discussion of Moore in "My earliest beliefs", *Collected Writings*, vol. X. Also Davis (1991) and Shioonoya (1991).

19   "It is difficult to see how we can establish a probability that by doing one thing we shall obtain a better total result than by doing another" (Moore 1959: 152).

20 This lack of a usable concept of subjective probability was potentially destructive of this line of philosophy; in Moore's words, "It will be apparent that it [an ethical probability] has never yet been justified – that no sufficient reason has ever yet been found for considering one action more right or more wrong than another" (1959: 152).

21 At this time the field of economics was only beginning to claim the status of an independent course of study. The qualifying examinations at Cambridge, until the death of Henry Sidgwick in the late nineteenth century, were still given under the title of Moral Philosophy. It was not until 1903 that the first independent examinations in economics were offered. See Skidelsky (1983: 42–6)

22 Keynes (1909: 78–81).

23 This conclusion follows from Keynes's use of the quantity theory fifteen years later in his *Tract on Monetary Reform* (1924).

24 Keynes (1909: 80–1).

25 For example, in the 1909 essay he states: "Because we know well enough what a particular price level is, we assume, somewhat too lightly, that we know also the meaning of a general price level" (p. 64). He continues in this vein on pp. 66–7: "While we have a price corresponding to each *particular* exchange value, it is not true, as it is sometimes assumed, that we have a price corresponding to *general* exchange value. General exchange value is a function of particular exchange values, but it does not possess all their properties" (his italics). A review of Keynes's critique of the idea of a general price level is in Carabelli (1991: Section 4.2, pp. 22–5).

26 The critique is of Walsh (1901). It occurs on pp. 67–8.

27 This is exactly the approach followed by interwar monetary theorists. See Robertson (1926), Hawtrey (1927) and Keynes (1930). An overview of the emergence of Cambridge monetary theory is provided in Bigg (1990) and Pascal (1987).

28 Keynes (1909: 99–104). This observation was true on another ground, namely the fixed weight index will always overstate an inflation by ignoring the substitution effect. However, the point that Keynes desired to make concerned the relative movement of different composite prices in different sectors over the course of the business cycle.

29 He never changed his opinion on the reduced or restricted value of indices for making long-term comparisons. "But the proper place for such things as net real output and the general level of prices lies within the field of historical and statistical description, and their purpose should be to satisfy historical or social curiosity, a purpose for which perfect precision – such as our causal analysis requires, whether or not our knowledge of the actual values of the relevant quantities is complete or exact – is neither usual nor necessary" (Keynes 1964: ch. 4, p. 40).

30 Keynes (1909: 126–7). These passages point to Keynes's early (and I believe sustained) interest in empirical matters. However, his view of the role and possibility of empirical work was not the same as that which was soon to sweep to ascendency within the economics profession. This different vision was at least partially responsible for the positions he took in his methodological debate with Jan Tinbergen.

31 See references in note 27.

32 This work is ably summarized in Bigg (1990) and Pascal (1987).

33 The Cambridge movement away from the quantity theory of money is discussed in Bigg (1990: chs 7, 8, 9).

34 Mitchell (1915); Fisher (1922).

35 Fetter (1965). A policy which placed a priority on internal stabilization over external stabilization was to be an early characteristic of Keynes's economic thinking on monetary affairs. See Keynes (1924: ch. 4). See also Harrod (1966: ch. 9, Section 2, pp. 338–45).

BIBLIOGRAPHY

Bateman, Bradley W. and Davis, John B. (1991) *Keynes and Philosophy: Essays on the Origin of Keynes's Thought*, Brookfield, VT: Edward Elgar.

Bigg, Robert J. (1990) *Cambridge and the Monetary Theory of Production: The Collapse of Marshallian Macroeconomics*, New York: St Martin's Press.

Bowley, A. L. (1926) *Elements of Statistics*, 5th edn, London.

Carabelli, Anna (1991) "Keynes's monetary theory of value: his choice of the units of quantity and of measure in The General Theory", Paper presented to the History of Economics Meetings, University of Maryland, June.

Davis, John B. (1991) "Keynes' critique of Moore", *Cambridge Journal of Economics* March: 61–78.

Edgeworth, Francis Ysidro ([1925] 1970) *Papers Relating to Political Economy*, New York: Burt Franklin.

Fetter, Frank W. (1965) *The Development of British Monetary Orthodoxy, 1797–1875*.

Fisher, Irving (1922) *The Making of Index Numbers: A Study of Their Varieties, Tests, and Reliability*, Boston, MA: Houghton Mifflin.

Friedman, Milton (1968) "The role of monetary policy", *American Economic Review* March: 1–17.

Griliches, Zvi (ed.) (1971) *Price Indexes and Quality Change*, Cambridge, MA: Harvard University Press.

Harrod, Roy (1966) *The Life of John Maynard Keynes*, London: Macmillan.

Hawtrey, Ralph G. (1927) *Currency and Credit*, 3rd edn, London: Longmans, Green.

Jevons, W. Stanley ([1884] 1964) *Investigations in Currency and Finance*, New York: Kelley.

Keynes, John Marynard (1909) "The method of index numbers with special reference to the measurement of general exchange value", *The Collected Writings of John Maynard Keynes*, ed. D.E. Moggridge, London: Macmillan, vol. XI, ch. 2, pp. 49–173.

—— (1924) *Tract on Monetary Reform*, in *The Collected Writings of John Maynard Keynes*, ed. D. E. Moggridge, London: Macmillan, vol. IV.

—— (1930) *A Treatise on Money*, vol. I; *The Pure Theory of Money*, London: Macmillan.

—— ([1936] 1964) *The General Theory of Employment, Interest and Money*, New York: Harcourt Brace Jovanovich.

—— (1972–1989) *The Collected Writings of John Maynard Keynes*. ed. D. E. Moggridge, London: Macmillan, vols I–XXX.

Marshall, Alfred (1887) "Remedies for fluctuations of general prices", *Contemporary Review* March; reprinted in Arthur C. Pigou (ed.) *Memorials of Alfred Marshall* (1925).

—— (1923) *Money, Credit and Commerce*, London: Macmillan.

Mitchell, Wesley Clair (1915) *Index Numbers of Wholesale Prices in the United States and Foreign Countries*, Washington, DC: Bureau of Labor Statistics.

Moore, George Edward (1959) *Principia Ethica*, Cambridge: Cambridge University Press.

Pascal, Bridal (1987) *Cambridge Monetary Thought*, New York: St Martin's Press.

Patinkin, Don (1965) *Money, Interest, and Prices: An Integration of Monetary and Value Theory*, 2nd edn, New York: Harper & Row.

Robertson, Dennis H. ([1926] 1949) *Banking Policy and the Price Level*, New York: Kelley.

Sauerbeck, A. (1886) "Prices of Commodities and the Precious Metals", *Journal of the Royal Statistical Society* 49.

Shioonoya, Yuichi (1991) "Sidgwick, Moore and Keynes: a philosophical analysis of Keynes's 'My early beliefs'", in Bradley W. Bateman and John B. Davis (eds) *Keynes and Philosophy: Essays on the Origin of Keynes's Thought*, Brookfield, VT: Edward Elgar.

Skidelsky, Robert (1983) *John Maynard Keynes*, vol. 1: *Hopes Betrayed, 1883–1920*, New York: Viking.

Walsh, Correa (1901) *The Measurement of General Exchange Value*, New York.

Chapter 10

The indicator approach to monitoring business fluctuations

A case study in dynamic statistical methods

Philip A. Klein

INTRODUCTION

When approaching the analysis of business fluctuations, conventional statistics courses are probably still organized so as to give the student the impression that the field consists of a stock of techniques. Acquire them and one is equipped for a lifetime of work in the statistical analysis of – in this case – business cycles. This chapter is devoted to demonstrating how wrong this conclusion would be. The approach taken in the early days of the National Bureau of Economic Research (NBER) by Mitchell, Arthur Burns, Geoffrey H. Moore and their associates is a monument to the cogency of the view that there is, in fact, a perennial need for statistical innovation in a dynamic research area such as cyclical instability. Here we shall focus on the recent past.

It is a cliché to note that the economy is dynamic and that interrelationships critical in one cyclical crisis may vary both in their impact and in their importance in other crises. What is seldom realized is that statistical techniques optimally effective in exposing these changing critical relationships may themselves need to be varied or changed altogether over time. The most obvious example, perhaps, would be seasonal adjustments, the use of which was recognized but which were made only sporadically a generation ago. They were arguably less critical in earlier times, when inflation rates were less significant in their day in, day out impact on the functioning of the economy. Today, there are relatively few time series used in cyclical analysis which are not initially and routinely adjusted for seasonal variation. But there are many other examples and this chapter will concern itself with some selected from Geoffrey Moore's work.

The bulk of his work is a testimony to the assertion that the assessment of cyclical developments over any substantial period of time with an unchanging arsenal of statistical techniques is likely to prove increasingly inadequate as the economy moves further away from the time in which the techniques were developed.

One of the strengths of the National Bureau of Economic Research in its

New York-based days was that the group charged with developing up-to-date lists of reliable leading indicators and with selecting business cycle peaks and troughs was also the group carrying on an active research program in the field of cyclical analysis. Out of their ongoing research came a steady stream of statistically innovative techniques enabling new insights to be gained into old relationships and uncovering newly critical relationships as they emerged. Measuring cycles and analyzing cycles thus bear a symbiotic relationship to each other which is too easily overlooked in situations where the monitoring of cycles with cycle indicators is attempted in the absence of an ongoing analytical research program concerning currently unfolding evidence of instability.

The penchant for statistical innovation spearheaded by Moore was evident in his first National Bureau publication "A significance test for time series and other ordered observations", co-authored with W. Allen Wallis and published in 1941 (Wallis and Moore 1941). This test was developed in response to a question raised by Wesley Mitchell about whether fluctuations in crop harvests were random and how they compared in this respect with business cycles.

STATISTICAL INNOVATIONS – EARLY CONTRIBUTIONS

Some of the early contributions by Moore's group both to statistical practice and to statistical innovation are now so widely used that it is difficult to realize that they are relatively recent contributions to our analytical arsenal, or that we have Moore's basic perspective to thank for them.

It was Moore, for example, who began (in 1950) what would now be considered to be the conventional practice of periodically reviewing and revising the "most reliable short list" of statistical indicators (Moore 1950a). In this case, Moore was reevaluating the indicators chosen by Mitchell and Burns for the first list of business cycle indicators, which had been published in 1938. The reason for revising the list, both originally and perhaps half a dozen times in the intervening years, is not so much that time series capriciously alter their timing classification. Neither is it that heretofore reliable leaders suddenly become laggers or vice versa. It is rather that data availability in the United States has been steadily widened and data quality has been steadily improved. The result has been that new series offering better coverage become available for monitoring interrelationships whose importance had previously been established. Another factor is that the character of the underlying economy changes so that new areas and types of activity need to be included. A recent example of this would be the development of the service sector, once considered to be cyclically relatively inert and now a significant part of gross domestic product. We shall return to this below.

An example of early statistical innovation is the diffusion index. We have already seen that Moore, virtually from the outset, was concerned with shaping statistical measures and techniques to the changing challenges of current thinking about instability. One of Wesley Clair Mitchell's original insights was that the degree to which indications of instability are pervasive throughout the economy has much to do with how severe the expansion or contraction will be. Pervasiveness is a critical cyclical characteristic.

The technique developed at the National Bureau in order to answer the question "How widespread is the cyclical disturbance being observed?" is called a diffusion index – a calculation based on the percentage of the components of any aggregate which is experiencing an increase. This simple notion, applicable to industrial concerns, to sectors of the economy, to geographic areas, to groups of indicators etc., constitutes a way of indicating in a summary fashion the pervasiveness of all sorts of changes in production, in income, in prices, in profits and in other dimensions of economic performance. It has proven to be of enormous help. Usually diffusion indices are not weighted and no effort is made to indicate the magnitude of the increase they record. Yet, even in this deceptively simple form, diffusion indices are widely used for the following reasons. First, they are often significant in their own right – they do indeed indicate the extent to which contraction or expansion may be said to be widespread. Second, they have the valuable property of leading the aggregates to which they contribute.

A very widely used set of surveys, conducted monthly by the National Association of Purchasing Management (NAPM), provide data which are a kind of diffusion index and which therefore are illustrative of the uses to which diffusion indices can be put (Moore 1955; Klein and Moore 1991). The NAPM surveys some 250 companies each month, asking them questions about their new orders, buying prices, vendor deliveries, inventories, production and employment. Questions in the survey require each respondent to report whether, for example, their new orders are increasing, decreasing or staying the same. The report on the surveys therefore shows the percentage reporting increases in their new orders and acts as a diffusion index answering the question: "How widespread is the reported increase in new orders among the respondents?" Failure to recognize the way in which the results of these surveys resemble a diffusion index has led to many inappropriate compar-isons of actual *levels* of new orders with survey-reported *changes* in new orders. There are, of course, many other examples of such diffusion indices among surveys – the Michigan consumer sentiment surveys, the Dun and Bradstreet entrepreneurial surveys etc.

There were many other statistical innovations in this early period, emerging from Moore's creative approach to the task of cyclical analysis. He suggested calculating the "average duration of run", that is, the length of time, on average, in which month-to-month changes in a given series are in the same direction. By comparing current changes from this perspective it is possible to consider, for series behaving very differently, how likely it is that the month-to-month changes currently being observed will prove to constitute a cyclical phase (Moore 1950b). Analyzing current changes from the perspective of past cyclical behavior of the same series is a technique inherited from Mitchell and diligently applied by Moore. It reflects the fundamental notion behind the National Bureau approach to cyclical analysis: measure carefully the average behavior of a given economic activity during past cycles so that the present behavior can be compared with the past pattern.

Another example of early innovation is the notion of amplitude adjustment in constructing indices. A problem in combining series with disparate amplitudes into an index is clearly how to keep the series with the greatest amplitude from dominating the movements in the index. Amplitude adjustment involves calculating the average month-to-month change, without regard to sign, in each component series over some fairly long period and then adjusting all the component series so that their average relative amplitude is the same. The targeted amplitude may be made equal to that of some basic time series such as the index of industrial production (or gross national product) (Moore 1958a). Much experimentation has been done, for example, in combining series in weighted as opposed to unweighted fashion, but because it is simple to equalize the amplitudes of individual series, thus enabling diverse series to be combined, this technique has been very widely used in subsequent years.

Finally, we should mention the development and use of recession–recovery patterns (Moore 1958b). Basic to Mitchell's approach to the business cycle, as noted above, was the notion that we must seek to understand current cycles by diligently studying past cycles in an effort to tease from the statistical record the pattern of interrelationships which constitute the "typical" cycles of recorded history. To understand the cycles of today we must ask how and why they are similar to, and different from, cycles of the past. Recession–recovery analysis constitutes a principal technique for furthering this understanding. It is basically a technique in which various measures are summarized for past cycles by tracking their relative change after peaks (for recession analysis) or troughs (for recovery analysis). The movements are converted into an index with the turning points set equal to 100. Hence, the changes in relative amplitude since the last turning point can be calculated for various groups of past cycles (all cycles, or cycles divided into "severe", "moderate" and "mild"). By tracking the current cycle phase against this record one gets a developing impression of which of the past patterns the current episode most resembles. If one looks at the pattern of leading indices for past cycles one may well get an early indication of whether the current recession or recovery is likely to be severe, moderate or mild. Obviously, one can use the technique for many different kinds of economic activity and, in so doing, enhance our understanding of current cyclical developments.

STATISTICAL INNOVATIONS IN THE 1970s

Because Mitchell's view of cycles is of "one phase merging into the next", the lagging indicators have special significance. Not only do they reflect the nature of final adjustments among significant economic variables to the most recent turning point; they can also be viewed as the earliest signals of the next turning point.

One of Moore's most interesting notions was to use the lagging indicators to generate leading indicators (Moore 1969a). Because indicator sequences (from leading through coincident to lagging) reflect economic processes responding sequentially to cyclical conditions, the timing relations are not simply statistical flukes, as might be the case with tea leaves or entrails, but a reflection of the logic of the underlying economic processes. Thus, in employment (for example) it makes economic sense that there is a measurable temporal relationship between hirings (a leading series), employment volume (a coincident series) and wage rate levels or labor costs per unit of output (a lagging series). The same sequence is visible among other sets of indicators (e.g. orders, sales and inventories).

Moore discovered that often the ratio of coincident to lagging indicators formed a useful leading indicator. Why? Because the rates at which indicators rise are themselves related to business cycle turning points. He concluded that when lagging indicators rise faster than coincident indicators (i.e. the ratio declines) this exerts a depressing influence on the leaders. Hence, the leaders follow the decline in this ratio at peaks and the rise in this ratio at troughs. Moore examined this relationship for production sequences, employment sequences, financial sequences and others. He found that the timing of the ratio of the coincident to the lagging series led the leaders in an overwhelming number of cases, at both business cycle peaks and troughs. This relationship is still discernible. In this simple way, careful reflection on the way in which measures of economic activity respond to the cycles, both in reflecting past turns and in anticipating future turns, can enable us to develop new tools with which to analyze and monitor cyclical changes. It took both understanding of how cycles evolve and an appreciation of the statistical implications of how indicators respond to the cycle to create this new and insightful statistical measure from previously existing measures. As such, it illustrates precisely a view which many who work in the Mitchell tradition hold. Those who are engaged in ongoing research concerning the nature of instability are in a particularly favorable position – provided they have a reasonably sophisticated appreciation of present statistical techniques – to make significant methodological contributions to our arsenal of monitoring and forecasting tools.

Another direction which this approach to statistical method took during this period was an attempt to develop specialized leading indicators. Two examples which emerged were a leading index of inflation (Moore 1971) and another indicator designed to forecast changes in the employment picture (Moore 1981; Moore and Cullity 1986, 1990). In both cases the fundamental notion was that, by combining all the indicators pertaining to a single critical macroeconomic dimension of economic performance, results would be more precise and, hopefully, produce a longer lead for forecasting.

The inflation index has been proven to be quite useful in anticipating subsequent changes in the inflation rate. Like most indices, the components have changed from time to time as research has uncovered new series or series with wider coverage have become available. Currently this index includes seven components: the percentage employed, the growth rate of debt, the growth rate of industrial materials prices, the growth rate of import prices (excluding fuels), the expected change in selling prices reported by entrepreneurs, the change in buying prices reported by purchasing managers, and the percentage of purchasing managers reporting slower deliveries. All these series reflect the degree of tightness in employment, financial, or domestic and foreign goods markets. As such, they could be expected to reflect very sensitively the changing conditions that bring about price fluctuations. Therefore, the leading inflation index is thoroughly grounded in economic theory and has, in fact, proven to be a highly useful way to monitor and forecast changes in the inflation rate. As mentioned earlier, the inflation rates of recent times, often considered to be unacceptably high, have greatly increased interest in measuring inflation, so as to develop better techniques for controlling it without incurring other unacceptable consequences for the economy.

In the case of the leading employment index, an initial problem has to do with ensuring that the indicators are reasonably comprehensive. In point of fact, two of the seven indicators in the current index (average workweek and overtime hours) concern the manufacturing sector alone. The rest of the indicators, however, pertain to the labor force viewed more broadly. Three are used in inverted form – the layoff rate, the short duration unemployment rate, and initial claims for unemployment insurance. The last general indicator of employment is the ratio of voluntary to involuntary employment. The index has proven its capacity to forecast short-run changes in both employment and unemployment (Moore 1981). One of its advantages is that it becomes available before most other leading indices, owing to the early release of employment data each month.

Over the years, economists and forecasters have focused more and more on the problems of forecasting, particularly the problem of forecasting turning points in measures of aggregate economic performance. Although clearly subsumed under the Burns–Mitchell rubric of measures of aggregate economic performance which turn "at about the same time", the cycles described in Burns and Mitchell's 1947 study do not, in fact, turn necessarily at precisely the *same* time. Forecasters have thus known for some time that forecasting continued movement though a cycle phase is less difficult than forecasting the turning points. Many years ago, Moore suggested that a major requirement for improving forecasts was to keep better records of the track records of forecasters. Accordingly, in his presidential address to the American Statistical Association in 1968 he proposed the utilization of the annual survey which the American Statistical Association and the National Bureau of Economic Research have long conducted as the basis for formally tracking forecasters' accuracy. Said Moore, "It seems to me that this survey could be developed so that it would become the vehicle for a scientific record of economic forecasts and hence be of far greater service both to the profession and to the public" (see Moore 1983, 1969b). The ASA–NBER survey was a direct response to this suggestion by Moore. More recently, the *Blue Chip Indicators*, which publish the forecasts of about fifty of the best known individual economists and the larger econometric models, have become an essential component of serious efforts at monitoring the cycle in the United States. It has been particularly useful to learn, for example, that the mean forecast by large numbers of forecasters (as in the *Blue Chip Indicators*) tends to be somewhat more accurate than most of the individual forecasts which it contains (see Zarnowitz 1978).

STATISTICAL INNOVATIONS IN THE RECENT PAST

In recent years, Moore and his associates have continued to refine old techniques for measuring instability and to forge new tools which are useful both diagnostically and in terms of forecasting and the formation of stabilization policy.

One of the most important of the relatively recent innovations which has emerged has been an attempt to deal with a very old issue. In examining rates of growth, a major difficulty has been that the price of achieving currency in estimating growth rates has often been great volatility in the rates computed. The most common procedure by which to view growth rates in time series has involved an examination of the year over year percentage changes. In considering a series in this way, the investigator could include the very latest monthly figure, but the percentage change series was extremely volatile because of the great variability which can often be found in the figures for individual months. The alternative might be to restrict the examination to, for example, changes in annual averages, but clearly a series averaging the past twelve months and comparing this to the previous twelve months is not "current", even though the most recent data would be included.

Moore began experimenting with growth rates derived from smoothed series of various durations. The most successful has now been widely employed and is known as the "six-month smoothed growth rate" (see Center for International Business Cycle Research 1980). This growth rate is derived by calculating the change in the latest month available compared with an average of the previous twelve months of data. Because twelve months are averaged together, the denominator of the ratio will be a good deal smoother than is the case when both numerator and denominator refer to single months. In effect, the ratio is a "six-month smoothed rate" because the twelve preceding months would be centered six months before the current month. Hence, the rates of change calculated in this manner are smoother than percentage changes calculated from the same month a year ago, but they are reasonably current and can readily be annualized. This deceptively simple refinement of our statistical techniques has proven to be enormously helpful in assessing current developments.

One of the interesting and useful ways in which these growth rates have been employed has been in devising a "signalling" system for both recessions and recoveries, based on growth rates in leading and coincident indices (Moore and Zarnowitz 1983). These indices have been carefully examined to determine their historical behavior at previous turning points and, in particular, the pattern they describe in falling below or rising above specified bands. It turns out that initial signals can be derived from the pattern thus described by relevant leading indices, which can be confirmed when it is repeated by the coincident index. Thus, preliminary and confirming signals of future turns can be monitored and the turns can be forecast, with the usual proviso that the longer ahead the turn is forecast, the less sure the forecaster must remain. On the other hand, the record of forecast turns confirmed by these signal systems, while not exhibiting very long leads, has been consistently quite good for the past quarter century.

By the late 1970s the National Bureau was moved from New York City to Cambridge. With this physical move the basic interest of Bureau researchers shifted from the business cycle to other areas of economic research.

At the same time Moore retired from the National Bureau and established his own Center for International Business Cycle Research (CIBCR) initially at Rutgers and later at Columbia University. It is at this center that much of the innovation summarized here has been carried out. It is here, too, that the Mitchellian perspective toward business cycles continues to shape the approach and the method of empirical analysis of business cycles from which analysts and forecasters alike have learned so much.

Recent research at the CIBCR reflects Moore's determination to continue to make these forecasting tools as up to date and explicitly useful as possible. A new leading index for the increasingly important service sector has been developed with considerable success, though this was an area earlier widely regarded as not exhibiting pronounced cycles (Moore 1990). Here, growth rate analysis has proven to be highly effective. Moreover, it is critical to keep indicator systems representative of the entire economy – a good example of why static analytic methods for a dynamic phenomenon like cyclical instability will not suffice.

Moore and his colleagues devised a coincident index for the service sector consisting of four series (employee hours, real labor income, real output and real consumption expenditures). All of these are now available as measures restricted to the service sector. For leading indicators of activity in the service sector a composite index was constructed, including the average workweek, commercial building, contracts and floor space, the stock price index and an index of service sector profit margins.

This by no means exhausts the list of recent innovations in statistical techniques and in cyclical coverage of indicators which Moore has spear-headed. Others include a weekly leading index (Moore 1983) and also a long leading index consisting of indicators exhibiting very long leads which should therefore enable us to predict turning points further into the future than the customary six to nine months thought possible with the usual leading index (see Cullity and Moore 1987). Other innovations are a system of indicators bearing upon prospects in the stock market that offers both "buy" and "sell" signals over the cycle (see Moore and Boehn 1988), and improvements in our ability to forecast international recessions through the use of leading indices for the major market-oriented countries (see Moore 1980; Klein and Moore 1985).

CONCLUSION

In the final analysis the most impressive characteristic of the modern adherents of the Mitchellian approach to cyclical research is that, if one examines the past record of accomplishment, one comes away convinced that new techniques, better coverage, and more insightful analytical approaches will continue to pour forth. As leader of the approach, Moore has always regarded statistical techniques not as a stock to be exploited, but as a flow from which we can always learn how to make our efforts at monitoring and forecasting more comprehensive and more precise.

NOTE

Another version of this paper was originally published by the *International Journal of Forecasting*, April 1993, under the title "Geoffrey H. Moore and dynamic statistical methods".

REFERENCES

Burns, A. F. and Mitchell, W. C. (1947) *Measuring Business Cycles*, Washington, DC: National Bureau of Economic Research, p. 3.
Centre for International Business Cycle Research (1980) "Inflation watch", New York: CIBCR, Columbia University.
Cullity, J. P. and Moore, G. H. (1987) "Developing a long-leading composite index for the United States", CIRET Conference, Zurich, September.
Klein, P. A. (1990) "Essays honoring Geoffrey H. Moore", in P. A. Klein (ed) *Analyzing Modern Business Cycles*, New York: Sharpe.
Klein, P. A. and Moore, G. H. (1985) *Monitoring Business Cycles in Market-Oriented*

Countries, NBER, Cambridge, MA: Ballinger.

────── and ────── (1991) "Purchasing management survey data: their value as leading indicators", in K. Lahiri and G. H. Moore (eds) *Leading Economic Indicators*, New York: Cambridge University Press.

Moore, G. H. (1950a) "Statistical indicators of cyclical revivals and recessions", reprinted in G. H. Moore (ed.) *Business Cycle Indicators*, Princeton, NJ: NBER, Princeton University Press.

────── (1950b) "A technique for summarizing the current behavior of groups of indicators", reprinted in G. H. Moore (ed.) *Business Cycle Indicators*, Princeton, NJ: NBER, Princeton University Press, ch. 20.

────── (1958a) "An amplitude adjustment for the leading indicators", reprinted in K. Lahiri and G. H. Moore (eds) *Leading Economic Indicators*, New York: Cambridge University Press, 1991, ch. 19.

────── (1958b) "Measuring recessions", reprinted in G. H. Moore (ed.) *Business Cycle Indicators*, Princeton, NJ: NBER, Princeton University Press, ch. 5.

────── (1969a) "Generating leading indicators from lagging indicators", *Western Economic Journal.*

────── (1969b) "Generating short-term economic changes", reprinted in G. H. Moore (ed.) *Business Cycles, Inflation and Forecasting*, 2nd edn, Cambridge, MA: Ballinger, ch. 25, p. 425.

────── (1971) "Inflation's turn, studies in the management sciences", *Forecasting* 12.

────── (1980) "The case for international business cycle research", *Atlantic Economic Journal.*

────── (1981) "A leading index of employment and unemployment", *Monthly Labor Review* 104: 44–7.

────── (1983) "A new weekly leading index", *Business Economics.*

────── (1990) "New economic indicators for the service industries", in G. H. Moore (ed.) *Leading Indicators for the 1900's* Homewood, IL: Dow Jones-Irwin, ch. 13.

Moore, G. H. and Boehn, E. (1988) "Signals of major stock price movements: five countries", 8th International Symposium on Forecasting, Amsterdam.

Moore, G. H. and Cullity J. (1986) "A new leading indicator: workers recently laid off", *Monthly Labor Review* May: 35–7.

────── and ────── (1990) "Leading indicators for the 1900's", in G. H. Moore, (ed.) *Leading Indicators for the 1900's*, Homewood, IL: Dow Jones-Irwin.

Moore, G. H. and Zarnowitz, V. (1983) "Sequential signals of recession and recovery", in G. H. Moore (ed.) *Business Cycles, Inflation and Forecasting*, 2nd edn, Cambridge, MA: Ballinger.

Solo, R. A. (1955) "The diffusion of business cycles", R. A. Solo (ed.) *Economics and the Public Interest*, reprinted in G. H. Moore (ed.) *Business Cycle Indicators*, Princeton, NJ: NBER, Princeton University Press, ch. 8.

Wallis, W. A. and Moore, G. H. (1941) "A significance test for time-series and other ordered observations", Technical Paper 1, National Bureau of Economic Research, New York.

Zarnowitz, V. (1978) "On the accuracy and properties of recent macroeconomic forecasts", *American Economic Review Papers and Proceedings* 68: 313–19.

Chapter 11

The delayed emergence of econometrics as a separate discipline

S. Ambirajan

INTRODUCTION

There has always been one strand of thought which claims that the past is strewn with so much of ignorance – especially in scientific pursuits – that it is fruitless to go back to it. But that approach would deny us the many insights into the present position of any discipline because there is no present that did not have a past. There is a particular danger that this type of myopic approach is adopted in the case of recently developed academic disciplines like econometrics because people assume that, as they are of recent origin, they are free from historical puzzles.

Econometrics, if looked at etymologically, is a combination of familiar words, namely economics and *metrics* (from the Greek word *metron*), meaning "theory of measurement". Joseph Schumpeter, one of the early supporters of this budding discipline, thought that the term was "exposed to objection on philological grounds" and that it should have been either *ecometrics* or *economometrics* (Schumpeter 1954: 209n.). Just as a rose is a rose by whatever name you choose to call it, econometrics is all about measurement and analysis of economic phenomena. Though in the present time all economists use mathematics and statistics in greater or lesser measure, in the 1930s it was thought necessary to adopt a distinctive name embodying a research programme in the manner of biometrics, as statistical biology is known.

The year 1930 is a particularly important year because it was only in that year that Ragnar Frisch christened this new discipline with this name. Hashem Pesaran informs us through the *New Palgrave* that one Pawel Ciompa used the phrase many decades earlier, but we do not have any other details about the context in which the word was used.[1] It was only after the foundation of the Econometric Society in 1930 that the subject acquired a separate discipline (at least a subdiscipline) status. Professor Irving Fisher – a student of the mathematician Willard Gibbs at Yale University – had tried as early as 1912 to organize a group to "stimulate the development of economic theory in its relation to statistics and mathematics" under the auspices of the

American Association for the Advancement of Science. But Fisher received no support because, as one of the founders of the Econometric Society, Charles F. Roos, put it: "the time was not ripe and the union of these three branches of learning failed to develop" (1948: 127). Apparently the situation had not changed even fourteen years later. Roos gives his own experience of trying to get an econometric paper published in 1926. He had written a paper introducing both the instantaneous rates of change (or derivatives) and the cumulative effects of past production and prices (or Integrals) into the Walras–Pareto equations of economic equilibrium. This made possible a transformation of static theories into a dynamic form, and needless to say it was somewhat technical. Roos had great difficulty in having this contribution accepted for publication. When it was offered to a leading economic periodical, the editor agreed to publish it provided that Roos left out the mathematical and statistical portions. Similarly, mathematical and statistical periodicals were prepared to publish the paper if the offending references to the other two disciplines were excised!

Of course this couldn't go on for ever. In 1930, Ragnar Frisch along with Charles Roos happened to meet Fisher and stressed upon him the need for a forum to bring mathematically and statistically inclined economists together. Fisher in turn challenged the two young enthusiasts to collect a hundred people who would be interested in such enquiries. Frisch and Roos were able to collect seventy names in only three days. Somewhat encouraged, in the III meeting of Section K of the American Association for the Advancement of Science held at Cleveland, Ohio, the Society was founded with twelve Americans and four Europeans in the organizing group (Roos 1948: 128–30).

The Econometrics Society was founded in 1930 and ample funding was provided by the philanthropist Alfred Cowles Jr for the encouragement of such studies. Despite Professor Tinbergen's statement that "This international association includes practically all workers in this field and counts its members in all civilized countries" (1951: 9), the total number in 1950 was well below 1,000 and the bulk of them came from two or three countries. Even this figure was barely 300 more than what it was ten years earlier. As late as 1950, Tinbergen had to admit that "As a young branch of science, econometrics can only be learned from periodical articles; as yet it has no textbooks" (1951: Preface).

By the 1950s econometrics had acquired an identity as a separate discipline from which it later became, as Robert Strotz expressed it, "nearly con-terminous with the entire field of economics".[2] Terence Gorman is even more emphatic: according to him econometrics *is* "the existing methodology of economics, tailored for the subject, and taught as such to graduate students almost everywhere" (1984: 261).

Looking at the rather prolonged period of gestation and sudden take-off of the discipline, we would like to pose two broad questions in a historical setting:

1   When did the basic tools required for the development of econometrics become available?
2   What was the reason for the delay in the emergence of this discipline or, in other words, what were the obstacles to the discipline's growth earlier?

THE FOUNDATIONS

The basic requirements for the learning and development of econometrics are mathematical/statistical methods, economic theory and economic data. When were they available to enable scholars to promote this discipline?

The mathematical foundations of econometrics were certainly available well before the middle of the nineteenth century.[3] Let us take the four most important mathematical ideas used by econometricians: (a) the least squares approach, (b) probability distributions, (c) simultaneous equations and (d) matrix algebra.

Regression analysis is perhaps the most important and widely used econometric technique and, notwithstanding the maximum likelihood method of estimation, nobody will deny that the staple food of regression analysis is the estimation of the coefficients of econometric models with the least squares technique. The least squares approach has a hoary past. While the word "regression" was first used by Francis Galton, the statistician-biologist, in 1886, the basic theory of least squares was dealt with satisfactorily in 1805 by the French mathematician Adrien Marie Legendre and by the great Carl Friedrich Gauss as early as 1796. Laplace gave his proof of the method of least squares in 1812. Thus the Gauss–Markov theorem which is referred to in most elementary textbooks of econometrics has a very long history.[4]

Probability theory is the central mathematical pillar of econometrics, and it too has a very long past.[5] The great French mathematicians Fermat and Pascal carried on a spirited correspondence in the seventeenth century about wagers in a game of chance: thus the mathematical theory of probability was born. Even before that, in medieval Europe some concept of probability was the basis for ship insurance and financial speculation. Whether for the consideration and formulation of developing techniques for solution of problems, or the enunciation of general theorems, mathematicians working on probability had achieved a good deal by the beginning of the nineteenth century. One can mention the work of Jakob Bernoulli and his law of large numbers (*Ars Conjectandi*, "Art of Conjecturing", published in 1713, has been referred to by Charles Boyer (1968: 458) as the "earliest substantial volume in the theory of probability"). Laplace (1814), Gauss (1794–5) and, earlier, De Moivre (1733) are other great mathematicians who did most for the development of the theory of probability. Laplace was also responsible for the rescue from certain oblivion of Thomas Bayes's work (1761) on inverse probability. Of course mathematicians like Gauss and Laplace were more concerned with observational errors of physical measurements than with what probability theory was used for later. De Moivre's contribution – his work on the normal or so-called Gaussian function was discovered by Karl Pearson only in the twentieth century – had a surprisingly modern ring about it.

Indeed Laplace not only contributed to the foundations of probabilistic thought, but also applied it to both physical and social sciences. Of the latter, he studied problems relating to vital statistics such as mortality, fertility, marriages and insurance as well as judicial procedures, credibility of witnesses and the probability of judicial pronouncements. However, it was left to the Belgian mathematician – astronomer L. A. J. Quetelet, in his *Sur l'Homme et le Développement de ses Facultés: Physique Sociale* (1835) – to draw our attention to the existence of social phenomena exhibiting a very remarkable statistical consistency. Quetelet can rightly be called the Father of social statistics.[6] Thus probability theory and its applications were understood by the first quarter of the nineteenth century and were available for economists to utilize for explaining economic phenomena.

While single-equation models in econometrics are no doubt interesting, in order to capture the complexity and interdependence of the real world it is necessary to resort to simultaneous equation models. No wonder, then, that a majority of the applications of econometrics are essentially simultaneous in nature. Both the microeconomic and the macroeconomic approaches are simultaneous. Now, simultaneous equations have been around for centuries. We are told that Thymarides of Paros solved simultaneous linear equations as early as 380 BC, and that Diaphantos solved quadratic simultaneous equations in AD 275. Certainly by the tenth century both simultaneous equations and quadratic equations were common knowledge. With the work of Jerome Cardan (whose *Ars Magna* published in 1545 was an important landmark), Ludovico Ferrari and Nicolo Tartaglia in the sixteenth century, the algebra of equations had achieved a high water mark. By the nineteenth century, algebra did not hold any terrors for the educated elite of society.

Matrix algebra, well utilized by econometricians for the last three or four decades, also has a hoary past. The development of linear algebra was the result of efforts to find general methods for the solution of systems of linear equations in several unknowns. The early result of such enquiries was the discovery of the concept of determinants by Gottfried Leibnitz, although the Chinese had done much work centuries before. In the eighteenth century, Gabriel Cramer (of Cramer's rule fame), Lagrange with his symmetric results, and Etienne Bezout (another mathematician like Cramer who gave artificial rules to solve *n simultaneous linear equations in n unknowns*) had all used determinants for algebraic elimination. The definitive theory of determinants was the work of Augustin-Louis Cauchy who published it in 1812. The word "matrix" was itself coined by J. J. Sylvester, and matrix algebra became formalized by the work of Sylvester and Sir Arthur Cayley.

Even this cursory glance at the history of mathematics shows that the basic mathematical tools necessary for the emergence of virtually all branches of econometrics were available by the first quarter of the nineteenth century. Had they wanted, budding econometricians would not have been handicapped by the absence of analytical techniques. It is no doubt true that correlation analysis and curve-fitting were developed by statisticians like Galton, Pearson, Edgeworth, Yule, Weldon and R. A. Fisher in the last two or three decades of the nineteenth century, but these methods were not absolutely essential for useful analytical work, because other less precise methods were still available. Or, these statistical techniques would have occurred to them in the process of econometric investigations.

Two other factors ought to be noted while looking at the non-use of mathematics by economists and the non-development of econometrics during the period (1775–1825) when economics became a separate and respected discipline. It was only much later, that is, in the last quarter of the nineteenth century, that mathematics branched off into specialist subdisciplines. As Professor Dirk J. Struik, the historian of mathematics, has pointed out: "By 1870 mathematics had grown into an enormous and unwieldy structure, divided into a large number of fields in which only specialists knew the way" (1967: 174). But half a century earlier, this was not so. There was no reason, then, to suppose that the whole available body of mathematics was closed to the educated men of the day. At the same time, during the half century referred to above, mathematicians were slowly departing from aristocratic salons and Royal courts for universities, technical schools, academies and Gymnasiums to teach ordinary students.[7] Again, while specialization was perhaps the ambition, most people believed the utilitarian approach of the mathematics of Fourier (1768–1830), that is, that the objective of mathematics was public usefulness and explanation of the mysteries of nature, rather than the approach of Jacobi (1804–51) for whom mathematics was simply "the honor of the human mind".[8]

THE MATHEMATICAL EQUIPMENT OF ECONOMISTS

The next question concerns the mathematical equipment of the economists. Could it be that economists were unaware of analogous developments in mathematics and could not have taken advantage of the powerful techniques? This doesn't seem probable. Economists – at least the more important ones – were all good to fair students of mathematics of the period.

The physiocrats as the earliest school of economists were not ignorant of mathematics and their contributions lent themselves to mathematical treatment. Indeed François Quesnay shifted to pure mathematical research – especially the geometry of the circle – after making his contributions to economics.[9] Another French economist-statesman of the day, Marquis de Condorcet, was probably one of the very few economists before 1914 to have achieved fame as a mathematician independent of his economics.

Coming to the acknowledged founding father of the discipline, Adam Smith, it is fair to say that he was quite well versed in mathematics, although he would not himself claim to have been a mathematician. He had studied mathematics under the Scottish mathematician Robert Simson (1687–1768), and his fellow student was another great mathematician, Matthew Stewart, who later became Professor of Mathematics at Edinburgh University. John Rae has pointedly said that during his student days Smith "acquired a distinct ardour for mathematics under the inspiring instructions of Simson", besides citing a tutor who spoke of Smith's "fondness for mathematics in those early days" (Rae 1895: 10, 11). Like his class-mate Stewart, Smith was interested in astronomy to the extent of writing a treatise on it. He was strongly influenced by Isaac Newton's scientific method and his admiration for Newton was very great. The French mathematician D'Alembert was among his long-time friends (Smith 1976: 124).

Among Smith's two immediate followers in the classical economic tradition, Malthus was a student of mathematics at Cambridge and secured a Wranglership. David Ricardo, certainly the greatest of the nineteenth-century economists, was a self-taught person and we need not dispute Schumpeter when he says that, though Ricardo was not a trained mathematician, "he was a born one" (1954: 957n.). Jacob Hollander, writing in 1910, notes that David Ricardo was from his early childhood much interested in "mathematics, chemistry, geology and mineralogy" (p. 35).

Nor was there a lack of knowledge of mathematics among other classical economists. Jean Baptiste Say refers to the mathematical works of D'Alembert[10] and others with easy familiarity. Contrary to the popular belief, John Stuart Mill was also quite knowledgeable about contemporary mathematics.[11] Similarly, Karl Marx was a serious student of mathematics and by assiduous self-study had worked through most of the mathematics subjects taught at that time in the German universities.[12] Thus when Frank Knight ([1935] 1956: 41) expressed the view that classical economists were "ignorant of mathematical concepts", he was totally wrong. During the period before 1870, most of the serious economists would have had some mathematical training – formal or self-taught. In any case, if any "normal and normally educated person" felt the want of it, he "could acquire what was needed of it by the spare-time work of about six months".[13] It should also be mentioned that actually there was a good deal of work as well in mathematical economics *per se* – the most famous being the work of Augustin Cournot.

As for the period after 1870, virtually all famous first rank economists, with rare exceptions such as Carl Menger, J. M. Clark and J. E. Cairnes, had varying levels of expertise in mathematics. Some economists were so mathematical that even sympathetic commentators were overwhelmed. For example, James Bonar in his obituary note on F. Y. Edgeworth (1845–1926) remarked how he displayed "the exuberance of algebraic foliage".[14]

Not only were economists not ignorant about mathematics, there has also been a tradition of careful collection of economic statistics. In the Western world, one of the earliest compilations of economic data was the *Domesday Book* – a sort of fiscal survey – of William the Conqueror. With the rise of the nation-states, the need for collection of taxes, trading activities and organization of economic activity resulted in the gathering of all kinds of data.[15] But such collection of statistics was not done in the same spirit as it was done in the natural sciences in the sixteenth and seventeenth centuries.

The collection of data was considerably stimulated in those centuries because of the philosophical-methodological developments in the natural sciences. The Baconian inductive empiricism that caught the imagination of the natural philosophers of the Royal Society infected students of society as well. The main difference was that, whereas the natural scientists collected data for demonstration and proof of some scientific hypothesis, students of society merely wanted to give a quantitative expression (i.e. in terms of measure) to socioeconomic phenomena of interest to them.

The most famous data-gatherer of the seventeenth century was Sir William Petty (1623–87) who gave the name *political arithmetick* to this genre of studies. In his words:[16]

> The Method I take to do this, is not yet very usual; for instead of using only comparative and speculative words, and intellectual arguments, I have taken the course ... to express myself in Terms of Number, weight or measure.

Both in England and on the Continent, practitioners of this discipline were numerous. John Graunt (1620–74), Gregory King (1648–1712), Marshall Sebastian Vauban (1633–1707), Charles Davenant (1656–1714), William Fleetwood (1656–1723) and Johann Sussimilch (1707–67) are some of the more famous gatherers of statistics of the seventeenth and eighteenth centuries. They collected all types of data – demographic, trade and natural resources – with a view to studying the economy.[17] Some of them also did very original work. For example William Fleetwood prepared the first systematic history of prices over six centuries, and concerned himself with the relative increases in prices and wages and the consequent fall or rise in welfare. On Marshall Sebastian Vauban as a collector of data, Schumpeter (1954) showered immense praise: "Nobody ever understood better the true relation between facts and argument" (p. 204). There was yet another statistician, William Playfair (1759–1823), who published in 1786 the course of prices of wheat and wages over two and a half centuries, and for the first time used visual presentation of data.[18] Mention should also be made of a German statistician, A. F. M. Crome, who was another early pioneer in the use of graphical presentation of economic statistics.[19] In the 1790s, David Davies and Frederic Morton Eden collected detailed survey data on the budgets of the poor workers of England. In the nineteenth century, there were many economic statisticians who assembled voluminous data, among them Thomas

Tooke, William Newmarch, Thorold Rogers, Robert Giffen, Charles Booth and Ernest Engel, to name but a few.[20]

Probably, we should add twentieth-century statisticians like W. C. Mitchell, F. C. Mills and A. F. Burns of the National Bureau of Economic Research (NBER) to the list. The founders of NBER cannot be strictly compared with the Restoration Period virtuosi who, to quote William Letwin (1963: 99), "continued, endlessly and pointlessly, to record, catalogue and count"; nevertheless, they belonged to the Brahe–Kepler tradition, as Tjalling Koopmans (1970: 112) has said, of "large scale gathering, sifting, scrutinizing of facts" which "precedes, or proceeds independently of, the formulation of theories and their testing by further facts". As this is "measurement without theory", the NBER economic statisticians belonged to the genus comprising Sir William Petty and his successors. The nineteenth century also saw the beginnings in most countries of systematic collection of economic statistics. For example, population censuses, price statistics and other statistics began to be systematically collected and published in many countries.

What we have said so far amounts to this.

1   The basic mathematical tools necessary for the development of econo-metrics were available at least by 1830, a hundred years before the foundation of the Econometric Society in 1931.
2   With few exceptions, from the 1750s onwards economists were not ignorant of mathematics, and it is a reasonable inference that they were capable of generating testable hypotheses.
3   The quantitative aspects of political economy were practised vigorously, not only by individuals but also by government institutions.

While the three elements that make up econometrics were available to economists at least a hundred years before the discipline took off, until the last ten years of the nineteenth century even the practising economists kept their economics and statistical work in tightly separated compartments. There were also statisticians like Ernest Engel (1821–96) who did not realize how important his work would have been to economic theorists. It was only with the work of Benini, Lenoir, Moore, Mackeprang and a few others before 1914 that we can talk of genuine econometric work.[21] During the next twenty years a certain amount of econometric analysis was done both in America and Europe, but Stigler (1965: 233) was certainly exaggerating when he said: "The speed and generality with which the new techniques (mathematical statistics) were adopted by economists left no occasion for complaint".

FACTORS IMPEDING THE USE OF ECONOMETRICS

No single reason can be given for the late emergence of econometrics. There is, first, the question whether the mathematical foundations – despite their availability – could easily have come to the aid of the economists. Schumpeter has remarked how Laplace and Gauss's

> law of error and method of least squares ... became the pride and at the same time the curse of applied statistics for more than half a century ... the curse because it induced an incidental belief to the effect that deviations in statistical material from the law of error are simply due to paucity of observations.
>
> (Schumpeter 1954: 960–1)

This prevented progress in the generalization of the frequency theory. Another reason for inadequate progress in mathematical statistics could be that Laplace left many of his results in the form of approximations.[22] Again, statistics was viewed with suspicion in many quarters because, among other things, Quetelet oversold the idea of stability of certain social phenomena like suicides per year. The idea of statistical regularity which Quetelet propounded and which was seen as inconsistent with free will was a source of much criticism as well as embarrassment for the nineteenth-century statisticians. They found to their dismay that the sort of criticism that Quetelet was subjected to "threatened to undermine the legitimacy of their science".[23]

Whereas the ideas of Gauss, Laplace and others were immediately found useful in the study of physical phenomena (i.e. astronomy) they could not be so easily adopted to analyse social phenomena notwithstanding the work of energetic and competent statisticians like Quetelet. Even Jevons with all his mathematical equipment and capacity for detailed empirical investigations could not successfully overcome the difficulties he met in his efforts to apply probability in his statistical work.[24] Until the creation of an entirely new statistical methodology suitable for social scientists, based of course on the work of earlier pioneers, by Galton, Karl Pearson, Edgeworth and Yule from the 1880s onwards, further developments in statistical economics were not possible.

Knowledge about what happens in the economy is transmitted to economists through statisticians who collect data. Naturally whatever the economist knows comes to him from the data-gatherer, and if the latter is ignorant of the theorist's requirements (something that may not always be clear to the theorists themselves) or is anti-theoretical, economists cannot comprehensively analyze the economy. The problem apparently is still unresolved, as Zvi Griliches lamented in 1985. Certainly economists of the nineteenth century failed to realize that economic functions and quantities could be determined empirically (as Stigler (1965: 232) points out), and until a way was shown to them by mathematical statisticians in the post-1880 period no econometric work of the modern type was done. And, in general, the nineteenth-century data-gatherers and their twentieth-century followers were not theoretically inclined. They believed that if sufficient data were gathered, they would bring illumination by themselves. Vast quantities of statistical data were generated both by governments and individual social researchers, but apart from use as illustrative examples statistics was not put to any systematic purpose. While economists made some simple manipulation of data such as averages, percentages and ratios, there was no question of hypothesis formation and statistical testing. Frank Knight ([1935] 1956) was not wrong when he remarked "To a large degree we find one group of students in possession of the problems and another in possession of the data and the two living in separate universes of discourse" (p. 90). Even those first-rate economists who were also eminent statisticians kept the two domains apart. For example, Edgeworth whose contributions to economic and statistical theory are well known never attempted to construct demand curves empirically. Again, Jevons, whose penchant for quantitative economics is not a matter of dispute, kept his economic theory purely deductive without validating it empirically. When Jevons tried his hand at empirical studies in, for example, *The Coal Question* (1865) and *Investigations in Currency and Finance* (1884), they were nowhere near proper econometric analysis. For example, his work on the coal question follows the approach of Malthus eighty years earlier by juxtaposing the non-increase in coal supply and the demand for coal which he showed to be increasing in geometric proportion. Faulty and inadequate though Jevons's empirical studies were, they represented (in the words of Lord Keynes) "a revolutionary change, for one who was a logician and a deductive economist, to approach the subject this way".[25] However, Jevons did not initiate any empirical tradition, as Keynes said: "It is remarkable, looking back, how few followers and imitators he had in the black arts of inductive economics in the fifty years after 1862".[26]

One reason why British economists kept statistical analysis separate is, perhaps, not because they did not know how to manipulate statistics, but because they were afraid that data – especially statistical data – could never be perfect and that if such data are used to confirm or reject theories they might lead to misconceptions. In other words, many economists were convinced that, while logical errors can be detected, statistical errors cannot be.

Such considerations appear to have been responsible for the non-development of econometrics in France. The three great and influential French economists of the nineteenth century, J. B. Say, Augustin Cournot and Léon Walras, about whose mathematical equipment one need not doubt, all resisted the intrusion of economic statistics in what they considered to be economics for different reasons.[27] They – Say in particular – regarded statistics as a descriptive subject whereas economics was an "experimental science". They were certain that statistics was too simplistic and could not take into account the immense complexity of the subject matter of economics. Even if exact statistics could be gathered, it would only yield a static picture of the social and economic reality and not explain the process. Another objection was that past data were uncertain whereas future data are unavailable. Finally they believed that statistics was essentially linked to the state apparatus and is always incomplete. Cournot did not take as extreme a position as Say, but nevertheless rejected in total Quetelet's conceptions of social statistics. Walras went a little further to accept the role of statistics in practical economics but it was not pure theory and hence not useful or relevant for economic science. John Stuart Mill, of course, was clear about the inadequacy of mathematics and statistics to help out economic theorists. He was aware of the danger of giving spurious precision to symbols by constructing simplified models. Besides, he knew that available data represented only a part of the reality, a reality of complex causal relations.[28]

Marshall's attitude to mathematics and statistics can be held responsible in considerable measure for the lack of progress in econometrics until the 1930s. There is no doubt that he conceived economics as "scientific and analytical" in the manner of physical sciences. But at the same time he was against the excessive use of mathematics in economics. More than that, he was worried that, by looking at statistics, statistically inclined economists could easily miss vital aspects of the problem because of their non-quantifiability. Marshall also did not think well of Henry Moore's pioneering econometric work, for he was most reluctant even to grant an interview to Moore when the latter came to England and wanted to see Marshall. In a letter to Edgeworth, he made the following comment about Moore's work: Moore had "reached results not nearly as helpful *practically* as those which he could have got by looking at the world with wide open eyes for a few minutes".[29]

Marshall was never clear about what economics should be.[30] Should it be a useful discipline or should it be an objective science? Obviously he wanted it to be both. Perhaps this ambivalence did not permit the sort of single-minded pursuit of refining and elaborating economic theory and statistical testing that was necessary for the development of econometrics. Narmadeshwar Jha, a close student of the economic thought of the period, has pointed out:

> Even though some attempts were made by the younger contemporaries of Marshall to measure economic phenomena, surprisingly little was done in the direction of what is now called econometric work.... Marshall seems to have discouraged progress on econometric lines and the achievements of British economists in this respect before the '30s perhaps for that reason do not add up to anything significant.
>
> (Jha 1963: 22)

Except for the odd scholar like Richard Stone very few of the best British economists took to econometrics. While British economists blazed many trails in economic thinking during the pre-war era, the cultivation of the quantitative aspects of the discipline took place mainly in Europe, and during the 1930s in the United States as well.

NOTES

This chapter began as a special lecture given to the Silver Jubilee Conference of the Indian Econometrics Society held at Bangalore in January 1988. I am grateful to the President of the Indian Econometrics Society, Professor N. Srinivasa Iyengar, for encouraging me to look at the history of econometrics. The original address was read carefully and commented upon by Professors Ingrid Rima and A. W. Coats, and Dr Eric Sowey. None of the above should be held responsible for what I have made of their suggestions.

1   See his article on "Econometrics" in *The New Palgrave* (1987).
2   "Econometrics", *International Encyclopaedia of the Social Sciences*.
3   See for references on the history of mathematics the following standard treatises: Smith (1951, 1953); Boyer (1968); Struik (1967); Bell (1937).
4   See Neyman (1976: 158–9).
5   For a knowledge about the hoary past of the literature on probability, one can do no more than refer to the following: David (1962); Pearson and Kendall (1970); Kendall and Plackett (1977).
6   This is not to deny the existence of other great social statisticians in the nineteenth century like Le Play, Charles Booth, to name two, but Quetelet was the pioneer. See Lazarsfeld (1961).
7   This process of the professionalization of mathematics in the nineteenth century has been dealt with at great length in the papers of Hodgkin, Schneider and Schubring in Mehrtens *et al.* (1981).
8   Dirk Struik (1981: 139–40n.). The utilitarian approach to mathematics cannot be minimized. Dr Struik in a recent paper has observed: "The search for information in connection with markets and imperial expansion brought scholars to explore the east. This brought Rosen, Woepcke and the Sedillots to the study of Arabic mathematics, Colebrooke and Strachey to the mathematics of the Hindus. With Biot and Aylie begins the modern study of Chinese mathematics." See Struik (1981: 20).
9   See Meek (1962: 375n.). It was not until 1955 that Quesnay's *Tableau Economique* was translated into the form of a three-industry closed Leontief model by arranging the conjectural data provided in the model. This was possible because of the close affinity between Quesnay's and Leontief's models both of which emphasize the union between theory and statistical data. See Phillips (1955: 137ff.).
10 See Say ([1821] 1964: xxvii n.).
11 See Schabas (1985).
12 See Smolinski (1973).
13 Schumpeter (1954: 955).
14 *Economic Journal* (December 1926): 651.
15 For an exhaustive survey of estimates and a statistical description of national income from Sir William Petty onwards, see Studenski (1958).
16 Hull (1899: 244).
17 See Enders (1985).
18 On Playfair, see Tufte (1983). See also Fitzpatrick (1960).
19 See Royston (1956).
20 See Stigler (1954).
21 See Stigler (1954; 1962), Humphrey (1973), Cargill (1974), Koergaard (1984), Christ (1985).
22 See Rietz (1927: 3).
23 Porter (1986: 164).

24 See Aldrich (1987: 251).
25 *Essays in Biography*, ed. Geoffrey Keynes, London, 1961, p. 278.
26 Ibid., p. 268.
27 See Menard (1980).
28 Quoted in Hollander (1985: 45).
29 Quoted in Stigler (1965: 353).
30 Maloney (1985: 52–4).

REFERENCES

Aldrich, John (1987) "Jevons as statistician: the role of probability", *Manchester School* September (3).
Bell, E. T. (1937) *Men of Mathematics*, London.
Boyer, Carl B. (1968) *A History of Mathematics*, New York.
Cargill, Thomas F. (1974) "Early applications of spectral methods of economic time series", *History of Political Economy* 6 (1).
Christ, Carl F. (1985) "Early progress in estimating quantitative economic relationships in America", *American Economic Review* 75 (6).
David, F. N. (1962) *Games, Gods and Gambling: The Origins and History of Probability and Statistical Ideas from the Earliest Times to the Newtonian Era*, London.
Enders, A. M. (1985) "The functions of numerical data in the writings of Graunt, Petty and Davenant", *History of Political Economy* 17 (2).
Fitzpatrick, Paul J. (1960) "Leading British statisticians of the 19th century", *Journal of the American Statistical Association* 55; reprinted in Sir Maurice Kendall and R. L. Plackett (eds) *Studies in the History of Statistics and Probability*, vol. II, London, 1977.
Gorman, Terence (1984) "Towards a better economic methodology?", in Peter Wiles and Guy Routh (eds) *Economics in Disarray*, Oxford.
Griliches, Zvi (1985) "Data and econometricians: the uneasy alliance", *American Economic Review* 75 (2): 196–200.
Hollander, Jacob (1910) *David Ricardo: A Centenary Estimate*, Baltimore, MD.
Hollander, Samuel (1985) "The relevance of John Stuart Mill: some implications for modern economics", Mimeo, March.
Hull, C. H. (ed.) (1899) *Economic Writings of Sir William Petty*, vol. I, Cambridge: Cambridge University Press.
Humphrey, Thomas M. (1973) "Empirical tests of the quantity theory of money in the United States, 1900–1930", *History of Political Economy* 5 (2).
Jha, Narmadeshwar (1963) *The Age of Marshall: Aspects of British Economic Thought 1890–1915*, Patna.
Kendall, Sir Maurice, and Plackett, R. L. (eds) (1977) *Studies in the History of Statistics and Probability*, vol. II, London.
Knight, Frank ([1935] 1956) "The Ricardian theory of production and distribution", *Canadian Journal of Economic and Political Science* February–May; reprinted in *On the History and Method of Economics*, Chicago, IL.
Koergaard, Niels (1984) "The earliest history of econometrics: some neglected contributions", *History of Political Economy* 16 (3).
Koopmans, Tjalling C. (1970) "Measurement without theory", *Review of Economics and Statistics* 29; reprinted in *Scientific Papers of Tjalling C. Koopmans*, Berlin.
Lazarsfeld, Paul (1961) "Notes on the history of quantification in sociology – trends, sources, problems", *Isis* 52; reprinted in Sir Maurice Kendall and R. L. Plackett (eds) *Studies in the History of Statistics and Probability*, vol. II, London, 1977.

Letwin, William (1963) *The Origins of Scientific Economics: English Economic Thought 1600–1776*, London.

Maloney, John (1985) *Marshall, Orthodoxy and the Professionalization of Economics*, Cambridge: Cambridge University Press.

Meek, R. L. (1962) *The Economics of Physiocracy*, London.

Mehrtens, Herbert, Bos, Henk, and Schneider, Ivo (eds) (1981) *Social History of Nineteenth Century Mathematics*, Boston.

Menard, Claude (1980) "Three forms of resistance to statistics: Say, Cournot, Walras", *History of Political Economy* 12 (4): 524–9.

Neyman, Jerzy (1976) "The emergence of mathematical statistics", in D. B. Owen (ed.) *On the History of Statistics and Probability*, New York.

Pearson, E. S. and Kendall, M. G. (eds) (1970) *Studies in the History of Statistics and Probability*, vol. I, London.

Pesaran, Hashem (1987) "Econometrics", in *New Palgrave Dictionary of Economics*, London: Macmillan.

Phillips, Alamarin (1955) "The Tableau Economique as a simple Leontief model", *Quarterly Journal of Economics* 69 (1): 137ff.

Porter, Theodore M. (1986) *The Rise of Statistical Thinking 1820–1900*, Princeton, NJ: Princeton University Press.

Rae, John (1895) *Life of Adam Smith*, London.

Rietz, H. L. (1927) *Mathematical Statistics*, Chicago, IL.

Roos, Charles F. (1948) "A future role for the Econometric Society in international statistics", *Econometrica* 16 (2): 127.

Royston, Erica (1956) "A note on the history of the graphical presentation of data", *Biometrika* 43; reprinted in E. S. Pearson and M. G. Kendall (eds) *Studies in the History of Statistics and Probability*, vol. I, London, 1970.

Say, J. B. ([1821] 1964) *A Treatise on Political Economy or the Production, Distribution and Consumption of Wealth*, New York.

Schabas, Margaret (1985) "Some reactions to Jevons's mathematical programme: the case of Cairnes and Mill", *History of Political Economy* 17 (3): 344ff.

Schumpeter, J. A. (1954) *History of Economic Analysis*, New York.

Smith, Adam (1976) *The Theory of Moral Sentiments*, Glasgow.

Smith, D. E. (1951, 1953) *History of Mathematics*, 2 vols, New York.

Smolinski, Leon (1973) "Karl Marx and mathematical economics", *Journal of Political Economy* 81 (5).

Stigler, George J. (1954) "The early history of empirical studies of consumer behaviour", *Journal of Political Economy* 42 (April); reprinted in his *Essays in the History of Economics*, Chicago, IL, 1965, pp. 198ff.

—— (1962) "Henry L. Moore and statistical economics", *Econometrica* 30; reprinted in his *Essays in the History of Economics*, Chicago, IL, 1965.

—— (1965) *Essays in the History of Economics*, Chicago, IL.

Struik, Dirk J. (1967) *A Concise History of Mathematics*, 3rd edn, New York.

—— (1981) "Mathematics in the early part of the nineteenth century", in Herbert Mehrtens, Henk Bos and Ivo Schneider (eds) *Social History of Nineteenth Century Mathematics*, Boston.

Studenski, Paul (1958) *The Income of Nations*, Part I, *History*, New York.

Tinbergen, Jan (1951) *Econometrics*, London.

Tufte, Edward R. (1983) *The Visual Display of Quantitative Information*, Cheshire.

Chapter 12

Some conundrums about the place of econometrics in economic analysis

Ingrid H. Rima

The era that began in the 1920s and lasted some twenty years until the beginning of the Second World War is often spoken of as the "high theory" era. It was so called because the innovative theoretical breakthroughs that were made had a potential for completely altering "the orientation and character of economics" (Shackle 1967: 5). The Robinson–Chamberlin theories of imperfect or monopolistic competition, Hicks's revival of Edgeworth's indifference curves, Keynes's theory of aggregate effective demand, the Morgenstern–von Neumann theory of games, and the *ex ante, ex post* construct of the Swedish School were chief among these breakthroughs. Each in its own way these innovations undertook to address the anomalies or "puzzles" inherent in the conventional model of an economic process driven by the maximizing choices of households and firms to determine the equilibrium prices that clear markets. It is thus a conundrum that, some sixty years later, the neo-Walrasian model of the contemporary mainstream is predicated on essentially the same "vision" (to use Schumpeter's indispensable term) of the real world that was dominant when the creative spasm of high theory began.

Expressed in terms of contemporary literature relating to scientific progress, it is now quite clear that, in spite of Shackle's expectations, the years of high theory did *not* bring forth either a new paradigm (Kuhn 1957, 1970) or a progressive SRP (Lakatos 1964, 1971).[1] J. M. Keynes *offered* a new SRP in economics that was intended to compete with that of "the classics". But it was not long before J. R. Hicks began the integration of Keynes's theory into the neoclassical SRP (Hicks 1937). This was accomplished by grafting microeconomic behavioral assumptions onto its "hard core" which, by leading to a general equilibrium conclusion, rendered Keynes's theory a special case within the "single paradigm ... of economic equilibrium via the market mechanism" (Coats 1969).

This chapter intends to focus on the question why neither Keynes's theory of aggregate effective demand nor the Swedish *ex ante, ex post* approach were successful in summoning forth either a Kuhnian scientific revolution or a Lakatosian theoretically progressive SRP? The answer, in brief, hinges on the coincidence of the neo-Walrasian marriage with the "formalist revolution" that made mathematical and econometric techniques the chief instruments of the discipline. Thus, the intellectual "end product" of the creative spasm of the high theory era that began in the mid-1920s is *methodological* rather than substantive. Though Hicks would say that his reformulation of the Keynesian system as a simultaneous equation system in three variables (income, the rate of interest and the volume of investment) was purely a matter of mathematical convenience (Hicks 1937: 160–2), the IS–LM model is in fact a general equilibrium representation of an economy predisposed to yield an optimizing outcome (Weintraub 1979: 25–6).

Yet, Hicks's IS–LM reformulation was only a first step in the direction of the contemporary neo-Walrasian paradigm. Two additional steps were essential. The first derives from the institutional environment in which economic research has been nurtured since the Second World War period. The second derives from the computer revolution of the 1950s which made large-scale macrodynamic models a technical possibility. Empirical research typically requires a large-scale research unit, often university related or government sponsored, to generate the requisite financial resources to bring together a research team to work on the kinds of problems for which large-scale computer capability is essential. Gone are the days of pure competition among academic scholars.

Economic research today is often the product of a "knowledge industry" that is characterized by "competition among the few", that is, by oligopoly rather than by pure competition. Much of this is concerned with hypothesis testing. On a microlevel, the chief concern is empirical research that follows from the premise of maximizing behavior within the framework of the theory of choice. On a macrolevel, the concern is to generate and test large-scale models that will predict economic variables critical to business and government policy. Thus, the secondary theme of this chapter will undertake to examine how econometrics extended and enhanced the classic Walrasian model, rendering it not simply a mathematical representation of inter-dependences among commodity and factor markets but a technique for selecting among explanatory hypotheses about the economic process.

Part I of this inquiry proceeds by recalling the "anomalies", or "puzzles", which were identified during the years that preceded those of high theory. The second part identifies the leading works of the high theory era for the purpose of establishing that the innovations which have had the greatest impact on economics are *not*, as one might expect, *The Economics of Imperfect Competition* (1933), *The Theory of Monopolistic Competition* (1933), Myrdal's *Monetary Equilibrium* (1939) or even Keynes's *General Theory* (1936). Rather, the books that have had the greatest long-term impact on economics are Hicks's *Value and Capital* (1939), Samuelson's *Foundations of Economic Analysis* (1947), and von Neumann and Morgenstern's *Theory of Games and Economic Behavior* (1944), Tinbergen's *Statistical Test of Business-Cycle*

Theories (1939) and Haavelmo's *The Probability Approach in Econometrics* (1944). These are not among the works which Shackle identified as "innovative" and they are titles that remain relatively unfamiliar to practising economists.

The third part examines the evolution of the "knowledge industry" in consequence of the interdependence between the computer revolution and economic research. Economic research is dominated by econometric technique and the emergence of econometrics as the sister discipline of economics has changed the economics profession as a knowledge industry. Thus the central argument of this chapter is that the economist's research agenda has been altered in a way that has substantially undermined the effectiveness of many of the innovations which Shackle found so persuasive.

I

The urgent intellectual puzzles that became apparent in the 1920s were (1) incompatibility between increasing returns and industry-wide equilibrium under pure competition, (2) the unreliability of flexible prices for achieving equilibria in labor, commodity and money markets, (3) uncertainty and imperfect knowledge about the future and their effect on economic behavior over time and (4) the related puzzle of incompatibility between imperfect knowledge and successful prediction of prices and levels of economic activity. The first two puzzles relate to the neoclassical tradition that flourished after Marshall and which was transmitted from Cambridge to Oxford, the London School and eventually to American scholars. The third and fourth relate more specifically to the general equilibrium tradition, though the problem of assessing the economic effect of uncertain knowledge and risk on market behavior made itself apparent in both the Marshallian and Walrasian traditions, albeit in very different contexts.

During the 1920s the "increasing returns–perfect competition" puzzle elicited the lion's share of attention both at Cambridge, where Marshall's tradition continued, and at Oxford where Harrod and others were concerned with empirical research to address the anomalies they perceived in Marshallian theory. These were brought into view by Sraffa's 1926 paper which challenged Marshall's attribution of increasing returns to external economies that are equally available to all firms. Less well known, but no less relevant is the concern, much of which centered at Oxford, about the question whether the size of a firm is limited by the tendency toward rising supply price (Kaldor 1934; E. A. G. Robinson 1931, 1941; Harrod 1936). The latter, which also provoked empirical study of the relevance of the behavioral assumptions economists made, bear on the tenability of the assumption of pure competition.[2] For Pigou (1922) consideration of increasing returns led in the direction of examining divergences between private and social returns and costs.

The post First World War unemployment problem brought several interrelated puzzles into focus. At the center, particularly in England, was the apparent attachment of workers to money rather than to real wages (money illusion) and the usefulness of trying to reduce real wages by means of monetary policy. This was an issue about which Pigou had already expressed reservations (Pigou 1914: 14–17). From a conceptual perspective the problem of worker responses to price level changes is part of the larger puzzle of understanding the process by which an economy changes over time. For Marshall and Pigou, concern about expectations was developed within the context of their concern about industrial fluctuations – the antecedent of contemporary macroeconomics. Although Pigou was attentive to the way in which expectations underlie fluctuations in business, he cannot be credited with substantial analytical advance for he effectively assumed the problem away by relying on the simplification of ignorance and uncertainty as "frictions" which can be abstracted, even though he was attentive to the expectations underlying the errors of optimism and pessimism inherent in business fluctuations (Pigou 1912: Part IV, ch. 7). Expectations and the state of confidence also play a role in J. M. Keynes's discussion on the speculative behaviors of stock market participants in his *Treatise on Money* (1931) and in his ongoing debate with Hubert Henderson about the effectiveness of public works (Winch 1970). This concern was expressed in the context of policy and had yet to be recast into an analytical framework which undertook to link "before" and "after". Dennis Robertson's attempt to analyze changes in investment and income over time by means of his conceptual construct of "the day" which enabled him to conceive income, savings and investment as variables whose values may be different "today" from what they were "yesterday" and from what they may become tomorrow, is another construct devised for the purpose of coming to grips with changes over time (Robertson 1933).

There were also puzzles that related to the Walrasian tradition that became apparent during the 1920s. Some fifty years had by then elapsed since the mathematician-economist Léon Walras conceived of the general equilibrium problem: what, he asked, are the output quantities supplied by industries and demanded by households and the input quantities supplied by households and demanded by industries and what are the relative prices at which such input and output transactions are consummated? By assuming that exchanges take place only at equilibrium prices and invoking the presence of an "all knowing" auctioneer who contracted (and recontracted) inputs and outputs, Walras was able to demonstrate mathematically the possibility of *tâtonnement*. In the context of the real world, a unique equilibrium solution to these equations is contingent on the unlikely premise that the behaviors of individual market participants are mutually compatible in a sense that is possible only if each participant "knows" *a priori* how others will behave.[3]

Oscar Morgenstern recognized the problem in his 1928 book *Wertschaft-sprognose* written while he was still engaged in business cycle research at his

Vienna Institute and concerned about supplying businesses with economic predictions. Morgenstern was emphatic that prediction is possible in nature because its variables are "dead". The matter is conceptually different when "live" variables are at issue, for these represent other "wills" which can be expected to impact on another's behavior in unpredictable ways (Morgenstern 1928: 806).[4] His now famous Holmes–Moriarty example (p. 98) illustrated why the premise that either man might out-think the other is not tenable and that the problem their interdependence posed was, essentially, one of strategy. Morgenstern's example made it clear that individual rational behavior is a determinate only if the behavior of "others" can be assumed known *a priori*. Without this assumption a logical impasse is reached which vitiates the possibility of prediction and thus a general equilibrium solution.[5]

II

The innovations which Shackle spoke of as "high theory" were a response, so to speak, to the kind of intellectual puzzles identified in the preceding section. One approach to examining the degree of their relevance for the ongoing development of economics may perhaps be evaluated in terms of the "great books" of the era. If the criterion of "greatness" is a book's impact on the direction and content of the subsequent development of economics, some surprises will (perhaps) become apparent in the selection to be offered here.

The place of Piero Sraffa's article (1926) as giving impetus toward the Chamberlin–Robinson reconstruction of Marshall's theory of value and distribution requires no elaboration. An important theoretical literature grew out of Sraffa's recommendation that the profession direct its attention to the subjective customer preferences that underlie a firm's sales curves and the offer curves of its nearest competitors. These insights led, on the one hand, toward analyses of business strategy and, on the other, in the direction of a new sub-field of economics now known as "industrial organization". Yet, neither *The Economics of Imperfect Competition* (1933) nor *The Theory of Monopolistic Competition* (1933) had a subsequent impact on the profession that is comparable with the unsettling effects of the increasing returns–costs of production and pricing controversies that preceded them. The impact of the so-called "monopolistic competition revolution" has chiefly refined Marshallian market conceptions. It is also clear that Keynes's *General Theory* has not generated a "Keynesian revolution" in the sense of having permanently changed the direction of economics. This conclusion is encapsulated in a recent observation by Alan Blinder (1988) that "It would be difficult to find any Keynesian under the age of forty".

Nor have the insights of the "Swedish School" which once enjoyed a separate, though very brief, identity borne fruit. Unlike Robertson's attempt to tame time by separating spending, savings and investing "today" from their counterparts "yesterday" in order to understand their magnitudes "tomorrow", the Swedish approach launched a tradition that built on the works of Knut Wicksell. The *ex ante, ex post* distinction made by Gunnar Myrdal (1927, 1932, 1933) and Erik Lindahl (1939) was a significant alternative approach to conceptualizing the puzzle of changes taking place over time, especially in relation to the relationship between savings and investment. This distinction was "one of the most transforming insights that theoretical economics has had" (Shackle 1972: 400). Flow-related magnitudes like savings, investment and income must always be conceived in two senses: the *ex ante* sense conceives of the value of variables at the beginning of a time period while the *ex post* sense refers to their values at the end of a process which their initial values set into motion. Thus, savings and investment may diverge from each other *ex ante*, but this divergence brings about changes in income which bring savings and investment into equality *ex post*.

The loss of interest in business cycle theory that followed on the heels of the *General Theory* and the shifting interests of Myrdal and his colleagues cut short the intellectual influence of Wicksell's successors (Hansson 1982). Thus it would appear that if the era of high theory has left *any* legacy it is to be found in J. R. Hicks's *Value and Capital* (1937), Paul Samuelson's *Foundations of Economic Analysis* (completed before the Second World War though not published until 1941), *Theory of Games and Economic Behavior* (1944) by John von Neumann and Oscar Morgenstern and Trygve Haavelmo's *The Probability Approach in Econometrics* (1944). These are the works that substantially shaped the post high theory era of economics.[4]

The analytical result of the counter-revolution that began with Hicks's "Mr Keynes and the Classics" and his later *Value and Capital* was to recast the *General Theory* into a Walrasian framework. What Hicks's reformulation (and a similar one offered by Alvin Hansen in 1953) accomplished was a static equilibrium postulation of economic activity "which wipes out the theory of effective demand in one stroke" (cf. Pasinetti 1974: 47). So completely did Hicks's interpretation eclipse the *General Theory* that Axel Leijonhvud was later able to observe that the "majority view on the theory of income determination" is the view one finds conventionally summarized in most textbooks in the familiar Hicks–Hansen IS–LM apparatus (1968: 4).

The success of the neo-Walrasian synthesis was not, however, the critical factor in undermining Keynes's theoretical revolution. The definitive factor was the emergence of mathematics and econometrics as indispensable techniques for research in economics. This outcome is largely the consequence of the development of game theory, the probability revolution and the perspective of economics as a predictive science. As it was for Morgenstern, the puzzle of prediction remained closely related to the phenomenon of the business cycle which also promoted the statistical verification of alternative hypotheses.

Tinbergen's work (1939, 1940) had already emphasized that the influence of unknown variables must be included in coming to grips with the causal relationships that underlie economic life. While the precise effect of an unknown causal factor is unpredictable, Trygve Haavelmo offered the thesis that it may be possible to make an empirically significant statement about the probability that a random variable will affect an outcome.[6] He argued that economists can provide themselves with a basis for testing hypotheses by adopting probability theory. In his view a theoretical model "will have an economic meaning only when associated with design of an actual experiment that describes and indicates how to measure – a system of 'true' variables (or objects) X_1, X_2, ..., X_n that are to be identified with the corresponding variables in the theory . . ." (Haavelmo 1943: 8). What follows is his argument that measurement errors, as evaluated by probability laws, can bridge the gap between the exactness of a "theory" and the accuracy of observational "fact". Under the direction of Jacob Marshak and his colleague Tjalling Koopmans econometric work at the Cowles Commission moved in the direction of a general equilibrium approach towards problem perception and a probability approach towards problem solution.

There is a substantial consensus that the Cowles Commission method offers an acceptable alternative to the experimental method in science by bringing theory and data together. This consensus holds sway despite the criticisms that the theory development role of applied econometrics has become downgraded relative to its theory testing role (Morgan 1990: 264) and that probability theory is not relevant under the conditions of uncertainty that characterize the real world (see Chapters 21 and 22).

III

Reliance on mathematics and econometrics as the chief vehicles for research in economics has characterized the discipline for only the last three or four decades. These reflect a clear line of descent from the macroeconomic modeling of Frisch and Tinbergen and the general equilibrium and game theoretical work of von Neumann, Morgenstern and Wald at Karl Menger's Vienna colloquium. The research environment of the professional economist has been modified to facilitate econometric research and to train graduate students to become proficient in mathematics and econometric techniques and to view prediction as the essence of economic science (Collander and Klammer 1991).

It has been urged that the history of the natural sciences, physics in particular, is something of a passkey for understanding both the neoclassical research program and the rise of econometrics. In particular, "The connections between the early Cowles Commission/Econometric Society group with contemporary physics has not yet received the attention which it deserves" (Mirowski 1989: 232). Given the antipathy which had developed by the 1930s against the deterministic aspects of neoclassical theory, which had largely been copied from nineteenth-century physics, the timing of the development of econometrics as a sister discipline of economics can certainly be read *à la* Mirowski as an intellectual movement to cut loose from deterministic models in much the same way as physicists had already relinquished determinism and embraced stochastic concepts.

Yet, without the change in the institutional environment of what may be termed "the economic knowledge industry" econometrics would simply coexist with other sub-fields of the discipline instead of achieving the place of dominance it, in fact, enjoys. The industry's "product" consists of economic models (micro as well as macro) that express interrelations in terms of dynamical equations whose coefficients are determined quantitatively by deriving statistically relevant information from real data. The computer revolution of the 1950s has made large-scale macrodynamic models a technical possibility. Hans Brems has recently described the setting of the period between the end of the Second World War and the Great Inflation as coinciding with "the third industrial revolution" which was set in motion by the advent of nuclear fission and the microchip (Brems 1986: 225–7). The former breakthrough launched the nuclear power industry, with its multiplicity of military and civilian applications; the latter is the foundation for high speed electronic computation. The long-term legacy of "high theory" for economics can only be understood in relation to the development of econometrics and the advent of the computer revolution. The modality of the computer determined, perhaps even dictated, the way in which analytical tools and concepts originating during the years of high theory would be harnessed into service in the task of economic model building. It changed the focus of the questions that economists asked and, more particularly, it changed the institutional environment within which economic research is undertaken. In responding to the resource allocation directives of grant availability and opportunities for contract research the "invisible college" of scientific practitioners in economics has principally bunched its "puzzle solving" activities to address problems that lend themselves to mathematization and econometric solution within a multi-equation framework.

Equally important is the perspective that prediction is the essence of science. The heuristic of the profession is that theoretical models acquire meaning only in terms of a properly specified stochastic model from which a set of values can be identified. Research efforts of this sort are typically the product of a large group effort. In contrast with the necessarily small-scale efforts of self-financed individual scholars working in a university setting, with only occasional internal or external support, today's economic knowledge industry is heavily dependent on research grants and contracts.[7] Its research style is one that was anticipated by the famous European colloquia and institutes that flourished, particularly in Germany and Austria, during the era of the Weimar Republic. These were typically separate from, or only loosely affiliated with, the old centers of higher learning, and also became intellectual magnates for visiting scholars (Szilard 1969: 36–7).

A predilection toward this research style was encouraged in America and England by the experiences of the First World War, which made the need for quantitative data apparent (Patinkin 1976) and gave impetus to funding the Brookings Institution (1916), the National Industrial Conference Board (1916) and the National Bureau of Economic Research (1920).[8] The symbiotic relationship that came into being between the Cowles program and its ability to generate funds made possible the employment of an extra-ordinarily talented group of researchers.[9] The move of the Cowles Commission to the University of Chicago in 1939 was important in establishing the economics knowledge industry as a large-scale operation. It marked the beginning of financial support by the Rockefeller Foundation, the National Bureau of Economic Research as well as the Social Science Research Committee of the University of Chicago and various sponsors in Canada and Europe. Thus the stage was set for the Cowles Commission to undertake a leading role in the American knowledge industry. Much of its early research related to the theory of resource allocation and was financed by the US Office of Naval Research, the Rand Corporation and the US Airforce, which gave rise to linear and nonlinear programming. By the 1950s the commission's objective became "to move gradually into the field of long run economics, while bringing to completion our attempts in the field of business cycle theory" and "to make possible discussions of specific issues of economic policies . . ." (Epstein 1987: 110).

Concern about the problem of less than full employment and the implementations of the Full Employment Act (1949) soon led to the construction of large Keynesian macroeconomic models. Laurence Klein became the chief advocate of the perspective that small models are inherently unsuited to the demands of economic policy (1986: 2067). Model builders of the 1950s, 1960s and 1970s had at their command the awesome capability information storage and processing facilitated by the microchip. The scope of their efforts has expanded steadily with the further development of econo-metric theory, improved data sets and the expanding capability of computer technology. These were spectacularly harnessed by several outstanding economist entrepreneurs – none more famous than Laurence Klein who together with Goldberger developed the Klein–Goldberger Macroeconomic Model (1953) which became the prototype for the Wharton Model, the Michigan Model, the Chase Econometric Model and the Data Resources Model developed by the late Otto Eckstein. Their commercial profitability was yet another step in the direction of establishing econometrics as the chief tool of the economics knowledge industry. The essential complementarity between forecasting and prediction shaped the economic knowledge industry by advancing prediction as the *sine qua non* of scientific economics. The prescribed method has become to express a hypothesis in terms of an equation, and to follow this by estimation to identify the best fit in order to adjust the theoretical argument to rationalize the hypothesis being tested

(Ward 1972: 146–52). Thus, the acid test of a "good" theory is how well it "predicts" rather than the tenability of its assumptions or the quality or relevance of the data to the hypothesis being tested and its usefulness as a policy tool.

Econometric tools have had their greatest impact on macroeconomic theory and policy. Friedman's 1956 paper "The quantity theory of money: a restatement" may be interpreted as "the second salvo" in the counter Keynesian revolution (i.e. if we think of Hicks's IS–LM as encapsulating the first). Whereas Hicks offered a purely theoretical rebuttal to Keynes, Friedman's "counter-revolution" is predicated on a substantial body of empirical work relating to the quantity of money (Friedman and Schwarz 1963). His chief finding, based on the study of price movements in the United States during the Civil War and the two World Wars is that price and income changes during each of three periods is more readily explainable by the quantity theory than by Keynes's income–expenditure theory (Friedman 1952: 621). Unemployment, Friedman argued, "cannot be attributed to an inherent flaw in the price system; it requires an explanation in terms of such other forces as requisites in adjustable external disturbances and the like" (Friedman 1959: 138). Thus by the 1970s the economics profession was fully conditioned, four decades after the years of high theory began, to *expect* empirically established theorems.

This mindset is especially apparent in the subsequent development of the so-called "New Classical" macroeconomics, which appeared in the late 1970s and which has substantially replaced the IS–LM model. So overwhelming was its progress that Alan Blinder encapsulated its remarkable success as follows:

> By about 1980 it as hard to find an American academic macroeconomist under the age of 40 who professed to be a Keynesian. That was an astonishing intellectual turnabout in less than a decade – an intellectual revolution for sure ... the young were recruited disproportionately into the new classical ranks.... By 1980 or so, the adage that there are no Keynesians under the age of 40 was part of the folklore of the (American) economics profession.
>
> (1988: 278)

The transformation was carried out within a framework which focused on constructing "microfoundations" for macroeconomic conclusions on the basis of rational expectations and equilibrium modeling techniques. These "new methods" are

> constructed so as to predict how agents with stable tastes and technology will *choose* to respond to a new situation (Lucas 1977: 220–1). These are "the main ingredients for a mathematically explicit theory of general equilibrium: an artificial system in which households and firms jointly

solve explicit, "static", maximization problems, taking prices as parametrically given.

(Lucas 1980: 277–8)

Thus it is quite clear that the research program for developing the microfoundations of macroeconomics has been built on theoretical constructs and
model building techniques that have their roots not in the innovations of "high
theory" but rather in the tradition that originated in Vienna, and which was
transplanted via the London School to Chicago and Yale from whence it
substantially commandeered and redirected the research effort of professional
economists towards a choice theoretic formalism. With benefit of hindsight,
it is clear that, contrary to Shackle's evaluation, the innovations of high theory
have by no means "altered the orientation and character of economics".

NOTES

1   Without intending to specifically invoke either a Lakatosian growth of knowledge framework (1964, 1971) or a Kuhnian puzzle-solving view of development
of science (1957, 1970) it is nevertheless useful to relate the innovations of high
theory to the problem areas that were identified in the 1920s and 1930s.
2   The cost controversy also had significant methodological implications; economists who were concerned about the question whether the size of a firm is limited
by the tendency toward rising supply price (Kaldor 1934; E. A. G. Robinson
1931, 1941) were also concerned with the importance of empirical verification
and the descriptive accuracy of the behavioral assumptions that economists
made. The latter were of central importance throughout the marginalist controversy (Hall and Hitch 1939, Lester 1946, 1947; Machlup 1946, 1947)
becoming blunted only after Friedman's *Essay on Positive Economics* (1953) by
the shift in the economics focus towards interest in the "goodness" of a theory's
prediction rather than the realism of the assumptions.
3   In view of E. Roy Weintraub's comprehensive exploration of the modern
development of general equilibrium analysis (1985) it is sufficient here only to
note the aforementioned facts which are germane to the argument about to be
developed.
4   It is also relevant that Arthur Marget, who reviewed Morgenstern's *Wirtschaft-
prognose*, noted that "the formal technique of probability analysis can only
rarely, if ever, be applied to economic data with any hope of obtaining reasonably
significant results" (Marget 1929: 315). Presumably he would make the same
comment in relation to the probabilistic approach that later became associated
with the Cowles Commission econometric technique.
5   The famous Bertrand examples are determinate only because of the conjectures
made about the behavior of the competing duopolists.
6   Ragnar Frisch's formulation of mathematical laws of economic behavior (1929)
stands as an important forerunner, less for being based on statistical data such as
Tinbergen's than for envisioning the possibility of establishing economics as a
predictive science. At the time of Frisch's early work, the relevance of
mathematical discourse for addressing questions arising in the "moral sciences",
like economics and psychology, had already been considered by J. M. Keynes in
a work that was unrelated to his interest in economics. Long before his *Treatise
on Money* and his later *General Theory*, Keynes had reached the now well known

conclusion in *Theory of Probability* (1921) that

> where our experience is complete, we cannot hope to derive from it judgements of probability without the aid of intuition or of some further *a priori* principle.

7 Mitchell's work on business cycles became the prototype for its research program whose objective was to collect statistical data and develop statistical techniques.
8 Britain had little organized economic research during the interwar period. Indeed, the National Institute of Economic and Social Research, the British counterpart of the National Bureau, was not founded until 1938 and little significant research was accomplished until after the war. Neither private nor public government funds were available to fund research in England on a scale comparable with what was available in the United States.
9 The story of the founding and early years of the Cowles Commission has been told by Carl Christ (1952) with due attention to both the technical aspects and the personalities involved. Other Europeans who joined with the Cowles Commission during the prewar period were Oskar Lange, George Katona, Leonid Hurwicz, Martin Beckman, Horst Mendershausen, Jacob Mosak, Gerard Titner, Abraham Wald (Christ 1952).
10 There was remarkable similarity between the formal structure of Koopman's model and the Air Force procurement and deployment models of George Dantzig, Marshall Wood and Murray Geisler. The insights which were derived from the von Neumann–Morgenstern *Theory of Games* led to the recognition that a two-person zero sum game is the mathematical equivalent of a linear programming problem. This work was a prelude to the Cowles Commission Monograph 13, edited by Koopmans and published under the title *Activity Analysis of Production and Allocation*.
11 Some degree of appreciation of the rapidly developing field of macroeconomic modeling shortly before the publication of the *General Theory* can be gleaned from a perusal of volume 3 of *Econometrica* (1935) which included three papers from the Lieden survey "Suggestions of quantitative business cycle theory", and Ragnar Frisch and Harold Holme on "The characteristic solution of a mixed difference and differential equation occurring in economic dynamics". Also relevant for establishing this rapidly emerging area is Charles Roos's "A mathematical theory of price and production fluctuations and economic crises".

REFERENCES

Allen, R. G. D. (1940) "Review of T. Haavelmo: *The Probability Approach in Econometrics*, *American Economic Review* 36: 161–3.
Anderson, R. L. (1945) "Review of T. Haavelmo: *The Probability Approach in Econometrics*", *Journal of the American Statistical Association* 40: 393–4.
Arrow, K. J. and Debrue, G. (1954) "Existence of an equilibrium for a competitive economy", *Econometrica* 22 (July): 265–90.
Arrow, K. J. and Hurwicz, L. (1958) "On the stability of the competitive economy", *Econometrica* 26 (October): 522–52.
Baumol, William J. and Goldfeld, Stephen M. (eds) (1968) *Precursors in Mathematical Economics*, LSE Series of Reprints of Scarce Works on Political Economy No. 19, London: London School of Economics.
Bennion, E. G. (1952) "The Cowles Commission's simultaneous equations approach: a simplified explanation", *Review of Economics and Statistics*: 49–56.

Begg, D. K. H. (1982) *The Rational Expectations Revolution in Macroeconomics*, Baltimore, MD.

Blaug, Mark (1980) *The Methodology of Economics*, Cambridge: Cambridge University Press.

Blinder, Alan (1988) "The rise and fall of Keynesian economics", *Economic Record* 64: 278–94.

Brems, H. (1986) *Pioneering Economic Theory 1630–1980*, Baltimore, MD: Johns Hopkins University Press.

Burns, Arthur, and Mitchell, Wesley (1946) *Measuring Business Cycles*, New York: National Bureau of Economic Research.

Casson, M. (1984) *Economics of Unemployment*, Cambridge, MA.

Chamberlain, E. H. (1933) *The Theory of Monopolistic Competition*, 6th edn, Cambridge, MA.

Christ, C. F. (1952) "History of the Cowles Commission 1932–67", in *Economic Theory and Measurement*, Chicago, IL: Cowles Commission, pp. 3–67.

——— (1967a) "A short-run aggregate demand model of the interdependence and effects of monetary and fiscal policies with Keynesian and classical interest elasticities", *American Economic Review* 57: 434–43.

——— (1967b) "A model of monetary and fiscal policy effects on the money stock, price level and real output", *Journal of Money, Credit and Banking* 4 (November): 683–705.

Clower, R. (1975) "Reflections on the Keynesian perplex", *Zeitschrift für Nationalökonmie* 35: 1–24.

Coats, A. W. (1969) "Research priorities in the history of economics", *History of Political Economy* 1 (1): 9–18.

Collander, D. and Klammer, A. (1991) "The education of economists from undergraduate to graduate study", *Journal of Economic Literature* September.

Dantzig, George B. (1951) "A proof of the equivalence of the programming problem and the game problem", in T. J. Koopmans (ed.) *Activity Analysis of Production and Allocation*, New York: Wiley, pp. 330–5.

Debreu, G. (1959) *The Theory of Value: An Axiomatic Analysis of Economic Equilibrium*, New Haven, CT, and London.

——— (1984) "Economic theory in the mathematical mode", *American Economic Review* 74 (3): 267–78.

De Vroey, Michael (1975) "The transition from classical to neoclassical economics: a scientific revolution", *Journal of Economic Issues* 9 (3).

Di Marchi, N. and Gilbert, C. (1989) "Introduction", *Oxford Economic Papers* 41: 1–11.

Duesenberry, J. S., Fromm, G., Klein, L. R. and Kuhn, E. (1965) *The Brookings Quarterly Econometric Model of the United States*, Chicago, IL.

Eckstein, O., Green, E. W. and Sinai, A. (1974) "The Data Resources Model: uses, structure and analysis of the U.S. economy", *International Economic Review* 15: 595–615.

Epstein, Roy (1987) *A History of Econometrics*, New York: Elsevier.

Friedman, Milton (1953) "The methodology of positive economics", *Essays on Positive Economics*, Chicago, IL: University of Chicago Press.

——— (1960) *A Program for Monetary Stability*, New York: Fordham University Press.

——— (1968) "The role of monetary policy", reprinted in *The Optimum Quantity of Money and Other Essays*, Chicago, IL: Aldine, pp. 97–110.

Friedman, Milton, and Schwarz, Anna J. (1963) *A Monetary History of the United States, 1867–1960*, National Bureau of Economic Research Studies in Business

Cycles No. 12, Princeton, NJ: Princeton University Press.

Frisch, R. (1929) "Correlation and scales in statistical variables", *Nordic Statistical Journal* 8: 36–102.

Garegnani, P. (1976) "On the change in notions of equilibrium in recent works on values and distribution", in M. Broron, K. Sato and P. Zaremba (eds) *Essays in Modern Capital Theory*, Amsterdam.

Goldberger, Arthur S. (1972) "Structural equation methods in the social sciences", *Econometrica* 40 (6): 979–1001.

Gordon, Robert J. (1976) "Some recent developments in the theory of inflation and unemployment", *Journal of Monetary Economics* 2: 185–219.

Haavelmo, T. (1943) "The statistical implications of a system of simultaneous equations", *Econometrica* 11: 1–12.

—— (1944) *The Probability Approach in Econometrics*, Supplement to *Econometrica* 12.

Haberler, G. (1937, 1941) *Prosperity and Depression*, Geneva.

Hahn, F. H. (1973) *On the Notion of Equilibrium Economics*, Cambridge: Cambridge University Press.

—— (1978) "Keynesian economics and general equilibrium theory: reflections on some current debates", in G. C. Harcourt (ed.) *The Microeconomic Foundations of Macroeconomics*, London.

Hall, R. L. and Hitch, C. J. (1939) "Price theory and business behavior", *Oxford Economic Papers* 2: 12–45.

Hansen, Alvin (1941) *Fiscal Policy and Business Cycles*, New York.

—— (1949) *Monetary Theory and Fiscal Policy*, New York.

—— (1951) *Business Cycles and National Income*, New York.

Hansson, B. A. (1982) *The Stockholm School and the Development of Economic Method*, London: Croom Helm.

Harrod, R. F. (1936) *The Trade Cycle*, Oxford: Clarendon.

Hawtrey, R. A. (1913) *Good and Bad Trade*, London: Constable.

—— (1926) "The monetary theory of the trade cycle and its statistical test", *Quarterly Journal of Economics* 41: 471–86.

von Hayek, F. A. (1931) *Preise and Produktion*, Vienna, translated as *Prices and Production*, London.

—— (1939) *Profits, Interest and Investment*.

Hendry, D. R. (1980) "Econometrics – alchemy or science?", *Econometrica* 5: 147–59.

Hicks, J. R. (1937) "Mr. Keynes and the 'Classics': a suggested interpretation", *Econometrica* 5: 147–59.

—— (1939a) *Value and Capital*, 2nd edn, Oxford: Clarendon.

—— (1939b) "Foundations of welfare economics", *Economic Journal* December: 696–712.

—— (1974) *The Crisis of Keynesian Economics*, Oxford.

—— (1983) "A skeptical follower", *The Economist*, June 18: 17–19.

Hildreth, Clifford (1986) *The Cowles Commission in Chicago 1939–1955*, Berlin: Springer.

Hotelling, H. (1929) "Stability in competition", *Economic Journal* 39 (March): 41–57.

Jaffe, William (1977) "The normative bias of the Walrasian model: Walras vs. Gossen", *Quarterly Journal of Economics*.

Kaldor, Nicholas (1934) "On the determination of equilibrium", *Review of Economic Studies*.

Kalman, R. E. (1982) "Dynamic economic models", in G.P. Szego (ed.) *New*

Quantitative Techniques for Economic Analysis, New York: Academic Press.

Keynes, J. M. (1921) *Theory of Probability*, London.

—— (1931) *A Treatise on Money, 2 vols*, London.

—— (1936) *The General Theory of Employment, Interest and Money*, London.

—— (1973) *Collected Works*, Vol. XIV, ed. D. Moggridge, London: Macmillan.

Keynes, J. M. and Tinbergen, Jan (1939, 1940) "Professor Tinbergen's method" (Review of J. Tinbergen, *League of Nations*, vol. 1, 1939), *Economic Journal*: 8–68. "A reply" by Tinbergen and "Comment" by Keynes, *Economic Journal*: 141–56.

Klein, L. R. (1947) *The Use of Econometrics as a Guide to Economic Policy*.

—— (1950) *Economic Fluctuations in the United States: 1921–1944*, New York.

Koopmans, T. C. (1937) *Linear Regression Analysis of Economic Time Series*, Haarlem: Netherlands Economic Institute.

—— (1945) "Statistical estimation of simultaneous economic relations", *Journal of the American Statistical Association* 40: 448–66.

—— (1947) "Measurement without theory", *Review of Economics and Statistics* 29: 161–72, reprinted in *Readings in Business Cycle Theory*, Blakiston: AEA.

—— (ed.) (1950) *Statistical Inference in Dynamic Economic Models*, Cowles Commission Monograph 10, New York: Wiley.

—— (1951) "Analysis of production as an efficient combination of activities", in T. C. Koopmans (ed.) *Activity Analysis of Production and Allocation*, Cowles Commission Monograph 13, New York: Wiley, pp. 33–97.

—— (1957) "Allocation of resources and the price system", in T. C. Koopmans (ed.) *Three Essays on the State of Economic Science*, New York.

Lange, O. (1944) *Price Flexibility and Employment*, Cowles Commission Monograph 8, Bloomington, IN: Princeton Press.

Lawson, Tony (1985) "Keynes, prediction and econometrics", in T. Lawson and H. Peseron (eds) *Keynes Economics Methodological Issue*, London: Croom Helm.

Lee, F. S. (1981) "The Oxford challenge to Marshallian supply and demand", *Oxford Economic Papers*: 339–49.

Leijonhvud, Axel (1968) *On Keynesian Economics and the Economics of Keynes*, New York: Oxford University Press.

—— (1983) "What was the matter with IS–LM?", in J. P. Fitousi (ed.) *Modern Macroeconomics*, Oxford: Blackwell.

Leontief, W. (1948) "Econometrics", in H. S. Ellis (ed.) *A Survey of Contemporary Economics*, Philadelphia and Toronto.

Lester, R. D. (1946) "Shortcomings of marginal analysis for wage employment problems", *American Economic Review* 37: 135–48.

Lucas, R. (1980) "Methods and problems in business cycle theory"; reprinted in *Studies in Business Cycle Theory*, Cambridge: MA: MIT Press, 1981, pp. 271–96.

—— (1983) Interview by Arjo Klamer in *Conversations with Economists*, Totowa, NJ: Rowman & Allanheld, 1984.

—— (1988) "Monetary demand in the United States: a quantitative review", Carnegie Rochester Series on Public Policy, pp. 137–67.

Machlup, F. (1946) "Marginal analysis and empirical research", *American Economic Review* 36.

Marchak, J. (1946) "Neumann's and Morgenstern's new approach to static economics", *Journal of Political Economy* 54 (2): 97–115.

—— (1947) "Quantitative research in agricultural economics: the interdependencies of agriculture and the national economy", *Journal of Farm Economics*.

—— (1950) "Introduction", in T. C. Koopmans (ed.) *Statistical Inference in Dynamic Economic Models*, Cowles Commission Monograph 10, New York: Wiley.

Marget, Arthur (1929) "Morgenstern on the Methodology of Economic Forecasting", *Journal of Political Economy* 37: 312–39.

Marshall, Alfred (1898) *Principles of Economics*, 8th edn, London: Macmillan.

McKenzie, L. W. (1959) "On the existence of general equilibrium for a competitive market", *Econometrica* 27: (January): 54–71.

Milgate, Murray (1988) "Equilibrium: development of the concept", in S. Eatwell, M. Milgate and P. Newman (eds) *The New Palgrave Dictionary of Economics*, vol. 2, London, Macmillan, pp. 179–82.

Mirowski, P. (1989) "The probabilistic counter revolution, or how stochastic concepts came to neoclassical theory", *Oxford Economic Papers* 41: 217–35.

Mitchell, Wesley C. (1913) *Business Cycles*, Berkeley, CA: University of California Press.

Morgan, Mary S. (1990) *The History of Econometric Ideas*, Cambridge: Cambridge University Press.

Morgenstern, Oscar (1928) *Wirtshaftsprognose: Eine Untersuchuno ihrer Voraussetzungen und Mocklichkeiten*, Vienna: Julius Springer.

——— (1941) "Professor Hicks on value and capital", *Journal of Political Economy* 49.

——— (1976) "Collaborating with von Neumann", *Journal of Economic Literature* 14 (3): 805–16.

Muth, J. F. (1961) "Rational expectations and the theory of price movements", *Econometrica* 29 (July): 315–35.

Myrdahl, G. (1939) *Monetary Equilibrium*, London: Hodge.

von Neumann, J. (1937) "Über ein ökonomisches Gleichungsstem und eine Verallgemeinerung des Brouwerschen Fixpunktsatzes", *Ergebnisse eines mathematischen Killoquiums 8*, Leipzig and Vienna, pp. 73–83; translated by G. Morgenstern in W. J. Baumol and S. M. Goldfeld (eds) *Precursors in Mathematical Economics: An Anthology*, London, 1968, pp. 296, 306.

von Neumann, J. and Morgenstern, O. (1944) *Theory of Games and Economic Behavior*, Princeton, NJ: Princeton University Press; second corrected edition, 1947.

Passinetti, L. (1974) *Growth and Income Distribution, Essays in Economic Theory*, Cambridge: Cambridge University Press.

Patinkin, D. (1956) *Money, Interest and Prices*, Evanston, IL, and White Plains, NY.

——— (1976) "Keynes and econometrics", *Econometrica* 44: 1091–1123.

Phillips, A. W. (1958) "The relations between unemployment and the rate of change of money wage rates in the United Kingdom, 1861–1957", *Econometrica* 25 (November): 283, 299.

Pigou, A. C. (1912) *Wealth and Welfare*, London: Macmillan.

——— (1914) *Unemployment*, New York: Holt.

——— (1922) "Empty economic boxes: a reply", *Economic Journal* 12: 463.

——— (1927) *The Economic Position of Great Britain*, London: Royal Economic and Cambridge Economic Service.

——— (1931) *Evidence: Minutes of Evidence taken before the Committee on Finance and Industry*, vol. II, London: His Majesty's Stationery Office.

Reder, Melvin (1988) "Chicago economics: permanence and change", *Journal of Economic Literature* (March): 1–38.

Rima, Ingrid (1988) "Keynes' vision and econometric analysis" in O. Hamouda and J. Smithin (eds) *Keynes and Public Policy After 50 Years*, Chichester: Edward Elgar.

Robbins, L. (1930) "On certain ambiguity in the concept of stationary equilibrium", *Economic Journal*.

Robertson, D. (1933) "Saving and hoarding", *Economic Journal* September: 399–443.

Robinson, E. A. G. (1931) *The Structure of Competitive Industry*, London: Cambridge University Press.

—— (1941) *Monopoly*, London: Cambridge University Press.

Robinson, Joan (1933) *The Economics of Imperfect Competition*, London.

—— (1953) "Imperfect competition revisited", *Economic Journal* 63: 579–93.

Rowley, Robin (1988) "The Keynes–Tinbergen exchange in retrospect", in O. Hamouda and J. Smithin (eds) *Keynes and Public Policy After 50 Years*, Chichester: Edward Elgar.

Samuelson, P. A. (1947) *Foundations of Economic Analysis*, Cambridge, MA.

Sargent, T. J. (1973) "Rational expectations, the real rate of interest and the natural rate of unemployment", *Brookings Papers on Economic Activity*: 429–72.

Schumpeter, J. A. (1928) "On the instability of capitalism", *Economic Journal*: 361–86.

—— (1936) "Review of general theory", *Journal of the American Statistical Association* 31 (December): 791–5.

Shackle, G. S. L. (1967) *Years of High Theory*, Cambridge: Cambridge University Press.

Shubik, M. (1983) *Game Theory in the Social Sciences*, Cambridge, MA: Cambridge Press.

Sraffa, P. (1926) "The laws of returns under competitive conditions", *Economic Journal* 36 (December): 535–50.

Szilard, Lev (1969) "Reminiscences", in Donald Fleming and Bernard Barlyn (eds) *The Intellectual Migration*, Cambridge, MA: Harvard University Press.

Tinbergen, J. (1939) *Statistical Test of Business-Cycle Theories: vol I, A Method and Its Application to Investment Activities: vol II, Business Cycles in the United States of America, 1919–1932*, Geneva.

—— (1940) "Econometric business cycle research", *Review of Economic Studies* 7: 73–90.

—— (1959) "Zur Theorie de Langfristigen Wirtschaftsentwicklung", *Weltw. Archiv* (May 1942), 55, 511, 549; translated in L. H. Klassen, L. M. Koyck and H. J. Witteveen (eds) *Jan Tinbergen, Selected Papers*, Amsterdam.

Vining, Rutledge (1949) "Koopmans on the choice of variables to be studied and of methods of measurement", *Review of Economic Statistics* 312 (2): 77–86. Reply by Koopmans, pp. 86–91; rejoinder by Vining, pp. 91–4.

Wald, A. (1935) "Über die eindeutige positive Losbarketi der neuen Produktionsgleichungen", *Ergebnisse eines mathematischen Kolloquiums* 6, Leipzig and Vienna, pp. 12–18; translated as "On the unique non-negative solvability of the new production equations" by W. J. Baumol in *Precursors in Mathematical Economics: An Anthology*, London, 1968, pp. 281–8.

Walras, L. (1954) *Elements d'Economie Politique Pure*, Lausanne, Paris and Basle, 1874–7; translated as *Elements of Pure Economics or the Theory of Social Wealth* by W. Jaffe, Homewood, IL.

Ward, Benjamin (1972) *What's Wrong With Economics?*, New York: Basic Books.

Weintraub, E. R. (1979) *Microfoundations*, Cambridge: Cambridge University Press.

—— (1983) "On the existence of a competitive equilibrium: 1930–1954", *Journal of Economic Literature* 21: 1–39.

—— (1985) *General Equilibrium Analysis*, Cambridge: Cambridge University Press.

Weintraub, S. (1982) "Money demand motives: a reconsideration", *Economie Appliqué*: 365–84.

Wells, P. (1981) "Keynes demand for finance", *Journal of Post-Keynesian Economics* 3: 586–9.

Wicksell, K. (1907) "The influence of the rate of interest on prices", *Economic Journal* 17 (June): 213–20.

Chapter 13

The right person, in the right place, at the right time
How mathematical expectations came into macroeconomics

Bradley W. Bateman

Two of the stylized facts about modern macroeconomics are that Maynard Keynes invented it in 1936 with the publication of his *General Theory of Employment, Interest and Money* and that this basic apparatus was supplanted by the rational expectations revolution in the 1970s. While there is just enough substance behind each of these two myths for them to have become widespread, they hide as much as they reveal about the true evolution of ideas that led to modern macroeconomics. In particular, they hide the fact that Keynes was the first theorist to introduce an explicit analytical model of expectations into macroeconomics. Contrary to the canard begun by Paul Samuelson, in his obituary notice of Keynes, that the *General Theory* "paves the way for a theory of expectation, but it hardly provides one" (1946: 320) it is actually the case that Keynes was the product of an intellectual tradition that had paved the way for a theory of expectation, but he ultimately had to provide it himself.[1]

EXPECTATIONS IN THE CAMBRIDGE TRADITION

The need for a theory of expectations in the explanation of aggregate economic behavior was always implicit in the Cambridge tradition in which Keynes was trained. From the time of the "founding" of the school in 1885, when Alfred Marshall returned to Cambridge to take the chair of Political Economy, Cambridge theorists routinely explained the business cycle as the result of errors of optimism and pessimism on the part of businessmen. This explanation of the cycle actually dated from at least 1837 with Lord Overstone, and was formally adopted by Marshall and his wife, Mary Marshall, in 1879 with the publication of their *Economics of Industry*. There the Marshalls describe how confidence and "her magic wand" (p. 155) can excite businessmen's expectations of profit and how these expectations ultimately end in a situation in which businessmen lose their confidence and a "trade storm" ensues.[2] Marshall repeated these arguments verbatim in his *Principles* (1890) and redeveloped them in *Money, Credit and Commerce* (1923) which was published shortly before his death.

A. C. Pigou, successor to the chair upon Marshall's retirement in 1908, continued this tradition in each of the books he published which dealt with the business cycle: *Wealth and Welfare* (1912), *Unemployment* (1913), *The Economics of Welfare* (1920) and *Industrial Fluctuations* (1927). Marshall referred approvingly to the arguments about confidence in *The Economics of Welfare* in his own *Money, Credit and Commerce*, and it was those parts of Pigou's book which dealt with "errors of optimism and pessimism" which were ultimately separated out to form the core of *Industrial Fluctuations*. Here he described how "the varying expectations of businessmen ... and not anything else, constitute the immediate and direct causes or antecedents of industrial fluctuations" (1927: 33–4).

But, as Robert Bigg (1990) has pointed out, there was a striking asymmetry in the writings of Marshall and Pigou on expectations. While both of Keynes's teachers posited "errors of optimism and pessimism" as the causes of macroeconomic fluctuations, both also argued that uncertainty in the micro-economic setting was "an *objective* property which all well informed persons would estimate in the same way" (Marshall 1964: 77n., italics in original). Neither Marshall nor Pigou ever addressed the question why people would act rationally and "objectively" in one context and not another, but both maintained the firewall between their arguments throughout their careers.[3] In fact, it is illustrative of the asymmetrical nature of their arguments that both were eventually to segregate their macroeconomic arguments into separate books.

Many feasible arguments can be adduced as to how and why two theorists of this stature could each propound such self-contradictory arguments. Nor can we doubt that contradiction exists in the argument for both Marshall and Pigou posited their objective uncertainty arguments in the context of investment activity, which is subject to repeated miscalculation. Both proceeded in terms of situation in which expectations were crucial to understanding macroeconomic phenomena. What they omitted was an *analytical* treatment of expectations. To paraphrase Samuelson, "Marshall and Pigou paved the way for a theory of expectation, but they had hardly provided one"; for one of the things which undoubtedly allowed them to persist in their inconsistency was the fact that they merely *talked about* expectations, but never formally introduced an explicit model to represent their ideas. Had they ever tried to *formalize* their statements, the incongruities would have been impossible to ignore.

INTELLIGENT ANTICIPATIONS AND THE MAGIC FORMULA MENTALITY

At first sight Maynard Keynes might appear to be the perfect candidate to resolve the conflict in Marshall's and Pigou's work. He was, after all, the author of *A Treatise on Probability* (1921) and his degree was in mathematics.

But despite the fact that he had advocated an objective theory of probability in *Probability*, Keynes was actually a bad bet to serve as the person who would provide an *analytical* underpinning for the treatment of expectations in Cambridge macroeconomics.

The reason for this is not far to seek, for in *Probability* Keynes had largely dismissed the possibility that uncertainty was a tractable problem. While he believed probability to be objective and the "guide of life" (1921: 321), he believed it was measurable in only a very limited number of cases.[4] Thus his well-known conclusion:

> The hope, which sustained many investigators in the course of the nineteenth century, of gradually bringing the moral sciences under the sway of mathematical reasoning, steadily recedes – if we mean, as they meant, by mathematics the introduction of precise numerical methods. The old assumptions, that all quantity is numerical and that all quantitative characteristics are additive, can be no longer sustained. Mathematical reasoning now appears as an aid in its symbolic rather than in its numerical character. I, at any rate, have not the same lively hope as Condorcet, or even as Edgeworth, "éclaire les Sciences morales et politiques par le flambeau de l'Algébre". In the present case, even if we are able to range goods in order of magnitude, and also their probabilities in order of magnitude, yet it does not follow that we can range the products composed of each good and its corresponding probability in this order.
>
> (1921: 316)

Keynes had postulated that probability is a real, objective entity akin to a Platonic essence, which he believed people intuited directly in order to make decisions, but he refused to allow that it is measurable. In this he reflected the influence of his mentor G. E. Moore, who believed that goodness is a directly intuited entity but not measurable. For better or worse, this made Keynes the wrong person to provide an analytical basis for expectations in economics.

In a nice irony, however, Keynes's first two works in macroeconomics provide two quite different resolutions to the problem of the asymmetry in Marshall's and Pigou's arguments. He achieved this by first rejecting the idea that businessmen make systematic errors and then later by rejecting altogether the traditional Cambridge explanation of business cycles.

In his first major work in macroeconomics, *A Tract on Monetary Reform* (1923), Keynes considers the effects of changes in credit conditions and prices on businessmen's expectations of profits (pp. 17–25) and on the expectations of "the investing class" (i.e. those who save money and provide the funds for investment), but he stops short of providing a theory of the business cycle. "[I]t is beyond the scope of this volume to deal adequately with the diagnosis and analysis of the credit cycle" (1923: 204). The reason why is not clear since he easily says as much as Marshall had about fluctuations in business expectations. It is conceivable that he wanted to extend the idea of an objective uncertainty to businessmen's macroeconomic behavior but preferred not to differ with Marshall in print.

Like Marshall, Keynes talks at length about the possibility that a rise in prices will stimulate expectations of greater profits among businessmen, but unlike Marshall he never refers to these expectations as being in *error*. Quite the contrary, using the example of recent inflation in Britain, Keynes develops an idea of "intelligent anticipation" (1923: 23).

> Take, for example the *Statist* index number for raw materials month by month from April 1919 to March 1920:

April 1919	100	October	127
May	108	November	131
June	112	December	135
July	117	January 1920	142
August	120	February	150
September	121	March	146

> It follows from this table that a man, who borrowed money from his banker and used the proceeds to purchase raw materials selected at random, stood to make a profit in every single month of this period with the exception of the last, and would have cleared 46 per cent on the average of the year. Yet bankers were not charging at this time above 7 per cent for their advances, leaving a clear profit of between 30 and 40 per cent per annum, without the exercise of any particular skill, to any person lucky enough to have embarked on these courses. How much more were the opportunities of persons whose business position and expert knowledge enabled them to exercise intelligent anticipation as to the probable course of prices of particular commodities!
>
> (1923: 23–4)

The real essence of Keynes's argument also comes through in "Changes in the value of money, as affecting production", the concluding section of his first chapter. Here he argues explicitly for a monetary policy that stops fluctuations in the price level since *it is the expectation of the continuation of such fluctuations which perpetuates the cycle*. Thus, it is the "intelligent anticipation" of fluctuations which causes their continuation and only a policy of *expected stability* can work to effectively stop this.

> It is one of the objects of this book to urge that the best way to cure this mortal disease of individualism is to provide that there shall never exist any confident expectation either that prices generally are going to fall or that they are going to rise; and also that there shall be no serious risk that a movement, if it does occur, will be a big one. If, unexpectedly and accidentally, a moderate movement were to occur, wealth, though it might be redistributed, would not be diminished thereby.

To procure this result by removing all possible influences towards an initial movement, whether such influences are to be found in the skies only or everywhere, would seem to be a hopeless enterprise. The remedy would lie, rather, in so controlling the standard of value that, whenever something occurred which, left to itself, would create an expectation of a change in the general level of prices, the controlling authority should take steps to counteract this expectation by setting in motion some factor of a contrary tendency.

(1923: 43)

In the most fundamental sense, Keynes's argument removes the *ground* for the inconsistency in Marshall's and Pigou's argument. It provides both an argument for removing the fluctuations that cause changes in expectations and, more importantly, a suggestion that such changes in expectation are really an "intelligent anticipation" of the course of things, rather than errors of optimism and pessimism.

By the time Keynes got to the conclusion of his *Treatise on Money* seven years later, however, his resolution of the inconsistency in Marshall's and Pigou's argument rested on a completely different ground. Expectations are present in the *Treatise*, especially in Keynes's discussion of the "two views", or how bulls and bears influence the stock market, but this is not central to his *theoretical apparatus* which compared with the *Tract* seems to dictate the relative unimportance of expectations. Don Patinkin has spoken of the "magic formula mentality" of the *Treatise* to describe Keynes's reliance on his "fundamental equations" to explain substantially everything (in a manner which is often quite mechanical). Keynes himself comes close to admitting that this is his perspective when he refers to his position as one of a person who believes in "some magic mathematical formula" (1930: 340).[5] The gist of this magic formula (i.e. the fundamental equations) is that business cycles are caused by interest rate disequilibria which lead to disequilibria between savings and investment and which, in their turn, cause fluctuations in employment and prices. The mathematical tightness of his formulas enabled Keynes to speak of his "scientific explanation of booms and slumps (and of much else, I should claim) which I offer you" (1931b, in *CW*, XIII, p. 354).

The "scientific" nature of Keynes's apparatus, and the certitude with which he spoke when employing it, allowed him to remove expectations as a cause of cycles; someone wanting to study the cycle need only look at differences between the natural and the market rates of interest to understand what was happening. Indeed, expectations are still explicit in his treatment of the economy, but they are minimized in two distinct ways. The first occurs in his chapter on fixed investment in which he again attributes new investment to the expectation of future profit. These expectations are tied explicitly to Schumpeter's theory of the introduction of inventions and innovations in productive techniques and thus are quite independent of the possibility of waves of confidence and trade storms. The second way of minimizing the role of expectations comes in Keynes's arguments manipulating long-run interest rates via changes in short-term rates (i.e. the bank rate). While Keynes acknowledges (1930: II, pp. 352–62) that bond holders and speculators often base their expectations on "mob psychology", this is actually a *deus ex machina* since it provides him with a convenient means of affecting rates on long-term bonds when the banking system's "main, direct influence" (1930: II, p. 352) is over short rates.[6] Thus, rather than bringing uncertainty into his analysis of what *causes* the cycle, it becomes a means to facilitate the authority's *control* of cycles. "We may carry away, therefore, to the next section of our argument the conclusion that short-term rates influence long-term rates more than the reader might expect, and that it is not difficult to find sufficient explanations for this observed behavior" (1930: II, p. 362).

Because it represents Keynes's prose at its best and most humorous, it would be a shame not to close this explanation of how Keynes displaced the Marshall–Pigou theory of the cycle without considering his one explicit allusion to it in the *Treatise*. In one of the draft chapters that has survived there is actually a reference to "Professor Pigou's somewhat mythical 'psychological errors of optimism and pessimism'" (*CW*, XIII, p. 89) but this passage does not survive into the final text. What does survive is an amusing account of how the causes of cycles can be misdiagnosed.

> For example, a change-over in the type of production from investment-goods to consumption-goods (or *vice versa*) does not, on account of the period occupied by the process of production, produce its results in the market until after an appreciable time has elapsed. Thus, as we have seen, the price stimulus to a change-over is apt to be continued until some time after the necessary steps have been taken. The result often is that the remedy is overdone. It is as though the family were to go on giving a child successive doses of castor-oil every ten minutes until the first dose had done its work. Or – to take a better parallel – it is as though different members of the family were to give successive doses to the child, each in ignorance of the doses given by the others. The child will be very ill. Bismuth will then be administered on the same principle. Scientists will announce that children are subject to a diarrhoea–constipation cycle, due, they will add, to the weather, or, failing that, to alternations of optimism and pessimism amongst the members of the family.
>
> (1930: II, p. 223)

REINTRODUCING EXPECTATIONS

By this point it might seem that there is little basis for the claim that Keynes ultimately introduced an *analytical* model of expectations to explain the swings in confidence which cause business cycles. This was accomplished in two stages: first, the abandonment of his "magic formula mentality" and, second, his conversion to a theory of tractable expectations. Neither story can be told in full in the space available, but both can be sketched in very easily.

The loss of Keynes's magic formula mentality took three years and was the result of the inadequacies which became apparent in its use. These were already apparent in the *Treatise* which drew a unanimously negative reaction. By 1931 Keynes was already working on revisions and corrections which led to *The General Theory*. Keynes was also stung by his failure to influence policy or policy makers.[7] His last grandiose exercise in the magic formula mentality, his *Means to Prosperity*, was published in 1933. Here he used Richard Kahn's newly developed multiplier to argue for a massive public works program to spur the economy. But neither his argument over the multiplier's validity nor his policy prescription were persuasive.[8] Thus it was that Keynes found himself by late 1933 out of magic formulas and without any noteworthy successes as a policy analyst.

It was during this general time period that Keynes admitted the failure of the objective theory of probability he had advocated in his *Probability*. In response to Frank Ramsey's criticism that the Platonic entities he had postulated did not exist, Keynes's recourse was to argue that probabilities are subjective reflections of individual beliefs.[9]

In his only published reply to the many critics of *Probability*, Keynes acquiesced.[10]

> Ramsey argues, as against the view which I had put forward, that probability is concerned not with objective relations between propositions but (in some sense) with degrees of belief, and he succeeds in showing that the calculus of probabilities belongs to formal logic. But the basis of our degrees of belief – or the *a priori* probabilities, as they used to be called – is part of our human outfit, perhaps given us merely by natural selection, analogous to our perceptions and our memories rather than to formal logic. So far I yield to Ramsey – I think he is right.
>
> (1931a, *CW*, X, pp. 338–9)

It was also a major point of Ramsey's essay, however, that these subjective probabilities could be *approximated* in many cases by using mathematical expectation to represent the bets that people would make on various possible outcomes.

> The question then arises how we are to modify this simple system to take account of varying degrees of certainty in his beliefs. I suggest that we introduce as a law of psychology that his behaviour is governed by what is called the mathematical expectation; that is to say that, if p is a proposition about which he doubtful, any goods or bads for whose realization p is in his view a necessary and sufficient condition enter into his calculations multiplied by the same fraction, which is called the

"degree of his belief in *p*". We thus define degree of belief in a way which presupposes the use of the mathematical expectation.

(1931: 174)

Thus there is no contradiction in representing each person's subjective probabilities by mathematical expectation even though there are no logical relations (or relative frequencies) upon which one could make unique calculated mathematical expectations. Such a representation was merely a snapshot of a person's behavior at any given moment and had no relation to any conception of probability other than the likelihoods implied by their actions.

So it was that in late 1933 Keynes found himself out of magic formulas and in possession of a new conception of probability which explicitly allowed for *measurement and tractable analysis*. The change in his attitude and his analytical structure immediately became evident in his lectures at Cambridge that Fall. Keynes was at this time giving a series of eight lectures every Michaelmas term. With the publication of Thomas Rymes's (1989) compilation of students' notes from these lectures, we have a fascinating record of the development of Keynes's thought between the *Treatise* and the *General Theory*. While all the elements of Keynes's pathbreaking model of aggregate demand were in place by late 1932, it was not until the 1933 lectures that he introduces business confidence as a crucial aspect of his theory and begins to animate his presentations with a mathematical expectations model to explain the world.

It was not a foregone conclusion, of course, that Keynes would have reverted to business confidence as an important explanation of macro-economic behavior when he abandoned the "scientism" of his fundamental equations, but it was also not an unreasonable choice given his training and the fact that, in his own mind, confidence must have seemed the primary alternative to the type of explanation he had worked so hard to develop in the *Treatise*. Two other things must certainly have contributed to his return to business confidence. One was his continuing dispute (from 1930 to 1933) about confidence with Hubert Henderson, his co-author of the famed pamphlet "Can Lloyd George Do It?" (1929). Henderson abandoned the pamphlet's position in support of public works in 1930, largely because he believed such programs would have deleterious effects on business confidence and investment. He engaged in a three-year debate with Keynes on exactly this point.[11] A set of letters between the two men in summer 1933 reflects the final recorded exchange. The other likely reason for Keynes's reconversion to confidence lies in the retrospective evidence provided by Matthews, Feinstein and Odling-Smee in their *British Economic Growth 1856–1973*. In this exhaustive and authoritative study, the authors find that the primary cause of the failure of investment to recover during the early 1930s was poor expectations on the part of businessmen (1982: 383–4).

Thus it was that in 1933 Maynard Keynes became the right person, in the right place, at the right time to introduce mathematical expectations into macroeconomic analysis. As a Cambridge economist he was trained to see confidence as a crucial dimension of macroeconomic activity. He was living in a nation in the midst of severely depressed business expectations, *and* he had a fresh theory at hand for representing expectations in a mathematical format. It had taken many years and many unexpected turns to get there, it was Keynes who led the way.[12]

THE GENERAL THEORY

From a purely analytical point of view, the role of expectations in the *General Theory* is paramount. Keynes employs a formal model of expectations in each of the book's major functions: aggregate demand, aggregate supply, the marginal efficiency of capital, liquidity preference, and the propensity to consume. He refers throughout to mathematical expectation and explains what he means in Chapter 3.

> An entrepreneur, who has to reach a practical decision as to his scale of production, does not, of course, entertain a single undoubting expectation of what the sale-proceeds of a given output will be, but several hypothetical expectations held with varying degrees of probability and definiteness. By his expectation of proceeds, I mean, therefore, that expectation of proceeds which, if it were held with certainty, would lead to the same behavior as does the bundle of vague and more various possibilities which actually makes up his state of expectation when he reaches his decision.
>
> (1936: 24)

This is exactly the model which he had described in *Probability*, though its usefulness was doubted in 1921.

> "Mathematical expectation" is a technical expression originally derived from the scientific study of gambling and games of chance, and stands for the product of the possible gain with the probability of attaining it. In order to obtain, therefore, a measure of what ought to be our preference in regard to various alternative courses of action, we must sum for each course of action a series of terms made up of the amounts of good which may attach to each of its possible consequences, each multiplied by its appropriate probability.
>
> (1921: 311)

It was this familiar model which Keynes introduced to *The General Theory* in order to model businessmen's expectations of aggregate demand and aggregate supply. Then, having introduced the model, he goes on in his other three principle behavioral functions to state an explicit role for expectations. In introducing investment demand he says, "The reader should note that the marginal efficiency of capital is here defined in terms of the *expectation* of yield and the *current* supply price of the capital asset" (p. 136, italics in original). His discussion of liquidity preference makes his focus on expectations equally clear.

> There is, however, a necessary condition failing which the existence of a liquidity-preference for money as a means of holding wealth could not exist. This necessary condition is the existence of uncertainty as to the future of the rate interest, i.e., as to the complex of rates of interest for varying maturities which will rule at future dates.
>
> (1936: 168)

Even the discussion of the propensity to consume contains explicit reference to the effect of expectations under the subheading "Changes in expectations of the relation between present and future income" (p. 95).

"THE WHOLE STRUCTURE OF CONFIDENCE"

There has been a tremendous amount of research during the last fifteen years by historians and economists which has clarified and redefined our understanding of Keynes's policy prescriptions (and of the transmission of these ideas into the policy arena). Given this wealth of information, and Keynes's vision of economic theory as a source for policy recommendations, it would seem necessary that any serious exposition of his analytical work to be compatible with his policy recommendations. Such an investigation also provides additional insight into the role that Keynes saw for the expectations he had incorporated in *The General Theory*.

Without undertaking a full survey of Keynes's post-1936 policy recommendations, it is nonetheless instructive to consider one of the best known episodes in this period. This is Keynes's advice in 1937, in a series of articles, speeches and letters, that government expenditure *not* be used to further stimulate the economy. Terence Hutchison (1977) first pointed out the pattern of Keynes's thought in the year immediately following the publication of *The General Theory*. Although unemployment was still at 11–12 percent, Keynes repeatedly pointed out the need to curtail further government expenditure and borrowing. This, of course, flies in the face of the textbook caricature of a man hell bent on the use of fiscal policy to alleviate unemployment.

It is not just his failure to endorse further government expenditure which is of significance, however. His rationale for this and the entire complex of policy ideas that he proffered make an interesting point: both fiscal and monetary policy are constrained by expectations. Part of his caution undoubtedly sprang from a desire to avoid creating inflationary pressure, but he was nonetheless resolute that "it is premature to abate our efforts to increase employment so long as the figures of employment remain so large"

(*CW*, XXI, p. 385). But if one is curtailing fiscal policy, just what effort is being made to reduce unemployment?

The answer is the creation of the expectations necessary for increasing and stabilizing private investment. This was to be carried out through *both* fiscal and monetary policy.

The limiting nature of subjective expectations with respect to fiscal policy is explicit in a letter to *The Times* on December 22, 1937.

> Public loan expenditure is not, of course, the only way, and not necessarily the best way, to increase employment. Nor is it always sufficiently effective to overcome other adverse influences. The state of confidence and of expectation about what will happen next, the conditions of credit, the rate of interest, the growth of population, the state of foreign trade, and the readiness of the public to spend are scarcely less important.
>
> (*CW*, XXI, pp. 429–30)

The rationale for this limitation had been explicit since his *Times* articles in January when Keynes spoke of the need to avoid "mistaken expectations" (*CW*, XXI, p. 388). His concern was that "the abnormal profits obtainable, during a too rapid recovery of demand, from equipment which is temporarily in short supply is likely to lead to exaggerated expectations from certain types of new investment, the disappointment of which will bring a subsequent reaction". The problem here is *not* rational expectations. It is *not* the case that on average investors correctly estimate the longer-term results of a temporary stimulus and act in accordance with their expectations of this long-run outcome; the problem is that some investors *do* react to the stimulus, in expectation of long-run profits, and their overreaction causes an eventual downturn.

The limiting effect of subjective expectations on monetary profit is even more explicit. This was the crux of Keynes's "cheap money" advice; if investors believe that long-run interest rates will vary with policy, their liquidity preference will fluctuate as their expectations of policy changes fluctuate. He worried over "what careful handling is necessary to develop a psychological state in the investment market which will accept a reduction in the long-term rate of interest" (ibid., p. 342). Again, the "problem" is not rational expectations. Nor is it the liquidity trap. The problem is "the whole structure of confidence and credit" (ibid., p. 389). If liquidity preference changes because people subjectively expect interest rate changes, then the mere possibility of high rates late in an expansion may lead to higher rates as investors switch to cash holdings in order to take advantage of expected high yields. Thus, the best advice for the authorities was to maintain an expectation of stable, low, long-run rates of interest.

In both cases, then, Keynes saw real limits to the use of activist policy. Overstimulus with fiscal policy could lead to a slump if "mistaken expectations" were formed. Activist monetary policy could cause an unstable demand for money and make the interest rates necessary for the desired levels of private investment difficult to obtain. The key to good policy was to use just enough stimulus to stabilize investor expectations and maintain growth without a "boom".

CONCLUSION

The story of how Maynard Keynes introduced mathematical expectation to macroeconomics is an excellent example of how progress in economics is dependent on the development of an analytical tool suited to the task at hand. Keynes's introduction of mathematical expectations to macroeconomics is, of course, not the only novel element of *The General Theory*, but it is inextricably bound up with his ability to conceptualize the book's model and to tie its component parts together. Only when he had a clear picture in his own mind of subjective evaluations of uncertain outcomes which could be represented by mathematical expectation did his overarching model of a capitalist economy come together. This is clear from his lectures in 1933, from the remaining drafts of *The General Theory* from 1934 (in which each function of the book has an independent variable, E, to represent expectations or the state of the news) and from his powerful restatement of the central message of his book in his well-known *Quarterly Journal of Economics* article (1937) "The General Theory".

Understanding this story of theoretical progress helps to illustrate both the nature of such progress and the peril of living by myths that are actually only half truths. The story of the development of *The General Theory*, for instance, reminds us that, while Keynes is responsible for several of the modern theoretical constructs of macroeconomics, he developed these tools as part of what is the true source of modern macroeconomics, namely nineteenth-century monetary theory. Likewise, the idea that expectations were introduced into macroeconomics in the 1960s and 1970s is a myth that hides too much. And finally, the canard about Keynes not employing a theory of expectations is simply wrong. The final moral of the story, thus, is not just that progress depends on new tools, but also that understanding this fact is made all the more difficult in the face of canards, myths and half-truths.

NOTES

1 Don Patinkin (1976: 142; 1990: 219) has repeated and endorsed this canard. Despite Patinkin's (1976: 24n) suggestion that a study of the connections between Keynes's *Probability* and his *General Theory* would be "worth while", he does not ever seem to have followed up on the suggestion.
2 Marshall and Marshall (1879: 153) quote Overstone (1837). "Thus the state of trade, to use the famous words of Lord Overstone, 'revolves apparently in an established cycle. First we find it in the state of quiescence, – next, improvement, – growing confidence, – prosperity, – excitement, – over-trading, – confidence,

– prosperity, – excitement, – over-trading, – convulsion, – pressure, – stagnation, – distress, – ending in quiescence.'"

3   Bigg (1990) makes the inconsistency of Marshall's and Pigou's position a tension in the "hard core" of the Cambridge School which was lead to its ultimate demise once it failed to generate new ideas.

4   See Bateman (1988) for an explanation of how Keynes came to advocate an objective theory of probability. Bateman (1987) explains why Keynes's objective probabilities cannot be confused with relative frequencies or stochastic probabilities.

5   See Patinkin (1976: 53, 126). Patinkin does not mention Keynes's use of the phrase. Keynes is actually quoting Benjamin Strong when he uses this passage, but he is using Strong to represent the position with which he (Keynes) disagrees and so Strong's statement is a characterization of Keynes's position.

6   Meltzer (1988: 56) says, "Nothing in the *Tract* or the *Treatise* ties anticipations to actual events or observables. Anticipations, or expectations, are a *deus ex machina* that enter or leave at convenient places." The explanation above of "intelligent anticipations" in the *Tract* is at odds with this statement, but Meltzer is clearly correct as regards the *Treatise*.

7   Peter Clarke has documented Keynes's failure in the Macmillan Committee to carry the day with his analysis based on the framework of the *Treatise* and Susan Howard and Donald Winch have likewise shown that he was unsuccessful at turning his position on the Economic Advisory Council into a successful platform for advancing his ideas.

8   That is to say, that his recommendation led to no discernible change in public policy. As Davis (1971) has explained, the advocacy of public works projects was widespread by this time among mainstream economists so it is not really possible to say that Keynes influenced economists with his argument for public works.

9   The person who dissuaded Keynes from his belief in objective probabilities was himself one of the founders of the modern theory of subjective probabilities. Frank Ramsey, a close friend and Cambridge philosopher, criticized Keynes's idea of objective probabilities based on logical relations in a 1926 essay which was published in his posthumous (1931) collection *The Foundation of Mathematics*.

10 See Bateman (1987) for a full account of Keynes's change of heart about the objective nature of probabilities. Carabelli (1988) and O'Donnell (1989) argue that Keynes's capitulation to Ramsey was not sincere and so neither discusses the story told in this essay about Keynes "borrowing" Ramsey's use of mathematical expectation.

11 Howson and Winch (1977: 66–70) explain the ongoing debate between Henderson and Keynes in 1930 on the Committee of Economists (a Committee of the Economic Advisory Council) and the role of confidence in that debate.

12 It seems a reasonable question to ask why Keynes's introduction of mathematical expectation as a part of his model escaped attention at the time. The simple answer would seem to be that economists simply did not recognize what was being put in front of them. One need only consider that the requirement of bounded utility for solution of the St Petersburg paradox was first noted in 1934 (Bassett 1987) or that in 1939 there were only three universities in the United States which offered course work in mathematical statistics (Frazer and Boland 1983) to get an idea of how little chance there was that economists would have had an acquaintance with what Keynes was intimately familiar with. Even more telling evidence comes in the form of J. R. Hicks's handling of expectations in *Value and Capital* (1939). Writing three years after the publication of *The*

General Theory, Hicks found it necessary (p. 125) not only to explicitly introduce mathematical expectations to his readers, but to do so in a very general way and *verbally*!

> Secondly, and perhaps more importantly, people rarely have *precise* expectations at all. They do not expect that the price at which they will be able to sell a particular output in a particular future week will be just so-and-so much; there will be a certain figure, or range of figures, which they consider most probable, but deviations from this most probable value on either side are considered to be more or less possible. This is a complication which deserves very serious attention.

(1939: 125)

REFERENCES

Bassett, Gilbert W. (1987) "The St Petersburg paradox and bounded utility", *History of Political Economy* 19: 517–23.

Bateman, Bradley W. (1987) "Keynes' changing conception of probability", *Economics and Philosophy* 3: 97–120.

—— (1988) "G. E. Moore and J. M. Keynes: a missing chapter in the history of the expected utility model", *American Economic Review* 78: 1098–1106.

Bigg, Robert J. (1990) *Cambridge and the Monetary Theory of Production*, London: Macmillan.

Carabelli, Anna (1988) *On Keynes's Method*, London: Macmillan.

Davis, J. Ronnie (1971) *The New Economics and the Old Economists*, Ames, IA: Iowa State University Press.

Frazer, William J. and Boland, Lawrence A. (1983) "An essay on the foundations of Friedman's methodology", *American Economic Review* 73: 129–44.

Hicks, J. R. (1939) *Value and Capital*, Oxford: Oxford University Press.

Howson, Susan K. and Winch, Donald (1977) *The Economic Advisory Council. 1930–1939*, Cambridge: Cambridge University Press.

Hutchinson, Terence W. (1977) *Keynes versus the Keynesians*, London: Institute of Economic Affairs.

Keynes, J. M. (1921) *A Treatise on Probability*, London: Macmillan.

—— (1923) *A Tract on Monetary Reform*, London: Macmillan.

—— (1930a) *A Treatise on Money*, vol. 1, *The Pure Theory of Money*, London: Macmillan.

—— (1930b) *A Treatise on Money*, vol. II, *The Applied Theory of Money*, London: Macmillan.

—— (1931a) "Review of F. P. Ramsey's *Foundations of Mathematics*", *The New Statesman and Nation* 2: 407.

—— (1931b) "An economic analysis of unemployment", in Quincy Wright (ed.) *Unemployment as a World Problem*, Chicago, IL: Chicago University Press.

—— (1933) *The Means to Prosperity*, London: Macmillan.

—— (1936) *The General Theory of Employment, Interest and Money*, London: Macmillan.

—— (1937) "How to avoid a slump", *The Times* January 12–14.

Marshall, Alfred (1923) *Money, Credit and Commerce*, London: Macmillan.

—— (1964) *Principles of Economics*, 9th edn (1st edn 1890), London: Macmillan.

Marshall, Alfred, and Marshall, Mary (1879) *The Economics of Industry*, London: Macmillan.

Matthews, R. C. O., Feinstein, C. H. and Odlin-Smee, J. C. (1982) *British Economic*

Growth 1856–1973, Stanford, CA: Stanford University Press.

Meltzer, Allan H. (1988) *Keynes's Monetary Theory*, Cambridge: Cambridge University Press.

O'Donnell, Rodney (1989) *Keynes: Philosophy, Economics and Politics*, London: Macmillan.

Overstone, Lord (1837) *Reflections Suggested by a Perusal of Mr. J. Horsley Palmer's Pamphlet on the Causes and Consequences of the Pressure on the Money Market*, London: Richardson.

Patinkin, Don. (1976) *Keynes' Monetary Thought*, Durham, NC: Duke University Press.

—— (1990) "On different interpretations of the *General Theory*", *Journal of Monetary Economics* 26: 205–43.

Pigou, Arthur C. (1912) *Wealth and Welfare*, London: Macmillan.

—— (1913) *Unemployment*, London: Williams & Norgate.

—— (1920) *The Economics of Welfare*, 1st edn, London: Macmillan.

—— (1927) *Industrial Fluctuations*, 1st edn, London: Macmillan.

Ramsey, Frank P. (1931) *The Foundations of Mathematics*, London: Routledge & Kegan Paul.

Rymes, Thomas K. (ed.) (1989) *Keynes's Lectures, 1932–35: Notes of a Representative Student*, Ann Arbor, MI: University of Michigan Press.

Samuelson, Paul A. (1946) "Lord Keynes and the *General Theory*", *Econometrica* 14: 187–200.

Chapter 14

The New Classical macroeconomics

A case study in the evolution of economic analysis

Sherryl D. Kasper

During the 1970s economists witnessed radical changes in orthodox macroeconomic theory as the New Classical model replaced the Keynesian model as the standard framework of analysis. The theoretical transformation comprised two fundamental changes – first, the replacement of the disequilibrium premise of Keynesian analysis with a general equilibrium orientation and, second, the extension of the rationality hypothesis to accommodate the formation of expectations. Equally striking was the policy change that New Classical macroeconomics engendered: the corollary policy recommendation from the Keynesian interventionist stance to the New Classical proposition that the institution of a *laissez-faire* framework of predictable rules would provide better for macroeconomic growth and stability.

Even though the New Classical economists failed to persuade policy makers of the superiority of rules, they succeeded in fomenting a technical revolution in macroeconomic analysis. Macroeconomists routinely build stylized mathematical models that incorporate the tool of rational expectations.[1] Furthermore, the new classical revolution forced Keynesian economists to replace *ad hoc* assumptions about rigid prices with complex models that use microeconomic theory to explain how price rigidities or market failure in the capital, goods or labor markets lead to economic fluctuations. Given its continuing technical impact, the New Classical revolution provides fertile ground for studying the role of technique in influencing the development of economic analysis.

One way to study the role of technique in the New Classical revolution is by means of an in-depth examination of the research of a leading proponent. The research of Robert E. Lucas Jr will serve as the case study. Lucas stands as one of the originators of New Classical macroeconomics. He presented the first new classical model in his 1972 paper "Expectations and the neutrality of money", and he has often served as a spokesperson for New Classical macroeconomics.[2] To accomplish the investigation of Lucas's work, the next section will outline his research method. The section following will explain how he built on this research method to develop the New Classical model and his accompanying critique of Keynesian econometric models. The concluding section will draw on Lucas's research to investigate the implications of having technique impel the development of economic analysis.

LUCAS'S RESEARCH METHOD

Lucas brings to his study of macroeconomic phenomena a definite view of the proper method for conducting economic research. Key elements include a method for theory development and assessment, the use of two fundamental postulates to derive economic behavior and the utilization of mathematical techniques for model building.

In essence, Lucas comprehends economic theory as a "fully articulated, artificial economic system", a "mechanical imitation economy" or a "robot imitation of people" (Lucas 1980a: 271, 272; Lucas, in Klamer 1983: 49).[3] In this form, economic theories "serve as laboratories in which policies that would be prohibitively expensive to experiment with in actual economies can be tested out at lower costs" (Lucas 1980a: 271). To perform this role well, Lucas believes that the "artificial 'model' economy [must] be distinguished as sharply as possible in discussion from actual economies" (Lucas 1980a: 271). As a result, economic theory "will necessarily be artificial, abstract, patently 'unreal'" (Lucas 1980a: 271).

Lucas acknowledges that not all artificial economies serve equally well as laboratories. As a result, he advocates that the analyst develop models that are amenable to econometric testing to facilitate comparison of rival theories. This method entails "subjecting them [models] to shocks for which we are fairly certain how actual economies, or parts of economies would react" (Lucas 1980a: 272).[4]

When using a positivistic method of this type, the facts that the analyst relies on to describe actual economies become crucial. They establish the benchmark for comparison among rival models. In Lucas's case he claims that "the basic source for 'my' facts, not very surprisingly, turned out to be Friedman and Schwartz's – *Monetary History* (1963).... [And] from Friedman and Schwartz, it is a short and direct step back to the work of Wesley Mitchell (1913)" (Lucas 1980a: 16).

Lucas maintains that progress in economic analysis "means getting better and better abstract, analogue models" (Lucas 1980a: 276). He suggests that economists have looked to two sources in order to improve these "analogue models" over time. First, they made use of "purely technical developments that enlarge our abilities to construct analogue economies" such as improvements in mathematical methods and computational capacity; second, they respond to "changes in the questions we want models to answer or in phenomena we wish to understand or explain" (Lucas 1980a: 272–3, 284).

Yet, when evaluating these potential catalysts for theory development, Lucas asserts that "purely technical developments" promote greater scientific progress. For example, when isolating the distinctive features of the Keynesian revolution, he judged Keynes's contribution as "a more political event than a scientific event.... The *General Theory* is a political response to the Depression and to the discrediting of conventional economics that resulted from it" (Lucas, in Klamer 1983: 56). Yet even though Keynes did not make a major scientific contribution, he "left an opening for younger econometricians and mathematical economists to take over and write down models.... So people like Klein and Tinbergen took over because they had the exciting new methods" (Lucas, in Klamer 1983: 56). Thus, in Lucas's estimation, the progressive element of the Keynesian revolution consisted of the technical developments it encouraged.

The context of Lucas's work is to be found in two fundamental postulates: "(a) that markets be assumed to clear, and (b) that agents be assumed to act in their own self-interest" (Lucas and Sargent 1978: 57). Lucas follows this approach because he believes that

> An equilibrium model is, by definition, constructed so as to predict how agents with stable tastes and technology will *choose* to respond to a new situation. Any disequilibrium model, constructed by simply codifying the decision rules which agents have found it useful to use over some previous sample period, without explaining *why* these rules were used, will be of no use in predicting the consequences of nontrivial policy changes.
>
> (Lucas 1977: 220–1)

In part he associates his emphasis on the postulates of market clearing and individual optimization with his graduate teachers at the University of Chicago. In particular, he cites Friedman as a "big influence" in his intellectual development, interestingly not as a macroeconomist but as a price theorist (Lucas, in Klamer 1983: 30). When explaining the decision he made with Leonard Rapping to model unemployment as a "side story" to a supply and demand model for employment and wages, Lucas states that

> In the tradition of Friedman and [Gregg] Lewis it is hard to think about labor markets without supply and demand. You have to tell how wages and employment arise from certain shifts in supply and demand curves. That was the rule we imposed on ourselves.
>
> (Lucas, in Klamer 1983: 36)

Lucas claims that he and Rapping were also influenced by the effort at that time by Keynesian economists to develop microfoundations for their model of the macro economy:

> We were modeling [the labor market] after the work of people like Modigliani and Jorgenson, who weren't Chicago people....
>
> See, this business of microeconomic foundations has been kicking

around for years. Rapping's and my paper is pretty conventional; that's what everybody was doing.

(Lucas, in Klamer 1983: 36)

But his view that the proper microfoundations for macroeconomic theory consist of both market clearing and individual optimization set him apart from his Keynesian contemporaries, who continued to explore disequilibrium solutions. This distinction between Lucas and Keynesian economists is made sharper in a later statement in which he recommends collapsing macro-economics into microeconomics:

> The most interesting developments in macroeconomic theory seem to me describable as the reincorporation of aggregative problems such as inflation and the business cycle within the general framework of "micro-economic" theory. If these developments succeed, the term "macro-economic" will simply disappear from use and the modifier "micro" will become superfluous. We will simply speak, as did Smith, Ricardo, Marshall and Walras, of economic theory. If we are honest we will have to face the fact that at any given time there will be phenomena that are well-understood from the point of view of the economic theory we have, and other phenomena are not. We will be tempted, I am sure, to relieve the discomfort induced by discrepancies between theory and facts by saying that the ill-understood facts are the province of some other, different kind of economic theory. Keynesian "macroeconomics" was, I think, a sur-render (under great duress) to this temptation. It led to the abandonment, for a class of problems of great importance, of the use of the only "engine for the discovery of truth" that we have in economics.

(Lucas 1987: 107–8)

Like many of his contemporaries Lucas emphasizes the importance of incorporating mathematical techniques of analysis. This approach derived from his reading of Paul Samuelson's *Foundations of Economic Analysis* (1947), a book Lucas deems as essential to his intellectual development as Friedman's price theory. While Lucas believes Friedman was instrumental in teaching him to think in price theoretic terms, "he wasn't good for teaching tools" (Lucas, in Klamer 1983: 30). Reading on his own, Lucas discovered that Samuelson's book filled that void:

> It's a "how-to-do-it" book, a great book for first-year graduate students. It says, "Here's the way you do it." It lets you in on the secret of how you play the game, as opposed to cutting you off with big words.

(Lucas, in Klamer 1983: 30)

Lucas also views mathematical modeling as a useful means to improve communication among economists during periods when professional con-sensus does not exist. For example, during the consensus of the 1960s, Lucas stated that, "it was possible to use a shared verbal shorthand to convey fairly complicated ideas" (Lucas 1981a: 17). But, "when consensus has broken down, such looseness becomes a barrier in professional debate, and it becomes impossible for the public to distinguish language that summarizes underlying analysis and language that is just talk" (Lucas 1981a: 17). As a result, Lucas contends that mathematical models are essential so that analysts can "get behind terms like *theory* or *equilibrium* or *unemployment* to get at the specific constructs or facts they are being used to summarize" (Lucas 1981a: 17).

Lucas's reading of Samuelson's *Foundations* also reinforced his preference for equilibrium modeling. For Lucas ascribed to this intellectual mentor the technical achievement of "advanc[ing] ... the main ingredients for a mathematically explicit theory of general equilibrium" (Lucas 1980a: 278).

LUCAS'S "NEW CLASSICAL" ECONOMICS

Lucas began the research that resulted in New Classical economics in a professional environment influenced by both external events and internal debates. In 1965 an escalation in the Vietnam War made economists more conscious of the problem of inflation (Johnson 1971: 59), a concern that was reinforced by an acceleration in the rate of inflation in the late 1960s (Gordon 1976: 197). In addition, during the 1960s, the monetarists and the Keynesians identified new evidence for their debate regarding the effectiveness of monetary versus fiscal policy. The results of the 1966 monetary squeeze and the 1968 tax surcharge indicated "that monetary effects on nominal income dominated fiscal effects when the two were operating in opposite directions" (Gordon 1976: 197). This evidence encouraged macroeconomists to evaluate monetarism more seriously than they had done previously (Gordon 1976: 197). Finally, in the 1970s, episodes of stagflation called into question theories of inflation based on the Phillips curve tradeoff between unemployment and inflation.

With respect to internal developments in macroeconomic theory, during the 1950s and 1960s economists had directed their research efforts toward developing microfoundations that were consistent with Keynesian macroeconomics. Macroeconomists worked from the neoclassical postulate of individual optimization to construct models of sectors of the economy such as the labor and product markets. In turn these sectoral models were joined to form a macroeconomic model of the economy. A continuing problem remained in rationalizing the equilibrium premise of microeconomic models with the disequilibrium premise of the Keynesian models. A variety of factors was postulated to explain this inconsistency, such as money illusion (Friedman 1968a) and imperfect information (Phelps 1970).

Development of the New Classical model

In his initial work in macroeconomics, Lucas collaborated with Leonard Rapping to aid Keynesian economists in the construction of a model of the labor market founded on individual optimization that could join with those of other sectors to form a comprehensive model of the macro economy (1969). This paper was selected by Edmund Phelps for inclusion in a volume he was editing about the microeconomic foundations of employment and inflation theory. In the introduction, Phelps presented a verbal argument for a general equilibrium reconciliation of the natural-rate hypothesis[5] and business cycle theory that relied on information imperfections (Phelps 1970: 1–6). At a conference for the contributors to this volume, Lucas stated that "much of the discussion ... involved questions that seemed to stand in the way of casting this argument in modern mathematical form" (Lucas 1981a: 7). Not surprisingly given his espousal of mathematical analysis, Lucas was intrigued by the theoretical puzzle of the possible relationship between market clearing and individual optimization. In an attempt to solve it, he developed the first of what came to be known as New Classical models of the economy presented in his paper "Expectations and the neutrality of money" (1972).

Lucas began his analysis "persuaded ... by the arguments of Friedman and Phelps that a natural-rate hypothesis was valid and consistent with the main features of the observed business cycle" (Lucas 1981a: 8). This assessment is not surprising given that the natural-rate hypothesis is premised on Lucas's favored notion of market clearing. At the same time, following from his views on theory development, Lucas stated that "the form this persuasion took was the conviction that an artificial, model society could be constructed in which these objectives were verifiably valid" (Lucas 1981a: 8). In constructing this artificial, model society, Lucas determined to reconcile the natural-rate hypothesis with an equilibrium theory of the business cycle (Lucas 1981a: 7; 1981b: 561).

In developing this model, Lucas's research agenda became to reconcile the notion of monetary neutrality, as a proxy for the natural rate, with that of money "as the principal source of instability", as a proxy for the business cycle (Lucas 1981b: 561). In order to cast this problem into a mathematical framework, Lucas brought together a variety of techniques developed by other analysts. To model a competitive equilibrium, he adapted the notion of a contingent-claims equilibrium developed by Kenneth Arrow and Gerard Debreu (1954, 1959).[6] To develop an econometrically testable model that incorporated individual optimization in an uncertain environment, he adopted John Muth's rational expectations hypothesis (1961) and Phelps's idea of an island economy (1970).[7] Lucas's novel combination of these techniques resulted in the archetypal New Classical model. A short discussion of Lucas's adaptation is relevant.

Lucas's concept of equilibrium, borrowed from Arrow and Debreu, was one in which "an economy follow[ed] a multivariate stochastic process ... [and] at each point in time" exhibited cleared markets (Lucas and Sargent 1978: 58). Arrow and Debreu developed the model of a contingent-claims equilibrium under the assumption that agents had complete information about the prices of goods in all future periods. But Lucas stated that

> it was soon recognized by many researchers that the idea of viewing a dated, contingent commodity as a function of stochastically determined shocks is an invaluable one also in situations in which information differs in various ways among traders.
>
> (Lucas 1980a: 285)

In the latter conception of a contingent commodity, the role of expectations became crucial in influencing the behavior of traders.

Lucas selected Muth's hypothesis of rational expectations to represent the process by which agents form expectations in a model society with a contingent-claims equilibrium. In adopting this technique, Lucas used a theory of expectations consistent with the postulate of individual optimization he had deemed essential to his concept of the proper research method. Individual optimization is maintained, because the rational expectations hypothesis simply extends the neoclassical assumption of optimizing behavior to encompass the economic agent's process of forming expectations regarding future labor supply and consumption.[8] When using the hypothesis the analyst assumes that rational agents will seek out all possible sources of information as they form their expectations and that they will learn from past mistakes rather than persisting in behavior once they realize it is detrimental.

The rational expectations hypothesis also permitted the econometric testing of the New Classical model essential to Lucas's advocacy of positivistic methods. When formalizing the rational expectations hypothesis, Muth assumed that the "expectations ... tend to be distributed, for the same information set, about the prediction of the theory (or the 'objective' probability distribution of outcomes)" (Muth 1961: 316). This technique allowed Lucas to identify an agent's subjective forecasts, since this hypothesis implied that agents' subjective probabilities are identified with "the predictions of the relevant economic theory" (Muth 1961: 315).

By using the rational expectations hypothesis, Lucas, in effect, converted uncertainty into a measurable magnitude. He maintained that this application was appropriate in situations characterized by "a fairly well defined recurrent event, situations of 'risk' in Knight's terminology" (Lucas 1977: 224). Thus, in order to apply the rational expectations hypothesis to business cycle theory, Lucas additionally had to assume that business cycles manifest a "*recurrent character*", that they represent "repeated instances of essentially similar events" (Lucas 1977: 224). Interestingly, in keeping with his view that progress in economic analysis derived from technical developments, Lucas discounted the role of stagflation in instigating the New Classical revolution.

Rather, he stressed the importance of reviving Wesley Claire Mitchell's concept of viewing "business cycles as a recurring event" (Lucas 1980a: 284).

The final tool Lucas adopted in constructing the New Classical model was Phelps's notion of an island economy. In this scheme, the analyst posits individual suppliers as unable to distinguish whether the causes of current price movements are relative or general impacts. As a rational economic agent, the individual supplier makes his best estimate of whether an observed price movement signifies a change in the relative demand for his good or a change due to movements in the general price level resulting from monetary impacts. Lucas assumed that, because of misperceptions about relative and general price changes, the individual supplier did not immediately incorporate the effects of monetary changes into his expectations. As a result, monetary changes could have the effect of distorting market price signals. Thus, the agent's misperceptions of relative prices could lead to fluctuations in real output (Lucas 1972, 1973; Lucas and Sargent 1978). With this technique Lucas was able to maintain the postulate of individual optimization, since any observed behavior classified as less than optimal resulted from differences in information among traders, rather than the agent's own actions.[9]

The New Classical model reconciled the natural-rate hypothesis with an equilibrium theory of the business cycle. The natural-rate hypothesis was maintained by "postulating agents free of money illusion, so that the Ricardian hypothetical experiment of a fully announced, proportional monetary expansion will have no real consequences" (Lucas 1972: 84). In a setting in which suppliers lack perfect information, policy makers can affect the variance of the monetary growth rate. As a result, unanticipated policy leads agents to alter their behavior in a manner consistent with observed time series data presented by Friedman and Schwartz in their history of the business cycle (Lucas 1972: 84; 1973: 141).

Econometric implications of New Classical economics

Even though Lucas included econometric testing as an important feature of a proper research method, he relied on other economists to complete the bulk of the tests of his New Classical model. He did complete a simple econometric test based on cross-country data which produced results that were consistent with his hypothesis (Lucas 1973). Other analysts devised time series tests using data from a single country and also produced results consistent with the implications of the New Classical model (see Barro 1977, 1978, 1979; Small 1979; Barro and Rush 1980).[10]

Lucas's greater contribution to the issues surrounding the econometric testing of New Classical economics is the so-called Lucas critique of Keynesian econometric theory and quantitative policy analysis. Lucas identified the Keynesian approach as the theoretical underpinnings for the large-scale econometric models such as the Wharton Model that were in use for both forecasting and testing of rival macroeconomic theories of the economy during the 1970s. According to Lucas's description, these models drew on techniques for building econometrically testable models developed by the Cowles Commission during the 1940s. In essence, this approach built on the principles of general equilibrium analysis to advocate that a properly testable economic theory contained a system of simultaneous equations with endogenous variables describing behavioral relationships in the economy, exogenous variables describing the structure of the economy, and error terms signifying random shocks to the economy (Christ 1952: 31–2). Lucas criticized this method because it assumed that the structure of the economy remained stable under alternative policies. In his estimation the New Classical approach to model building *"indicate[s] that this presumption is unjustified"* (Lucas 1976: 111). Rather, in a general equilibrium framework with rational expectations, a modification in policy would alter the values of the exogenous variables describing the structure of the economy because rational agents would change their behavior as they learned about the policy change (Lucas 1981a: 11). Thus in a general equilibrium framework with rational expectations, Lucas asserted that a policy must become an endogenous variable, so that a change in policy could alter both time series behavior and the behavioral parameters governing the rest of the system (Lucas 1976: 125).

Lucas pointed out that practitioners using the large-scale econometric models implicitly recognized that a change in policy variables altered the structure of the economy, because they routinely modified equations to improve their short-term forecasts (Lucas 1976: 108). However, Lucas stated that this adjustment would not work "for longer term forecasting and policy simulations" ... because "ignoring the systematic sources of [exogenous variable] drift will lead to large, unpredictable errors" (Lucas 1976: 111).

Policy implications of New Classical economics

Lucas brought together an innovative combination of techniques to construct a theoretical case for the superiority of rules over authority that was even more radical in its implications than those cases developed earlier in the century.[11] When individual suppliers anticipate monetary policy in the artificial, model society of New Classical economics, they immediately incorporate that information into their wage–price expectations and do not alter their supply of labor or real output. In contrast, unanticipated monetary policy creates misperceptions of relative price changes, thus causing changes in labor supply and real output. Despite his model's predictions of the momentary effectiveness of unanticipated monetary policy, Lucas asserted that the more frequently policy makers exploit their ability to induce price variability, the more difficult it is for individuals to interpret the signals sent by price changes. Eventually, individual agents would disregard the information implicit in observed price movements and would not change their supply behavior. Hence, the monetary authority would lose its ability to affect the level of real output (Lucas 1973: 141; Lucas and Sargent 1978: 60).

Lucas provided additional support for his advocacy for policy rules in his critique of econometric policy evaluation. He asserted that the method of initiating the policy change had a crucial effect on the behavioral patterns of the agents in the system. If policy makers did not pre-announce a change, the new policy "bec[a]me known to agents only gradually" and movements to new behavioral patterns "will be unsystematic and econometrically unpredictable" (Lucas 1976: 125). If policy makers made changes according to pre-announced rules, "there is some hope that the resulting structural changes can be forecast on the basis of estimation from past data of [behavioral patterns]" (Lucas 1976: 125).[12] Thus, given the present state of knowledge regarding econometric forecasts, policy rules were superior to discretionary policy because "the only *scientific* quantitative policy evaluations available to use are comparisons of the consequences of alternative policy rules" (Lucas 1976: 125–6). Lucas's implicit interpretation of the term "scientific" derives from his notion of the proper foundation for theory development, that is, the tools of general equilibrium analysis founded on the postulates of market clearing and individual optimization.

CONCLUDING REMARKS

When Lucas began his macroeconomic research in the late 1960s, macroeconomists were concerned with both the social problem of inflation and the theoretical problem of inadequate microfoundations. Lucas brought together the techniques of general equilibrium analysis, the rational expectations hypothesis and Phelps's notion of an island economy to solve the *theoretical* gap in macroeconomic analysis. Ultimately, because New Classical economics solved complicated technical problems, the majority of macroeconomists chose it to replace Keynesian theory as their standard framework of analysis. New Classical economics incorporated the most advanced use of the techniques that macroeconomists had been developing during the postwar years. For example, by adopting the rational expectations hypothesis Lucas extended the rationality postulate to the analysis of the formation of expectations. By adopting the contingent-claims equilibrium he was able to apply general equilibrium analysis to macroeconomic phenomena; this modeling choice represented a logical extension of the microfoundations research initiated by Keynesian economists. His rigorous mathematical format exemplified a further development of the patterns of model building started by Lucas's intellectual mentor Samuelson and other Keynesian economists after the Second World War. While many older Keynesian economists engaged Lucas and his fellow New Classical economists in strident debates regarding the unrealistic assumptions of rational expectations and market clearing,[13] younger economists trained in the method of positive economics accepted that the true test of a theory is the conformity of its outcomes, not its initial assumptions, to reality. Thus, in many respects New Classical economics provided the best, logical progression of modeling techniques that many economists had been taught by both teachers and colleagues as those to emulate when undertaking theoretical research. In addition, due to the technical skills required to extend New Classical theory, by adopting this approach many young economists discovered a means to more quickly advance their professional prestige.[14]

Clearly the ascendancy of New Classical economics demonstrates the crucial role of technique in effecting the development of economic analysis. What implications does this mode of development have for the body of economic knowledge? First, when economists use technique as the motivating force in the development of economic analysis, they are often uncritical about the tools with which they are attempting to establish new or refined generalizations. As a result, an avenue opens whereby ideology can enter analysis. Nobel Laureate and Keynesian economist James Tobin suggested this possibility in a discussion about Reaganomics:

> Free market ideology is an extravagant version of the central paradigm of economic theory. The modern theory of general competitive equilibrium and its theorem that such an equilibrium is in some sense a situation of optimal social welfare make rigorous the intuitive conjectures of Adam Smith and subsequent classical and neoclassical economists. Economists know the restrictive conditions of these proofs; they can list the standard caveats and qualifications. These are lost in the arena of politics and public opinion, and they are increasingly glossed over by economists themselves. At the same time and for the same reasons that conservative ideology was gaining public favour, its counterpart in economic theory was being more uncritically accepted throughout the economics profession.
>
> (Tobin 1987: 70)

The same observation can be made about macroeconomists' acceptance of New Classical economics. Lucas clearly acknowledges the strong influence of conservative economist Milton Friedman in his work. For example, when developing New Classical economics, Lucas uncritically accepted Friedman's preference for market clearing solutions and his general equilibrium notion of the natural-rate hypothesis; when testing the New Classical model, he uncritically recommended the acceptance of Friedman's facts about the behavior of time series data; and when offering policy recommendations, he explicitly borrowed Friedman's program for monetary stability (Friedman 1960) rather than develop his own policy agenda (Lucas 1980b: 248–9). The positivistic methodology embraced by Lucas and the majority of his fellow economists ideally enables the analyst to rank competing "analogue" economies. Yet, empirical tests failed to falsify Friedman's hypotheses and their concomitant case for policy rules. Given this unsettled state of affairs, Friedman's observation that a scholar's values can influence scientific judgments becomes relevant: "A scholar's basic values undoubtedly affect the way he resolves the inevitable uncertainties in his scientific judgments when he comes to recommend policies" (Friedman 1968b: 7). Friedman explicitly stated that "there is little to be said in theory for [the money-growth] rule"; rather his theoretical work suggested the superiority of discretionary monetary policy (Friedman 1960: 106). But his "preferences for limited government and, where government is essential, for limiting government so far as possible by clearly specified rules" led him to recommend the money growth rule (Friedman 1968b: 9). Thus when Lucas uncritically accepted Freidman's tools and policy pronouncements, he constructed New Classical economics on a theoretical edifice clearly biased by Friedman's ideological preference for limited government involvement in the economy. In turn, when macroeconomists used technical sophistication as the criterion for selecting New Classical economics as the superior framework for analysis, the high degree of formalism made it appear as if they had removed the effect of ideology on the process of theory development. Yet when they uncritically accepted Lucas's borrowed tools, the ideological influence of Friedman re-entered analysis on the ground floor.[15]

A second consequence of economists' reliance on technique as the motivating force in the development of analysis is that the scope of economic inquiry is circumscribed by what can be done with the preferred set of tools. Lucas illustrates this outcome when he draws on his econometric critique to argue that economists can only test models that recommend policy rules; by implication, models that recommend discretionary policy remain outside the scope of inquiry because no scientific technique exists to test them.

Not only does technique-driven development dictate the type of models economists build, it also influences the questions they seek to answer with their inquiries. For when they set up research problems they seek to close theoretical gaps that inhibit the construction of "analogue" economies rather than attempt to build models that aid in the understanding of problems in the actual economy. As a result economists cannot provide policy makers with professional guidance about the problems affecting the actual economy. In a recent survey of the state of macroeconomics, N. Gregory Mankiw confirmed this lack of relevance. He observed that business and government economists continue to use the supposedly outdated and flawed Keynesian theoretical and large-scale econometric models. Further, he acknowledged that New Classical macroeconomics has "had relatively little impact on applied macroeconomics" (Mankiw 1990: 1646). His hope was "that recent developments in macroeconomics ... [would] ultimately ... point the way to a deeper understanding" of the actual economy (Mankiw 1990: 1658). But in the meantime a generation of talented economists have devoted much energy and ingenuity to building "analogue" economies while pressing problems of the actual economy remain unaddressed and unsolved.

NOTES

The author wishes to thank Hans E. Jensen, Jean Gauger and Charles E. Staley for helpful comments on an earlier draft of this essay.

1   Early examples of Keynesian research using the rational expectations hypothesis include Fischer (1977), Phelps and Taylor (1977) and Blinder and Mankiw (1984).
2   For example, in describing his early years as a New Classical economist, Lucas stated:

> I guess when we first got going it was kind of exciting because the people who were interested in this rational expectations model were a tiny minority at first. We were pretty confident of what we were doing, but we were regarded as very far out by other people. I had a lot of fun going to Yale and other places to talk in these chaotic seminars where I stand up and people throw darts at me.
>
> (Lucas, in Klamer 1983: 34)

3   Lucas did "not know the background of this view of theory" but states, as "an immediate ancestor" to his own, the argument of Herbert A. Simon (1969) (Lucas 1980a: 292n.). Though Lucas acknowledged that Simon, a colleague of his at Carnegie-Mellon, was often critical of the outcome-focus of the neoclassical analysis of decision-making, Lucas contended that "for some questions [Simon believed] a superficial view of process is safe enough" (Lucas, in Klamer 1983: 48). In support, Lucas cited Simon's example discussing arctic animals with white fur. The theorist observed that the development of white fur was a useful outcome for arctic animals; thus he can incorporate this information in his analysis without being able to explain the reasons for this turn of events (Lucas, in Klamer 1983: 47).
4   Lucas does not state from whom he learned this positivistic method for choosing among competing theories of the economy. Yet two individuals he has claimed as intellectual mentors played leading roles in introducing positivistic methods to mainstream economics since the Second World War. Paul Samuelson presented a version termed operationalism (1947). Milton Friedman introduced an instrumental version of positivism (1953). Thus it is likely that Lucas absorbed his mentors' commitment to positivistic methods along with other more overt lessons.
5   Phelps (1967) and Friedman (1968a) independently developed the natural-rate hypothesis. In his interpretation, Friedman postulated that a natural rate of employment existed at a "level that would be ground out by the Walrasian system of general equilibrium equations, provided there is imbedded in them the actual structural characteristics of the labor and commodity markets" (Friedman 1968a: 102).
6   In their model, Arrow and Debreu posited that commodities possess four attributes: physical characteristics, location, date of delivery and the state of nature in which the commodity was available. Goods of this type were called dated, contingent commodities, since their availability was contingent upon the occurrence of certain events. Arrow and Debreu assumed that contingent commodities were traded in markets that had (1) a complete set of future markets so that agents possessed the price information necessary to make production and

consumption plans for all time and (2) insurance markets so that agents were able to insure themselves against all possible events. By bringing together the concept of a dated, contingent commodity with a restrictive set of properties regarding the agent's preferences and production sets, Arrow and Debreu demonstrated the existence of a competitive equilibrium (see Arrow and Debreu 1954; Debreu 1959).

7   Lucas attributed the idea of using imperfect information to reconcile the hypotheses of monetary neutrality and monetary-induced instability to the "verbal tradition of business cycle theory" which originated in Wesley C. Mitchell who had suggested that agents react to imperfect signals in a way which, after the fact, appears inappropriate (Lucas 1980a: 286). Phelps followed the same tack in his verbal argument for a general equilibrium reconciliation of the natural-rate hypothesis and business cycle theory (Phelps 1970: 1–6).

8   See Begg (1982), Sheffrin (1983) and Persaran (1987) for further discussion about the rational expectations hypothesis.

9   In a critique of the New Classical model, Benjamin Friedman also noted the importance of the assumptions made regarding which actors had what information and at what time. He argued that Lucas's presentation of the aggregate supply function is valid only if agents perceived that the relative prices of their outputs had changed before they perceived that the relative prices of their inputs had changed. If it was assumed that perceptions changed in an opposite sequence, agents would alter the supply of labor in a fashion exactly opposite from the observed time series describing business cycles (see Friedman 1978: 76). James Tobin made a similar point in his 1978 Jahnsson lectures (Tobin 1980: 42).

10 These tests have not received universal acceptance. Critics faulted Barro's two-step estimation procedure primarily because it forced rationality on the system, permitting only a test of the neutrality proposition (Mishkin 1982). In addition they have cited incorrect specifications of the money forecasting equation due to the omission of crucial information, such as the interest rate, to which rational agents would realistically have access (Mishkin 1982). They further have criticized these tests for assuming short lag lengths (Gordon 1979; Mishkin 1982). Subsequent empirical studies that address these criticisms suggest that, counter to the predictions of the New Classical model, anticipated monetary changes do affect real output (see Mishkin 1978, 1981, 1982; Gordon 1979).

11 Note that the implications of Lucas's model are more radical than those cases for policy rules developed earlier in the century. For example, Henry Simons advocated the institution of a legislated monetary rule to minimize the "uncertainty for enterprisers and investors as to monetary conditions in the future" (Simons 1936: 181), to provide automatically for downward adjustment of commodity prices as technical efficiency increased, and to serve as an alternative rallying point for the obsolete gold standard (Simons 1936: 164). Simons appealed to Irving Fisher's version of the quantity theory of money as the theoretical base for his recommendation (Simons 1936: 164, 166), but his analytic case for policy rules was weak at best. Friedman's version of the natural-rate hypothesis demonstrated that discretionary policy could cause real output changes in the short run. Hoover also argues that New Classical economics is distinct from monetarism. He emphasized methodological differences – Friedman's use of the partial equilibrium method of Marshall and the New Classicals' application of the equilibrium method of Walras (1984).

12 Lucas attributed "this point of view toward conditional forecasting" to Knight as presented in *Risk, Uncertainty and Profit* (1921) and Muth in "Rational expectations and the theory of price movements" (1961).

13 See, for example, Tobin (1980: 20–48).
14 Harry G. Johnson described the Keynesian revolution in similar terms. He said
    it appealed to the younger economists due to "the opportunity it offered to bypass
    the system of academic superiority by challenging senior colleagues with a new
    and self-announced superior scientific approach" (Johnson 1971: 57). In addition,
    David Colander has argued that part of the success of New Classical macro-
    economics was due to the numerous dissertations topics it suggested (1986).
    Similarly Mankiw states that work incorporating and explaining the effect of the
    rational expectations hypothesis "replaced the large-scale macroeconometric
    models as the primary focus of research" (Mankiw 1990: 1649).
15 See Kasper (1990) for a detailed study of the effect of ideology on the
    development of recent American macroeconomic theory.

REFERENCES

Arrow, Kenneth, and Debreu, Gerard (1954) "Existence of equilibrium for a
competitive economy", *Ecta* 22: 265–90.

Barro, Robert (1977) "Unanticipated money growth and unemployment in the U.S.",
American Economic Review (March): 101–15.

—— (1978) "Unanticipated money growth and unemployment in the United
States", *Journal of Political Economy* (August): 549–80.

—— (1979) "Unanticipated money growth and unemployment in the United States:
reply", *American Economic Review* (December): 1004–9.

Barro, Robert, and Rush, Mark (1980) "Unanticipated money and economic activity",
in Stanley Fischer (ed.) *Rational Expectations and Economic Policy*, Chicago, IL:
University of Chicago Press (for the National Bureau of Economic Research).

Begg, David K. H. (1982) *The Rational Expectations Revolution in Macroeconomics:
Theory and Evidence*, Oxford: Phillip Allan.

Blinder, Alan S. and Mankiw, N. Gregory (1984) "Aggregation and stabilization
policy in a multi-contract economy", *Journal of Monetary Economics* 13: 67–86.

Christ, Carl (1952) "History of the Cowles Commission 1932–1952", in *Economic
Theory and Measurement*, Chicago, IL: Cowles Commission for Research in
Economics.

Colander, David (1986) "The evolution of Keynesian economics", Paper presented at
the Conference on Keynes and Public Policy after Fifty Years, Glendon College,
York University.

Debreu, Gerard (1959) *The Theory of Value*, New York: Wiley.

Fischer, Stanley (1977) "Long-term contracts, rational expectations, and the optimal
money supply rule", *Journal of Political Economy* (February): 191–205.

Friedman, Benjamin (1978) "Discussion", in *After the Phillips Curve: Persistence of
High Inflation and High Unemployment*, Boston, MA: Federal Reserve Bank of
Boston, pp. 73–80.

Friedman, Milton (1953) "The methodology of positive economics", reprinted in
Essays in Positive Economics, Chicago, IL: University of Chicago Press,
pp. 117–32.

—— (1960) *A Program for Monetary Stability*, New York: Fordham University Press.

—— (1968a) "The role of monetary policy", reprinted in *The Optimum Quantity of
Money and Other Essays*, Chicago, IL: Aldine, pp. 97–110.

—— (1968b) "Why economists disagree", in *Dollars and Deficits: Inflation,
Monetary Policy and the Balance of Payments*, Englewood Cliffs, NJ: Prentice
Hall, pp. 1–16.

Friedman, Milton, and Schwartz, Anna J. (1963) *A Monetary History of the United*

States, 1867–1960, National Bureau of Economic Research Studies in Business Cycles 12, Princeton, NJ: Princeton University Press.

Gordon, Robert J. (1976) "Some recent development in the theory of inflation and unemployment", *Journal of Monetary Economics*, 2: 185–219.

—— (1979) "New evidence that fully anticipated changes influence real output after all", Paper 368, Center for Mathematical Studies in Economics and Management Science, Northwestern University.

Hoover, Kevin D. (1984) "Two types of monetarism", *Journal of Economic Literature* 22: 58–76.

Kasper, Sherryl Davis (1990) "The revival of *laissez faire* in American macro-economic theory", Ph.D. Dissertation, University of Tennessee.

Knight, Frank H. (1921) *Risk, Uncertainty and Profit*; reprinted New York: Augustus M. Kelley, 1964.

Lucas, Robert E., Jr (1972) "Expectations and the neutrality of money"; reprinted in *Studies in Business Cycle Theory*, Cambridge, MA: MIT Press, 1981, pp. 66–89.

—— (1973) "Some international evidence on output–inflation tradeoffs"; reprinted in *Studies in Business Cycle Theory*, Cambridge, MA: MIT Press, 1981, pp. 131–48.

—— (1976) "Econometric policy evaluation: a critique"; reprinted in *Studies in Business Cycle Theory*, Cambridge, MA: MIT Press, 1981, pp. 104–30.

—— (1977) "Understanding business cycles", reprinted in *Studies in Business Cycle Theory*, Cambridge, MA: MIT Press, 1981, pp. 215–39.

—— (1980a) "Methods and problems in business cycle theory"; reprinted in *Studies in Business Cycle Theory*, Cambridge, MA: MIT Press, 1981, pp. 271–96.

—— (1980b) "Rules discretion and the role of the economic advisor"; reprinted in *Studies in Business Cycle Theory*, Cambridge, MA: MIT Press, 1981, pp. 248–61.

—— (1981a) "Introduction", in *Studies in Business Cycle Theory*, Cambridge, MA: MIT Press, 1981, pp. 1–18.

—— (1981b) "Tobin and monetarism: a review article", *Journal of Economic Literature* (June): 558–67.

—— (1983) Interview by Arjo Klamer, in *Conversations with Economists*, Totowa, NJ: Rowman & Allanheld, 1984.

—— (1987) *Models of Business Cycles*, New York: Basil Blackwell.

Lucas, Robert E., Jr and Rapping, Leonard A. (1969) "Real wages, employment, and inflation", reprinted in *Studies in Business Cycle Theory*, Cambridge, MA: MIT Press, 1981, pp. 19–58.

Lucas, Robert E., Jr and Sargent, Thomas J. (1978) "After Keynesian Macro-economics", in *After the Phillips Curve: Persistence of High Inflation and High Unemployment*, Boston: Federal Reserve Bank of Boston, pp. 49–72.

Mankiw, N. Gregory (1990) "A quick refresher course in macroeconomics", *Journal of Economic Literature* 28 (December): 1645–60.

Mishkin, Frederic S. (1978) "Efficient-markets theory: implications for monetary policy", *Brookings Papers on Economic Activity* 3: 702–57.

—— (1981) "Monetary policy and long-term interest rates: an efficient markets approach", *Journal of Monetary Economics* 7 (January): 29–55.

—— (1982) "Does anticipated monetary policy matter? An econometric investigation", *Journal of Political Economy* 90: 22–51.

Mitchell, Wesley C. (1913) *Business Cycles*, Berkeley, CA: University of California Press.

Muth, John F. (1961) "Rational expectations and the theory of price movements", *Econometrica* 29 (July): 315–35.

Pesaran, M. Hashem (1987) *The Limits of Rational Expectations*, Oxford: Basil Blackwell.

Phelps, Edmund S. (1967) "Phillips curves, expectations of inflation and optimal employment over time", *Economica* (August): 254–81.

—— (1970) "Introduction: the new microeconomics in employment and inflation theory", in Edmund S. Phelps (ed.) *Microeconomic Foundations of Employment and Inflation Theory*, New York: Norton.

Phelps, Edmund S. and Taylor, John B. (1977) "Stabilizing properties of monetary policy under rational expectations", *Journal of Political Economy* 85: 163–90.

Samuelson, Paul A. (1947) *Foundations of Economic Analysis*, Cambridge, MA: Harvard University Press.

Sheffrin, Steven A. (1983) *Rational Expectations*, Cambridge: Cambridge University Press.

Simon, Herbert A. (1969) *The Science of the Artificial*, Cambridge, MA: MIT Press.

Simons, Henry (1936) "Rules versus authority in monetary policy", reprinted in *Economic Policy for a Free Society*, Chicago, IL: University of Chicago Press, 1948, pp. 40–77.

Small, David H. (1979) "Unanticipated money growth and unemployment in the United States: comment", *American Economic Review* 69 (December): 996–1003.

Tobin, James (1980) *Asset Accumulation and Economic Activity*, Chicago, IL: University of Chicago Press.

—— (1987) *Policies for Prosperity*, Brighton: Wheatsheaf.

Chapter 15

Experimenting with neoclassical economics
A critical review of experimental economics

Shaun Hargreaves Heap and Yanis Varoufakis

INTRODUCTION

Experimental economics has a long history, but in the last decade there has been a proliferation of dedicated laboratories yielding a large body of experimental results (see Roth (1988) for a review of this history). This chapter assesses the contribution of the experimental approach to the neoclassical canon. We set the scene in the next section with a brief discussion of the methodological role of experiments in economics. The third section focuses on the experimental evidence with respect to one aspect of neoclassical economics: its theory of decision-making. These two sections feed directly into the final sections which is concerned with the implications of these results for both method and neoclassical economics.

THE PROMISE OF EXPERIMENTS

Neoclassical economics has empiricism to thank for a strong defense of its often puzzling assumptions and concepts.[1] By referring the critic to the "tribunal of the facts", it blunts all deductive criticism, asking instead the simple question: "Does the theory predict well?" If to predict is also to explain, then *any* theory which is consistent with its own premises can be good and proper depending entirely on its predictive capacity.

Many a criticism has stumbled on this empiricist defense, and yet there has been an undeniable and growing discomfort with its use over the last forty years. For example, econometrics may have prospered as a result of the commitment to empiricism, but the doubts have been growing at the same time. Unlike statisticians working in natural scientific or biomedical fields, economists have failed to make their statistics equally respectable. Instead, there is more than a hint of fool's gold and the whiff of alchemy as the regressions pile up (see Hendry 1980). Indeed, we may laugh at the suggestion of "lies, more lies and statistics", but it is a slightly nervous laugh because few economists will not at one time or another have been frustrated by the failure of the econometric evidence to throw any real light on a major theoretical controversy (famously, of course in macroeconomics where the econometric evidence seems uncannily to favor one's theoretical predisposition). In other words, we laugh nervously precisely because, however exaggerated the suggestion may be, we know the boundary between lies and statistics in economics is not as hard and fast as we would like.

Whatever the complete explanation for this failure, it is clear that at least one important difference between disciplines in which statistics are respectable and econometrics is that the latter relies on field observations which are generated in a very complicated way by a world which is quite indifferent to the question of providing tests for particular bits of economic theory. Thus our best efforts at empirical testing are stymied in part by the poor quality of our evidence.

Against such a background, it is easy to appreciate the attractions of experimental economics. In a manner reminiscent of "proper" science, the economist can *generate* data in the controlled environment of a laboratory, under conditions that are determined through careful experimental design to yield precise tests of hypotheses. Remarkable feats well beyond the econometrician's reach become feasible. The practitioner can, for example, impose demand and supply functions on a sample of randomly selected buyers and sellers (thus doing away with the problem of identification) and then sit back and observe the speed of convergence to equilibrium. Indeed, it is possible to test the bulk of economic theory which is grounded on comparative statics without having to worry too much about whether the *ceteris paribus* assumptions have been satisfied. Furthermore, one can give particular kinds of information to subjects and, for example, test a theoretical hypothesis that only a certain type of information is relevant to economic behavior under specific circumstances; and so on.

In short, non-observable variables and parameters cease to be a problem. The possibilities seem boundless and, indeed, a great deal of research using experimental techniques is genuinely exciting. Nonetheless there is a serious danger that the prospects are exaggerated; and it will be helpful for the later discussion to record some doubts.

The first signs of trouble appear at the outset when subjects are selected. For instance, it is often noted that the bulk of participants are university undergraduates; and the immediate worry is over how "representative" such samples are. There are two aspects to the disquiet. One concerns whether the sample provides a fair test of the theory. It is quite possible, for instance, that the MBA and economics students, who form the usual fodder, have been *trained* to think in a manner sympathetic to the predictions of neoclassical theory. The more interesting test, perhaps, would be to see whether, say, a group of nurses from a publicly (under-) funded hospice would also confirm the theory's predictions.

This problem might seem to arise simply because it is, quite naturally, easier to use your own students in a test. So the remedy is equally simple, if a little more costly: draw subjects from a wider population. However, the selection problem runs deeper. Consider the Forsyth *et al.* (1991) experimental study of the likelihood of industrial disputes. The theory's main empirical prediction (namely that strikes will not occur when a so-called incentive efficiency condition does not hold) performed less well than was hoped. The authors offered as an explanation the fact that the sample was "heterogeneous". What does this mean? According to the authors, a significant proportion of "altruists" and "risk-averse" players was detected. In a poignant footnote they write: "One might reduce the problem of heterogeneity by conducting the experiment in two phases, using the first phase to screen out *undesirable subjects*" (our italics).[2]

Nor is this an isolated example of an experimenter seeking to place constraints on the sample. Even when the experimenter is not actively soliciting homogeneity, sometimes it is difficult not to do so unwittingly. For instance, in an interesting study of the determinants of bargaining outcomes, Roth *et al.* (1981) asked agents to bargain with each other over the probability of winning a certain prize, rather than on outcomes *per se*. Before the experimental sessions got under way, participants were subjected to a "brief review of probability theory". They were also instructed that "your objective should be to maximise your own earnings by taking advantage of the special features of each session".

This type of restriction on the sample can be traced to a perfectly legitimate desire to remove "impurities" from the sample. The experimental natural scientist does this all the time; and likewise it would not be fair to test a theory of rational behavior on a group of irrational subjects. However, there is no problem when a microbiologist rejects a sample if she thinks it is impure because "impurity" in natural science is usually defined objectively, that is, independently of the theory the experimenter is testing. The worry with social science is that there is frequently no independent way of selecting our impurities. Too often, the only way of detecting an impurity is the failure of a subject to conform with the theory; and in this way the desire to provide a fair test actually turns the test into no test at all.[3] In other words, "fact" and theory can mingle unhealthily when sample selection is guided by theory.

There is a further twist to this problem. Sample biases can arise as a direct result of the material of the experiment itself because, in some degree, a sample selects itself on the basis of what is offered by the experiment. Consider, for instance, the vexed issue of whether to pay the subjects. Psychologists frequently refrain from offering money as they distrust the effect of financial incentives on behavior. Cognitive dissonance, for example, is a real phenomenon that disappears when subjects have monetary reasons by which to explain what it is they are doing.[4] On the other hand, payment linked to effort keeps subjects on their toes and allows economists to assume that their behavior is self-interested. This is a strong argument as anyone who has been bored playing poker without money will readily testify. On the other hand, does the payment of money encourage a particular kind of subject to come forward? Indeed is it really so unfair to suspect that the kind of person who is attracted to an experiment offering money is also the kind of person who conforms more generally to the theory of instrumental motivation which the neoclassical experimenter wishes to test?

The second aspect of the worry about "representativeness" concerns the applicability of the laboratory results to other settings. In other words, MBA and economics students may not only fail to represent a wider population, their behavior in a laboratory may fail to represent their behavior in markets, firms and the like. Since there has never been any suggestion that experiments in economics are designed to throw light on how people behave in experimental settings alone, the second concern with "representativeness" is a real one. It is an issue which we take up more fully in the fourth section.

A SURVEY OF SOME NEOCLASSICAL EXPERIMENTS

Parametric choice

We take the neoclassical theory of choice to be synonymous with the hypothesis that action follows from an exercise in constrained optimization. Agents choose so as (or "as if") to maximize some objective function. This is the instrumental model of rational agency which associates rationality with the calculation of the most efficient means for achieving given ends. Thus, in conditions of certainty, individuals, when they act on a well-behaved preference ordering, act as if they maximize utility. Likewise, since von Neumann and Morgenstern (1947) and Savage (1954), individuals, acting on appropriately defined preference orderings for conditions of uncertainty, act as if they were maximizing expected utility.

To be specific with respect to uncertain decision-making, let us define an *option* as comprising a distribution of payoffs and a distribution of probabilities with which each of the payoffs will be won. Consider an example: option O_i will yield \$100 with probability 30 percent and \$20 with probability 70 percent whereas O_j will yield \$80 with probability 40 percent and \$18 with probability 60 percent. In general, we denote an option O as $O[v, p]$ where v is the payoff vector and p the probability vector associated with it. For simplicity let us take an example where each option to be considered has three possible outcomes v_1, v_2 and v_3. Then, von Neumann and Morgenstern demonstrated that, when the choice over options satisfies various conditions, it is "as if" the individual selected the option which maximized expected utility as given by

$$E(U) = p_1 u_1 + (1 - p_1 - p_3)u_2 + p_3 u_3 \qquad (15.1)$$

where u_i is a cardinal utility index representation of the choice of v_i under conditions of certainty (see Hey 1979).

This hypothesis of rational decision-making has been tested experimentally in both parametric and strategic settings of uncertainty: that is, in situations where the uncertainty attaches respectively to the state of nature and the actions of others. Allais (1953) provides a famous first illustration of one type of test of this theory under parametric uncertainty. To illustrate this generic test, suppose that an individual is told that the potential payoffs are $v_1 = \$1000$, $v_2 = \$500$ and $v_3 = -\$500$ respectively and that there are four options (A, B, C and D) to be considered which each offer different probability combinations of these v_i. The options are summarized in Figure 15.1. The right-hand side of this figure sets the options out in a conventional fashion, while the left-hand side exploits the fact that each option contains the same set of outcomes and that probabilities sum to one, and so represents each option by a point in the probability triangle.

It will be noted that the slope of the line AB in this triangle is the same as the slope of the line CD. This is important. It means that expected utility theory predicts that if A is preferred to B then C must be preferred to D, or if B is preferred to A then D must be preferred to C. To appreciate this implication, differentiate (15.1) to obtain the slope of the indifference curves with respect to these options in $[p_3, p_1]$ space:

$$\frac{dp_1}{dp_3}\bigg|_{dU=0} = -\frac{\partial U/\partial p_3}{\partial U/\partial p_1} = \frac{u_2 - u_3}{u_1 - u_2} \tag{15.2}$$

Thus, since the cardinal utility indices of each outcome do not change with the probability attached to them, the indifference curves are straight lines in this space, and they have been drawn in as the broken lines in Figure 15.1. We also know that $u_1 > u_3$ (since $\$1000 > \$500$), so that vertical movement takes one to higher indifference curves. Hence, the preference relation between A and B depends solely on the relative slope of AB compared with the slope of the indifference curves given by (15.2), and likewise the

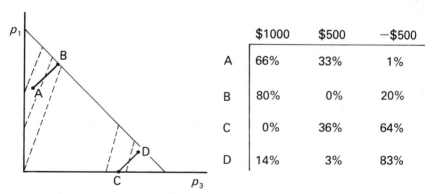

	$1000	$500	−$500
A	66%	33%	1%
B	80%	0%	20%
C	0%	36%	64%
D	14%	3%	83%

Figure 15.1

preference between C and D. And since the slope of the indifference curve is always the same and the slope of AB is the same as that of CD, the particular prediction of expected utility theory follows.

However, Allais's (1953) and many subsequent experiments have demonstrated that when individuals face such a choice they often choose "inconsistently" in the sense that A is preferred to B while D is preferred to C (see Machina 1987). One possible interpretation of these inconsistencies is that option A attracts more subjects than option B for the simple reason that it involves an extremely low probability of losing $500 while still retaining a heartening expectation of winning $1000. However, when it comes to a choice between C and D, option C may prove far less popular than the theory predicts because both C and D are "bad" options as, more likely than not, they will lead to a loss of $500. Perhaps in such situations agents have a tendency to throw caution to the wind, a tendency that they do not have when choosing between "good" options such as A and B. Simply put, there is a distinct possibility that different decision rules are employed when the context/description of what is the "same" choice (from the perspective of expected utility) switches from gains to losses.

More formally the slope of the indifference curve reflects risk aversion and if this changed between losses and gains then the indifference curves fan out, creating the possibility that the slope of the curve is less than CD in this vicinity while the slope is greater than AB in this vicinity. This idea has been explored within generalized expected utility models by a number of authors who have posited preference functions which are nonlinear in probabilities. These efforts are noteworthy, but from the perspective of this chapter what is perhaps more interesting is the fact that none of these fanning explanations is capable of explaining another anomaly which has surfaced in the experimental literature: that is, preference reversals (see Machina 1987). To illustrate this phenomenon, consider the options in Figure 15.2 which are taken from Machina (1987).

In experiments, people are asked both how much they would sell each bet for when they owned the right to it (call these selling prices SP(P) and SP($)) and which bet they would prefer when given the choice between the two. Typically people prefer the P bet, while assigning a higher price for the $ bet (that is SP($) > SP(P)). In other words, such people say they are indifferent between P and SP(P), P is preferred to $, and they are also indifferent between $ and SP($); this entails an inconsistency with what we presume, since SP($) > SP(P), to be their preference of SP($) over SP(P).

One of the leading attempts at explaining such intransitivities is regret theory (see Bell 1982; Loomes and Sugden 1982; Loomes *et al.* 1989). With this theory, an option is evaluated not just in terms of its expected return but also in terms of the regret which might be experienced if another option should prove to be superior once the outcome is known. This immediately makes context matter again, but in a slightly different way than before. The

$$
\text{P bet} \left\{ \begin{array}{l} p \text{ chance } \$X \\[1em] 1 - p \text{ chance } \$x \end{array} \right. \qquad \text{\$ bet} \left\{ \begin{array}{l} q \text{ chance of } \$Y \\[1em] 1 - q \text{ chance of } \$y \end{array} \right.
$$

X and Y are greater
than x and y
respectively and p is
greater than q and Y
is greater than X.

Figure 15.2

context does not come from ordinary language descriptions which signal a difference which expected utility theory denies, as it did before. Instead the important context now is that afforded by the other options from which the individual must choose and once this is an important factor in decisions it is not so surprising to find that pairwise choices prove inconsistent because this aspect of the context of choice varies between the pairs.

To appreciate how this dependence on context is more broadly plausible than a simple matter of regret and how it helps explain intransitivity, consider an example where x, y and z are political parties. Why should we assume transitivity here? Might not a person plausibly reason thus:

> When I am asked to act politically, my experience of that action depends not only on the nature of what I choose, but on the nature of what I forgo as well. When I am offered the choice between x and y, I choose x rather than y. When I am asked to choose between y and z, I prefer y. But when I am asked to choose between z and x, I prefer z to x simply because of a certain linkage between x and z that is incommensurable in terms of y. Since the element of the feasible set *that I do not* choose matters, there is no inconsistency.

Consider another where a person's feasible set is (x, y, z) and her ranking is x > y > z. Does this mean that she would still choose x from the smaller set (x, y)? There are situations in which a rational A may experience a reversal of preference just because a less desired member of the feasible set is no longer available.[5] Suppose that x= stay at home, y= go to the theatre, z= attend a political meeting, when A's ranking is still x > y > z. Suddenly the military authorities of the land ban the political meeting. Is it irrational for A to alter her preferences and to lift z from the bottom of her ordinal ranking? Suppose further that the same authorities declare martial law commanding everyone to stay indoors for the next three hours. Recalling that staying at home was A's initial first preference when the feasible set was (x, y, z), is it irrational for A to drop x from the top of her ranking after the feasible set has been cut down? A pointed example this may be, yet it helps demonstrate the relevance of context (see also Sugden 1991).

The other major approach to explaining preference reversals comes from a psychological literature. It makes context matter again, but in a way which is closer to the earlier example. This literature emphasizes that individuals who are not all knowing and calculating (that is, who are boundedly rational), and who use decision rules, may have different rules for processing information when "choosing" compared with when "setting" prices. Not unsurprisingly, the application of different rules can yield different and inconsistent results (see Slovic and Lichtenstein 1983). Thus the context matters here because it can contribute to the definition of what sort of problem the individual faces, and then a "choice" problem triggers a different decision rule then does a "valuation" problem.

In this brief review of the experimental literature we have emphasized that the context of choices influences decisions, where context has been broadly construed as various aspects of the decision problem which agents take to be relevant in their choices in a way that expected utility theory denies. We have emphasized this for several reasons. First, it reminds us that the violations of expected utility theory are not just random; they seem to follow a systematic pattern (that is, "context" exercises a predictable influence). Second, it helps explain why no single alternative theory of choice seems to fare better in the experimental literature than all others (see Appleby and Starmer (1987) Battalio *et al.* (1990) for surveys). After all, since each theory of choice highlights a different aspect of the context of each decision problem and since not all choice problems will necessarily have the same contextual factors, there should be no expectation that a theory based on one aspect of context could explain all violations of expected utility theory. Finally, as we shall argue in the next section, the appreciation of context provides a source of continuity in the experimental literature because it appears to be important in strategic settings as well.

Strategic choice

The neoclassical analysis of decision-making in interactive settings relies on game theory. This theory is based on the assumption that agents are expected utility maximizers. In addition, it assumes there is common knowledge that agents are rational in this instrumental sense. There is some controversy over precisely what is entailed by these assumptions (see Binmore 1990), but the conventional wisdom on the matter suggests that we should expect behavior which conforms with a Nash equilibrium (or the related concept of a perfect equilibrium in games with a dynamic structure – see Selten 1975).

This prediction has been extensively tested experimentally in one particular game: a bargaining game. The evidence from these tests reinforces the early conclusion because it seems to suggest that context, in the form of shared views on justice, the presence or otherwise of face-to-face contact and so on, affects significantly the outcome of these games (see Roth 1988). Some care is required here, since the tests typically involve two different Nash hypotheses. There is the axiomatic Nash (1953) solution to a bargaining game and there is the Nash equilibrium concept for non-cooperative games. It is the latter which is our concern, although much of the evidence relates to whether the former solution obtains in these games. However, the two are connected because it is often argued that the Nash solution emerges as the unique Nash equilibrium when the bargaining game is played non-cooperatively. Thus, if these arguments are correct, then the tests for the Nash solution are also a test of the prediction that agents behave according to the prediction of a Nash equilibrium.

Many theorists now believe that this argument is flawed and there are multiple Nash equilibria in the bargaining game. Thus the evidence against the Nash solution does not tell unambiguously against the Nash equilibrium prediction. Indeed, it might be argued that the evidence with respect to the role of context fits well with this picture because agents facing multiple Nash equilibria must base their choice of which Nash equilibrium to guide their actions on something. By definition that "something" will have to be a source of distinction which is not ordinarily recognized by game theory, since this theory is unable to single out one equilibrium when there are multiple Nash equilibria.

Against the view that context is unavoidably influential when there are multiple Nash equilibria, it is sometimes argued that equilibrium selection in such games need not rely on such sources of extraneous information. Instead, it is argued that principles like Pareto dominance follow from a presumption of common rationality and that they can be used to select an equilibrium (see Harsanyi and Selten 1988). Whether these arguments are right or not, there have been several tests of the hypothesis. For instance, Van Huyck et al. (1990) report a revealing experiment. Each subject in every session was asked to choose a number between 1 and 7. If everyone chooses 7 then each wins $1.30. If on the other hand each chooses number 6, every subject wins $1.20. And so on. Finally if each chooses the lowest integer (i.e. 1), then each gets only $0.7. To introduce the coordination problem, suppose one participant chooses integer k while the lowest integer chosen within this group is m ($m < k$). Then the person who chose k receives what she would have received had they both chosen k minus ($k - m$) times $0.2. The person who chose m receives what she would have received had they both chosen m minus, again, ($k - m$) times $0.2. Thus, this is a pure coordination problem with multiple Nash equilibria which can be Pareto ranked; and at the top of the list, everyone can walk away with the top prize provided each chooses 7. Moreover, everyone knows this and no one benefits by choosing a lower number than others. As the authors explain, the game is designed in a way that "the players have complete information about the payoff function and strategy space and know that the payoff function and strategy space are common knowledge".

Under such conditions, if the Pareto principle was used to select the equilibrium then everyone should opt for number 7.

The results are striking. The first time this game was played, only 31 percent chose number 7. The most popular choices were numbers 4 and 5. Were the participants plain irrational? Before making their choice, they were asked to predict the overall outcome. The average range of predictions was about 4. Although they failed to coordinate their actions and beliefs between themselves, in most cases each subject's actions were compatible with his or her beliefs. Each of the seven classes of subjects played the same game ten times. Was there convergence to an equilibrium? Indeed there was, albeit the direction of the dynamics took the players further away from the theoretical prediction. In the authors' own words, "rather than converging to the payoff-dominant equilibrium or to the initial outcome ..., the most inefficient outcome obtains in all seven experiments.... Since the payoff-dominant equilibrium would have paid all subjects $19.50 ... and the average earnings were only $8.80, the observed behaviour cost the average subject $10.70 in lost earnings."

We can illustrate a further finding from the experimental literature on the role of extraneous information with an experiment of our own. Consider the games in Figure 15.3. Game 1 represents the simplest possible form of bargaining: strategy 1 is the "tough" choice for the row players and the "weak" option for the column players. Similarly, strategy 2 is the "weak" ("strong") strategy for the row (column) player. The element of coordination comes into the picture via the off-diagonal elements of the payoff matrix, which exact a price from each when they fail to choose the same strategy. However, unlike the Huyck et al. (1990) games, there is antagonism now since coordination means that one of the two will earn $5 while the other ends up with nothing. Furthermore as there is no unique equilibrium (and they cannot be Pareto ranked), the general theory does not predict a specific outcome. The purpose of making subjects play this game was threefold: (a) to give them a simple 2 × 2 game in order to get them used to reading payoff matrices; (b) to check the consistency between their expectations about their opponents' behavior and their own choices;[6] and (c) to use the results from

	1	2
1	5, 0	−1, −1
2	−1, −1	0, 5

	1	2	3
1	5, 0	−1, −1	10, −1
2	−1, −1	0, 5	−1, −2
3	−1, 10	−2, −1	6, 6

Game 1   Game 2

Figure 15.3

this game as the "control" by which to test neoclassical game theory's main hypothesis: namely that game 2 is strategically equivalent to game 1 or, put differently, that rational agents will play game 2 as if it were game 1. It is the last hypothesis which interests us here.

The hypothesis comprises the subhypotheses that players will neither expect their opponent to play strategy 3 nor themselves opt for strategy 3. This may seem paradoxical at first sight as it is clear that, if they both choose strategy 3, then the outcome will be Pareto superior to both the Nash equilibria ((5,0) and (0,5)). Nevertheless, it is true to say that strategy 3 is dominated by strategies 1 and 2. In other words, there is no expectation that a player can entertain that will motivate strategy 3 on instrumental grounds. Even if you predict that your opponent will play strategy 3 (because he or she is non-instrumental, or plain foolish, or whatever), you are better off playing strategy 1.

In an ongoing experimental project,[7] we observed large deviations from the theory's predictions. From a sample of sixty individuals (six sessions each involving ten subjects) who anonymously played game 2 four times each (twice as row players and twice as column players), three things became clear. First, strategy 3 was observed at a rate exceeding 30 percent and, significantly, cooperation (that is, outcome (6,6)) was achieved in more than one out of six occasions. Second, the third strategy was anticipated approximately half of the time. Clearly the decisions to attempt cooperation by playing strategy 3 were based on an expectation that the opposition would also prove cooperative. Third, the second strategy was almost totally eclipsed. That is, even column players who had no cooperative streak (that is, who neither expected cooperation, in the form of strategy 3, from their opponent nor wished to cooperate themselves in order to attain the $6 outcome) did not attempt to reach the Nash equilibrium that favored them. On the other hand, row players exhibited remarkable confidence in that they predicted cooperation from the column players 30 percent more often than the column players predicted cooperation from them. Row players predicted that strategy 2 would be used only three times out of 120. They were right: column players played strategy 2 only three times (out of a maximum of 120).

The latter result is indeed surprising in view of the fact that the roles were rotated from repetition to repetition so that the column and the row players were the same people playing an utterly symmetric game! It seems that the players bought some background convention which gave priority to the row player in this game. The earlier reported result on the use of strategy 3 is equally surprising. It suggests that the Pareto principle may play a role in guiding individual behavior, but in circumstances where the theory suggests that it could have no role since its use confounds a more basic presumption that individuals are instrumentally rational and so will not use dominated strategies.

In other words, we conclude from this experiment that context matters again in the playing of games, but in an even more radical way than is suggested by the bargaining literature, where it plausibly helps select a Nash equilibrium when there are many. It seems context may actually activate a different form of decision-making altogether.

THE IMPLICATIONS OF EXPERIMENTAL ECONOMICS

At first glance the implications of these experiments seem straightforward. Decision-making does not seem to conform to neoclassical theory in either strategic or parametric settings and consequently the behavioral core of neoclassical economics is in trouble. Of course, no alternative theory sweeps the board yet. Each has its own failures and problems, and so perhaps a case can be made for keeping expected utility theory, at least until one of the new theories achieves ascendence. In any event, whether we decide to drop expected utility theory now or later, the road for future research seems clear: it is paved with more labs and more experiments devoted to discovering the best model of decision-making.

But is this really where the future lies? There seem to be two problems with drawing such an inference. They relate directly to the two problems of "representativeness" distinguished above. First, the problem of facts mingling with theory is part of a general philosophical criticism of empiricism – usually known as the Duhem–Quine criticism after the two philosophers who are held responsible for the insight (see Hollis and Nell (1975) and Hargreaves Heap and Hollis (1987) for further discussion and references). In other words, the subject selection difficulties are reminders that the experimental type of empirical work does not escape from this criticism. It attaches to all empirical methods and ought to caution against an *exclusive* reliance on empiricism as a method. Thus, the future road ought not to be paved *exclusively* with more labs and experiments.

Second, the broad finding from the experimental evidence that "context matters" is potentially rather damaging with respect to the applicability of these laboratory results to non-laboratory settings. After all, if context seems to affect behavior, as the experimental results show, then there can be no general presumption that the results generated in the contexts of laboratories have any relevance for a behavior outside the laboratory. It is therefore tempting to conclude, and indeed somewhat ironically, that the message of experimental economics is actually a self-denying ordinance. In short, not only have we discovered that there is a warrant for building something other than laboratories in the future, we also find that there should be a moratorium on all future lab building.

It may be difficult to avoid this temptation because the conclusion is so strikingly opposed to what seemed to be the case on a first glance. Nevertheless, it should perhaps be more cautiously stated. The discovery that "context matters" could always be construed as an invitation to develop a theory of context within the laboratory setting. Indeed, there seems to be no reason why it should not be interpreted in this way. However, the experimental work in this direction can only be a step towards a theory of context because any theory of context which is designed to apply in non-laboratory contexts will have to be tested in non-laboratory contexts. This is a matter of definition since no one has ever proposed as good practice the testing of a theory over domains to which it does not apply.[8]

Another temptation to be avoided is the reinstatement of expected utility theory. We may have reason to doubt the significance of experimental results but that does not mean that the adverse results with respect to expected utility theory should be wholly discounted. First, it is *not* obvious that the interdependence between theory and facts will have worked against the acceptance of expected utility theory. The more usual worry is that the theory becomes self-fulfilling through its influence on the facts; and indeed the examples of unfortunate mingling in the second section were all of this sort. Of course, defenders of the faith may be able to provide counter examples, so this argument is at best suggestive. Nevertheless, the point remains. We are still interested in empirical evidence, even if the Duhem–Quine argument counsels caution, and at the moment the evidence reflects badly on neoclassical decision theory.

There are two further, and perhaps more substantial, reasons for rejecting the expected utility theory as a general model of decision-making. They come from the methodological space which is created once empiricism ceases to be the exclusive method. This is not the place to develop these observations and the points will be baldly stated.

In effect, the methodological warrant for empiricism comes from a correspondence theory of truth and it is the failure of facts to be clearly distinguishable from theory which undermines the correspondence test. There remains, of course, a coherence account of truth; and there is also the possibility of slanting the interdependence between fact and theory in a more positive way. First, consider briefly the criterion of coherence. This demands that the hypotheses (which, notice, you may still want to test) logically follow from the theory, and there must be some doubt regarding whether this condition is satisfied – at least as far as the conventional wisdom's use of expected utility maximization in game theory is concerned, because there is some doubt over whether Nash behavior is entailed by this and common knowledge assumptions (see Bernheim 1984; Pearce 1984).

The difficulty for expected utility theory is that a move to something like rationalizable strategies, which comes from these discussions, typically expands the number of admissible behaviors. This, in turn, compounds the problem which arose with multiple Nash equilibria, namely, that the theory may simply, say, turn out to be close to vacuous because almost every possible behavior conforms with it. Or to put this slightly differently, if we want a theory to be coherent in the different sense of generating "meaningful" statements, then it must be possible for the statement not to correspond with some state of the world. The problem for expected utility theory is that in many settings it may court the danger of failing the test of being "meaningful" because it will admit too many types of behavior.

Second, since the mingling of fact and theory means that theory helps in part to create the world in which we live, we may wish to be guided in our choice of theories by our preferences between the worlds which are thereby created. In other words, there are legitimate normative considerations which enter into theory selection because theory is not simply an attempt to explain what is going on in a pre-existing world. Of course, there may be strict limits on the scope which exists for theory to create the world, but nevertheless there seems to be some scope and this licenses a normative component to the discussion of theory selection. The problem for expected utility theory which arises from this thought is simply that this model of rational agency does not obviously equip us to engage in this type of normative discussion. For instance, it is well known from discussions in welfare economics (and political theory) that there is no general formula for constructing a social welfare ordering from individual preferences. In Sen's (1976) words, it seems that we need to have a bit more "room up top" than the conventional utility maximizing model allows if we are to engage in this sort of discussion. This is not the place to develop a discussion of what might be involved in equipping us motivationally to deliberate in this way, but if the users of theory might want to exercise such faculties (whatever they may be), then surely our theory ought also to take account of the possibility that our behavior in the economy may also be influenced by the use of these faculties.

CONCLUSION

This chapter has argued that experimental economics has made a very significant contribution to the discipline. It has undermined the claim of expected utility theory to be a general theory of decision-making. However, the way it has done this is not, as some might suppose, by providing irrefutable evidence against the hypothesis. Although it has generated contrary evidence which has contributed to the doubts over expected utility theory, this has not been its only contribution. The experimental approach has also helped to remind us of the problems associated with all empiricist methods. Thus, it contributes to the creation of space for other methodological considerations – and it has been argued briefly that these other considerations seem likely to reinforce the empirical evidence by telling against the general adoption of expected utility theory.

Of course, the problems with empiricism do not spell the end of all empirical testing. Indeed, such testing will remain important and it is here that there is a further and somewhat paradoxical conclusion to be drawn from the laboratory experimental approach: it is that such testing will have to take place in some degree outside the laboratory. Thus, laboratory experimental economics has had an extremely important impact on economics but, in contrast, its future role is likely to be more modest.[9]

NOTES

1   Of course, there are other methodological defenses of neoclassical economics. For example, there are those who claim it is simply an exercise in logic. But, there are few people who would deny that most neoclassical economists subscribe to some form or other of empiricism as a methodological support.

2   The authors did not, however, pursue that line. Yet it is instructive to note why: "there are additional strategic complications in the screening phase of the game, since some players who should be screened out might dissemble if they desire to play the second phase of the game".

3   Of course, this problem is related to the strategy of immunizing a theory from contrary empirical evidence by claiming that the theory is normative and not descriptive.

4   A simple example of cognitive dissonance is when a subject alters her views on some political or moral issue as a result of a contradiction between (a) her original beliefs on the matter and (b) an opposing view that she was asked to advocate in front of a large number of people (as if it was her own) as part of the experiment. In such experiments it has been observed that, when money was paid, the original beliefs remained intact (presumably because payment was conceived as an internal explanation of the dichotomy between one's views and one's speech), whereas when money was not paid subjects' original beliefs became increasingly shaky. For a discussion of objections to payment of experimental subjects see Kahneman and Tversky (1979), Wright and Abdul-Ezz (1988) and Scott et al. (1988).

5   This is the possibility that John Nash's infamous axiom of the independence from irrelevant alternatives was meant to outlaw.

6   For example, if a row player expects the column player to choose strategy 2, then the only action by the row player consistent with this expectation is also to choose strategy 2.

7   References to our work are available on request. The data referred to herein come from a data set that will be augmented shortly. Nevertheless, the reported results are statistically significant and the sample size is comparable with those of other experimental projects. See for example Cooper et al. (1990) whose work is along similar lines.

8   Of course, this argument would not preclude an extension of the experimental method to venues outside the laboratory – and we are indebted to Chris Starmer for making this point to us. However, the conduct of experiments outside the laboratory immediately reintroduces the kind of problem with respect to controlling for a plethora of influences which was partially responsible for the original switch away from econometrics to laboratory experiments as a means for empirical testing. In addition, there is an ethical problem which may arise concerning the conduct of experiments on subjects who are not aware that they are being experimented upon. In so far as this is an ethical problem, then it cannot be overcome simply by telling the people that they are participating because this will recreate in a weaker form the problem regarding the applicability of experimental results to other settings.

9   This is unlikely to be immediately obvious for some time because the labs have been built and the dynamics of our profession are such that the experiments will fill them (and the journal pages) for some time to come.

REFERENCES

Allais, M. (1953) "Le comportement de l'homme rational devant le risque, critique des postulates et axiomes de l'ecole americain", *Econometrica* 21: 503–46.

Appleby, L. and Starmer, C. (1987) "Theories of choice under uncertainty: the experimental evidence past and present", in J. Hey and P. Lambert (eds) *Surveys in the Economics of Uncertainty*, Oxford: Basil Blackwell.

Battalio, R., Kagel, J. and Jiranyakul, R. (1990) "Testing between alternative models of choice under uncertainty: some initial results", *Journal of Risk and Uncertainty* 3: 25–51.

Bell, D. (1982) "Regret in decision making under uncertainty", *Operations Research* 30: 961–81.

Bernheim, B. (1984) "Rationalisable strategic behaviour", *Econometrica* 42: 1007–28.

Binmore, K. (1990) *The Foundations of Game Theory*, Oxford: Basil Blackwell.

Cooper, R., DeJong, D., Forsythe, R. and Ross, T. (1990) "Selection criteria in coordination games: some experimental results", *American Economic Review* 80: 218–33.

Forsythe, R., Kennan, J. and Sopher, B. (1991) "An experimental analysis of strikes in bargaining games with one-sided private information", *American Economic Review* 81: 253–78.

Grether, D. (1992) "Testing Bayes rule and the representative heuristic: some experimental evidence", *Journal of Economic Behaviour and Organization* 17: 31–57.

Hargreaves Heap, S. and Hollis, M. (1987) "Epistemological issues in economics", in J. Eatwell, M. Milgate and P. Newman (eds) *The New Palgrave*, London: Macmillan.

Harsanyi, J. and Selten, R. (1988) *A General Theory of Equilibrium Selection in Games*, Cambridge, MA: MIT Press.

Hendry, D. (1980) "Econometrics: alchemy or science?", *Economica* 42: 387–406.

Hey, J. (1979) *Uncertainty in Microeconomics*, Oxford: Martin Robertson.

Hollis, M. and Nell, E. (1975) *Rational Economic Man*, Cambridge: Cambridge University Press.

Kahneman, D. and Tversky, A. (1979) "Prospect theory: an analysis of decision under risk", *Econometrica* 47: 263–92.

Loomes, G. and Sugden, R. (1982) "Regret theory: an alternative theory of rational choice under uncertainty", *Economic Journal* 92: 805–24.

Loomes, G., Starmer, C. and Sugden, R. (1989) "Preference reversal: information processing effect or rational non-transitive choice", *Economic Journal* 99 (Supplement): 140–51.

Machina, M. (1987) "Choice under uncertainty: problems solved and unsolved", *Journal of Economic Perspectives* 1: 121–54.

Nash, J. (1953) "Two person cooperative games", *Econometrica* 21: 128–40.

Pearce, D. (1984) "Rationalizable strategic behaviour and the problem of perfection", *Econometrica* 52: 1029–50.

Roth, A. (1988) "Laboratory experimentation in economics: a methodological overview", *Economic Journal* 98: 974–1031.

Roth, A., Malouf, M. and Murnighan, J. (1981) "Sociological versus strategic factors in bargaining", *Journal of Economic Behaviour and Organization* 2: 153–77.

Savage, L. (1954) *The Foundations of Statistics*, New York: Wiley.

Scott, W., Farg, J.-L. and Podsakoff, P. (1988) "The effects of 'intrinsic' and 'extrinsic' reinforcement contingencies on task behaviour", *Organizational Behavior and Human Decision Processes* 41: 405–25.

Selten, R. (1975) "A re-examination of the perfectness concept for equilibrium in extensive games", *International Journal of Game Theory* 4: 22–55.

Sen, A. (1976) "Rational fools: a critique of the behavioural foundations of economic theory", *Philosophy and Public Affairs* 6: 317–44.

Sugden, R. (1991) "Rational choice: a survey of contributions from economics and philosophy", *Economic Journal* 101: 751–86.

Tversky, A. and Kahneman, D. (1986) "Rational choice and the framing of decisions", *Journal of Business* 59: S251–78.

Van Huyck, J., Battalio, R. and Beil, R. (1990) "Tacit coordination games, strategic uncertainty and coordination failure", *American Economic Review* 80: 234–48.

von Neumann, J. and Morgenstern, O. (1947) *Theory of Games and Economic Behaviour*, 2nd edn, Princeton, NJ: Princeton University Press.

Wright, W. and Abdul-Ezz, M. (1988) "Effects of extrinsic incentives on the quality of frequency assessments", *Organizational Behavior and Human Decision Processes* 41: 143–52.

Chapter 16

The Carnot engine and the working day

Murray Wolfson

INTRODUCTION

What is the proper domain of applicability of the neoclassical utility maximization model? For the University of Chicago's George Stigler and Gary Becker (1977), it is a philosopher's stone, a framework for resolving all social problems in or out of economics' traditional realm. Mirowski (1989) carries to its outer limits Veblen's criticism ([1898] 1934, [1899–1900] 1946) that it fails to describe evolutionary processes. He sees neoclassical economics as an anachronism imported from physics generating "more heat than light".

Actually, proponents as well as critics of neoclassical economics have built their theories around the fact that utility theory has the same structure as field theories in physics (Edgeworth [1881] 1961; Samuelson 1947, 1972). In much the same way as the force of gravity attracts objects in three-dimensional space, utility maps the attraction of individuals to higher levels of satisfaction in a space of commodities. In this chapter we will explore both the power and the limitation of field theory and attempt to arrive at a balanced judgment as to its applicability.

Field theory is a staple of contemporary physics and engineering from microwave transmission to chemical diffusion. Nevertheless, not all problems can be treated in this fashion. One need not appeal to Einstein's failed search for a grand unified field theory to realize that the method does not solve all problems. Many dynamic processes cannot be integrated in this way. They have come to play a leading role in theoretical physics, but have only begun to find their way into economics.

Field theories work beautifully as long as the objects are at rest. They work less well when the objects are driven by external forces over the field. They run into serious trouble when the path traversed changes the field itself, and they fail completely when the changes induced are so great as to call into question its long-term existence.

The Carnot heat engine will serve as a physical analogue to the economic dynamics induced over a utility field. As a cycling process it may fruitfully be compared with two repeating economic cycles: labor performed by the owners of human capital, and the generation of capital services by the owners of the material instruments of production.

Engines evolve like everything else. While their history may be ignored for some applications, machines do wear out and run out of fuel unless repaired and replenished. Eventually they fail. As irreversible historical processes become successively more important both in physics and economics, field theory becomes a more unreliable and misleading guide to policy as the field itself is altered over time.

When can we use field theory and when must we abandon it? When should neoclassical conclusions be rejected as dogma, and when would such an approach discard a useful tool of analysis? In practice this becomes a central question of public policy: when should society rely on "economic" motivations through the manipulation of prices and incomes, and when ought it to turn to "sociological" means such as conditioning, education and emulation.

If the utility field is spanned by the price–income instruments but remains exogenous, unaffected by their application, teaching and preaching is pointless meddling in the choices of individuals who are the best judges of their own welfare. If utility is itself endogenous to the social process and concomitant economic feedback upon it, then the traditional instruments that rely on the manipulation of individual motivation are doomed to failure.

Milton Friedman (1962) and the Chicago tradition reflect the widest application of the exogenous utility field concept. A negative income tax should replace the intrusive social worker; voucher-supplemented free enterprise in education should take the place of the traditional public school system; rather than invoke legislation, racial discrimination can be safely allowed to die of its own accord since firms are confronted with competitive conditions that make bias in employment unprofitable.

Yet even if Friedman takes the exogeneity of utility too far, say in the educational voucher proposal, does it follow that price motivations can be ignored? Can we rely on exhortation alone to induce individuals to enter the teaching profession? How shall educators' services be allocated? With what theoretical underpinning might econometrics forecast the demand for education?

How far is too far in field theory? The story we shall tell suggests that Freidman–Stigler–Becker take utility theory too far and Veblen–Mirowski not far enough.

It all began with the Industrial Revolution.

THE CARNOT ENGINE

The first half of the nineteenth century was the creature of the reciprocating steam engine (Usher [1929] 1954). This wonder of the age combined three elements which had been seen before, but never in combination. It was constructed of moving parts. It operated in a repeating cycle. It transformed heat into mechanical work.

The theoretical consequences of steam power launched the science of thermodynamics with Carnot's celebrated essay, *Reflections on the Motive Power of Fire* ([1824] 1986).[1] Its certainties were soon challenged by a still unresolved question. How can we understand changing, evolutionary, irreversible processes in terms of the postulate of the uniformity of nature which lies at the heart of the inductive scientific method?[2]

Despite Marshall's attempts (1890) to include time and historical evolution in his system, neoclassical economics followed Jevons's (1871) narrower focus on equilibrium. Inspired by the Maxwell equations, Edgeworth translated Jevons's mechanical notions of equilibrium into a field theory: "As electro-magnetic force tends to a maximum energy, so also pleasure force tends toward a maximum energy. The energy generated by pleasure force is the physical concomitant and measure of the conscious feeling of delight" (1881: 25). Individuals are attracted by the marginal utility gradient of the scalar utility function toward its (constrained) maximum value (Samuelson 1947; Georgescu-Roegen 1966, 1971; Tisaz 1966; Truesdell 1980, 1984; Wolfson 1981, 1985, 1987; Proops 1984; Bródy *et al.* 1985; Mirowski 1988, 1989).[3]

The specification that a variable is defined by a scalar function is not trivial. It makes the dependent, state variable determined solely by the current state of the independent variables, regardless of their previous values or the order in which they appeared over time. Since this state variable is independent of the path traversed, any closed loop of independent variables returns the scalar state variable to its original level. A special case of the closed loop is reversibility, which simply retraces the original path. For a state variable, the most important thing about history is that it is over.

Economists will recognize this requirement as the assumption of extended transitivity in utility theory. If bundle of goods A is preferred or indifferent to B, and B is preferred to C, then A is preferred or indifferent to C. Since A is indifferent to itself, if the consumer proceeds from C to A, he is in no way influenced by the succession of trades that have taken place A, B, C, A. To be sure, this transition can be understood as a logical sequence rather than in real time. Yet if the utility function is to have empirical content and actually explain events rather than simply rationalize them after the fact, this closed loop must apply over real time as well as instantaneously (Wolfson 1994).

Unlike Edgeworth's utility-maximizing consumer, the Carnot engine does not come to equilibrium unless it runs out of fuel. It is not a closed system, but operates by importing heat energy and exporting mechanical energy – work. If the machine is not a closed system, neither are workers and capitalists. They are not at a position of equilibrium in real time, but are engaged in a daily cycle of expenditure of work and regeneration through rest and consumption that raises and lowers their utility in a repeating cycle. To understand human actions in this light, we first review the physics of the Carnot engine. Then we consider an individual in a similar closed path in real time over a utility field. We then extend the analysis to the labor and capital cycles in reversible and irreversible form.

THE REVERSIBLE CARNOT ENGINE IN THE MECHANICAL PLANE

The Carnot engine was an idealized steam engine. Abstraction from the "historical" dissipative effects of friction, leakage and wear and tear made it reversible. It could be driven backward, so the parameters describing its state would recover their original values at the end of each cycle (Zemansky 1957; Truesdell 1980).[4]

Gas (steam) is enclosed in a cylinder and held under pressure by a piston, which is coupled to a mechanical device such as the flywheel in Figure 16.1. Mechanical work is done as the injection of heat causes the gas to expand, driving the piston and the flywheel.[5] Cooling the gas returns the piston to its original position, permitting the cycle to be repeated.

The principles that make the engine work are the first and second laws of thermodynamics. The first law is the conservation of energy E. It is nothing but the statement that E is a state variable, a scalar function of temperature T, pressure P and volume V. A closed loop in these values implies zero net

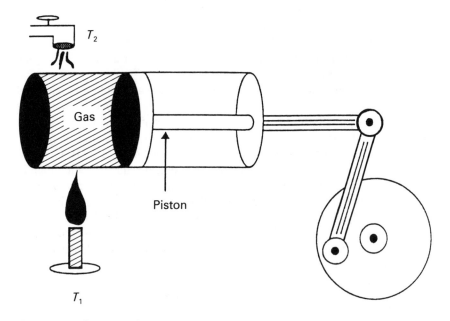

Figure 16.1 Carnot engine

change in E over the cycle no matter how rapidly or long the machine has operated. The heat Q, and work W, transferred by the engine do not describe the state of the engine at an instant of time, but rather the flows of energy it imports and exports over time. Flows are not conserved, but depend on the path of the state parameters as the machine operates. The change in the state variable E is the algebraic sum of the flows of heat and work.[6] Since the change in E is zero over the closed cycle, the flow of heat applied is equal and opposite to the work performed. The engine converts heat to work.[7]

The second law of thermodynamics requires that the engine operate between differing temperature levels.[8] This principle is illustrated in the "mechanical plane" of gas pressure and volume. Initially (1) the gas is at high temperature (T_1) and held in the small volume (V_1) by high pressure (P_1). It is then allowed to expand, driving the piston and losing pressure until it reaches (2). Expanding gas tends to cool, but a constant temperature (isothermal) expansion is achieved by adding heat from an outside source.[9] Mechanical work done by the machine is equal to the area under the "isotherm", (1)–(2). Phase (2)–(3) of the expansion of the gas is carried out "adiabatically", that is to say, insulated from heat flows. Further work is done as the gas expands and cools to T_2.[10] The work that the machine exports is equal to the area under these curves.[11]

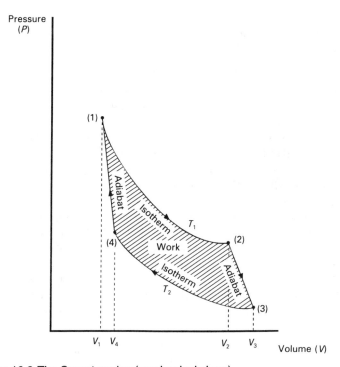

Figure 16.2 The Carnot engine (mechanical plane)

After exporting work, the machine returns to its initial condition by importing work. In phase (3)–(4), the turning flywheel drives the piston back into the cylinder as long as the gas is prevented from heating up by compression. Cooling prevents the temperature from rising by removing heat in this isothermal phase. Further work is added in a second, adiabatic, compression phase without cooling; path (4)–(1) allows the temperature to return to T_1. The cycle is complete. The net flow of work is the "circulation", the area within the closed paths.[12] The significance of the second law is apparent: if expansion and contraction were on the same isotherm, the circulation would be zero.

Since state variables are independent of path, the Carnot engine can be operated in reverse as a refrigerator. Instead of being a net importer of heat and a net exporter of mechanical work, it can import work and export heat. Starting from (1) the gas is allowed to expand to (4) adiabatically lowering its temperature; it then expands isothermally to (1), losing heat but held at a constant temperature; then it is compressed adiabatically by mechanical work to (2), raising the temperature; and finally it is further compressed iso-thermally, losing heat to the surrounding environment as it returns to (1). Since net imported mechanical energy is work done on the refrigerator, conservation of energy requires that it be a net exporter of heat.

THE REVERSIBLE CARNOT ENGINE IN THE ECONOMIC GOODS PLANE

Static equilibrium under utility theory puts each individual in a position of rest on the highest attainable indifference curve. If we hope to draw an analogy with the Carnot engine, we must consider that individuals would not voluntarily reduce their level of utility. They must be driven by externally applied income and substitution effects from utility U_2 to U_1 (Figure 16.3). Such a combination of taxes and subsidies would be akin to the work and heat flows imposed on the Carnot engine. Just as the engine gains or loses energy as it moves between the two isotherms, income transfers can move the consumer between higher and lower indifference curves.

Imagine, somewhat fancifully, a system of taxes reducing the consumer along the income effect line from (2) to (3), followed by price changes with further compensating taxation to keep him on the lower indifference curve path (3)–(4); then suppose a subsidy takes him to (1), followed by compensated price changes returning him finally to (2). The resulting circulation would be a negative welfare flow, because the utility level of the consumer is reduced during his journey through time at lower indifference levels.

The terms need careful definition. Under neoclassical assumptions, utility is a state variable and independent of the path followed. Welfare is an integral, an area, and does depend on path. Utility does not have a time

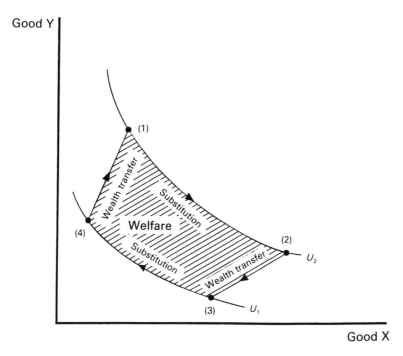

Figure 16.3 Welfare under compulsion

dimension, while welfare is measured as a flow over the time required for each cycle.[13]

The cycle is reversible. The individual can always be brought back to his original state by reversing taxes with subsidies (Jevons [1871, 1879] 1970: 77). Then the consumer would be moved in the opposite direction and would experience a positive flow of welfare. Instead of being driven down to a lower level of utility before returning to the initial condition, the individual would be raised to a higher level and then reduced to the former circumstances.

There are differences between the heat engine and the consumer. In the case of the engine, the integral of pressure with respect to volume is precisely equal to the mechanical work done. But, due to the ordinal nature of utility, the welfare circulation integral is necessarily only an ordinal measure as well. Consequently, there is no conservation law of welfare in utility theory. We can describe the direction of welfare flows, the reverse path regains what was lost during the first circulation. It is not possible to claim that the welfare loss to one individual is equal to the welfare gain by another.[14]

THE REVERSIBLE ENGINE IN THE THERMAL AND UTILITY PLANES

Some of the difficulty in attempts to apply the physical analogy to economics derives from Edgeworth's identification of utility with energy. Energy is an integral, the sum of the product of variables like force and distance. To be sure it is a state variable, but it acquires this status as the result of the law of conservation of energy.

Heat and work flows are integrals of an "intensive" parameter like force, with respect to an "extensive" one like distance. Intensive parameters measure the condition of the system at each point, and are homogeneous of degree zero. Extensive parameters represent the "size" of the system, and are homogeneous functions of the degree of its dimensions. They are said to be conjugate variables that make up the energy integral.

In general, parameters may or may not be state variables. Distance is clearly a state variable because it is a reversible characteristic of the geometry of the system itself. If the coordinates of a point are changed and then returned to their initial condition, the distance moved from the first point to the second is simply reversed. But force might not be a state variable. By definition, an external force applied from outside the system is not a state variable, since reversing the coordinates of the system does not necessarily recreate the system. But a force generated as the gradient of a system's field is a state variable because the reversal of coordinates does reproduce the original condition.

If we concern ourselves with the special case where the system is defined broadly enough to be closed – to include the heat engine and the mechanical device to which it is coupled – the system as a whole is said to be conservative. Then if one variable is a state variable, the other must be one as well so that energy changes will always sum to zero. But this need not be so in the case of open systems, where the applied force is external.

When Clausius (1850 *et seq.*) set out to describe the Carnot heat engine, temperature was the obvious candidate for the intensive variable, but what might the conjugate extensive variable be? Since temperature is a state variable, the extensive variable in a conservative system must be a state variable as well. But what is it? Clausius suggested the term entropy (S), for the unobservable theoretical construct. As a state variable, entropy is independent of path and is returned to its initial value at each cycle of the Carnot engine.[15] Later we will discuss the awkward but important problem of irreversible processes during which entropy may increase. The increase in entropy in irreversible systems should not obscure the fact that, as a state variable, it is defined in terms of reversible processes for which its net change is zero over a closed path.

We can display the same Carnot engine in the entropy–temperature "thermal plane". In Figure 16.4, heat flows into the system, increasing entropy

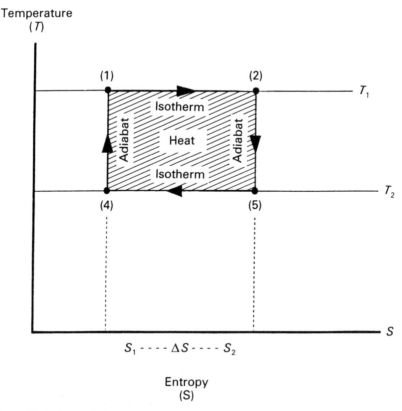

Figure 16.4 Thermal plane

under the isothermal path (1)–(2). The second path (2)–(3) is adiabatic, so temperature falls as the gas expands; since no heat has been transferred, the change in entropy must be zero, making this path a vertical line.[16] the second isothermal path (3)–(4) permits heat to escape from the system, so that entropy is reduced. Finally, the adiabatic path (4)–(1) raises the temperature of the system and returns it to its original state. The circulation integral is the net heat injected into the system, equal and opposite to the work extracted.

Following Jevons, we transfer this concept to the welfare flow (H) by identifying utility as the intensive variable and time spent at each utility level as the conjugate extensive variable. In the utility–time plane (Figure 16.5) the welfare integral is the area of the closed loop of income and substitution effects carried out in real time.[17]

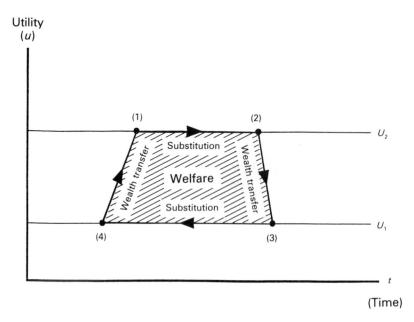

Figure 16.5 The utility–time plane

SOCIAL CHANGE AND DISEQUILIBRIUM PROCESSES

Thus far we have not addressed the myriad of unspecified parameters operating in our subjects. Convection, turbulence, electrical and chemical effects are at work in Carnot's gas-filled cylinder. Unless we are prepared to make the metaphysical statement that an individual's utility function is a Leibnizian monad formed at the moment of conception (Wolfson 1994), individual tastes are shaped by ongoing biological, psychological and social processes. How can we be sure that we have really described a reversible process when only the commodities consumed identified as parameters in the utility function have returned to their original state?

One pragmatic answer is the physicist's distinction between "internal" and "external" parameters. External parameters are those macroscopic data used to model the system. For the Carnot engine they are temperature, pressure and volume, and for the individual they are goods currently consumed. Internal parameters are the remaining forces unspecified in any finite-dimensional model. In the mechanical Carnot model, the unspecified internal parameters include chemical and electrical effects. In the utility function they are the psychological, biological and social influences that economists impound in their *ceteris paribus* assumption.

For a system to be described completely in terms of external parameters, it must be assumed that the internal parameters are completely adjusted, in equilibrium with the external ones. In a dynamic process the adjustment must be incomplete. Consequently, at any condition other than static equilibrium, the true state of the system cannot be completely defined by the external parameters. For discrete changes in the external parameters, the physicists tell us, a "long time" must elapse for the system to settle down to equilibrium so that the external parameters can once again define the system with tolerable accuracy.[18]

For this reason, the term thermodynamics has been regarded as a misnomer by physicists who feel it more properly should be called "thermostatics". Dynamic analysis requires an *ad hoc* solution. They have recourse to the uneasy term "quasi-static" to describe states of "slow" change for which the discrepancy between the true state and that given by the external parameters is small. During rapid changes, the discrepancies are not the least bit negligible and classical thermodynamics breaks down.

Utility is likewise properly defined only at equilibrium. The consumer must be adjusted in his internal mental, physical and social parameters to the palpable bundle of consumer goods taken to be the external parameters of his state.[19] Asking whether consumers maximize their utility is now seen to beg the question: the existence of a utility function presupposes maximizing equilibrium and has no meaning otherwise. If the system does tend toward rest, and if the disturbances are small, utility is a useful theoretical construct. If not, then we cannot be so sure.

Frequently the internal parameters are only imperfectly in equilibrium with the external ones. Then the system cannot be returned to its original state by reversing the same path of external parameters. The system is then said to be irreversible. We cannot measure irreversible processes directly in terms of reversible external parameters. Nevertheless it can be done indirectly by imputing the effects of irreversible processes to their effect on the reversible state variables. That is to say, we impute the effect of irreversible physical and economic changes to changes in the reversible variables entropy and utility.

Even though it is not possible to measure entropy or utility with complete accuracy along the disequilibrium path between two states, a comparison can be carried out between initial and terminal static states of equilibrium. This is an extension of the method of comparative statics to irreversible processes which is as useful in economics as it is in physics. The actual path between initial and terminal states may be irreversible, but we may be able to describe the change in terms of another, hypothetical, reversible path (Katchalsky and Curran 1965: 33).[20]

The utility change imputed to an irreversible process can be estimated as the utility gained by a reversible exchange or transfer of goods that would return an individual to his initial state. The assumption that such a continuous path exists amounts to the assertion that the domain of the state variable is simply connected. Connectedness is, in turn, a necessary condition for the existence of a scalar function (Henderson and Quandt 1980: 12–13). Therefore one may only estimate the effect between two equilibrium states of an irreversible process in terms of a reversible scalar function provided that the changes are small enough to ensure that there are no cumulative effects or catastrophic discontinuities which prevent a return (Arrow 1963: 8–9; cf. Knight 1935).

Expressed with fewer misgivings, George Stigler and Gary Becker (Stigler and Becker 1977; Becker 1988) subsume into the comparative statics utility-maximizing paradigm such irreversible processes as the acquisition of information, the accumulation of human capital, the acquisition of tastes for fine music and drug addiction. They interpret these changes as the free choices of rational utility-maximizing individuals.

This line of reasoning is not inappropriate as long as it is clearly understood that it is applicable only to circumstances where (1) the individual is at rest before and after these changes, and no attempt is made to deal with the intervening disequilibrium transition; (2) no fundamental irreversible changes have taken place in the person or his social environment that threatens the connectedness of the space over which he makes his choices; and (3) from a policy point of view it is more effective to move along utility surfaces than to try to change the attitudes that govern them.

DISEQUILIBRIUM IRREVERSIBILITY: THE LABOR PROCESS IN THE GOODS–ACTIVITIES PLANE

We now are able to turn our attention to the labor process. Clearly it is irreversible. The laborer cannot un-work, and therefore must refresh himself along other paths of consumption and rest to complete the daily work cycle. The process is also a disequilibrium one. The worker is unable to simply come to optimizing equilibrium for one obvious reason. Human beings are perishable. In so far as the laborer owns only his own stock of perishable human capital (Jorgenson and Griliches 1967: 254; Winston 1982: 52–4), he must enter into a contract specifying that he spend part of his day providing labor services and the remainder in consumption and rest in order to be able to work again.

Something of the same is true of capitalists. While their physical assets may depreciate only slowly, their consumption disappears into their individual maintenance. If their cycle is to repeat without gain or loss of wealth, they also must throw their wealth into economic activity to survive.[21]

Neither of these processes is closed. As we shall see in some detail, the worker receives a welfare flow from goods and the environment, and exports labor. The capitalist allows his property to be used in production while receiving the welfare flow of goods and services.

We wish to describe those flows as the agents proceed on their disequilibrium path that traverses utility levels in the course of the working day.

To analyze such open disequilibrium systems we follow Prigogine's lead in biochemistry and push further on the limitations of the use of scalar functions. Prigogine suggested that for changes close to equilibrium we could record the change in dissipative effects as an entropy flow resulting from energy transfers. In a similar fashion we study open cyclic processes in which the utility-dissipating effects of work are compensated by flows of goods. We consider changes sufficiently close to equilibrium for utility to remain meaningful (Prigogine 1955; Georgescu-Roegen 1971: ch. X).

This approach leads us away from the traditional view of the labor market as a pure exchange of labor for leisure. The restoration of the capacity of the worker to work another day must be part of a disequilibrium unidirectional cycle in which the worker loses utility through fatigue in the course of his work and regains it during the rest of the day (Jevons [1871, 1879] 1970: 192–3; Wolfson *et al.* 1986). It consists of three paths in a goods–activities space, where the activities are measured in units of time (Figure 16.6). The worker labors (Ω) and is then paid in money; he purchases goods and services (π) with his wages; and he rests and recovers (θ) and is ready to work again. Phases Ω and θ are irreversible for biological reasons, while π is a reversible market transaction.

For the cycle to repeat, four "conservation laws" have to be imposed as feasibility conditions:

1 *Physiological and psychological feasibility* It must be possible to maintain and restore the worker after labor through man-made goods and the effects of the environment.
2 *Production possibility* Labor, combined with natural and capital resources, must be able to provide the restorative goods and services.
3 *Conservation of natural and capital resources* The stock of resources must be reproduced with each cycle.
4 *Conservation of money* The stock of money must be constant between cycles.

In Figure 16.6, indifference curves are shown for the worker's stock of consumer goods ($G(t)$) compared with $A(t)$, the time-consuming activities of the three phases of the cycle.[22] The irreversible work path (Ω) starts at the beginning of the work day at α and ends at β. It consists of the labor activity $L(t)$ over the time interval AB, and the consumption (reduction of stock) of goods $G(t)$ to sustain the worker on the job. So to speak, he works and eats his lunch. At the end of the day, the employee is paid, adding to his stock of money. The worker then engages in time-consuming market activity π that increases his supply of $G(t)$ as he takes time to buy goods $B(t)$. He uses all his wages, reducing his money stock to its initial level in a phase that starts at β and reaches ε over the time interval BE. Finally, in the recovery activity phase θ, he rests ($R(t)$) and consumes $G(t)$ which returns him to α in time EA. He is now ready to begin the cycle over again.[23] Utility is reduced along

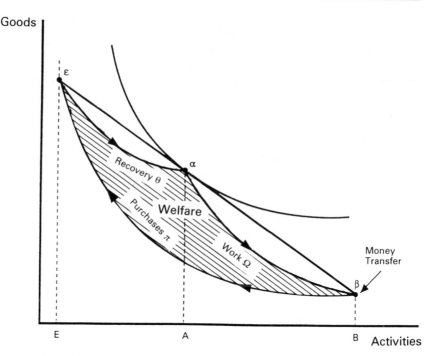

Figure 16.6 Work cycle in the goods–activities plane

Ω from U_2 to U_1, held constant along π, and increased along θ.

The concavity of the work and recovery paths can be justified by comparing the actual irreversible paths outlined above with the hypothetical reversible paths of market transactions posited by the traditional neoclassical model of the labor market. The received doctrine has it that, at the beginning of each day, the worker is endowed at β with a stock of human capital which translates into the maximum time during which he might carry on work activity. He is taken to make an instantaneous market transaction at the going wage rate (w), which takes him to α, where he provides labor services AB and keeps the rest of the day for himself. Presumably the worker is in static equilibrium at α all day, spending no time at β or anywhere else.

In fact, the non-working hours are not simply leisure time retained by the worker. They are the activities he must perform to retain his job. He has an implicit contract with his employer to engage in activities today which will enable him to present himself ready for work again tomorrow. The forward labor contract requires the worker to bring the renewed stock of human capital back to the work place. The employer agrees to provide wages and working conditions that will make that possible.

Nevertheless, we can fruitfully utilize the neoclassical description to evaluate the irreversible process in reversible terms. The market transaction is the line segment βε along which money can be exchanged for work. The worker's real income is $M = G + wL$, where M and w are stated in terms of the price of goods. Given that income, the worker chooses α. Even though $L(t)$ has a time dimension, the points on the budget line are simply alternatives offered by the market. They have no time directionality and are therefore reversible.

We impute the change in utility over the actual irreversible paths by comparison with the reversible ones.

Work path Ω   Since the utility function is taken to be quasi-concave, the fact that the workers choose α over β shows that the latter is at a lower utility level. Therefore utility falls over time $(\partial U/\partial t\,|_{\,\Omega} < 0)$ over the actual work path.

Purchasing path π   If shopping is not pleasurable, the path π lies on or below its indifference curve $(\partial U/\partial t\,|_{\,\pi} \leq 0)$. (In Figure 16.6 utility is drawn as constant.)

Rest path θ   Since workers choose α over ε, utility increases during the recovery phase $(\partial U/\partial t\,|_{\,\theta} > 0)$.

It remains to show that paths Ω and θ are convex. Except at their end points, they lie below any budget line which might be generated by a given stock of human capital and market wage.[24] This must be the case if the worker is to operate in a repetitive cycle between the two indifference curves. Suppose the contrary, that either path crosses above the budget line. Then by arbitrage the worker could strike a better bargain than α; at some positive wage rate he could achieve a higher utility level by hiring somebody else to do his work for him. Alternatively, suppose the paths merely touched the budget line before the ends of the present work cycle. The workers would not have to work the whole day from A to B to earn their income, and would complete the cycle at a higher utility level than the one shown. Either way, the cycle would not repeat, contrary to hypothesis.

The circulation area H represents the loss of welfare to the worker each day from the implicit contract he must accept.[25] He may gain from the opportunity to trade labor for leisure as standard theory suggests, but he loses over the whole cycle. Since the circulation is path dependent, the problem becomes one of minimizing the loss subject to the completion of the cycle.[26]

Subsistence, which has bulked so large in the development of economic thought, is not a fixed bundle of goods, but the completion of the work cycle. Consequently, subsistence wages only acquire meaning with respect to the path followed over the cycle. Arrangements such as "flex-time" can serve to minimize the circulation and to influence the required subsistence wage. Labor welfare, properly conceived, depends on the whole circulation including the natural and social environment. It is more than the direct wage bargain, but the arrangements over all phases of the cycle which enforce the conservation laws.

WORKER SURPLUS: IRREVERSIBILITY IN THE UTILITY–TIME PLANE

We now study the worker's welfare circulation in the utility–time plane (Figure 16.7). Here the individual operates between the intensive utility levels U_2 and U_1, for various extensive time periods.

First consider the fanciful case of carrying out the cyclical transit by market operations. Then the outermost triangle $\alpha\beta\varepsilon$ represents the hypothetical welfare circulation that the worker would give up if he moved between points on the cycle by market transactions. Starting at utility level U_2 at α, he hires somebody else to perform the work that he is obligated to complete for his employer, and arrives at β.[27] He would have to be under legal compulsion to provide the service, and would be like one of Henry Rossovsky's (1965) serf

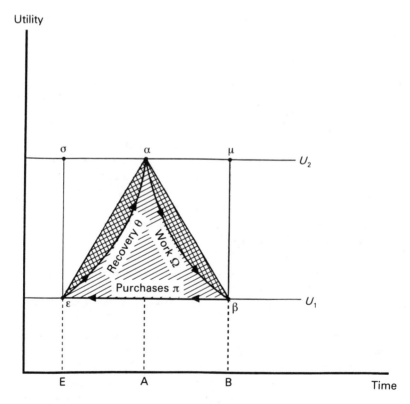

Figure 16.7 Work cycle in the utility–time plane

entrepreneurs or a modern jailhouse manipulator of other inmates. The loss of money leaves him at a lower level of utility, U_1. He then is reimbursed by his employer and proceeds to take the time to buy consumer goods (say) along the same level of utility until he arrives at ε.[28] Finally he does not physically consume those goods, but sells them to hire someone to make him feel better – this is written in California where such possibilities might exist. In this way he returns to α, his initial state.

The reason that this is so absurd is that the employee has another option: he can work and feed himself. By the convexity argument, for any chosen path, it must be that the work and recovery paths lie within the market cycle, so the circulation represents a lesser loss of welfare. The result is the inverse to the consumer–producer surplus, which we might call the worker surplus. Instead of the gains from trade, traditionally assigned to the ability of the worker to trade leisure for income, the worker surplus arises because the individual has the option of not trading and doing the work himself.

Worker surplus is easily portrayed in the utility–time plane. The innermost (light shaded) area is the negative welfare circulation arising from the actual irreversible three-phase cycle. The area within the straight sided triangle $\alpha\beta\varepsilon$ is the hypothetical market circulation. The worker surplus is the dark shaded area equal to the difference between them. It is in the interest of capitalists, workers and the general public to maximize this offset against the inevitable negative welfare effect of labor.

THE CAPITAL CYCLE

We can describe the capitalist's cycle as a counterclockwise welfare-enhancing rotation for those who earn property income. The capitalist's utility depends on his current consumption $C(t)$ and on his stock of wealth $W(t)$. As long as he is operating in a repeating cycle, we may treat his "permanent consumption" as fixed at subsistence. His wealth takes the form of money $M(t)$ and goods $G(t)$, both measured in value terms. For ease of exposition, we assume a single good. It can be used for consumption, sale or as productive capital. Therefore his utility function is $U = U(M,G;C)$, all variables being functions of time. Utility depends on his current consumption and on the value and liquidity of his stock of wealth. The indifference curves in the money–goods plane (Figure 16.8) display the portfolio tradeoff between liquid money and potentially income-earning goods.

Start the cycle at point M, on indifference curve U. The capitalist engages in a time-consuming activity F to purchase goods to be used as factors of production. This brings him to C. The loss of liquidity, as well as the effort expended in making these purchases, entails a loss of utility, so C lies on U'.[29] These factors go to work in the production process along path S, increasing the value of the stock of commodities he now owns, but holding his stock of money constant. He is then at C' on the higher utility level U''. Then the goods

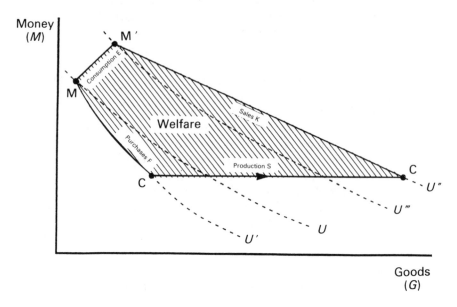

Figure 16.8 The capital cycle

must be sold for money in marketing activity K. Liquidity increases, but the sales activity requires effort. The balance of these effects is unclear *a priori*, but we will take it that the net effect is to reduce utility to *U'''* at point M'.[30] Finally, in the consumption phase E, the capitalist buys consumer goods with money and uses them up to maintain himself. He has returned to M and is ready to start the cycle again.

This is the simple cycle of reproduction of the capitalist. Like the labor process, it is irreversible due to the nature of production and consumption. But here the shaded circulation integral is a positive gain of welfare. To be sure the gain is not certain. There can be short-term losses in the production and selling transactions which involve a loss of welfare, and which can exceed the gains from production. In the long term, this loss has a lower bound since bankruptcy allows the capitalist the option of free disposal of his property and becoming a worker.

The welfare-losing worker and welfare-gaining capitalist circulation are necessary for each other's survival. Marx-like though this account of opposite welfare flows may be, it is not a story about capitalist exploitation of workers, but of the welfare-producing capacity of capital assets. The welfare gain to the capitalist, and the welfare loss to the worker, do not come out of a common fund, and are not necessarily antithetical to each other. Nevertheless, there is a fundamental difference which seems to have gotten lost with the abandonment of the classical version of subsistence wages as a bushel of corn. Workers work because they have to, and therefore endure a negative welfare flow. Capitalists invest because their capital generates a positive welfare flow.

THE RIGHT-HAND RULE

The results achieved thus far can be generalized in terms of the ordinary vector calculus which is the bread and butter of physical field theory (Hildebrand 1962: ch. 6). Figure 16.9 shows the intensive and the extensive parameters on their respective horizontal axes, and the welfare flow vertically. Placing the origin inside the cycle, a radius vector is drawn to the path traversed. Each point is located in polar coordinates as the length of the radius r and the angle Φ as shown in the horizontal plane. Both r and Φ are functions of time, so Φ sweeps through 360° in each cycle. The direction of the flow of welfare (the so-called curl of the vector) is perpendicular to the plane of rotation, and its orientation obeys the right-hand rule.[31] For labor the rotation is clockwise, and the welfare flow is negative; for capital the rotation is counterclockwise, and the welfare flow is positive.

For any path on the same indifference surface, the curl of the vector is zero. This is the neoclassical case, where the only force at work is the gradient of the utility field. Another way of saying this is that in the absence of external income transfers the process is said to be conservative. The fact that the curl of a scalar function like utility is zero is a standard result of vector analysis.

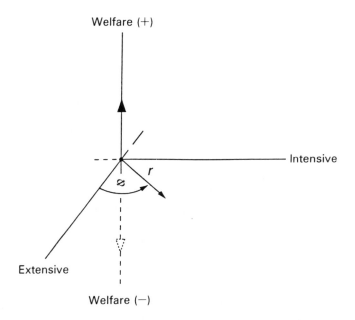

Figure 16.9 The right-hand rule

The fact that the curl of the labor and capital cycles is non-zero tells us that these economic activities cannot be represented as motion in a closed system, induced by the gradient of the utility function. Rather, they are induced in an open system by the circumstances in which these economic agents earn their livelihood.

THE EVOLUTION OF THE UTILITY FUNCTION

Thus far we have considered repeating cycles in which the effect of the curl is to import or export welfare as individuals are driven in a closed path over a given utility field. Now we must consider that the circulation curl may have a component that affects the field itself by altering the internal parameters of the individual. What happens if the flow of welfare generated by the repetition of the cycle affects an individual's preferences?

The simplest place to start is to relate utility to objective levels of well-being. It is likely that subjective utility is related to such negative elements as fatigue in the course of the repeated work cycle. Similarly, there can be a progressive accumulation of wealth when saving is conducted over the course of the capital cycle.

Assume a fatigue index $a(n)$ for the labor process, where n is the number of repeated cycles. Then $U = U\{a[n(t)], G(t), A(t)\}$, and $\partial U/\partial n < 0$. Clearly n is an increasing function of time. Therefore unless it is possible to compensate for the fatigue, the individual runs down, just as a machine wears out. The worker may accumulate human capital in the form of skills acquired through experience. When the individual's utility evolves in this fashion, it is no longer possible to speak of the same person – the same utility field (Wolfson *et al.* 1986). In tractable cases, $a(n)$ is continuous, so that it is possible to retain the utility function as a field but make it endogenous to a time-dependent evolving process. Yet that cannot always be done when the irreversibility is catastrophic or discontinuous.

What we say about the time path dependence of individuals applies to the conservation laws as well. They are also time dependent as a consequence of cumulative interactions within the environment, stock of technical knowledge and social institutions. Again, if these changes are continuous then we can retain an amended neoclassical model with endogenous utility functions (Hammond 1976). But if the induced changes in the system violate these conservation laws, or make them incompatible with each other, then we have reached the limits of utility maximization (Nickelsburg and Wolfson 1990).

Eventually we must face up to the reality that the utility-maximizing approach will not deal with all the cases we must confront. The extended transitivity doctrine of the theory of consumer demand, independence of path, irrelevance of history, absence of a circulation integral, zero curl, equality of second-order cross partial derivatives of utility (reciprocity conditions), and indeed the existence of a scalar utility function all mean the same thing:

utility, like any other scalar function, defines a conservative field in which there are no consequences to a closed trajectory over time.

This makes perfect sense in dealing with a closed reversible system such as the pure, timeless, hypothetical paths in commodity space which Houthakker (1950), Samuelson (1950) and Georgescu-Roegen (1935–6) defined forty years ago in their integrability discussion. Nevertheless it is not an ontological proof that the economy is in fact reducible to individual decisions. Reviewing the progression of models presented in this chapter, we see that the further we got from static equilibrium, the greater were the limitations which we had to place upon utility maximization. In the final analysis, it became clear that we could not force all economic processes into the mold. Utility theory is a convenient and powerful tool of analysis, but like any other scientific explanation it is not a universal truth.

There is some consolation in this outcome. It appears that utility analysis is not an empty tautology. It contains non-trivial falsifiers which make it meaningful within its proper domain of definition. It also means that it is only approximately correct. There is a "gray area" in which we must decide whether utility maximization is the correct paradigm or whether it must be replaced by a time-dependent behaviorist dynamic process. Inevitably both models contain elements that can be described as *ad hoc* – indeed that is their claim to realism.

CONCLUSIONS: POLICY ISSUES AGAIN

We must look to economic theory to guide public policy. But which theory? Let us conclude with four cases where the competing theories, utility maximization and dynamic social conditioning, lead to radically different policy prescriptions.

1 Should government attempt to influence macroeconomic variables to maintain full employment? Rational expectations and real business cycle theorists argue the negative. They point to markets linking utility-maximizing individuals. Are they right to explain unemployment as the result of imperfect labor markets, voluntary idleness, information breakdown or technological instability, all the while insisting that individual utility functions remain rock solid? Or is there sense to the Keynesian alternative with its behaviorist account of dysfunctional propensities to consume, hold cash and illusory money wages?

2 What is the correct policy toward drug abuse? Should we follow the utility-maximizing approach and stress law enforcement in order to impose costs on drug users? Or, should we stress education, moral suasion and social services to reduce demand by changing the tastes and attitudes that lead to drug use? If we were to choose the latter, by what warrant do we claim that it is morally

justifiable to mold the choice functions of individuals in a free society?

3 Is the women's liberation movement a result of technical progress which reduces the opportunity cost of traditional female roles, or is it a change of social attitude? If tastes have changed, then the movement should be supported by policies such as affirmative action. If it is technical change that is at work, then public policy would be best served by leaving career choice to individuals operating in the labor market.

4 Is the cause of poverty the result of individual choice of lifetime income paths or imperfections in the human capital market? Or is it the result of social conditioning? If the first explanation applies, market incentives under more nearly perfectly competitive human capital markets will deal with the question. If not, deeper social changes aimed at raising aspiration levels may have to be employed.

In all these cases, we are torn between simply accepting individual preferences as if they were the primary microfoundations of the economy, or dealing with much more complex, macroeconomic and social aggregate interactions direction human dynamics. If the latter is involved, economic policy makers cannot simply manipulate individual behavior through prices and incomes, but must consider conditioning and motivations that were traditionally relegated to the other social sciences.

The inclusion of changing the attitudes of others inevitably places a heavy normative burden on us all. If utility is endogenous, we can no longer simply adopt the view that even self-destructive individuals make their own choices which are best treated as their own private affair. We are all in the unenviable, and easily abused, position of being forced to make moral and value judgments, and by various manners and means influencing the choices of others. Would that it were not so, but it is.

NOTES

This chapter was drafted when I was Visiting Fellow at the History of Ideas Unit at the Australian National University. I appreciate the help and encouragement of Eugene Kamenka of that university as well as Richard Day (University of Southern California), Shalom Groll (Haifa), Gerald Nickelsburg (McDonnell-Douglas Co.), Ulrich Witt (Freiburg), Paul G. Wolfson (Texas Instrument Co.) and David Wong (California State University, Fullerton). They are not responsible for my opinions or errors.

1   A brief history of thermodynamics is to be found in Tisza (1966: 3–52) and Truesdell (1980, 1984: 1–48). Original papers are reprinted in Magie (1899).
2   The inspiration for the present work is the illuminating treatise on the thermodynamics of irreversible processes in biology by Katchalsky and Curran (1965, 1975). Like the life sciences, economics must deal with both uniformity

and evolution. This wonderful book mirrors economics in a revealing and often startling way.

3   The focus of this chapter is on welfare changes during the labor process. As such it is closest to Brody and his associates (1985) who studied net gains and losses from the circulation process in terms of capital accumulation. Other literature compares entropy increase and environmental decay (Georgescu-Roegen 1971; Faber *et al.* 1983, 1987). Still others compare cycling heat engines with macroeconomic and monetary circulations (Bryant 1982).

4   Dissipation makes perpetual motion machines "of the first kind" impossible.

5   Mechanical work (W) equals the integral of force (F) with respect to the displacement of the device (dX), and pressure (P) with respect to change in volume (dV): $W = \int F\,dX = \int P\,dV$.

6   $dE = dQ + dW$.

7   Integrating over the path of the whole cycle we get $\oint dE = 0 = \oint dQ + \oint dW$. We will explain the circulation integral momentarily.

8   The impossibility of operating at one temperature rules out perpetual motion machines "of the second kind" even without dissipation.

9   The isotherm is a rectangular hyperbola, since for an "ideal gas" where k is constant, $PV = kT$.

10 Since the adiabat must connect the two isotherms, its slope must be steeper than theirs.

11 Work is the integral of force with respect to distance. In the geometry of a cylinder it is the integral of pressure with respect to volume.

12 The circulation area is the line integral taken along the closed curve: $W = \oint dW = \oint P\,dV$. By Green's theorem the line integral is equal to the enclosed area.

13 Jevons saw this point quite clearly when he argued that to consider pleasure or pain as magnitudes one must take into account intensity and duration. He went on to measure time on the horizontal axis and intensity on the vertical, making pleasure an area (Jevons [1871, 1879] 1970: 94–5).

14 This consequence of the ordinal nature of utility is not simply the denial of interpersonal comparisons of utility.

15 Carathéodory finally showed in 1909 that the existence of entropy as a state variable was a consequence of the fact that not all states could be reached from a given state without the transfer of heat. While utility is an intensive variable, it is obvious to economists that the parallel existence of a utility function depends on the impossibility of moving from one level of utility to another by pure substitution without an income effect.

16 Since $dQ/T = dS$, and since $dQ = 0$ and $T > 0$, then $dS = 0$.

17 Designating income and substitution activities $A(t)$ as functions of time, the ordinal welfare circulation is strictly speaking an increasing function of $H = \oint U(A)A'(t)dt$.

18 Physicists are comforted by dissipative processes which permit them to believe that their systems will return to equilibrium given slow enough changes and long enough time (Fermi 1936: 4; Kestin and Dorfman 1971).

19 Nickelsburg and Wolfson (1990) describe the regime switches that can result from the information-destroying effects of rapid changes in monetary policy.

20 In an isolated system without external sources of heat, it is impossible to carry out that reversal and therefore the change in entropy is non-negative, $dS \geq 0$. During irreversible processes $dS > 0$, until at equilibrium entropy is maximized at $dS = 0$. Conceiving the universe to be an isolated system, Clausius (1865) predicted heat death: "*Die Energie der Welt ist konstant. Die Entropie strebt einem Maximum zu.*"

21 Irreversibility applies to the production of goods as well as people. As a natural process, neither can be un-made in a land of Cockaigne by retracing the path of production, even though they (both!) can be scrapped for parts and recycled with the addition of other resources (Koopmans 1957: 23–35, 56, Arrow and Hahn 1971: 64, 73–4n.)

22 In terms of the definitions in the next paragraph $A(t) = L(t) \cup B(t) \cup R(t)$.

23 The space curves Ω, π and θ in three dimensions consist of U and its arguments G and the appropriate activity L, B or R. All of the components of the space curves are functions of t. For instance $\Omega(t) = \{G(t), L(t), U[G(t), L(t)]\}$. Over the cycle the rest and work phases are measured from left to right, while the purchases phase is measured from right to left. The directional day is the clockwise cycle parametrized by the passage of time over the sum of the intervals $AB + BE + EA$.

24 A formal proof of convexity follows from the strict positivity of the wage rate. Choose any (G_0, L_0) on Ω so that $L_0 = mA + (1 - m)B$ and $0 < m < 1$. Points on Ω can be written as $G(L)$. $G(L)$ is strictly convex if, for all m, $G(L_0) < mG(A) + (1 - m)G(B)$. Assume the contrary, that $G(L_0) \geq mG(A) + (1 - m)G(B)$. But the expression on the right-hand side is the budget constraint $M = G + wL$, which takes on the value $M = G_0 + wL_0$. Then $G(L_0) \geq G(L_0) + wL_0$. For positive L_0, $w \leq 0$ contrary to $w > 0$. The proof for the convexity of θ is similar.

25 $H = \oint U = \oint_{\Omega} U dt + \oint_{\pi} U dt + \oint_{\theta} U dt$.

26 This becomes a problem in the calculus of variations. For all cycles, maximize H such that Ω, π, θ satisfy the conversation laws.

27 In the figure, he pays out the funds over time although he could do so instantaneously.

28 Notice that in this plane we are trading money for labor services not for goods. Therefore, no path is shown for converting money into goods, only money into the services of buying goods. Having assumed that purchasing was not painful, there is no reason to believe that an agent would be hired for this purpose. If this were the case, then the actual purchase path would dip below the indifference curve and might be truncated by the employment of a purchasing agent.

29 The consumer-worker might not have experienced a loss of utility as a result of shopping for consumer goods, but the same cannot be said of the capitalist.

30 We do not care whether utility increases or decreases during K, as long as it does not decrease to the point that the amount of money at the end of K is not enough to permit capitalist consumption and the renewed purchase of commodities.

31 If the fingers of the right hand show the direction of rotation, the thumb shows the direction of the curl vector.

REFERENCES

Arrow, K. (1963) *Social Choice and Individual Values*, 2nd edn, New York: Wiley.

Arrow, K. and Hahn, F. H. (1971) *General Competitive Analysis*, San Francisco, CA: Holden–Day.

Becker, G. S. (1965) "A theory of the allocation of time", *Economic Journal* 75: 493–517.

—— (1988) "Family economics and macro behavior", *American Economic Review* 78 (1): 1–13.

Boyce, W. E. and DiPrima, R. C. (1965) *Elementary Differential Equations and Boundary Value Problems*, New York: Wiley.

Brody, A., Martinas, K. and Sajo, K. (1985) "An essay in macroeconomics", *Acta Oeconomica* 35 (3–4) 337–43.

Bryant, J. (1982) "A thermodynamic approach to economics", *Energy Economics* 4: 36–50.

Carnot, S. [1824] (1986) *On the Motive Power of Fire*, New York: Barber.

Edgeworth, F. Y. [1881] (1961) *Mathematical Psychics*, New York: Kelley.

Faber, M., Niemes, H. and Stephen, G. (1983, 1987) *Entropy, Environment and Resources, an Essay in Physico-Economics*, trans. I. Pellengahr, Berlin: Springer.

Fermi, E. (1936) *Thermodynamics*, New York: Dover Books.

Friedman, M. (1962) *Capitalism and Freedom*, Chicago, IL: University of Chicago Press.

Georgescu-Roegen, N. (1966) *Analytical Economics* Cambridge, MA: Harvard University Press.

—— (1971) *The Entropy Law and the Economic Process*, Cambridge, MA: Harvard University Press.

—— (1935–6) "The pure theory of consumer behavior", *Quarterly Journal of Economics* 49: 544–93.

Gleick, J. (1987) *Chaos, Making a New Science*, New York: Penguin.

Haken, H. (1977) *Synergetics, An Introduction*, Berlin: Springer.

—— (1983) *Advanced Synergetics*, Berlin: Springer.

Hammond, P. J. (1976) "Endogenous tastes and stable long-run choice", *Journal of Economic Theory* 13: 371–9.

Heiner, P. (1989) "The origin of predictable dynamic behavior", Working paper 2, Russell Sage Foundation.

Henderson, J. M. and Quandt, R. E. (1980) *Microeconomic Theory, A Mathematical Approach*, 3rd edn, New York: McGraw-Hill.

Hicks, J. R. and Allen, R. G. D. (1934) "A reconsideration of the theory of value", *Economica* 1 (52–76): 196–219.

Hildebrand, F. B. (1962) *Advanced Calculus for Applications*, Englewood Cliffs, NJ: Prentice Hall.

Hirsch, M. W. and Smale, S. (1974) *Differential Equations, Dynamical Systems and Linear Algebra*, New York: Academic Press.

Houthakker, H. S. (1950) "Revealed preference and the utility function", *Economica* 17: 159–74.

Jevons, W. S. ([1871, 1879] 1970) *The Theory of Political Economy*, 2nd edn, Harmondsworth: Pelican.

Jorgenson, D. W. and Griliches, Z. (1967) "The explanation of productivity change", *Review of Economic Studies* 34: 249–83.

Katchalsky, A. and Curran, P. F. (1965) *Nonequilibrium Thermodynamics in Biophysics*, Cambridge, MA: Harvard University Press.

Kestin, J. and Dorfman, J. R. (1971) *A Course in Statistical Thermodynamics*, New York: Academic Press.

Knight, F. H. [1935] (1956) "The Ricardian theory of production and distribution", in *On the History and Method of Economics*, Chicago, IL: University of Chicago Press.

Koopmans, T. (1957) *Three Essays on the State of Economic Science* New York: McGraw-Hill.

Magie, W. F. (1899) *The Second Law of Thermodynamics: Memoirs by Carnot, Clausius and Thomson*, New York: American Book.

Marshall, A. (1890) *Principles of Economics*, London: Macmillan

Mirowski, P. (1984) "Physics and the marginalist revolution", *Cambridge Journal of Economics* 8: 361–79.

—— (1989) *More Heat Than Light*, New York: Cambridge University Press.

Nickelsburg, G. and Wolfson, M. (1990) "The destruction of information and economic behavior", Working Paper 1–90, Department of Economics, California State University at Fullerton.

Prigogine, I. (1955) *Introduction to Thermodynamics of Irreversible Processes*, 3rd edn, New York: Wiley.

Proops, J. L. R. (1984) "Thermodynamics and economics: from analogy to physical functioning", in W. van Gool and J. J. C. Bruggink (eds) *Energy and Time in the Economic and Physical Science*, Amsterdam: North-Holland.

Rossovsky, H. (1965) "Serf entrepreneurs in Russia", in H. G. J. Aitken (ed.) *Explorations in Enterprise*, Cambridge, MA: Harvard University Press, pp. 341–70.

Samuelson, P. A. (1947) *Foundations of Economic Analysis*, Cambridge, MA: Harvard University Press.

—— (1950) "The problem of integrability in utility theory", *Economica* 17 (68): 355–85.

—— (1972) "Maximum principles in analytical economics", *American Economic Review* 62 (3): 249–62.

Stigler, G. J. and Becker, G. S. (1977) "De gustibus non est disputandum", *American Economic Review* 67: 76–90.

Tisza, L. (1966) *Generalized Thermodynamics*, Boston, MA: MIT Press.

Truesdell, C. (1984) *Rational Thermodynamics*, 2nd edn (1st edn 1969), New York: Springer.

—— (1980) *The Tragicomical History of Thermodynamics 1822–1854*, New York: Springer.

Usher, A. P. ([1929] 1954) *A History of Mechanical Inventions*, Cambridge, MA: Harvard University Press.

Veblen, T. ([1898] 1934) "Why is economics not an evolutionary science", in L. Ardzooni (ed.) *Essays in Our Changing Order*, New York: Viking.

—— ([1899–1900] 1946) "The preconceptions of economic science", in *The Place of Science in Modern Civilization*, New York: Russell & Russell.

Winston, G. C. (1982) *The Timing of Economic Activities*, Cambridge: Cambridge University Press.

Wolfson, M. (1981) "An exploratory specification of the role of history in economic theory", Waseda Economic Papers, XX.

—— (1985) *Thermodynamics and Economics*, Proceedings l'Association Charles Gide pour l'Etude de la Pensée Economique, Montpelier.

—— (1987) "Science and history: economics and thermodynamics", Papers and Proceedings, History of Economics Society, Mimeo.

—— (1994) "*Eligo ergo sum*: classical concepts of the self in neoclassical economics", *History of Political Economy* 26(2): 297–326.

Wolfson, M., Orzech, Z. B. and Hanna, S. (1986) "Karl Marx and the depletion of human capital as an open access resource", *History of Political Economy* 18 (3): 497–514.

Zemansky, M. W. (1957) *Heat and Thermodynamics*, 4th edn., New York: McGraw-Hill.

Chapter 17

The problem of interpersonal interaction
Pareto's approach

Vincent J. Tarascio

During the nineteenth-century development of economics, there was an intellectual interregnum during which the procedures used by economists were vague, shifting and tentative. As economics developed, economists, as well as sociologists, felt the need to "rationalize" their aims and procedures. The result was methodological controversy among various schools of thought. The controversies involved such issues as ethical neutrality, the scope of economics and method and methodology in the social sciences and economics. All of these issues became embodied in what eventually was known as the "economic model of man". It had its origins in classical economics, was refined by the neoclassical economists, and has become the paradigm of modern orthodox economics. Along the way, the model has had many critics, starting with Comte, the German Historical School, Marx, the American institutionalists, and others. But it was the critique of two philosophers, Benedetto Croce in 1901 and Martin Hollis in 1977, which gave us the greatest insights into the nature and limitations of the economic model of man, and these two writers will be discussed in the relevant parts of the chapter.

Pareto plays a central role in the controversy, first as a defender of the economic model of man, and later as one who replaced that model with his own more general model. The purpose of this chapter is to examine the nature of the economic model of man and Pareto's contribution in dealing with the problem of interpersonal interaction, which the standard model ignores. I begin with Croce and an elaboration of his critique of the economic model of man, then I go on to present Pareto's contribution to the subject in a utility theory framework, and finally I introduce Hollis's more recent discussion and critique of models of man and compare his models with Pareto's. It will be shown that Pareto's contribution was pathbreaking and consistent with new directions in the biological and physical sciences today.

CROCE'S CRITIQUE OF THE STANDARD ECONOMIC MODEL

In December 1898, Pareto read a paper to the *Société Stella* entitled *Comment se pose le problème de l'économie pure*, wherein he attempted to explicate the nature of economic theory. He sent a copy of his paper to Benedetto Croce, perhaps the greatest contemporary Italian philosopher in Italy, requesting his comments. Croce responded (1901) with a critique of the model of man implicit in economic theory. This model, according to Croce, consisted of four conceptions which rendered the economic model inappropriate for investigations of human societies. These he called the *mechanical*, the *hedonistic*, the *technological* and the *egoistic*. He argued that the mechanical conception of the economic principle is untenable, because this principle confines economics only to what is measurable, and what is not measurable is ignored, thus depriving economics of a wide range of human actions which have a bearing on economic behavior. He rejected the hedonistic hypothesis because of the utilitarian tendency to equate pleasure with economic behavior; instead he preferred the more scientific concept of choice, without the metaphysical aspects of hedonism. Croce argued that the economic principle (model) confused the technological with the economic, by treating the two as though they were the same. Since a technical error is an error of knowledge and an economic error is an error of will, economics presumes that errors are acts of ignorance rather than the results of wilful behavior. Economists dealt with the problem by assuming perfect knowledge, thus eliminating errors of the first type and at the same time ignoring errors of the second type. Finally, the egoistic aspect of the economic principle (model) assumes that the economic agent only looks to his own self-interest and is not aware of, or concerned with, those of others.

Pareto's response to Croce (1901) was uncompromising in that he defended the standard neoclassical paradigm minus the hedonistic hypothesis, which he had eliminated in his own work earlier by defining economics as the science of choice. Pareto's disagreement with Croce was in his adherence to the *economic* model of man which he considered as a first approximation at best. When Pareto went on to develop his sociological analysis he developed a new model of man which dealt with most of Croce's criticisms.

What is important for my purposes, Pareto called attention to the limitations of marginalism for solving concrete problems. The limitation was largely the consequence of its *mechanical* nature. The mechanical nature of pure economics was seen by Pareto not as a "fault" (contrary to many critics of marginalism) but merely as a limitation which could be resolved by (1) taking into account complexities through a process of successive approximations (at the theoretical level), (2) considering the effects of institutional factors that is, market structure etc. (applied economics), and (3) a synthesis of the respective social sciences (sociology). Pareto worked in all these areas, but he undoubtedly attached the greatest importance to (3):

For the past ten years I have been perpetually repeating that in order to study a phenomenon, one must first separate out its elements, analyze, and then, in order to solve a concrete case, one must bring together the conclusions of the various sciences and make a synthesis.

(1900: 186)

He argued that human action is essentially synthetical in nature: *homo œconomicus, homo ethicus, homo religiosus* exist only as abstractions, since concrete human action involves some combination of them.

What Pareto worked with in pure economies was the theory of static equilibrium. What movements occurred were movements or tendencies towards a state of equilibrium. The external forces were tastes and obstacles, and these are the only ones explicitly considered in the *Manuale*. Pareto realized that, in reality, the system moves continuously under the action of internal and external forces. The internal forces, largely non-economic, influence the external forces so that economic dynamics really merges into sociology.

Pareto's sociology also represented a counterweight to the mechanistic nature of his pure economics. In pure economics, individuals are constrained to act in a particular way. The parameters at the individual level were prices, tastes (given utility functions) and technology (given production functions). A change in any of these resulted in a new configuration of equilibrium. The ability of individuals to influence each other or to act collectively to alter the parameters in the system (that is through interpersonal interaction) is assumed away. In reality, individuals do act collectively to alter conditions in order to maximize their interests (say wages and profits) either privately or politically. Not only is this propensity, and its economic consequences, recognized in Pareto's sociology, but it becomes a central theme; the political process is examined in such a general way that an important part of the sociology becomes an analysis of *interpersonal* interaction (in contrast to the impersonal interaction characteristic of "pure" economics). The former type of interaction involves subjective and dynamic considerations, while the latter focuses attention on objective and static aspects. In Pareto's pure economics, economic man resembles a mechanical man. This is the point Pareto was making when he stated, "For the determination of equilibrium, the individual can be replaced just as well by curves" (1911: 62). In his sociology, Pareto was dealing with synthetical man, whose actions stem from economic, political, ethical etc. motives. These motives represent a complex of sentiments and interests.

So much for the background. We now are in a position to see how Pareto dealt with the problem of interpersonal interaction in his utility theory, and how his approach is reflected in a model of man quite distinct from the standard economic model of behavior.

SOME INITIAL CONCEPTIONS

Before going into Pareto's theory, it will be necessary to distinguish between types of utilities. Pareto coined the term ophelimity to designate satisfaction deriving from economic sources, whereas he used the term "utility" as satisfactions deriving from any source including economic. "Utility" has a broader meaning in Pareto's usage than the current use of the term in economics. Also, Pareto distinguished between the individual and collective in the case both of ophelimity and of utility. Table 17.1 summarizes these distinctions, and compares them with terms in current usage. Now let us examine Pareto's terms.

Individual "ophelimity" is well known to economists, although not under that label, having derived from Pareto. Here we have the familiar indifference curve analysis where individual equilibrium is given by the condition that the marginal rates at substitution are equal to price ratios of goods. Community ophelminity can be understood within the familiar Pareto–Edgeworth box diagram, in this case a community of two individuals, possessing two goods, in an exchange framework. Within this context a Pareto optimum is defined. All this is familiar to economists and we need not devote more space to it. Suffice it to say that both individual and community ophelminity involved

Table 17.1 Pareto's terms and terms in current usage

Pareto's term	Current usage	Reference	Source of satisfaction
1 Individual ophelimity	Personal utility	Individual	Economic
2 Community ophelimity	Social utility	Any group of individuals, but without consideration of collective apart from individual interest	Economic
3 Individual utility	Personal utility	Individual	Any source
4 Social utility	Social utility	Any group of individuals, but without consideration of collective apart from individual interest	Any source
5 Utility of society	Social utility	Any structurally integrated group, with consideration of collective apart from individual interest	Any source

impersonal interaction, since each actor is not aware of or does not care about the gains or losses experienced by others. In other words, ophelimities are independent, not dependent.

PARETO'S SOCIOLOGICAL MODEL OF MAN

In his sociology, Pareto broadened the concept of satisfactions to include not only economic satisfactions but those deriving from all sources, and utilities are now "dependent" in that the individual's welfare is made to depend not only on his own satisfactions but also on those of others.

The framework developed below follows Pareto and my elaboration of his work.[1] Suppose that each individual in the social system possesses certain precepts regarding what is "best" for himself and for others. That is to say, each individual in the social system has a subjective social welfare function:

$$w_i = f_i(u_1, u_2, \ldots, u_i, \ldots, u_n). \tag{17.1}$$

In this expression the u_i are the utilities of the individuals in the social system as the ith individual imagines them. The term "utilities" here is used in a broader sense than economic satisfaction; it designates satisfactions deriving from all sources, economic, political, religious, ethical, moral etc.

Suppose for the ith individual an ideal social state is one which satisfies the following condition:

$$0 = \alpha_{i1} du_{i1} + \alpha_{i2} du_{i2} + \ldots + \alpha_{ii} du_{ii} + \ldots + \alpha_{in} du_{in} \tag{17.2}$$

The α_{ij} represents the ith individual's subjective interpersonal comparison of the u_{ij}, and the du_{ij} are indices of changes in the u_{ij}. Expression (17.2) is quite general and it allows heterogeneous types of individuals. For example if the ith individual is a pure egoist, then all the α_{ij} will be zero except α_{ii}, which will have a high positive value. In other words such an individual pays attention only to his own interests. For an altruist, the α_{ii} will be near or equal to zero, while the remaining α_{ij} will have a higher positive value. A misanthrope would place a high negative value on the α_{ij}, so that a positive increase in the du_{ij} would result in a decrease in social welfare (and vice versa) as he imagines it. For the lover of mankind, the α_{ij} would have high positive values. For the martyr egoist the α_{ii} would be negative, reflecting his belief that his sacrifices (negative du_{ii}) are a benefit to society. For the egalitarian the α_{ij} would be equal, whereas for the lover of inequality they would not be so. In reality, one would expect that the α_{ij} will be positive (but not equal), and we shall assume that the situation best defines the representative case. Since the α_{ij} are positive some of the dus must be negative and some positive in order that condition (17.2) be satisfied. In other words they cannot be all positive or all negative. This result, due to Pareto, is important as we shall see, since it calls attention to the differential effects of social action or policy.

If individuals' precepts regarding justice are influenced by their class positions, interests etc., we have heterogeneous individuals and heterogeneous conceptions of justice. More formally, for n individuals we have

$$
\begin{aligned}
O &= \alpha_{11}du_{11} + \alpha_{12}du_{12} + \ldots + \alpha_{1n}du_{1n} \\
O &= \alpha_{21}du_{21} + \alpha_{22}du_{22} + \ldots + \alpha_{2n}du_{2n} \\
&\vdots \\
O &= \alpha_{n1}du_{n1} + \alpha_{n2}du_{n2} + \ldots + \alpha_{nn}du_{nn}
\end{aligned}
\tag{17.3}
$$

Since individuals' subjective views of what is just for themselves and others are heterogeneous, then in most cases $\alpha_{11} \neq \alpha_{21} \neq \ldots \neq \alpha_{n1}; \alpha_{22} \neq \ldots \neq \alpha_{nn};$ etc.

The question of the existence of a solution for system (17.3) is not an issue, since no individual in the social system possesses the data for solving the problem objectively.

We are faced with the problem of individual heterogeneity and its resolution. It is at this point that an important and often neglected function of government enters the scene. A government makes subjective interpersonal comparisons of individuals' subjective interpersonal comparisons. In terms of Paretian analysis, it multiplies the α_{ij} by β_{ij}, where the β_{ij} are its own interpersonal comparisons. With the introduction of government, we have for each individual in the system

$$
\begin{aligned}
M_1 &= \alpha_{11}\beta_{11} + \alpha_{21}\beta_{21} + \ldots + \alpha_{n1}\beta_{n1} \\
M_2 &= \alpha_{12}\beta_{12} + \alpha_{22}\beta_{22} + \ldots + \alpha_{n2}\beta_{n2} \\
&\vdots \\
M_n &= \alpha_{1n}\beta_{1n} + \alpha_{2n}\beta_{2n} + \ldots + \alpha_{nn}\beta_{nn}
\end{aligned}
\tag{17.4}
$$

The M_i are the weighted individual subjective welfare functions. The government's (political) welfare function is given by the expression

$$
W + G(U_1, U_2, \ldots, U_i, \ldots, U_n)
\tag{17.5}
$$

A political (social) optimum is obtained when the following condition is met:

$$
O = M_1 dU_1 + M_2 dU_2 + \ldots + M_i dU_i + \ldots + M_n dU_n
\tag{17.6}
$$

The above condition is general, and does not depend on any particular system. What is important for my purposes is to establish an important function of government, namely reconciling the problem of heterogeneity. Individuals are willing to submit to higher authority (government) to overcome the problem of heterogeneity, in order to create a determinate social system.

Equation (17.6) is analogous to equation (17.2), with the exception that the government actually pursues the path leading to the conditions in expression (17.6), to the benefit of some and the detriment of others. In other words, it imposes its political welfare function upon individuals. Individuals reasoning from the point of view of their own subjective welfare functions may be dissatisfied with the government's course, but then, one could conceive of very few instances of unanimity because of the heterogeneity of individual welfare functions. This is not to suggest that individuals passively allow governments to pursue their own optimum paths. The interaction of individuals and governments and the process of determination of social welfare functions in Paretian theory will be discussed below. Before going on to Pareto's approach to the problem, I should like to add an additional dimension, namely, "social utility" in contradistinction to "utility of society", since Pareto attached some significance to the distinction.

Social utility is a concept which is *individualistic* in orientation, referring to any group of individuals but without consideration of the collective apart from the individual interests. Utility of society refers to any structurally integrated group with consideration of collective apart from individual interests. The social welfare functions deriving from each of these references may not correspond.

It might be worthwhile to examine the distinction between social utility and utility of society in greater detail, since the distinction is particularly relevant to current discussions on social welfare functions. Pareto's analysis is very general, and he abstracts from various political institutions which attempt to deal in one way or another with the problem of heterogeneous utilities. All government policy, regardless of the form of government, involves a social welfare function, W. Nevertheless, the manner in which W is determined is extremely important, depending on whether the norm chosen is social utility or utility of society. A quotation from Pareto makes the distinction quite clear:

> Let us imagine a community so situated that a strict choice has to be made between a very wealthy community with large inequalities in income among its members and a poor community with approximately equal incomes. A policy of maximum utility of the community may lead to the first state, a policy of maximum utility for the community to the second. We say may, because results will depend upon the coefficients that are used in making the heterogeneous utilities of the various social classes homogeneous. The admirer of the "superman" will assign a coefficient of approximately zero to the utility of the lower classes, and get a point of equilibrium very close to a state where large inequalities prevail. The lover of equality will assign a high coefficient to the utility of the lower classes and get a point of equilibrium very close to the egalitarian condition.[2]

Social utility, then, has an individualistic orientation, whereas utility of society considers the well-being of society quite apart from the individual interests. The welfare function of a government which sets out to maximize social utility will be quite different from a welfare function deriving from considerations of maximization of utility of society. In reality a government often reasons from both points of view. Its domestic policies may be oriented toward social utility, whereas its foreign policies may involve considerations of utility of society. Or during national emergencies, individual interests may be sacrificed in consideration of the utility of society. In order to simplify the analysis in what follows, the main concern will be with social utility, although the discussion can be extended to include utility of society. Also, the social utility reference is more in keeping with the individualistic orientation of Western civilization.

INDIVIDUAL UTILITY IN RELATION TO SOCIAL UTILITY

From what has been said thus far, there need not be a coincidence of individual utility and social utility, even in cases in which the individual does not stand in conflict with the norms obtaining in society. In such cases one might find that the points of maximum individual utility and social utility do not coincide. Suppose an individual possesses certain precepts regarding what is "beneficial" for himself and others (i.e. a subjective social welfare function), and these precepts are reflected through his observances of norms obtaining in society. In such cases one might find that the points of maximum individual utility and social utility do not coincide. In Figure 17.1, A is the extreme point representing strictest observance of every norm obtaining in society by an individual, and B is another extreme point representing violation of norms that are not recognized as absolutely indispensable.[3]

The mnp curve indicates the utility curve of the individual, who suffers a "damage" at A (due to obstacles he encounters, that is, the social preferences of other individuals with whom he has interpersonal relations) and attains a maximum benefit at n, which thereafter diminishes and becomes a loss at B (again due to the effects of interpersonal relations). The srv curve is the utility

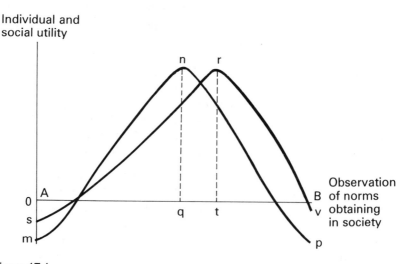

Figure 17.1

deriving to society from the point of view of, say, public authorities or other informed members of the community, from the fact of the individual's faithful observance of norms. The government (public authority) has no knowledge of mnp, but it does have some idea of srv. Social utility is greatest at point r. At point q, the maximum individual utility is obtained, while point t is the maximum social utility deriving through the individual's conduct. Society, then, would derive a maximum utility from the individual if he were to observe those norms corresponding to t. But from the individual's viewpoint, t would not represent a maximum of utility for him; he would prefer to observe those norms q, at which his utility is at a maximum. Therefore, even when the individual is not at odds with the norms obtaining in society, the social utility resulting from his preferred position may not be at a maximum.

THE INTERACTION OF INDIVIDUAL AND SOCIAL OR POLITICAL WELFARE FUNCTIONS AND THE POLITICAL PROCESS

A government observes an individual at q and it knows, or thinks it knows, that, from the point of view of social utility, society will gain if he moves from q to t. In other words, it has assigned to the individual's utility U a coefficient M reflected in the political welfare function W. The problem then is to move the individual from q to t. The individual may be forced to move to t, with the direct consequence that his utility declines. It may be the case that he later experiences an indirect gain in utility at t equal to or greater than qn. In such a case, the movement from q to t was warranted both from the individual's subjective view and from the view of "social utility". This case implies a transformation of the individual's subjective welfare function. Or the government may wish to induce the individual to move from q to t voluntarily. This is where "derivations" enter the scene in Paretian utility theory. The term "derivations" was coined by Pareto to designate arguments intended to spur individuals to action. The form of the arguments used to move the individual in a desired direction – scientific arguments, appeal to emotions and so on – may be important from certain points of view. Regardless of the form, the purpose of the "derivations" is to convince the individual that a movement from q to t is to his advantage. In order to induce the individual to make the movement, it may be necessary to offer a promise of a gain, or even a fantastic gain, in utility. In short, the function of the derivation is to blend the individual's social preferences with those deriving from social utility. If the individual refuses to move in a "desired" direction, he is judged as ignorant, irrational etc. These are also "derivations" which attempt to objectify the political welfare function W by suggesting that such persons are unworthy of consideration.[4]

The above can be viewed in another way. Instead of mere violations of norms, transformation and reforms of norms obtaining in society may be considered (Pareto 1935: IV, 1474). Individuals observing someone at t may attempt to convince public authorities or other individuals that social utility will be at a maximum if public policy induced movements from t to q. Again derivations enter the scene, in this case to transform the political welfare function W to the individuals' subjective views of what is best for society, that is, what is best according to their subjective welfare functions.

In the above examples, the utility of one individual or a group of individuals having similar subjective welfare functions was examined. In reality, the government encounters many different individual welfare functions, so that the situation is much more complex. Nevertheless, the above examples serve to show the role that the Paretian theory of derivation plays in the determination of W. In other words, the Paretian theory of derivation shows how public authority acting on the basis of a political welfare function W influences individual welfare functions and how, in turn, individuals exert themselves to transform their welfare functions into the social welfare function W through the political process. This interaction describes in a very general way the nature of the political process, without any particular reference to specific political institutions.

The Paretian analysis also suggests the limitations of studies which describe the political process in a voting framework. Voting may serve to reveal social preferences with regard to a limited number of proposals of a specific nature. But within the broader framework of state and national government, all that individuals can do is elect representatives and administrators. Once a government is constituted, the problem of complex individual utilities manifests itself in the slogans, creeds, ideals etc. of individuals and governments in their reciprocal attempts to influence movements in directions deemed "desirable". Hence, we are in a Paretian world.

Pareto insisted that the problem of interpersonal interaction which had been ignored in the social sciences was in fact central to those sciences. Through his utility approach he conceptualized the problem in a manner which lent itself to rigorous analysis. As Pareto argued, "From what we have been showing it also follows that the problem of utility is quantitative and not qualitative, as is commonly believed" (1935: II, p. 1500). Nevertheless, he realized that quantification in sociology was difficult because of the nature of the subject matter: "If we would deal with them [concepts] scientifically, we must be able to define them rigorously, and if we would introduce them into the determination of the social equilibrium, we must find some way, be it by mere indices, to make them correspond to quantities" (ibid., p. 1457). Thus Pareto provided the framework suitable for quantification, but actual quantification had to wait for the availability of numerical data. As concerns Pareto's work, this development never took place since his *social utility* approach to the problem of interpersonal interaction was unknown to economists and not understood by sociologists.

HOLLIS AND MODELS OF MAN

In his pathbreaking book *Models of Man* (1977), Martin Hollis distinguishes between two models of man: a passive conception of man, which he calls *Plastic Man* and an active conception to which he attaches the term *Autonomous Man*. Although the distinction seems simple, Hollis's discussion makes it clear that each of these models is quite complex, the former being more familiar and therefore more easily discernible, the other more vague and tentative. For my purpose it will be sufficient to make a crude distinction by describing the polar cases, leaving it to the reader to explore the subtleties in the book.

Those who use the Plastic Man conception, "are inclined to treat men as super-rats or super-pigeons, armed with stimulus-response theories and hypothetico-deductive tests for causal regularities" (p. 16). This model is by far the most characteristic model of the social sciences in general, and especially economics. On the other hand, "Autonomous Man is to be self-caused and self-explanatory", whose actions cannot be wholly explained by causal laws and conditions (pp. 14–15). Autonomous Man is not satisfied merely to react to stimulus in a mechanical manner, but instead attempts to understand the nature of the environment in which he makes decisions in order to achieve his goals. His behavior is purposive.

Hollis does not go far enough in his development of Autonomous Man, since he limits its actions to a single actor. This constrains the actor to accepting given institutions (and/or rules) since he cannot count on being helped or hindered by others in changing those constraints (p. 187). So neither the Plastic Man or the Autonomous Man framework adequately deals with the problem of change in general or social change in particular.

Hollis confines himself to conceptualization of the two models of man. Yet his criticism of Plastic Man seems to be that in their bias towards quantification the social sciences have been led to an arid mechanical model of man. He seems to suggest that Autonomous Man captures the essence of human action, although not lending itself easily to quantification. Therefore, his distinction between the two models of man is based on mechanism and quantification.

Hollis paints with a very broad brush, which renders his analysis too ambiguous. Also by its very nature, important exceptions are often over-looked. In economics, both models prevail so that we can give more precise meaning to his concepts. For example, the neoclassical theories of utility and of the firm, with their assumption of perfect competition are examples of the Plastic Man model, whereas game theory serves as an example of the Autonomous Man model of behavior. So in economics we have some familiar specific theoretical examples which serve as illustrations of the two models of man posed by Hollis, examples which are *both* mechanistic in nature. Therefore the basis for his distinction between the two models of man is misplaced. The more interesting problem is the one which neither model as developed by Hollis deals with nor which the modern economic model of man deals with, namely the human problem at interaction. Such a model exists in Pareto's sociology and is cast in terms of utility theory.

CONCLUSION

It should be clear that Pareto's sociological model of man differs fundamentally from the Plastic and Autonomous models of man discussed earlier. Plastic Man is comparable with Pareto's ophelimity theory whereas Autonomous Man is similar to that of modern game theory. But neither represents a model of interpersonal interaction where the goal is to *alter* the environment (or rules) as is the case with Pareto's model, in keeping with individuals' desires to maximize welfare. In this sense, Hollis's Autonomous Man stops where Pareto began sixty-four years earlier.[5] It is also remarkable that the dynamic process of interaction presented by Pareto has much in common with the "New Physics" of today with its emphasis on nonlinear dynamics in biological systems and the new field in molecular biology which has discovered that bacteria seem to act as groups and communicates with each other, leading to a sociological approach to research. Once again the physical and biological sciences may lead the way for economics to follow, away from nineteenth-century classical mechanics.

NOTES

1   See Pareto (1913) and Tarascio (1969, 1978). The analysis of Pareto's utility theory in this chapter follows that presented in the two prior works.
2   Pareto (1935: IV, 1473); see also the Reference column in Table 17.1.
3   Figure 17.1 is essentially Pareto's diagram, with minor modifications for purposes of clarity; see Pareto (1935: IV, 1473–4).
4   Pareto gave many examples of such situations (see Pareto (1935: IV, 1617–22) for a notable example pertaining to the concept of "public needs").
5   One might argue that there are similarities between Autonomous Man and Pareto's sociological man since both attempt to use "reason" in their desire to understand. The similarity ends there because for Pareto "reasonings" are mere rationalizations of sentiments on an individual basis and "derivations" in interpersonal interaction situations. Also Pareto stressed the *uncertain* nature of the social process from the point of view of individuals. Belief creates certainty, but that was not the kind of world the utilitarians and modern day economists had or have in mind. It is the lack of certainty in the economic and social process which makes individuals so susceptible to beliefs and ideologies. See Pareto (1907).

REFERENCES

Croce, Benedetto (1901) "Replica all'articolo del Professore Pareto", *Giornale delgi economisti* 22 (February): 121–30; trans. as "On the economic principle",

International Economic Papers 3 (1953): 172–9.

Hollis, Martin (1977) *Models of Man*, Cambridge: Cambridge University Press.

Pareto, Vilfredo "Sul fenomeno economico, Lettera a Benedetto Croce", *Giornale degli economisti* 21 (August): 139–62; trans. as "On the economic phenomenon", *International Economic Papers* 3 (1953): 180–96.

—— (1901) "Sul principio economico", *Giornale degli economisti* 22 (February): 131–8; trans. as "On the economic principle", *International Economic Papers* 3 (1953): 203–7.

—— (1907) Letter to Antonio Antonucci, November 24: in *Alcune lettere di Vilfredo Pareto publicate e commentate da A. Antonucci*, Rome: Maglione, 1938.

—— (1911) "Economie mathématique", *Encyclopédie des Sciences mathématiques*, tome 1, vol. 4, fasc. 4, Paris; trans. as "Mathematical economics", *International Economic Papers* 5 (1955): 58–102.

—— (1913) "Il massimo di ulitiaá per un collectivitia in sociologia", *Giornale degli economisti* 46 (April): 338–41.

—— (1935) *The Mind and Society*, trans. and ed. A. Livingston, 4 vols, New York: Harcourt, Bruce: trans. from *Trattato di sociologia generale*, 4 vols, Florence: Barbera, 1916.

Tarascio, Vincent J. (1969) "Paretian welfare theory: some neglected aspects", *Journal of Political Economy* 77 (January–February): 1–20.

—— (1978) "Theories of justice, social action, and the state" *Eastern Economic Journal* 4 (January): 41–9.

Chapter 18

Is emotive theory the philosopher's stone of the ordinalist revolution?

John B. Davis

In the latter half of the twentieth century economics has come to be regarded as a science little different in its use of scientific methods from the longer established natural sciences. In good part this has been due to economists' adoption of sophisticated mathematical models and state-of-the-art econometric techniques that permit empirical testing of formally expressed causal relationships. Science since Newton has been understood to be mathematical in nature, and good science has for an even longer time depended upon evaluating theory according to its ability to explain and predict observable events. But is economic behavior truly governed by causal laws? The foundation of modern economics is the theory of individual choice, and while we say that circumstances often occasion the choices individuals make, it seems inappropriate to make the stronger claim that choices are actually caused. Given this, it seems odd that economic behavior is modeled in terms of relationships between independent and dependent variables, where the former cause or bring about the latter. Indeed one might go so far as to say that the reliance on mathematical functions to represent human behavior is a misuse of mathematics, and that economics should return to an earlier practice of producing more descriptive, qualitative analysis.[1]

The argument in this chapter is somewhat more modest. Here it is argued that there are significant limitations on the use of mathematics in economics on account of the nature of choice behavior, and that these limits have been generally overstepped by economists anxious to legitimate social science thinking in the wider scientific community. The immediate thesis of the chapter is that an important problem in contemporary economics is its systematic misapprehension of the nature of practical reasoning or practical inference. This misapprehension, it is argued, principally derives from the widespread acceptance of Lionel Robbins's critique of value judgments and ethics advanced more than a half century ago in his influential methodological tract *An Essay on the Nature and Significance of Economic Science* (1932, 1935). Value judgments and ethical argument of course are only one species of practical reasoning. Indeed, pragmatic reasoning without ethical implication is an equally if not more pervasive form of practical inference. However,

Robbin's treatment of value judgments and ethics, which we will see in key respects followed the logical positivists' emotivist critique of ethics of the 1920s and 1930s, applies equally to other forms of practical reasoning. Thus Robbins was in effect responsible for a more general critique of practical reasoning and inference which, it will be argued here, subsequently encouraged a mistaken understanding of economic behavior among later economists. In essence, Robbins's *Essay* convinced most economists that economics was properly thought a natural science in its scientific methodology, when a reasonable assessment of the nature of practical reasoning in which economic agents engage should have produced the view that economics possessed distinctive characteristics as a social science.

The chapter develops these conclusions in several stages. In the next section, the principal differences between deductive or demonstrative reasoning and practical reasoning are set forth with special attention to the significance of these differences for understanding economics as a social science. In the third section, Robbins's characterization of value judgments and the connection between his arguments and those of the logical positivists A. J. Ayer and C. L. Stevenson are examined. The principal implication of Robbins's critique, it will be seen, is the idea that economics is a natural science that focuses on truth and causality. In the fourth section, we look at the importance of choice behavior in economics and the reasons for saying that economics cannot be treated as a natural science but must rather be understood as a social science. Finally in the concluding section, the topics of measurement, quantification and the empirical work in economics are briefly discussed with the aim of outlining the limits of quantitative methods in economics.

FORMS OF REASONING

Economists do not always appreciate that the choice behavior they study falls within a broader domain of practical reasoning whose logic has been long investigated by philosophers, logicians and, more recently, decision theorists. Yet it is important to see choice behavior as being part of this larger framework, since this serves to distinguish it as a specific form of reasoning with its own particular requirements. Perhaps the easiest way to see what this involves is to allude briefly to Aristotle who, in a basic distinction since maintained by philosophers and logicians, distinguished reasoning by its subject matter as either scientific or practical. Scientific or demonstrative reasoning, first of all – i.e. what is now characterized as deductive reasoning in formal logic – concerns the relation of entailment, whereby valid inferences from true premises entail true conclusions. The relation of entailment, it should be emphasized, is a relation of necessity, such that should one profess belief in the truth of the premises of a valid syllogism, then one can fairly be accused of inconsistency should one deny the truth of its conclusion. Thus, for Aristotle, demonstrative reasoning was scientific in that the natural world, which he took to be the sole domain of science, was constituted of invariable relationships or laws whose investigation demonstrative reasoning assisted. On this view, given some generalization from experience that all x's are A's, should we find some entity we know to be an x, we would then be entitled to infer with certainty that this x was also an A.

The importance of demonstrative or deductive reasoning to the expansion and development of natural science can hardly be exaggerated. Its model of science is of a nomological and verificationist form of investigation, the object of which is to elaborate highly confirmed generalizations, sometimes referred to as laws of nature, which may function as major premises of theoretical syllogisms. Indeed, attendant to this logical conception there has also developed a philosophy of the meaning of general relationships, namely, that they reflect causal connections or causal laws that operate in the world itself. That a is always followed by b tells us that b is necessary for a and thus a cause of a. Natural scientists have thus made one of their chief preoccupations the empirical substantiation of general relationships. While the empirical testing of such relationships is a complicated matter – something made increasingly evident in debates in recent decades in the philosophy of science – in the main, natural scientists still take as their principal task the explanation of causal connections in the world through the use of demonstrative reasoning and empirical analysis.

In contrast, practical reasoning or inference, though it may also be represented in syllogistic form, is fundamentally different from demonstrative reasoning on account of the fact that its conclusion is something that one ought to do (in either moral or pure pragmatic terms), not something said to be true. That is, practical reasoning prescribes, and is reasoning leading toward action, whereas demonstrative reasoning describes, and is reasoning toward the truth of a conclusion. This difference is significant with respect to our different relations to the respective conclusions of theoretical and practical syllogisms. As noted, in demonstrative reasoning one cannot consistently deny the truth of a conclusion validly inferred from true premises. One is compelled to accept the truth of such a conclusion on pain of being inconsistent. With practical syllogisms, however, the conclusion of an argument, say, that one ought to perform some action does not in itself compel one to perform that action. Suppose, for example, that some practical argument produces the conclusion that a certain action is desirable. We all recognize that an individual may accept such an argument yet still fail to desire the action called for. Nor, moreover, are we inclined to say that this involves some sort of inconsistency. Thus, whereas demonstrative reasoning concerns relationships which are necessitous and invariable, practical reasoning concerns relationships which are contingent and variable.

This distinction has functioned in one form or another throughout much of the history of modern science, with causal relationships being central to natural science reasoning, and social science making individuals' practical reasoning behavior central to the examination of society. Indeed social scientists have often emphasized that their fields differ from the natural sciences by their assumption that social agents engage in purposive behavior and intentional action, so that the explanation of human conduct – both of individuals and groups of individuals – requires analysis of the processes of practical inference this presupposes.[2] As might be expected, however, this creates significant difficulties for causal analysis in social science. While a few have argued that mental events are a part of nature and can both cause and be caused in a law-like manner (Davidson 1980), most seem to agree that when one is asked why an intentional act was performed, the answer is not to be defined in terms of natural or psychological processes but in terms of a request for reasons (Anscombe 1957). In essence, intentions are characteristically cognitive phenomena, and as such cannot be understood in terms of patterns of cause and effect, which have very little if anything to tell us about the psychological world of motives, reasons and intentions.

Certainly, then, much more might be said on the subject of the character of practical reasoning. What needs to be emphasized here, however, is that the practice of employing natural science methods in economics – whereby economic choices are modeled as cause and effect relationships – implicitly makes specific assumptions about what must pass as practical reasoning in the realm of economic behavior. In the natural science model, the economist's principal task is to establish law-like generalizations about economic behavior that predict future behavior on the basis of past experience. This assumes, however, that economic agents are governed by causal relationships rather than engage in a practical reasoning that may redirect the future away from the pattern of past events. Suppose it is thought that the proposition that all x's are A's constitutes a law-like generalization in economic life. Then an economic agent who encounters an entity said to be truly an x must act in accordance with the proposition that all x's are A's. Since economic behavior is thought to involve reasoning capacity, an individual's failure to observe laws that pertain to economic life might indeed be considered a failure of rationality. In the language used above, a reasoning agent able to recognize true propositions and understand valid inference is thus compelled to act as demonstrative reasoning and economic laws dictate.

We will return to this argument below. Here it only needs to be noted that the obviously unacceptable implication of this interpretation of economic choice is that it makes economic behavior deterministic. On the natural science model of explanation, we seek law-like generalizations, because they are believed to reflect underlying causal relationships. Yet it is the consensus among philosophers, most social scientists and everyday individuals that human behavior is inadequately explained on this model. Though it may be possible to inject causal thinking into our accounts of human behavior, this is only done by ignoring the vast tide of intentional phenomena that appear to obey and be ruled by an altogether different logic. Aristotle sought to capture this distinct component of human behavior by the notion that practical reasoning does not compel its conclusions as does theoretical reasoning. Modern thinking understands practical reasoning as purposive behavior and intentional action. Agents' actions are informed by their intentions in that they act in accordance with their intentions, while their intentions themselves are formed according to their goals and ends. These goals and ends are then themselves evaluated and redetermined as we observe how well our actions fit our intentions.

Given all this, the assertion that most economists employ the methods of natural science as their model for explaining economic behavior might well seem paradoxical. The theory of price determination that constitutes the main body of current economic theory stems from an analysis of what economists term agent choice behavior. Central to the idea of choice, however, is the assumption that individuals are not compelled to act in certain ways. Thus how could it have been thought by Robbins that economics was best thought to be – as he explicitly insisted – a natural science? This puzzle is important for more than historical reasons. At issue is the contemporary understanding of economic method and the conception of economics as a science. To better approach these larger issues, we turn to Robbin's own thinking and the influences upon it during his time from the logical positivists.

ROBBINS AND THE EMOTIVISTS

To understand Robbins's critique of ethics and value judgments in his *Essay*, it is valuable to have some basic acquaintance with arguments that the logical positivists advanced regarding ethical statements in the same decade as the *Essay* was written. The logical positivists were a group of philosophers and scientists that formed in Vienna in the 1920s and 1930s to argue for a rigorously empiricist approach to science.[3] Though Robbins did not make special reference to the views of the logical positivists in his own works, the assumption here is that his thinking was indirectly influenced by their arguments, because their ideas had wide appeal, were widely discussed at the time and offered the promise of scientific respectability which Robbins valued. Irrespective of the question of influence, however, Robbins's own views bear striking resemblance to many of those adopted by the logical positivists. First and foremost was a common commitment to the project of demarcating science from non-science. For both Robbins and the logical positivists, science by the 1930s still suffered from undesirable admixtures of ethics and metaphysics. Second, there was a conviction on behalf of both that non-scientific ideas could be purged from science by the conscious adoption of the psychological causes and effects that tended to be associated with their utterance. "The emotive meaning of a word is the tendency of a word, arising through the history of its usage, to produce (result from) affective responses in people" (Stevenson 1937: 14). As a theory of ethical language, emotivism was thus an early form of what ethics philosophers now characterize as non-cognitivism. Ethical language is non-cognitive on this view, because it is an incidental, in itself meaningless, accompaniment to an underlying causal process involved in individuals' efforts to pursue their interests through psychological manipulation. This underlying causal process could be explained in standard natural science terms using deductive logic and empirical analysis, but ethical language in itself is meaningless. Thus, whereas scientific statements possessed descriptive meaning in virtue of their (empirically verifiable) representation of the causal connections we find in the world, ethical statements had what Stevenson distinguished as causal meaning in that we use this kind of language purely because psychological circumstances stimulate us to do so.[4]

Given this, it is not difficult to see that the emotivist doctrine provided valuable support for the logical positivists' main contention that science could be demarcated from non-science. It was commonplace that people argued a great deal about ethical questions, and this might well suggest philosophers were right to think that ethical argument obeyed unique rules of reasoning. However, the emotivist doctrine struck at the very root of this notion in asserting that ethical language was intrinsically meaningless. Not denying that people engaged in disputes about ethics, the logical positivists were able to argue that the only thing of significance in such arguments fell squarely within the province of science. Ayer drew this conclusion quite clearly.

> For we certainly do engage in disputes which are ordinarily regarded as disputes about questions of value. But, in all such cases, we find, if we consider the matter closely, that the dispute is not really about a question of value, but about a question of fact.
>
> (Ayer 1946:110)

Generally, then, objective intellectual inquiry corresponds to scientific investigation, and science is identical with the nomological, verificationist natural science that employed the tools of deductive logic. The logical positivists thought that these were particularly important conclusions to draw, because they feared science was in danger of incorporating a host of irrational, spiritualist notions that might set back the human progress science had assisted over the last two centuries.

Robbins was very sympathetic to this concern.[5] In his view economics had also suffered as a science on account of its failure to define its subject matter properly. He disparaged past attempts to describe economics as "the study of the causes of material welfare" (Robbins 1932, 1935: 9), and also insisted that as the study of resource allocation decisions economics only investigated ends–means relationships, not the ends of economic activity themselves.

[T]he subject matter of Economics is essentially a series of relationships

– relationships between ends conceived as the possible objectives of conduct, on the one hand, and the technical and social environment on the other. Ends as such do not form part of this subject-matter. Nor does the technical and social environment. It is the relationships between these things and not the things in themselves which are important for the economist.

(p. 38)

These relationships, Robbins went on to argue, existed in economics in a small number of essentially incontrovertible generalizations upon experience. In the simple theory of value and exchange where production is not at issue, the "main postulate" concerned individuals' capacity for arranging their preferences in order.

The propositions of economic theory, like all scientific theory, are obviously deductions from a series of postulates. And the chief of the postulates are all assumptions involving in some way simple and indisputable facts of experience related to the way in which the scarcity of goods which is the subject-matter of our science actually shows itself in the world of reality. The main postulate of the theory of value is the fact that individuals can arrange their preferences in an order, and in fact do so.

(pp. 78–9)

The "main postulate in the theory of production", Robbins continued, was the law of diminishing returns. There was then a law of dynamics. From these foundations, all "the complicated theorems of advanced analysis ultimately depend". And though "the more complicated applications of these propositions involves the use of a great multitude of subsidiary postulates ... [t]he truth of the deductions from this structure depends, as always, on their logical consistency" (p. 79).

Clearly, then, though Robbins characterizes economics in the seemingly practical terms of means and ends, his view of its subject matter bears little relation to the traditional view of practical reasoning. Two things make this especially apparent. First, his insistence that the structure of economic argument employs postulates, theorems and logical consistency demonstrates that Robbins placed considerable weight on using traditional deductive reasoning in economics. Indeed, the desire to employ straightforward deductive argument in economics seems to have played an important role in Robbins's project of redefining economics, since his elimination of the material causes of welfare and the ends of economic activity from the domain of economics effectively serves to restrict its subject matter to sets of generalizable relationships that then readily function as propositions in deductive arguments. Second, though Robbins refers to ends–means relationships, his ends–means relationships explicitly exclude any consideration of the ends of action. Yet practical reasoning, as the investigation of purposive behavior and intentional action, examines both how individual actions are informed by intentions and how the intended ends of action are re-evaluated according to the success of our actions. The ends of action cannot thus be excluded from consideration of ends–means relationships if one is concerned to explain individuals' processes of practical reasoning, and Robbins's willingness to do this consequently betrays a commitment to a different approach to explaining economic behavior.

Why, then, did Robbins think that the ends of action fell outside the domain of economics? Here the influence of logical positivist thinking in the 1930s seems to have been crucial. Like the logical positivists, Robbins believed that the topic of the ends of action belonged to the domain of ethics, and that ethics and economics are "two fields of inquiry ... not on the same plane of discourse" because ethics concerned values and economics – as a science – concerned facts (p. 148). This difference, he emphasized, gave the propositions of economics a special advantage over those in ethics. Because factual propositions are susceptible to empirical verification, true propositions can be thought objective. The propositions of ethics, in contrast, must be thought subjective, because they lack an evaluation procedure comparable with empirical verification. Indeed, this conclusion was central to Robbins's famous critique of interpersonal utility comparisons. Earlier (cardinal) utility theorists had thought it possible to compare changes in one individual's well-being with those of another's. Robbins insisted that this involved value judgments, because "There is no means of testing the magnitude of A's satisfaction as compared with B's" (pp. 139–40). Value judgments, however, were subjective, and this implied that interpersonal comparisons of utility should be excluded from economics.

Robbins thus followed the logical positivists both in demarcating science and non-science and in regarding ethics as non-science. Yet the objections of Robbins and the logical positivists to ethics applied no less to other forms of practical reasoning, so that on their understanding social science had to be a deductive nomological form of investigation that had as its object the explication of causal connections in the social world. It was for this reason that Robbins termed economics a natural science, and asserted that "the propositions of Economics are on all fours with the propositions of all other sciences" (p. 104). But, surely, this conclusion also must strike many as a curious one, since Robbins's *Essay* is most well known for its conclusion that "Economics is the science which studies human behaviour as a relationship between ends and scarce means which have alternative uses" (p. 16). How can a science of behavior in which individuals must make decisions over resource use be a natural science? The simple answer to this question is that it cannot. The more complicated answer is that while Robbins was correct to emphasize the choice as central to economics, he was mistaken in thinking that this did not require a conception of the methodology of economics distinct from the model offered by natural science.

SOCIAL SCIENCE AND PRACTICAL REASONING

On the assumption that contemporary economics largely follows Robbins in employing natural science methods of thinking and analysis, just how, then, is practical reasoning in economic life misrepresented? When we consider a demand relationship, the quantity demanded of a good is termed a dependent variable and the good's price is termed an independent variable. Economists sometimes hasten to add that this does not imply that price and quantity demanded are causally connected, with changes in the former necessitating changes in the latter. Yet this assertion, it seems, is at odds with the practice of attempting empirically to verify demand (and other) relationships in economics. Presumably the goal of empirical work is to show that there exist true relationships between whatever variables are the subject of investigation. But if such relationships truly obtain, then it follows that changes in independent variables are responsible for bringing about changes in dependent variables, and this is the idea of causal connection. True relationships, that is, are causal relationships, and thus the goal of empirical work in economics is to uncover causal laws governing economic phenomena, despite the fact that this implies that economic behavior is deterministic.

Note that this conclusion is not undermined by saying that whatever demand behavior was in the past, it might be different in the future. If a demand relationship is said to have obtained in the past as a matter of fact, then it has already been asserted that price changes caused changes in quantity demanded. It is true that the world might well be different in the future, but if one later establishes a different set of empirically true relationships between variables, then one has only shown that different causal connections then obtained between those variables. Moreover, since we suppose that the laws of nature do not change, the establishment of a new causal relationship between variables seems to imply that the original specification of the model involved in the initial testing was somehow mistaken. Essentially, then, once one begins the project of finding true general relationships in economic behavior one commits oneself to the idea that causal relationships govern that behavior.

Thus, although most economists believe that empirically established relationships in economics are meant to explain choice or decision behavior, the idea that these relationships display causal connections means that there is not only no need to refer to such behavior in the description of these relationships, but moreover to do so betrays a misunderstanding of the nature of choice behavior itself. A true empirical relationship between two variables implies that these variables will always be associated in a particular manner. But if they are to be invariably associated in some particular manner, then it cannot be the case that an agent has chosen to respond in the way this relationship requires, because choice presupposes the ability to act otherwise than one has. That is, that such a relationship obtains implies that agents must always behave in accordance with it. At bottom, then, the idea of there being empirically established relationships in economics is incompatible with the idea of individuals exercising genuine choice or decision behavior in economic life, this despite the fact that economists generally believe themselves to be explaining choice behavior.

Economists who accordingly model economic behavior functionally to permit empirical investigation must implicitly employ a theoretical under-standing of behavior that precludes the exercise of agent choice.[6] One way that this occurs is through a violation of the central assumption underlying practical reasoning as a distinct form of reasoning, namely, that the conclusion to a practical argument does not compel action or, as it was put above, that the demonstrated desirability of something does not entail its being desired by any given individual. From this perspective, economists wedded to the natural science model of explanation rule out choice behavior by effectively requiring that desirability does imply desire. That is, should some item be shown to be desirable for an individual, that individual must also desire that item, or else (as the theoretical syllogism has it) be charged with acting inconsistently. In economics, of course, failure to act as the model requires is termed irrational behavior, and only "acting" as one's preferences and opportunity sets dictate is regarded as rational. True, economists do not deny that individuals sometimes fail to act as their models require, but they do deny that there is a logic or form of reasoning that might render this behavior rational.[7] In this way they demonstrate their implicit commitment to a natural science interpretation of economic behavior.

How, then, should economic behavior be described so as to be said purposive and intentional? The difficulty with the standard model is that the so-called goal or end, utility maximization, is not really a goal in the sense of being an end determined by the agent. Rather, the agent maximizes utility, because he or she possesses an unchosen preference structure that, upon being confronted with a set of stimuli designated as that agent's opportunity set (prices, income etc.) which defines the relevant setting and circumstances, dictates a rational "choice". A reasonable characterization of behavior that is purposive and intentional, however, would involve agent determination of goals, followed by subsequent action in accordance with those goals, followed by the evaluation of the appropriateness of the actions selected to the task of achieving the chosen goals, finally followed by reconsideration of goals that may be chosen in the future. In essence, purposive behavior involves an interaction between actions and goals that involves a process or series of steps in reasoning. The domain of practical reasoning, as investigated by philosophers (e.g. Anscombe 1957; Gautier 1963; Edgely 1969; Norman 1971; Von Wright 1971; Korner 1974; Raz 1975, 1978), represents the field of logic that attempts to systematize the rules of inference involved in this form of reasoning. Without looking into this literature, it is possible to say briefly how the standard model of behavior used in economics circumvents the sort of analysis that would be involved in an account of the interaction of actions and goals.

In the standard model of economic behavior, preferences are both complete and stable (Stigler and Becker 1977). Thus, if we examine behavior over a period of time, we can assume that action does not modify intention and that the goal of action, namely, to maximize utility, is constant. On this view, desirability dictates desire or preferences dictate action (given an opportunity set), essentially because the agent has a single, unchanging behavior function. In contrast, were agents to engage in goal-determining behavior on account (at least in part) of the actions they undertook, then the analysis of their behavior as agents would need to assume that their objectives at any one point in time were incompletely determined, else they would be incapable of change. In effect, that our ends or goals may be reevaluated in light of actions performed tells us that our ends or goals at any one point in time do not fully represent us. This incomplete determination is both incompatible with a functional analysis of behavior and also necessary to any theory of practical reasoning based on an interaction of actions and goals. The standard theory of economic behavior, then, achieves its results – and excludes a genuine theory of choice – by exhaustive definition of the agent's goals in a well-defined objective function. Clearly, too, it is determinacy at this level which underlies the natural science approach in economics, since the project of discovering causal connections in any sphere depends upon treating behavioral relationships in functional terms.

A genuine choice theory of economic behavior, accordingly, needs to avoid functional analysis and preserve an element of indeterminacy in the goal-setting behavior of the economic agent. Practical inference as a logic of ends–means interaction, it might also thus be said, turns on recognizing an important asymmetry between the effects of ends on means (how our actions are informed by our intentions) and the effects of means on ends (how we revise our goals in light of the results of our actions). While how our means address our ends is usually a relatively straightforward, technical matter, how our ends are revised in light of the results of our actions is by comparison quite obscure, if only because of the difficulty in seeing clear patterns in our changing goals. The implication of this is that goals and ends possess an element of ambiguity that we may be mistakenly inclined to minimize to achieve more concrete results in social science. This was something that Robbins and the logical positivists seem to have concluded in judging ends as valuational (which is correct) and as such irrational (which is disputable).[8]

There have been, it should be noted, many economists who have resisted this conception of the nature of economics, and some who have addressed the role Robbins's thinking has played in bringing it about. Among Austrian economists, Israel Kirzner (1960) has argued that Robbins's thinking about the nature of economics was particularly responsible for the confused view of economic decision-making held by so many contemporary economists. For

Kirzner, this approach led economists to over-appreciate static equilibrium methods and under-appreciate the active role of the entrepreneur in the economy. From the English Marshallian tradition, J. M. Keynes attacked Robbins's view of economics, precisely because he thought it led to a mistaken characterization of economics as a natural science. Adopting an older English political economy designation of social science as moral science, Keynes argued that the intentional nature of human behavior necessitated an altogether different methodology for economics.

> I also want to emphasise strongly the point about economics being a moral science. I mentioned before that it deals with introspection and with values. I might have added that it deals with motives, expectations, psychological uncertainties. One has to be constantly on guard against treating the material as constant and homogeneous.
>
> (Keynes 1971–89: XIV, p. 300)

However, neither Kirzner nor Keynes have had much influence on economic methodology, whatever their influence on economic theory itself. Indeed, the tremendous explosion of econometric techniques and methods that has occurred in recent decades dates from about the time of Keynes's criticisms of Robbins, when individuals such as Jan Tinbergen first began to apply multiple correlation techniques to macroeconomic data (1939).[9] Perhaps in the case of Keynes, whose influence on economic theory has been considerable, it may have been that, though he distanced himself from traditional deductive logic in his own early work on probability theory (Keynes 1971–89: VIII), he never systematically went on to work out his thoughts about practical logic. Thus, though his emphasis on "motives, expectations, and psychological uncertainties" was entirely appropriate to an investigation of purposive behavior and intentional action, his failure to provide a clear rationale for this emphasis left his message muted.

IMPLICATIONS FOR EMPIRICAL AND QUANTITATIVE WORK IN ECONOMICS

What are the implications of the analysis above for empirical economic methodology and for the use of quantitative methods in economics? The argument here has been that the behavior of agents in economic life must be understood as exhibiting practical reasoning, and that economics needs to avoid representing agent behavior in natural science terms, that is, as a behavior explainable in terms of generalizable relationships that imply causal laws. This argument does not imply, it should be emphasized, that economics does not aim at producing true propositions about economic behavior. As a social science, of course, economics aims no less at producing truth than does natural science. Thus, while strict causal laws of the sort that are sought in natural science have no place in economics on the argument here, facts are still very much an object of economic analysis. A classification of the kinds of factual propositions compatible with the assumption that individuals exercise practical reason in their economic behavior should accordingly provide guidelines for empirical economic research in economics. There seem to be two sorts of factual propositions in economics and social science.

First, there are those general factual propositions that might be said to describe non-causal, "structural" relationships in the economy. Even though intentional, economic behavior in many contexts seems lethargic in the sense that slowly changing circumstances are often associated with little variation in individuals' ends and actions. Moreover, many economic categories and concepts involve a level of aggregation that typically obscures the intentional component in individual economic behavior. Thus, relationships that are "structural", in the sense that they largely omit reference to individual choice behavior and describe patterns of events that are simply highly confirmed rather than explainable as the products of agent choice behavior, are reasonably given mathematical and statistical treatment. Note that this has implications for our interpretation of the error term involved in probabilistic analysis. If we assume that behavioral equations tested possess at most an implicit reference to agents' intentional behavior, then the error term in such equations should no longer be said to reflect random elements in underlying agent behavior (since the idea of the true model being deterministic is contrary to our view of choice). Rather the error term should be thought to reflect the degree to which our "structural" equations fail to approximate agents' underlying intentional behavior. That is, the error term seems better understood as a measure of our failure to capture the essential variability of choice behavior in our effort to produce reasonably well confirmed but not exact characterizations of aggregate activity.

Second, there are those particular factual propositions that aim only at explaining specific historical events. Since actions have causal impact, a large body of information may potentially be integrated and organized to produce a knowledge of past economic behavior and relationships. Economic history in this sense aims to explain unique historical occurrences as a result of the particular choices made by particular economic agents in particular circumstances. That is, economic history, by making the historical process its subject of investigation, focuses directly upon individuals' practical reasoning, or how intention informs action and is revised in light of its results. Put differently, this domain of economic investigation places its chief emphasis on documenting the development and change in agents' motivations for action, and thus it is the traditional historian's methodologies rather than statistician's techniques that are what are required for this portion of empirical economics.

These two kinds of factual propositions, however, appear to exhaust the allowable domain for empirical research in economics and social science. Only the former, however, allows for the use of contemporary quantitative and statistical methods, and even in this connection considerable caution must be exercised in interpreting econometric results. It would thus be going too far to say that mathematical representation of economic relationships is an altogether misconceived enterprise. Rather the proper conclusion seems to be that mathematics is often misused in economics due to a failure to recognize the limitations placed on explanation in social science. Too much of contemporary economics can indeed be characterized as natural science masquerading as social science. What, then, it seems fair to recommend is that economists devote less effort to functional representation of economic behavior and more effort to investigating the dynamic and variable character of economic choice. This no doubt would diminish the value of much contemporary equilibrium analysis – a mainstay of modern economics. But it presumably would lead to better economic analysis and, perhaps, better explanation and prediction of economic events.

NOTES

1   Among contemporary economic theorists with this view are the Austrians, who treat economic decision-making as a process of creative discovery, and traditional institutionalist economists, who emphasize the complex role an economy's institutional fabric plays in influencing choice.

2   Gordon's (1992) monumental study of the history and philosophy of social science continually emphasizes this fundamental divide between natural and social science.

3   See Gordon (1992: 590ff.) for an account of the rise and fall of logical positivism.

4   Neither Robbins nor the logical positivists, it turned out, were really consistent on this last, central point. In particular, their methodological strictures themselves clearly lacked empirical foundations.

5   To be sure, Robbins drew very much upon the Austrian school of economics for his principal inspiration, and this in important respects meant that his methodology was more *apriorist* than would have suited the logical positivists. The argument here concerns their common commitment to deductivist reasoning.

6   A good example here is Elster (1989). Elster insists that the proper method for the social sciences is one that investigates causal mechanisms. When he comes to the analysis of choice and explanation of action his expedient is to speak of "two successive filtering operations" in our constraints and opportunities (p. 13). Nowhere in his discussion is he able to persuasively demonstrate that this analysis of behavior permits us to explain the real phenomena of choice behavior.

7   Indeed, originally some of the most innovative work attempting to explain this apparently widespread "irrational" behavior as reasonable invoked the notion of a bounded or procedural rationality (Simon 1957). Such an analysis, however, still presupposes the natural science orientation in economics.

8   Robbins is sometimes taken to have purged the remaining classical political economy elements from the neoclassical revolution in economic theory of the later nineteenth century, where the essence of that revolution was to make choice behavior central to economic analysis. On the interpretation here, that revolution was more responsible for making a deterministic functional analysis based on the

differential calculus the cornerstone of economics. Marshall's two blades of the supply-and-demand scissors, then, were the determinations of psychology and technology.

9   Keynes also, it is worth noting, advanced one of the first major critiques of econometrics.

REFERENCES

Anscombe, G. E. M. (1957) *Intention*, Oxford: Basil Blackwell.

Ayer, A. J. (1936, 1946) *Language, Truth and Logic*, New York: Dover Publications.

Davidson, D. (1980) *Essays on Actions and Events*,

Edgley, R. (1969) *Reason in Theory and Practice*, London: Hutchinson.

Elster, J. (1989) *Nuts and Bolts*, Cambridge: Cambridge University Press.

Gautier, D. (1963) *Practical Reasoning*, Oxford: Oxford University Press.

Gordon, S. (1992) *The History and Philosophy of Social Science*, London: Routledge.

Keynes, M. J. (1971–89) *The Collected Writings*, ed. D. Moggridge, London: Macmillan.

Kirzner, I. (1960) *The Economic Point of View*, Kansas City, KS: Sheed & Ward.

Korner, S. (ed.) (1974) *Practical Reason*, Oxford: Blackwell.

Norman, R. (1971) *Reasons for Action*, Oxford: Blackwell.

Raz, J. (1975) *Practical Reasons and Norms*, London: Hutchison.

—— (ed.) (1978) *Practical Reason*, Oxford: Oxford University Press.

Robbins, L. (1932, 1935) *An Essay on the Nature and Significance of Economic Science*, London: Macmillan.

Simon, H. (1957) *Models of Man: Social and Rational*, New York: Wiley.

Stevenson, C. L. (1937) "The emotive meaning of ethical terms", *Mind*.

Stigler, G. and Becker, G. (1977) "De gustibus non est disputandum", *American Economic Review* 67 (2): 76–90.

Tinbergen, J. (1939) *A Method and Its Application to Economic Activity*, Geneva: League of Nations.

Von Wright, G. H. (1971) *Explanation and Understanding*, Ithaca, NY: Cornell University Press.

Chapter 19

If empirical work in economics is not severe testing, what is it?

Robert S. Goldfarb

There is a substantial case made by serious scholars that, despite a methodological rhetoric that often seems to imply and require sustained attempts to falsify economic theories, economists as a group do not take seriously this "responsibility". Some scholars, such as Mark Blaug (1980), subscribe to this description of the behavior of economists, and bemoan it. Others, such as Donald McCloskey (1983), appear to accept the description but reject the appropriateness of a falsificationist attitude. Still others, such as E. Roy Weintraub (1988), seem to take issue with the description itself.[1] This chapter attempts to shed light on this debate by focusing on the actual practice of empiricism in economics. Is it reasonable to characterize the typical objective of empirical work in economics as severe testing of theories ("falsification") or simply "verification", or something quite different?[2]

One well-known participant in the methodological debate, Mark Blaug (1980: 254) asserts that "the central weakness of modern economics is, indeed, the reluctance to produce the theories that yield unambiguously refutable predictions, followed by a general unwillingness to confront these implications with the facts". This proposition is put forward after quoting like-minded criticisms by Leontief (1971), Ward (1972) and others. Blaug elaborates on the lack-of-empirical-testing part of this proposition by observing that economists do "engage massively in empirical research", but "unfortunately, much of it is like playing tennis with the net down: instead of attempting to refute testable predictions, modern economists all too frequently are satisfied to demonstrate that the real world conforms to their predictions, thus replacing falsification, which is difficult, with verification, which is easy" (pp. 256–7).

An empirically oriented economist, reacting to my verbal description of Blaug's complaint, indicated that the complaint had some appeal to him based on his own experience. In particular, he reported that when he had strong *a priori* sign expectations based on theory, he would tend to go on doing additional statistical estimation so long as his results displayed "incorrect" signs. That is, his "stopping rule" was based on finding the "right" signs. His "stopping rule" procedure is surely *not* designed to severely test the theory in question by trying to refute its predictions. It is far more consistent with an attempt to provide numerical support for the theory, and with Leamer's well-known (1983) critical description of econometric practice.[3]

While I believe that the conversation reported above describes what many competent and well-intentioned researchers do, Denton (1988), in a highly insightful article about what he calls "information filtering" problems, shows that the same kinds of problems can arise even if individual researchers behave like "classical statisticians" in their hypothesis testing. Denton presents the following case:

> (A)ssume a population of researchers ... working with a common set of data. Each member of the population is a confirmed classical statistician. Working independently, each chooses a single specification for his or her regression equation, estimates the equation, and does the hypothesis testing exactly as planned. If the researcher is lucky enough to obtain significant t-statistics and to satisfy the other requirements for acceptability, he or she writes a paper and sends it to a journal. Otherwise the researcher gives up.... On no account would he or she consider trying a different model specification.
>
> (pp. 177–8)

Denton points out that the aggregate effect of this kind of individual behavior is "as if" each individual had been experimenting with repeated runs (or "data mining", in Denton's terminology) until he got the "right" signs. "If only those equations that have high t-statistics and other desirable characteristics ... get published ..., the effect is essentially the same ... as individual mining" (p. 178).

But why are these procedures, in which data and specification are extensively manipulated (by one individual in my example, or in the aggregate, in Denton's) until the desired results are found and disseminated, apparently so widespread? Surely a major contributing factor is the researcher's expectations about the criteria used by journals for acceptance of manuscripts. An article with an interesting empirical application of standard price theory whose empirical results fail to support the application is unlikely to be seen as a valuable contribution by reviewers. More specifically, it will be seen as a failed attempt to apply price theory, and therefore not worthy of attention, rather than being seen as a worthwhile piece of evidence because it casts doubt on standard theoretical approaches. The researcher, worried about publishability, is likely to work long and hard to get the statistical runs to come out "right". Or the researcher obtaining "wrong" results often will not send them to journals. It seems intuitively clear that these behaviors, if widespread, will bias the empirical evidence available to the profession towards consistency with standard, received theory.

If the profession really believed deeply in and practised the severe testing of theories with the aim of rejecting them, then estimated results counter to standard price theory applications would be viewed as "newsworthy" – that is, as valuable rejection evidence – and researchers would expect such results to be far more often published.[4] Thus, if the alleged existence of these reviewer and journal editor attitudes is correct, it provides presumptive evidence in favor of Blaug's assertion that economists do not seriously practise severe testing of their theories.[5]

Examination of particular empirical undertakings can deepen our understanding of these issues about the existence or nonexistence of testing, and the function(s) of empirical work in economics. Does empirical activity in particular applied areas in economics in fact display the alleged lack of "severe testing of theories"? And if severe testing is largely absent, what is the purpose of all this empirical work, found in enormous quantity in the profession's leading journals, that seems to focus on testing sign predictions?

The chapter proceeds as follows. Section I proposes an interpretation of sign-testing activity in the absence of severe theory testing, relating this interpretation to a discussion by the historian and philosopher of science Thomas Kuhn about the nature of empirical activity in the physical sciences. The interpretation is developed in the context of recent empirical research in labor economics, a field displaying an exceptional level of empirical activity. Section II examines the extent to which this interpretation is relevant to an empirical episode in another applied area of economics, industrial organization. Section III considers some philosophy of science issues and interpretations raised by the two cases. Section IV contains conclusions.

I

This section proposes an interpretation of sign-testing activity in economics that is consistent with the Blaug assertion that economists do not single-mindedly practise severe testing of their theories. The question of what all this sign-testing activity is really about actually requires a two-part answer. It must first be decided what all this journal-filling statistical activity might really be intended or designed to do; that is, what is the *purpose or purposes* of the overall activity? Once a provisional answer about *purpose* is provided, one must then indicate how sign-testing activity which is not severe hypothesis testing might contribute to this claimed purpose(s).

Empirical research in the physical sciences

It is instructive to start considering these issues by reviewing Thomas Kuhn's classification of the kinds of "normal science" empirical research done in the physical sciences. Kuhn's term "normal science" refers to operating within an accepted paradigm, and performing the kinds of intellectual activities that are regularly observed in that setting and fit into it.

Kuhn identifies three categories of empirical activities "neither always nor permanently distinct" (p. 25), which might be labeled measurement, theory-testing and paradigm articulation. He describes the "measurement" category as follows:

> First is that class of facts that the paradigm has shown to be particularly revealing of the nature of things. By employing them in solving problems, the paradigm has made them worth determining both with more precision and in a larger variety of situations. At one time or another, these significant determinations have included: in astronomy – stellar position and magnitude . . .; in physics – the specific gravities and compressibilities of materials, wave lengths and spectral intensities . . .; and in chemistry . . . boiling points and acidity of solutions. . . . Attempts to increase the accuracy and scope with which facts like these are known occupy a significant fraction of the literature of experimental and observational science.
>
> (p. 25)

"Theory testing", Kuhn's second category, involves testing the predictions from the "paradigm theory" in which the researcher is operating.

> A second usual but smaller class of factual determinations is directed to those facts that, though often without much intrinsic interest, can be compared directly with predictions from the paradigm theory. . . . There are seldom many areas in which a scientific theory, particularly when it is cast in a predominantly mathematical form, can be compared directly with nature. . . . Furthermore, even in those areas where application is possible, it often demands theoretical and instrumental approximations that severely limit the agreement to be expected. Improving the agreement or finding new areas in which agreement can be demonstrated at all presents a constant challenge to the skill and imagination of the experimentalist and observer.
>
> (p. 26)

This category seems analogous to Blaug's falsificationism, or what this chapter calls the "severe" testing of theories. It is interesting to note that Kuhn describes this class of empirical activity as less frequent ("smaller") than other empirical activities, even in the physical sciences.

Khun's third category, which we have labeled "paradigm articulation", "consists of empirical work undertaken to articulate the paradigm theory, resolving some of its residual ambiguities and permitting the solution of problems to which it had previously only drawn attention" (p. 27). Kuhn regards this category as "the most important of all", and he subdivides it into several categories: the determination of the numerical values of physical constants; the determination of quantitative laws; and "a third sort of experiment which aims to articulate a paradigm". This "third sort of experiment" might arise when "a paradigm developed for one set of phenomena is ambiguous in its application to closely related ones. Then experiments are necessary to choose among the alternative ways of applying the paradigm to the new area of interest" (p. 29).

If Blaug is right that Kuhn's category two, serious testing of the predictions of the paradigm theory, is relatively rare in economics, is it possible that much of the empirical activity we observe in the guise of theory testing is in fact aimed at something different, perhaps analogous to Kuhn's other two categories of "measurement" or "paradigm articulation"? If the answer turns out to be "yes", then we can investigate how sign testing might be relevant to these "other" aims of empirical work.

To get a handle on what the "something different" might be, it is certainly helpful and perhaps essential to focus on concrete examples from specific areas of research. Since this writer's perceptions about the nature of empirical activity in economics derive in substantial part from familiarity with empirical studies in labor economics, my argument about the nature of empirical activity will be developed in that context. Section II below will consider how the arguments might apply or fail to apply to another applied economics area, industrial organization.

Recasting empiricism in labor economics into "Kuhnian categories"

There has been a very major empirical component to research in labor economics in the last several decades. The central focus of much of this empirical work has been labor supply behavior.[6] How might this body of labor supply research be classified in terms of Kuhn's three categories of empirical work?

Recent interpretations of reasons for interest in empirical labor supply studies can help inform our discussion. Killingsworth, in his 1983 survey of the labor supply literature, provides four reasons why "(e)mpirical studies of static labor supply models are of interest" (p. 67):

First, they may be used to test the predictions and implications of theoretical models: for example, is the own-substitution effect of a wage increase on labor supply positive? Second, such studies may provide information on the signs and magnitudes of effects about which theoretical models make no *a priori* predictions: For example, is leisure a normal good and is the labor supply schedule backward bending? Third, such studies may shed light on a variety of important labor market developments, such as the phenomenal increase in the labor force participation of women ... in the past quarter century. ... Fourth, empirical studies are an important tool for evaluation of proposed government policies.

(p. 67)

Which of the four items on the Killingsworth list have actually played major parts in generating the empirical labor supply literature? Two historical examples suggest that Killingsworth's items three and four, "shedding light on labor market developments" and "evaluation of government policies" were very important. The first example involves the fact that the focus of Jacob Mincer's seminal 1962 article was on explaining an important "labor market development", the labor supply behavior of married women. The second example stresses the fact that an important source of interest in the pressure for labor supply studies in the 1960s and 1970s were policy discussions of income maintenance schemes and welfare reform.[7] These historical examples examined in more detail also support the central importance of item two, discovery of signs and especially magnitudes of effects. This follows because explanations for historical developments and the evaluation of government policies frequently turn out to depend on the actual magnitudes of income and substitution effects, and measuring the size of these effects has been a central focus of this literature. Thus, one of the major thrusts of the entire literature can be viewed as *measurement* of crucial labor supply parameters. In this sense the literature falls into Kuhn's measurement category.[8]

Thus, one clear conclusion from examining the actual history of empirical labor supply research is that a central focus is *measurement*, and this measurement effort in turn helps shed light on labor market developments and on policy choices. A second clear conclusion from examining the history is more negative. Neither our historical examples nor a more in-depth consideration of the history of empirical research in labor supply economics provides any support for the proposition that serious continuing efforts were single-mindedly devoted to severe testing of the "predictions and implications" of the underlying labor supply model.[9] Thus, Killingsworth's item one, while it is a potential reason for interest in empirical work, did not seem to be a driving force behind the empirical literature that was generated.

That severe testing of the underlying theory was not a major force driving labor supply research is recognized with varying degrees of explicitness by several major surveys of the literature. Killingsworth's summary observation about what he calls "first generation" empirical studies gives implicit support to the proposition that testing was not the central focus or use of this literature: "All in all, then, use of results of first-generation studies to support simple propositions of the simple static labor supply model is not to be recommended to those whose main concern is peace of mind" (p. 128). Killingsworth does *not* go on to say that this evidence of the received model's poor predictive power has led to a groundswell of demands for abandoning the model; nor has such a groundswell arisen. We would argue that this is because the focus of empirical attention has *not* been on testing the underlying modeling framework.[10]

More explicit focus on the relative absence of severe testing as a driving force underlying this literature is provided by Pencavel (1986). "(T)he overwhelming proportion of the empirical work has not questioned the validity of the conventional model; this model has been treated as a maintained hypothesis. Empirical research has concentrated on quantifying the magnitude of the presumed relationships.... In male labor supply research, very little formal testing of the standard model has been undertaken ... it can be described as 'measurement without testing'" (p. 5). Pencavel provides several surmises about reasons for this lack of testing, and then fires off the following broadside in his conclusion. "It is not as if the model has already survived many different attempts to refute it.... (F)ew scholars have conducted their research with the aim of testing the theory; most have been interested in quantifying a relationship whose existence is presumed to be true. As a by-product of this concern with measurement, they have turned up a number of ... (violations of) ... the theory's predictions. Under these circumstances, the scientific procedure is surely to regard the theory as it has been formulated and applied to date as having been refuted by the evidence" (pp. 94–5). As we indicated above, such a groundswell in favor of rejecting the model has not in fact emerged; this is a mute testimonial to the lack of sustained interest in and attention to severe testing of theories.[11]

Having documented that the focus of a major empirical literature in labor economics is on measurement rather than severe testing of theories, we can now address a central question of this chapter: if empirical work has not focused on severe testing of theories, why is there attention to testing predictions about particular coefficients?

There seems a simple and plausible answer to this question in the context of empirical labor supply research. Sign testing performs two functions when the aim is measurement, with additional goals of explaining labor market developments and evaluating public polity options. First, it provides a way of helping to evaluate the "quality" or "believability" of the labor supply elasticity estimates produced by a particular study. If measurement is in fact the aim, sign tests may aid the observer in forming an opinion as to how "good" or "believable" the measurement effort actually is. Second it can help identify which "control" variables are needed to explain labor market developments or for estimating/simulating the effects of alternative policies. Each use needs to be explained more fully.

To understand how sign results might help an observer come to grips with the "believability" of a particular set of elasticity estimates, consider the following scenario. A labor economist encounters a new empirical estimate of the elasticity of labor supply for a particular demographic group. How is this labor economist to decide how seriously to take this new estimate? We would not be surprised to find the following two "checks" conducted. First, the new estimate is compared with the stock of other available estimates. Sizable differences will give the evaluator cause for concern and further investigation. A second check is to examine the estimating equation to see if the signs and perhaps the sizes of various other (i.e. nonwage) coefficients meet prior expectations. The presence of "disturbing" signs, especially if they do not show up regularly in other studies, may represent a cause for concern about the "believability" of the estimate being offered. In this context, sign testing of other coefficients helps the observer evaluate the "believability" of the new labor supply estimate.[12]

A second function of sign testing in which measurement is the focus is to establish which "control" variables need to be used in explaining labor market developments or in estimating/simulating the effects of alternative policies. Suppose, for example, we are trying to explain historical patterns of labor force growth. In order to see how well an empirically estimated model "tracks" historical patterns, it is necessary to know whether our empirical estimates indicate that labor supply is affected by income, lowered prices and greater availability of home service goods (vacuum cleaners etc.), the presence of children in the household and so forth. The significance or lack of significance of the signs on these nonwage variables affect how we do the relevant historical simulation.[13] Similar comments apply to simulating the effect on labor supply of various alternative public policy options. Thus, there are several reasons to expect attention to sign testing even in settings where the focus is on measurement rather than severe theory testing.

In summary, the empirical labor supply literature can be characterized as directed primarily at the measurement of labor supply elasticities (or income and substitution effects). Sign testing can have a particular role to play in such a measurement-directed effort, a role not directly and strongly linked to attempts to severely test theories. Indeed, this empirical labor supply literature does not devote sustained attention to testing the underlying model.

If our interpretation of empirical work in labor supply economics is at least provisionally accepted, an interesting question concerns its generality. Do other applied areas in economics display empirical efforts primarily directed at measurement (with the attendant functions for sign testing), or are there important research areas in which there is significant empirical activity to which our interpretation does not apply? How is empirical research, especially sign testing activity, in these other areas to be interpreted? Comprehensive consideration of these issues would seem to call for in-depth reviews of a large number of applied areas, a task far beyond the scope of the present chapter and author. However, if may be possible to shed some light on the issues involved by considering one of many possible comparison cases.

II

We take as a comparison case a particular body of empirical work in industrial organization.[14] The body of empirical work to be considered flourished in the 1960s and early 1970s, and focused on the effects of industry concentration on measures of industry performance such as profits and prices. It provides some striking and instructive contrasts to the labor supply example discussed above. In particular, unlike the labor supply literature, the literature on concentration seems to have contained a serious theory-testing component. Moreover, this testing component itself seems to shed light on issues about how, and how "well", falsificationism can actually be practised.

Recent commentaries (Schmalensee 1982, 1989; Bresnahan and Schmalensee 1987) attempt to characterize from the vantage point of the 1980s the concentration–performance–profits–price literature (hereafter denoted "the CP literature") in terms of the broad sweep of empirical work in industrial organization. To paraphrase Bresnahan and Schmalensee (1987), industrial organization emerged as a separate field in the 1930s. Under the influence of the so-called "Harvard School", practitioners focused on book-length industry case studies which "made relatively little use of formal economic theory or econometric techniques". The focus of the field was substantially altered by the work of Joe Bain (1951, 1956) who showed "the apparent power of statistical studies of industry-level cross-section data". The Bain-inspired cross-sectional econometric approach so dominated the literature by the 1960s that William Comanor could write in 1971 that "To a large extent, therefore, a review of econometric studies of industrial organization is a review of much of the content of the field". However, criticism of this approach escalated in the 1970s. "By the end of the decade, the critics had generally prevailed. The study of industry-level cross-section data had fallen from fashion." The result was that, in the early 1980s, "relatively little exciting empirical work was being done in industrial organization.... The main action was on the theoretical front" (Bresnahan and Schmalensee 1987: 372–3).

This historical account suggests that a major empirical approach generating much of the research in industrial organization in the 1960s and 1970s was no longer of significant interest to researchers by the late 1970s. From the point of view motivating this chapter, this history raises a number of issues. Did the empirical approach include a sizable component of theory testing, or was its focus on something else, such as measurement? If there was a sizable component of theory testing, was the apparent demise of the approach brought on in part by an empirical testing which resulted in rejection of its theoretical underpinnings? More generally, how can we account for the downturn in popularity of this empirical approach, and how does an appropriate explanation relate to its apparent purposes (theory testing, measurement etc.)?

The CP literature as propounded by leading proponents does seem to contain a theory-testing element. Leonard Weiss's two survey articles (1971, 1974) are excellent sources of what practitioners believed the CP approach entailed, both because Weiss is one of its major proponents and because he states his views with admirable clarity.[15] In both his 1971 and 1974 surveys, Weiss argues that there is some basis in oligopoly theory for expecting a link between concentration and profits, since concentration increases the ability to collude and collusion might be expected to raise joint profits. While "a common statement of economists in general is that oligopoly theories yield an almost limitless range of predictions ... I feel this badly understates the guidance that theory can give" (1974: 192). Of the major "regularly cited and plausible" oligopoly theories that Weiss explicitly reviews, he finds that "most predict a positive effect of concentration on profits" (p. 192).

The argument thus far seems to be that "theory" suggests a link running from higher concentration to higher profits. Thus, an empirical investigation of the link might be viewed as one test of the variety of oligopoly theories which (according to Weiss) seem to yield the prediction. Note that the test is not a particularly demanding or severe one: all it requires is a positive concentration effect rather than some stronger result such as a particular "shape" to the positive relationship or a particular numerical value of a coefficient.

But the idea that investigating the concentration–profits link is somehow viewed in large part as a test of some specified subset of oligopoly theory does not seem consistent with the focus of the CP practitioners. Instead, for the proponents, *the very existence of the postulated link between concentration and profits is of interest for its own sake.* While a rigorous derivation from received oligopoly theory (or micro theory in general) would certainly have enhanced the claim of the CP prediction to be taken seriously, it seems to have been of interest to proponents quite independently of the microeconomic theory "legitimacy" of its parentage.[16] Thus what was being "tested" was the "theory" (in the sense of the "postulated relationship") that concentration affects profits.

But why were proponents particularly interested in this postulated relationship "for itself", regardless of the legitimacy of its exact links to or derivation from received microeconomic theory? Even if such a relationship happens to exist, why not treat it as no more interesting than the well-known correlation between temperature and frequency of cricket chirps? One possible reason for interest in the relationship independent of its theoretical derivation is that it seemed to have important implications for appropriate government policies for regulating business. There are any number of examples illustrating this link to policy concerns. One is the title of Weiss's 1974 survey: "The concentration–profits relationship and antitrust". A second example is the search by those exploring the concentration–profits relationship for a "critical concentration ratio" which, if found, could conceivably guide antitrust and merger policy.[17] A third example is Paul Pautler's 1983 article in the *Antitrust Bulletin*. Pautler examines the changing results of empirical work, contrasting the view in 1968 (his article contains a section heading "What did we think we knew in 1968?") to how views had changed by the early 1980s ("Revisionist views and debate, 1970–?"). His underlying goal is to evaluate what the empirical results imply for government policy towards horizontal mergers. Thus, the CP literature can be viewed as attempting to investigate the postulated existence of a link between concentration and profits. It does not seem a misuse of language to say that the literature "tested" for the existence of this relationship.

As we indicated above, the CP approach had fallen out of favor by the late 1970s. What led to this "defeat"? Was the apparent demise of the approach brought on in part by empirical testing which resulted in rejection of the postulated relationship? More generally, how can we account for the decline in this line of empirical research in industrial organization?

Some of the historical features of the fall from grace of the CP approach are quite striking. For one thing, at least according to the adherents, a large number of empirical studies seemed to *support* rather than refute the relationship. Weiss's 1971 survey reviews "32 tests of some form of the classic profit-determination hypothesis" appearing over an eighteen-year period, while his 1974 survey reviews forty-six studies. He describes the overall result of the studies as follows. "The bulk of the studies show a significant positive effect of concentration on profits or margins." Moreover, for any period "overlapped" by a number of studies, "the relationship was quite robust" (1974: 202). Weiss further argues that biases in the data are likely to lead to understatement of the strength of the relationship.[18] The "bottom line" in Weiss's view is that the studies *support* the postulated relationship.

How well does this "bottom line" result hold up from the vantage point of the late 1980s? Schmalensee's 1989 survey of "Interindustry studies of structure and performance", whose basic focus is to report "useful stylized facts" revealed by cross-section studies, notes that many studies published after Weiss "found no statistically significant linear relationship between domestic concentration and profitability" (p. 974). Moreover, non-US studies "have also produced negative results" (p. 975). Schmalensee concludes as follows, with what he labels a "stylized fact": "The relation, if any, between seller concentration and profitability is weak statistically, and the estimated concentration effect is usually small. The estimated relation is unstable over time and space and vanishes in many multivariate studies" (p. 976).

How can one explain this quite striking apparent reversal of empirical results? Why did those writing prior to the mid-1970s seem to find in the data confirmation of the postulated relationship, while those writing after the mid-1970s found refutations? There are several conflicting possible explanations. This may simply be a case of severe testing leading to empirical refutation of a "theory" or postulated relationship. As empirical studies became more sophisticated, it was revealed that the proposed empirical relationship in fact did not hold. If this turns out to be the correct interpretation, then Blaug's critique is incorrect in this instance; falsificationism (of the very simplest kind) lives, at least in this one area of industrial organization.[19]

A second possible explanation for the reversal of results makes the reversal appear far more consistent with Blaug's concerns, and therefore antithetical to the falsificationist interpretation provided above.[20] It turns out that a theoretical attack, as opposed to empirical testing, was a major contributor to the fall from favor of the view that concentration actually *causes* higher profits or collusion. Harold Demsetz (1974) argued that higher accounting profit rates might be due to superior efficiency rather than concentration. As one example, suppose a persistently concentrated industry has a mix of large and small firms. Perhaps because of economies of scale, the large firms are differentially efficient. More generally, existing large firms might "possess superior characteristics that are difficult to imitate. Their methods of organizing production, of providing service, and of establishing buyer confidence must yield lower cost than can be obtained by newer or smaller firms" (1974: p. 179). Small firms can coexist in the industry because demand is not sufficiently large to support one more large firm. But to make these smaller firms viable, "Price will need to be high enough to cover their unit cost, and this means that price will need to be high enough for accounting profits to be recorded by the large firms in these industries" (p. 177). In short, the theoretical attack suggested that, even if a robust statistical relationship were found between concentration and profits, it would not imply causation; it did not mean that the higher profits were caused by collusion or related undesirable monopolistic practices. Instead, differential efficiency "caused" the profits–concentration link.

An important feature of the "defeat" of the profits–concentration relationship is the fact that the empirical evidence seemed to be interpretable as largely favoring the "concentration causes profits" view before Demsetz, but then became less and less favorable after Demsetz launched his theoretical attack. This apparent reversal of the empirical evidence after Demsetz might of course just be a remarkable coincidence. Alternatively, it might be due to the fact that Demsetz's theoretical framework suggested (to Weiss (1974: 225), for example) the inclusion of market share as an additional variable in concentration–profit regressions. If entering market share became common practice, and turned out to greatly weaken the statistical significance of the concentration variable, this would help explain the switch from positive to negative results post-Demsetz.[21]

However, there is an alternative explanation of the switch that is not favorable to interpreting the PC literature as a successful falsificationist episode. It seems not only possible but plausible that Demsetz's theoretical attack on the earlier literature led researchers to look harder for results inconsistent with the "concentration causes profits" view (or made them more willing to submit such results, once found). Such a possibility would probably not surprise Demsetz himself, who wrote as follows about the concentration–profits view that he was attacking: "When a profession accepts a new system of belief, research is guided by that belief to rationalize observed phenomena in ways that confirm it. The belief in a self-sufficient theory of monopoly power offers no exception" (p. 167). If this phenomenon, which Demsetz (1974: 164) dubs "believing is seeing", is an important part of the explanation for the reversal of empirical results beginning in the mid-1970s, then Blaug's concerns about the insufficiency of testing efforts is supported by this empirical episode.

What does this example suggest about feasibility of falsificationism? The very possibility that "believing is seeing", that what is in fact published is conditioned on what seems to be theoretically acceptable, casts a long and dark shadow over the very possibility of falsificationism based on the weight of cumulative empirical evidence. If fifty studies all show result X (supporting rather than refuting the theory in question), we cannot necessarily conclude that this theory deserves to be treated as difficult to refute. It may be that the hundred studies showing not-X, studies that would have refuted the theory, were all still-born and never saw the light of day because of researcher perceptions about what referees and journals were likely to accept. The relative dearth of negative studies before Demsetz, versus the relative abundance of such studies afterwards, is at least superficially consistent with this concern.

A related conclusion is less discouraging. It seems plausible that meaningful falsificationism is more likely when two or more seriously competing alternative theories exist; in that situation, empirical researchers are more likely to think about doing their research in a way that can discriminate among competing explanations, journals are more likely to be interested in empirical work which supports one theory versus the other(s), and the juxtaposition of the alternative theories may itself suggest measurable phenomena that can distinguish between the competitors.

III

The two case studies examined above suggest a number of issues about how economists do empirical work. Why was there not more explicit attention to testing in the labor supply literature? Why does a testing focus appear to emerge in the PC literature, when it was absent in the labor supply literature? More thorough answers to these questions may emerge if we first go back and consider more abstract explanations for the alleged paucity of severe testing in economics, and then consider how well these explanations fit the cases examined.

The question is, why don't economists more consistently practice severe testing of their theories? It may be, as Blaug seems to urge, that they ought to practice a lot more of it than they do. It is possible to argue, however, that the general case in favor of severe testing is not as overwhelming as one might initially think. There are at least two distinct lines of argument that might be pursued. The first derives from the philosophy of science literature. The way that Kuhn and Lakatos look at research efforts in the physical sciences, scientists work in "paradigms" (Kuhn) or "scientific research programs" (Lakatos). Within these research programs certain assumptions or principles are taken as fundamental to the approach, and are simply not subject to test or empirical refutation. If you want to do "normal science" (Kuhn's term) within a research program, some assumptions are inviolate. Lakatos dubs these fundamental, unattackable tenets "hard core assumptions". If you cannot stand the hard core assumptions, you must get out of that paradigm or research program. Indeed a major issue for this kind of philosophy-of-science approach involves what causes paradigms or research programs to be abandoned, and how the "weight of empirical evidence in the large" contributes to sustaining or defeating a research program or paradigm.[22]

The Kuhn–Lakatos kind of approach has another important corollary about empirical work. As Albert Hirschman (1970: 68) once paraphrased a Kuhnian idea, "a model is never defeated by facts, no matter how damaging, but only by another model". The idea is that a model or theory (actually, a research program) is only abandoned if there is some arguably superior alternative conceptual scheme to take its place. Moreover, "facts" or empirical work only become compelling as tests of theory when competing theories (paradigms) are available, and the weight of empirical work can help distinguish the empirical applicability of the two theoretical approaches.[23]

A second line of argument as to why we might expect to have only limited amounts of severe testing activity in economics stresses some differences between economics and the physical sciences. The argument in essence is that the predictions produced by economic theory are in an important sense less "concrete" than some physical science predictions, making the economic predictions less amenable to severe and definitive tests. As Latsis (1976) puts it,

> (u)nfortunately, in economics the degree of specificity that may be attained is limited by the kind of predictions economists strive for. Neoclassical economists have tended to subscribe, explicitly or tacitly, to the testing technique of qualitative comparative statics.... According to this method, a simplified and idealized economic model is considered at some equilibrial position. This new position is then compared with the previous one in terms of the direction but not the *amount* of change. This means that *any amount* of change, *provided it is in the right direction*, would corroborate the hypothesis. Thus the range of potential falsifiers is severely reduced and the possibility of "severe testing" – in the sense of exact quantitative specification of the potential falsifier – becomes very remote. Moreover, it is often the case that no unambiguous prediction of the direction of change is available.
>
> (p. 8)

In contrast, writers such as Kuhn describe situations in the physical sciences in which the theory predicts *particular shapes* for orbits of planets, or *particular values* for weights of chemical elements.[24]

How well do these general explanations apply when we turn to the concrete features of the labor supply case? Are there additional explanations suggested by that case? Pencavel provides two possible explanations for the lack of attention to testing in the labor supply literature. First, "we hesitate even to test a theory until an alternative, behavioral hypothesis is available" (pp. 5–6). Second, "A more substantive reason for the lack of hypothesis testing ... is that many economists view such tests as tantamount to questioning whether a consumer's income-compensated demand curve for a commodity slopes downwards with respect to its price ... if the theory of consumer behavior had been found to be an apt description of the demand of apples, oranges, cherries, bananas and many other fruit, an economist will wager it also applies to the demand for pears" (p. 6).[25] Pencavel's second reason, which might be paraphrased "economists don't question (test) the theory if it has the status of motherhood and apple pie", seems the more fundamental of his two explanations.[26] Note that it can be interpreted as a specific version of the Kuhn–Lakatos idea of working in a paradigm or scientific research program, within which certain fundamental "hard core" propositions are not to be challenged or tested. We have suggested a third explanation for the relative lack of testing in the labor supply literature. A literature driven by policy concerns is apt to use the existing theory for guidance as to how to evaluate policy, not as an occasion to test the theory providing that guidance.

There is a quite different set of reasons why there might be only limited attention to testing in the labor supply setting. The view that data can "refute" a theory appears to presuppose data which meets a reliability standard. Indeed, in the physical sciences immense attention seems to be devoted to producing and/or insuring the quality of important data. Suppose instead that the data are known to be seriously flawed, and the setting is such that "much less flawed" data are (practically speaking) unattainable. In such a situation, sensible empirically oriented researchers might be heard to utter the following statements.

1   "When considering whether a meaningful data-based test of the theory is possible, I ask myself 'do I have more faith in the theory or in the (reliability of) the data?' I only go ahead and test when the data appear to be reliable enough."

2   "Because the data are so unreliable, it may be relatively easy to get statistical results counter to a theory which reliable data would fail to refute, and relatively hard to make the (unreliable) data appear consistent with the theory."[27]

The individual uttering statement (1) would go on to list the ways in which the underlying labor supply data sets are badly deficient.[28] The individual uttering statement (2) might use this as a basis for arguing in favor of (to use Blaug's terms) "verification", rather than "falsification", since it may be "hard" to get confirmation out of badly flawed data. And both of them would undoubtedly sympathize with Lakatos's much more general point that one's interpretation of experimental (for our case, read "testing") data and results depends crucially on one's underlying theory of observation. Of course, if the reason for not testing is that the data are unreliable, this same reasoning would seem to call into question the measurement results of the labor supply literature. If the data are too unrealiable for testing, doesn't this suggest that the measurements being produced might also be badly biased because of the poor underlying data?

A second issue raised by our two case studies concerns why a testing focus appears in the CP literature when it is absent in the labor supply literature. The labor supply literature focused on measurement issues (measuring elasticities) from the very beginning, while the CP literature concentrated on providing support for, or evidence against, a conceptual approach.

The presence of a testing mentality in the CP literature versus its relative scarcity in the labor supply literature may be connected to the disparity between the two literatures in the degree to which each is grounded in orthodox microeconomic theory. The labor supply literature applies the economist's standard theory of choice to the labor market. As we suggested above, a probable reason for the dearth of a sustained testing component in this literature is that the underlying model rests on fundamental tenets or Lakatosian "hard core assumptions" of neoclassical economics. The CP literature, on the other hand, is not a direct extension of widely held propositions from microtheory. The viewpoint that concentration is likely to generate collusion, and that market processes (as opposed to government intervention) may in a significant number of industries lead to economically undesirable market outcomes, is counter to the belief-proclivities of a sizable proportion of the profession (for example those with "Chicago"-type views). Indeed, Demsetz's (1974) article specifically attacks the "system of belief" the lies behind the "concentration causes high profits" position.[29]

The suggestion is that testing of the economic theory equivalent of "motherhood and apple pie" is far less likely than is testing of propositions that some percentage of the profession find troublesome. On the one hand, this finding surely adds empirical weight to Blaug's complaint about the insufficiency of severe theory testing in economics. It implies that the profession neglects to severely test exactly those propositions that it finds most congenial. On the other hand, the fact that this "uncritical" posture about accepting "hard core assumptions" appears consistent with Kuhn's and Lakatos's views of how the natural sciences proceed suggests that Blaug may be asking economists to behave in a way not consistent with actual procedures in the natural sciences.

Some recent work in the philosophy of science supports the idea that economists' restricted testing is closer to practice in the natural sciences than Blaug's stance implies. In his wide-ranging review of recent developments in the philosophy of science, Suppes (1977) offers the following view of the relation of empirical work to the paradigms or research programs to which they are linked.

Although observation and theory figure centrally in Lakatos's, Toulmin's and Shapere's accounts of the growth of scientific knowledge, it is significant that there is virtually no talk of "verification", "inductive confirmation", or "refutation" of theories or hypotheses. This is no accident.... (W)hen one looks at how observation and experiment are employed in evaluating sophisticated theories within these larger units [such as research programs] one finds that the focus typically is not what philosophers of science have characterized as inductively confirming a theory as true or refuting it as false. When a sophisticated theory is undergoing active development, it is commonplace for scientists working on it to suppose that the present version of the theory is defective in various respects, which is to say it is literally false, at best being only an approximation to the truth or a promising candidate ... (so) ... it would be pointless to attempt to either refute or inductively confirm the theory. What *is* to the point is to use observation and experiment to discover short-comings..., to discover how to improve the theory, to eliminate known artificialities, distortions, oversimplifications and errors in the descriptions, explanations and predictions of reality that the theory affords. It is to these ends that science ordinarily uses observation to "test", its current theories – and not ... (for) ... refutation of them which has so occupied the attention of philosophy of science in the past.

(p. 706)

It is quite intriguing that empirical work on the sciences described by Suppes bears a strong resemblance to the way in which Schmalensee (1989) proposes that cross-section (inter-industry) empirical studies in industrial organization be used, and to quite a different description in Stafford (1986) of procedures in labor economics. Schmalensee first notes that some students of industrial organization "feel that the cross-section approach is inherently incapable of producing anything useful", and that he himself believes that "cross-section studies rarely if ever yield consistent estimates of structural parameters". However, he feels they have a role to play in producing "useful stylized facts to guide theory construction and analysis of particular industries" (p. 952). Indeed, a major theme of his summary article is to identify those "stylized facts" produced by the cumulation of inter-industry empirical studies in industrial organization. Stafford describes current practice in labor economics as "the maintained or restricted hypothesis testing approach to empirical work" (p. 419). While Stafford is not satisfied with this approach,[30] such an approach is quite consistent with Suppes's description of using testing to "discover how to improve the theory" at the margin.

IV

Concluding comments seem called for on three topics: evaluating the validity and importance of Blaug's claim about the absence of severe theory testing in the face of our empirical examples; categorizing empirical work that is not severe theory testing; and implications about how economists come to "believe" things.

Blaug's claim that economists as a profession do not seriously attempt to severely test their theories is surely supported by the labor supply economics example. A sustained severe testing component is not an important feature of that literature. The industrial organization example seems to have more of a testing component associated with it, but a plausible case can be made that the "defeat" of the original hypothesis was largely due to a theoretical attack, rather than a compelling empirical refutation. Moreover, the very presence of a sustained attack on the initial hypothesis seems to be attributable in good part to the fact that the hypothesis itself flies in the face of the cherished beliefs of a powerful segment of the profession. One is tempted to conclude (based admittedly on what is far too small a sample of cases) that the profession can be relied on to try to test those propositions that somehow gain professional visibility but seem misguided to a significant proportion of the profession; it cannot be relied upon to try in a sustained manner to severely test those propositions that the profession holds to be fundamental to its "world view". This tempting conclusion is supported not only by the two empirical examples explored in this chapter, but also by the "information filtering" problems discussed initially.

As suggested in the previous section, however, Blaug's claim about the lack of severe empirical testing may have only limited force as an all-encompassing and overwhelming criticism of practice in economics. First, even if the profession exhibited collectively the testing tenacity of a very determined bulldog, telling results might be extremely hard to come by. Kuhn's discussion of the physical sciences indicates the great difficulty in defining and carrying out meaningful tests of a particular paradigm or research program (see the quotation above, p. 336). The difficulties are even more severe in economics due to the largely nonexperimental context of testing in economics and the fact that fluctuations in economic regimes suggest less stability in individual human behavior over time (and "regime–space") than in the behavior of atoms over time and space. Second, our Kuhn–Lakatos discussion suggested that it is an arguable proposition that the physical sciences *do not* in fact proceed by constantly trying to severely test the underlying basic assumptions of particular research programs. In a Lakatosian framework, for example, those in a particular scientific research program treat certain "hard core" propositions as immune from attack. Under this kind of conception, the relations between empirical evidence and the viability of a particular research program is far subtler and more problem-atical than is implied by the Blaug view of how we "ought" as a profession to proceed.

Finally, the juxtaposition of Blaug's and Lakatos's views suggests the following proposition: the underlying fundamental question should be "what set of procedures or methodological stance(s) produces the most sustained and productive growth of knowledge?" The philosophers of science seem to be unable to definitively answer this question for the physical sciences, suggesting that we as economists cannot answer it for economics. That is, we quite simply do not know whether behaving as Blaugian empirical-testing bulldogs would turn out to yield better growth-of-knowledge results than would other methodological stances. Suppose that a large percentage of the profession, having read Blaug, began to devote themselves to looking for and carrying out fundamental empirical tests of neoclassical theory. Given the difficulty of carrying out meaningful tests of particular paradigms or research programs, this massive effort might turn out after several decades to yield few definitive results. Under such a scenario, it is quite conceivable that knowledge would have grown faster if this massive testing effort had not been undertaken, and the large majority of these researchers had instead devoted themselves to trying to find extensions of economic theory, or to empirical measurement activities.

Turning to the issue of categorizing empirical work, Blaug observed that economists do "engage massively in empirical research", but "unfortunately, much of it is like playing tennis with the net down: instead of attempting to refute testable predictions, modern economists all too frequently are satisfied to demonstrate that the real world conforms to their predictions, thus replacing falsification, which is difficult, with verification, which is easy" (pp. 256–7). This stress on the "verification versus testing" aspect of empirical work has the danger that it seems to fail to recognize other possibly important foci of empirical activity. We cited Kuhn to argue that testing is only one (and the "smallest") class of empirical work in the physical sciences, and then showed that the empirical labor supply literature in fact focused on one of these other classes of empirical activity, namely measurement.

Our claim is that major portions of the empirical work that economists do should not be dismissed merely because it is not severe testing. If this claim is accepted, what needs to be done is for the profession to become more self-conscious about its range of empirical activity. Kuhn's list, suggestive though it is, is surely a very incomplete categorization when applied to economics. A more adequate characterization of the range of empirical work would allow more sophisticated evaluation of what all this empirical work is (or is not) "good for", and how these functions relate to our evaluation of underlying theoretical approaches.

This author would not presume to provide such a categorization, but would like to offer up an example of a kind of empirical research that seems pregnant with interesting implications for categorizing empirical approaches. One finds papers in economics that start with an empirical "fact" or observation and then try to test among alternative explanations for this "fact". An example might be a paper focusing on the behavior of the ratio of earnings of black individuals or families to earnings of white individuals or families (for an example of this kind of paper, see Vroman 1989; see also Heckman and Payner 1989). "Contributing" or "alternative" explanations might include changes in stocks of human capital by race, shifts in labor demand by geographical region, changes in supply due to demographic changes or to changes in transfer program availability, and effects of affirmative action initiatives.

How might one characterize such a paper, and what relationship might it have to the "testing" of the underlying economics approach? Depending on the researcher's orientation, the paper might be directed at any of the following issues. If the researcher is interested in policy issues, the paper might aim at shedding (indirect) light on policy issues ("has schooling acted to widen or narrow the racial income gap?"; "have affirmative action initiatives had effects in the desired direction?"; "have transfer payments succeeded in narrowing racial income gaps?"). If the researcher is a student of the determinants of the income distribution, the paper might instead focus on trying to understand what factors actually affected the income distribution over a particular period. If the researcher is a labor market analyst, the paper might focus on investigating whether labor market changes tend to swamp the effects of those transfer policies that have in fact been adopted. Notice that, for any one of the three orientations described, it is inappropriate to characterize this research as having to do with "verification versus falsifica-tionism" (*à la* Blaug), nor does this research seem to fit well into any of the Kuhnian empirical categories. The suggestion is that a different categorizing scheme is needed.

Part of the interest in such research is to see whether we can "explain" history in terms of factors sometimes claimed as potentially having an effect. Yet a finding that (say) human capital factors or demand shifts did not play a sizable part is not in any simple sense a "test" and refutation of human capital theory or supply–demand analysis. Indeed, there is a subtler relation-ship between the esteem in which one holds a theory or paradigm and that paradigm or theory's performance in repeated "historical" or "factual" explanation exercises of the type just described. If supply and demand explanations (relative to, say, "sociological" explanations) consistently fail to help illuminate relevant historical or other factual developments, then one's faith in the empirical power of supply–demand analysis might well be severely shaken. In this sense, the cumulative weight of studies like the one just described do provide an empirically based "testing" of the received paradigm, even though the studies are not designed as falsificationist "tests" in the Blaug sense.

Our final topic concerns the following question: what implications does the analysis in this chapter have for how economists come to "believe" things? If severe testing of theories (falsificationism) were unfailingly practised, one could say "economists believe propositions that have been subjected to and withstood severe empirical tests". Indeed, Friedman's famous 1953 methodology article seems to offer a slightly modified version of this claim.[31] Despite Friedman's assertions, however, the profession does not appear to continuously and unflinchingly practise severe testing. Thus, a "falsificationist" answer to the question of how economists come to believe things is not available. The issue remains open and important, since it is central to understanding how economists actually proceed.

There are, of course, a series of other competing candidates for answers to this question. Two of them neatly capsulized by Hausman (1989) are what he calls "deductivism" and an "eclectic" view associated with McCloskey among others. Deductivism derives from the views of John Stuart Mill; Hausman believes that orthodox economists typically subscribe to it, "regardless of what they say in methodological discussion" (p. 117). In deductivism, one first inductively establishes "basic psychological or technical laws – such as 'people seek more wealth' or the law of diminishing returns – and then ... deduce their economic implications given specifications of relevant circumstances. Empirical confirmation ... has an important role in whether the deductively derived conclusions are applicable ... but such testing does not bear on one's commitment to the basic 'laws'" (p. 117). McCloskey uses the tools of rhetoric and literary analysis to understand what economists do and believe. "He is skeptical that there are any detailed standards for what counts as good argument in economics apart from whatever in fact persuades economists" (p. 123).

My purpose in reciting these capsulized views is to leave the reader very uncomfortable with (and therefore provoke him or her to think hard about) the state of our understanding of how economists come to believe things, and how empirical work contributes to these beliefs. As a final try at increasing this discomfort level, I offer some thoughtful though incompletely convincing comments of Koopmans (1979) about how economists come to believe things. Koopmans sets out to comment on

> the empirical basis of quantitative economic knowledge in general.... (A)ny statement resulting from such studies retains the form of an "if ... then ..." statement. The set of "ifs," sometimes called "the model," is crucial to the meaning of the "thens," usually but somewhat inaccurately called the "findings." ... The "if ... then ..." statements are similar to those in the formal sciences.... The heart of substantive economics is what can be learned about the validity of the "ifs" themselves.... "Thens" contradicted by observation call, as time goes on, for modification of the list of "ifs" used. Absence of such contradiction gradually conveys survivor status to the "ifs" in question. So I do think a certain record of noncontradiction gradually becomes one of tentative confirmation. But the process of confirmation is slow and diffuse.... I have not found in the literature a persuasive account of how such confirmation of premises can be perceived and documented. How do we keep track of the contradictions

and confirmations? How do we keep the score of surviving hypotheses. . . .
(U)nresolved issues, sometimes important and mostly quantitative . . . drag
on and remain unresolved. Do they have to?

(pp. 11–12)

What is useful here is Koopmans's (implicit) stress on the idea that any
refutation– confirmation process may be far subtler and more indirect than a
set of explicit severe tests specifically designed for falsificationist purposes.
What is missing is an explicit recognition of the difficulties imposed on the
meaningfulness of "keeping score" by the existence of "filtering problems",
so that counts of confirmations or refutations may be highly biased measures
of the true explanatory power of the "ifs" in question.

NOTES

In the course of thinking about the issues considered in this chapter I have benefited
from conversations with or written comments from Steven Allen, Steve Baldwin, Jeff
Biddle, Bryan Boulier, Michael Bradley, Timothy Brennan, Gary Burtless, Vincy Fon,
Marsha Goldfarb, David Greenberg, William Griffith, Arjo Klamer, John Kwoka,
Fred Joutz, Sar Levitan, David Lindauer, Len Nichols, John Pencavel, David Pritchett,
Ingrid Rima, Robert Rogers, Charles Stewart, Harry Watson, Tony Yezer and
participants at a seminar at George Washington University. The usual statement that
remaining errors are not attributable to these individuals applies with special force,
since some of them have never seen a complete version of the chapter and others
disagree with some of my assertions.

1   A very recent and useful broad-brush categorization and evaluation "in a
    nutshell" of alternative methodological positions is Hausman (1989). A useful
    discussion of Weintraub's position is Diamond (1988).
2   The position espoused by Blaug is hardly unique to him, and is undoubtedly
    shared by many economists, including a goodly number who avoid reading the
    methodology literature in which Blaug writes. I focus on Blaug because he is a
    leading exponent of this critique in the methodology literature, and has clearly
    stated his position. The view that Blaug is a Popperian is widely held; Hausman
    (1989) indicates that Blaug argues "that neoclassical economics does not meet
    Popperian or positivist standards for science (p. 118)", and the Introduction to
    The Popperian Legacy in Economics classifies Blaug, who is an author of one of
    the papers in the volume, as using "Popper's methodological to criticize
    economic practice" (p. 4).
3   Leamer (1983) notes that

    > The econometric art as it is practiced at the computer terminal involves fitting
    > many, perhaps thousands, of statistical models. One of several that the
    > researcher finds pleasing are selected for reporting purposes. This searching
    > for a model is often well-intentioned, but there can be no doubt that such a
    > specification search invalidates the traditional theories of inference. The
    > concepts of unbiasedness, consistency . . . in fact, all the concepts of
    > traditional theory, utterly lose their meaning by the time an applied researcher
    > pulls from the bramble of computer output the one thorn of a model he likes
    > best, the one he chooses to portray as a rose.

    (pp. 37–8)

Our description stresses in addition the peculiarly one-sided nature of the hypothesized "stopping rule" which our story alleges is used by the researcher at the computer terminal. Later in his paper, in discussing what he calls "Sherlock Holmes inference", Leamer produces an example in which the researcher adds variables to try to get the "right" sign. He then suggests a statistical evaluation method for this procedure, but notes that it requires "a discipline that is lacking even in its author" (p. 40).

4 The analogy to news coverage comes from Denton (1988). He suggests that it is no surprise that journals select "interesting" results to publish: "I do not expect the journals to report vast numbers of uninteresting statistical results – and 'interesting' in the applied econometrics context very often means 'statistically significant.' (Surely nobody would long subscribe to a journal containing article after article in which authors stated novel theories and then reported that attempts to find empirical support for them were dismal failures)" (p. 179). He then makes the analogy to news coverage, in which interesting events ("fires") are reported; one cannot get a good estimate of the probability of fires from news reports, since they provide no data about "nonfires", which are not "newsworthy" events (pp. 178–9). But our stress, as opposed to Denton's, is on the underlying professional attitudes that *determine* what economist readers find interesting, which in turn allows a somewhat different "twist" to Denton's analysis. If the profession believed deeply in severe testing, then empirical rejection would in fact be of great interest to journal readers.

In this context of what is "newsworthy", a comment in Leamer (1985) is interesting: "After all, the finding that a data set does not admit a sturdy inference is news worthy of publication. On the other hand, current institutions clearly encourage, and have produced, either delusion or deceit" (p. 312).

5 Some of those who are skeptical about the seriousness with which the profession treats empirical endeavors will raise a quite different line of criticism. It has recently been carefully documented in an article in one of the profession's most prestigious journals (DeWald 1986) that a sizable percentage of a sample of published journal articles contain empirical work whose results cannot be replicated. While our version of the Blaug criticism does not depend on the absence of replicability, it does seem plausible that the alleged procedure of repeated statistical runs to make the signs come out "right" increases considerably the danger that results cannot be easily replicated. The larger the number of iterations with slight variations in the treatment of observations and variables, the more likely that fallible human beings will forget exactly what it was that they did to "finally" get the signs right. The more of such iterations there are, the greater the care in documentation that would be required to allow another researcher to replicate particular published results. But standard price theory seems to suggest that the higher the price of careful documentation, the less of it will be employed (other things equal).

6 One useful source that documents these claims is Stafford (1986).

7 With respect to the first historical example, Pencavel (1986) indicates that "Modern research on labor supply ... dates from Mincer's (1962) paper on the labor force participation rate of married women" (p. 5). A major focus of that paper was to show that an apparent "paradox" about the behavior of female labor force participation rates in cross-section versus time series data could be resolved (explained) by using the tools of microeconomic theory, in particular income and substitution effects.

As for the second historical example, a major historical impetus to labor supply research during part of the 1960s and 1970s were policy discussions of income maintenance schemes and welfare reform. Empirical labor supply studies could in principle provide important information for these discussions because the cost of various income maintenance schemes, and their ability to affect the incomes of target groups, depended on how the schemes affected labor supply behavior. As one indication of the link between interest in income maintenance issues and interest in empirical labor supply studies, a very intellectually influential collection of empirical papers was published as a book in 1973 with the telling title *Income Maintenance and Labor Supply* (Cain and Watts 1973). A second indication of the link is the carrying-out of a series of major "negative income tax" social experiments; a major aim of these experiments was to measure labor supply responses to income maintenance schemes (see, for example, Rees 1974). In short, a major focus of the labor supply literature was on policy applications of empirical research, rather than on severe testing of labor supply theory.

8   Alternatively, measurement of labor supply elasticities might be put into Kuhn's "paradigm articulation" category, if such activity is seen as analogous to measurement of what Kuhn calls "physical constants". At a more general level, it might be concluded instead that Kuhn's classification scheme, designed as it is for physical sciences, may need some modification in the form of addition of categories to improve its applicability to the labor economics case and, more broadly, to economics. For example, explaining (observed historical) patterns of market activities (such as the growth in female labor force participation) and doing policy evaluations may need new and separate categories in addition to those identified by Kuhn.

9   Consider again our two historical examples. The focus of Mincer's seminal article was on explaining a set of seemingly puzzling empirical phenomena, *not* on setting up a severe test of the existing theory of labor supply. As for our second historical example, a major focus of the labor supply literature in the 1960s and 1970s was on policy applications of empirical research, not on setting up severe tests of labour supply theory. To put the point more strongly, an empirical literature provoked by the focusing on policy evaluation and policy design – how particular policies work, and how they might be redesigned to work better – is unlikely to devote serious attention to theory testing. Theory is used as an analytical framework to *inform and guide* the empirical analysis, rather than itself serving as a major target for investigation.

10   There is another possible reason why there has been no outcry for rejecting the entire literature. Several individuals with considerable expertise about the labor supply literature have pointed out to me that the income maintenance experiments seem to provide evidence that the substitution effect of a wage change does in fact have the predicted sign. My strong sense of this literature, however, is that it simply is not focused on severe testing. This view is shared by these same commentators. Because the focus is on measurement and not testing, the experimental results do not in fact seem to play a central role as critically important testing findings. (For what it is worth, my own guess is that, had the experimental findings displayed the "wrong" signs, we would have been treated to sophisticated discussions of why the experimental setting was flawed, so that a "real" test of the theory was not performed. As it is, there is an interesting literature about why the experimental setting is highly imperfect. A useful discussion with references is Pencavel (1986: 73–83).) In addition, not everyone agrees that the experimental results provide definitive evidence about the sign of the own-substitution effect. "(I)f the estimates are interpreted as tests of the static model of labor supply (and no doubt some would not want to take this step), then the frequency of negative values for the income-compensated wage elasticity of

hours of work casts serious doubt on its empirical relevance" (Pencavel 1986: 83).

11   Another explanation of the failure to perform severe tests is that the data just aren't there. Stafford (1986) observes that "One can be skeptical about the prospects for a substantial synthesis of the various elements of the second generation work. This is not surprising since the data actually available and perhaps even potentially available do not contain enough information to abandon the maintained or restricted hypothesis testing approach to empirical work" (p. 419).

12   This stress on the primacy of measurement should not be taken to mean that measurement efforts have been "successful" in the sense of limiting the possible range of measured parameters within an acceptable range. Topel (1988) in his review of the *Handbook* observes that "(o)ne message that runs through the labor supply reviews (and the rest of the volume) is the lack of consensus on magnitudes and even signs of important effects" (p. 1791). Hamermesh (1988) observes that "(i)t is not clear that the efforts of the 1970s and 1980s ... at refining our knowledge of labor supply elasticities (or their component income and substitution effects) have done anything to narrow the agreed-upon range of estimates" (pp. 10–11). See also the quote from Stafford in note 11 above.

13   Indeed, one sometimes finds use of the word "testing" in a context suggesting that measurement is in fact a large component of the objective of the "testing". Thus Stafford (1986), in discussing the uses of cross-section versus panel data, gives the following example as part of a discussion of the design of survey instruments: "If we were gathering data for the single purpose of testing the hypothesis of the effect of transfer income of individuals on their time in market ..." (p. 409). But the term "testing" here seems aimed at an interesting *measurement* issue – does transfer income lower hours or speed retirement – rather than a crisp "test" capable of falsifying a strong theoretical prediction and therefore a basic theoretical approach. Stafford seems to indicate earlier in the paper (p. 403) that the theory is consistent with a wide range of possible results because of complexities associated with the features of the social security system.

14   While I believe strongly that careful knowledgeable examination of the general "thrust" and "shape" of empirical work in various areas of economics can significantly raise our profession's self-knowledge about how we actually proceed and how we come to establish beliefs and change them, a large and serious warning about my discussion of the industrial organization literature is in order. Having kept a reasonably careful eye on labor economics (and even practised some myself) for several decades, I feel some confidence about my impressions of the field. I am not similarly confident of my impressions – developed in the course of preparing this chapter – of the industrial organization literature. Thus, I offer these interpretations as provisional.

15   Evidence of Weiss's status as a major proponent is the fact that Demsetz, a leading critic of the literature, chooses Weiss's 1974 exposition as the formulation to take issue with (Demsetz 1974).

16   Weiss (1971) notes in a footnote that "The assumptions of the concentration–profits model are often not spelled out. I am following Bain who was much more explicit than most of us" (p. 363, n. 2). A look back at Bain (1951) suggests that his "inspiration" to examine empirical relations came from some questions that arose out of the Mason case study research program. Bain notes in his opening sentence that "Students of industrial price behavior have recently shown much interest in the concept of workable competition and the potential association between the workability of competition and the structure of the industry. Their

evident uncertainty about the nature of such a relationship suggests the need for detailed empirical studies which would formulate specific hypotheses on the relations of market structure to market performance and would then test such hypotheses with available evidence" (p. 293). Bain states "the hypothesis to be tested" as "the average profit rate of firms in oligopolistic industries of a high concentration will tend to be significantly larger than that of firms in less concentrated industries or in industries of atomistic structure". He notes in a footnote that "the size of the profit rates for a firm or industry should not be regarded as a sole or infallible index of the workability of competition. . . . We are thus essentially unable here to discover any net relation of concentration to the workability of competition; we seek simply the relation of concentration to the profit rate, whatever its ultimate significance" (p. 294).

17   Weiss (1974) observes that

> Bain and Chamberlin point to some critical level of concentration. . . . I have spent a great deal of time and money trying to answer such questions as whether there is a critical concentration ratio, and if so, where it falls. Also, does the sixth or eighth firm in a market make any difference in market performance? I never really reached a convincing conclusion and I now doubt that we will without much better data. These are important issues. We can probably agree that General Motors shouldn't be allowed to merge with Ford and that a merger among two feed mills is harmless. The real questions have to do with mergers by middle-sized firms in moderately concentrated markets.
>
> (p. 193)

18   Weiss (1974) also examines in detail a number of studies yielding no significant effect of concentration on profits to try to ferret out why the expected relationship did not show up. Some weak results "are undoubtedly due to bad methodology" (p. 203), or collinearity between concentration and measures of capital requirements or plant-level scale economies. Other studies "yield a weak relationship during periods when the concentration–profits relation was apt to be weak". This includes periods of price controls and, more generally, periods of "open inflation". "There is good evidence that concentrated industries do not raise prices as rapidly as competitive industries do in time of open inflation" (p. 200).

19   Another possible explanation, which is logically possible but seems to this author to be far-fetched, is that the "facts" actually changed! It is conceivable that, as the US economy became more open, the link between domestic concentration and profits actually did attenuate. This possibility could be checked by running consistently specified cross-section equations for a number of different years (one regression for each separate year) in the 1960s, 1970s and 1980s. Notice that, if the facts had changed, the CP literature would still qualify as a legitimate falsificationist episode.

20   Not only are there competing explanations for the "reversal of results" reported in the text, but there is also an important complication about how well established the reversal itself is. The underlying hypothesis is that concentration may allow collusion. But *measured* profit may be a very defective measure of effective collusion. This measurement problem has led researchers to look for other indicator variables. Price level can be interpreted as such a variable. In reviewing the evidence on the link between concentration and price levels (as opposed to measured profits), Schmalensee gives as a "stylized fact" that "In cross-section studies involving markets in the same industry, seller concentration is positively related to the level of price" (p. 988). He further notes that, "Since studies of price

have fewer obvious weaknesses than studies of profitability, Stylized Fact 5.1 seems to provide the best evidence in support of the concentration–collusion hypothesis" (p. 988). Thus, this bit of empirical evidence, based on what is arguably a superior measure of the link, seems to support that link rather than lead to its rejection. At the very least, it is certainly arguable that the "facts" remain deliciously ambiguous. Note that there are any number of reasons for thinking that profits are not the most appropriate measure of monopoly power. The difficulties are not limited to the well-known problems with using accounting profits to measure economic profits. As an example of a different kind of difficulty, it is perfectly possible for a monopoly with considerable monopoly power, in the sense (following Abba Lerner) that its price is considerably above its marginal cost, to have normal or below-normal profits.

21   For a discussion which seems to imply that the reversal of results was due largely to "the availability of better data and more careful use of statistical techniques" (p. 292), see Langenfeld and Scheffman (1986).

22   While Kuhn and Lakatos focused on the physical sciences, there is an interesting similarity between their view of science and some features of Melvin Reder's (1982) description of Chicago economics – in the Chicago approach assumptions of rationality are simply not to be questioned; they are hard core assumptions, not available to be subjected to empirical testing in any simple direct way. Reder actually cites Kuhn and Lakatos in his discussion: "Were it not for fear of becoming involved in side issues, I would have suggested that Chicago economics is a scientific sub-culture in the Kuhnian sense, and spoken of the 'Chicago Paradigm' . . . or the 'Chicago Scientific Research Program' (*pace* Imre Lakatos)" (p. 19).

23   At quite a different level of generality, it is useful to keep in mind that theories or paradigms gain their explanatory power from abstracting from some features of complex reality. This "fact" of abstracting suggests that no theory can ever explain "everything" about complex reality. It is only a small step from this proposition to the assertion that virtually all theories will have anomalies (since no theory can explain "everything"). If the latter assertion is correct, then it follows that the existence of a fact that "refutes" a theory is not enough *in isolation* to torpedo a theory, since (by the proposition just given) *every* theory is likely to have refuting facts. This line of argument also supports the idea that the defeat of a theory requires the presence of a competing theory, one which seems to have "fewer" crucial anomalies.

24   A statement with a quite different focus from Latsis's analysis, but that has the same implication about the dearth of concrete theoretical predictions generated by economic theory, is in Stafford's (1986) discussion of empirical work in labor economics. Stafford notes that a number of controversies "arise based on maintained hypotheses brought about by the fact that there is a very limited set of restrictions one can place on preferences based on theory *per se*" (p. 419).

25   In making this statement, Pencavel puts aside "the issue of whether that basic proposition of consumer theory has itself been corroborated" (p. 6).

26   One sense in which Pencavel's first reason is less fundamental than his second is that it leaves unanswered the question of why an alternative theory does not emerge. His second reason provides an answer: if the profession treats the existing theory as sacrosanct, there is little inclination or incentive to spend time developing a competing theory, especially since it is likely to be met with extreme skepticism.

27   I received a number of like-minded comments from others with whom I have discussed these issues. The basic point was that the data itself were often

unreliable ("relative to the theory"), or the ability to "hold constant" relevant variables was severely limited by the available data sets. Most of these individuals are very serious-minded empirical researchers. As one of them put it, in some settings he had considerably greater confidence in the theory than he did in the data he was using. One can find echoes of this kind of view in very diverse literatures, ranging from industrial organization to macro. In the industrial organization literature, Brennan (1989) espouses a similar position from a less statistical orientation: "when 'data' and 'theory' conflict in economics, 'data' will often lose, *and deserve to*, because after the processes the 'data' have been put through to test a theory, they end up less deserving of confidence than the theory they were designed to test. Economic theory is predicated upon assumptions that often possess a legitimate grounds for acceptance on the basis of experience; data often lack that legitimacy" (pp. 23–4). The "experience" Brennan refers to is "our own experience, viewed from within" (p. 22). In the macro literature associated with real business cycles, Prescott (1986), in an article tellingly entitled 'Theory ahead of business cycle measurement", asserts that "The match between theory and observation is excellent but far from perfect.... An important part of this deviation could disappear if the economic variables were measured more in conformity with theory. That is why I argue that theory is now ahead of business cycle measurement and theory should be used to obtain better measures of the key economic time series" (p. 21). In the real business cycle case, others think that the disagreement between theory and data is due to imperfections in Prescott's version of the theory (see, for example, Summers 1986; Christiano and Eichenbaum 1988).

28 For a particularly troubling critique of the data underlying many labor supply studies, see Lillard *et al.* (1986). They point out that, "(i)n the most frequently used microdata sets, over a quarter of all respondents now refuse to answer some questions about their incomes" (p. 489). The Census's imputation procedures for dealing with this problem leave the authors "with a real concern about the accuracy of the income data that underlie a good deal of empirical economic research" (p. 505).

Lest the reader think that statement (1) is just another excuse for shielding economics from severe testing, let me assure the reader that the individual being paraphrased believes in a refutationist stance and practises it, but only in those areas where he thinks the data is dependable enough to warrant being taken seriously. In fact, his major gripe about economists' empirical practices is their inattention to the issue of the adequacy of the underlying data.

29 Another interesting contrast between the two empirical episodes concerns the continuing high volume of empirical research in labor economics versus the downturn in interest in such work in industrial organization in the late 1970s. The literature attempting to measure labor supply parameters generated any number of important econometric-statistical issues about the appropriate statistical way to proceed. These interesting econometric issues drew into the research area individuals with interests in these matters. Thus labor economics became a haven for quantitative researchers with a strong econometric bent. This was reinforced by the growing availability of micro-data sets usable for labor supply research and the growing availability and increasing capacity of computer facilities. As Hamermesh (1988) put it, "labor economics has become a leader among subspecialities in economics in linking empirical work and theory, in acquiring large amounts of data, and in making strides in analyzing those data" (p. 1). A significant proportion of the ongoing research in labor economics became describable as an applied econometrics research program, with particular focus

on problems arising in large micro-data sets. It can even be claimed that labor economics "applications have generated important advances in econometric theory that have been used elsewhere in economics" (Hamermesh 1988: 7).

It appears that the CP literature did not produce any comparable proliferation of fascinating econometric problems. Moreover, there did not appear to be an analogous growth of micro-data sets peculiarly well suited to the empirical issues facing CP researchers. Stafford (1986) observes, for example, that "The contrast between data available on the supply side of the labor market versus the demand side is striking. No national probability samples exist for industrialized countries at the establishment level which can be used to characterize the microeconomic choice processes of firms in a fashion analogous to the way in which the choice process of households and individuals can be characterized" (p. 388). Thus, there does not appear to have been the development of an ongoing "self-sustaining" applied econometrics research program within industrial organization.

In response to the above interpretation of the continuing high volume of research in labor supply economics, Jeff Biddle has suggested two other possible factors that, if they turned out to be correct and important, would lead to implications alternative to the ones I suggest. Biddle asks whether the move to build ever more involved econometric models for estimating labor supply parameters might have been in part a response to the failure of so-called "first generation" models to produce results in accordance with theory. If this turned out to be a correct interpretation, it would suggest more of a theory-testing attitude than I find among researchers. He also has the impression that in some cases there was a problem with the early elasticity estimates from the policy-oriented labor economist's point of view. Such economists want to convince policy makers of the importance of economic incentives. But the practical importance of such incentives depends on "large enough" supply elasticities. This perception of a "problem" could have led to further empirical research to get larger and therefore "better looking" elasticity estimates. I leave as an open question for future investigation sorting out the possible correctness and importance of these intriguing suggestions.

30   See note 11 above.

31   "An even more important body of evidence for the maximization-of-returns hypothesis is experience from countless applications of the hypothesis to specific problems and the repeated failure of its implications to be contradicted. This evidence is extremely hard to document; it is scattered in numerous memorandums, articles and monographs concerned primarily with specific concrete problems rather than with submitting the hypothesis to test. . . . The evidence for a hypothesis always consists of its continuing failure to be contradicted, continues to accumulate so long as the hypothesis is used, and by its very nature is difficult to document at all comprehensively" (Friedman 1953: 22–3).

BIBLIOGRAPHY

Bain, Joe S. (1951) "Relation of profit rate to industry concentration: American manufacturing, 1936–1940", *Quarterly Journal of Economics* 65 (August): 293–324.
—— (1956) *Barriers to New Competition*, Cambridge, MA: Harvard University Press.
Blaug, Mark (1980) *The Methodology of Economics*, Cambridge: Cambridge University Press.

Brennan, Timothy (1989) "Economic theory in industrial policy: lessons from U.S. v. AT&T", Working Paper 1989-1, Graduate Institute for Policy Education and Research, George Washington University.

Bresnahan, Timothy, and Schmalensee, Richard (1987) "The empirical renaissance in industrial economics: an overview", *Journal of Industrial Economics* 35 (June): 371–8.

Cain, Glen, and Watts, Harold (eds) (1973) *Income Maintenance and Labor Supply*, Chicago, IL: Markham.

Christiano, Lawrence, and Eichenbaum, Martin (1988) "Is theory really ahead of measurement? Current real business cycle theories and aggregate labor market fluctuations", Mimeo, August.

Comanor, William S. (1971) "Comments", in M.D. Intriligator (ed.) *Frontiers of Quantitative Economics*, Amsterdam: North-Holland, pp. 403–4.

De Marchi, Neil, and Gilbert, Christopher (1989) "Introduction" (to special issue on the "History and Methodology of Econometrics"), *Oxford Economic Journal* 41 (January): 1–11.

Demsetz, Harold (1974) "Two systems of belief about monopoly", in H.J. Goldschmid, H.M. Mann and J.F. Weston (eds) *Industrial Concentration: The New Learning*, Boston, MA: Little, Brown, pp. 164–84.

Denton, Frank (1988) "Significance of significance: rhetorical aspects of statistical hypothesis testing in economics", in Arjo Klamer, Donald McCloskey and Robert Solow (eds) *The Consequences of Economic Rhetoric*, Cambridge: Cambridge University Press, pp. 163–83.

DeWald, William, Thursby, Jerry, and Anderson, Richard (1986) "Replication in empirical economics", *American Economic Review* 76 (September): 587–603.

Diamond, Arthur (1988) "The empirical progressiveness of the general equilibrium research program", *History of Political Economy* 20: 119–35.

Epstein, Roy J. (1987) *A History of Econometrics*, Amsterdam: North-Holland.

Friedman, Milton (1953) "The methodology of positive economics", in his *Essays in Positive Economics*, Chicago, IL: University of Chicago Press, pp. 3–43.

Hamermesh, Daniel (1988) "Data difficulties in labor economics", NBER Working Paper 2612; in E. Berndt, E. Diewert and J. Triplett (eds) *Fifty Years of Economic Measurement*, Chicago, IL: University of Chicago Press, forthcoming.

Hausman, Daniel (1989) "Economic methodology in a nutshell", *Journal of Economic Perspectives* 3 (Spring): 115–27.

Heckman, James, and Brook, Payner (1989) "Determining the impact of federal antidiscrimination policy on the economic status of blacks: a study of South Carolina", *American Economic Review* (March): 138–77.

Hirschman, Albert (1970) *Exit, Voice and Loyalty*, Cambridge, MA: Harvard University Press.

Killingsworth, Mark (1983) *Labor Supply*, Cambridge: Cambridge University Press.

Koopmans, Tjalling (1979) "Economics among the sciences", *American Economic Review* 69 (March): 1–13.

Kuhn, Thomas (1970) *The Structure of Scientific Revolutions*, 2nd edn, Chicago, IL: University of Chicago Press.

Lakatos, Imre (1978) *The Methodology of Scientific Research Programmes*, Cambridge: Cambridge University Press.

Langenfeld, James, and Scheffman, David (1986) "Evolution or revolution – what is the future of antitrust?", *Antitrust Bulletin* (Summer): 287–300.

Latsis, Spiro (1976) "A research programme in economics", in S. Latsis (ed.) *Method and Appraisal in Economics*, Cambridge: Cambridge University Press, pp. 1–42.

Leamer, Edward (1983) "Let's take the con out of econometrics", *American-*

Economics Review 73 (March): 31–43.

––––– (1985) "Sensitivity analyses would help", *American Economic Review* 75 (June): 308–13.

Leontief, Wassily (1971) "Theoretical assumptions and nonobserved facts", *American Economic Review* 61: 1–7.

––––– (1982) "Academic economics" (Letter to the Editor), *Science* 217: 104–7.

Lillard, Lee, Smith, James, and Welch, Finis (1986) "What do we really know about wages? The importance of nonreporting and census imputation", *Journal of Political Economy* 94 (June): 489–506.

McCloskey, Donald (1983) "The rhetoric of economics", *Journal of Economic Literature* 21 (June): 481–517.

Mincer, Jacob (1962) "Labor force participation of married women", in *Aspects of Labor Economics*, NBER Conference Series 14, Princeton, NJ: Princeton University Press, pp. 63–97.

Morgan, Mary (1988) "Finding a satisfactory empirical model", in Neil De Marchi (ed.) *The Popperian Legacy in Economics*, Cambridge: Cambridge University Press, pp. 199–211.

Pautler, Paul (1983) "A review of the economic basis for broad-based horizontal merger policy", *Antitrust Bulletin* 28 (Fall): 571–651.

Pencavel, John (1986) "Labor supply of men: a survey", in O. Ashenfelter and R. Layard (eds) *Handbook of Labor Economics*, vol. I, Amsterdam: Elsevier, pp. 3–101.

Prescott, Edward (1986) "Theory ahead of business cycle measurement", *Federal Reserve Bank of Minneapolis Quarterly Review* 10 (Fall): 9–22.

Reder, Melvin (1982) "Chicago economics: permanence and change", *Journal of Economic Literature* 20 (March): 1–38.

Rees, Albert (1974) "An overview of the labor supply results", *Journal of Human Resources* 9: 158–80.

Schmalensee, Richard (1982) "The new industrial organization and the economic analysis of modern markets", in W. Hildenbrand (ed.) *Advances in Economic Theory*, Cambridge: Cambridge University Press, pp. 253–85.

––––– (1989) "Inter-industry studies of structure and performance", in R. Schmalensee and R. Willig (eds) *Handbook of Industrial Organization*, vol. II, Amsterdam: Elsevier, pp. 951–1004.

Stafford, Frank (1986) "Forestalling the demise of empirical labor economics: the role of microdata in labor economics research", in O. Ashenfelter and R. Layard (eds) *Handbook of Labor Economics*, vol. I, Amsterdam: Elsevier, pp. 387–423.

Summers, Lawrence (1986) "Some skeptical observations on real business cycle theory", *Federal Reserve Bank of Minneapolis Quarterly Review* 10 (Fall): 23–7.

Suppes, Frederick (1977) "Afterwards – 1977", in F. Suppes (ed.) *The Structure of Scientific Theories*, 2nd edn, Urbana, IL: University of Illinois Press, pp. 617–730.

Topel, Robert (1988) "Review of *Handbook of Labor Economics*", *Journal of Economic Literature* 26 (December): 1790–2.

Vroman, Wayne (1989) "Industrial change and black men's relative earnings", Mimeo, The Urban Institute, May.

Ward, Benjamin (1972) *What's Wrong with Economics*, London: Macmillan.

Weintraub, E. Roy (1988) "The neo-Walrasian program is empirically progressive", in Neil De Marchi (ed.) *The Popperian Legacy in Economics*, Cambridge: Cambridge University Press, pp. 213–27.

Weiss, Leonard (1971) "Quantitative studies of industrial organization", in M.D. Intriligator (ed.) *Frontiers of Quantitative Economics*, Amsterdam: North-Holland, pp. 362–403.

—— (1974) "The concentration–profits relationship and antitrust", in H.J. Gold-schmid, H.M. Mann and J.F. Weston (eds) *Industrial Concentration: The New Learning*, Boston, MA: Little, Brown, pp. 185–233.

Chapter 20

Econometrics and the "facts of experience"

John Smithin

INTRODUCTION

In an important recent paper, Summers (1991) explores the question of why "formal econometric work" has been so apparently unpersuasive in settling macroeconomic controversies and in setting the agenda for research, in spite of the huge volume of intellectual and other resources which have been devoted to it. He makes the case that an alternative approach, "pragmatic empirical work", has been and will be more fruitful.

In one sense, of course, Summers has simply written down explicitly in an academic journal what has been tacitly known, if not acknowledged, by much of the economics profession for some time. Given the incentive structure of contemporary academia the implicit goal of a large percentage of publication activity is mainly to demonstrate "technical virtuosity" (Summers 1991: 146) rather to advance knowledge or engage in substantive debate on the issues.[1] Summers contribution, nonetheless, is doubly significant in that it comes from a leading scholar at a major university, whose own research clearly meets or exceeds the peer-defined technical standards of the day.

In this chapter, however, it will be argued that in order to fully understand the linkages between economic theory and the "facts of experience"[2] (linkages which formal econometrics is supposed to provide but has failed to do) it is necessary to push the debate on beyond the position taken by Summers – specifically that, in practice, the major examples of instances in which the macroeconomics research agenda has been seriously affected by empirical evidence have occurred when the prevailing theory of the day has failed to correspond with some very crude large-scale empirical generalizations which are nonetheless widely accepted. These empirical generalizations have typically been such that little or no formal technique, even at the level of Summer's "pragmatic empirical work", has been necessary to apprehend them, and have had maximum impact in situations when some competitor theory was in the wings which could (apparently) explain the empirical anomaly when the prevailing orthodoxy could not.

In making this case the chapter will draw on the work of Pheby (1988:

68–80), who has argued that economists can profitably apply the approach of the philosopher-of-science Laudan (1977) to these questions, and on arguments made previously in Smithin (1990a, b). A byproduct of this line of argument is that use can be made of Laudan's distinction between empirical and conceptual problems (see Pheby 1988: 69) which allows for a more comprehensive discussion of the role of economic theory.[3]

WHAT COUNTS AS "EMPIRICAL EVIDENCE"?

According to Summers (1991: 133–4) two alternative approaches to formal econometrics dominate the contemporary scene (at least in the United States). One approach, originally championed by Sargent (1981), seeks to use formal technique to identify "deep structural parameters" (Summers 1991: 129) in rational expectations models. The other, associated with the name of Sims (1980, 1982), attempts to identify causal relationships between economic variables using the technique of vector autoregressions (VARs) while imposing little or no theoretical structure on the data. Sargent (1984) has himself provided an overview of the differences between the two approaches. Summers takes the view that neither approach has really been influential in either changing or confirming the views of economists on the important substantive questions in macroeconomics.

Summers's critique of the first approach is essentially along the lines of the Duhem–Quine thesis.[4] If a hypothesis is "falsified" using this methodology it is never clear whether this is because of the failure of some assumption which is central to the theory under investigation or of one of the myriad auxiliary assumptions which are necessarily made in the course of empirical implementation. Moreover, in these circumstances, falsification of a hypothesis does nothing to suggest what alternative lines of inquiry, if any, might be fruitful (Summers 1991: 133). The critique of the VAR methodology, on the other hand, has to do precisely with the lack of theoretical structure in these methods. Empirical results in the genre (almost by definition) contribute little to economists' ability to explain or predict[5] (1991: 137–9). Finally, both approaches to formal econometrics are implicitly criticized for a lack of rhetorical persuasiveness in the sense of McCloskey (1983).

In contrast to formal econometrics, Summers characterizes empirical work which *is* persuasive as "pragmatic" or "informal" (1991: 140). Where Summers draws the line between "formal" and "informal" work is perhaps a little surprising[6] as the latter includes such contributions as Solow (1957), Friedman (1957) and the literature surveyed by Fama (1970). However, his references to Friedman and Schwartz (1963), Phillips (1958) and Denison (1967), for example, seem to make clear what is meant. Pragmatic empirical work seeks to establish "stylized facts" or regularities, uses many different types of data including discussion of historical episodes and natural experiments, applies commonsense, and ultimately is persuasive in changing the minds of economists on substantive issues (not necessarily permanently, as is obvious from many of the quoted examples) and suggesting new directions for research (Summers 1991: 140–3).

Summers is surely correct as to the relative merits of this type of work and the various "high-tech" approaches in terms of their contribution to the growth of economic knowledge. However, if the objective is to identify the major turning points in the development of macroeconomics in the twentieth century, episodes that really changed the "hearts and minds" of economists in a serious way, it will be argued here that the decisive "empirical evidence" has usually been apprehended by even *less* formal methods than those discussed by Summers. It has been suggested elsewhere (Smithin 1990a, b) that these episodes seem to correspond to Laudan's (1977) notion of an "empirical problem" as expounded in the context of economics by Pheby (1988).

According to the Laudan approach, "scientific progress" can be viewed as a process of finding solutions to both *empirical* and *conceptual* problems which arise in the course of the development and articulation of competing theories. The status of alternative theories at any time depends on how effective they are perceived to be in providing acceptable solutions to problems according to the peer-defined standards of the day. In the case of empirical problems, particular difficulties arise for an entrenched theory when an empirical problem becomes "anomalous", that is, when the theory cannot solve the problem but another competitor theory can.

Pheby (1988: 70–1) stresses that an advantage of the general approach is its clear recognition that there is really no objective standard as to what constitutes an empirical problem or an acceptable solution to it. What appears to be a generally acceptable solution at one point in time may not be so later on. The theory-bound nature of "facts", difficulties of perception and cognition etc. are therefore taken into account.[7] For an empirical generalization to count as an "empirical problem" what appears to be required is simply that it is widely accepted as such by the relevant audience in a particular epoch. This is evidently a descriptive rather than a prescriptive approach to methodology. It is relevant to the present discussion because the observations which do seem to have counted in practice as empirical problems in the development of macroeconomics have most often not been those made in the course of scholarly research, but rather the much more prosaic "facts of experience" available to the population generally. The next section will go on to provide some examples of this phenomenon.

EMPIRICAL PROBLEMS IN MACROECONOMICS

The most obvious example of a decisive empirical problem in macroeconomics is the impact of the mass unemployment of the 1930s on the status of the pre-1930s "classical school" (using that term in the sense of Keynes (1936: 3)[8] which maintained that any deviation from full employment would be short-lived and quickly corrected by market forces. The apparent distress of the 1930s was such a blatant contradiction to the predictions of the accepted economic teachings of the day that academic research was hardly required to make contemporaries aware of the problem. It is noteworthy also that the status of the 1930s experience as an empirical problem continues to this day in spite of numerous sophisticated academic attempts to rewrite the history of the period. These have been uniformly unpersuasive.[9]

It is an important point that even such a glaring discrepancy was only a *potential* problem for existing doctrine until a rival theory emerged which was able to "solve" the empirical problem by the subjectively determined scientific standards of the day. In the 1930s, the apparently successful competitor theory was that of Keynes. In the 1940s, the existence of some such alternative then magnified the impact of the next crude empirical problem for orthodox theory. This was the observation that the massive government spending associated with the Second World War did apparently restore at least the North American economies to health, if not those of the nations on whose territory combat was actually taking place. As Galbraith (1987: 237–50) puts it, this was "affirmation by Mars".

Having mentioned Keynes, it must be recognized that the doctrines which eventually became the new orthodoxy as "Keynesian economics" in the 1950s and 1960s owed more to Hansen, Samuelson, Hicks, Modigliani, Lerner and their contemporaries than to anything which Keynes actually wrote. There is an influential view, expressed forcefully by Joan Robinson (e.g. 1975: 126–8), which continues to be held by many post-Keynesian economists, that these developments represented a serious distortion and betrayal of the original Keynesian message. In this chapter, however, the concern is primarily with the doctrines which most influenced the economics profession at large and the expression "Keynesian economics" will therefore refer to the orthodoxy of the post war years.

For present purposes, the main point is that in the 1970s "Keynesian economics", in the above sense, was also eventually challenged and defeated, not by sophisticated econometric analysis but by very basic empirical problems which seemed obvious to the relevant audience at the time.

To recapitulate the two serious empirical problems which faced orthodox Keynesianism in the 1970s, in what is now a rather familiar story, the first was simply that double-digit inflation had emerged as an apparently intractable problem in the Western industrial nations. The second was the new phenomenon of "stagflation". In what seemed like the worst of all possible worlds, episodes occurred in which already high inflation rates actually rose during serious recessions and periods of low growth. Note that, as with the different economic problems of the 1930s, both of these difficulties were immediately apparent from the raw data or even everyday experience.

The experience of inflation itself was a problem for Keynesian economics because of both the widespread view that the standard Keynesian model was not well equipped to deal with inflationary problems and a deep-seated suspicion that the Keynesian policies themselves were actually the cause of inflation. Stagflation was a problem to the extent that Keynesian economics had become identified with the large-scale econometric models in the Klein–Goldberger tradition. The demand side of these models was based on the IS–LM framework, with the supply side consisting of a Phillips curve type of relationship with a postulated negative tradeoff between inflation and unemployment. So constrained they clearly could not predict the opposite occurrence of stagflation.[10]

Again, the impact of empirical problems on the entrenched orthodoxy of the day was greatly enhanced by the existence of competitor theories which could potentially fill the breach. The inflationary environment of the 1970s, for example, provided a climate in which monetarism suddenly became intellectually attractive. Monetarism explicitly placed inflation at the center of the stage, and had an extremely simple and understandable explanation of the phenomenon via the resurrection of the quantity theory of money. Moreover, crucially, by restricting the quantity-theoretic element to the long run and allowing for the short-run non-neutrality of changes in the rate of monetary growth, monetarism, at least in the version provided by Friedman and Schwartz (1963) and Friedman (e.g. 1974, 1983), was also able to provide an alternative explanation of the empirical problem which had given rise to Keynesianism in the first place, namely the Depression of the 1930s. Note that, contrary to Summers, the contribution of the monetarists is interpreted here as primarily providing a plausible *theoretical* explanation of the two crude empirical problems of inflation and unemployment (by blaming them both on the activities of the central bank) rather than of establishing the "stylized facts" *per se*. It was the alternative intellectual framework, rather than the money–income correlations, which was the main attraction.

The original "monetary misperceptions" version of New Classical theory, as in Lucas (1981), provided an even more formidable competitor for orthodox Keynesianism than did monetarism. Via the combination of Muthian rational expectations, continuous market clearing, and a sharp analytical distinction between the "anticipated" and "unanticipated" components of macroeconomic policy, the theory seemed to be able to reconcile a number of what were believed in the 1970s to be the key "stylized facts". Specifically, the theory was able simultaneously to retain the main propositions of monetarism about the long-run determinants of inflation, explain the standard Phillips curve correlations as the impact of *unanticipated* demand shocks, and even provide a demand-side explanation of stagflationary episodes in terms of confidently expected increases in aggregate demand which do not transpire.[11]

Continuing the story into more recent times, say the past decade and a half, there are also numerous examples of crude empirical problems causing difficulties for established theories and provoking serious adjustments and reconsideration of those theories. Due to the lack of historical distance it is necessary to be increasingly circumspect the closer we approach our own era, but it is now obvious, for example, that the original "monetary misperceptions" version of New Classical theory was itself an early casualty of empirical implausibility during the 1980s. One of the main planks of that theory was the so-called "policy irrelevance proposition" according to which only unanticipated policy changes could affect real economic variables such as output and employment, whereas correctly anticipated changes would be neutral. This not only ruled out the possibility of Keynesian activism, but also, and probably more importantly in the political climate of the late 1970s and early 1980s, held out the promise of a painless disinflation if only the public understood the determination of the authorities to achieve this. According to the New Classicals, as long the proposed "tight money" policy was fully anticipated and credible there need be no short-run real effects.

Obviously, the experience of the severe tight money recessions in the United States, the United Kingdom and elsewhere in the 1979–82 period seriously damaged this view. It could not be convincingly argued that the switch in policy regimes was not widely discussed and understood, nor (in particular) could the determination of Mrs Thatcher in Britain or Fed chairperson Paul Volcker in the United States be in doubt. Yet in the process of disinflation there were nonetheless severe recessions on both sides of the Atlantic. The policy irrelevance proposition demonstrably did not hold. The later fiscal or monetary policy induced recoveries in the mid-1980s and the renewed tight-money recessions of the early 1990s simply provided further confirmation of this. In any event, by the mid-1980s one prominent participant and commentator (McCallum 1986: 1) was able to refer simply to "the recent downturn in popularity of the Lucas–Barro theory of cyclical fluctuations induced by monetary misperceptions".

If the prototype versions of New Classical economics soon ran into empirical difficulties in the early 1980s, traditional monetarism fared little better. The experiences of the early 1980s (and our later experience) have certainly demonstrated that central banks can reduce inflation via high real interest rates, a tightening of credit conditions and an enforced slowdown of economic activity. However, in the 1980s it was also the case that the preferred monetarist description of this process, in terms of relationships between the growth rates of statistically defined monetary aggregates and nominal incomes, broke down, as logically it might have been expected to do in a period of rapid financial innovation.

Unlike the earlier episodes, it was not the case in the 1980s that a prominent competition theory was waiting in the wings to profit from the disarray of the erstwhile orthodoxy. The journals were full of ongoing disputes between "real business cycle" theorists and "New Keynesians" and at the end of the decade Blanchard and Fischer (1989: 27), in their graduate level text, summed up the situation as follows: "no new theory has emerged to dominate the field and the time is one of explorations in several directions...." Even where there is no outstanding or obvious rival on the horizon, however, we can at least see how the emergence of empirical problems, in the sense in which that term is used here, is a significant milestone in the gradual loss of influence of a set of ideas which were previously dominant.

Smithin (1990a: 85–6) further argues that one of the popular successor theories to the first wave of New Classical theory, that relating to so-called "real business cycles", already seems to be facing severe empirical problems. In that theory the driving force of the cycle is supposedly "technology shocks" which immediately implies that the theory is hard pressed to explain severe downturns such as those of the 1930s and the early 1980s as well as booms. In other words, these episodes automatically present empirical problems for the theory. An even more significant difficulty actually derives from the starting point of the real business cycles view, the denial of any causal role to monetary factors. Ironically, the first versions of real business cycle models began to appear in the literature in the early 1980s at a time when the consensus of observers of the practical situation was precisely that the activities of central banks in the disinflation experiment were the key to understanding current events. From this point of view the timing could not have been worse to introduce a new theory that "money does not matter". Although it is true that the events of the past decade and a half have called into question the monetarist understanding of *how* monetary policy actually works, they provide no support at all for the view that the activities of central banks have no real effects.

Smithin (1990a: 80–3) discusses a number of other instances of the process of adjustment to empirical problems within the discipline of macroeconomics in the past few years, but there is little point in multiplying examples in the present chapter. As with the observation that "money mattered" in the two most recent recessions, the leading theorists of the day may well try to dismiss the views of practitioners and commonsense observers of the policy process as "anecdotal" (Mankiw 1990: 1653–4).[12] Repeatedly, however, in practice it has proved to be evidence of this kind, rather than that derived from technically impressive econometric work, which has ultimately proved to be decisive.

THE ROLE OF THEORY

In addition to his critique of formal econometric work, Summers (1991: 143–6) is also highly critical of much contemporary economic theorizing in which the main objective is to construct "models" which are mathematically rigorous and internally consistent but are not closely connected with efforts to establish empirical generalizations and make predictions. Most participants would presumably agree that this type of theorizing is a notable feature of the contemporary academic scene, to an extent that would amaze the general public (whose idea of an "economist" more closely resembles the practitioners employed by, say, financial institutions or brokerage houses) if it were generally known.

This tendency appears inexplicable from the point of view of what Pheby (1988: 72) calls "a naive empiricist bias" in most methodological prescriptions. However, he goes on to argue that another advantage of Laudan's approach to methodological issues is precisely that equal weight is placed on the ability of theories to solve "conceptual problems" (Pheby 1988: 71–3; Laudan 1977: 48–54) in addition to the empirical problems discussed above. As Pheby points out, this is particularly important once it is recognized that much empirical evidence (in any discipline) can simply be ignored for much the same reasons put forward by Summers in his critique of formal econometrics (i.e. the Duhem–Quine thesis).

The suggestion that the ability to solve conceptual problems may be an important factor leading to the acceptance or rejection of theories certainly seems to strike a chord in economics. Even a passing acquaintance with the contents of most contemporary academic journals in the subject would reveal an obsessive concern on the part of theorists, not with the actual subject matter of the discipline, but with finding solutions to the conceptual problems which arise in the development and articulation of theory itself.

As Laudan (1977: 50) seems to suggest, in the case of the natural sciences it may well be the case that the *external* conceptual problems, the cross-disciplinary challenge, has been historically the most significant. In economics, however, it seems clear that the twists and turns of the theoretical debate in the mainstream literature of the modern period have revolved around *internal* conceptual problems, specifically the extent to which the competing theories can be reconciled with the central axiom of neoclassical economics, the hardcore proposition that economic agents are rational (self-interested) maximizers.[13] Contemporary mainstream economic theory is notable for the extreme tenacity with which it adheres to this principle and, as argued by Tobin (1986: 350) by the late 1980s this had hardened into the view that there can be no valid economic theory that is not consistent with it.[14] For macroeconomics, this means that the behavioral functions of macroeconomic models are considered suspect unless it can be demonstrated that they are consistent with "rational maximizing behavior" at the microeconomic level, with firms maximizing profits, consumers maximizing utility and so on. This is the point of the vast literature on the microeconomic "underpinnings" of macroeconomics.

The best example of the significance of this issue in macroeconomics is the way in which "Keynesian economics", broadly defined, has always been on the defensive in terms of methodological purity, even during periods when it was apparently empirically successful.

The professed purpose of what was called the "neoclassical synthesis" of the 1950s and 1960s was, of course, precisely to reconcile Keynesian macroeconomic ideas with neoclassical microeconomics. Indeed, this objective was the reason why the post-Keynesians, who claim a more faithful adherence to the original writings of Keynes, regarded the whole exercise as a betrayal of the original Keynesian revolution. In any event, the effort was not particularly successful, and it quickly became apparent that the mainstream Keynesian economics of the era could only "work" (in the sense of proving a theoretical explanation for the real effects of fluctuations in aggregate demand) by abandoning the cherished first principle in certain key areas. It was always necessary, for example, to invoke wage or price rigidity or adaptive expectations. The point is that the crucial assumptions were never based on convincing microtheoretical arguments as to why "rational optimizing agents" would set wages and prices or form expectations in this way. Hence, key elements in the model would always be under attack by methodological purists. It goes without saying that, in debate at this conceptual level, observations that (for example) nominal wages *do* tend to be sticky in practice are no defence. There must also be an explanation of *why* wages tend to be sticky which is consistent with the basic methodological presupposition of rational maximizing agents.

In spite of these attitudes, however, it would not be correct to suggest that there is no connection between the abstract conceptual debate and the "facts". Identifying this connection will then directly illustrate the interaction between conceptual and empirical problems in determining the fate of individual macroeconomic theories. In the case of the orthodox Keynesian macroeconomic models it would be more accurate to say that in their heyday they were accepted *on sufferance* by the methodological purists in the economics profession. They were marginally acceptable because they seemed to work in the sense of being broadly consistent with the facts, because Keynesian macroeconomic policies based on those models also seemed to work and, crucially, because there was nothing better. As soon as the empirical problems of the Keynesian models became obvious in the 1970s, however, the patience of neoclassical theorists with Keynesianism quickly wore thin, and there were very few who were inclined to defend it.

The ideas of Lucas and his colleagues in the first wave of New Classical economics therefore fell on fertile ground. Orthodox economists had long been unhappy with the "micro underpinnings" of the conventional Keynesian models presented to them, but could do little about this as long as these models were empirically successful in a crude sense, and when there was nothing else on the horizon. It was this awkward situation, however, which set the stage for the rise of the New Classical school. The later empirical problems of the Keynesian models meant that they could now be dispensed with by a profession which had become increasingly skeptical. Then, what Lucas and others seemed to be able to do was to provide an alternative explanation of economic phenomena which was much more firmly based on the preferred methodology. At the time, the Lucas theory apparently solved the empirical problems of *both* the original "classical" school of the 1930s and the latter-day Keynesians of the 1970s, in a way which satisfied the desire of academic economists to bring the awkward discipline of macroeconomics safely back within the fold of orthodox neoclassical theory. Indeed, the ultimate logic of the approach would finally promise to abolish macroeconomics as a separate field of study altogether (Lucas 1987: 107–8; Hoover 1988:87), a development which would not be entirely unwelcome in certain theoretical circles.

It has proved to be somewhat more difficult to similarly abolish macroeconomic problems in the real world, and the empirical problems which, in turn, were faced by the early versions of New Classical theory have been discussed above. The methodological imperative that macroeconomic models should have what are called "sound" optimization underpinnings nonetheless continues to have an extraordinary influence. For example, the most basic common characteristic of the broad spectrum of work that currently falls under the rubric "New Keynesian" is simply the attempt to provide new optimizing "microfoundations" for the market imperfections and rigidities which concerned the earlier Keynesian literature, in accordance with the peer-defined technical standards of the day. Their contribution is almost entirely *internal* to the academic discipline of economics, the attempt to solve the conceptual problem of providing explanations for the various kinds of rigidities in terms acceptable to the current theoretical establishment in academia.

THE ROLE OF ECONOMETRICS

As Summers (1991: 1) puts it: "formal econometric work ... virtually always fails". In the light of the foregoing discussion what explanation can be offered for this phenomenon?

Part of the explanation may be that it is not seriously expected to succeed. If a large part of scholarly activity in economics is devoted to purely theoretical effort for its own sake, the ongoing effort to solve internal conceptual problems within a given research tradition,[15] there will clearly be incentives for researchers to shrug off adverse empirical findings. Because of Duhem–Quine considerations, this is particularly easy to do in the case of formal econometric evidence, as Summers demonstrates. The volume of intellectual resources devoted to such endeavours would then only be explicable in terms either of a perceived need to maintain the methodological proprieties or, as Summers suggests, the necessity for demonstrating technical virtuosity in the academic job market.

However, it has also been argued that the relative lack of success of formal econometric testing does not mean that there is no relationship between economic theory and the facts. As the examples quoted above have demonstrated, what seems to have been decisive in practice in determining the acceptability of individual theories at different periods is their ability to solve empirical problems in the sense of Laudan. The argument differs from that of Summers primarily in suggesting that the decisive turning points have involved even cruder and more basic empirical generalizations than in his examples of "pragmatic empirical work". The most important empirical problems in macroeconomics seem to have been those which could be readily apprehended by the general public, such as mass unemployment in the 1930s or stagflation in the 1970s.

It is not suggested that this implies that economists should refrain from empirical work, particularly in the pragmatic tradition favored by Summers, or even from econometrics. Given the existence of the contemporary "toolkit" of statistical and econometric techniques, there will presumably continue to be numbers of potentially interesting research projects which seem to require some kind of econometric method, including method which is "informal" by Summers's standards. It would be nihilistic to suggest that all these future projects should not go ahead. What is implied, however, is that empirical researchers should be under no illusions about the likely impact of their efforts on the overall research agenda, certainly compared with the impact of the more obvious major empirical anomalies of the type discussed above. At best their efforts are incremental, adding to the weight of evidence for one proposition or another, but rarely proving decisive in themselves. The implications for the more formalistic type of research discussed by Summers are, of course, relatively more serious.

CONCLUDING REMARKS

Pheby's (1988) suggestion that economists might usefully employ Laudan's (1977) approach to descriptive methodology does appear to be fruitful. The relative status of alternative macroeconomic theories seems to depend on the extent to which they can solve both empirical problems and internal conceptual problems. Internal conceptual problems are those which arise in the development and articulation of theory itself. Empirical problems are posed by fairly crude empirical generalizations which are nonetheless widely accepted (the "facts of experience"), arising out of real-world macroeconomic events.

Consistent with the views of Summers (1991) formal econometric work plays a limited role in this process, for the reasons set out above. The pragmatic empirical work championed by Summers is certainly more defensible. However, the most significant empirical problems in macro-economics, in the sense of those which have genuinely influenced the research agenda, seem to have been those which could be readily apprehended from the raw data in the course of the various "natural experiments" thrown up by macroeconomic history. This chapter has given several examples of this process.

NOTES

1 Summers (1991: 133) makes the telling point that attempts to replicate the work of others, which play a major role in other disciplines, are negligible in econometrics except for the purposes of audit (1991: 133).
2 This is a phrase used by Keynes (e.g. 1936: 3).
3 Summers (1991: 143–5) describes his own discussion of the role of theory as "tentative reflections".
4 Summers, however, does not use this terminology. See Pheby (1988: 30–1) for an explanation of the Duhem–Quine problem.
5 It is, of course, highly debatable whether the latter is at all a feasible objective in economics. See McCloskey (1983: 487–8).
6 At least to any remaining "poets" in the economics profession, as Harcourt (1972: 14) calls non-quantitative types.
7 See Hodgson (1988: 86–93) for a discussion (in a somewhat different context) of the inherent difficulties involved in the interpretation of empirical evidence.
8 Keynes (1936: 3n.) admitted that this usage was a "solecism". Historians of thought typically distinguish between the "classical school", including Smith, Ricardo *et al.*, and the "neoclassicals" of the generation after the marginalist revolution of the 1870s. Keynes's terminology included both of these groups.
9 On the contemporary status of the concept of "involuntary unemployment" see Blinder (1987: 131).
10 In terms of broad intellectual history it is by no means clear why the name of Keynes should be so firmly associated with the later work of Phillips or, even more incongruously, with econometric work in the direct line of descent from the pioneering work of Tinbergen which Keynes (1939) had so harshly criticized. Nonetheless, the large-scale econometric models had certainly come to be regarded as "Keynesian" by the majority of the economics profession in the 1970s, and hence empirical problems for the econometricians were empirical problems for Keynesianism also.
11 For a clear intermediate level textbook treatment of these issues see the first edition of Parkin (1982).
12 This is not to suggest that the cited author would himself dismiss this evidence. On the value of "anecdotal" (i.e. historical) evidence see also Kindleberger (1989: xii, 243).
13 See Hamouda and Smithin (1988: 277–85) for an elaboration of what is meant by the term "rational" in contemporary economic analysis.
14 See also Hodgson (1988: x–xiv).
15 The term "research tradition" in Laudan is analogous to the "paradigm" of Kuhn and the "research programme" of Lakatos. See Pheby (1988: 73).

REFERENCES

Blanchard, O.J. and Fischer, S. (1989) *Lectures on Macroeconomics*, Cambridge, MA: MIT Press.
Blinder, A. (1987) "Keynes, Lucas and scientific progress", *American Economic Review, Papers and Proceedings* 77 (May).
Denison, E. (1967) *Why Growth Rates Differ*, Washington, DC: Brookings Institution.
Fama, E.F. (1970) "Efficient capital markets: a review of theory and empirical work", *Journal of Finance* 25 (May): 383–417.

Friedman, M. (1957) *A Theory of the Consumption Function*, Princeton, NJ: Princeton University Press.

—— (1974) "A theoretical framework for monetary analysis", in R.J. Gordon (ed.) *Milton Friedman's Monetary Framework*, Chicago, IL: University of Chicago Press.

—— (1983) "Monetarism in rhetoric and in practice", *Bank of Japan Monetary and Economic Studies* 1 (October): 1–14.

Friedman, M. and Schwartz, A.J. (1963) *A Monetary History of the United States, 1867–1960* Princeton, NJ: Princeton University Press.

Galbraith, J.K. (1987) *Economics in Perspective: a Critical History*, Boston, MA: Houghton Mifflin.

Hamouda, O.F. and Smithin, J.N. (1988) "Rational behaviour with deficient foresight", *Eastern Economic Journal* 14 (July–September): 277–85.

Harcourt, G.C. (1972) *Some Cambridge Controversies in the Theory of Capital*, Cambridge: Cambridge University Press.

Hodgson, G.M. (1988) *Economics and Institutions: a Manifesto for a Modern Institutional Economics*, Cambridge: Polity Press.

Hoover, K.D. (1988) *The New Classical Macroeconomics: a Sceptical Inquiry*, Oxford: Basil Blackwell.

Keynes, J.M. (1936) *The General Theory of Employment, Interest and Money*, London: Macmillan.

—— (1939) "Mr. Tinbergen's method", *Economic Journal* 49 (September): 558–58.

Kindleberger, C.P. (1989) *Manias, Panics, and Crashes: a History of Financial Crises*, revised edition, New York: Basic Books.

Laudan, L. (1977) *Progress and its Problems: Toward a Theory of Scientific Growth*, London: Routledge & Kegan Paul.

Lucas, R.E. Jr (1981) *Studies in Business-Cycle Theory*, Cambridge, MA: MIT Press.

—— (1987) *Models of Business Cycles*, Oxford: Basil Blackwell.

Mankiw, N.G. (1990) "A quick refresher course in macroeconomics", *Journal of Economic Literature* 28 (September): 1645–50.

McCallum, B.T. (1986) "On 'real' and 'sticky-price' theories of the business cycle", *Journal of Money, Credit and Banking*, 18 (November): 397–414.

McCloskey, D.N. (1983) "The rhetoric of economics", *Journal of Economic Literature* 21 (June): 481–517.

Parkin, M. (1982) *Modern Macroeconomics*, Scarborough, Ontario: Prentice-Hall Canada.

Pheby, J. (1988) *Methodology and Economics: a Critical Introduction*, London: Macmillan.

Phillips, A.W. (1958) "The relation between unemployment and the rate of change of money wage rates in the United Kingdom, 1861–1957", *Econometrica* 25 (August): 283–300.

Robinson, J. (1975) "What has become of the Keynesian revolution?", in M. Keynes (ed.) *Essay on John Maynard Keynes*, Cambridge: Cambridge University Press.

Sargent, T.J. (1981) "Interpreting economic time series", *Journal of Political Economy* 89 (April): 213–48.

—— (1984) "Autoregressions, expectations, and advice", *American Economic Review, Papers and Proceedings* 74 (May): 408–15.

Sims, C.A. (1980) "Macroeconomics and reality", *Econometrica* 48 (January): 1–48.

—— (1982) "Policy analysis with econometric models", *Brookings Papers on Economic Activity* 1: 107–64.

Smithin, J.N. (1990a) "Empirical and conceptual problems in contemporary macroeconomics", *British Review of Economic Issues* 12 (June): 73–95.

—— (1990b) *Macroeconomics after Thatcher and Reagan: the Conservative Policy Revolution in Retrospect*, Aldershot: Edward Elgar.

Solow, R.M. (1957) "Technical change and the aggregate production function", *Review of Economics and Statistics* 39: 312–20.

Summers, L.H. (1991) "The scientific illusion in empirical macroeconomics", *Scandanavian Journal of Economics* 93: 129–48.

Tobin, J. (1986) "The future of Keynesian economics", *Eastern Economic Journal* 12 (October–December).

Chapter 21

Simultaneous economic behavior under conditions of ignorance and historical time

Donald W. Katzner

Economists recognized long ago, indeed, at least as far back as Cournot (1960: 127), that simultaneity is a fundamental fact of economic life. At present, their most sophisticated expression of this idea is represented, perhaps, by so-called general equilibrium analysis. In its microeconomic form, a fully developed general equilibrium analysis involves the construction of a dynamic mathematical model whose equations characterize, at each moment, the behavior of consumers, the behavior of firms and the operation of markets. (A government may also be included.) Consumer and firm behaviors emerge from distinct decision-making mechanisms. For each vector of equilibrium and nonequilibrium price values, announced, perhaps, by an auctioneer, the unique solution of the relevant equations of the model at a moment on the model's time-clock (assuming such a solution exists) represents the result of the simultaneous interaction of the consumers, firms and markets at that moment in light of the endowments and the history of the interactions of previous moments already determined by the model. A sequence of these solutions starting with a fixed initial endowment and generated by changing prices is called a time path. A time path along which there is neither change in economic behavior by any consumer or firm nor change in economic value in any market is an equilibrium path. It is frequently supposed in general equilibrium analysis not only that an equilibrium exists and is (globally) stable, but also that at this equilibrium all markets clear and that trade takes place only after market-clearing equilibrium is achieved.[1] As parameters and other "fixed" elements modify, the equilibrium changes. The presence of fixed-element variation across a succession of given dates thus generates a sequence of equilibria and resulting trades at those dates. Such a model is often referred to as a sequence economy.[2]

However, the general equilibrium approach to simultaneity carries with it certain methodological assumptions that severely limit its applicability to real-world phenomena.[3] First, time is "logical" as opposed to historical. It can be restarted over and over again by repeatedly placing the same, fixed dynamic equations at their initial values. Moreover, the equilibrium itself, when it exists, is timeless, that is, the relations that determine the equilibrium values do not depend on time. Second, all decision-makers have "perfect" knowledge in the sense that they know all of the possible outcomes in their opportunity or budget sets that can result from their actions, they know the probabilities of future occurrences of those outcomes when actual outcomes are uncertain, and they know their evaluations of each of their actions (in light of the probabilities if relevant) in a manner that is invariant over time. Third, learning, novelty and the unimagined are precluded. Only things that are consistent with the working out over time of the fixed equations of the model can happen and, of course, upon reaching equilibrium, all change must cease. It is clear, then, that these assumptions remove general equilibrium analysis, along with the simultaneity it depicts, from the realities of ignorance and historical time.

To face up to the presence of ignorance and historical time requires, in part, the recognition that functions describing individual behavior, to the extent that they can be given economic meaning, have to be defined separately at each moment of time by asking the individual how he would behave under various hypothetical circumstances in which everything that does not explicitly vary is held rigidly fixed.[4] Such functions, often called "behavioral" or "notional" functions, are valid only for the instant at which they are constructed. Actual behavior takes place in real historical time and, since persons always acquire new knowledge and react to new and unique situations as time passes, decisions to act are made independently at each moment. Thus, if an individual says that were he presented with situation A today he would do α, there can be no presumption that he would do α were he presented with A, or some facsimile thereof, tomorrow. Indeed, the individual could not say today with any confidence what he would do tomorrow because he cannot have any prior awareness of what his knowledge tomorrow will be. It follows that observation of the individual's behavior today and tomorrow furnishes a single point on each of two distinct behavior functions. In other words, the individual cannot be thought of as moving along a behavior function through historical time.[5]

Another aspect of notional or behavioral functions worthy of mention is that they reflect the planned activity of the individual under the assumption that he is able to carry out these plans. That is, if, under a particular price regime, say, an individual's behavioral functions indicate that he wants to sell some of his initial endowment and use the funds obtained to buy a certain basket of commodities, these plans make sense only if the individual believes that, at the given prices, he will be able to sell the intended endowment, thereby permitting him to buy the intended basket of goods. But just because plans are made does not mean they can be carried out. In the swirl of simultaneous economic activity of the moment, as the individual interacts with other individuals and with firms, if markets do not clear, then the assumption that he can buy and sell what he wants at prevailing prices may turn out to be incorrect and he may be frustrated in achieving the intentions expressed in his behavioral functions.[6]

A second element that has to be accounted for, if ignorance and historical time are to be fully recognized, is that in making decisions individuals look not only to the past and present for knowledge and experience but also contemplate and evaluate the future possible outcomes of various present choices. Unlike general equilibrium analysis, in this process the individual has only imperfect and usually nonprobabilistic knowledge of the past and present, and no knowledge at all of the future.[7] Thus contemplations and evaluations of future outcomes necessarily fall in the realm of informed, albeit nonprobabilistic, conjecture and guesswork.

In the absence of logical time and perfect knowledge, that is, outside the domain of general equilibrium analysis and the sequence economy, individuals still make decisions, simultaneous activity still occurs and sequences of events can still be discerned. Individual behavior across time, either from the perspective of the person making decisions or the analyst trying to understand them, can still be analyzed in the tradition of Marshall. And the interaction of the behaviors of two or more individuals taking place simultaneously through time can still be examined in the tradition of Walras. Of course, the analytical visions of Marshall and Walras need careful reconstruction in this context and, consequently, the results of such analyses are decidedly quite different from those of traditional partial equilibrium and general equilibrium analyses and the sequence economy. Models of sequences of simultaneous and interacting behaviors that emerge may be called, to use Shackle's (1974) term, "kaleidic" economies. As Shackle put it (1974: 42), a kaleidic economy is an expression of

the view that the expectations, which together with the drive of needs or ambitions make up the "springs of action," are at all times so unsubstantially founded upon data and so mutably suggested by the stream of "news," that is, of counter-expected or totally unthought-of events, that they can undergo complete transformation in an hour or even a moment, as the patterns in the kaleidoscope dissolve at a touch....

Even the structures of kaleidic models themselves need not remain stable over time. In any event, it is the character of expectations arising from the uncertainty created by the presence of ignorance and historical time that ultimately colors the sequences of simultaneous actions and their outcomes. Uncertainty, then, is the "kaleidic factor".

Clearly, to deal with economic simultaneity under conditions of ignorance and historical time requires specification of the particular behaviors that are to be viewed as occurring simultaneously. These behaviors, as indicated above, necessarily emerge from decision-making that takes place in the face of genuine uncertainty, and require some sort of resolution at each moment of (historical) time. There are many options. At one extreme, all relevant actions happen together at every instant (as occurs along the equilibrium path in general equilibrium analysis); at the other, each act has its own moment at the center of the stage while all others watch and wait. Of course, the precise specification employed will depend on the intent of the investigation.

The purpose of the present chapter is to show how simultaneity can be represented and analyzed under conditions of ignorance and historical time. This is accomplished by providing an example in which a model of simultaneous economic activity is constructed without the limiting methodological assumptions described above, and hence in which the equilibrium of general equilibrium analysis, even without the extra requirement that all markets clear, cannot be expected to be achieved. Of course, models of present-day economic reality that account for ignorance and historical time are exceedingly complex. Not only do such models have to describe simultaneous behavior, but they must also include a realistic concept of money and be applicable to an arbitrary number of persons, goods and firms. Although models of this sort are the ultimate aim of the line of inquiry proposed here, the analysis that follows, being an initial step, is necessarily more modest. Indeed, the present strategy is to invoke enough simplifying assumptions to be able to focus exclusively, under conditions of ignorance and historical time, on the most elementary version of the phenomenon of simultaneity alone. Since these assumptions, in part, exclude both production and money, and reduce the number of persons and goods to a minimum, the model obtained cannot be said to represent true economic reality. Nevertheless, the role of simultaneity in the understanding of situations of ignorance and historical time, and the problems that arise when attempting to model simultaneity in such a context, can still be meaningfully explored.

On subsequent pages, then, the example considered concerns a simple exchange economy in which two individuals trade from real initial endowments. Time, that is, historical time, is measured in discrete moments. Before actually presenting the example, preliminary discussion examines some of the characteristics and implications of ignorance and historical time and alludes to an alternative perspective on decision-making that acknowledges their presence.

I

All economic events in the world take place in historical time. Historical time, moreover, is unidirectional and irreversible; it flows in a single continuous stream along which every moment is unique. The distinctive history that each moment carries necessarily imparts its own peculiar knowledge, and the objects of this knowledge may be perceived differently by different people. When considered in their relevance for economic decisions and behavior, successive moments in real historical time bring with them their own unique institutional structures and environments, and their own totality and distribution of resource endowments. They also come with their own unique implications for perceptions of the future possibilities that time, at each moment, conceals from view. Models based on historical time can never be started over again by returning to initial values because it is impossible for history to repeat itself without change.[8] A model that is constructed at a given moment and that recognizes historical time, then, whether employed by an actor in the making of a decision or by an outside investigator studying those decisions, generally diverges from all other models having the same purpose but constructed at other moments.

Ignorance arises, in part, because time is historical and reality is overwhelmingly complicated. As historical time passes, the present separates the past from the future. Only the present and the past, however, are capable of observation and description. By looking at present and past events, the decision-maker can gain perceptions of what is presently happening and what has previously occurred. These perceptions may find expression in the form of a theoretical model "explaining" that which is and was seen. But it is important to recognize that perceptions are only perceptions, and no more. They are fraught with errors and gaps. The same is true of intellections and knowledge. The world is just too complex to know and to understand everything.[9] Moreover, as indicated above, knowledge, intellections and perceptions are unique to each individual: everyone thinks different thoughts and knows different things. Thus the decision-maker always remains partially ignorant of the present and the past. Even after all information available about prior events is taken into account, after all imaginable inferences are drawn, at least a kernel of impenetrable ignorance remains. And this ignorance cannot be assumed away in the formulation of a probabilistic event-generating mechanism or a theoretical model because the decision-maker has no idea of what he does not know.

Matters are even worse with respect to the future. Because the future cannot be known until it has arrived, the decision-maker is unable to obtain information about coming economic events. Knowledge of natural laws and knowledge of human intentions is hardly knowledge of future economic outcomes. In Shackle's words (1972: 3), "What does not yet exist, can not now be known." Nor do human beings have the capacity to see novelty in advance. Even the totality of all possibilities is unknowable: the unexpected can and does occur. Thus the decision-maker is in real ignorance about the future. But this does not mean that, based on his faulty and incomplete perceptions of the present and the past, he cannot guess and imagine possible future contingencies. And such "educated" guesses and imaginings well may serve as the springboard for decisions that are made in the present.[10]

Clearly, then, the decision-maker arrives at each moment of decision with a unique background and with unique thoughts derived from that background. The environment in which the decision-maker decides is also unique because it, too, has its own singular history. In other words, the decision-maker has his own perceptions of the moment with regard to history, his own perceptions of the moment concerning the things that he takes as given and his own epistemic abilities of the moment to bring to bear on the issue at hand. The same background, the same environment and the same decision opportunity can never occur again.

The existence of a residual ignorance of the present and the past and of a more pervasive ignorance of the future means that the decision-maker is confronted by genuine uncertainty in the carrying out of his activities. Although knowledge removes some (but never all) uncertainty about the present and past, since (as noted above) no relevant knowledge of the economic future is ever available, the future is always uncertain. To use the idea of probability to describe present, past or future events (or errors), however, is to assume certain knowledge about those events.[11] Furthermore, the knowledge that the assumption of probability requires rests on the possibility of replication. But because historical time rules out replication (since it implies an inability to hold other things constant into the future), and because the presence of ignorance precludes the possession of knowledge of future outcomes, the application of probability in dealing with these issues has to be discarded.

The Shackle–Vickers model of decision-making does not employ the notion of probability and takes into account the ignorance and historical time described here. It may be quickly summarized as follows. The decision-maker constructs a potential surprise function over sets of possible future outcomes.[12] Using utility evaluations of these outcomes, this potential surprise function is transformed into a potential surprise density function defined for all possible utility outcomes (i.e. utility evaluations of outcomes). Maximizing an attractiveness function subject to the potential surprise density function then provides a characterization of each choice option that allows its comparison to other choice options in terms of a decision index. Lastly, the decision-maker selects the choice option that maximizes this decision index.[13] All of the elements of the Shackle–Vickers model – the choice options, the imagined future outcomes that emerge from them, the potential surprise function, the attractiveness function and the decision index – are unique to the moment of historical time at which the decision is made, unique to the decision-maker and, except for the set of all choice options and the decision index, unique to a particular choice option. This model will be employed as the basis for decision-making in the example that follows.

II

Consider, now, the problem of exchange in an economy with neither production nor money. Individuals come together, each with an initial endowment, seeking to improve themselves through trade. But trade requires negotiation (i.e. offers and counter-offers), and negotiation takes time. It is assumed that each person involved in negotiations can make only one offer at any given moment. While negotiating, individuals and situations change. Uncertainty is present in at least three forms. First, at any negotiating moment, since individuals are unable to peer into the minds of others they cannot know in advance the offers that will be presented to them, and hence the trading possibilities, at that moment. Second, because historical time precludes any knowledge of what individuals will be like in the future, subsequent offers and trading possibilities to be faced are shrouded in mystery. Therefore the final outcome of the negotiating process is also uncertain. And third, as a special case of the above, no individual can know what he himself will be like in the future. Thus individuals are even uncertain of what their own preferences will be when trade, if it occurs, takes place. Assume that decisions of offers to propose are made so as to account for these forms of uncertainty in a Shackle–Vickers manner. Thus, in constructing a potential surprise function over outcomes, the individual takes cognizance of the first two forms of uncertainty by looking to his past experience and accumulated knowledge up to the moment of decision as well as to his conjectures of possible future outcomes at, and perhaps even beyond, the cessation of negotiation and trade. And he recognizes and accounts for the third form of uncertainty in his translation of this potential surprise function over outcomes into a potential surprise density function over utility outcomes.[14]

To begin with, imagine a world with only two goods and two persons. In this simplified circumstance, offers made are not contingent on potential trades involving a third commodity or a third person. Quantities of one of the goods can only be swapped for quantities of the other, and possible trading prices are irrelevant to the making of offers. Since actual trading prices are defined by trades if and when they occur, and since the individual has no knowledge of which trades might eventuate, actual trading prices and their associated budget constraints cannot be known to him. It follows that there is no reason to subject maximization to budget constraints. Maximization is constrained instead by the limited quantities in the individual's initial endowment. Assume further that both individuals propose offers simultaneously at each moment, and that each person's offer proposal is a set that contains many acceptable trades from his initial endowment. With proposals stated at moment t, a specific mechanism (two examples are given below) determines which trade, if any, takes place at t. To the extent that trade occurs, a relative trading price is determined for moment t, and the traders' real initial endowments are modified accordingly. Actual trading thus effects subsequent offers. The process continues until the individuals involved in negotiating decide to stop.

More precisely, let x_{ik} denote quantities of good i for person k, where i, k = 1, 2, and write $x_k = (x_{1k}, x_{2k})$ for each k. Suppose these individuals have initial endowments $\hat{x}_1$ and $\hat{x}_2$, respectively, from which they may be willing to trade. Each person is assumed to have his own perception or expectation of the other's initial endowment. Symbolically, $\hat{x}_1^{e2} = (\hat{x}_{11}^{e2}, \hat{x}_{21}^{e2})$ is person 2's perception of person 1's endowment, and $\hat{x}_2^{e1} = (\hat{x}_{12}^{e1}, \hat{x}_{22}^{e1})$ is person 1's perception of person 2's. Note that $\hat{x}_{i1} \gtreqless \hat{x}_{i1}^{e2}$ and $\hat{x}_{i2} \gtreqless \hat{x}_{i2}^{e1}$, for $i = 1, 2$. Negotiation for trade is initiated when one individual, say person k, offers to move from his initial endowment $\hat{x}_k$ to other baskets of commodities x_k, thus suggesting exchanges such as $|x_{1k} - \hat{x}_{1k}|$ for $|x_{2k} - \hat{x}_{2k}|$. As indicated above, the present approach is to take offers to be independent of the exchange values of the initial endowments as defined by the implied rates of exchange and to be proposed in sets; that is, person k offers to move to any one of a collection of baskets B_k. All trades are constrained by the facts that what is given up by one person is received by the other, and that there are no more than $\hat{x}_{i1} + \hat{x}_{i2}$ units of good i available, where $i = 1, 2$. Since each person has a perception of the other's initial endowment, this may be interpreted to mean, in part, that in any single offer one person cannot ask for more in exchange than he thinks the other possesses.

Focus next on a moment in time t at which person k determines a collection of offers B_k^t to propose. Take person k to be a Shackle–Vickers type of decision-maker as described in Section I. His collection of choice options is

$$X_1 = \{x_1 : x_1 = (x_{11}, x_{21}) \le (\hat{x}_{11} + \hat{x}_{12}^{e1}, \hat{x}_{21} + \hat{x}_{22}^{e1})\}$$

if $k = 1$, or

$$X_2 = \{x_2 : x_2 = (x_{12}, x_{22}) \le (\hat{x}_{11}^{e2} + \hat{x}_{12}, \hat{x}_{21}^{e2} + \hat{x}_{22})\}$$

when $k = 2$. Observe that X_k contains person k's initial endowment. In addition, because X_k depends on the expectations of person k, it can vary from moment to moment even though initial endowments remain fixed. For each option x_k, and in light of the uncertainty about his preferences, about the current offer proposal he may face and about the end result of trade, let person k contemplate the (incomplete) collection of possible future outcomes, along with the preference ordering he might have at the end of trade, and determine his corresponding collection of utility outcomes, his potential surprise density function defined over those outcomes and his attractiveness function. These elements are all time dependent. Recall that, as envisaged in Section I, to conjure them up the decision-maker has to ponder what he has learned in the past and present as well as the possibilities that may arise in the future as the effects of the various decision choices play themselves out. Also, in the manner outlined in Section I, let person k build this time-dependent decision index $D^{kt}(x_k)$ over X_k. Finally suppose that person k independently selects, at each t, a "base point" $\tilde{x}_k^t$ such that $D^{kt}(\tilde{x}_k^t) \ge D^{kt}(\hat{x}_k)$ from which he determines his offers, and define his proposal of offers at time t as

$$B_k^t = \{x_k : x_k \text{ is in } X_k, \text{ and } D^{kt}(x_k) \ge D^{kt}(\tilde{x}_k^t)\} \tag{21.1}$$

Thus, with time starting at $t = 0$, say, person k produces a sequence of offer proposals B_k^0, B_k^1, B_k^2, ... Note that, as mentioned earlier, trading prices do not figure in the individual's decisions. Furthermore, because initial endowments change when trade occurs, and because other elements of the construction determining the B_k^t vary with time, no relation between any pair $B_k^{t'}$ and $B_k^{t''}$ can be known before both t' and t'' have passed.

The selection of a base point by an individual may be thought of as setting his "negotiating strategy" at the relevant moment of time. It is also possible to characterize behavior B_k^t as a function of strategies $\tilde{x}_k^t$, for each k at every t. Such a behavioral function would indicate the set of proposed offers that are associated with each strategy $\tilde{x}_k^t$. But as suggested at the outset, these behavioral functions are valid only for the moment t at which they are defined; nor is it possible to move along them through time in any way.

Suppose both individuals propose offers simultaneously at each moment t = 0, 1, 2, ... Write the proposals of person 1 in terms of his own coordinate system as described in (21.1), i.e.

$$B_1^t = \{x_1 : x_1 \text{ is in } X_1, \text{ and } D^{1t}(x_1) \geq D^{1t}(\tilde{x}_1^t)\}$$

It is possible to look at the trading possibilities and the potential outcomes from a perspective akin to that of the traditional Edgeworth box analysis. For this purpose, one might assume that each person knows the initial endowment of the other with complete accuracy and certainty, that is, $\hat{x}_1 = \hat{x}_1^{e2}$ and $\hat{x}_2 = \hat{x}_2^{e1}$. Under such conditions, all trade offers would satisfy the vector equation

$$x_2 = \hat{x}_1 + \hat{x}_2 - x_1$$

and the proposals of person 2 could be expressed in the coordinate system of person 1. Denote person 2's proposals in this form by B_1^{*t}, for all t, so that

$$B_2^{*t} = \{x_1 : \hat{x}_1 + \hat{x}_2 - x_1 \geq 0, \text{ and } D^{2t}(\hat{x}_1 + \hat{x}_2 - x_1) \geq D^{2t}(\tilde{x}_2^t)\}$$

Then the feasible trades that the two individuals could make at time t would be given by the intersection $B_1^t \cap B_2^{*t}$. Were $B_1^t \cap B_2^{*t} = \varnothing$, no trade would be possible at t. In these circumstances, however, due to the continued presence of historical time and the other manifestations of ignorance set out above, the analytical apparatus that emerges (as will be described subsequently) is quite different from that which generally corresponds to the standard Edgeworthian construction.

Return now to the general situation in which neither person is sure of the other's endowment. To complete the model, it remains to specify what it means to say that agreement is reached at any moment t. If agreement is reached at t, then the individuals trade at t and, should they negotiate further at $t + 1$, they necessarily bargain from a new initial endowment. If agreement is not reached at t, then trade does not take place at t. In this case, too, the individuals have the option of continuing to negotiate at $t + 1$.

Consider, first, a highly restricted and simplified characterization of reaching agreement. A more general approach is discussed later on. Suppose that agreement is said to be reached at a moment t provided there exists unique vectors $\bar{x}_1 = (\bar{x}_{11}, \bar{x}_{21})$ in B_1^t and $\bar{x}_2 = (\bar{x}_{12}, \bar{x}_{22})$ in B_2^t such that

$$\left| \bar{x}_{11} - \hat{x}_{11} \right| = \left| \bar{x}_{12} - \hat{x}_{12} \right|$$

and

$$\left| \bar{x}_{21} - \hat{x}_{21} \right| = \left| \bar{x}_{22} - \hat{x}_{22} \right|$$

In the special Edgeworthian-type case introduced above in which both initial endowments are known, this is equivalent to the statement that $B_1^t \cap B_2^{*t} = \{\bar{x}_1\}$. At any rate, upon reaching agreement, $\left| \bar{x}_{11} - \hat{x}_{11} \right|$ is exchanged for $\left| \bar{x}_{21} - \hat{x}_{21} \right|$, and the individuals move from their initial endowment positions to $\bar{x}_1$ and $\bar{x}_2 = \hat{x}_1 + \hat{x}_2 - \bar{x}_1$, respectively. Moreover, the trading price or rate of exchange, that is, the relative price of good 1, for example, is established as

$$\frac{\left| \bar{x}_{11} - \hat{x}_{11} \right|}{\left| \bar{x}_{21} - \hat{x}_{21} \right|}$$

If agreement cannot be reached in finite time, then no agreement is possible: it makes no sense in historical time to let t approach infinity.

It also does not make any sense to ask, when $t = 0$ is the present, say, whether the parameters and functions of the model are such that agreement can eventually be reached. One cannot know in advance if agreement can be secured because one cannot know in advance how the parameters and functions of the model, indeed how the model itself, will evolve as historical time moves on. And anyway, with hindsight it is always possible to tell through observation if agreement had been obtained. Of course, one could always ask, if functions and parameters were stable over time, under what conditions agreement would always be reached. But in practically all situations such a question would not be interesting because it would not have any relevance for what is happening in historical time.

Thus the model developed here is, in a very real sense, both open and closed. On the one hand, it is open in that there is not enough information available to the individual traders or the investigator for the model to determine a unique time path along which, in the absence of parameter shifts, future negotiation (i.e. subsequent values of the B_k^t) will proceed. One cannot tell in advance if and when trade will take place. On the other hand, the model is closed in that the simultaneous behavior of each moment t is "resolved" at t to determine if trade actually occurs at t. The simultaneous behavior resolved at each moment consists of the contemplations and determinations of offers by each person, the investigation of compatibility of those offers, and the occurrence of trade should agreement be reached. The simultaneity described by the model, then, is only a "partial" simultaneity. Even if agreement were reached, it could still, unlike traditional general equilibrium analysis, leave both individuals desirous of further trade. This illustrates a fundamental methodological property of models of simultaneous economic behavior under conditions of ignorance and historical time: that behavior which is seen as occurring simultaneously at each moment must be resolved in some way in a closed submodel valid only at that moment while, at the same time, the overall model itself necessarily remains open to allow for the unforeseen novelty that the future hides. And, as the kaleidics of uncertainty unfold, the model (assuming its own internal structure does not change) generates an unpredictable sequence of outcomes across time.[15]

For the particular Edgeworthian-type case in which both individuals know both endowments, that is, in which a significant part of the uncertainty facing them is assumed away, the geometry of the offer proposals and possible trades that emerge at any moment of time can be illustrated in the familiar Edgeworth box diagram of Figure 21.1. Person 1's origin is in the lower-left corner and person 2's origin is in the upper right. The initial endowment appears at the point labeled ε and determines the dimensions of the box. Assume, for the purposes of the diagram only, that each $D^{kt}(x_k)$ is (like individual utility functions in the traditional theory of demand) differentiable, increasing and strictly quasi-concave. Then level contours through ε of the decision indices exist and may be identified as d_1^t and d_2^t respectively. (Clearly, these contours are valid only for the particular moment of time t under consideration. At any other moment of negotiation, the decision index, and

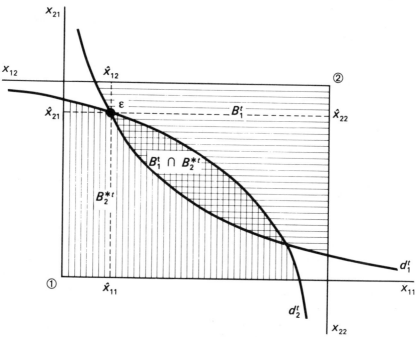

Figure 21.1

hence the level contours, are different.) Furthermore, with $\tilde{x}_k^t = \hat{x}_k$ at moment t for each k, B_1^t is the horizontally shaded region, B_2^t or, in the coordinate system of person 1, B_2^{*t} is the vertically shaded region, and $B_1^t \cap B_2^{*t}$ is the crossed-hatched area between the two contours.[16] Clearly, for these $\tilde{x}_1^t$ and $\tilde{x}_2^t$, agreement is not reached since $B_1^t \cap B_2^{*t}$ contains more than one point. For other values of $\tilde{x}_1^t$ and $\tilde{x}_2^t$, agreement might be reached at t and, if so, then the vector to which the individuals would trade, namely $(\bar{x}_1, \bar{x}_2)$, would necessarily (due to the extreme speciality of the assumptions made in this case) appear in the diagram at a tangency between a level contour for person 1 and a level contour for person 2. (One or the other of these level contours can be the same as, respectively, d_1^t or d_2^t, but not both.) Observe that under the specialized conditions imposed in Figure 21.1, this $(\bar{x}_1, \bar{x}_2)$ would be pairwise Pareto optimal in the sense that, given the decision indices at the moment of agreement and exchange, it is impossible through further trading *at that moment* to push higher up on one person's decision index without sliding lower on the other's. However, although the slope of the straight line connecting $(\bar{x}_1, \bar{x}_2)$ to the initial endowment in a suitably redrawn version of Figure 21.1 is the trading price as defined above, the line itself need not be tangent to the tangent level contours at the point of tangency $(\bar{x}_1, \bar{x}_2)$. That is, $(\bar{x}_1, \bar{x}_2)$ together with the established trading price is not necessarily a momentary "equilibrium" and, if not, trading out of equilibrium or "false trading" has occurred.[17]

It is important to recognize that the analogy of trading to the tangency between level contours of the two decision indices arises in this special case only because of the particular characterization of reaching agreement employed above. Moreover, there are at least three reasons why a person might be willing to participate in trading that involves a different characterization of reaching agreement, and hence be willing to accept a trade to a nontangency point where two level contours only intersect. First, the individual might have, or think that he has, relevant information that the other person does not possess. Second, he might hold expectations of the future that would render such a move appropriate. And third, he may misperceive the other person's intentions or decision index. In any event, an alternative way to characterize the reaching of agreement is in terms of some random mechanism whose outcome at time t reflects these possibilities and determines, when $B_1^t \cap B_2^{*t} \neq \emptyset$, whether trade takes place and, if it does, which $\bar{x}_1$ in $B_1^t \cap B_2^{*t}$ is secured. (As before, when $B_1^t \cap B_2^{*t} = \emptyset$ no trading occurs.) A similar characterization could be expressed in the context in which each person is only able to guess at the other's initial endowment. With such a characterization in either situation, although individuals are still trying to improve their positions, the resulting vector to which they trade if agreement is reached at t, namely $(\bar{x}_1, \bar{x}_2)$, will not, in general, even be pairwise Pareto optimal. That is, pairwise Pareto optimality can arise only by accident.

In the presence of more than two goods and two persons, a more general model is needed. One of the added requirements is that each person conjures up in his own mind estimated or perceived trading prices with which to value his initial endowment.[18] For one person's willingness to propose an offer to another may now depend on, say, the relative value he perceives of the two goods that he is attempting to exchange for a third, or on the terms of trade he expects to secure in a different trade with a third party. Each choice set X_k is thus defined by a budget constraint, and maximization effectively takes place subject to that constraint. Another added requirement is to determine who trades with whom. A simple, if not entirely realistic, possibility here is to assume that, at every t, some specified rule such as a random drawing assigns a trading partner to each individual desiring one. (If there were an odd number of persons, then one of them would not trade at time t.) Note, however, that under the conditions of Figure 21.1, although pairwise Pareto optimality may be achievable among all pairs of traders at some moment t, such a situation, when it obtains, might still not be Pareto optimal with respect to all traders simultaneously. Moreover, the introduction of a generally acceptable medium of exchange (money) that allows purchasing power command over commodities to be transported and temporarily stored, will facilitate the possible movement toward an overall Pareto optimum.[19] In that case, an individual might, for example, accept more of the medium of exchange now, hoping to trade it away to someone else (or even the same person) at a later date. In any event, if trade takes place between two partners, their initial endowments change for the next moment, $t + 1$. Then, at moment $t + 1$, those individuals wishing to find new trading partners participate in the drawing at that moment, and the process continues.

Observe that when trade takes place between two persons with more than two goods, the established rates of exchange are necessarily consistent in that the rate at which good i exchanges for good j is the same as the product of the rate at which good i exchanges for good n, say, and the rate at which good n exchanges for good j. But in the presence of more than two individuals, since each pair of persons establishes, if they trade, their own rates of exchange, such consistency usually does not extend to the market level. Indeed, in a kaleidic world where exchanges take place in historical time, it is not generally possible to define the market rates of exchange to which such consistency might relate. A similar statement applies to the comparison of rates of exchange across time even in the two-person case.

Even in its generalized form, however, the model suggested above still describes a highly specialized situation. Clearly, markets that do not function in terms of pairwise negotiation and trade, that provide for the sale of newly produced commodities or that possess true monetary intermediation, in other words most markets in the real economic world, cannot be modeled in this way. But in any market that is viewed from the perspective of ignorance and historical time, to the extent that simultaneity in individual (and firm) decision-making or behavior is present, such simultaneity has to be handled in a manner analogous to that depicted here.

III

To glimpse how simultaneous microeconomic behavior can be modeled in general, consider very briefly a world with production and many consumers, firms and goods. As in the above example it is first necessary to determine the forms of uncertainty that are introduced by the presence of ignorance, the simultaneous decisions (and hence behaviors) that arise in their milieu, and the mechanism that resolves this (partial) simultaneity at each moment of time. One possibility is as follows. Let markets operate on the basis of short-side trading rules and associated rationing schemes.[20] Let each consumer decide on quantities of commodities to buy, amounts to save in the form of the purchase of IOUs issued by firms, and quantities of factors to sell. Let each firm estimate the demand for its output and plan its investment in real capital and financial assets. Then, based partly on these estimates and decisions, let it determine the quantities of inputs it demands (and hence the output it wants to produce), the price at which it sells its output and the quantity of IOUs it will try to sell (positive or negative) to finance these operations. All market allocations and consumer and firm decisions are made simultaneously at each moment, and each decision requires the relevant decision-maker to face appropriate forms of uncertainty. Such uncertainty may arise, in part, from ignorance about preferences or technology, and ignorance of the extent to which plans and intentions will turn out to be realized. And, as before, this uncertainty imparts a kaleidic quality to the model. In consequence, the resolution of the simultaneous behavior produced by these decisions necessitates consideration of the possibility that, at any moment, not all markets clear, and hence that consumers might not have enough income to purchase what they originally intended, that firms might not be able to secure sufficient quantities of inputs so as to meet the demand for their output, that firms' revenues might not be enough to cover their costs and so on. The ability, or lack thereof, to realize plans and intentions at one moment is one of many elements that influences the decisions made at the next. Thus, as in the example of Section II, the model is closed in its resolution of the simultaneity of each moment and open in its awareness of kaleidic change across time.

In general, it is clear that models of simultaneous economic activity accounting for ignorance and historical time have a different conceptual basis than their full-knowledge, logical-time counterparts. Their main focus necessarily is on the possibility of a unique and independent coherence among appropriately specified activities at each moment that is unrelated to the possibility of coherence at any other moment. Such coherence, if it exists, is a nonequilibrium solution notion. That is, it can be described as the solution of a system of equations valid only at that moment. Furthermore, the solution itself is not an equilibrium (i.e. a position from which no change over time takes place), nor can it be a part of a time path that converges to one.[21] By contrast, the standard full-knowledge, logical-time, Walrasian microeconomic model is a system whose equations are fixed over time, and whose solutions lie either on an equilibrium path along which no change occurs or on a time path that stands in some relations (e.g. converging) to the equilibrium path.

Any of these models can be used to explain what is seen. This is accomplished in the Walrasian case by interpreting observations taken over time either as separate equilibria that arise from variations in functions and parameter values (in which case dynamic movement such as convergence toward an equilibrium path is hidden from view) or as points along a time path that is converging, say, toward the equilibrium path (in which case the equilibrium itself cannot be seen). In the latter situation, of course, functions and parameters could modify in time, and subsequent observations would then lie on a different time path converging to a different equilibrium path. However, there is no such choice of interpretation when using kaleidic models that recognize ignorance and historical time. Nor can there be any interpretation of observations in reference to equilibrium. The only possibility in these circumstances is to identify what is seen with the unique coherence of the moment in the model, as the model itself evolves through historical time. In terms of the example presented earlier, the model of Section II explains an observed process of negotiation that may or may not end in agreement. Thus, rather than trying to clarify particular states, these kinds of models attempt to illuminate an ongoing and changing process.[22]

NOTES

Thanks are due to Douglas Vickers for numerous and insightful comments and suggestions.

1 For a discussion of equilibrium without market clearing see, for example, Benassy (1982).
2 For example, Hahn (1973: 230).
3 See, for example, Loasby (1976: 217–20).
4 One of the problems that arises in asking such questions is discussed momentarily.
5 Vickers (1989–90).
6 Ibid.
7 Only knowledge of the past, not of the present or the future, can be probabilistic in form, and only in the following way. Because observations of the past necessarily require abstraction and the omission of numerous details, it might appear that certain happenings reoccur in certain repeated situations. In that case, a probability of occurrence over the time-frame of the observations might be inferred. However, the presumption is that as soon as the present moves into the past and provides a new observation, this probability changes. History, that is, does not establish probability distributions that are stable over time. In Davidson's terminology, our world is "nonergodic" (1982–3: 187).
8 History may, on occasion, give the impression of repetition. But upon closer

examination of details, such impressions generally turn out to be illusory. See note 7 above.

9   Loasby (1976: 2).

10   It is interesting to note that in this context Shackle defines expectation as "imagination constrained to congruity with what seems in some degree possible ..." (1969: 13).

11   Shackle (1972: 15–18) and Vickers (1978: 140; 1987: 214).

12   The potential surprise of a set of outcomes is the surprise the individual imagines now that he would experience in the future were an outcome in the set to actually occur.

13   This model is attributable to both Shackle and Vickers in that it follows Shackle up through the constrained maximization of the attractiveness function and then switches to Vickers in its use of the decision index instead of Shackle's gambler's preference map. See Shackle (1969), Vickers (1978: Part 3; 1987: ch. 12) and Katzner (1989, 1989–90).

14   In this translation, the utility function itself depends on the outcome state of the world that eventuates. See Katzner (1989–90: 248).

15   Clearly, in the present scheme, trades will be contemplated and may take place at successive time dates. In this sense, the sequential decision-making that occurs captures the true meaning of what is, in effect, a "sequence" economy. But the sequence economy as it is here understood is different from the vision that has frequently been presented in the literature because of its considerations of historical time and uncertainty, and because of the decision processes it involves. Indeed, such an economy has already been characterized above as a kaleidic economy.

16   Note that there is still uncertainty in this diagram in that neither person knows the basket of commodities with which he will wind up and the decision index that he will have at the conclusion of the negotiations.

17   In more general models, of course, neither trading nor false trading necessarily takes place at the equivalent of tangency points.

18   Due to the kaleidic uncertainty in which individuals operate, such estimates are likely to vary across persons and bear little relation to actual trading prices.

19   Cf. Starr (1989) and the papers following it.

20   See, for example, Benassy (1982: chs 1, 2).

21   It could of course, be part of what Bausor calls "historical equilibrium" (1982–3: 174).

22   See Loasby (1976: 220).

REFERENCES

Bausor, R. (1982–3) "Time and economic analysis", *Journal of Post Keynesian Economics* 5: 163–79.

Benassy, J. P. (1982) *The Economics of Market Disequilibrium*, New York: Academic Press.

Cournot, A. (1960) *Researches into the Mathematical principles of the Theory of Wealth*, trans. N. T. Bacon, New York: Kelley.

Davidson, P. (1982–3) "Rational expectations: A fallacious foundation for studying crucial decision-making processes", *Journal of Post Keynesian Economics* 5: 182–98.

Hahn, F. H. (1973) "On the foundations of monetary theory", in M. Parkin and A. R. Nobay (eds) *Essays in Modern Economics*, London: Longman. pp. 230–42.

Katzner, D. W. (1989) "The 'comparative statics' of the Shackle–Vickers approach to decision-making in ignorance", in T. B. Fomby and T. K. Seo (eds) *Studies in the Economics of Uncertainty*, New York: Springer, pp. 21–43.

—— (1989–90) "The Shackle–Vickers approach to decision-making in ignorance", *Journal of Post Keynesian Economics* 12: 237–59.

Loasby, B. J. (1976) *Choice, Complexity and Ignorance*, Cambridge: Cambridge University Press.

Shackle, G. L. S. (1969) *Decision Order and Time in Human Affairs*, 2nd edn, Cambridge: Cambridge University Press.

—— (1972) *Epistemics and Economics*, Cambridge: Cambridge University Press.

—— (1974) *Keynesian Kaleidics*, Edinburgh: Edinburgh University Press.

Starr, R. M. (1989) Introduction to a paper by A. M. Feldman, in R. M. Starr (ed.) *General Equilibrium Models of Monetary Economics*, San Diego, CA: Academic Press, pp. 83–4.

Vickers, D. (1978) *Financial markets in the Capitalist Process*, Philadelphia, PA: University of Pennsylvania Press.

—— (1987) *Money Capital in the Theory of the Firm*, Cambridge: Cambridge University Press.

—— (1989–90) "The illusion of the economic margin", *Journal of Post Keynesian Economics* 12: 88–97.

Chapter 22

Liapounov techniques in economic dynamics and classical thermodynamics
A comparison

Randall Bausor

Many disciplines articulate their internal structure mathematically. Both classical thermodynamics and general competitive analysis are such, for each applies mathematics to define equilibria and to assess an equilibrium's stability. Both fields employ strikingly similar reasoning, as opposed to mechanics, to construct stability arguments. In particular, both depend upon Liapounov's second or direct method rather than solving for disequilibrium trajectories. By comparing these two applications, this essay demonstrates that, although the logic in both fields is the same, the meaning attached to that logic and the metaphors it voices in each diverge profoundly. Indeed, their respective allegories of natural processes are antithetical. By examining the similarities and differences in these two cases. I hope to elucidate the role of applied mathematics in each. I conclude that although the lens of mathematical argumentation tints one's concepts – in this case most notably one's notion of time itself – it does not impose a unique story.

LIAPOUNOV'S DIRECT METHOD IN ECONOMICS AND IN CLASSICAL THERMODYNAMICS

As is well known, tracing the solution of a system of nonlinear differential equations is, in general, intractable. Consequently, scientists widely rely upon qualitative techniques to acquire information about systemic behavior. Liapounov's stability theorems (1947) are prominent among these alternatives. His method is particularly helpful because it avoids the need to solve the differential equations.

Following La Salle and Lefschetz (1961), for an autonomous system of differential equations

$$\frac{\partial x}{\partial t} = F(x) \qquad F(0) = 0 \tag{22.1}$$

where x is a real vector and t a real variable representing continuous time, the origin is a steady state equilibrium. Its stability within a spherical region $S(A)$

$= \{x \mid \|x\| < A\}$ is to be investigated. Assuming that existence and uniqueness conditions hold within $S(A)$, and that the partial derivatives of $F(x)$ all exist and are continuous within this region, each point in $S(A)$ generates a unique path (forward for $t > 0$ and backward for $t < 0$) through $S(A)$. The origin is stable if, for every $R < A$, there is an $r \leq R$ such that the forward path initiating at $x_0 \in S(r)$ is contained within $S(R)$. That is, it never reaches the sphere bounding $S(R)$. If, in addition, every forward path initiating within some $S(R_0)$, $R_0 > 0$, tends to the origin as time increases, then the origin is said to be asymptotically stable. Now consider a scalar function $V(x)$. If $V(x)$ is positive definite (i.e. (i) it and its first partial derivatives are continuous in an open region about the origin, (ii) $V(x) \geq 0$ and (iii) $V(x) = 0$ if and only if $x = 0$) and if $\dot{V} = F(x)$ grad $V(x) \leq 0$, then $V(x)$ is called a Liapounov function. If a Liapounov function exists on a region containing the origin, then the origin is stable, and if, in addition, $-\dot{V}$ is positive definite, then the origin is asymptotically stable.

Liapounov's theorem dramatically shifts attention from traditional dynamics, in which equations are solved for forward paths, to the examination of qualitative systemic behavior. Rather than tracing moment-by-moment progress, equilibria emerge as those special phenomena naturally attracting nonequilibrium states. Rather than mapping the journey, Liapounov's second method concentrates on the attractor at journey's end.

Precisely this liberation from needing to solve dynamic systems with significant nonlinearities in $F(x)$ empowers this method to advance many analyses. When one cannot know where one is going next, as it were, isolating a Liapounov function does reveal where one is going ultimately. For classical thermodynamics this approach formalizes the second law in simple cases of heat flow, and in general competitive analysis it reflects the sense that equilibria spontaneously arise from nonequilibria. The strictly mathematical arguments of both are identical;[1] referring to specific models illustrates the similarities.

Classical thermodynamics addresses macroscopic problems of heat flow.[2] The rate at which heat flows through a membrane is proportional to the surface area and the temperature differential across it, and varies inversely with its thickness. Assessed over infinitesimal distances, at a point in the simplest case of an orthotropic material whose conductivity is unaffected by temperature, this yields the classical Fourier equation:

$$\frac{\partial \tau}{\partial t} = \alpha \frac{\partial^2 \tau}{\partial x^2} \tag{22.2}$$

where τ is temperature, t is time, α is the thermal conductivity of the material relative to its thermal capacity and x is the direction of heat flow. That is, the time rate of change in temperature is proportional to the second derivative of temperature in the direction of flow. In steady state thermal equilibrium $\partial \tau / \partial t = 0$. The temperature at a point is constant; it neither warms nor cools.

Moreover, since $\alpha > 0$, in thermal equilibrium the temperature gradient is constant. In addition, since external energy is required to maintain a nonuniform thermal gradient, for an isolated system in thermal equilibrium $\partial \tau / \partial x = 0$, i.e. temperature is uniform through space. An obvious question is whether or not the flow of heat eventually produces equilibrium. Following Prigogine (1980),

$$G(\cdot) = \int \left(\frac{\partial \tau}{\partial x}\right)^2 dx \geq 0 \qquad (22.3)$$

is a Liapounov function for this problem. Its time derivative is nonpositive, and the function decreases to a minimum at thermal equilibrium. Consequently, systems subject to (22.2) approach equilibrium with the passage of time. In isolation, a uniform temperature distribution attracts all other thermal distributions. We may not be able to trace the route, but we recognize the terminus.[3]

Compare this with the analysis of competitive equilibrium.[4] Identical methods organize the demonstration of global stability here as in thermodynamics. Following Arrow et al. (1959) we introduce $f_k(p)$, where $k = 0, \ldots,$ m. That is, excess demand in each market is a function of the vector of relative prices $p = (1, p_1, \ldots, p_m)$, where p_0 is the numeraire. Market-clearing equilibrium prices $\bar{p}$ are determined by

$$f_k(\bar{p}) = 0 \qquad \text{all } k = 0, \ldots, m \qquad (22.4)$$

Change enters through

$$\frac{dp_j}{dt} = h_j[f_j(p)] \qquad \text{for } j = 0, \ldots, m \qquad (22.5)$$

in which each h_j is presumed continuous and sign-preserving. Given $\bar{p} > 0$. positive homogeneity of excess demand functions and an appropriate substitutability condition assure uniqueness of $\bar{p}$, so that the question of systemic stability is one of convergence of nonequilibrium price vectors to $\bar{p}$ as t increases. However, the particular form of the functions $h_j(\cdot)$ remains general, and is usually unspecified. Interpretations in terms of the auctioneer's *tâtonnement* are also not usual.

Arrow et al. write

To establish the stability of the normalized process (II), we shall show that the distance $D(t)$ from the variable point $p(t) = \psi^{II}(t, p^0)$ to the (unique) normalized equilibrium price vector $\bar{p}$ tends to zero as time tends to infinity. Where the distance has a continuous time derivative $D(t)$, the convergence $p(t) \to \bar{p}$ is established by showing that $\dot{D}(t) < 0$ unless $f(p(t)) = 0$, i.e. when $p(t)$ is the equilibrium vector.

(1959: 93–4)

The distance to equilibrium must serve as a Liapounov function. In Lemma 7 (pp. 100–1) and Theorem 1 (p. 95) Arrow *et al.* demonstrate the global stability of $\bar{p}$ by following Liapounov's logic. Their argument hinges on the existence of a continuous, nonnegative real-valued function with time derivative of the opposite sign. As the value of such a function approaches zero with increasing t, the system converges to its unique equilibrium.

Thus, mathematical arguments for stability in general competitive economics and in classical thermodynamics mirror each other. Their logic is identical, and the common method is justified by Liapounov's proofs. This striking commonality offers a rare opportunity to examine the role of mathematics in economics. Comparing these two applications enhances appreciation of each.

CONTRASTING STABILITY IN ECONOMICS AND THERMODYNAMICS

We begin with similarities which reveal ways in which the mathematics may jointly affect the conceptualizations in each, and proceed to differences which delineate the domain over which the needs of the mathematics dictate analysis. Perhaps the most fundamental attribute common to these stability arguments is their concept of time. Both represent time as a real-valued variable, an image inherited from mechanics. Each instant is denoted by a scalar, so that temporal ordering follows from the organization of the real numbers. Thus, time appears as exactly analogous to a dimension of space.

This notion of time produces problems for both thermodynamics and economics, for it entails a future at t_0 distinguishable from the past only by the sign of $t - t_0$. This "time" can proceed in either "direction" from t_0, for no inherent qualitative difference between past and future exists. History has two, not one, possible destinations. The contrast between an imagined and presumably changeable future balanced at the present against a remembered and unalterable past vanishes. Past and future are essentially identical. Time is reversible, and events are revocable.[5] Such an idea of time obstructs stability analysis, for the one thing an asymptotically stable system must *not* be is dynamically reversible. Something fundamental must separate future from past, but a forward trajectory is all but qualitatively indistinguishable from its backward twin. Ironically, the very failure of classical dynamic techniques for most nonlinear systems saves this concept of time by profoundly changing its analytics. Liapounov's method reformulates the problem from tracing the system's tail into the past and future to assuring that, regardless of where you are, your destination is an equilibrium. Concern for the route to the future dissolves in the certainty of arrival. Rather than solving for the direction of motion given initial conditions, one shows that all paths achieve the set of equilibria. Showing a unique equilibrium to be stable by Liapounov's second method thus reduces anxiety about how and when you get there, and about where you start, to insignificance. When all roads lead to

Rome, only Rome matters. Since the particular path followed is unimportant (they all get there) then reversibility along the path appears unimportant also.

This shift in emphasis implies two further aspects of economics and thermodynamics. First, it inserts a sort of temporal irreversibility into nonequilibrated behavior. The Liapounov function cannot be constant along all approaches to an asymptotically stable equilibrium set. In the terms of Arrow *et al.*, for example, the distance from the current price vector to the unique vector of equilibrium relative prices must be falling. Similarly, in simple heat transfer models, heat flows from the warm to the cool. Since, in both cases, the direction of flow is uniquely specified, a sense of systemic irreversibility, not implicit in "time" itself, is attained. In equilibrium, however, even this disappears. In both economics and thermodynamics the attractor lies at one end, the "forward" end, of time, and any state lies at the opposite extreme. The asymmetry arises only through the existence of a Liapounov function.[6]

Second, a profound amnesia of initial conditions results from concentrating on the equilibrated attractor. This is forgetfulness in the sense that they are lost to the analysis. Where one starts is analytically unimportant and neglected as long as it is within the domain of the Liapounov function. Unlike classical dynamics, the initial conditions do not hold past and future captive, since the ultimate future transcends any particular initial conditions to encompass them all. Such models ultimately achieve the same states irrespective of initial conditions, for asymptotic stability brings them all to the same thing in the end. Competitive economies are drawn to the same vector of relative prices and simple isolated physical systems achieve thermal uniformity regardless of the initial heat distribution.

Spontaneously "forgetting" initial conditions profoundly colors both classical thermodynamics and general competitive analysis. In classical dynamics (such as is used in mechanics), in contrast, the route is fundamental, so that, in systems obeying the Lipschitz conditions, where you are uniquely specifies where you go. Liapounov's qualitative arguments stand this on its head: where you go is *independent* of where you are. Current conditions shrink to minor significance. Thus, this qualitative approach directs the meaty business of analysis onto the attractor, onto equilibrium. In Lakatosian terms, demonstrating global stability "hardens" a "hard core" of equilibrium concepts.[7]

In thermodynamics this forgetfulness has been crucial. For example, consider Prigogine's remarks regarding Poincaré's theorem that most interesting problems in classical dynamics do not lead to integrable systems:

> it should be noted that, in consideration of the relation of dynamics and thermodynamics, Poincaré's theorem is most fortunate. In general, if physical systems belonged to the class of integrable systems, they could not forget their initial conditions; if the action variables, $J_1, \ldots, J_s$, had

prescribed values initially, they would keep them forever, and the distribution function could never become uniform over the microcanonical surface corresponding to a given value E of the energy. Clearly, the final state would drastically depend on the preparation of the system, and concepts such as approach to equilibrium would lose their meaning.

(1980: 32)

Similarly in economics, return to a stable equilibrium allows, as in Samuelson's correspondence principle (1947), one to concentrate on the equilibrium rather than on the particular perturbation from it. Thus, the *tâtonnement* in a normalized model with substitutability (ensuring a unique equilibrium) licenses the economist to gaze only at equilibrium. By comparison, models of "false" trading at nonequilibrium prices emphasize the particular intertemporal trajectory which itself affects the final outcome. Liapounov's liberation of stable equilibria from initial conditions characterizes the classic models of both thermodynamics and competitive economics. It constitutes one of their most notable common features.

Despite these similarities, however, economics and thermodynamics depict strikingly different innate processes. Indeed, their basic phenomenological stories deeply diverge. This metaphorical chasm must now be addressed.

ANALYTICAL DIFFERENCE BETWEEN THERMODYNAMICS AND COMPETITIVE ECONOMICS

Classical thermodynamics and competitive economics present wildly different pictures of spontaneous processes. Whereas one approaches entropic disintegration, the other assembles an efficient socially coherent organization. Whereas one articulates decay, the other finds constructive advance.

The second law of thermodynamics demolishes differences between components. In thermally isolated systems the spatial temperature gradient erodes until, in equilibrium, it vanishes and heat flow ceases. Kinetically, the average motion of each molecule becomes the same, forbidding macroscopic perpetual motion. Eventually all machines stop. The image of degeneration also associates with entropic phrasing of the second law. Here $dS/dt \geq 0$, where S is entropy and t is time. In equilibrium S is maximized, so $ds/dt = 0$. Since entropy production is not limited to heat transfer, its other mechanisms color one's image of the second law. Everyday experiences of iron that rusts, coal that becomes ashes and walls that fall carries powerful metaphorical baggage into one's understanding of what the mathematics says.

This sense of depletion conflicts dramatically with the economist's impression of progress toward equilibrium. Here the process embodies the spontaneous assembly of an efficient and highly coordinated state; it manifests the "invisible hand's" fabrication of a formidable organization from decentralized behavior. Rather than disintegrating into chaos, markets generate efficiency and coherence.

That applications of Liapounov's direct method should attain diametrically opposed interpretations is striking, and suggests that each discipline involves much more than mathematization. Formal mimicry alone renders neither conceptually or theoretically a derivative of the other. Explaining the difference lies not so much in the logic of stability as in the formulation of equilibrium itself. For in making equilibria attractors, one's conception of the manifestation of attraction necessarily reflects equilibrated properties.

The most fundamental distinction between these two conceptions of equilibrium reflects the scale at which they are formulated. Classical thermodynamics, although it speaks for heat flow at a point, is essentially macroscopic. In particular, it addresses aggregate, not atomic, behavior. In terms of entropy, equilibrium conditions require the system to have attained maximum entropy; in terms of heat flow, change in temperature, an aggregate notion, must cease. Relating these macroscopic ideas to the kinetics of atomic motion remains one of the thorniest questions in physics, for no straightforward link between the macroscopic and the microscopic is possible.[8] Precisely this difficulty of connecting microstructure to macrotheory has made Boltzmann's (1964, 1974) probabilistic interpretation of kinetics so powerful. Unable to trace each atom's motion, one estimates the probability of various possible states. The macroscopic production of equilibrium reflects an increasingly probable microscopic configuration. In equilibrium the most probable microscopic state pertains; i.e. although individual atomic trajectories cannot be traced, in an isolated system, on average, they all behave alike. Thus, through probabilistic disaggregation, the average uniformity of the small reflects macroequilibrium, which absorbs a sense of homogenized dissipation. Economists, on the other hand, begin with the microscopic, with individual agents. From their preferences, endowments and technologies optimizing behavior leads to excess demand functions, and through additive aggregation to the large. Thus, an efficient economy rises from rational behavior. It is precisely this construction of the large from the small that classical thermodynamics cannot do.

The scale reversal in equilibrium concepts profoundly colors both fields, for it governs the survivability of individuality at the attractor. Following Boltzmann's (1964, 1974) interpretation of the second law, increasing entropy means greater microscopic randomness. Initial differences decline on average so that at equilibrium no systematic distinction between atoms remains. Their motion appears to be random, and they become profoundly undifferentiated. The details of individual motion and history are swamped amidst the chaotic milieu into which they have degenerated.

For competitive analysis, with its tethering of the large to the small, approaching equilibrium appears very differently. Although important differences between agents disappear in perfectly competitive equilibrium – the marginal rates of substitution for all consumers equal relative prices, which also reflect the marginal rates of technical substitution in production for all firms – agents retain their essential individuality unaltered. Thus, although prices reflect much about everybody's state, the system has not degenerated into a microscopic chaos of indistinguishable atoms. Far from it, for differentiation between individuals according to preferences, technologies and endowments all persist. In equilibrium I may still consume coffee and you tea, one can tell a blast furnace from a dairy, and the distribution of income need not be uniform. All the basic markers of microscopic individuality survive equilibration. Consequently, economists view equilibration not as a disintegrated chaos, but as the coherent coordination of individually differentiated agents. This image of equilibrium endows stable economic processes with the sense of constructing order, an impression antithetical to classical thermodynamics.

Thus, the opposing notions of stable processes in economics and thermodynamics can be attributed to their distinct interpretations of equilibria. One is essentially macroscopic, so that microscopic differentiation vanishes into chaos at equilibrium, whereas the other is essentially microscopic and congeals into an efficiently coherent order at equilibrium. That identical mathematical arguments formalize both versions of "natural" processes attests to the generality of Liapounov's second method. Precisely because it focuses attention on equilibria in both fields, differences of equilibrium concepts explain the profoundly conflicting metaphors used to interpret spontaneous convergence.

I conclude from this comparison that although mathematical argument imposes substantial form to analysis, it, *per se*, does not dictate theory. In particular, arguments for stability entail no unique descriptive interpretation of the processes enforcing stability, just as the concept of equilibrium does not, in itself, impose any necessary attribution of particular characteristics to a particular equilibrium.

NOTES

1   Although the historical development of these two applications is of considerable interest, its telling is not our objective here.
2   A complete discussion of heat transfer is to be found in Gebhart (1971).
3   Solving (22.2) may lead one to believe the Liapounov argument superfluous. Equation (22.2) however, is valid only for the simplest cases. If the conductive material is not orthotropic (equally conductive in all directions), for example wood, if the thermal conductivity depends upon temperature, if the generation of heat is not spatially uniform, as in living tissue, or if the material is subject to turbulence, then the classical Fourier equation is inadequate, significant non-linearities emerge, and explicit solvability is lost.
4   These arguments follow Arrow *et al.* (1959). Samuelson (1941, 1942, 1947) studied similar issues without Liapounov's method. A superb discussion of stability appears in Arrow and Hahn (1971). Although Arrow *et al.* introduced

Liapounov arguments to Western economics, it should be noted that their significance was recognized earlier by Yasui. See Weintraub (1987).

5   Irreversibile time is unidirectional and admits no returning to earlier dates. In irrevocable systems the state at any instant cannot be duplicated later. Each moment is uniquely embedded in time. Since economic decisions depend upon expectations imagined over a future uniquely bounded by the present, all decisions are temporally irrevocable and economic time must be irreversible. See Bausor (1983, 1987), Georgescu-Roegen (1971), Shackle (1968, 1972, 1974, 1979) and Vickers (1978, 1987).

6   Note that this fails to provide irrevocability. Any singleton attractor, for example, reproduces itself eternally; historical time still eludes analysis.

7   See Weintraub (1985) on the role of equilibrium in the "hard core" of Walrasian economics, and on its "hardening".

8   It has been known for generations that directly solving the dynamics of atomic motion utterly fails even for the minutest quantities of a gas. The Poincaré–Misra theorem also shows that the difficulty requires substantive generalization of the dynamic methods of mechanics. See Prigogine (1980).

REFERENCES

Arrow, Kenneth J. and Hahan, Frank H. (1971) *General Competitive Analysis*, San Francisco, CA: Holden-Day.

Arrow, Kenneth J., Block, H. D. and Hurwicz, Leonid (1959) "On the stability of competitive equilibrium, II", *Econometrica* 27: 82–109.

Bausor, Randall (1983) "Time and the structure of economic analysis", *Journal of Post Keynesian Economics*, 7 (Winter): 1–10.

—— (1987) "Time and equilibrium", in Philip Mirowski (ed.) *The Reconstruction of Economic Theory*. Amsterdam: Kluwer-Nijhoff.

Boltzmann, Ludwig (1964) *Lectures on Gas Theory*, Trans. Stephen G. Brush, Berkeley, CA: University of California Press.

—— (1974) "The second law of thermodynamics", in *Theoretical Physics and Philosophical Problems, Selected Writings*, trans. Paul Foulkes, Boston, MA: Reidel.

Gebhart, Benjamin (1971) *Heat Transfer*, 2nd edn. New York: McGraw-Hill.

Georgescu-Roegen, Nicholas (1971) *The Entropy Law and Economic Process*, Cambridge, MA: Harvard University Press.

La Salle, Joseph, and Lefschetz, Solomon (1961) *Stability by Liapounov's Direct Method with Applications*, New York.

Liapounov, Aleksandr Mikhailovich (1947) *Problème Général de la Stabilité du Mouvement*, trans. from Russian by E. Davaux, Princeton, NJ: Princeton University Press.

Prigogine, Ilya (1980) *From Being to Becoming, Time and Complexity in Physical Sciences*, San Francisco, CA: W.H. Freeman.

Samuelson, Paul A. (1941) "The stability of equilibrium: comparative statics and dynamics", *Econometrica* 9 (April): 97–120.

—— (1942) "The stability of equilibrium: linear and nonlinear system", *Econometrica* 10, (January): 1–25.

—— (1947) *Foundations of Economic Analysis*, Cambridge, MA: Harvard University Press.

Shackle, G. L. S. (1968) *Uncertainty in Economics, and Other Reflections*, Cambridge: Cambridge University Press.

———— (1972) *Epistemics and Economics: A Critique of Economic Doctrines*, Cambridge: Cambridge University Press.

———— (1974) *Keynesian Kaleidics: The Evolution of a General Political Economy*, Edinburgh: Edinburgh University Press.

———— (1979) *Imagination and the Nature of Choice*, Edinburgh: Edinburgh University Press.

Vickers, Douglas (1978) *Financial Markets in the Capitalist Process*, Philadelphia, PA: University of Pennsylvania Press.

———— (1987) *Money Capital in the Theory of the Firm*, Cambridge: Cambridge University Press.

Weintraub, E. Roy (1985) *General Equilibrium Analysis: Studies in Appraisal.* Cambridge: Cambridge University Press.

———— (1987) "Stability theory via Liapounov's method: a note on the contribution of Takuma Yasui", *History of Political Economy* 19 (Winter): 615–20.

Chapter 23

The Hamiltonian formalism and optimal growth theory

Nancy J. Wulwick

Hamiltonian calculus originated as the mathematical counterpart of the physics of energy in the mid-nineteenth century. Economists have recently adopted the Hamiltonian formalism to develop the theory of optimal growth.[1] To what extent, the essay asks, have economists remarked upon the formal analogy between dynamic optimization in economics and in energetics? To what extent has the fact that the discourses of energetics and economics both translate into a common mathematical language served to legitimize economics? Have economists good reason to think that the analogy is empirically justified? Has the Hamiltonian formalism given economists the power to think freshly about problems of economic growth? Do economic growth theorists attempt to use the formalism adopted from energetics in ways that conflict with restraints imposed by the formalism? Is the calculus overly constrictive? That is, has the calculus, in inducing economists to ignore what it cannot handle, too narrowly circumscribed the issues that economists can treat in dealing with growth?

To answer those questions, the essay introduces the Hamiltonian dynamic system as presented originally by Hamilton (1834) and in the form of modern control theory (Pontryagin *et al.* 1962). The essay then examines three applications of the Hamiltonian dynamic system to problems of economic growth. The applications appeared in papers by Samuelson and Solow (1956) and Cass (1965), two precursors of New Classical growth theory, and the New Classical economist P. M. Romer (1990). The history of the Hamiltonian in economics is retrospective in that the focus of interest of the essay is on the New Classical growth models; thus the essay emphasizes the economics that the New Classical economists extracted from the Samuelson–Solow and Cass models. The conclusion of the essay suggests that the New Classical economists have adopted a formalism that is inappropriate to help economists better answer the old question, "What are the engines of growth?" (Rebelo 1987: 2).

In order to develop its argument, the essay contains more mathematical exposition than most essays in the history and the methodology of economics. Most readers who suffer from mathematics anxiety will be comforted to learn that to follow the mathematical exposition of the essay in detail merely requires aptitude in elementary differential calculus. Readers who are ignorant of calculus will be able to grasp the essential mathematical argument from six tables that expose the syntax, or linguistic patterns, underlying the formalisms of energetics and economics.

A standard criterion of success in the modern empirical sciences is whether a science is accessible to mathematical methods. As mathematics increasingly has penetrated physics, so the formalisms of physics have increasingly permeated chemistry and biology (Browder 1988: 279). Thus the dominance of mathematical techniques imported from physics is not special to economics. Yet a vocal minority of economists have repudiated the infiltration of economics by mathematical physics. Mirowski has recently taken up the cudgels of the anti-physics economic school. Mirowski has argued that the principles of microeconomic statics spring from the formalisms of energetics. Mirowski further has argued that the adoption of the formalisms of energetics unduly constrains and distorts how economists think about the real micro-economy (Mirowski 1986, 1989a, b; De Marchi 1993). This essay begins where Mirowski stopped. The essay from a historical perspective explores the implications of the importation of the formalisms of energetics into macro-economic dynamics.

Economists of the pro-physics school have responded to their critics that the use of mathematical techniques, whatever their origin, is neutral with regard to the content of economics. Mathematics in the view of the pro-physics economic school is synonymous with logic. In logic the sentence "if all A are B and all B are T, then all A are T" is true no matter what words or phrases one may substitute for the letters, A, B, T. If mathematics is logic, in the case of mathematics too a statement can be made identically in any number of arbitrary formal languages. It is common in the natural sciences for one science to adopt the mathematical techniques used in other sciences. In that context, let us imagine a formal language L_0 that expresses the notions that "x is the sum of y and z" and "x is the product of y and z". Now imagine some other formal language L_i. It is possible to translate the terms of L_i into the notions of L_0. Then – the gist of the argument goes – L_i must be valid in L_0 *and* valid in L_i no matter what the language L_i happens to be (Putnam 1971: 9, 16–17). The formal language that economists typically accept as the universal language L_0 in economics is the mathematics of minimization and maximization, on the grounds that such mathematics most economically solves all problems in all domains of nature and social action (Samuelson 1972: 251). Say that the problem of minimization and maximization in terms of the language L_0 is written as "if ζ, θ, ψ such that $\zeta = \theta(\psi)$ and θ is a continuously differentiable function, then $\theta'(\psi^*) = 0$ gives the extremum of ζ, at ψ^*, ζ". Because it is possible to translate the terms of economic discourse L_1 into L_0, then the optimization scheme L_0 is valid in economics.

The formalist argument above acknowledges that scientific discourse like economics is composed of symbols that refer to reality. According to the formalists, mathematical syntax is purely abstract, while the posture of science is realistic. What happens is that scientists agree on the principles of their field and then express those principles in mathematical terms (von Neumann 1963: 483). Thus science independently assigns meaning to mathematical symbols.[2] But the critics of the formalists counter that it is impossible to be a realist in science and a formalist in applied mathematics. For example, the critics argue, Newton's law of universal gravitation $F_{grav} = Gm_1m_2/d^2$ presupposes the existence of gravitational force, the masses of two particles and the distance between the particles, if not as real entities, at least as things measurable by rational numbers (Putnam 1971: 36–7; 1979: 74). Newton's law is logical because the law is consistent with other Newtonian principles. But Newton's law is true because it holds approximately for real-world things at nonrelativistic distances and velocities. The truth of laws depends on extralogical knowledge. Thus the realist critics charge that economists who use mathematical formalisms as representations without adequate knowledge of the relevant real-world economic subject matter are prone to do poor applied mathematics or – the same thing – poor economics.

The critics of formalism argued that the developments of mathematics and physics have been interdependent. The way we think about numbers influences how we think about the physical world. And the way we think about numbers depends upon how the quantities arise in the real world (Krauss 1993: 27). The interaction between developments in mathematics and physics dominates the history of mathematics since the seventeenth century (Archibald 1989: 29). Physical questions stimulated and channeled mathematical research in certain directions. Newton's (1642–1727) calculus of fluxions was part and parcel of the study of natural philosophy. The theory of partial differential equations had its origins in problems such as how to explain motion in resisting mediums (Guicciardini 1989: 29). Problems like that of the brachistochrone prompted the development of the calculus of variations in the eighteenth century. W. R. Hamilton (1805–65) invented the Hamiltonian formalism as part of the mathematical theory of physical optics. Still, many mathematical ideas originated to solve purely abstract problems and only became useful after a lapse of time. The application of mathematical ideas required that the techniques be appropriate to the study of the subject matter at hand. So non-Euclidean geometry suggested directions that Einstein took in the theory of relativity, which abandoned the Euclidean metric. The theory of relativity then promoted the further development of the tensor calculus associated with non-Euclidean geometry (Struik 1989: 99). Heisenberg, starting with nineteenth-century matrix algebra, designed matrix mechanics, which provided the basis for the first complete form of quantum mechanics (Segré 1976: 154, 156). During the Second World War, complex weapons systems called for mathematical expertise and promoted the development of new mathematical tools for use in statistics, the theory of shock waves and operational research (Owens 1989: 289). Advances in numerical analysis and the electronic computer went hand in hand. Industrial laboratories, engineering schools, physics departments and the electrical engineering profession have served as loci of invention in applied mathematics (Aspray 1989).

Different fields within science share mathematical formalisms. Sharing mathematical formalisms implies a rational analogy between the laws of one science and those of another. The principle of analogy reached maturity in Maxwell's discussion of the transfer of the equation of motion from mechanics to the theories of electricity and magnetism. The use of analogies intensified the concern of Maxwell, trained as he was to take the Cambridge tripos in "mixed mathematics" (the mixing of concepts from mathematics and physics), that scientists would exaggerate what is to be learned from formalisms alone. As the historian of science P. M. Harman wrote,

> "[f]or Maxwell, any symbolic representation had to provide a physical interpretation of nature. A purely symbolic theory employing "the machinery with which mathematicians have been accustomed to work problems about pure quantities" was inadequate and the mathematical symbolism had to be "clothed with the imagery ... of the phenomena of the science itself". In the *Treatise* Maxwell ... contrasts Lagrange's method, which he considers to be a formalism of generalized equations of motion conceived as "pure algebraic quantities" in a manner "free from the intrusion of dynamical ideas," with the method [that kept] ... "constantly in mind the ideas appropriate to the fundamental science of dynamics, ... [c]oncepts of energy, momentum and velocity. Wary of the dominance of formalism, Maxwell admonished his colleagues that "[W]e must have our minds imbued with these [physical] dynamical truths as well as with mathematical methods".
>
> (Harman 1989: 288–9)

By the turn of the century scientists hammered out formal analogies covering elementary phenomana of the largest branches of physics. Table 23.1 presents the analogy between the laws of the conservation of energy in mechanics and electromagnetics. The four concepts in electricity, L, I, C, Q, and the four concepts in mechanics, m, v, k, x, each have the same algebraic function. The same general principle and structure of organization governs the two expressions of the conservation law. Discovering such isomorphisms was part and parcel of the process of scientific discovery. The analogies transferred terminology from the familiar (mechanics) to the unfamiliar domain (electricity). The viability of the translations (as realists emphasize) required empirical testing. The empirical exploration exposed negative as well as positive analogies. Some failed, but those that were deployable were theory-constitutive (Wulwick 1990).

Let us now turn to the formal analogy between the law of energy

Table 23.1 The laws of conservation in mechanics and electromagnetics

$\frac{1}{2}mv^2 + \frac{1}{2}kx^2 = \bar{c}$	Mechanics
$\frac{1}{2}LI^2 + Q^2/2C = \bar{c}$	Electromagnetics
$T + V = \bar{c}$	Energy

Mechanics: A block of mass m slides from left to right on a frictionless, horizontal surface with constant velocity v. The block collides with a light coiled spring, which exerts a constant force k on the block as it compresses the spring. Initially the energy in the system is the kinetic energy $T = \frac{1}{2}mv^2$ of the moving block. After it hits the spring at position x_0, the energy is the kinetic energy of the block plus the elastic potential $V = \frac{1}{2}kx^2$ ($i = 0, \ldots, n$) stored in the spring. When the block cannot slide any further, all the energy is potential. Total energy remains constant.

Electromagnetics: When a capacitor of capacitance C is fully charged (to charge Q), the total energy in the circuit stored in the field of the capacitor is $V = Q^2/2C$. As the capacitor discharges current I, the magnetic field of the inductor stores moving charges, or $T = \frac{1}{2}LI^2$ (L, constant inductance). When the current is maximum, all the potential energy of the conductor has been transferred into kinetic energy of the inductor.

Sources: Bachelard 1975: 162–3; Serway 1982: 145–7

conservation and the theory of optimal economic growth, as implied by their common expression in terms of Hamiltonian calculus. Table 23.2 defines the symbols used in the rest of the essay.

The origins of the Hamiltonian calculus lie in the calculus of variations. One of the earliest problems in the calculus of variations was the problem of the brachistochrone (from the Greek *brachistos*, shortest; *chrone*, time). The problem consisted in finding which curve joining two points that do not fall on a vertical line has the property that a massive particle acted on only by gravity slides down this curve in the shortest time (Elsgolc 1962: 11).[3] Basically, the problem came down to finding the function $x = f(t)$ that gave the action integral

$$J(x, \dot{x}; t) = \int_{t_1}^{t_2} L(x, \dot{x}; t) dt \qquad (23.1)$$

a minimum value during the time period $t_2 - t_1$. The solution, the Euler–Lagrange equation, a second-order differential equation in terms of the position and velocity of the particle.

$$\delta J = \frac{\partial L}{\partial x} - \frac{d}{dt}\frac{\partial L}{\partial \dot{x}} = 0 \qquad t_1 \leq t \leq t_2 \qquad (23.2)$$

meant that the quickest descent occurred along the path of the particle on which J was stationary.[4] Along the path, the tradeoff of the position and the velocity of the particle would be optimal.

In the eighteenth century, a new analytic tradition of mechanics was

Table 23.2 Definition of symbols

B	bliss		
$C\,(c)$	consumption (per head)	$s \equiv \dfrac{\dot{k}}{f(k)}$	investment ratio
$\bar{c}$	constant		
F	force	t	time
f	function	T	kinetic energy
G	balanced per capita economic	$T-V$	kinetic potential
	growth	$U\,(u)$	social utility index (per person)
h	Hamiltonian, a scalar	V	potential energy
$\dot{k}$	net investment per head	w	control function
$K;\,k$	capital; capital per capita – a	x	displacement from the original
	state variable		position, a state variable
L	Lagrange integrand		
m	mass	$\dot{x} \equiv \dfrac{dx}{dt} \equiv v$	velocity
N	number		
n	constant rate of growth of	$\ddot{x} \equiv g$	gravitational acceleration
	population/labour force	Ψ	responses of system to
p	imputed price of a unit of		changes in w, a costate
	consumption, a costate		variable
	variable	$*$	optimal
q	momentum, a costate variable	ρ	social rate of time-discounting

developing that centered on the notion of an energy scalar rather than on a vector of force (Mirowski 1989: ch. 2, pp. 402–3). The concept of energy crystallized with the calculus of Hamilton as a byproduct of his study of the variational properties of the optical system. Energetics introduced the theories of energy conservation and the physical field, the two kinds of energies belonging to particles that move in the earth's gravitational pull – potential and kinetic energy – and two kinds of dynamics, statics (the action of forces in maintaining rest) and kinetics (the action of forces in maintaining states of motion) (Harman 1982: 69).

The basic idea behind energetics was as follows. According to Newton's second law, $F_x = mg$.[5] Total force was the sum of forces associated with displacements along the path: $\int_{x_1}^{x_2} dx = m\dot{x}_{x_1} - m\dot{x}_{x_2}$. During the Lagrangian era of the eighteenth century, the natural philosophers thought that $m\dot{x}$, or *vis viva*, was conserved. But given the definition of kinetic energy as $T = \int_{x_1}^{x_2} F_x dx$, if $F_x dx$ is an exact differential, then one can define a scalar potential function V which expresses mechanical work able to be done by a system of forces $F_x = -dV/dx$. And the assumption of an exact differential $F_x dx$ implies that it is $T + V$ that is conserved in closed systems. Thus the basis for the conservation law lay in the mathematics, though it took a century for natural philosophers to discern the physical significance of the mathematics (Mirowski 1989: 31, 210, 231, 272–3).

The workings of the law of energy conservation become clear from the following simple example. A massive particle thrown without friction above the surface of the earth stores potential energy in the gravitational field between the earth and the raised object. The amount of potential energy in a closed system depends only on the height of the particle. Say that you throw a ball up to height x_1. In that position, the potential energy V relative to the ground is mgx_1. At height x_1 the system is at rest and kinetic energy is zero. The energy the ball possesses as it falls is kinetic energy, the work actually done to set the particle in motion, which depends on velocity. When the particle is at a distance x_2 from the ground, the energy of the system is $T = \frac{1}{2}m\dot{x}^2$ plus $V = mgx_2$. The total energy of the system is constant, so that $mgx_1 = \frac{1}{2}m\dot{x}^2 + mgx_2$ (Serway 1982: 146).[6] The conservation law holds whether the particle falls vertically or takes a horizontal-cum-vertical path. In the closed system, the original and final states of the system are independent of the path.[7] Nature minimizes the kinetic potential, or the action integral:

$$\min L(x, \dot{x}; t) = \min (T - V) \qquad (23.3)$$

The principle of energy conservation resembles bookkeeping. There is a total amount of energy. The only visible form is kinetic energy. When the conversion is totally reversible with no loss the form of energy the kinetic energy is converted into is potential energy. Energy in a closed system is a state variable, purely a function of the present position and velocity, not the path or time the system took to get into that state. The Hamiltonian function

$$H = \int_{t_1}^{t_2} (T + V)dt = \bar{c} \qquad \frac{\partial H}{\partial t} = 0 \qquad (23.4)$$

as Hamilton explained, means that "the quantity H is independent of time, and does not alter in the passage of the points of the system from one set of positions to another" (Hamilton 1834: 250). In contrast, open, nonconservative systems which have friction or other dissipative forces are necessarily time dependent and work depends upon the path taken (Serway 1982: 138–9)[8]

Hamilton mathematically simplified the solution of the problem of how to explain motion. He defined the auxiliary variable, momentum

$$q \equiv \frac{\partial L}{\partial \dot{x}} \equiv m\dot{x} \qquad \dot{q} \equiv mg = F_x \qquad (23.5)$$

Since kinetic energy is the integral of F_x,

$$T \equiv \frac{1}{2}m\dot{x}^2 \equiv \frac{1}{2}q\dot{x} \qquad (23.6a)$$

Given (23.3), we can see that the Hamiltonian can be derived from the Lagrangian, and vice versa:

$$H = -L + q\dot{x} \qquad (23.6b)$$

Given the definition of potential energy,[9]

$$V \equiv mgx \qquad \frac{dV}{dx} = F_x \qquad\qquad (23.6c)$$

the Hamiltonian could be rewritten as

$$H(x, \dot{x}, q) \equiv mgx + \tfrac{1}{2}q\dot{x} = q\dot{x} - [(q^2/2m) - mgx] \qquad (23.7)$$

Differentiating the Hamiltonian with respect to its two parts and setting each differential to zero gave two simultaneous first-order equations in two variables, known as the canonical equations. q gave the extreme value of $H(x, \dot{x}, q)$ holding x constant

$$\frac{\partial H(x, \dot{x}, q)}{\partial q} = \dot{x} \qquad\qquad (23.8a)$$

and x gave the extreme value of $H(x, \dot{x}, q)$ for fixed q

$$\frac{\partial H(x, \dot{x}, q)}{\partial x} = -\dot{q} \qquad\qquad (23.8b)$$

which is equivalent to Newton's second law.[10] The physical system was stationary when $\dot{q} = \dot{x} = 0$. The system of first-order differential equations according to Hamilton achieved the goal of a "general solution of the general problem of dynamics" (Hamilton 1834: 252).

A more general energy conservation law applied to isolated systems when scientists took other forms of energy and energy transformations into account. Applying Hamilton's principle, physicists found laws of reflection and refraction of light, and elementary phenomena of electricity, magnetism, heat and hydrodynamics. The program of energetics showed that events in different branches of physics satisfied one mathematical law and that conclusions arrived at in one field were to be reinterpreted for use in other fields (Wulwick 1987: 217–18). Hamilton's principle, "the pinnacle of mathematical physics", played an essential part in consolidating nineteenth-century physics (Klein 1959: 441).

The energetics movement was not without opposition. Critics saw too many scientists ignoring the major purpose of the energetics analogy, i.e. to describe natural phenomena by a quantitative method based on the energy principle. According to the critics, the analogical method often produced research which embedded physics in a mechanical picture, which chiefly interested mathematicians. And scientists too often overlooked disanalogies. The dynamics of the Hamiltonian system were reversible; irreversible events characterized observed physical reality. Mathematicians could accept the closed system imposed by the Hamiltonian formalism; physicists should not

(Jungnickel and McCormmach 1986: 211–27). Proponents of energetics responded that it was useful to think of certain small systems (like a pendulum) as closed, as if no external forces acted on them and energy was conserved within them. The trick was convincingly to identify isolated systems.[11]

Hamiltonians were not particularly useful in solving practical problems (Klein 1972: 745). But the weight of experimental evidence supported the physical principles underlying Hamiltonian physics. The properties of physical matter were directly accessible to experimenters (Lindley 1993: 36–7). Experimenters constructed numerous gadgets to test the convertibility of mechanical work, electrical energy, heat and kinetic energy (Harman 1982: 51–63). Not all experimentation went easily. For example, Clausius found problems in electricity too complicated to permit a rigorous comparison between theory and experiment. "But where the comparison was possible, he found a reasonable agreement, which encouraged him to view his results as a new conformation of the mechanical theory of heat" (Jungnickel and McCormmach 1986a: 167). In 1905 the physicist Poincaré could say without much overstatement that he knew of "no one who does not know that it [energy conservation] is an experimental fact" (Poincaré 1905: 129). The theory of special relativity introduced the law of conservation of energy and momentum (Krauss 1993: 157). Modified Hamiltonians played a foundational role in the development of quantum mechanics (1990–20) and wave mechanics in the 1920s, and modern experiments confirmed the revised conservation laws (Yehuda 1974: 14; Rothman 1972: 101–30). Textbooks in elementary physics remain organized around a notion of the conservation of energy.

Economists soon adopted the analogical method by which scientists generalized the principles of physics. Founders of neoclassical economics such as Jevons (1879), Edgeworth (1881: 1–15), Fisher (1925) and Walras (1909) expanded upon the shared properties of energetics and economics (Mirowski 1989: 217–61; 1990; Wulwick 1987: 217–21). Fisher, a student of the physicist J. W. Gibbs, provided a table of "mechanical analogies" (Fisher 1925: 85–6). In the table, potential energy translates into utility (utility is conserved along an indifference curve) and kinetic energy into the budget constraint.[12] The mechanical and the economic systems reach an optimum state when the objective function (the kinetic potential to be minimized or the utility to be maximized) attains a stationary value. In the stationary state, following Fisher's table, the law of conservation of energy is analogous to the law of conservation of utility plus the budget constraint.

The mathematician F. P. Ramsey (1928) implicitly applied the conservation law to the problem of dynamic optimization in economics (Wulwick 1990: 13–17). Basically, Ramsey sought to define for each point in time the rate of tradeoff of current consumption for current saving that maximized – subject to a production function with diminishing returns – the sum of social utility in the time interval from now to "bliss" – or, in mathematical terms,

$$\min J = \int_0^\infty \frac{B - U(C)}{\dot{\kappa}} \, dK \qquad U'(C) > 0, \, U''(C) < 0 \tag{23.9}$$

Ramsey solved the minimization problem by setting the derivative of the integrand with respect to the independent variable $\dot{\kappa}$ equal to zero. This yielded the rule

$$U'(C) \, \dot{\kappa} = -[B + U(C)] \tag{23.10a}$$

which meant that, as the economy neared bliss, the marginal utility that resulted indirectly from investment in any period (the left-hand side) was just sufficient to make up for the difference between bliss and the instantaneous level of utility (the right-hand side). Expressing the Ramsey rule in terms of the conservation law gives

$$H = B = U(C) + U'(C)\dot{\kappa}$$

(see equation (23.7)), i.e. $\qquad\qquad\qquad\qquad\qquad\qquad\qquad$ (23.10b)

$$H = B = -L + U'(C)\dot{\kappa}$$

(Sato 1990: 72–3). Ramsey's now famous paper had virtually no impact at the time on economists, who found the mathematics terribly difficult to read (Keynes 1933: 35–6).[13]

Samuelson first explicitly applied the law of energy conservation to dynamic optimization in economics. Samuelson's training in the 1930s as a graduate student at Harvard in mathematical physics profoundly impressed his future work in mathematical economics. Samuelson formed a "master"–student relationship with E. B. Wilson who, as a favorite student of Gibbs, wrote a textbook (1912) in mathematical physics and advocated a strong program in American universities in applied mathematics (Owens 1989: n.34). From Wilson, Samuelson gained a faith in the unity of science. "[O]ne of the most joyful moments of my life", Samuelson recalled, "Was when I was led by listening to E. B. Wilson's exposition of Gibbsian thermodynamics to infer an eternal truth that was independent of its physics or economics exemplification. (A student who studied only one science would be less likely to recognize what belongs to *logic* [to the language L_0] rather than to the nature of *things*)" (Samuelson 1983: pp. xviii–xix). Samuelson laid the groundwork for the adoption of the mathematical formalisms of energetics into economics in his doctoral thesis, published as *Foundations of Economics* (1947).[14] There Samuelson contrasted systems that are nonconservative because of the presence of friction or disturbing external forces to conservative physical systems where the sum of the potential and kinetic energies is constant. Nonconservative systems are nonstationary, historical and time dependent with the result that motion is nonreversible. Conservative systems are stationary, nonhistorical and autonomous of time with the result that motion is reversible. Knowledge of the initial state of the system and the time that has elapsed is sufficient to determine the final state of the system. The path of the conservative economic system is always an equilibrium path, just as, Samuelson maintained, one may "think of a cannon ball at equilibrium, not only when it has fallen to the ground at rest, but also at every point in its flight ..." (1947: 331–2).

Samuelson and R. M. Solow, Samuelson's junior colleague at MIT, wrote out the formal correspondence between the conservative energy system and the optimal theory of capital (Samuelson and Solow 1956).[15] The authors explained that they would use "the fashionable Hamiltonian formalisms", although the method was computationally disadvantageous, to solve the dynamic optimization problem (1956: 554). The baroque style of the paper leaves it unclear exactly what dynamic optimization problem concerning heterogeneous capital the authors sought to solve.[16] The formal analogies between energetics and economics drawn explicitly by Samuelson and Solow appear in Table 23.3. The Hamiltonian dynamic system in economics like mechanics was "time-free", reversible – that is, one could work via a sequence of solutions backwards from the terminal time or forwards from the

Table 23.3 Explicit isomorphisms, Samuelson and Solow (1956)

Hamilton's principle	$H(x, \dot{x}, q) = -L + q\dot{x} = \bar{c}$ where $q\dot{x} = 2T$	
Capital theory	$H(K_i, q_j) = -L(K, K_j') + \sum_2^n q_j K_j' = \bar{c}$ where $\sum_2^n q_j K_j' = 2T$	

Term	Energetics	Capital theory
Potential energy	$V = V(x)$	$V = V(K_i), i = 1, \ldots, N$
Kinetic energy[a]	$T = \frac{1}{2}m\dot{x}^2$	$T = \frac{1}{2}\sum\sum \alpha_{jk}(K_i)\,\dot{K}_k \dot{K}_j$
Momentum	$q \equiv \dfrac{\partial L}{\partial \dot{x}}$	$q_j = \dfrac{\partial L}{\partial K_j'}$ where $K_j' \equiv \dfrac{dK_j}{dK_1}$, $j = 2, \ldots, N$
Kinetic potential	$L = T - V$	$L = T - V$
Conservation	$H(x, \dot{x}, q) = T + V = \bar{c}$	$H(K_i, q_j) = T + V = \bar{c}$
Canonical equations	$\dfrac{\partial H(x,\ \dot{x},\ q)}{\partial q} = \dot{x}$	$\dfrac{\partial H(K,\ q)}{\partial q_j} = \dfrac{dK_j}{dK_1}$
	$\dfrac{\partial H(x,\ \dot{x},\ q)}{\partial x} = -\dot{q}$	$\dfrac{\partial H(K,\ q)}{\partial K_j} = \dfrac{dq_j}{dK_1}$

Note: [a] α_{jk} was undefined in the Samuelson–Solow paper. It might stand for the Lagrangian multiplier.

initial time – and conservative. A central planner with perfect foresight would find the quantitative solution to the Hamiltonian dynamic system. Fully informed line officials would make decisions about the allocation of output at each point along the economic trajectory. The amount of information required would be, in the words of the authors, "a tall order" (Samuelson and Solow 1956: 554–9).

The authors offered little argument, beyond the isomorphisms themselves, in support of the analogies between energetics and capital theory. How the problem they posed was pertinent to economics, what was conserved and why such conservation mattered were questions that remained unanswered (Northrop 1941: 10).[17] The applied economist T. Mayer recently recalled his "reaction when the paper came out. It was that Samuelson and Solow had written it purposely so that it would be completely obscure to those with [relatively] little mathematics."[18] Yet E. Burmeister and A. R. Dobell, two former students of Samuelson and Solow, concluded in their survey of optimal growth theory that the paper turned out to be "a remarkable anticipation of the maximization principle and of a literature to burgeon a decade later" (1970: 404).

So few economists in the 1950s knew the calculus of variations – which universities typically offered to students in mathematics, science and engineering only at the senior undergraduate or first-year graduate levels – that the Samuelson–Solow paper received few citations until recently. Currently graduate students in economics at the major universities learn the calculus of variations (Dixit 1990: v). As P. M. Romer reflected, "in the years between 1970 and 1980, the discussion of the theory of aggregate consumption moved from a point where it would have been impolite to mention Euler equations to a point where it was impossible to carry on a discussion without them" (1989: 52). Textbooks show how to solve a large variety of economic problems by means of the calculus of variations or its modern version, optimal control theory (Dorfman 1969: 817 n.3; Manuelli and Sargent 1987; Blanchard and Fischer 1989; Chiang 1992).

The emigration of German scientists to the United States in the interwar years, the military problems during the Second World War and the missile race with the Soviet Union during the Cold War intensified US research in optimal control theory. The Air Force, having gained independence of the Army in 1947, funded much of the US research. The control theories that became familiar to economists, one by R. Bellman, whose research was funded by the US Air Force, and the other by L. S. Pontryagin, the celebrated blind mathematician of the Soviet Union, differed only in detail from Hamiltonian methods (Kalman 1963: 315). Ever since the Russian Revolution, the Soviet Union had specialized in applied mathematics and engineering control theory. It was at the height of the Cold War that Pontryagin and three engineers wrote a textbook on optimal control theory. The textbook, which received the Lenin prize for Science and Technology, was translated quickly into English (Pontryagin *et al.* 1962).[19]

Pontryagin and his colleagues modified the Hamiltonian to solve dynamic optimization problems that included the explicit specification of a control variable (in the case of a missile, fuel, temperature, voltage etc.) and constraints (on, say, the missile's range). The modified Hamiltonian provided a general basis upon which to program explicit missile guidance (MacKenzie 1990: 318–19). The basic problem at hand for Pontryagin and his colleagues was the optimal path of a missile through the two fixed positions x_0, x_1 in real space. The law of motion of the missile was

$$\dot{x} = f[x(t), w(t)] \qquad x(t_0) = x_0 \qquad x(t_1) = x_1 \tag{23.11}$$

The choice of an admissible control, given the initial conditions, determined the motion of the missile from x_0 to x_1. The problem was to find among all the admissible controls which transferred the missile from position x_0 to x_1 that control which minimized the objective function

$$J = \int_{t_0}^{t_1} f[x(t), w(t)] \mathrm{d}t \tag{23.12}$$

(Figure 23.1). The trajectory of the vehicle was path-independent since the value of the optimal control depended only on the missile's current position in space. The analogies between Hamilton's principle and Pontrayin's maximum principle appear in Table 23.4.[20]

American economists in the 1960s were impressed by the maximum principle, prompted as it was by the requirements of space technology. Before a seemingly arcane subject, "the calculus of variations is called optimal control theory. It [became] ... the central tool of capital theory and [gave] the latter a new lease of life" (Dorfman 1969: 817). The maximum principle

Table 23.4

Maximum principle	$H(\Psi, x, w) = f_0(x, w) + \Psi\dot{x} \qquad = 0$
	$= f_0(x, w) + \Psi f(x, w) = 0$
Hamilton's principle	$H(x, \dot{x}, q) = mgx \quad + \frac{1}{2}q\dot{x}$

Translations		
Hamilton's principle		*Maximum principle*
q	$\partial L/\partial\dot{x}$	Ψ
mgx	V	$f_0(x, w)$
$\frac{1}{2}q\dot{x}$	T	$\Psi\dot{x}$
	$T + V = 0$	

Canonical equations	
$\partial H(x, \dot{x}, q)/\partial q = \dot{x}$	$\partial H(\Psi, x, w)/\partial\Psi = \dot{x}$
$\partial H(x, \dot{x}, q)/\partial x = -\dot{q}$	$\partial H(\Psi, x, w)/\partial x = -\dot{\Psi}$

suggested to the younger mathematical economists in the 1960s how to integrate the constraints imposed by resources and the price of capital into the dynamic optimization problem.[21] Progenitors of the Hamiltonian system in economics such Cass (1965), Uzawa (1965), Ryder (1967), Arrow (1968) and Shell (1969) all acknowledged their debt to Pontryagin *et al.* Cass, Shell and Ryder, Arrow recalls, were amongst the two or three students annually who received Ph.D. degrees from the economics department at Stanford University around 1960 (1987: 651; 1988: xii). Arrow had used a research grant from the office of Naval Research to bring the mathematician Uzawa from Japan to Stanford. Uzawa's research in optimal growth theory, which stemmed from his interest in social planning, caught the attention of Cass, Shell and Ryder. The optimal growth models of Cass and Shell assumed – though only in a loose, literary sort of way – as a condition of the optimal trajectory of capital the existence of an intertemporal Arrow–Debreu model.

The seminal Cass (1965) model began with the teleological problem of maximizing social utility over the life of the economy:

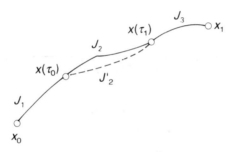

Figure 23.1 Figure 4 of Pontryagin *et al.*

[L]et $w(t)$, $t_0 \leq t \leq t_1$ be an optimal control which corresponds to a transition from x_0 to x_1, and let $x(t)$ be the corresponding optimal trajectory. Then, if $t_0 \leq \tau_0 \leq \tau_1 \leq t_1$, the control $w(t)$, considered on the interval $\tau_0 \leq t \leq \tau_1$, is an optimal control corresponding to the transition from $x(\tau_0)$ to $x(\tau_1)$ and $x(t)$, for $\tau_0 \leq t \leq \tau_1$, is the corresponding optimal trajectory. ... J_1, J_2, and J_3 denote the values of the integral [23.12] taken with respect to the intervals. ... Then $w(t)$, $t_0 \leq t \leq t_1$, which transfers the phase point from x_0 to x_1, imparts the value $J = J_1 + J_2 + J_3$ to the functional (23.12).

If the control $w(t)$ is optimal then J' such that $J' < J$ does not exist (Pontryagin *et al.* 1962: 16–17).

Readers who wonder why the path from x_0 to x_1 is not a straight line may recall how light travels in the least time. Imagine a day so sultry that the air down at the road is hot. How will light travel from points A to B, which lie well above the road? Instead of taking a straight line AB, the light will take a semicircular path that arches down to the road where the air is less dense (Krauss 1993: 51).

$$\max J = \int_0^\infty u[c(t)]e^{-\delta t}dt \quad u'(c) > 0, u''(c) < 0 \quad \delta \equiv \rho - n > 0 \quad (23.13)$$

The utility function expressed either the preferences of the central planner or the identical preferences of consumers for the one good produced in the economy. The objective function (23.13) was subject to constraints imposed by the scarcity of resources, as expressed by the static production function, which yielded constant returns to scale and diminishing returns to inputs:[22]

$$y(t) = f[k(t)] \qquad f'(k) > 0, f''(k) < 0 \qquad (23.14)$$

$$f[k(t)] \equiv z(t) + c(t)$$

$$z(t) \equiv \dot{k}(t) + nk(t)$$

The problem was to find the growth path that maximized (23.13) subject to (23.14). The current-valued Hamiltonian function given the auxiliary variable p was [23]

$$H(c, p, z) = u(c) + pz \qquad (23.15)$$

$H(\cdot)$ stood for the maximum current value of net national product measured in utility units. The formal analogies between optimization in engineering and

Table 23.5

Maximum principle	$H(\Psi, x, w) = f_0(x, w) + \Psi\dot{x} = 0$
Cass/Shell	$H(c, z, p) = u(c) + pz = 0$
or	$H(c, k, s, p) = u(c) + p[sf(k)] = 0$
Hamilton's principle	$H = V + T = \bar{c}$

Formal translations	
Maximum principle	*Cass/Shell*
x	k
w	s
$f_0(x, w)$	$(1 - s)f(k) = c$
$f(x, w)$	$sf(k)$
Ψ	$p = u'(c)$
	$[\partial H(c, k, p)/\partial c = u'(c) - p = 0]$

Canonical equations		
$\partial H(\Psi, x, w)/\partial \Psi = \dot{x}$	$\partial H(k, p)/\partial p = z, \dot{k} = 0$	
$\partial H(\Psi, x, w)/\partial x = -\dot{\Psi}$	$\partial H(k, p)/\partial k = -\dot{p} + \rho p$	$p = f'(k^*)$

Note: For the derivation of $\partial H(k, p)/\partial k = -\dot{p} + \rho p$, see note 21 and Chiang (1992: 178–81, 210–11, 287–90). For ρ not sufficiently near zero, $\partial H(k, p)/\partial k$ produces a "perturbed" Hamiltonian dynamic system which may exhibit complex dynamic behavior, including a limit cycle in p, k space (Burmeister 1980: 243–7, 253; Shell 1988: 589). For the derivation of $p = f'(k)$, see Phelps (1961) and Koopmans (1963).

in economic growth drawn by Shell appear in Table 23.5 (Shell 1969: 246, 254).[24] The stationary solution of the Hamiltonian dynamic system appears in the phase plane (Figure 23.2, Cass's Figure 1). The state k^*, p^* had properties of optimal, balanced, stationary growth.[25] The capital–labor ratio was consistent with full employment. The net national product per capita was maximized given constraints. Per capita capital, consumption and output were all constant. And utility was conserved throughout its conversions, from utils (however measured) in terms of which investments in future enjoyments of the representative consumer were priced, into utils to be enjoyed currently by the consumer. Burmeister and Dobell concluded, in light of the Cass solution, that "Academician Pontryagin and his colleagues have thus enunciated a newer and more powerful principle of an invisible hand; the maximum principle of Pontryagin is seen to be the culmination of a logical sequence originating in the maximum principle of Adam Smith" (1970: 404).

Yet, economists left unacknowledged the important disanalogies between

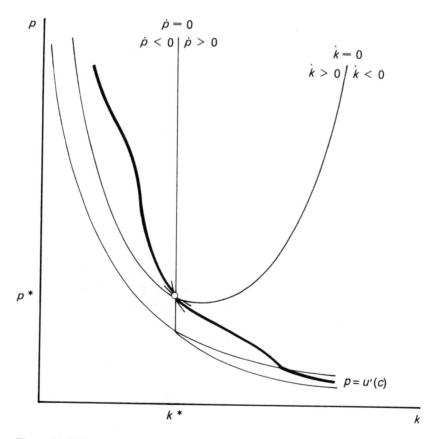

Figure 23.2 The optimum growth path

the maximum principle and dynamic utility optimization. The engineering objectives in launching a missile, such as the efficient use of fuel (minimizing the kinetic potential), were measurable. In contrast to economists, defense strategists recognized the gap between mathematical and physical models. The Hamiltonian offered strategists a very general system with which to think out certain problems of flight control given the limitations of the precision instruments available to them. It would be impossible to adopt the Hamiltonian dynamic system as the sole mathematical principle behind flight guidance because it was impossible to store on board the missile a model of the earth's gravitational field which covered all possible trajectories. Engineers performed tests with real missiles of the hypothesized link between the control function and the missile's motion. Tests confirmed the link between the controls and the missile's motion. Ballistic missiles, having traveled hundreds of thousands of miles, "hit right in the pickle barrel" (MacKenzie 1990: 1, 343).

In contrast to optimization in aeronautical engineering, the objective function in economics lacked an empirical counterpart. The economists' objective is to maximize the utility of the representative consumer. The measurability of utility has eluded economists. The preferences of the representative consumer are purely mathematical constructs; the deductions from representative agent models relate to aggregate data and do not reflect the preferences of individuals (Hoover 1993: xx; Kirman 1992). Dynamic economic optimization did not permit empirical validation, through either prediction or the realism of assumptions. The necessary conditions for dynamic optimization in the absence of the ideal central planner included perfect competition, market clearing, efficient pricing and perfect foresight. The current saving behavior of economic agents took all future saving decisions as given. The economy remained always in equilibrium and equilibrium was fully anticipated by everybody in the general equilibrium context. Those conditions manifestly did not mimic the real world. In retrospect Cass and Shell admitted that "[t]he success of the Hamiltonian approach in decentralized and descriptive growth theory has so far been very limited" (Shell 1988: 589). In the 1980s, the New Classical economists R. E. Lucas, P. M. Romer and S. Rebelo agreed that the optimal capital models of the past "ignored the fundamental questions and concentrated on abstraction and formalism. Therefore growth theory came increasingly to be viewed as a sterile exercise" (Romer 1989: 51; Sala-i-Martin 1990; Lucas 1985; Romer 1986; Rebelo 1987, 1991).[26]

The interest of New Classical economists in optimal growth models has constituted a natural extension of their research agenda. As the "fundamentalist wing" of the neo-Walrasian general equilibrium school, New Classical economists have taken the old problem of the microfoundations of macroeconomics seriously, seeking as they have to ground aggregate events in the optimization framework of individual choice expressed via prices and based on preferences and technology (Hoover 1993: xiv). New Classical economists have assumed that agents maximize utility and evince perfect foresight, and that markets continuously clear. Business cycles, which in the neoclassical model represented deviations from an exogenous trend of output governed by technical progress, in the New Classical models have reflected optimal jumps of the trend following technology shocks. In the 1970s New Classical economics developed a theory of the business cycle to explain how agents responded as the trend jumped. New Classical growth theory seeks to explain the trend itself.

New Classical economists have resurrected Kaldor's stylized facts of growth, which neoclassical economists found difficult to explain (Kaldor 1961; Wulwick 1992, 1993; Romer 1989: 54–5). Two important facts are the continued growth of labor productivity and the absence of evidence of a tendency for country growth rates to converge. Economists have never found satisfactory the mathematically convenient assumption of neoclassical models that technical progress is exogenous. The neoclassical model has predicted that the income levels and the growth rates of countries will converge over time. According to the model, rich countries which have a high capital–labor ratio and a low marginal product of capital experience an outflow of capital and thus slow growth. Poor countries which have a high marginal product of capital see capital inflows and rapid growth. Romer (1989) using a sample of 115 countries (drawn from the Summers–Heston data, 1984) showed that growth rates during 1960–1980 showed no tendency to converge. Taking all countries together, Lucas concluded, the correlation between their "income levels and rates of growth . . . would not be far from zero" (1988: 4; 1990).

To explain the stylized facts of growth, new growth economics has harnessed the line of research that expands the theory of neo-Walrasian general equilibrium to cover imperfect competition and incomplete markets, including externalities. The renewed interest in externalities is far from novel. There is a large overlap between the developments in trade theory since the later 1970s and New Classical growth theory. Trade theorists challenged the neoclassical model based on comparative advantage and constant returns to scale. Increasing returns due to the division of labor and specialization became as important as comparative advantage as a source of trade: while comparative advantage explained why countries with different endowments traded, increasing returns could explain why similar countries traded. The problem was that increasing returns conflicted with the assumption of perfect competition. Trade theorists defined increasing returns as a positive external effect to preserve the assumption of competition (Helpman and Krugman 1985: 45). New Classical economists, for the same reason, have treated increasing returns as a positive externality (Lucas 1988: 19; Wulwick 1992: 43).

Increasing returns due to externalities lead to general equilibria which are Pareto suboptimal.[27] Hence the New Classical growth models with externalities have invited New Classical proposals of taxation to "internalize" the externality and increase the rate of economic growth. It seems paradoxical that New Classical economists should propose government intervention in light of their well-known opposition to demand management. Their opposition to government intervention rested on three tenets: the Lucas critique, policy ineffectiveness, and policy inconsistency (Hoover 1992: 86–8). The Lucas critique (an idea which was not original to Lucas) says that the effects of policy changes cannot be predicted on the basis of reduced form models which do not take into account changes in technology and tastes. But the Lucas critique is irrelevant to policies to increase the growth rate that are based on the solution of the Hamiltonian dynamic system, which takes tastes (the objective function) and technology (the production function) into account. The policy ineffectiveness tenet says that agents with rational expectations who grasped the thrust of policy would prevent policy from raising employment above its natural rate. The policy ineffectiveness tenet is irrelevant to policies to increase the rate of growth of the economy at the natural rate of employment. The problem of inconsistent policies says that policies will be inconsistent over time unless the whole future course of policy is considered. But the Hamiltonian system solves for the optimal time-path (Petit 1990: 272, 292–6).

Of the optimal growth models of the 1980s, the Romer model with productive externalities has attracted much attention (Sala-i-Martin 1990b: 19–21; Romer 1989: 92–5).[28] The Romer model embeds Kaldor's idea that capital investment explains technical progress within an aggregative neo-Walrasian general equilibrium framework.[29] The model also suggests that increasing returns to scale are insufficient to generate economic growth. We begin with the standard problem of maximizing intertemporal social welfare, here defined by the tractable form $u(c) = \ln(c)$, $u'(c) = 1/c$:

$$\max J = \int_0^\alpha \ln[c(t)]e^{-\rho t}\, dt \tag{23.16}$$

The production function of each firm has two components, the Cobb–Douglas function, consistent with prices in a perfectly competitive equilibrium, and a function of the aggregated capital stock, which as a proxy for society's know-how acts like a productive externality. The externality arises because private knowledge can neither be patented nor kept secret (Romer 1986:1015). Not only the firm that itself invests in technology but also other firms in the industry directly benefit from the investment (Marshall 1926: 220–1, 262; Arrow 1962). With the productive externality, the aggregate production function yields increasing returns to scale.[30] The production function in per capita terms is

$$f(k, K) = k(t)^{\alpha}K(t)^{v} \qquad 0 < \alpha < 1 \qquad v > 0 \qquad \alpha + v \lessgtr 1 \tag{23.17}$$

$$k^{\alpha}(t)K^{v}(t) \equiv \dot{k}(t) + c(t)$$

Table 23.6

Hamilton's principle	$H(x, \dot{x}, q) = mgx + q\dot{x}/2$
Romer	$H(c, \dot{k}, p) = \ln c + p(k^{\alpha}K^{\nu} - c)$

Translations

Hamilton's principle		Romer
q		p
mgx	V	$\ln c$
$q\dot{x}/2$	T	$p\dot{k}$
	$T + V = 0$	
		$\partial H(c, \dot{k}, p)/\partial c = 1/c - p = 0$

Canonical equations

$\partial H(x, \dot{x}, q)/\partial q = \dot{x}$	$\partial H(c, \dot{k}, p)/\partial p = \dot{k}$
$\partial H(x, \dot{x}, q)/\partial x = -\dot{q}$	$\partial H(c, \dot{k}, p)/\partial k = -\dot{p} + \rho p$

The economy in the model maintains a competitive equilibrium with a constant number of N firms and workers. Hence $K \equiv kN$. Table 23.6 presents the formal analogies between the Hamiltonians of classical mechanics and of New Classical growth economics.

Romer deduced from the Hamiltonian dynamical system two conclusions about the time-path of investment and its price:[31]

$$\dot{k} = k^{\alpha + \nu}N^{\nu} - (1/p) \tag{23.18a}$$

$$\dot{p}/p = \rho - f'(k) = -G \qquad f'(k) = \alpha k^{\alpha + \nu - 1}N^{\nu} \tag{23.18b}$$

The conclusions are consistent with five cases, presented in Table 23.7. In *case 1*, the rate of economic growth G is unbounded (equation (23.18a)) and the Hamiltonian dynamic system is incomplete (Xie 1991). *Cases 2 and 3* correspond to the Pareto-suboptimal stationary state ($\dot{k} = \dot{p} = G = 0$). There is an upper bound on advances in knowledge induced by k. Utility is maximized in a stationary system. These two cases contradict the purpose of the model, which is to generate persistent economic growth induced by capital investment. In *case 4*, investment is not worthwhile and the life of the

Table 23.7 The five cases of the Romer model

Case	$\alpha + \nu$	Returns to scale	$f''(k)$	$f'(k) - \rho$	$\dot{k}$[a]
1	> 1	Increasing	> 0	> 0	> 0
2	< 1	Indeterminate	< 0	0	0
3	1	Increasing	0	0	0
4	1	Increasing	0	< 0	—
5	1	Increasing	0	> 0	> 0

Note: [a]We assume $p > 0$.

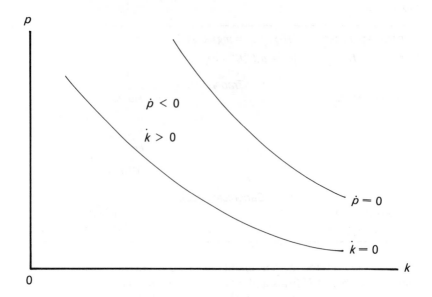

Figure 23.3 The growth path of the competitive equilibrium with constant returns to capital and $f'(k) > \rho$. The equation of the path is

$$p = \frac{\dot{p}}{\rho - f(k)} = u'(c)$$

Source: Based on Romer 1986: Figure 2

disequilibrium system is finite. It is case 5 upon which Romer focuses. *Case 5* yields a steady rate of per capita endogenous growth $G = \alpha N^v - \rho$. The model in case 5 fulfills two efficiency conditions $-p = u'(c)$ and $G = f'(k) - \rho -$ (Figure 23.3) and is consistent with balanced growth (Romer 1986: 94).

Case 5 answers the quotation, what sort of economic framework generates growth as we know it? The proferred answer to the question is a framework that includes not only perfect foresight, efficient pricing, continuous equilibrium and utility maximization, but also a relatively slight preference for the present compared with the future and capital investment at a rate to engender moderately strong increasing returns to scale.[32] What the Hamiltonian dynamic system represents as growth as we know it balances on a sharp knife-edge.[33, 34]

CONCLUSION

The New Classical economists have acknowledged that the application of the Hamiltonian formalism to the problem of growth has not generated new facts about growth. The stylized facts of growth are known. The contribution of the new growth theory, so the New Classical economists have stressed, consists of putting old ideas about increasing returns into an acceptable formal framework, thereby replicating and offering an alternative interpretation of the stylized facts. As Lucas stated, "[W]e want a formalism that leads us to think about individual decisions to acquire knowledge [in an optimizing context], and about the consequences of these decisions for productivity" (1988: 5). Mathematics, as Lucas implied, is no mere neutral language. Rather, mathematics provides the problem-solving techniques to forge ahead in certain directions. Some mathematical formalisms have superior heuristic power. They let economists say more than other mathematical syntaxes. But each syntax also imposes its own restrictions on what economists can and cannot say.

The formalisms of the New Classical growth theory admit an interpretation in terms of realistic, institutional detail about which the neoclassical growth model had nothing to say. Within the neo-Walrasian paradigm itself, New Classical growth theory offers an improvement over the stationary, capital-theoretic models of the 1960s. Optimal growth theory now has more general models, which can produce steady per capita growth. What one is intended to learn from the New Classical model is the answer to the question, what sort of economic structure generates growth as we know it? The preferred answer is intertemporal Arrow–Debreu models with moderately strong increasing returns to scale based on advances in public knowledge that result from capital investment. Given that answer, another thing that one wants to learn is what policies promote growth. The models suggest an answer.

At the same time, the New Classical model restricts economic thinking about growth to a framework that assumes a competitive economy with agents who have perfect foresight that is marching along an endogenous optimal path that is entirely predetermined given the community's original constrained objective and that is guided by fully reversible equations. The source of the teleological treatment of the growing economy lies in the representation of growth by the Hamiltonian dynamic system, which assumes the conservation of whatever is the analogue of energy in economics. It is impossible in the context of such a teleological system to think of a growing economy as open to the influence of history. The objective of the New Classical growth models, to maximize utility yielded by consumption in an infinite time horizon, has no obvious empirical counterpart given the problem economists have faced in measuring utility. The constraints of the formalism may suggest that the New Classical economists have adopted a formalism that is inappropriate to help economists better answer the old question, "What are the engines of growth?"

We have seen that the economists who introduced the Hamiltonian method into economics remarked on the analogy between dynamic optimization in mechanics and economics. But economists generally have neglected to pose the questions that arose when economics imported the formalisms of energetics. In particular, economists have not discussed the substantial negative analogies between the Hamiltonian dynamic system which represents energy conservation and the theory of per capita growth. The energetics analogy has not played the cognitive role in economics that it had across the physical sciences in the nineteenth century. In physics, hypothetical analogies inspired explorations of positive and negative analogies. The viability of positive analogies was subject to testing. Some analogies failed, but those that were deployable were theory-constitutive. The presence of substantial negative analogies between the Hamiltonian dynamic system which represents energy conservation and the theory of per capita growth would explain why research projects that have attempted to use the Hamiltonian to represent sustained economic growth have encountered difficult obstacles.

NOTES

The author thanks the Economics Department Seminar at SUNY-Binghamton, T. Mayer, M. Deedy, K. D. Hoover, R. L. Basmann, R. Backhouse, P. Mirowski, R. W. Clower, D. Colander and I. H. Rima for their comments. The Jerome Levy Institute at Bard College financed the research.

1   The Hamiltonian that is the topic of the essay deals with conservative systems. The essay does not discuss modified Hamiltonians used in the natural sciences to deal with nonconservative systems. The criticisms in the essay of the application by economists of the Hamiltonian formalism which implies the conservation law to capital theory and New Classical growth theory do not extend necessarily to the use of Hamiltonians in other subfields of economics.

2   In economics, the traditional formalist condition of a meaningful mathematical hypothesis is that economists conceivably could test the hypothesis against reality under ideal circumstances which may not exist (Samuelson 1983: 4). Thus for practical purposes, the major if not the sole criterion of a valid scientific argument for the formalists in economics come down to logical validity.

3   The shortest distance between the two points in the absence of gravity is a straight line. In the presence of gravity the particle that moves down a straight line gathers speed relatively slowly. A nonlinear curve that is steeper near the starting point is longer than the straight line, but the particle traverses the greater part of the nonlinear curve at greater speed than it traverses the straight line.

4   The derivation of the Euler–Lagrange equation from (23.1) appears in most books on the calculus of variations, e.g. Weinstock (1974: 20–3).

5   x here is a shorthand for three coordinates.

6   Hence the speed $\dot{x} = [2g(x_1 - x_2)]^{\frac{1}{2}}$.

7   The potential energy at the top of a child's curved slide in the absence of friction is the same whether the child mounts the steps or walks up the slide. The speed of the child at the bottom of the slide depends only on the height of the slide and is independent of the shape of the slide (Serway 1982: 145).

8   The Hamiltonian function can be extended to cover nonconservative systems (Weinstock 1974: 88–90).

9   The direction of the vector force $dV/dx = F_x$ is suppressed.

10 See equation (23.6). The Euler–Lagrange equation corresponding to equation (23.5) is

$$-\frac{\partial V}{\partial x} - \frac{d}{dt}\frac{\partial T}{\partial \dot{x}} = 0$$

where

$$\frac{d}{dt}\frac{\partial T}{\partial \dot{x}} = mg$$

Thus the Euler–Lagrange equation like the canonical equation (23.8b) is equivalent to Newton's second law (Elsgolc 1982: 58).

11   Here is a modern example. When a car smashes into a wall, the isolated system, defined by the system that conserves momentum, is composed of the car, the wall *and* the earth (Krauss 1993: 156).

12   The translation of kinetic energy assumed the following reasons (Mirowski 1989: 226–7). Given that prices and changes in the quantity of commodity bought are analogous in mechanics to force and displacements of position, then expenditure is $\sum F_x dx$. Work done by a conservative force equals the negative of the change in potential energy associated with that force: $-\Delta V/\partial x = \sum F_x dx$. If we start from a system at rest at t_0, then $-\Delta V/\partial x = T$ at t_1. Then $T = \sum F_x dx$ and kinetic energy is equivalent to expenditure, or the budget constraint.

13   Ramsey also solved the minimization problem (equation (23.9)) by means of the calculus of variations. This yielded the Lagrange–Euler equation $F'(K)\,U'(C) + U'(C) = 0$, which is known today as the "Keynes–Ramsey" rule (Blanchard and Fisher 1989: 40).

14   Most of *Foundations* treated problems in the theory of static general equilibrium. The thesis was part of the project of P. A. Samuelson, K. Arrow, G. Debreu, T. Koopmans and others during 1930–60 to supply the mathematical tools able to show the conditions in which the competitive price equilibrium exists mathematically and is stable at any point in time (Weintraub 1980). The 1950s found Samuelson and the next generation of mathematical economists faced with the problem of showing the optimal time-path of the general competitive equilibrium.

15   Solow, as the Ramsey models that he introduced burgeoned in the 1980s, disavowed the models as "far-fetched", stating that "the dynasty is supposed to solve an infinite-time utility-maximization problem. . . . The next step is harder to swallow in conjunction with the first. For this consumer every firm is just a transparent . . . device for carrying out intertemporal optimization subject only to technological constraints and initial endowments. Thus any kind of market failure is ruled out from the beginning, by assumption" (1988: 310).

16   The problem seemed to be to maximize, subject to the diminishing returns, the aggregate of heterogeneous capitals (with K_1 the numeraire) between time t and "bliss" in conditions of utility saturation. Two papers by Samuelson that apply the law of conservation to a von Neumann model without consumption were reprinted in the Sato (1990) volume.

17   Paradoxically Samuelson in his Nobel Prize lecture remarked after discussing thermodynamics, "Now what in the world has all this to do with economics? There is really nothing more pathetic than to have an economist or a retired engineer try to force analogies between the concepts of physics and the concepts of economics. How many dreary papers have I had to referee in which the author is looking for something that corresponds to entropy or to one or another form of energy. Nonsensical laws, such as the law of conservation in purchasing

power, represent spurious social science imitation of the important physical law of the conservation of energy ..." (1972: 254).

18   Letter to the author from Tom Mayer dated November 4, 1993.

19   The maximum principle is the subject of a priority dispute. According to Chiang, "the same technique was independently discovered by Magnus Hestenes, a mathematician at the University of California, Los Angeles". Hestenes's findings appeared in a Rand report, which was not easily available (Chiang 1992: 19 n.2, 167). Bellman saw in the work on constrained trajectories of Valentine in the 1930s, Hestenes, and Berkovitz (in 1961) the actual origin of the maximum principle (Bellman 1965: 252).

20   Some writers refer to what Pontryagin called the maximum principle as the minimum principle. We shall use the original name.

21   The older generation of mathematical economists like Samuelson and the former physicist T. Koopmans knew how to set up the constrained dynamic optimization problem with imputed prices without reading the textbook by Pontryagin *et al.* (Samuelson and Solow 1956: 561; Koopmans 1963).

22   This essay, unlike Cass (1965), assumes a zero rate of depreciation of the capital stock.

23   The present-value Hamiltonian takes the general form

$$H_{pv} = [f_0(k, t) + \lambda f_n(k, t)]e^{-\rho t}$$

The current-value Hamiltonian is

$$H = H_{pv}e^{\rho t} = f_0(k, t) + pf_n(k, t) \qquad \lambda = pe^{-\rho t}$$

(Chiang 1992: 210–11).

24   In terms of the energetics metaphor, the time derivative of the costate variable price (or marginal utility) is formally analogous to the force and potential energy is analogous to utility. The formal analogue of $F_x \mathrm{d}x = -\mathrm{d}V/\mathrm{d}x$ (equation (23.6c)) given the Hamiltonian (equation (23.15)) is $u'(c)\, \mathrm{d}k = -\mathrm{d}u(c)/\mathrm{d}k$.

25   The balanced growth property of the model follows Solow (1956).

26   Lucas helped supervise Romer's Ph.D. dissertation, and Romer and the New Classical economist R. G. King supervised Rebelo's dissertation (Letters to the author from S. Rebelo dated December 4, 1989, and from P. M. Romer dated October 12, 1993). Sala-i-Martin wrote his lecture notes on economic growth when he assisted the New Classical economist R. J. Barro at Harvard in 1988–90.

27   All agents may optimize, in the sense of being in equilibrium, even when the macroeconomic equilibrium situation is Pareto suboptimal, so that reallocating resources will promote a net increase in welfare.

28   The evidence for the existence of externalities using US post-Second World War data is mixed (Benhabib and Jovanovic 1989; Cabellero and Lyons 1989).

29   "The 'Romer' externalities model" is somewhat of a misnomer. The model draws heavily on the work of Arrow (1962; Letter to the author from P. M. Romer, October 12, 1993).

30   For a more formal discussion of the problem of consumption optimal growth with productive externalities, see Romer (1986: 1003, 1018–27) and the commentaries of Conlisk (1989: 793, 814–15) and Xie (1991).

31   To deduce the path of capital (23.18a), we have

$$\frac{\partial H(c, \dot{k}, p)}{\partial p} = \dot{k} = k^\alpha K^\nu - c$$

since $\partial H(c, \dot{k}, p)/\partial c = 1/c - p = 0$,

$$\frac{\partial H(c, \dot{k}, p)}{\partial p} = k^{\alpha}K^{\nu} - \frac{1}{p}$$

Koopmans (1963) explained the rationale for the derivation of $-G = \rho - f'(k)$ (in (23.18b)).

32 Romer and Sala-i-Martin stress that persistent growth requires "VERY increasing returns on scale" (Sala-i-Martin 1990b: 20). Case 2 permits slight increasing returns to scale. But case 1 involves very, very increasing returns to scale.

33 Neoclassical economists since Solow's (1956) seminal paper have criticized the Harrod–Domar model because of this "knife-edge" property.

34 The precarious solution may suggest that the model, that is, the specification of the objective function and the constraints (equations (23.16) and (23.17)), are causing the problem. Chiang worked out the implications of one of Romer's alternative models of a Hamiltonian dynamic system with increasing returns to scale due to endogenous technical progress (Chiang 1992: 269–74; Romer 1986: 100–4). Chiang found that the alternative model too has properties other than that of balanced growth equilibrium; also, the rate of balanced growth may take on negative values (Chiang 1992: 273–4). So alternative specifications of the model might not eliminate the knife-edge character of the endogenous growth models expressed in terms of Hamiltonian dynamics.

We can solve the Romer problem of maximizing utility given constraints (equations (23.16) and (23.17)) by means of the Lagrangian method (equations (23.1) and (23.2)). The result is identical to equation (23.18b) which resulted from using the Hamiltonian method. That may suggest that the problem with the Romer model is not the mathematical method *per se*, but the conservation law. Indeed, economists normally see the Hamiltonian as purely a mathematical technique that does not affect the substance of the economics to which the technique is applied. However, the Lagrangian derives from the Hamiltonian and vice versa (equations (23.1)–(23.7)). The use of the variational principle in the form of the Lagrangian or the Hamiltonian implies the conservation law.

REFERENCES

Archibald, T. (1989) "Physics as a constraint on mathematical research: the case of potential theory and electrodynamics", in D. E. Rowe and J. McCleary (eds) *The History of Modern Mathematics II: Institutions and Applications*, Boston, MA: Academic Press.

Arrow, K. J. (1962) "The economic implications of learning by doing", *Review of Economic Studies* 29: 155–73.

—— (1968) "Applications of control theory to economics growth", in G. B. Dantzig and A. F. Veinott (eds) *Mathematics of the Decision Sciences*, Part 2, Providence, RI: American Mathematical Society.

—— (1987) "Arrow on Arrow: an interview", in G. R. Feiwel (ed) *Arrow and the Foundations of the Theory of Economic Policy*, New York: New York University Press.

—— (1988) "Foreword", in *Preference, Production and Capital, Selected Papers of Hirofumi Uzawa*, New York: Cambridge University Press.

Arrow, K. J. and Debreu, G. (1954) "Existence of an equilibrium for a competitive economy", *Econometrica* 22: 265–90.

Aspray, W. (1989) "The transformation of numerical analysis by the computer: an example from the work of John von Neumann', in D. E. Rowe and J. McCleary (eds) *The History of Modern Mathematics II: Institutions and Applications*, Boston, MA: Academic Press.

Bachelard, G. (1975) *Le Rationalism Appliqué*, Paris: Presses Universitaires de France.

Barro, R. J. (1991) "Economic growth in a cross section of countries", *Quarterly Journal of Economics* 106: 407–43.

Barro, R. J. and Sala-i-Martin, X. (1991) "Convergence across states and regions", with commentaries, *Brookings Papers on Economic Activity* 1: 107–82.

Bellman, R. (1965) "Review of *The Mathematical Theory of Optimal Processes* by L. S. Pontryagin . . .", *Econometrica* 33: 252–5.

—— (1987) *Dynamic Programming*, Princeton, NJ: Princeton University Press.

Benhabib, J. and Jovanovic, J. (1989) "Externalities and growth accounting", *American Economic Review* 81: 82–113.

Blanchard, O. J. and Fischer, S. (1989) *Lectures on Macroeconomics*, Cambridge, MA: MIT Press.

Browder, F. E. (1979) "Mathematics and the sciences", in W. Aspray and P. Kitcher (eds) *History and Philosophy of Modern Mathematics*, Minneapolis, MN: University of Minnesota Press.

Burmeister, E. (1980) *Capital Theory and dynamics*, New York: Cambridge University Press.

Burmeister, E. and Dobell, A. R. (1970) *Mathematical Theories of Economic Growth*, New York: Macmillan.

Caballero, R. J. and Lyons, R. K. (1989) "The role of external economies in U.S. Manufacturing", Columbia University.

Cass, D. (1965) "Optimal growth in an aggregative model of capital accumulation", *Review of Economic Studies* 32: 233–40.

Chiang, A. C. (1992) *Dynamic Optimization*, New York: McGraw-Hill.

Conlisk, J. (1989) "An aggregate model of technical change", *Quarterly Journal of Economics* 104: 787–821.

De Marchi, N. (1993) *Non-natural Social Science: Reflecting on the Enterprise of More Heat than Light*, Durham, NC: Duke University Press.

Dixit, A. K. (1976) *The Theory of Equilibrium Growth*, New York: Oxford University Press.

—— (1990) *Optimization in Economic Theory*, New York: Oxford University Press.

Dorfman, R. (1969) "An economic interpretation of optimal control theory", *American Economic Review* 59: 817–31.

Edgeworth, F. Y. (1981) *Mathematical Psychics*, New York: Kelley, 1967.

Elkana, Y. (1974) *The Discovery of the Conservation of Energy*, Cambridge, MA: MIT Press.

Elsgolc, L. E. (1962) *Calculus of Variations*, Wokingham, Berks: Addison Wesley.

Fisher, I. (1925) *Mathematical Investigations in the Theory of Value and Prices*, New Haven, CT: Yale University Press (originally Fisher's 1895 Ph.D. thesis).

Guicciardini, N. (1989) *The Development of Newtonian Calculus in Britain 1700–1800*, Cambridge: Cambridge University Press.

Hamilton, W. R. (1834) "On a general method in dynamics", *Philosophical Transactions of the Royal Society* Part 1: 247–308.

Harman, P. M. (1982) *Energy, Force, and Matter*, Cambridge: Cambridge University Press.

—— (1987) "Mathematics and reality in Maxwell's dynamical physics", in R. Kargon and P. Achinstein (eds) *Kelvin's Baltimore Lectures and Modern*

Theoretical Physics, Cambridge, MA: MIT Press.

Helpman, E. and Krugman, P. R. (1985) *Market Structure and Foreign Trade*, Cambridge, MA: MIT Press.

Hoover, K. D. (1988) *The New Classical Macroeconomics*, New York: Blackwell.

—— (1992) "The rational expectations revolution: an assessment", *Cato Journal* 12: 81–96.

—— (1993) "Introduction", in K. D. Hoover (ed.) *The New Classical Macroeconomics I*, Aldershot: Edward Elgar.

Jevons, W. S. (1879) *The Theory of Political Economy*, New York: Kelley, 1965.

Jungnickel, C. and McCormmach, R. (1986a) *Intellectual Mastery of Nature*, vol. I, Chicago, IL: University of Chicago Press.

—— and —— (1986b) *Intellectual Mastery of Nature*, vol. II, Chicago, IL: University of Chicago Press.

Kaldor, N. (1957) 'A model of economic growth', *Economic Journal* 67: 591–624.

—— (1961) "Capital accumulation and economic growth", in F. A. Lutz and D. C. Hague (eds) *Theory of Capital*, London: Macmillan.

Kalman, R. E. (1963) "The theory of optimal control and the calculus of variations", in R. Bellman (ed.) *Mathematical Optimization Techniques* Berkeley, CA: University of California Press.

Keynes, J. M. (1933) *Essays in Biography*, New York: Macmillan.

Kirman, A. P. (1992) "Whom or what does the representative individual represent?", *Journal of Economic Perspectives* 117–36.

Klein, M. (1959) *Mathematics and the Physical World*, New York: Dover Publications.

—— (1972) *Mathematical Thought from Ancient to Modern Times II*, New York: Dover Publications.

Koopmans, T. (1963) 'On the concept of optimal economic growth", in *Study Week on the Econometric Approach to Development Planning*, October 7–13, Amsterdam; reprinted in T. D. Koopmans (ed.) *Econometric Approach to Development Planning*, Amsterdam: North-Holland, 1965.

Krauss, L. M. (1993) *Fear of Physics*, New York: Basic Books.

Lindley, D. (1993) *The End of Physics*, New York: Basic Books.

de Long, B. (1988) "Productivity growth, convergence and welfare: a comment", *American Economic Review* 78: 1138–54.

Lucas, R. E. (1988) "On the mechanics of economic development", 1985 Marshall Lecture, *Journal of Monetary Economics* 22: 3–42.

—— (1990) "Why doesn't capital flow from rich to poor countries", *American Economic Review* 80: 92–6.

MacKenzie, D. (1990) *Inventing Accuracy: a Historical Sociology of Nuclear Missile Guidance*, Cambridge, MA: MIT Press.

Manuelli, R. E. and Sargent, T. J. (1987) *Exercises in Dynamic Macroeconomic Theory*, Cambridge, MA: Harvard University Press.

Marshall, A. (1926) *Principles of Economics*, 8th edn, Philadelphia, PA: Porcupine Press (reprinted 1990).

Mirowski, P. (1986) "Mathematical formalism and economic explanation", in P. Mirowski (ed.) *The Reconstruction of Economic Theory*, Boston, MA: Kluwer-Nijhoff.

—— (1989a) *More Heat than Light*, New York: Cambridge University Press.

—— (1989b) "How not to do things with metaphors: Paul Samuelson and the science of neoclassical economics", *Studies in the History and Philosophy of Science* 20: 175–91.

Mirowski, P. and Cook, P. (1990) "Walras' 'Economics and mechanics': translation, commentary and context", in W. J. Sameuls (ed.) *Economics as Discourse*, Boston, MA: Kluwer Academic.

Northrop, F. S. C. (1941) "The impossibility of a theoretical science of economic dynamics", *Quarterly Journal of Economics* 56: 1–17.

Owens, L. (1989) "Mathematics at war: Warren Weaver and the Applied Mathematics Panel, 1942–1945", in D. E. Rowe and J. McCleary (eds) *The History of Modern Mathematics II: Institutions and Applications*, Boston, MA: Academic Press.

Petit, M. L. (1990) *Control Theory and Dynamic Games in Economic Policy Analysis*, New York: Cambridge University Press.

Phelps, E. (1961) "The golden rule of accumulation: a fable for growthmen", *American Economic Review* 638–43.

Poincaré, H. (1905) *Science and Hypothesis*, New York: Walter Scott.

Pontryagin, L. S., Boltyanskii, V. G., Gamkrelidze, R. V. and Mishchenko, E. F. (1962) *The Mathematical Theory of Optimal Processes*, New York: Wiley.

Putnam, H. (1971) *The Philosophy of Logic*, New York: Harper & Row.

—— (1979) *Mathematics, Matter and Method*, New York: Cambridge University Press.

Ramsey, F. P. (1928) "A mathematical theory of saving", *Economic Journal* 38: 543–59.

Rebelo, S. (1987) "Long run policy analysis and long run growth", Unpublished paper, available from N. J. Wulwick.

—— (1991) "Long run policy analysis and long run growth", *Journal of Political Economy* 99: 500–21.

Romer, P. M. (1986) "Increasing returns and long-run growth", *Journal of Political Economy* 94: 1002–37.

—— (1989) "Capital accumulation in the theory of long-run growth", in R. J. Barro (ed.) *Modern Business Cycles Theory*, Cambridge, MA: Harvard University Press.

Rothman, M. A. (1972) *Discovering the Natural Laws*, New York: Dover Publications.

Ryder, H. (1967) "Optimal accumulation and trade in an open economy of moderate size", in K. Shell (ed.) *Essays on the Theory of Optimal Economic Growth*, Cambridge, MA: MIT Press.

Sala-i-Martin, S. (1990a) "Lecture notes on economic growth", vol. I, Working Papers 3563, National Bureau of Economic Research.

—— (1990b) "Lecture notes on economic growth", vol. II, Working Paper 3564, National Bureau of Economic Research.

Samuelson, P. A. (1972) "Maximum principles in analytical economics", *American Economic Review* 62: 249–62.

—— (1983) *Foundations of Economic Analysis: Enlarged Edition*, Cambridge, MA: Harvard University Press (first published 1941 as a Ph.D. thesis).

—— (1990a) "Law of conservation of the capital–output ratio in closed von Neumann systems", in R. Sato and R. V. Ramachandran (eds) *Conservation Laws and Symmetry: Applications to Economics and Finance*, Boston, MA: Kluwer Academic (originally published in *Applied Mathematical Science* 67 (1972): 1477–9).

—— (1990b) "Two conservation laws in theoretical economics", in R. Sato and R. V. Ramachandran (eds) *Conservation Laws and Symmetry: Applications to Economics and Finance*, Boston, MA: Kluwer Academic (originally distributed as an MIT Department of Economics mimeo, 1970).

Samuelson, P. A. and Solow, R. S. (1956) "A complete capital model involving heterogeneous capital goods", *Quarterly Journal of Economics* 70: 537–62.

Sato, R. (1990) "The invariance principle and income–wealth conservation laws", in

R. Sato and R. V. Ramachandran (eds) *Conservation Laws and Symmetry: Applications to Economics and Finance* Boston, MA: Kluwer Academic.

Segré, E. (1976) *From X-rays to Quarks*, Berkeley, CA: University of California Press.

Serway, R. A. (1982) *Physics: for Scientists and Engineers*, New York: Saunders College Publishing.

Shell, K. (1969) "Applications of Pontriagin's maximum principle to economics", in H. W. Kuhn and G. P. Szego (eds) *Mathematical Systems Theory and Economics I*, New York: Springer.

—— (1988) "Hamiltonians", in J. Eatwell, M. Milgate and P. Newman (eds) *The New Palgrave*, New York: W. W. Norton.

Solow, R. S. (1956) "A contribution to the theory of economic growth", *Quarterly Journal of Economics*: 65–94.

—— (1988) "Growth theory and after", *American Economic Review* 78: 307–17.

Struik, D. J. (1989) "Schouten, Levi-Civita, and the emergence of tensor calculus", in D. E. Rowe and M. McCleary (eds) *The History of Modern Mathematics II: Institutions and Applications*, Boston, MA: Academic Press.

Summers, R. and Heston, A. (1988) "Improved international comparisons of real product and its composition, 1950–1980", *Review of Income and Wealth* 30: 207–62.

Tobies, R. (1989) "On the contribution to mathematical societies to promoting applications of mathematics in Germany", in D. E. Rowe and J. McCleary (eds) *The History of Modern Mathematics II: Institutions and Applications*, Boston, MA: Academic Press.

Uzawa, H. (1965) "Optimal technical change in an aggregate model of economic growth", *International Economic Review*, 6: 18–31.

Walras, L. (1909) "Economics and mechanics", trans. P. Mirowski and P. Cook, in W. J. Samuels (ed.) *Economics as Discourse*, Boston, MA: Kluwer Academic.

Weinstock, R. (1974) *Calculus of Variations with Applications to Physics and Engineering*, New York: Dover Publications.

Weintraub, E. R. (1980) *Microfoundations*, Cambridge: Cambridge University Press.

Wilson, E. B. (1912) *Advanced Calculus*, New York: Dover Publications.

Wulwick, N. J. (1990a) "Comment on Walras' 'Economics and mechanics' by P. Mirowski and P. Cook", in W. J. Samuels (ed.) *Economics as Disclosure*, Boston, MA: Kluwer Academic.

—— (1990b) "'New Growth Theory: Some Methodological Issues'", *Methodus* 2: 40–2.

—— (1991) "Comment on Hoover", in N. De Marchi and M. Blaug (eds) *Appraising Economic Theories*, Aldershot: Edward Elgar.

—— (1992) "Kaldor's growth theory", *Journal of the History of Economic Thought* 14: 36–54.

—— (1993) "What remains of the growth controversy", *Review of Political Economy* 5: 321–43.

Xie, D. (1991) "Increasing returns and increasing rates of growth", *Journal of Political Economy* 99: 429–35.

Yehuda, E. (1974) *The Discovery of the Conservation of Energy*.

Chapter 24

The impact of John von Neumann's method

M. H. I. Dore

Economics purports to be a science about reality, about real entities such as production processes, firms, prices, consumers and so forth, all of which are real and finite entities. Mathematical theorems have no intrinsic empirical content; yet the growing use of mathematical theorems to portray and represent economic entities and their interrelations requires a greater attention to *method*. John von Neumann's growth model (1937), translated in 1945, was the first major attempt to use mathematical structures and their related theorems to develop an economic analysis. To use mathematical results in this way, it is necessary to establish a strict one-to-one correspondence between mathematical object and entities. Without such correspondence, the economic interpretation lacks credibility.

The plan of this chapter is to examine the aspects of mathematical philosophy and method that are relevant to the use of mathematics in economics. Section II deals with a specific mathematical result and its economic interpretation: this mathematical result is von Neumann's minimax theorem of rectangular games, and the growth model is its economic interpretation. A well-known feature of the growth model is the duality of prices and outputs; however, when seen in terms of the minimax theorem, this duality is in fact the *bilinearity* of prices and outputs. It will be argued that this bilinearity is very special, and was rejected by Sraffa in 1926.

The linear methods of von Neumann have been adopted by both the neoclassical school and the reformulated classical school based on Ricardo and Marx. Because linear methods are dynamically unstable they are appropriate only for "snapshots" of the economy, as carried out, for example, by Sraffa.

The instability of linear methods suggests the need for nonlinear methods if mathematics is to be useful for dynamic economic analysis. But unfortunately nonlinear methods require the use of even more complicated mathematical structures and theorems, with the added danger of a growing distance between the mathematical structures and the economic interpretation. von Neumann's growth model is reexamined from the above perspective, and his method is contrasted with that of Sraffa.

I

John von Neumann was a friend and fellow countryman of the late Nikolas Kaldor, who can be judged to have had a material influence on him. When von Neumann became interested in economics, Kaldor recommended that he read Cassel. He did, but he claimed not to have been impressed by it. Yet his formulation of the model is remarkably like that of Cassel, as both Kaldor (1988) and Arrow (1989) have noted. The fixed coefficient technology assumed by von Neumann is also Cassel's, who modeled a uniformly growing economy which was an obvious generalization of Marx's schema of extended reproduction. But Cassel's "principle of scarcity", which governs economic value and so prices, is given an extreme binary interpretation whereby a resource has either a positive economic value if it is fully utilized or a value of zero. (This is the principle we now call complementary slackness.) To quote Koopmans's judgment of the John von Neumann model as a whole, "this is not very good economics". Unless every single man and woman is fully employed, the social value of labor is zero; this is indeed extreme. Why did von Neumann resort to this formulation? There appears to be no simple answer; but in order to appreciate a possible answer let us consider the model as a whole and the role of prices in particular.

Reference has already been made to von Neumann's saddle point theorem in the theory of two-person zero-sum games, which he had proved in 1928, which is itself a generalization (to an arbitrary number of strategies) of Borel's saddle point theorem which we shall refer to as "the minimax theorem". It will be shown below that von Neumann's growth model is a straightforward reinterpretation of his minimax theorem. This is indeed apparent from von Neumann's paper itself, and the close relationship between the growth model and the minimax theorem has been noted by others, e.g. Gale (1960) and Nikaido (1970). However, looking at the growth model in the light of the minimax theorem helps draw attention to bilinearity, which is of some importance.

Let us first restate the fundamental equations of the growth model:

$$\alpha A x \leq B x \qquad (24.1)$$

and if, for some i, the "less than" relation holds, then $p_i = 0$.

$$\beta p A \geq p B \qquad (24.2)$$

and if, for some j, the "greater than" relation holds, then $x_j = 0$. Here α is the expansion factor, β is the interest factor, A is the matrix of input coefficients, x is the vector of activity levels, B is the matrix of output coefficients and p is the vector of prices.

In equilibrium, loss-making processes and free goods are abandoned, and $\alpha = \beta$, so that

$$(B - \alpha A) x = 0 \qquad (24.3)$$

$$p\,(B - \alpha A) = 0 \tag{24.4}$$

John von Neumann's growth model is perhaps the first major attempt to use mathematical structures and their concomitant mathematical theorems to be given an economic interpretation. It should be noted that the mathematical theory has its own independent existence, devoid, of course, of any empirical content. This section is a note on aspects of mathematical philosophy that impinge on methods appropriate for economic analysis.

In so far as economics attempts to understand reality, its objective is to acquire empirical content. Mathematical theories and mathematical objects (such as sets, rings, fields etc.) have no empirical content. When such an object can be used consistently, that is, when a given interpretation is not contradictory in two different instances, then a one-to-one correspondence must be established between the mathematical object and the economic entity such as a price, or a consumer, or a growth rate. For example, in the Leontief matrix, the smallest eigenvalue is the reciprocal of the rate of economic growth, and the associated right and left-hand eigenvectors are interpreted as the price and quantity vectors. In these cases of eigenvectors and eigenvalues, the one-to-one correspondence is established and the resulting interpretation is consistent. However, the use of such mathematical entities might involve additional assumptions or implications not intended by the user from the point of view of economics. We shall return to this issue below.

von Neumann's model, formulated in discrete time, captures the real-time dependence of production and the consequent production lags. However, the use of matrices has some advantages as well as some disadvantages. The advantage is economy of notation, and the potential or possibility of exploiting the theorems of nonnegative matrices in inferring further properties of the model. But there are two perhaps unintended consequences of the matrix formulation.

Examine equations (24.3) and (24.4) above. Mathematically the output vector x and the price vector p are hyperplanes.[1] First note that both x and p are determined uniquely only up to a factor of proportionality. While conventionally this is described as being "independent of scale" it does mean that the production process is homogeneous of degree one, that is, doubling all inputs will double all outputs. Hence independence of scale really means constant returns to scale. Sraffa (1960) did not wish to make this assumption in his "snapshot" of the economy. He therefore avoided a matrix formulation of his system.

Second, the matrix formulation implies that if process j and process k are feasible processes, then all linear combinations of processes j and k are also feasible. But this implies an infinity of processes – an impossibility. Hence the one-to-one correspondence cannot be maintained.

The final objection to von Neumann's mathematical method is his use of a fixed-point theorem to prove the existence of a solution p^*, x^*, α^* and β^*

in which $\alpha^* = \beta^*$ in equations (24.3) and (24.4). In view of the fact that the use of fixed point theorems in order to establish existence is now standard, it deserves comment.

In the proof of his minimax theorem in his 1928 paper, von Neumann had also used a fixed-point theorem, a theorem which was both difficult and highly involved (Gale 1960: 211). Ten years later, Ville (1938) proved the minimax theorem using the ideas of separating hyperplanes, thus showing the fixed-point theorem to be redundant. von Neumann and Morgenstern (1944) adopted Ville's proof in their book.

In his economic growth paper, von Neumann proved a generalization of Brouwer's fixed-point theorem. Indeed, von Neumann's title for his original paper indicates that for him, *qua* mathematician, this generalization is the most novel aspect of his paper. This is an example of embedding a particular problem within a much larger mathematical structure, a technique frequently used in mathematics. It is a way of solving a particular problem by embedding it in a family of problems and solving the latter to obtain a solution of the former. This is what Richard Bellman (1957) did in developing dynamic programming. While this technique works well for special problems, such as the intertemporal planning problem,[2] it shifts the focus from a particular problem to a larger family of problems. It is no longer clear whether the one-to-one correspondence has been preserved or lost. The technique of embedding solves the larger mathematical family of problems. The particular problem is solved only implicitly. Naturally, no insight into the nature of the solution of the particular problem is obtained.

Once again the fixed-point theorem is unnecessary overkill and is, in fact, redundant. As Georgescu-Roegen (1951) has argued, convexity and the resulting separating hyperplanes could be used to establish existence. In other words, Ville (1938) method would again be sufficient.

It is interesting to note that in later generalizations of von Neumann's model only constructive proofs of existence were given. Thus in Kemeny *et al.* (1956), the generalized von Neumann model is formulated as a parametrized matrix game, and existence of solutions for the economy (and its subeconomies, as the input–output matrix is not assumed to be irreducible) is shown by linear programming methods. The same constructive proof is used in the two papers by Morgenstern and Thompson (1967, 1969).

Quite apart from overkill, there is a more fundamental objection to the use of fixed-point theorems, based on Brouwer's rejection of proof by double negation, a foundation stone of intuitionist and constructivist philosophy of mathematics.

In classical mathematics, the proof of existence may take the following form: nonexistence of a solution will involve a contradiction. At best, a fixed-point theorem is a negative statement; it indicates that it is impossible that there can be no solution, given the assumptions of compact subspaces and topological mappings. Such a classical proof gives no hint of how the solution may be found. In contrast, a constructive proof of the existence of a solution will give a general outline of how a solution may be found. It may be longer, but it contains more information. Consider a well-known example, the fundamental theorem of algebra. The classical proof of this theorem states that every polynomial with complex coefficients has at least one complex root. In contrast, Brouwer's proof of this theorem indicates how the root may be found.

In 1941, Kakutani published a further generalization of von Neumann's fixed-point theorem to cover point-to-set mappings. This theorem has now become the standard method of establishing existence of solutions both in the neoclassical school (Arrow, Debreu) and the neo-Keynesian school (e.g. Benassy 1976). Hence an unnecessary bad habit has been acquired by the economics profession from John von Neumann.

However, as noted earlier, one of his central objectives – as a mathematician – was to publish the generalized proof of the fixed-point theorem. Was the economics merely a convenient vehicle for an essentially mathematical exercise for von Neumann? Genius that he was, perhaps that is all that he wanted to do at that time. Later, after meeting Oscar Morgenstern, he returns to economics, but only through their joint interest in the theory of games. As far as is known, there is no further elaboration by von Neumann of his growth theory, a challenge that was taken up by Hicks, Kemeny, Morgenstern, Thompson, Mackenzie, Samuelson, Arrow, Solow, Dorfman, Morishima, Pasinetti, Koopmans, Chakravarty and Brody, to name the best known.

Finally, let us return to the central concern of this section, namely, mathematical structure and its economic interpretation. To repeat, abstract mathematical structures have no empirical content; the economics is as good as the interpretation given to the mathematical structure. Debreu (1959) is very explicit on this; in his *Theory of Value*, he states of his use of convex analysis and his economic interpretation'

> Allegiance to rigor dictates the axiomatic form of the analysis where the theory ... is logically entirely disconnected from its (economic) interpretations.

> (p. viii)

Hence one would be justified in concluding that Debreu's main objective was the systematic exposition of convex analysis, and the validity of the economic interpretation is very much a secondary question. For that further tests would be necessary. In the light of the criterion stated above, is there a well-identified one-to-one correspondence between the mathematical objects and economic entities? In Debreu, the set of producers as well as the set of consumers is convex, and the separating hyperplane is interpreted as representing prices.

For the set of consumers the one-to-one correspondence test fails, because convexity implies that if x and y are consumers then so are all linear combinations, that is, $\alpha x + (1 - \alpha)y$ are also consumers, which is an infinity of consumers. However, mankind is decidedly finite. It could therefore be argued that only finitary methods avoid these kinds of difficulties in economics.

There is no doubt that this would be one of the reasons why Sraffa (1960) in his remarkable classic eschews such methods and instead chooses finitary methods, although the Sraffa system can be equally presented by using methods akin to those of John von Neumann. Sraffa does not express his results by using matrix methods. A methodological purist, and philosophically inclined towards constructivism, Sraffa could not possibly compromise his inquiry by embedding his theory in a more general mathematical structure which could raise the possibility of additional assumptions, a baggage that he did not need. For instance, expressing the Sraffa system by matrix methods would imply that he was assuming constant returns to scale, an assumption which he did not wish to make. As argued earlier, embedding entails the potential danger of a loss of focus, unless the one-to-one correspondence between mathematical objects and economic entities is carefully preserved, with no loss of economic intuition.

II

In the previous section emphasis was placed on the philosophical implications of a mathematical structure, together with its logical implications which are usually stated as theorems, and its economic interpretation. Here the focus is on a specific mathematical result and its economic interpretation. The mathematical result is the minimax theorem, and the growth model is its economic interpretation. This will enable us to discuss two crucial issues: the bilinearity of prices and outputs, and the equality of the interest rate and the growth rate.

In Appendix 24A the growth model is derived from the minimax theorem. This is implicit in von Neumann's original growth paper, especially his paragraph 5, and so no originality is claimed and only a brief verbal statement is given.

The essential fact about the minimax theorem is that it applies to a two-person zero-sum game. Suppose there are two players, I and II. Player I's payoff (in a game) depends on the action, or choice, of player II. Player I *must* expect that player II's choice will be something that is the least favorable to player I; i.e. player I expects the worst possible outcome and maximizes I's payoff on the assumption that player II will make such a choice with certainty. Thus player I maximizes the minimum payoff that I can expect. This is called a *maximin* policy.

Reciprocally, player II will expect player I's choice to be the worst possible outcome for player II. Thus player II minimizes the maximum that the latter can expect. This is called a *minimax* policy. If the game is two-person zero sum, then the maximin and minimax policies mean that the value of the game is the same to both players. But each player must assume that the choice of the other is *given* – given by the worst possible response each can expect from the other. (As is stated below, in mathematics this is called *bilinearity*.)

Now enrich the game by introducing probabilities for each player, so that the payoff to each player is weighted by the probability of choosing a particular strategy. This is all that is required.

This enriched structure can now be interpreted in terms of economics: the probability vectors of the two players can be renamed the vector of prices and the vector of outputs. The value of the game to the two players is now called the growth factor and the interest factor. However, in an equilibrium, the value of the game is the same for both players. Hence the growth factor is equal to the interest factor. The one-to-one correspondence between mathematical objects and economic concepts is strictly maintained. In other words, the minimax theorem of rectangular games is reinterpreted as an economic growth model. (In order to appreciate how von Neumann did this, the reader is urged to read the Appendix.) In terms of the criterion stated above, the reinterpretation is consistent and convincing. Finally, to prove the existence of the solution to equations (24.3) and (24.4), von Neumann resorts to his fixed-point theorem, a position that has already been criticized in Section I above.

To repeat, because the game is zero sum, the interest factor is equal to the growth factor, and the payoff function takes the *bilinear form*,[3] that is, the payoff function is linear in the quantity vector x if the price vector p is fixed, and linear in p if x is fixed. This bilinearity is a reflection of the convexity assumptions: the probability distributions p and x are then reinterpreted as prices and quantities respectively in the growth model. (Mathematically, both the sets S and T, that is, the sets of prices and quantities, are supporting hyperplanes, as should be apparent from the mathematical definition of S and T given in the Appendix.) The bilinearity of p and x, and hence the duality of p and x, emerges as a consequence of the maximin strategy of player I and the minimax strategy of player II. Let us refer to the two strategies taken together as the *minimax principle*.

It is easy to see that the minimax principle implies bilinearity, since it requires that each player optimize by taking the worst possible play of the opponent as *given* with certainty. That is, player I chooses the best possible x assuming that player II will choose a p that is the worst possible choice for player I. That is, *player I can take it as given and therefore treat it as constant.* The converse is also true, that is, bilinearity implies the minimax principle. Thus bilinearity and the minimax principle are equivalent. We may therefore focus on one or the other. Let us consider bilinearity in detail.

To repeat, bilinearity means that the payoff function is linear in x if p is fixed, and linear in p if x is fixed. This is acceptable in a two-person zero-sum game. But if quantities of goods are x and their respective prices are p, does bilinearity make economic sense? If the quantities of, say, the first m goods increase by a factor λ, can their respective prices be assumed to be fixed?

Consider the mathematical definition of bilinearity. Let the two vectors x and y be points in $\mathbb{R}^n$. Then the inner product $\langle x, y \rangle$ is a function of two points in $\mathbb{R}^n$. By fixing y, it may be considered a function of x alone. Thus if λ is some scalar, then

$$\lambda \langle x, y \rangle = \langle \lambda x, y \rangle \tag{24.5}$$

and

$$\langle x^1, y \rangle + \langle x^2, y \rangle = \langle x^1 + x^2, y \rangle$$

similarly if x is fixed, then

$$\langle x, \lambda y \rangle = \lambda \langle x, y \rangle \tag{24.6}$$

and so

$$\langle x, \lambda y \rangle = \langle \lambda x, y \rangle \tag{24.7}$$

Now consider the inner product of prices p and quantities x:

$$\langle p, x \rangle = \text{real value of output}$$

But (24.7) would imply that a 10 percent increase in prices is the same as a 10 percent increase in real output; bilinearity would make it indistinguishable. However, in economics, one is primarily interested in distinguishing between price changes and (real) quantity changes. Thus bilinearity of prices and output does not make sense.

Bilinearity sets aside the crucial interrelationship between quantity and price, an issue that concerned Sraffa (1926). Although the main trust of his article was to focus on imperfect competition, Sraffa clearly argued that prices and outputs cannot be separated, either because of demand limitations or because of rising costs.

It might be argued that there exists a similar duality between prices and quantities in the Sraffa system. Nothing can be further from the truth: there is no bilinearity in Sraffa (1960). Even Pasinetti, who presents the Sraffa system using matrix methods, does not in any way rely on the minimax theorem and therefore no bilinearity is involved. Considering the autonomy of the price system and the quantity system, Pasinetti (1977) states:

it must now be emphasized that, all the similarities and formal analogies notwithstanding, the system of prices and the system of physical quantities are two separate systems, neither of which carries any implications from the other. The standard system, for example, is a logical construction which relates to physical quantities and which implies nothing about the price system. Although from a formal point of view, the particular system of prices ... appears as "dual" to the standard system, the former in no way implies the latter and, similarly, the latter in no way implies the former.

(p. 111)

Furthermore, one might ask, under what conditions would the bilinearity between prices and quantities make sense? In a Walrasian *tâtonnement*, quantities remain fixed, while the auctioneer raises or lowers prices in order to balance supply and demand. In such a model bilinearity might even be said to be necessary, but in a growing economy bilinearity is not acceptable.

To summarize, bilinearity requires the independence of prices and outputs from each other, a condition that never holds. It would hold only in a simple *tâtonnement* economy of pure exchange. In a production economy, it would not hold.

Finally let us consider the equality of the growth factor and the interest factor, in equilibrium. As noted earlier in the minimax theorem, the value of the game for player I (call it the growth factor) is equal to the value of the game for player II, which can be called the interest factor. von Neumann thus seems to prove Schumpeter's earlier conjecture that in a stationary state the rate of interest would be zero. But as interest is in some sense a price, there would be a multiplicity of interest rates; for this reason, Sraffa's concept of own rates of interest is much more profound (see Pasinetti 1981).

We have demonstrated in this section that von Neumann's growth model is an interpretation of his minimax theorem. The vectors of probabilities of the two players become the vectors of prices and quantities, and the common value of the game is the growth factor (equal to the interest factor). The minimax principle on which the strategies of the two players are based is equivalent to bilinearity of prices and output. However, bilinearity implies the independence of prices and outputs from each other, which is questionable. The equality of the growth rate and the interest rate follows from the fact that the value of the game is the same to the two players at the saddle point. Thus on the rate of interest there is very little economic analysis.

Nevertheless, in terms of the criterion of a one-to-one correspondence between mathematical objects and economic entities, the model is meticulous and maintains its focus very clearly. von Neumann's use of a mathematical structure has clearly revolutionized modern economics. His methods are borrowed and extended by the neoclassical school.[4] This is the subject of the final section.

III

It was stated that von Neumann was the first to introduce convex mathematical structure into economics to which he gave a consistent and convincing economic interpretation in his growth model. His mathematical tools, as well as his proof theory, revolutionized the neoclassical school.

Once this revolution in technique occurred, it was possible to abandon

Cassel and reformulate Walras's model of general economic equilibrium and replace the principle of scarcity with the principle of marginal utility, by exploiting von Neumann's convex methods and turning to the supporting hyperplane as the theoretical basis for prices. This task was essentially completed by Arrow and Debreu. A further defect in Walras was the assertion of a determinate solution based on the equality of the number of equations and the number of unknowns, a condition which is neither necessary nor sufficient for the existence of a solution. This issue was resolved by appealing to Kakutani's fixed-point theorem, as stated before. It gave new life to Walras's model of pure exchange and succeeded in integrating the marginal utility analysis of Jevons and Carl Menger. The neoclassical school thus became rigorous, resorting to any mathematical theory that seemed useful: first calculus, and then, after von Neumann, set theory, and most recently differential geometry. The theory established the existence and uniqueness of a competitive equilibrium. Indeed, competitive analysis celebrated Adam Smith's invisible hand in the guise of Walras. Arrow then established the optimality of the competitive equilibrium through the first and second theorems of welfare economics.

While the existence, uniqueness and optimality of the competitive equilibrium were established, its stability remained unsatisfactorily resolved, as has been admitted by Hahn (1982). All the main approaches to stability analysis (the assumption of gross substitutability of all goods, the assumption of the weak axiom of revealed preference, or the assumption of diagonal dominance) are singularly unappealing when translated into their respective economic meanings. It has been suggested that the least objectionable approach to stability is diagonal dominance (Arrow and Hahn 1971: 295). The economic meaning of diagonal dominance is that the excess demand or supply of each good is more sensitive to a change in its own price than to a change in the prices of all other goods combined. But even with the assumption of diagonal dominance there is a problem: stability depends on the choice of the numeraire. Thus for some numeraire the equilibrium will not be stable. In his recent review of stability, Hahn (1982) does not minimize the difficulties of establishing stability. The general conclusion of this survey is:

> while some special . . . models exist, we shall have to conclude that we still lack a satisfactory descriptive theory of the invisible hand.
>
> (p. 746)

Space does not permit a full critique of the assumptions and the results of stability analysis in neoclassical general equilibrium models.

The instability can be traced to the notion of equilibrium, which is a "chosen position", that is, chosen by optimizing agents, rather than *a position of rest*. The idea of an equilibrium as a chosen position is Hicksian, but Hicks's (1965) concept of equilibrium has two essential properties, which are an adjustment rule and rapid convergence to equilibrium. The latter property reflects Hicks's dissatisfaction with Samuelson's (1947) stability analysis, in which prices converge to equilibrium prices *as time approaches infinity.* Rapid convergence is an important property because in static analysis the given tastes, given technology and so on are locked up in the Marshallian "pound of *ceteris paribus*" (Hicks 1965: 49). The longer it takes prices to converge to equilibrium the longer the *ceteris paribus* assumption must hold. Consequently convergence as time approaches infinity is logically inconsistent with the *ceteris paribus* assumption (Dore 1984–5).

It is indeed remarkable that even John von Neumann evaded the issue of the stability of the growth path in his growth model. The balanced growth path is highly unstable: even the slightest deviation of even one commodity from balanced growth proportions (such as a slight variation in the output of corn due to the weather) would for ever veer the economy away from the balanced growth path. For illuminating numerical examples as well as a mathematical proof of instability, see Blatt (1983: 111–46). Hence the dynamics of the von Neumann model are spurious. Needless to add, the same issue plagues the neoclassical school.

CONCLUSION

In this chapter we have argued that von Neumann's growth model and his method have had a major impact on modern neoclassical economic thought. His paper introduced for the first time a mathematical structure and its implied theorems and gave it an economic interpretation. However, he established a strict one-to-one correspondence between mathematical objects and economic entities, and he succeeded in presenting a consistent and convincing interpretation. The mathematical result that he used was his minimax theorem of two-person zero-sum games. He reinterpreted the two vectors of probabilities as the vectors of prices and quantities. The value of the game, which is the same for the two players in equilibrium, is interpreted as the growth factor, equal to the interest factor. To establish existence he used a fixed-point theorem, an exercise in unnecessary overkill from the point of view of constructivist mathematics. A logical implication of the reliance on the minimax theorem is the bilinearity of prices and outputs, which implies that quantities and prices are independent. Such independence would hold only in a simple Walrasian *tâtonnement* economy of pure exchange: this independence was rejected by Sraffa.

The use of mathematical structures entails the possibility of unintended assumptions. It was perhaps for this reason that Sraffa avoided a matrix formulation of the Sraffa system. Indeed, there is good reason to suppose that Sraffa was a methodological purist and a constructivist.

The linear methods of von Neumann have been adopted by the neoclassical school as well as by others. But as linear methods are dynamically unstable, they are appropriate only for instantaneous "snapshots" of the economy, such as were carried out by Sraffa.

The well-known limitations of linear methods obviously suggest the use of nonlinear mathematical methods for dynamic analysis. However, nonlinear methods require the use of even more complicated mathematical structures and theorems, with the added danger of a growing distance between the mathematical structure and its economic interpretation. There are signs that this is already occurring, with increasing interest in differential geometry, differential inclusions, bifurcation theory and chaos theory. In using these mathematical techniques it will be necessary to establish a strict one-to-one correspondence, as von Neumann did; and use constructive proofs, which von Neumann did not.

Mathematical objects have no empirical content; if economics aspires to be a science with empirical content, it must use, as far as possible, only discrete and finitary methods, and its implied proof theory must necessarily be constructivist.

APPENDIX

In Section II it was stated that von Neumann's growth model is an economic interpretation of his minimax theorem. This Appendix demonstrates this by deriving the growth model from the minimax theorem. It must be emphasized that this is implicit in von Neumann's original growth paper, especially his paragraph 5, and so no originality is claimed.

Suppose that sets S and T are convex. Two players, I and II, acting independently of each other, choose a strategy x in S and a strategy p in T. Player I obtains a payoff $K_1(x, p)$ and player II obtains the payoff $K_2(x, p)$. As the game is zero sum,

$$K_1(x, p) + K_2(x, p) = 0 \tag{24A.1}$$

Let us take player I's payoff as a basis, and write

$$K(x, p) \equiv K_1(x, p)$$

This means that player II's payoff is $-K(x, p)$.

Now player I has no control over how $p \in T$ will be chosen. Rationality demands that each player would do the *best* for himself. But as the game is zero sum, player I expects II to choose the *worst* possible choice for player I. This would mean a choice of p by II that minimizes I's gain. Thus

$$F(x) \equiv \min_{p \in T} K(x, p) \tag{24A.2}$$

That is,

$$F(x) \leq K(p, x) \tag{24A.2a}$$

The maximum that player I can obtain by an appropriate choice of x is given by

$$v_1 \equiv \max_{x \in S} F(x) = \max_{x \in S} \min_{p \in T} K(x, p)$$

(24A.3)

That is, player I follows a *maximin* policy.

Symmetrically, player II must follow a *minimax* policy, given that II's choice is

$$G(p) = \max_{x \in S} K(x, p)$$

(24A.4)

That is,

$$G(p) \geq K(x, p)$$

(24A.4a)

which leads to

$$v_2 \equiv \min_{p \in T} G(p) = \min_{p \in T} \max_{x \in S} K(x, p)$$

(24A.5)

Combining (24A.2a) and (24A.4a), we have

$$F(x) \leq K(x, p) \leq G(p)$$

(24A.6)

Note that v_1, by definition, is the maximum of $F(x)$ for any $x \in S$, and v_2 is the minimum, by definition, of $G(p)$. But given (24A.6) above

$$v_1 = \max F(x) \leq \min G(p) = v_2$$

Therefore

$$v_1 \leq v_2$$

(24A.7)

Next we show that $v_2 \leq v_1$. From the minimax theorem, the saddle point of the payoff function $K(x, p)$ exists; then at the saddle point

$K(x, p^*)$ as a function of x attains a maximum on S at $x = x^*$
$K(x^*, p)$ as a function of p attains a minimum on T at $p = p^*$

which implies that

$$K(x, p^*) \leq K(x^*, p^*) \leq K(x^*, p) \text{ for all } x \in S \text{ and } p \in T$$

(24A.8)

By definition,

$$\max_{x \in S} K(x, p^*) \equiv G(p^*)$$

and

$$\min_{p \in T} K(x^*, p) \equiv F(x^*)$$

Substituting into equation (24A.8),

$$G(p^*) = F(x^*) \tag{24A.9}$$

But

$$v_1 \equiv \max_{x \in S} F(x) \geq F(x^*) \tag{24A.10}$$

$$v_2 \equiv \min_{p \in T} G(p) \leq G(p^*) \tag{24A.11}$$

But (24A.9), (24A.10) and (24A.11) imply that

$$v_1 \geq v_2 \tag{24A.12}$$

Taking equations (24A.7) and (24A.12) together, we have

$$v_1 = v_2$$

(at the saddle point).

Next let the (convex) sets S and T be specified by

$$S = \{x \mid x \in \mathbb{R}^m, \sum_{i=1}^{m} x_i = 1, x_i \geq 0, i = 1, 2, \ldots, m\}$$

$$T = \{p \mid p \in \mathbb{R}^m, \sum_{j=1}^{n} p_j = 1, p_j \geq 0, i = 1, 2, \ldots, n\}$$

Also, let the payoff matrix $C = [c_{ij}]$ be an (m, n) matrix. As the x_i and p_j each sum to 1, they can be interpreted as probability distributions. Then player I's expected payoff, assuming I selects probability vector x, *given that II selects* p, is $\sum_{i=1}^{m} x_i c_{ij} p_j$.

From the minimax theorem, C must have a saddle point on the cartesian product $S \times T$.

Next define a matrix B to be

$$B \equiv C + \sigma A \tag{24A.13}$$

where B can be treated as an affine transformation of C and A. Now interpret

matrix B to be the output matrix
matrix A to be the input matrix

From (24A.13), we may write in terms of components

$$[c_{ij}] = [b_{ij}] - \sigma[a_{ij}] \tag{24A.13a}$$

von Neumann had earlier proved that (x^*, p^*) is the saddle point of the payoff function and that $v_1 = v_2 = v$. However, now the value of the game is a function of σ in equation (24A.13a); denote this by $v(\sigma)$. Then, as von Neumann showed, the saddle point (x^*, p^*) exists if

$$v(\sigma) = 0 \tag{24A.14}$$

and $\sigma = \alpha$ in equation (24A.14) $\tag{24A.15}$

From the minimax theorem we know that

$$v(\sigma) \le \max_i \sum_{j=1}^{n} c_{ij}p_j \le 0 \le \min_j \sum_{i=1}^{m} x_i c_{ij} \le v(\sigma) \tag{24A.16}$$

Substitute (24A.13) and (24A.14) into (24A.16) to get

$$v(\sigma) \le \max_i \sum (b_{ij} - \sigma a_{ij}) p_j \le 0 \le \min_j \sum (b_{ij} - \sigma a_{ij}) x_i$$
$$i = 1, 2, \ldots, m, j = 1, 2, \ldots, n \tag{24A.17}$$

In fact, the inequality sign holds as an equality and (x, p), where $x \in S$ and $p \in T$, is a saddle point. Also $\alpha = \beta = \sigma$.

Now rearrange terms in (24A.17), and using matrix notation and noting equation (24A.15) we get

$$\alpha A x \le B x$$

$$\alpha p A \ge p B$$

That is, we obtain the fundamental equations of von Neumann's growth model, stated as equations (24.1) and (24.2) in the text.

Introduce complementary slackness, and von Neumann's balanced growth mode is complete.

What we have demonstrated is that the growth model is a straightforward reinterpretation of his minimax theorem of rectangular games. Because the game is zero sum, the interest factor is equal to the growth factor, and the payoff function takes the *bilinear* form, that is, the payoff function is linear in x if p is fixed the linear in p if x is fixed. This bilinearity is a reflection of the convexity assumptions: the probability distributions p and x are then reinterpreted as prices and quantities respectively in the growth model. The economic implications of bilinearity are discussed in the text.

NOTES

I have benefited from discussions with Richard Goodwin on the subject of this paper. I am also grateful to Jim Mayberry for checking and improving the Appendix. However I alone am responsible for any remaining deficiencies.

1   The general equation of a hyperplane is $m \cdot z = k$, where k is a constant. See any book on linear algebra, e.g. Lang (1968).
2   See, for example, Arrow and Kurz (1970) or Dore (1977).
3   For a discussion of bilinearity and bilinear forms, see Lang (1968: 142–6). More advanced treatment is given in Birkhoff and MacLane (1966: 187–8, 247–9).
4   Of course convex methods are being used also by the neo-Ricardian as well as the neo-Marxian schools. However, this aspect is beyond the scope of the chapter.

REFERENCES

Arrow, K. J. (1989) "Von Neumann and the existence for general equilibrium", in M. H. I. Dore, S. Chakravarty and R. M. Goodwin, (eds) *Von Neumann and Modern Economics*, Oxford: Oxford University Press.

Arrow, K. J. and Hahn, F. (1971) *General Competitive Analysis*, Amsterdam: North-Holland.

Arrow, K. J. and Kurz, M. (1970) *Public Investment, the Rate of Return, and Optimal Fiscal Policy*, Baltimore, MD: Johns Hopkins University Press.

Bellman, R. (1957) *Dynamic Programming*, Princeton, NJ: Princeton University Press.

Benassy, J. P. (1976) "The disequilibrium approach to monopolistic price setting and general monopolistic equilibrium", *Review of Economic Studies* 43: 69–81.

Birkhoff, G. and MacLane, S. (1966) *A Survey of Modern Algebra*, New York: Macmillan.

Blatt, J. M. (1983) *Dynamic Economic Systems: a Post-Keynesian Approach*, Armonk, NY: M. E. Sharpe.

Debreu, G. (1959) *Theory of Value: an Axiomatic Analysis of Economic Equilibrium*, New York: Wiley.

Dore, M. H. I. (1977) *Dynamic Investment Planning*, London: Croom Helm.

—— (1984–5) "On the concept of equilibrium", *Journal of Post-Keynesian Economics* 7 (2): 193–205.

Dore, M. H. I., Chakravarty, S. and Goodwin, R. M. (eds) (1988) *Von Neumann and Modern Economics*, Oxford: Oxford University Press.

Gale, D. (1960) *The Theory of Linear Economic Models*, New York: McGraw-Hill.

Georgescu-Roegen, N. (1951) "The aggregate linear production function and its applications to von Neumann's model", in T. C. Koopmans (ed.) *Activity Analysis of Production and Allocation*, New York: Wiley.

Hahn, F. (1982) "Stability", in K. Arrow and M. Intriligator (eds) *Handbook of Mathematical Economics*, vol. 2, Amsterdam: North-Holland.

Harsanyi, J. C. (1983) "Mathematics, the empirical facts and logical necessity", *Erkenntnis* 19: 167–92.

Hicks, J. (1965) *Capital and Growth*, Oxford: Clarendon.

Kakutani, S. (1941) "A generalization of Brouwer's fixed point theorem", *Duke Mathematical Journal* 8.

Kaldor, N. (1988) "John von Neumann: a personal recollection", in M. H. I. Dore, S. Chakravarty and R. M. Goodwin, (eds) *Von Neumann and Modern Economics*, Oxford: Oxford University Press.

Kemeny, J. G., Morgenstern, O. and Thompson, G. L. (1956) "A generalization of the von Neumann model of an expanding economy", *Econometrica* 24: 115–35.

Lang, S. (1968) *Linear Algebra*, Reading, MA: Addison-Wesley.

Morgenstern, O. and Thompson, G. L. (1967) "Private and public consumption and savings in the von Neumann model of an expanding economy", *Kyklos* 20: 387–409.

—— and —— (1969) "An open expanding economy model", *Naval Research Logistics Quarterly*, 16: 443–57.

von Neumann, J. (1937) "Über ein Ökonomisches Gleichungssystem und eine Verallgemeinerung des Brouwerschen Fixpunktsatzes", *Ergebnisse eines Mathematischen Kolloquium 8*, ed. K. Menger; trans. as "A model of general equilibrium", *Review of Economic Studies* 13 (1945–6): 1–9.

von Neumann, J. and Morgenstern, O. (1944) *Theory of Games and Economic Behavior*, Princeton, NJ: Princeton University Press.

Nikaido, H. (1970) *Introduction to Sets and Mappings in Modern Economics*, Amsterdam: North-Holland.

Pasinetti, L. (1977) *Lectures on the Theory of Production*, London: Macmillan.
—— (1981) "The rate of interest and the distribution of income in a pure labor economy", *Journal of Post-Keynesian Economics* 3(2): 170–82.
Samuelson, P. (1947) *Foundations of Economic Analysis*, Cambridge MA: Harvard University Press.
Sraffa, P. (1926) "The laws of returns under competitive conditions", *Economic Journal*, December.
—— (1960) *Production of Commodities by Means of Commodities*, Cambridge: Cambridge University Press.
Ville, J. (1938) "Sur la théorie générale des jeux'', in E. Borel (ed.) *Traité du Calcul des Probabilités*, vol. 4, Paris, Part 2, pp. 105–13.

Index